TRAINING & REFERENCE

murach's
structured
COBOL

Mike Murach

Anne Prince

Raul Menendez

MIKE MURACH & ASSOCIATES, INC.

2560 West Shaw Lane, Suite 101 • Fresno, CA 93711-2765

Writers:	Mike Murach
	Anne Prince
	Raul Menendez
Editor:	Judy Taylor
Cover design:	Zylka Design
Production:	Tom Murach

Other books for COBOL programmers

DB2 for the COBOL Programmer, Parts 1 & 2 by Curtis Garvin and Anne Prince

CICS for the COBOL Programmer, Parts 1 & 2 by Doug Lowe

MVS JCL by Doug Lowe

MVS TSO, Parts 1 & 2 by Doug Lowe

Library of Congress Cataloging-in-Publication Data
Murach, Mike.
  Murach's structured COBOL : training & reference / Mike Murach, Anne Prince, Raul Menendez.
      p. cm.
    Includes index.
    ISBN 1-890774-05-7
    1. COBOL (Computer program language) 2. Structured programming. I. Prince, Anne.
  II. Menendez, Raul. III. Title.

  QA76.73.C25 M859 2000
  005.13'3--dc21

                                                    00-061285

Contents

Expanded contents

Chapter 3 How to write a program that prepares a report

Section 2   Other COBOL essentials

Chapter 6   How to define, move, and initialize fields

Chapter 7   How to use intrinsic functions and arithmetic statements

**Chapter 18   How to compile and test a program on an
IBM mainframe**

Chapter 22 Introduction to object-oriented COBOL

Introduction

If you're new to COBOL, this is the right book for you. Whether you use it in a class or on your own, you'll learn faster and more thoroughly than you will with any other book. Beyond that, though, this is also the right reference book for the professional programmer on the job. Each page is packed with the kind of information you'll use every day, presented in a way that lets you get answers quickly, whenever you need them.

How can one book be the best choice for both beginner and professional? It has to be better than the other books in more ways than one.

9 ways this book outperforms the rest...for training AND reference

- If you're a beginner, you'll learn how to code, compile, test, and debug simple interactive programs in the first two chapters. No other book gets you started that fast.

- In chapters 4 and 5, you'll find practical techniques for designing and coding structured programs. These techniques are essential to productive programming on the job, and they have been making life easier for programmers ever since we pioneered them back in the 1970s.

- Besides teaching standard COBOL, which can be run on any computer system, our book covers the specifics that you need for developing COBOL programs for IBM mainframes...because that's where the job market is.

- 14 full programs and dozens of coding segments illustrate the best coding practices currently available. Whether you're a beginner or a professional, you'll boost your productivity by using these as models when you code your own programs.

- The exercises at the end of each chapter use the source code and data on the companion CD ROM to give you a maximum amount of practice in a minimum amount of time...on your own PC. This leads to dramatic improvements in training efficiency.

- Because Micro Focus Personal COBOL is an inexpensive product that is also a terrific training tool, we have integrated it into our book and its exercises. That too improves training efficiency. *Note, however, that you can also use our book and the exercises with other compilers.*

- All of the information in this book is presented in "paired pages" with the essential details and examples on the right and the perspective on the left. This lets you learn faster by reading less...and you won't find anything like it in competing books.

- After you read the five chapters in the first section of this book, you can read the other chapters in whatever sequence you prefer. That's because the chapters in the other sections are designed as independent modules. We refer to this as "modular organization," and it makes our book more flexible and useful than any other.

- After you use this book to learn COBOL programming, the coding models, the paired pages, and the modular organization make it the best on-the-job reference you'll ever use.

What this book does

Section 1 presents the essential skills of COBOL programming. In chapters 1 and 2, you'll learn how to code, compile, test, and debug simple interactive programs. In chapter 3, you'll learn how to write programs that prepare reports. And in chapters 4 and 5, you'll learn how to use structured techniques for designing, coding, and testing programs. When you complete this section, you'll be able to develop report-preparation programs in a thoroughly professional way.

From that point on, you can read the chapters in sections 2 and 3 to learn how to use other COBOL features. In section 2, for example, the chapters show you how to use intrinsic functions, how to work with dates, how to work with characters, and much more. In section 3, the chapters show you how to work with sequential, indexed, and relative files. When you complete these sections, you will know how to use all of the features of standard COBOL.

On the job, though, you need to know more than just the standard features. That's why the first five chapters in section 4 present coding and development skills for specific platforms. In chapter 17, for example, you can learn some non-standard COBOL for developing interactive programs. This is typical of the code that you'll use on networked PCs or UNIX systems. Then, chapters 18 through 20 present the specifics you need for developing programs on IBM mainframes. And chapter 21 shows you how to maintain old programs on all platforms, because maintenance programming represents a major portion of the job market.

The last chapter in this book introduces you to object-oriented COBOL, which will become available with the next set of COBOL standards. To take this from the theoretical to the practical, this chapter compares a 9-page object-oriented program with a structured program for the same purpose. This helps you learn to think in terms of objects, which is fast becoming a desirable job skill.

As you use this book, please remember that we designed the chapters so you don't have to read them in sequence. This makes the book better for both training and reference. In particular, you can read the chapters in sections 2 and 4 in whatever sequence you prefer. You can also read the chapters in section 3 anytime after you finish section 1, although we do recommend that you read the section 3 chapters in sequence.

What the prerequisites for this book are

If you're new to programming, the prerequisites for using this book are minimal. You just need to be familiar with the operation of the Windows 95 or 98 interface. That means you should be able to use the menus and toolbars for a Windows program as you perform tasks like opening, saving, printing, and closing a file. So if you've used programs like Word or Excel, you definitely have the starting skills that you need for this book.

Remember, though, that this book isn't just for beginners. If you're a programmer on the job or an advanced student who wants to develop the professional skills that are needed on the job, this book is also for you.

What compiler you need

Because COBOL is a standard language, it can be used on any computer system. All you need is a COBOL compiler for that system. Since the first three sections of this book present standard COBOL, you can use this book with any system that has a COBOL compiler that conforms to the 1985 standards…and all of the current compilers do.

To practice on your own, though, we recommend that you use Micro Focus Personal COBOL on your own PC. That's why chapter 2 presents everything you need to know for compiling and testing your COBOL programs with this compiler. In addition, the exercises at the end of each chapter are specifically designed for use with Personal COBOL. If you're using this book for a course that you're taking, you can probably buy this compiler in your school's bookstore. Otherwise, the last page in this book shows you how you can buy it from us.

If you want to use this book with some other PC compiler, though, you can do that too. In that case, you can print and use the generic exercises that are included on the CD ROM. These get the same training results as the exercises in the book; they just don't include the specific operational procedures for Micro Focus Personal COBOL.

Remember, though, that most COBOL programming is done on IBM mainframes. That's why our book also presents everything you need to know for developing COBOL programs on those systems. In particular, chapter 18 shows you how to compile and test your programs using one of the three compilers that are in use today on IBM mainframes. So if you have access to a mainframe, you can do the generic exercises on that platform.

What the bound-in CD ROM contains

The CD ROM that comes with this book contains all the source programs and data that you need for doing the exercises in this book. That way, you don't have to start every exercise from scratch. The CD ROM also contains the data and copy members that you need for the student projects in the appendix, as well as the source code and test data for the illustrative programs used in the book.

Because the source programs are in standard COBOL, you can easily modify them for use with any COBOL compiler. Because the data files are standard ASCII files, you can also use them on any PC. When you need to create non-standard PC files like indexed or relative files, the exercises and projects guide you through their creation from the standard files.

Besides the source code and data, the CD ROM contains a program called LISTMODS that develops a structure listing from the source code in a COBOL program. This is a program that we developed 20 years ago in COBOL, and we've been using it ever since. Why? Because it provides the quickest and best documentation for a structured program that we've ever seen.

1

Introduction to COBOL programming

The quickest and best way to *learn* COBOL programming is to *do* COBOL programming. That's why this chapter shows you how to code two simple but complete programs. Before you learn those coding skills, though, this chapter introduces you to COBOL.

COBOL platforms, standards, and compilers

COBOL is an acronym that stands for COmmon Business Oriented Language. Starting in 1959, this language was designed by representatives from business, government, and the U.S. Department of Defense. Their goal was to design a programming language that could be used on all business computers.

COBOL platforms

Today, COBOL is available on all of the major computer platforms. In general, you can think of a *platform* as a unique combination of computer hardware and operating system. Figure 1-1, for example, illustrates typical mainframe and PC hardware configurations and describes the operating systems that run on them.

In terms of hardware, all computer systems have the same basic components, including display screens, keyboards, disk drives, printers, processors, and internal storage. It's just the terminology and scale that differ from one computer to the next. On a *mainframe* or *mid-range computer*, for example, the display screen is a *terminal*; the processor is a *central processing unit*, or *CPU*; and the *internal storage* is *main memory*. On a *PC*, the comparable terms are *monitor*, *processor*, and *RAM (random-access memory)*.

The primary difference between a mainframe computer and a PC is that a mainframe computer serves dozens or hundreds of users from a single processor, while a PC serves only one user. Like a mainframe computer, a mid-range computer serves more than one user, but usually far fewer than a mainframe.

Today, the IBM mainframe computer running under the OS/390 operating system is a widely used COBOL platform. The AS/400 running under the OS/400 operating system and mid-range systems that run under the UNIX operating system are two other common COBOL platforms. And PCs that run under DOS and Windows are two more COBOL platforms.

With this book, you'll learn how to develop COBOL programs on your own PC because that's the easiest way to get started. However, you're also going to learn how to write COBOL programs for IBM mainframes because that's by far the most popular COBOL platform. You should also be able to transfer the skills you learn in this book to any other COBOL platform.

Keep in mind, though, that writing COBOL programs for mainframes is by far the largest job market. Today, billions of lines of COBOL code are in use on this platform. During the 1990's, tens of billions of dollars were spent fixing these programs so they would work correctly when the year changed from 1999 to 2000. And many billions more will be spent to keep these programs up-to-date in the next 20 years.

A typical mainframe configuration

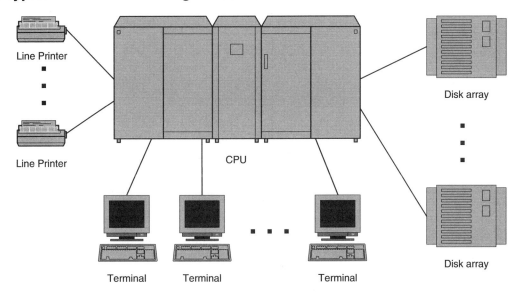

A typical PC configuration

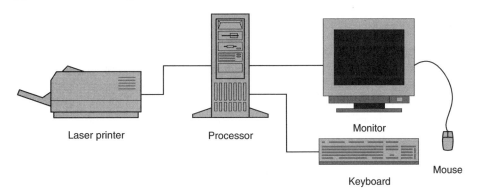

Description

- The most widely-used COBOL *platform* is the *IBM mainframe* running under the OS/390 or MVS operating system. IBM AS/400 systems that run under the OS/400 operating system and *mid-range computers* that run under the UNIX operating system are two other common COBOL platforms. A *PC* running under the Windows operating system is another COBOL platform.

- The biggest difference between a mainframe and a PC is that a mainframe serves dozens or even hundreds of users from a single processor, while a PC serves only one user. A mid-range system usually serves many users, but not as many as a mainframe.

Figure 1-1   COBOL platforms

COBOL standards and compilers

In an effort to make COBOL work the same way on all computer platforms, several sets of *COBOL standards* have been published since 1968. These are summarized in figure 1-2. The first three sets were developed by the American National Standards Institute (ANSI), and the latest set is being developed by ANSI/ISO (International Standards Organization).

The first set of specifications, referred to as COBOL-68, got the process of standardization going, but had some serious limitations. In particular, these standards didn't provide for the use of indexed files. In contrast, the COBOL-74 standards provided language for most of the capabilities that were in common use, thus reducing COBOL variation from one computer system to another.

The next set of standards, called *COBOL-85*, added language that makes it easier to adhere to the principles of structured programming. Then, in 1989, an addendum to the COBOL-85 standards introduced intrinsic functions. In this book, you'll learn how to use all of the COBOL-85 features because that's the standard that's in common use today.

Right now, we're awaiting the *COBOL-2000* standards, which are scheduled for release in 2002. The primary enhancement of these standards is that they will provide for object-oriented programming (see chapter 22). Otherwise, the improvements are expected to be minimal.

With all this standardization, you may think that the COBOL language is the same on all computer systems. But it's not, for two major reasons. First, the COBOL standards still don't provide effective language for displaying data on the interactive screens of computer users and for receiving data that has been entered through their keyboards. Second, the COBOL standards still don't provide language for working with databases, even though databases are commonly used on all types of computer systems.

Before a COBOL program can be run on a specific computer system, the COBOL language must be *compiled* into the machine language that will run on that computer. This is done by a *COBOL compiler*, a program that's written specifically for that computer. For a mainframe, the computer manufacturer develops the compiler. For a PC, independent software companies develop the compilers. For a mid-range computer or a UNIX-based system, either the manufacturer or an independent company develops the compiler.

In figure 1-2, you can see the four compilers that are in common use on IBM mainframes today. In addition, you can see some of the Merant compilers for other platforms. Merant is a leading supplier of tools that let you offload mainframe program development to a PC.

When the standards that a compiler is based upon don't provide for a needed capability, the developer of the compiler can add non-standard *extensions* to the language. The resulting compiler can still be called a standard compiler. To be a COBOL programmer, then, you need to know the standard language as well as the extensions that apply to the compiler you're using. In this book, you'll learn the compiler specifics for Micro Focus Personal COBOL, as well as the specifics for the three IBM mainframe compilers that are based on the 1985 standards.

COBOL standards

Year	Description
1968	Although these standards were limited, they showed that a language could be standardized from one type of computer to another.
1974	These standards were much more complete than the 1968 standards so they led to a high degree of COBOL standardization from one computer to another.
1985	These standards provided enhanced language for developing structured programs. A 1989 addendum added intrinsic functions to these standards.
2000	These standards will add a number of features to the previous standards, including object-oriented language. They are scheduled for publication in 2002.

COBOL compilers for IBM mainframes

Compiler	Standard	Description
OS/VS COBOL	1974	This compiler has been phased out of most shops.
VS COBOL II	1985	This compiler is still used in many COBOL shops.
COBOL for MVS & VM	1985	This compiler runs under the MVS and VM operating systems.
COBOL for OS/390 & VM	1985 plus 1989 functions	This compiler runs under the OS/390 and VM operating systems.

COBOL compilers developed by Merant

Compiler	Description
Micro Focus Personal COBOL	An inexpensive COBOL compiler that is an excellent tool for learning COBOL on a PC. Developed by Micro Focus, now part of Merant.
Net Express	A development environment that takes core business processes written in COBOL and extends them to the Web and other distributed platforms.
Mainframe Express	A complete workbench for developing COBOL programs for mainframes. By setting an option, the compiler can emulate any mainframe compiler.
Object COBOL Developer Suite for UNIX	Provides an integrated environment for developing client/server and standalone applications for UNIX platforms and the leading relational databases.

COBOL compilers

- Before a COBOL program can be run on a computer, the COBOL language must be converted to machine language. This is called *compiling* a program, and it's done by a program called a *COBOL compiler*.

- Some COBOL compilers are based on the 1974 standards, some on the 1985 standards, and some on the new 2000 standards.

- If a compiler meets the specifications of a specific standard (like COBOL-85), it is called a standard COBOL compiler, even if it has non-standard *extensions*.

Figure 1-2   COBOL standards and compilers

An interactive COBOL program

With that as background, you're now going to learn how to write a simple interactive program. Before you see this program, though, you should understand the difference between an interactive and a batch program. In addition, you should understand the difference between the interactive program presented here and interactive programs developed for business.

An *interactive program* interacts with the user by displaying information on the screen and accepting data in response. This type of program is easy to start with because it doesn't require the use of files. That way, you can focus on the overall structure, content, and logic of the program rather than on the statements for handling files. Then, in chapter 3, you'll see a simple batch program that works with files. In contrast to an interactive program, a *batch program* runs without interacting with the user and typically processes the data in one or more disk files.

When you develop professional interactive programs, you probably won't use the techniques illustrated in this chapter. Instead, you'll use non-standard extensions. If you're developing programs for an IBM mainframe, for example, you'll probably use CICS (Customer Information Control System) as shown in chapter 19. And if you're developing programs for other platforms, you'll use non-standard COBOL that's designed for those platforms as shown in chapter 17. So keep in mind as you read this chapter that the programs are for training purposes only.

An interactive session

Figure 1-3 presents an interactive session as it's displayed on a PC monitor. Here, the shaded data is data that has been entered by the computer user. All of the other data is displayed by the COBOL program.

As you can see, this program calculates and displays the sales tax for the amount of a purchase. The sales tax rate in this case is 7.85%. When the user enters 100.00, for example, the program displays the number 7.85. And when the user enters 10.00, the program displays the number .79, which is the sales tax rounded to the nearest penny. If the user continues to enter numbers, the program will continue to display the sales tax for each number.

To end the session, the user enters 0 instead of another number. Then, after it displays END OF SESSION, the program ends.

An interactive session on a monitor or terminal

```
-------------------------------------------------
TO END THE PROGRAM, ENTER 0.
TO CALCULATE SALES TAX, ENTER THE SALES AMOUNT.
100.00
SALES TAX =      7.85
-------------------------------------------------
TO END THE PROGRAM, ENTER 0.
TO CALCULATE SALES TAX, ENTER THE SALES AMOUNT.
10.00
SALES TAX =       .79
-------------------------------------------------
TO END THE PROGRAM, ENTER 0.
TO CALCULATE SALES TAX, ENTER THE SALES AMOUNT.
29.99
SALES TAX =      2.35
-------------------------------------------------
TO END THE PROGRAM, ENTER 0.
TO CALCULATE SALES TAX, ENTER THE SALES AMOUNT.
0
END OF SESSION.
```

Description

- The shaded numbers above are the entries made by the computer user. All of the other characters are displayed by the COBOL program.

- When the user enters a sales amount other than zero, the program calculates the sales tax, displays the result, and asks for the next amount.

- When the user enters a zero, the program displays END OF SESSION and ends.

Figure 1-3   An interactive session for calculating sales tax

The COBOL code

Figure 1-4 presents the complete COBOL code for the interactive program. This code will run on any standard COBOL compiler. In the rest of this chapter, you'll learn how this program works.

For now, though, please notice that the program is divided into four divisions: the Identification Division, the Environment Division, the Data Division, and the Procedure Division. You'll learn more about the code in each of these divisions later in this chapter and throughout this book. For now, just realize that the division headers are required in every COBOL program.

Please notice also how the periods are used throughout the program. As you can see, they are used at the ends of division and section headers. They are used at the ends of paragraph names like 000-CALCULATE-SALES-TAX and PROGRAM-ID. They are used at the ends of the data descriptions in the Working-Storage Section of the Data Division. And they are used at the ends of the statements in the Procedure Division.

When a computer runs a COBOL program, it starts with the first executable statement in the Procedure Division. The computer then executes the statements that follow in sequence, unless this sequence is changed by a Perform or Perform Until statement. In this figure, the first statement is a Perform Until statement, which performs procedure 100-CALCULATE-ONE-SALES-TAX.

In this program, procedure 000 performs procedure 100 until the value in the field named END-OF-SESSION-SWITCH equals Y. Since this field starts with a value of N in the Working-Storage Section, the Perform Until statement always performs the 100-CALCULATE-ONE-SALES-TAX paragraph the first time through the code.

When a Perform Until statement performs another paragraph, the computer executes all of the statements in that paragraph, from the first to the last. When it's finished, it returns to the Perform Until statement, which is executed again. This continues until the condition in the Perform Until statement becomes true. The program then executes the statements that follow the Perform Until statement. In this program, the first statement that follows displays this message: END OF SESSION. The next statement ends the program.

If you have any experience with other programming languages, you should be able to understand how this code works without further help. In the Working-Storage Section, you can see the definitions of the fields that are used by the program. In the Procedure Division, you can see the statements that use these fields.

If, on the other hand, you don't have any programming experience, the pages that follow present everything you need to know for writing a program like this. As you read on, please refer back to the program in figure 1-4 whenever you need to see how the parts of the program fit together.

The interactive program

```
IDENTIFICATION DIVISION.
*
PROGRAM-ID. CALC1000.
*
ENVIRONMENT DIVISION.
*
INPUT-OUTPUT SECTION.
*
DATA DIVISION.
*
FILE SECTION.
*
WORKING-STORAGE SECTION.
*
77  END-OF-SESSION-SWITCH       PIC X          VALUE "N".
77  SALES-AMOUNT                PIC 9(5)V99.
77  SALES-TAX                   PIC Z,ZZZ.99.
*
PROCEDURE DIVISION.
*
000-CALCULATE-SALES-TAX.
*
    PERFORM 100-CALCULATE-ONE-SALES-TAX
        UNTIL END-OF-SESSION-SWITCH = "Y".
    DISPLAY "END OF SESSION.".
    STOP RUN.
*
100-CALCULATE-ONE-SALES-TAX.
*
    DISPLAY "-----------------------------------------------".
    DISPLAY "TO END PROGRAM, ENTER 0.".
    DISPLAY "TO CALCULATE SALES TAX, ENTER THE SALES AMOUNT.".
    ACCEPT SALES-AMOUNT.
    IF SALES-AMOUNT = ZERO
        MOVE "Y" TO END-OF-SESSION-SWITCH
    ELSE
        COMPUTE SALES-TAX ROUNDED =
            SALES-AMOUNT * .0785
        DISPLAY "SALES TAX = " SALES-TAX.
```

Identification
Division

Environment
Division

Data
Division

Procedure
Division

Description

* The Identification Division identifies the program by giving the program name.

* The Environment Division includes the Input-Output Section, which identifies the input and output files used by the program.

* The Data Division includes the File Section and the Working-Storage Section. The File Section describes the files identified in the Input-Output Section, and the Working-Storage Section defines other data items used by the program.

* The Procedure Division contains the program logic. It is typically divided into procedures that contain the statements that do the functions of the program.

Figure 1-4   The COBOL code for the sales tax program

Basic coding rules

Figure 1-5 presents some of the basic coding rules for COBOL programs. To start, you should realize that the first six columns (or positions) in each coding line are left blank when you're using a COBOL compiler. Then, when you compile the program later on, the compiler adds sequence numbers in these positions.

The seventh column in each coding line can be used to identify a line as a *comment*. If there is an asterisk in column 7 (the *indicator column*), this means that the rest of the line is ignored by the compiler. If the rest of the line is left blank, the line can be referred to as a *blank comment*, and blank comments can be used to provide vertical spacing in the COBOL code. In this program, that's the only way that comments are used, but you'll soon see other uses for them.

Columns 8 through 11 in each coding line are referred to as the *A margin*, and columns 12 through 72 as the *B margin*. This is significant because some coding elements have to start in the A margin, and some have to start in the B margin. Although you can start an element anywhere in the A or B margin when that's required, it's customary to start A margin elements in column 8 and B margin elements in column 12.

The last eight positions in each coding line (73-80) aren't used by modern COBOL compilers. These positions originally were used for the name of the program. That was back when COBOL programs were punched into 80-column cards so they could be read by the card reader of a computer system. In the COBOL-2000 standards, the limitation of 80 positions per line will be dropped.

Although the code in this program is in all uppercase (capital) letters, COBOL isn't case sensitive. As a result, you can code a program in capital letters, lowercase letters, or any combination of the two. In practice, though, you usually use one or the other throughout since that's the most efficient way to type code. On mainframes, it's customary to use all capitals; on PCs, it's customary to use all lowercase letters.

When you need to use quotation marks in a coding entry, you can use double quotes (") or single quotes ('). On mainframes, single quotes (or apostrophes) are normally used, but that can be changed by a compiler option. On mid-range computers and PCs, double quotes are normally used. In this book, double quotation marks are used in all the programs.

To separate two coding elements like the words in a Procedure Division statement, you use one or more spaces. This means that you can use spacing to align or indent coding elements. In the Working-Storage Section, for example, you can see how extra spacing is used to align the Pic clauses. In the Procedure Division, you can see how extra spacing is used to indent the Until clause to show that it's part of the Perform statement that starts on the line above.

The A and B margins of a COBOL program

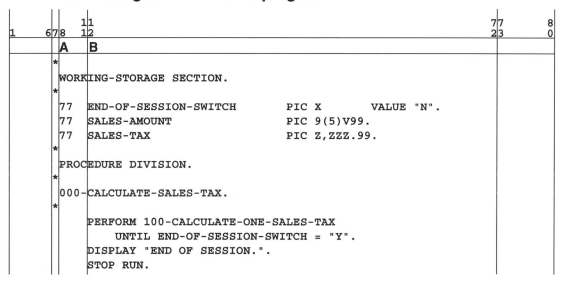

```
                11                                       77        8
1      678      12                                       23        0
         A  B
       *
          WORKING-STORAGE SECTION.
       *
          77  END-OF-SESSION-SWITCH        PIC X         VALUE "N".
          77  SALES-AMOUNT                 PIC 9(5)V99.
          77  SALES-TAX                    PIC Z,ZZZ.99.
       *
          PROCEDURE DIVISION.
       *
          000-CALCULATE-SALES-TAX.
       *
             PERFORM 100-CALCULATE-ONE-SALES-TAX
                 UNTIL END-OF-SESSION-SWITCH = "Y".
             DISPLAY "END OF SESSION.".
             STOP RUN.
```

The components of each line of code

Columns	Purpose	Remarks
1-6	Sequence	A sequence number is added to each coding line when the program is compiled. As a result, the programmer doesn't enter anything in these positions.
7	Indicator	If you code an asterisk in this column, the entire line is treated as a *comment*, which means it's ignored by the compiler. You can also use a slash (/) in this column to force the program listing to start on a new page when it is compiled or a hyphen (-) to continue the code from the previous line (see chapter 6).
8-11	A margin	Some coding elements (like division names, section names, procedure names, 77 level numbers, and 01 level numbers) have to start in this margin.
12-72	B margin	Coding lines that don't start in the A margin have to start in this margin.
73-80	Identification	These positions originally were used to identify a program, but they're not used today.

Coding rules

- You can use capital or lowercase letters when you code a COBOL program since the compilers treat them the same.

- When quotation marks are used, double quotes (") are required by most compilers. On IBM mainframes, though, single quotes (') are commonly used, although this can be changed to double quotes by a compiler option.

- One space is treated the same as any number of spaces in sequence. As a result, you can code more than one space whenever you want to indent or align portions of code.

Figure 1-5   Basic coding rules

How to code the Identification Division

Figure 1-6 shows how to code the Identification Division. The only required lines in this division are the division header and the Program-ID paragraph followed by the program name. Often, though, the Program-ID paragraph will be followed by a series of comments like those shown in this figure. These comments give more information about the program.

In standard COBOL, the program name can be up to 30 characters long, so a name like

```
CALCULATE-SALES-TAX
```

is a legal name. Many COBOL compilers, though, require names that are more restrictive than that. On an IBM mainframe, for example, you should keep the program name to eight characters or less using the rules presented in this figure. If you don't, the compiler will convert your name to one that does obey these rules. That's why the program in this example is named CALC1000.

In a mainframe COBOL shop, you usually are given the program name when a program is assigned to you so you don't have to create your own name. In addition, you usually are given specifications for what information you should provide through comments in the Identification Division.

Incidentally, the term *syntax* refers to the structure of a language. So the syntax at the top of this figure gives the structure that the Identification Division requires. In a syntax summary like this, the capital letters represent the COBOL words that are required. The lowercase letters represent entries made by the programmer. In the figures that follow, you'll learn the other conventions that are used in syntax summaries.

How to code the Environment Division

The Environment Division is used to identify any disk files that are used by the program. Since the sales tax program in this chapter doesn't use any, you don't have to write any code for this section. However, you still need to include the Environment Division header and the Input-Output Section paragraph that are shown in figure 1-4. In chapter 3, you'll learn how to develop programs that use disk files.

The syntax of the Identification Division

```
IDENTIFICATION DIVISION.
PROGRAM-ID. program-name.
```

An Identification Division with the minimum code

```
IDENTIFICATION DIVISION.
PROGRAM-ID.    CALC1000.
```

An Identification Division that contains comments

```
IDENTIFICATION DIVISION.
*
 PROGRAM-ID.       CALC1000.
*PROGRAMMER.       MIKE MURACH.
*COMPLETION-DATE.  MARCH 28, 2000.
*REMARKS.          THIS IS A SIMPLE INTERACTIVE PROGRAM THAT'S
*                  DESIGNED TO ILLUSTRATE THE USE OF COBOL.
*                  IT CALCULATES THE SALES TAX ON AN AMOUNT
*                  THAT HAS BEEN ENTERED BY THE USER.
```

The rules for forming a program name in standard COBOL

- Use letters, the digits 0 through 9, and the hyphen.
- Don't start or end the name with a hyphen.
- Use a maximum of 30 characters.

The rules for forming a program name on a mainframe compiler

- Start the name with a letter.
- Use letters and digits only.
- Use a maximum of 8 characters.

Typical comment entries in the Identification Division

- Who created the program and when it was completed.
- Who maintained the program and when that maintenance was completed.
- The purpose of the program.
- Any notes that will make the program easier to understand.

Figure 1-6   How to code the Identification Division

How to code the Working-Storage Section

Figure 1-7 gives the basic rules for coding the entries in the Working-Storage Section of the Data Division. When there are only a few entries, you can code them using 77 level entries as shown in this figure. To do that, you start by coding the number 77 in the A margin. Then, you code a *data name* starting in the B margin, usually in column 12. This is the name that will be used in the Procedure Division to refer to the *data item* that you're defining.

After the data name, you code a Picture clause that defines the format of the data item. Last, you can code a Value clause that gives a starting value to the item. One of the most important coding rules is that the Value clause should be consistent with the Picture clause. If it isn't, an error may occur when the program is compiled.

If your program requires more than just a few data items, you probably won't use 77 level numbers. Instead, you'll want to group related items to make them easier to find. You'll learn how to do that later in this chapter, after you learn how to create data names and code Picture and Value clauses.

How to create data names

Figure 1-7 gives the rules for forming data names. In brief, use letters, numbers, and hyphens with a maximum of 30 characters in each name. If you follow these rules, your names will be acceptable to the COBOL compiler.

However, it's also important to create data names that are easy to remember and understand. That's why long names like SALES-AMOUNT and SALES-TAX are better than short names like A1 and B2. Since a typical COBOL program contains dozens of data items, this is a critical factor for efficient programming. And the more data names a program uses, the more important this is.

Incidentally, one naming rule that isn't included in the summaries in this chapter is that a name created by a programmer can't be the same as a COBOL *reserved word*. Reserved words are those that are part of the COBOL language, like DATA, DIVISION, SECTION, WORKING-STORAGE, DISPLAY, ACCEPT, and PERFORM. If you follow our naming recommendations, though, you won't accidentally use a reserved word as one of your names.

Although the COBOL standards refer to *data items* and *data names*, you also can refer to a data item as a *variable* and to its name as a *variable name*. In addition, you can refer to a variable as a *field* because your data definitions are actually defining fields within internal storage. These terms are commonly used in other programming languages. In this book, we'll use all of these terms because a COBOL programmer should be able to use them all.

The Working-Storage Section of the interactive program

```
WORKING-STORAGE SECTION.
*
77   END-OF-SESSION-SWITCH        PIC X        VALUE "N".
77   SALES-AMOUNT                 PIC 9(5)V99.
77   SALES-TAX                    PIC Z,ZZZ.99.
```

Coding rules

- Code the level number (77) in the A margin, and code the data name, its Picture (PIC) clause, and its Value clause (if any) in the B margin.

- Code the Value clause so it is consistent with the Picture clause for each data item (see figure 1-9 for more information).

- Code a period at the end of each data item.

- You can use other level numbers when you want to group the items in working storage (see figure 1-10 for more information).

The rules for forming a data name

- Use letters, the digits 0 through 9, and hyphens only.

- Don't start or end the name with a hyphen.

- Use a maximum of 30 characters.

- Use at least one letter in the name.

Figure 1-7   How to code the Working-Storage Section

How to code Picture clauses

The Picture clause is used to define the data items that a program requires. When you code this clause, you normally code the abbreviation Pic followed by the characters that define the data item. In figure 1-8, you can learn how to code the pictures for the three types of data items you'll use the most.

When you code the characters in a picture, a number in parentheses means that the character is repeated that number of times. As a result, X(3) is equivalent to XXX, S9(3)V9(2) is equivalent to S999V99, and Z(4).9(2) is equivalent to ZZZZ.99.

When you define an *alphanumeric item*, you use X's to indicate the number of characters that can be stored in the item. Each of these characters means that one letter, digit, or special character can be stored in the item. Thus, a data item that's defined as X(3) can store values like 123, ABC, X2$, or just Y. If an alphanumeric item contains fewer characters than the picture provides for, unused positions to the right are filled with spaces. Thus, the data for the third example of an alphanumeric item is followed by five spaces.

When you define a *numeric item*, you use 9's to indicate the number of digits that can be stored in the item. You can also code a leading S to indicate that the item can have a plus or minus sign, and you can code one V to indicate where the decimal point is assumed to be. Thus, a data item that's defined as S999V99 can store values like +.05 and –999.95. If a numeric item contains fewer digits that the picture provides for, the unused positions to the left are set to zeros. As you will see later, it is the numeric items that you use in arithmetic operations.

When you define a *numeric edited item*, you use characters that make the data in the item easier to read. For instance, you can code a Z when you want a zero to the left of a number to be changed to a space, and you can use a comma or decimal point when you want to insert a comma or decimal point into a number. Then, when the program moves a numeric item to a numeric edited item, the data is converted to the more readable form. You'll learn more about this in figure 1-14.

When you code the pictures for the data items, you are actually defining the internal storage fields that are going to be used when the program is run. In general, each character or digit that you define in a Pic clause requires one *byte* of internal storage so an alphanumeric field that's defined as X(20) requires 20 bytes of storage, and a numeric edited field that's defined as ZZ,ZZZ.99- requires 10 bytes of storage.

For a numeric item, the V just marks the position of the decimal point so it doesn't require a storage byte. Similarly, the S indicates that the data item can include a sign, which is usually carried in the rightmost byte of the field along with the rightmost digit, so it doesn't require a separate storage byte. As a result, a numeric item that's defined as S999V99 usually requires just 5 bytes of internal storage. For more information about how data is defined and stored, please refer to chapter 6.

Some of the characters that can be used in Picture clauses

Item type	Characters	Meaning	Examples
Alphanumeric	X	Any character	PIC X
			PIC XXX
			PIC X(3)
Numeric	9	Digit	PIC 99
	S	Sign	PIC S999
	V	Assumed decimal point	PIC S9(5)V99
Numeric edited	9	Digit	PIC 99
	Z	Zero suppressed digit	PIC ZZ9
	,	Inserted comma	PIC ZZZ,ZZZ
	.	Inserted decimal point	PIC ZZ,ZZZ.99
	-	Minus sign if negative	PIC ZZZ,ZZZ-

Examples of Picture clauses

Alphanumeric items

Value represented	Picture	Data in storage
Y	X	Y
OFF	XXX	OFF
714 Main Street	X(20)	714 Main Street

Numeric items

Value represented	Picture	Data in storage	Sign
-26	999V99	02600	(no sign)
+12.50	999V99	01250	(no sign)
+.23	S9(5)V99	0000023	+
-10682.35	S9(5)V99	1068235	-

Numeric edited items

Value represented	Picture	Data in storage
0	Z(4)	(spaces)
0	ZZZ9	0
87	ZZZ9	87
+2,319	ZZ,ZZZ-	2,319
-338	ZZ,ZZZ-	338-
+5,933	Z,ZZZ.99-	5,933.00
-.05	Z,ZZZ.99-	.05-

Description

- The Picture clause (PIC) defines the format of the data that can be stored in the field.
- When coding a Picture clause, a number in parentheses means that the preceding character is repeated that number of times.
- When data is stored in an alphanumeric item, unused positions to the right are set to spaces. When data is stored in a numeric item, unused positions to the left are set to zeros.

Figure 1-8   How to code Picture clauses

How to code Value clauses

Figure 1-9 shows how to use a Value clause to assign a starting value to an alphanumeric or numeric data item. One way to do that is to code a *literal* in the Value clause. If the data item is defined as alphanumeric, you can code an *alphanumeric literal* in the Value clause by enclosing the characters in quotation marks. If the data item is defined as numeric, you can code a *numeric literal* in the Value clause by using the digits, a leading plus or minus sign, and a decimal point.

Another way to assign a value to a data item is to code a *figurative constant* in the Value clause. Although COBOL provides for a number of these, the two you'll use the most are ZERO (or ZEROS or ZEROES), which can be used to assign a value of zero to a numeric item, and SPACE (or SPACES), which can be used to assign all spaces to an alphanumeric item.

When you code a Value clause, it should be consistent with the data type that's defined by the Picture clause. For instance, a Value clause for a numeric item must contain a numeric value. Although it's okay to define a value that is shorter than the maximum entry for a data item, you can't define a value that is too large to be stored in the data item.

The use of literals in Value clauses

Type	Characters	Meaning	Examples
Non-numeric literal	Any	Any character	`VALUE "Y"` `VALUE "END OF SESSION"`
Numeric literal	0-9	Digit	`VALUE 100`
	+ or -	Leading sign	`VALUE -100`
	.	Decimal point	`VALUE +123.55`

The use of figurative constants in Value clauses

Type	Constant	Meaning	Examples
Numeric	`ZERO`	Zero value	`VALUE ZERO`
	`ZEROS`		`VALUE ZEROS`
	`ZEROES`		`VALUE ZEROES`
Non-numeric	`SPACE`	All spaces	`VALUE SPACE`
	`SPACES`		`VALUE SPACES`

Examples of data entries with consistent Picture and Value clauses

Alphanumeric items

```
77   CUSTOMER-ADDRESS    PIC X(20)       VALUE "213 W. Palm Street".
77   END-OF-FILE-SWITCH  PIC X           VALUE "N".
77   SEPARATOR-LINE      PIC X(20)       VALUE "--------------------".
77   BLANK-LINE          PIC X(30)       VALUE SPACE.
```

Numeric items

```
77   INTEREST-RATE       PIC 99V9        VALUE 12.5.
77   UNIT-COST           PIC 99V999      VALUE 6.35.
77   MINIMUM-BALANCE     PIC S9(5)V99    VALUE +1000.
77   GRAND-TOTAL         PIC S9(5)V99    VALUE ZERO.
```

Description

- The Value clause defines the value that is stored in the field when the program starts. As a result, the value should be consistent with the type of item that's defined by the Picture clause.

- In contrast to the rest of the program, the characters between the quotation marks in an alphanumeric literal are case sensitive. So the value of "End of Session" is: End of Session.

- If the Value clause defines a value that is smaller than the field defined by the Picture clause, an alphanumeric field is filled out with spaces on the right; a numeric field is filled out with zeroes on the left.

- If the Value clause defines a value that is larger than can be stored in the field defined by the Picture clause, a compiler error will occur.

- Because a numeric edited item typically receives a value as the result of a Move statement, it usually is not defined with a Value clause. See figure 1-14 for more information on the Move statement.

Figure 1-9   How to code Value clauses

How to code group items

A 77 level number in a data definition means that the item is independent of all other items. As the number of these items increases in a program, it becomes more difficult to find an item. If, for example, a program has 30 independent items, it's hard to find the one you're looking for when you need to check the spelling of its name or the way it's defined.

As some point, then, it makes sense to group related items as shown in figure 1-10. Here, the names used at the 01 level indicate how the subordinate items are related. In this case, the first group contains the fields that are going to receive the data entered by the computer user; the second group contains work fields that are needed by the program.

You also can use group items to show the structure of the data that you're defining. This is illustrated by the field named TODAYS-DATE. Here, the date is made up of three fields that represent the month, day, and year. In chapter 3, you'll see how grouping can be used to show the structure of the fields within a record.

When you group items, the item at the top is called a *group item* and the items that it's made up of are called *elementary items*. In this figure, USER-ENTRIES, WORK-FIELDS, and TODAYS-DATE are group items, and all the others are elementary items.

Because all but the simplest programs require a dozen or more working-storage fields, we recommend that you group the data items in all of your programs. That means that you shouldn't use 77 levels at all. We presented them in the first program only because you're likely to see them in other people's code.

A Working-Storage Section that contains group items

```
WORKING-STORAGE SECTION.
*
01  USER-ENTRIES.
*
    05  NUMBER-ENTERED          PIC 9         VALUE 1.
    05  INVESTMENT-AMOUNT       PIC 99999.
    05  NUMBER-OF-YEARS         PIC 99.
    05  YEARLY-INTEREST-RATE    PIC 99V9.
*
01  WORK-FIELDS.
*
    05  FUTURE-VALUE            PIC 9(7)V99.
    05  YEAR-COUNTER            PIC 99.
    05  EDITED-FUTURE-VALUE     PIC Z,ZZZ,ZZZ.99.
    05  TODAYS-DATE.
        10  TODAYS-MONTH        PIC 99.
        10  TODAYS-DAY          PIC 99.
        10  TODAYS-YEAR         PIC 9(4).
```

Description

- To code group items, you use the level numbers 01 through 49. Typically you will start with 01, and then use multiples of 5, such as 05 and 10. This allows you some room to add other levels later if you need to.

- Level 01 items must begin in the A margin. Other level numbers can begin in either the A or B margin.

- Whenever one data item has higher level numbers beneath it, it is a *group item* and the items beneath it are *elementary items*.

- In the example above, USER-ENTRIES, WORK-FIELDS, and TODAYS-DATE are group items. All of the others are elementary items.

- You can't code a Picture clause for a group item, and you have to code a Picture clause for an elementary item.

- A group item is always treated as an alphanumeric item, no matter how the elementary items beneath it are defined.

- To make the structure of the data items easy to read and understand, you should align the levels as shown above. However, this indentation isn't required.

Figure 1-10   How to code group items

How to code the Procedure Division

Figure 1-11 gives the basic rules for coding the Procedure Division. As you can see, the procedure names start in the A margin, and the statements start in the B margin. To make a statement easier to read, you can code extra spaces to indent portions of the statement. This is illustrated by the Perform and If statements.

In the pages that follow, you'll get detailed information about each of the statements used in the Procedure Division of the interactive program. But first, you need to know how to create valid procedure names.

How to create procedure names

Figure 1-11 gives the rules for forming *procedure names*. In brief, use letters, numbers, and hyphens with a maximum of 30 characters in each name, and don't start or end the name with a hyphen. If you follow these rules, your names will be acceptable to the COBOL compiler.

However, it's also important to create procedure names that have meaning rather than names like P5 or MY-PROCEDURE-1. In a program with only two procedures, this doesn't matter much, but the more procedures a program contains, the more it matters.

That's why we recommend that each procedure name consist of a sequence number, a verb, an adjective, and an object. This is illustrated by the procedure names in this figure and in all the programs throughout this book.

In this book, the Procedure Divisions of all the illustrative programs are divided into paragraphs. As a result, you also can refer to a procedure name as a *paragraph name*. You should think of the code within each paragraph, though, as a *procedure* that represents one functional module. You'll understand this better when you learn how the Perform and Perform Until statements work.

The Procedure Division of the interactive program

```
PROCEDURE DIVISION.
*
000-CALCULATE-SALES-TAX.
*
    PERFORM 100-CALCULATE-ONE-SALES-TAX
        UNTIL END-OF-SESSION-SWITCH = "Y".
    DISPLAY "END OF SESSION.".
    STOP RUN.
*
 100-CALCULATE-ONE-SALES-TAX.
*
    DISPLAY "----------------------------------------------".
    DISPLAY "TO END PROGRAM, ENTER 0.".
    DISPLAY "TO CALCULATE SALES TAX, ENTER THE SALES AMOUNT.".
    ACCEPT SALES-AMOUNT.
    IF SALES-AMOUNT = ZERO
        MOVE "Y" TO END-OF-SESSION-SWITCH
    ELSE
        COMPUTE SALES-TAX ROUNDED =
            SALES-AMOUNT * .0785
        DISPLAY "SALES TAX = " SALES-TAX.
```

Margin use

- Code all procedure names starting in the A margin, and code all statements in the B margin.

Period use

- Although it isn't required with a COBOL-85 compiler, we recommend that you end each statement with a period. In chapter 5, you'll learn about the alternatives to this practice.

The rules for forming a procedure name

- Use letters, the digits 0 through 9, and hyphens only.
- Don't start or end the name with a hyphen.
- Use a maximum of 30 characters.

Description

- The Procedure Division of a program should be divided into paragraphs like the one above, where each paragraph represents one *procedure* of the program. The name of each paragraph can then be referred to as either a *paragraph name* or a *procedure name*.
- The name of the first procedure should represent the function of the entire program. The names of the procedures it calls should represent the functions performed by those procedures.

Figure 1-11   How to code the Procedure Division

How to code Accept statements

Figure 1-12 shows how the Accept statement works. It gets a value that the user has entered on the keyboard and stores the value in the data item named in the statement. If you look at the syntax for this statement, you can see that you just code the word ACCEPT followed by the data name for the item. Because the Accept statement doesn't display anything on the screen, it is usually issued after a Display statement to tell the user what to enter.

As the table in this figure shows, the data that's stored depends on the Picture of the data item that the entry is stored in. If, for example, the user enters a negative number but the Picture doesn't include an S, the sign isn't stored. If the user enters a numeric value that is larger than the data item can hold, the value is truncated on the left. And if the user enters an alphanumeric value that is larger than the data item can hold, the value is truncated on the right.

Although Accept statements work well when you're using a PC, they present a few problems when you're using a mainframe. As a result, you rarely use Accept statements to get user entries on a mainframe. In chapter 18, though, you can learn how to run programs that use Accept statements on a mainframe. And in chapter 19, you can learn the right way to code interactive programs on a mainframe.

The syntax of the Accept statement

```
ACCEPT data-name
```

An example of an Accept statement

```
ACCEPT SALES-AMOUNT.
```

The operation of some typical Accept statements

Picture	User entry	Value stored	Notes
S999	10	10	
S999	787	787	
S999	-10	-10	
S999	5231	231	Truncated on the left
999	-100	100	Sign dropped
9(3)V99	458.12	458.12	
9(3)V99	45812	812.00	Truncated on the left
9(3)V99	4735.26	735.26	Truncated on the left
X	Y	Y	
X	Yes	Y	Truncated on the right

Description

- When the Accept statement is run, the computer waits for the user to type an entry on the keyboard and press the Enter key.
- When the user presses the Enter key, the entry is stored in the variable identified on the Accept statement, and the cursor moves to the next line on the screen.
- The user entry should be consistent with the Picture of the variable. If it isn't, it will be truncated or adjusted as shown in the table.

Mainframe note

- On an IBM mainframe, the Accept statement gets its data from the SYSIN device. As a result, this device must be set to the terminal keyboard if you want this program to work interactively. Also, you have to enter the data more precisely when you use a mainframe than you do when you use a PC. In chapter 18, you'll learn how to run this type of program on a mainframe.

Figure 1-12   How to code Accept statements

How to code Display statements

Figure 1-13 shows how the Display statement works. If you look at the syntax for this statement, you can see that it consists of the word DISPLAY followed by a series of data names or literals. Here, the braces {} mean that you have a choice between the items separated by a vertical bar (|), and the ellipsis (…) means that you can code as many data names or literals as you need.

When the Display statement is executed, the values represented by the data names and literals are displayed on the screen in the sequence that they're coded. In the examples, you can see that the first four statements display one literal value each. The fifth statement displays the value in a data item. The sixth and seventh statements display an alphanumeric literal followed by the value in a data item followed by another alphanumeric literal.

The syntax of the Display statement

```
DISPLAY {data-name-1 | literal-1} ...
```

Examples of Display statements

```
DISPLAY " ".
DISPLAY 15000.
DISPLAY "------------------------------------".
DISPLAY "End of session.".
DISPLAY SALES-AMOUNT.
DISPLAY "THE SALES AMOUNT IS " SALES-AMOUNT ".".
DISPLAY "THE SALES TAX IS " SALES-TAX ".".
```

The data displayed by the statements above

```
(one space or a blank line)
15000
------------------------------------
End of session.
100.00
THE SALES AMOUNT IS 100.00.
THE SALES TAX IS  7.85.
```

Note: The last three display lines assume that SALES-AMOUNT has a Pic clause of ZZZ.99 and a value of 100.00 and that SALES-TAX has a Pic clause of ZZ.99 and a value of 7.85.

Description

- The Display statement displays one or more literal or variable values on the screen of a monitor or terminal. After it displays these values, the cursor moves to the next line on the screen.

- After the word DISPLAY, you can code one or more literals or variable names. For instance, the first statement above displays an alphanumeric literal value of one space (it looks like a blank line on the screen); the second statement displays a numeric literal value of 15000.

- If you code more than one literal or variable name after the word DISPLAY, you must separate them by one or more spaces. For instance, the last two statements above display an alphanumeric literal, a variable value, and another alphanumeric literal (the period).

Mainframe note

- On an IBM mainframe, the Display statement sends its data to the SYSOUT device. As a result, this device must be set to the terminal screen if you want this program to work interactively. You'll learn more about this in chapter 18.

Figure 1-13   How to code Display statements

How to code Move statements

Figure 1-14 shows you how to code Move statements. If you look at the syntax for this statement, you can see that you code a data name or literal after the word MOVE and a second data name after the word TO. Then, when the statement is executed, the value in the first data name or literal (the *sending field*) is stored in the data item represented by the second data name (the *receiving field*). Note that the original data remains in the sending field after the move operation.

If you look at the table of legal and illegal moves in this figure, you can see that the sending field and the receiving field need to be compatible. So you normally send alphanumeric data to an alphanumeric receiving field and numeric data to either a numeric or a numeric edited receiving field. Other types of moves may work if the items consist of unsigned integers, but you shouldn't need to use them.

When you move a numeric field to a numeric edited field, the data is *edited* before it is stored in the receiving field. This means that it is converted to the more readable form represented by the picture of the receiving field. If you look at the examples of this type of move, you can see that lead zeros are suppressed, commas and decimal points are inserted into numbers, and a minus sign is printed after a number to show that its value is negative. Although this is enough information to get you by for the next few chapters, you'll learn more about moving data to numeric edited fields in chapter 6.

The syntax of the Move statement

```
MOVE {data-name-1 | literal} TO data-name-2
```

Examples of Move statements

```
MOVE "Y" TO END-OF-SESSION-SWITCH.
MOVE 1 TO PAGE-NUMBER.
MOVE NUMBER-ENTERED TO EDITED-NUMBER-ENTERED.
```

Legal and illegal moves

Type of move	Legal?
Alphanumeric to alphanumeric	Yes
Numeric to numeric	Yes
Numeric to numeric edited	Yes
Alphanumeric to numeric	Only if the sending field is an unsigned integer
Alphanumeric to numeric edited	Only if the sending field is an unsigned integer
Numeric to alphanumeric	Only if the sending field is an unsigned integer

Examples of numeric to numeric edited moves

Picture of sending field	Data in sending field	Sign of sending field	Picture of receiving field	Edited result
S9(6)	000123	+	ZZZ,ZZ9-	123
S9(6)	012345	-	ZZZ,ZZ9-	12,345-
S9(6)	000000	(no sign)	ZZZ,ZZ9-	0
S9(4)V99	012345	+	ZZZZ.99	123.45
S9(4)V99	000000	(no sign)	ZZZZ.99	.00

Examples of truncation

Picture of sending field	Data in sending field	Picture of receiving field	Result
X(3)	Yes	X	Y
S9(6)	012345	S9(3)	345

Description

- The Move statement moves data from a literal or a sending field to a receiving field. However, the original data is retained in the sending field.
- If the sending field is a numeric item and the receiving field is numeric edited, the Move statement converts the data from one form to the other.
- If the receiving field is larger than the sending field, the receiving field is filled out with trailing blanks in an alphanumeric move or leading zeros in a numeric move.
- If the receiving field is smaller then the sending field, the data that's moved may be truncated. In general, you should avoid this type of move because you may not get the result that you expect.

Figure 1-14   How to code Move statements

How to code arithmetic expressions

Figure 1-16 gives you more information about the coding and evaluation of arithmetic expressions. To start, it gives the *order of precedence* of the arithmetic operations. Unless parentheses are used, this means that the exponentiation operations are done first, from left to right in the expression. Then, the multiplication and division operations are done from left to right. Last, the addition and subtraction operations are done from left to right.

If this isn't the sequence in which you want the operations done, you can use parentheses to change that sequence. Then, the operations in the innermost sets of parentheses are done first, followed by the operations in the next sets of parentheses, and so on until the operations in all the sets of parentheses have been done. Within a set of parentheses, though, the operations are still done in the order of precedence.

If that sounds complicated, the examples in this figure should help you understand how this works. There you can see how the use of parentheses can affect the result. In general, you should use parentheses to clarify the sequence of operations whenever there's any doubt about how the expression will be evaluated.

The order of precedence for arithmetic operations

1. Exponentiation (**)
2. Multiplication and division (* and /)
3. Addition and subtraction (+ and -)

The use of parentheses

- When you use parentheses within an arithmetic expression, the operations in the inner sets of parentheses are done first, followed by the operations in the outer sets of parentheses.

Examples of arithmetic expressions

Expression	A	B	C	D	Result
A + B + C	2	3	2		7
A + B + C	2	-3	2		1
A - B - C	2	3	2		-3
A + B * C	2	3	2		8
(A + B) * C	2	3	2		10
A + B * C ** D	2	3	2	2	14
(A + B) * C ** D	2	3	2	2	20
(A / (B * C)) ** D	12	3	2	2	4
A - B / B	125	100			124
(A - B) / B	125	100			.25
(A - B) / B * 100	125	100			25

Examples of Compute statements

Statement	A (After) S9(3)V9	A (Before) S9(3)V9	B S9(3)	C S9(3)
COMPUTE A = A + B	5.0	2.0	3	
COMPUTE A = A + 1	3.0	2.0	1	
COMPUTE A ROUNDED = B / C	.3	?	1	3
COMPUTE A = B / C * 100	66.6	?	2	3
COMPUTE A ROUNDED = B / C * 100	66.7	?	2	3
COMPUTE A = 200 / B - C	37.0	?	5	3
COMPUTE A = 200 / (B - C)	100.0	?	5	3
COMPUTE A = 10 ** (B - C)	Size Error	?	5	1
COMPUTE A = A + (A * .1)	110.0	100.0		
COMPUTE A = A * 1.1	110.0	100.0		

Description

- Unless parentheses are used, the operations in an expression take place from left to right in the *order of precedence*.
- To clarify or override the sequence of operations, you can use parentheses.

Figure 1-16   How to code arithmetic expressions

How to code Add statements

Figure 1-17 presents the basic syntax for the two formats of the Add statement. You use this statement for simple additions that can be coded as easily with this statement as they can be with the Compute statement.

When you use the first format of this statement, the result is stored in the data item named in the To clause. If, for example, YEAR-COUNTER has a value of 7 when this statement is executed

```
ADD 1 TO YEAR-COUNTER
```

it has a value of 8 after the statement is executed. In this case, the receiving field has to be a numeric item.

When you use the second format, the result is stored in the data item named in the Giving clause. With this format, you can use either a numeric or a numeric edited item as the receiving field. If you use a numeric edited item, the result is edited when it is sent to the receiving field.

The optional clauses of the Add statement are like those of the Compute statement. If the result may have more decimal places than the receiving field provides for, you can code a Rounded clause. If the result may be larger than the receiving field provides for, you can code an On Size Error clause. In most cases, though, you won't need either of these clauses with Add statements.

In addition to the Add statement, COBOL provides Subtract, Multiply, and Divide statements. These statements, which are presented in chapter 7, have formats that are similar to those for the Add statement. In general, though, the Compute statement is easier to use and its code is easier to read, so you may never need those statements.

The syntax of the Add statement

Format 1

```
ADD {data-name-1 | literal} TO data-name-2 [ROUNDED]
    [ON SIZE ERROR statement-group]
```

Format 2

```
ADD {data-name-1 | literal-1} {data-name-2 | literal-2} ...
    GIVING data-name-3 [ROUNDED]
    [ON SIZE ERROR statement-group]
```

Examples of Add statements

Format 1

```
ADD 1 TO YEAR-COUNTER.

ADD CUSTOMER-SALES TO GRAND-TOTAL-SALES.
```

Format 2

```
ADD OLD-BALANCE NEW-CHARGES
    GIVING NEW-BALANCE.

ADD JAN-SALES FEB-SALES MAR-SALES
    GIVING FIRST-QUARTER-SALES.
```

Description

- When you use format 1, the value in data-name-1 or a literal value is added to the value in data-name-2, and the result is stored in data-name-2. As a result, data-name-2 must be defined as a numeric item.

- When you use format 2, two or more values are added together and the result is stored in the data item that's named in the Giving clause. As a result, that item can be defined as either a numeric or numeric edited item.

- You can code the Rounded clause whenever the result can have more decimal places than is specified in the picture of the result field.

- You can code the On Size Error clause when there's a chance that the result may be larger than the receiving field. If it is, the statements in this clause are executed.

Figure 1-17   How to code Add statements

How to code If statements

Figure 1-18 shows you how to code an If statement. After the word *If*, you code a condition followed by one or more statements that are executed if the condition is true. After the word Else, you code one or more statements that are performed if the condition isn't true. You also can code an End-If *delimiter* to mark the end of the statement.

To code a simple condition within an If statement, you use a *relational operator* to set up a comparison between two data names or between a data name and a literal. If you want the negative of a condition, you code the word NOT before the operator. For instance, NOT > (not greater than) is the same as <= (less than or equal to).

As the syntax for the If statement shows, the Else clause and the End-If delimiter are optional. This is illustrated by the first two examples in this figure, which don't include these items. Here, the first statement executes a Move statement when the SALES-AMOUNT is zero. The second statement executes a Compute and a Display statement when the SALES-AMOUNT isn't equal to zero.

The next example is an If statement that includes both an Else clause and the End-If delimiter. This statement gets the same result as the two statements without the Else clauses.

The last example shows that you can code If statements within If statements. The result can be called *nested If statements*, and this nesting can continue many levels deep. Although End-If delimiters are used in this example, this nest of If statements would work the same without them. Sometimes, though, End-If delimiters are required for the logic to work correctly.

Note in all of the examples that periods aren't used to mark the ends of the statements within the If statement. Instead, one period is coded at the end of an entire nest of If statements. If you code a period within an If statement, the compiler assumes that the statement is supposed to end, which is a common coding error. That's why you use an End-If delimiter whenever you need to mark the end of an If statement within an If statement.

The syntax of the If statement

```
IF condition
    statement-group-1
[ELSE
    statement-group-2]
[END-IF]
```

The syntax of a simple condition

```
{data-name-1 | literal} relational-operator {data-name-2 | literal}
```

The relational operators

Operator	Meaning	Typical conditions
>	Greater than	`NUMBER-ENTERED > ZERO`
<	Less than	`999 < NUMBER-ENTERED`
=	Equal to	`END-OF-SESSION-SWITCH = "Y"`
>=	Greater than or equal to	`LINE-COUNT >= LINES-ON-PAGE`
<=	Less than or equal to	`SALES-THIS-YEAR <= SALES-LAST-YEAR`
NOT	The negative of the operator that follows	`NUMBER-ENTERED NOT = 0`

Examples of If statements

If statements without Else and End-If clauses

```
IF SALES-AMOUNT = ZERO
    MOVE "Y" TO END-OF-SESSION-SWITCH.
IF SALES-AMOUNT NOT = ZERO
    COMPUTE SALES-TAX ROUNDED = SALES-AMOUNT * .0785
    DISPLAY "SALES TAX = " SALES-TAX.
```

An If statement with Else and End-If clauses

```
IF SALES-AMOUNT = ZERO
    MOVE "Y" TO END-OF-SESSION-SWITCH
ELSE
    COMPUTE SALES-TAX ROUNDED = SALES-AMOUNT * .0785
    DISPLAY "SALES TAX = " SALES-TAX
END-IF.
```

Nested If statements

```
IF SALES-AMOUNT >= 10000
    IF SALES-AMOUNT < 50000
        COMPUTE SALES-COMMISSION = SALES * COMMISSION-RATE-1
    ELSE
        COMPUTE SALES-COMMISSION = SALES * COMMISSION-RATE-2
    END-IF
END-IF.
```

Description

- The If statement executes one group of statements if the condition it contains is true, another group of statements if the condition is false and an Else clause is coded.
- When coding an If statement within an If statement, you are coding *nested If statements*.
- The End-If *delimiter* can be used to mark the end of an If statement. This can be useful when you are nesting If statements.

Figure 1-18   How to code If statements

How to code Perform statements

The top portion of figure 1-19 shows how to code the Perform statement to execute a procedure. When the Perform statement is executed, the program skips to the first statement in the procedure named in the statement. Then, the computer executes the statements in this procedure. When the last statement in the procedure is executed, control returns to the first statement after the Perform statement.

This is an important COBOL statement because it lets you divide a large program into a number of manageable procedures. You'll see this statement illustrated in the interactive program presented at the end of this chapter. And you'll appreciate the value of this statement when you study the programs in later chapters.

How to code Perform Until statements

The lower portion of figure 1-19 shows how to code the Perform Until statement. With this statement, a procedure is performed until a condition becomes true. To code the condition in the Until clause of this statement, you use the same relational operators and syntax that you use for If statements.

If you look back to the Procedure Division code in figure 1-11, you should now understand what the Perform Until statement does. It performs the procedure named 100-CALCULATE-ONE-SALES-TAX until the value of the data item named END-OF-SESSION-SWITCH becomes equal to Y. This happens after the Accept statement gets a value of zero from the keyboard and the If statement that follows moves a Y to the switch field. When the condition becomes true, the computer continues with the next statement after the Perform Until statement.

How to code the Stop Run statement

The Stop Run statement stops the execution of a program. Each program should include just one Stop Run statement, and it is usually coded as the last statement in the first procedure of a program.

The syntax of the Perform statement

```
PERFORM procedure-name
```

An example of a Perform statement

```
PERFORM 100-GET-USER-ENTRIES.
```

The operation of the Perform statement

- The Perform statement skips to the procedure that's named and executes the statements in that procedure. Then, it returns to the statement after the Perform, and the program continues.

The syntax of the Perform Until statement

```
PERFORM procedure-name
    UNTIL condition
```

An example of a Perform Until statement

```
PERFORM 100-CALCULATE-ONE-SALES-TAX
    UNTIL END-OF-SESSION-SWITCH = "Y".
```

The operation of the Perform Until statement

- The Perform Until statement tests a condition to see whether it is true. If the condition isn't true, the statement performs the procedure that it names. This continues until the condition becomes true. Then, the program continues with the statement after the Perform Until statement.

- The execution of a Perform Until statement is often referred to as a *processing loop*, or simply a *loop*.

- If the condition never becomes true, the program will continue until the operator interrupts it. This is a programming error.

- The condition in a Perform Until statement is formed the same way it is formed in an If statement.

Figure 1-19   How to code Perform and Perform Until statements

Another interactive COBOL program

This chapter ends by presenting another interactive program. That will give you a chance to see how the COBOL you've learned in this chapter can be applied to another application.

An interactive session

Figure 1-20 presents an interactive session that is controlled by another COBOL program. Here, the program prompts the user to enter three values: investment amount, number of years, and interest rate. Then, the program calculates the future value of the investment and displays the result. The program repeats this until the user indicates that the program should end.

In this example, the future value is the value of an investment of $10,000 that is held for 10 years and gets 10.5 percent yearly interest. In other words, the program calculates how much the $10,000 investment will be worth if it draws 10.5% interest for 10 years. In this case, the result is $27,140.81.

To get the result, the program calculates the interest on the investment one year at a time using this formula:

```
Interest = Investment * Interest / 100
```

Here, the interest rate is divided by 100 so an entry of 10.5 gets treated as .105. As a result, the interest for the first year is $10,000 times .105, or $1050. The program then adds the interest for the year to the principal so the investment value at the end of one year is $11,050.

The program continues in this way for nine more years. For each year, the interest is calculated the same way, but the investment amount keeps increasing. That's the way compound interest works. By the end of the ten years, the investment amount has grown from $10,000 to $27,140.81.

Another interactive session on a monitor or terminal

```
----------------------------------------
To end the program, enter 0.
To perform another calculation, enter 1.
1
----------------------------------------
Enter investment amount (xxxxx).
10000
Enter number of years (xx).
10
Enter yearly interest rate (xx.x).
10.5
Future value =     27,140.81
----------------------------------------
To end the program, enter 0.
To perform another calculation, enter 1.
0
----------------------------------------
End of session.
```

Description

- The shaded numbers above are the entries made by the computer user. All of the other characters are displayed by the COBOL program.

- This program calculates the future value of an investment amount that accumulates interest at a given rate for a given number of years. This can be referred to as compound interest.

Figure 1-20   An interactive session for calculating the future value of an investment

The COBOL code

Figure 1-21 presents the Working-Storage Section and Procedure Division for the interactive session shown in figure 1-20. Unlike the program in figure 1-4, which is coded in capital letters, this one is coded in lowercase letters. Instead of blank comments, this program uses blank lines (with no asterisk in column 7) to provide spacing within the code. This is the style that is commonly used when developing COBOL programs on a PC.

In the Working-Storage Section, you can see how 01 levels are used to group the data items into fields that receive user entries from Accept statements and fields that are required by calculations. Although the 05 levels could be coded as 77 levels, the grouping makes it easier to find the fields you're looking for.

In procedure 100, you can see a Perform statement that performs procedure 110-get-user-values. This puts six related statements in a separate procedure, which makes the program easier to read and understand. The alternative is to code these statements in procedure 100 in place of the Perform statement (without the periods that end these statements).

Also in procedure 100, you can see a Perform Until statement that performs procedure 120 until a field named year-counter is greater than a field named number-of-years. Note that the field named year-counter is set to 1 before this Perform Until statement is executed and that this field is increased by 1 each time procedure 120 is executed. That means procedure 120 will be performed once for each year that the investment amount is held. Note also that the investment amount that has been entered by the user is moved to a field named future-value before this procedure is performed.

Now, if you study procedure 120, you can see that a single Compute statement calculates a new future value each time this procedure is executed. In effect, this statement says: The new future value equals the old future value plus the interest that is calculated for the year. Because the investment amount is moved to the future-value field before this procedure is performed, the interest for the first repetition is based on the original investment amount. But after that, the interest is compounded.

When the Perform Until statement in procedure 100 ends, a Move statement moves the future value into a numeric edited field and a Display statement displays the edited future value. The program then returns to the Perform Until statement in procedure 000, which performs procedure 100 again.

If you're new to programming, this should give you a pretty good idea of what programming is like. Every detail matters. And even in a simple program like this, the logic can get complicated in a hurry.

Do you understand exactly how this program works? If not, you don't need to worry about that right now. In the exercises for the next chapter, you'll step through this program one statement at a time and see how the data changes after each statement is executed. That should clear up any questions you still have about how this program works.

The future value program

```
working-storage section.

01  user-entries.

    05  number-entered          pic 9           value 1.
    05  investment-amount       pic 99999.
    05  number-of-years         pic 99.
    05  yearly-interest-rate    pic 99v9.

01  work-fields.

    05  future-value            pic 9(7)v99.
    05  year-counter            pic 999.
    05  edited-future-value     pic z,zzz,zzz.99.

procedure division.

000-calculate-future-values.

    perform 100-calculate-future-value
        until number-entered = zero.
    display "End of session.".
    stop run.

100-calculate-future-value.

    display "----------------------------------------".
    display "To end the program, enter 0.".
    display "To perform another calculation, enter 1.".
    accept number-entered.
    display "----------------------------------------".
    if number-entered = 1
        perform 110-get-user-values
        move investment-amount to future-value
        move 1 to year-counter
        perform 120-calculate-next-fv
            until year-counter > number-of-years
        move future-value to edited-future-value
        display "Future value = " edited-future-value.

110-get-user-values.

    display "Enter investment amount (xxxxx).".
    accept  investment-amount.
    display "Enter number of years (xx).".
    accept  number-of-years.
    display "Enter yearly interest rate (xx.x).".
    accept  yearly-interest-rate.

120-calculate-next-fv.

    compute future-value rounded =
        future-value +
            (future-value * yearly-interest-rate / 100).
    add 1 to year-counter.
```

Figure 1-21   The COBOL code for the future value program

Perspective

The goal of this chapter has been to get you started with COBOL programming as quickly as possible. If this chapter has succeeded, you now should understand how the code in the two illustrative programs works. You may even be ready to code simple interactive programs of your own.

Before you can actually run a COBOL program, though, you need to enter it into the computer, compile it, and test it. That's why the next chapter shows you how to do these tasks when using Micro Focus Personal COBOL on your own PC. When you complete that chapter, you'll be able to develop programs of your own.

Summary

- COBOL is a standard programming language that can be run on any computer that has a COBOL compiler to create the machine language that will run on the computer. Most COBOL compilers today are based on the 1985 standards.

- An *interactive program* gets its input data from the keyboard of a mainframe *terminal* or PC, and it displays its output data on the screen of a terminal or PC *monitor*. In contrast, a *batch program* processes the data in one or more disk files without interacting with the user.

- A COBOL program consists of four divisions: Identification, Environment, Data, and Procedure.

- When you code a program, some lines must start in the A margin and some in the B margin. If a line has an asterisk in column 7, it is treated as a *comment*, which means that it is ignored by the compiler. To make a program easier to read, you can use *blank comments* or blank lines for vertical spacing and extra spaces for horizontal spacing.

- The Working-Storage Section in the Data Division defines the *data items* that are used by the program. For each item, you code a Picture clause to define the format. You can also code a Value clause to give the item a starting value. A data item can also be referred to as a *field* or *variable*.

- The Procedure Division consists of *procedures*, or *paragraphs*. When a program is run, the computer executes the statements in this Division in sequence starting with the first one in the first procedure, unless a Perform or Perform Until statement changes this sequence by performing one of the other procedures.

- The Accept and Display statements are input and output statements. The Move statement moves data from one field in storage to another, sometimes with *editing*. The Compute and Add statements are arithmetic statements. The If statement is a logical statement. And the Stop Run statement ends the execution of a COBOL program.

Terms

platform	interactive program	alphanumeric literal
mainframe computer	batch program	numeric literal
mid-range computer	comment	figurative constant
terminal	indicator column	group item
central processing unit	blank comment	elementary item
CPU	A margin	procedure name
internal storage	B margin	paragraph name
main memory	syntax	procedure
PC	data name	sending field
monitor	data item	receiving field
processor	reserved word	editing
RAM	variable	arithmetic expression
random-access memory	variable name	arithmetic operator
COBOL standards	field	order of precedence
COBOL-85	alphanumeric item	delimiter
COBOL-2000	numeric item	relational operator
compile	numeric edited item	nested If statements
COBOL compiler	byte	processing loop
extension	literal	loop

Objectives

- Given a COBOL listing for a simple interactive program like the ones in this chapter, explain what each statement in the program does.

- Identify the primary difference between a mainframe computer and a PC.

- Distinguish between these sets of terms: terminal and monitor; CPU and processor; main memory and RAM.

- Distinguish between a set of COBOL standards and a COBOL compiler.

- Identify the location and use of these portions of a line of COBOL code: indicator column, A margin, B margin.

- List three rules for forming any name in a COBOL program.

- Describe the purpose of a Picture clause and a Value clause.

- Distinguish between a group item and an elementary item.

- Describe the operation of any of the statements presented in this chapter:

Accept	Compute	Perform
Display	Add	Perform Until
Move	If	Stop Run

Questions

The questions that follow are designed to test whether you can do the tasks defined by the chapter objectives. Although questions aren't included after the other chapters in this book, objectives are included so you'll know what you should be able to do when you complete a chapter.

1. What is the primary difference between a mainframe computer and a PC?

2. What is the difference between a terminal and a monitor? A CPU and a processor?

3. In a line of COBOL coding, where is the indicator column located and what is it used for?

4. List three rules for forming any COBOL name.

5. What does a Picture clause do? A Value clause?

6. What's the difference between a group and an elementary item?

7. What does each of the following statements do when it is run?

Accept	Move	Perform	Compute
Display	If	Perform Until	Stop Run

Refer to figure 1-4 as you answer the questions that follow. These are designed to make sure that you know how this program works.

8. What are the first six statements that are executed when the program is run? (Just list the verbs of these statements in sequence.)

9. If the user enters a zero when the first Accept statement is run, what statements are run before the program ends? (Just list the verbs.)

10. If the user enters 25 when the first Accept statement is run, what statements are run before the Accept statement is run again? (Just list the verbs.)

11. What happens if the user enters 100000 and the entry is truncated?

12. If the Value clause for the END-OF-SESSION-SWITCH mistakenly sets the value to Y instead of N, what statements will be executed before the program ends? (Just list the verbs.)

Refer to figure 1-21 as you answer the questions that follow.

13. If the investment amount that's entered by the user is $125 and the interest rate is 10 percent, what is the value of the future-value field after procedure 120 has been executed one time?

14. If the picture of the future-value field is changed to S9(7), what does this field contain after procedure 120 has been executed one time?

2

How to compile
and test a program
with Personal COBOL

In this chapter, you'll learn how to enter, compile, test, and debug a program when you're using Micro Focus Personal COBOL on a PC. When you finish this chapter, you'll be able to develop programs on your own using that compiler.

In addition, this chapter will give you a good background for learning how to develop programs on other platforms or with other compilers. Even if you use a different compiler on the job or at your school, though, we recommend that you use Personal COBOL to learn on your own PC. It is an inexpensive product that is a terrific training tool.

If you do use a different compiler on the job or at your school, you will of course have to learn how to compile and test programs with that compiler too. If, for example, you're going to develop programs for an IBM mainframe, chapter 18 shows you how to compile and test programs on that platform. You can read that chapter any time after you complete this one.

Introduction to Micro Focus Animator

To develop a program using Micro Focus Personal COBOL, you use the Micro Focus Animator. This Animator works essentially the same way for all versions of Micro Focus COBOL, including the versions for developing PC, UNIX, and mainframe applications. As a result, you'll be able to transfer the skills that you learn in this chapter to any of the other Micro Focus COBOL products.

The Integrated Development Environment

When you start Personal COBOL, an application window like the one shown in figure 2-1 is displayed. This is the *Integrated Development Environment*, or *IDE*, of Personal COBOL. The key component of this IDE is the Animator because you use it for entering, compiling, and testing code.

Within the application window are one or more *document windows*. By default, an empty document window is displayed when you start the Animator. However, you can open additional document windows to display existing program files or to create new files.

As in most Windows programs, you can use the menus in the Animator to issue commands. In the File menu, for example, you'll find commands for opening, saving, and printing files. You can also issue some of the most common commands by using the buttons in the toolbar. The first button on the toolbar, for example, lets you open an existing file.

Before you go on, you should know that Personal COBOL was written for Windows 3.1 systems. So if you're using a more recent operating system, such as Windows 95 or Windows 98, the Animator interface may seem somewhat dated. Nevertheless, you shouldn't have any trouble using Personal COBOL with one of these operating systems because this chapter presents everything you need to know.

The starting window for the Micro Focus Animator

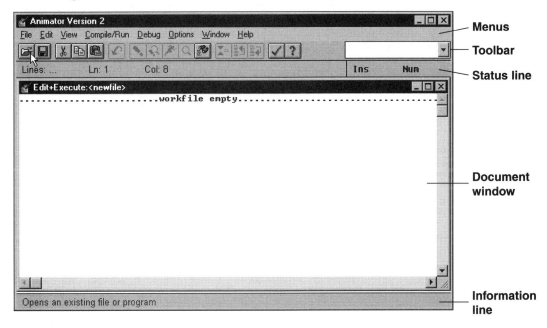

Description

- When you first start the Animator, an empty *document window* is displayed where you can enter the code for a new program. Usually, though, you'll start a new program from an existing program as shown in figure 2-5.

- You can use the menus or the toolbar buttons to issue commands. To find out what a toolbar button does, place the mouse pointer over it and a description is displayed in the *information line* at the bottom of the window. The information line is also used to display status information about various operations.

- The *status line* indicates the number of lines in the current file and the current location of the cursor in that file. At the right side of the status line is the *key status area*, which indicates the status of the Insert, Caps Lock, and Num Lock keys.

Figure 2-1   The Integrated Development Environment for the Animator

The two operating modes

When you use the Animator, you can open a file in two different modes. When you use the Open for Edit command in the File menu, the file is opened in *edit mode*. When you use the Open for Execution command, the file is opened in *execute mode*.

In either case, the mode of the file is indicated by the title bar of its document window. In figure 2-2, for example, the active window is opened in edit mode. In contrast, the inactive window is in execute mode (this is the empty document window that's opened by default when you start Animator).

When you work with a file in edit mode, you can only enter, edit, and compile the code in the file. Then, after the program compiles with no errors, you need to open the file in execute mode so you can test it. In this mode, you have access to all of the debugging tools that the Animator provides. Although you can open up to 50 programs in edit mode, you can open only one document at a time in execute mode.

The Animator with two open windows

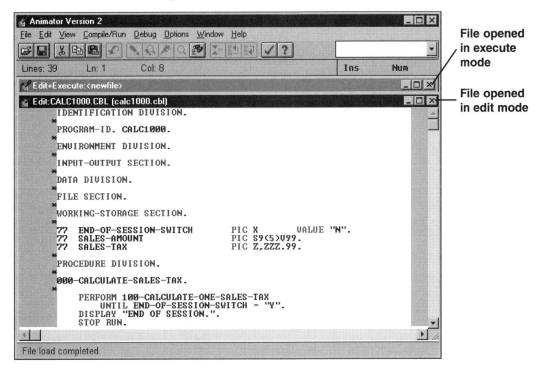

File opened in execute mode

File opened in edit mode

Description

- An Animator window can be opened in either *edit mode* or *execute mode*. The mode is indicated in the title bar of the window along with the name of the file that's displayed in the window.

- You use edit mode to enter and compile the code for a program. To open a program in edit mode, select the Open for Edit command from the File menu or click on the Open button in the toolbar.

- You use execute mode to test and debug a program after it has been compiled. To open a program in execute mode, select the Open for Execution command from the File menu.

- You can open up to 50 windows in edit mode, but you can open only one window in execute mode.

- If you select the New command from the File menu, a new document window is opened in edit mode.

Figure 2-2   The two operating modes of the Animator

A basic procedure for developing programs with the Animator

To develop a COBOL program with the Animator, you follow a procedure like the one outlined in figure 2-3. In step 1, you use edit mode to enter the *source code* for the program. This result is a *source program* that's stored in a *source file.* In step 2, you compile the source program to create an *intermediate file* that the Animator can execute.

At this point, you open the intermediate file in execute mode so you can do the next two steps. Then, in step 3, you *test* the program to see whether it works correctly. Here, your job is to test all possibilities until you're sure the program works correctly. For most programs, though, you'll find one or more errors. So in step 4, you *debug* the program, which means that you find and correct the causes of the errors.

As you develop COBOL programs, you'll run into three types of errors. A *compile-time error* occurs when the compiler can't convert a statement into machine language because its syntax is incorrect. Even if a program compiles without errors, though, the Animator may not be able to execute some of the statements in the program. In that case, a *run-time error* occurs. Finally, a *logical error* occurs when the program runs successfully, but the results aren't as expected.

An intermediate file opened in execute mode

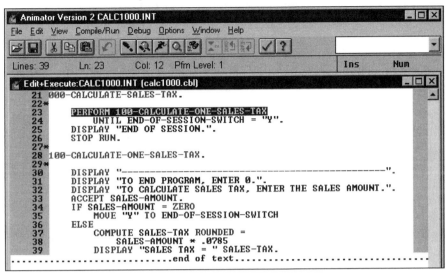

A basic program development procedure

1. Use edit mode to enter the *source code* for the program, and save this *source program* in a file with *cbl* as the extension (the default). This file can be referred to as the *source file*.

2. Compile the program to check its syntax, and correct any errors that are detected. When the program compiles without errors, an *intermediate file* is created. This file has the same name as the source file, but has an *int* extension.

3. Open the intermediate file in execute mode, and run it to see whether it works. This is known as *testing* a program.

4. If the program doesn't work correctly, find the errors, correct them, recompile the program, and test the program again. This is known as *debugging* a program.

Description

- The COBOL compiler compiles a program into machine language that the computer can understand. If a statement can't be compiled into machine language, a *compile-time error* occurs. See figure 2-10 for information on correcting compile-time errors.

- If a statement compiles cleanly but can't be executed, a *run-time error* occurs when you run the program. See figure 2-12 for information on correcting run-time errors.

- Even if a program runs without encountering any errors, the results of the program may not be as expected. This type of programming problem is referred to as a *logical error*.

- The Animator provides debugging tools that help you find and correct the run-time and logical errors.

Figure 2-3   A basic procedure for developing programs with the Animator

How using Personal COBOL
differs from developing production programs

When you use Personal COBOL, the Animator always controls the execution of the programs that you develop. As a result, you can't use Personal COBOL to develop *production programs* that are used on the job because those programs have to run by themselves.

To illustrate the difference, figure 2-4 shows how a production program is developed. After the programmer uses an interactive editor to create the source program, the programmer initiates a three-step procedure that's run by the computer. As you can see, the output of the second step is an *executable* that is run by itself in the third step. In contrast, Personal COBOL isn't able to produce an executable, so you always have to run your programs through the Animator.

In step 1 in this figure, the COBOL compiler compiles the source program into an *object module* (or *object program*). If the source program uses any Copy statements (see chapter 11), the compiler copies the source code from the related copy members into the program as part of this process. The compiler also produces output like a compiler listing and a list of the compile-time errors (often called *diagnostics*). Sometimes, this output is printed, but it is often reviewed on the monitor or screen without ever printing it.

In step 2, the *linkage editor* program *link edits* (or *links*) the object module with any subprograms that the program requires into an executable. On most platforms, one or more system subprograms are required in this step. These subprograms do some of the specific types of processing that the program requires. In addition, the linkage editor can link the object module with user subprograms (see chapter 11). Although the linkage editor also produces some printed output in this step, programmers rarely need to refer to it.

In step 3, the executable version of your program is executed. This is the test run of your program. As a result, the program gets the input that it requires including keyboard or disk data, and the program produces the output it requires including display, disk, or printer data.

With minor variations in the terminology, this is the way a production program is prepared on all platforms: compile, link edit, and test. If you want to see how this is done on an IBM mainframe, please read chapter 18.

The three-step procedure that's done by the computer

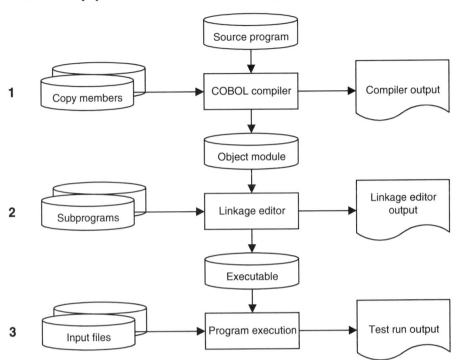

Description

- Before the three-step procedure shown above can be run by the computer, the programmer enters the source program using an interactive editor like Micro Focus Animator.

- When the source program is ready, the programmer initiates a three-step procedure that's done by the computer. In step 1, the COBOL compiler compiles the source program into an *object module*. In step 2, the *linkage editor* link edits the object module into an *executable*. In step 3, the executable is run so the programmer can see whether the program works.

- During step 1, the COBOL compiler inserts the source code that's in the copy members that are referred to by any Copy statements in the program (see chapter 11). The compiler also produces output like a compiler listing or a list of any compile-time errors.

- During step 2, the linkage editor link edits the object program with any system subprograms or user subprograms that it needs (see chapter 11). The linkage editor also produces linkage editor output.

- Step 3 is the test run for the program. It gets whatever input the program specifies and produces whatever output the program specifies. In contrast to the way you test a program with Micro Focus Personal COBOL, this test run is independent of the development environment.

Figure 2-4   How a production program is compiled, link edited, and tested

How to enter and edit a program

Now that you have a general idea of how to use the Animator to develop COBOL programs, you're ready to start working on your own programs. So the topics that follow show you how to enter and edit a program and how to use some of the Animator features that will save you time as you work.

How to start a new program

If you want to start a new program, you can enter code into the empty document window that's displayed when you first start the Animator. Or, you can open a new document window in edit mode using the New command on the File menu. Because every COBOL program requires some of the same coding, though, you should rarely, if ever, start a new program from scratch.

Instead, you should start a new program from an old program that is similar to the one you're going to develop. At the least, the old program will have the required division and section headers in it. And it may have a lot of other code that you can modify for use in the new program.

Figure 2-5 shows you how to start a new program from an old one with Personal COBOL. In step 1, when you use the Open for Edit command to open an old program, the Open dialog box is displayed. Since Personal COBOL originally was written for use with Windows 3.1, though, this dialog box uses the Windows 3.1 interface. In case you aren't familiar with this interface, this figure shows you how to use it to set the current folder to the one that you use for your programs. Later in this chapter, you'll learn how to change the default folder so it's displayed whenever you open a file.

As soon as you open the file, you should use the Save As command to save it with a new name. That way, you won't forget to do that later on and accidentally save the changes you make to the original file. Here again, the Save dialog box uses the Windows 3.1 interface, so you can change the current folder using the techniques shown in this figure. In addition, you have to use eight or fewer characters in the new file name with no intervening spaces because that's what Windows 3.1 required. This is true even if you're using Personal COBOL with Windows 95 or 98.

After you've saved the file, we recommend that you close it, then open it again to edit it. That's because of a quirk in the way Personal COBOL works. If you bypass this step, you can't compile the program immediately after editing it. Instead, the Animator closes the file and returns you to the old program you opened in step 1. So closing and re-opening the file as suggested in step 3 will save you some frustration later on.

Once you've saved the old program with the new name, you can delete the statements you don't need, modify the statements you do need, and add all the new statements that you need. Often, you can pick up dozens of statements from an old program when you start a new program this way. That's why this is one of the keys to increased programmer productivity.

The Open dialog box

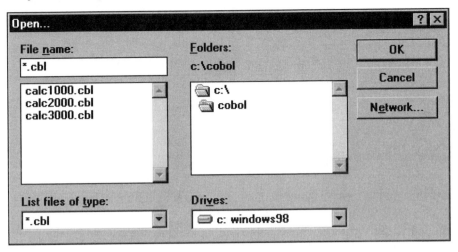

How to start a new program from an old program

1. Use the Open for Edit command in the File menu to open an old program that is similar to the new one that you're going to develop.

2. Use the Save As command in the File menu to save the file with a new name that contains eight or fewer characters.

3. Close the file, then open it again for editing.

4. Delete the portions of the old program that you don't need.

5. Modify the portions of the old program that are appropriate for the new program.

How to change the current folder in the Open or Save dialog box

1. To change the drive, choose a new drive from the Drives drop-down list.

2. To change the folder, double-click on the top-level folder in the Folders list box (c:\ in the example above) so all of its subfolders are displayed. Then, double-click on the first subfolder in the path that you want to establish, and continue double-clicking on subfolders until you reach the folder you want.

Figure 2-5   How to start a new program from an old program

How to enter and edit code

Before you learn how to enter code, you should know that you typically compose a program right at the keyboard. In other words, you don't write it down on paper before you enter it, although that used to be common practice. Today, interactive compilers make it easy to change program code on the fly, so it's more efficient to just enter the program code directly at the keyboard. Although this may take some practice at first, that's the way professional programmers work.

Figure 2-6 shows you how to enter COBOL code into the document window. Notice that the left and right margins are set the way you want them for a COBOL program because that's how the *COBOL profile* for the Animator is set. In addition, this profile provides for tab stops every fourth position so it's easy to align and indent your code.

If you've ever used a word processor, you shouldn't have any trouble using the Animator since the basic editing techniques are the same. The main difference is that you enter COBOL programs one line at a time, and you press the Enter key at the end of each line to start the next line. With a word processor, you have to press the Enter key only when you want to start a new paragraph.

Because this book assumes that you are already familiar with the way Windows programs work, it doesn't present detailed operational instructions for entering and editing code. As a result, this figure just summarizes some of the typical editing operations. Later, when you experiment with the Animator, you'll see that entering and editing a program isn't too much different from entering and editing a document, although the Animator features aren't quite as slick as those of a word processor.

The Animator while a program is being entered into it

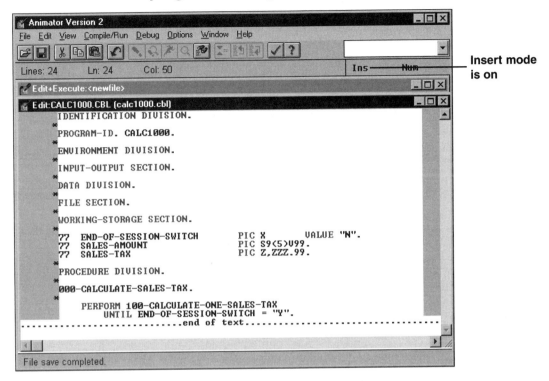

Insert mode is on

Description

- The Animator uses colors to identify various elements of code. By default, the COBOL reserved words are displayed in green and the programmer entries are displayed in black.

- The *COBOL profile* is set so the white area of the document window represents positions 8 through 72 with tab stops at every fourth position. The gray areas represent positions 1-7 and 73-80.

How to enter code

- To move to the next tab stop, press the Tab key. To move to column 7 so you can enter an asterisk into it, use the left arrow key or click on it with the mouse. To start a new line, press the Enter key.

- To turn insert mode on or off, press the Insert key. This controls whether you insert new code or type over existing code when you type.

How to edit code and undo the last editing operation

- To delete one or more lines of code, highlight the lines and press the Delete key. To move or copy lines of code, highlight them and use the standard Windows Cut (Ctrl+X), Copy (Ctrl+C), and Paste (Ctrl+V) commands.

- Click on the Undo toolbar button to undo up to 100 operations (Ctrl+Z doesn't work).

Figure 2-6   How to enter and edit code

Special features for working with code

Figure 2-7 presents some of the time-saving features you can use as you enter and edit your program. To start, this figure shows you how to display the *button bar* because its buttons are easier to use than the toolbar buttons. However, this bar isn't displayed by default. As a result, you need to do this procedure so the button bar is displayed in all of your coding sessions.

Once you've got the button bar displayed, you can use its buttons to start many of the common Animator functions. One of these buttons is the Find button, which can be used to start the Find feature. You can use this feature to find one or more occurrences of the text that you enter. If you check the Replace box in this dialog box, you can also enter the text for a find and replace operation.

When you click on the All button to find all the occurrences of the text, the lines that contain those occurrences are tagged and highlighted as shown in this figure. Then, you can move from one *tagged line* to another as described in this figure. You can also *compress* all of the tagged lines so only those lines appear in the document window, after which you can *expand* the tagged lines so all of the lines appear again.

If you find yourself having to scroll back and forth between two or more procedures or statements in a long program, you may want to mark them with a generic *tag* so you can move to them more easily. To do that, you can right-click on a line number and select the Tag command from the shortcut menu. Then, this tag appears in the left margin of the statement:

```
Tag->
```

Once the statements are tagged, you can move from one tag to another the same way that you move from one Find tag to another. You can also compress and expand these tags.

If more than one type of tag is displayed at the same time, you can move from one type of tag to another by placing the cursor in a line that has the type of tag you want to move to before you start the move operation. If, for example, both Tag and Find tags are displayed, you can move the cursor to a Tag line before you press the F8 key to move to the next Tag line. If you start a move operation when the cursor isn't in a tagged line, the Animator displays a small menu that lets you choose the type of tagged line that you want to move to.

Similarly, you can compress all the lines except those that have a certain kind of tag. To do that, place the cursor on a line that has that type of tag and click on the Compress button. Or, select the tag type from the shortcut menu that's displayed when you click on the Compress button.

The easiest way to remove all of the tags in a program is to compile the program, which you'll soon learn how to do. Otherwise, you can right-click on a generic tag and choose the Unset command in the shortcut menu to remove that tag. Or, to remove all Find tags, you can use the Clear Finds command in the Edit menu. Most of the time, though, you'll just compile the program to remove all tags.

The Find dialog box and the highlighted lines that result from its command

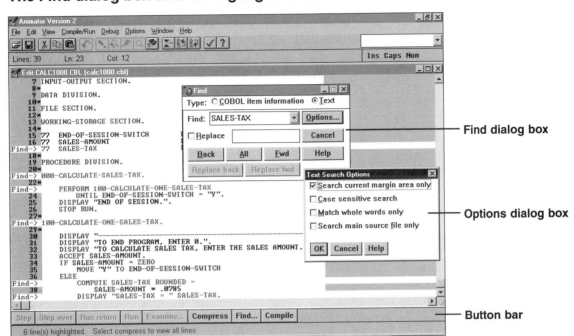

Find dialog box

Options dialog box

Button bar

How to display the button bar

- Pull down the Options menu and choose the Configure Interface command. In the dialog box that's displayed, click on the Button Bar icon at the far left (the second one from the top) so its options are displayed. Then, check the Bar Visible option, click on the Save button, click OK on the message that's displayed, and click on the Close button.

How to use the Find command to find and replace text

- To display its dialog box, click on the Find button and select the Text option. Then, after you enter the text for what you want to find and replace, you click on the buttons to set options, to find or replace one occurrence of the text, or to find or replace all occurrences. When you click on the All button, all of the lines that contain the occurrence are tagged.

How to move to, compress, and expand tagged lines

- To move from one tagged line to another, click on the Previous or Next toolbar button or press the F7 or F8 key.
- To compress the display so only the tagged lines are shown, click on the Compress button (which then turns into an Expand button). To redisplay all the lines of code, click on the Expand button.

How to remove tagged lines

- Compile the program as shown in figure 2-9. Or, to remove Find tags, choose the Clear Finds command in the Edit menu.

Figure 2-7   Special features for working with program code

As you experiment with the Animator, you'll discover that it has many other features. You'll also discover that you can start most features in more ways than figure 2-7 shows, including using regular menus, shortcut menus, toolbar buttons, and button bar buttons. This figure, though, presents some of the most useful features and the most efficient ways to work with them.

How to set the default folder

By default, when you save a file, the Animator saves it in the same folder where Personal COBOL is installed. And when you open an existing file, the default is to look in that folder for the file. In most cases, though, you'll want to save the files you create in a different folder. Although you can switch to the appropriate folder every time you save a new file or open an existing file, it's easier to just change the default folder. Figure 2-8 shows you how to do that.

As you can see in this figure, you change the default folder from the Properties dialog box for Personal COBOL. The easiest way to display this dialog box is to locate Personal COBOL on the Windows Programs menu, right-click on it to display its shortcut menu, and choose the Properties command from that menu. Then, you can enter the path for the folder you want to use as the default in the Start In box. In this case, the default folder has been changed to C:\cobol. (Since this isn't case sensitive, you don't have to worry about the capitalization.)

How to print a source program

To print the source code for a program from the Animator, you can use the Print command in the File menu. This can be useful when you're debugging a long program or correcting its compile-time errors. Unfortunately, there is no way to print selected pages, so you have to print the entire program even if you make just a minor change to it. As you get used to working with programs on the screen, though, you'll find that you rarely need printed listings.

Another way to print a source program is to use a text editor like NotePad or a word processing program like Word. After you open the source file, you can change its formatting and print the entire program or selected portions. Often, this works better than using the Animator to print the program.

The Properties dialog box for Personal COBOL and how to display it

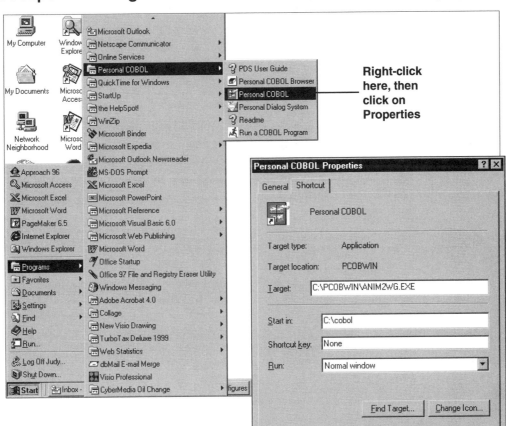

How to display the Properties dialog box

- Click on the Start button in the Windows taskbar and locate the Personal COBOL entry in the Programs menu. Right-click on the entry to display the shortcut menu, and choose the Properties command.

How to change the default folder

- Change the Start In option in the Properties dialog box to the folder that will contain your program files and click on the OK button. The folder you specify will be displayed by default each time you open or save a file. This change will take effect the next time you run Personal COBOL.

Figure 2-8   How to set the default folder

About the exercises in this book

If you're new to programming, the best way to master COBOL is to practice on a PC. That's why this book provides practice exercises that guide you through the process of developing COBOL programs. These exercises are designed for use with Micro Focus Personal COBOL because it's an inexpensive product that is an excellent training tool.

If you don't already have Micro Focus Personal COBOL, the last page in this book shows you how to order and install it. That page also shows you how to copy the programs and data from the CD ROM in this book to the C drive on your PC. Once you've installed Personal COBOL and copied the programs and data, you're ready to start the exercises.

Exercise 2-1   Get started with the Animator

This exercise helps you get started with Animator by guiding you through some common operations. It also guides you through the process of setting the defaults so the Animator is easier to use.

Set the default folder for the Animator

1. Click on the Windows Start menu, locate the Personal COBOL entry in the Programs menu as shown in figure 2-8, and right-click on it. Then, click on the Properties option in the shortcut menu that appears.

2. In the dialog box that appears, enter c:\cobol in the Start In text box as shown in figure 2-8, and click on the OK button. We recommend that you use this folder for all of the programs that you develop.

Start Personal COBOL and review its buttons

3. Start Personal COBOL, maximize its window, and close the window for the new file.

4. Use your mouse to point to one of the toolbar buttons, and look at the description that appears in the information line at the bottom of the screen. Then, use this technique to review the other toolbar buttons.

5. Use the procedure in figure 2-7 to display the button bar. Then, move the mouse pointer to one of the buttons and note the description in the information line.

Start a new program from an old program

6. Click on the Open toolbar button to start the Open command. If you did steps 1 and 2 right, the folder should be set to c:\cobol, and several files should be listed. Then, double-click on calc2000 to open that file.

7. Use the Save As command in the File menu to save the file as int0000. Then, close the file and open it for edit again (this is necessary due to a quirk in the way Personal COBOL works).

Navigate through the program

8. Press the Page Up or Page Down key to move through the program one screen at a time. Next, press the arrow keys to move one line or character at a time. Then, click on the vertical scroll bar to move through the program.

9. Press the Ctrl key plus the left or right arrow key to move from word to word in the program. Then, press the Ctrl key plus the up or down arrow key to move from paragraph to paragraph.

Edit the program

10. Press the Insert key and notice how this turns insert mode on or off as indicated by *Ins* in the status line. With insert mode off, move to the Program-ID paragraph and change the program name to INT0000.

11. Move to the start of procedure 120. Next, hold down the Shift key as you press the right arrow key to highlight the procedure name. Then, press the Delete key to delete the highlighted text. To restore that text, click on the Undo button in the toolbar.

12. Drag the mouse over two characters or lines so you can see that the mouse only lets you highlight complete lines. Next, drag the mouse over all the lines in procedure 120 including the procedure name. Then, press Ctrl+C to copy the lines, move the cursor to the start of procedure 110, and press Ctrl+V to paste the copied lines into the text. Last, undo the operation.

13. Repeat step 12, but cut the lines instead of copying them and use the toolbar buttons instead of the shortcut keys for cutting and pasting. Then, undo that operation.

Use the Find command and generic tags

14. Use the Find command as shown in figure 2-7 to find each occurrence of FUTURE-VALUE. Next, use the Previous and Next toolbar buttons or the F7 and F8 keys to move from one occurrence to another. Then, compress and expand the source code. Last, use the Clear Finds command in the Edit menu to clear the find tags.

15. Repeat step 14 with the "Match whole words only" option on.

16. Tag the line in working storage that defines FUTURE-VALUE and the first line in procedure 120 that refers to this field. To do that, right click on each line number and select the Tag command from the shortcut menu. Next, use the F7 and F8 keys to move from one tag to another. Last, remove the tags by using the shortcut menus again.

Continue to experiment, then close the program

17. Review the commands in the File, Edit, and View menus to see that you can also use these menus to start commands. Then, experiment on your own until you feel comfortable with the way the Animator works.

18. Save your changes and close the file using the Save button in the toolbar and the Close command in the File menu.

How to compile and test a program

Once you've entered the source code for a program, you're ready to compile and test it. During these steps of program development, you'll find and correct any errors in your program.

How to compile a program

Figure 2-9 shows how to compile a program. The easiest way to start the compile is to click on the Compile button in the button bar. Then, you respond to any dialog boxes that are displayed until the compile is finished.

When you compile a program, the Animator checks the syntax of the code to be sure it's correct. When it's done, the Animator displays a window that lists all the errors it found as shown in the next figure. In addition, each line of code that contains an error is highlighted in the document window, and an Error> tag is placed in the left margin so the errors are easy to locate.

The first time you compile a program, sequence numbers are added in the left margin. These numbers are updated each time you compile the program so they're always in sequence. In addition, various elements of the code are displayed in different colors so they're easy to identify. For example, all the data names are displayed in red.

The Animator window after a compile with errors

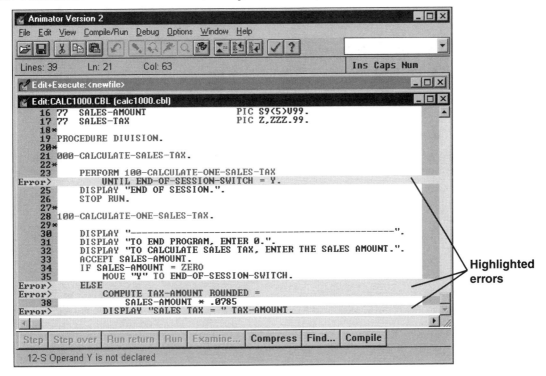

Highlighted errors

Description

- The easiest way to start a compile is to click on the Compile button.

- If you make changes to a program, you must save it before you compile it. If you don't, the Animator will prompt you to save the changes.

- If errors occur during the compile, a dialog box is displayed that describes each error (see the next figure), and the errors are highlighted in the document window.

- After you compile a program, sequence numbers appear in the left margin. Reserved words, variable names, literals, procedure names, and comments also appear in different colors so they're easy to identify.

Figure 2-9   How to compile a program

How to correct compile-time errors

When the Personal COBOL compiler comes to a statement that it can't compile into machine language, it displays the dialog box shown at the top of figure 2-10. From this box, you can continue checking the code with or without displaying additional error messages, or you can cancel the compilation. When the compile ends, all of the errors that were found are listed in a window like the one in this figure. You can use this window along with the highlighted statements in the document window to correct the errors.

Most of the time, you can find the errors without much trouble by studying the error messages and the source code. If, for example, you study the messages in this figure and the code in the previous figure, you should be able to tell what caused the errors in just a minute or two. If you can't do that, though, the exercises at the end of this section will guide you through the corrections.

This figure also describes some techniques that you can use to work with the list of errors and the highlighted statements in the document window. For example, you can double-click on an error in the list to move to the statement that's in error in the source code. And you can use the F7 and F8 keys or the Previous and Next buttons in the toolbar to move between errors in the document window.

After you correct the errors, you need to save the program and compile it again. Then, if additional errors are detected, you need to repeat the correction process until the program compiles without any errors. That can be referred to as a *clean compile*. When the program compiles with no errors, the compiler creates an intermediate file, which you can open in execute mode to test the program.

The dialog box that's displayed when a compile-time error occurs

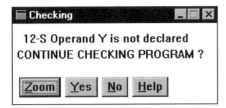

The window that describes all the compile-time errors

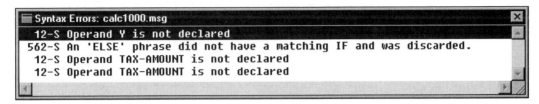

The four buttons in the Checking dialog box

Zoom   Completes the compile without displaying any additional errors

Yes   Completes the compile and displays additional errors

No   Cancels the compile

Help   Displays a description of the error

Description

- When an error occurs during a compile, the Checking dialog box is displayed with a description of the error. Then, you usually click on the Zoom button so that dialog box isn't displayed any more but the compiler keeps on checking for errors. When the compiler finishes, the Syntax Errors window is displayed and the error lines are highlighted as shown in figure 2-9.

- If you double-click on an error in the Syntax Errors window, the cursor moves to the line of code that contains the error.

- To move from one error to another in the document window, click on the Previous or Next toolbar button or press the F7 or F8 key.

- To compress the display so only the error lines are displayed, click on the Compress button (which then changes to an Expand button). To expand the display, click on the Expand button.

- If you study the error messages and the source code, you should be able to figure out what's wrong with each highlighted statement. Then, you can correct the errors and compile again.

- If you need more information on an error, you can right-click on the highlighted statement and choose the Error Help command from the shortcut menu that's displayed.

Figure 2-10   How to correct compile-time errors

How to test a program

Figure 2-11 shows you how to run a program so you can test whether it works right. If you've been working in edit mode and you've just gotten a clean compile, you first need to open the program for execution. When you do that, you'll notice that the first executable statement in the program is highlighted. Then, you can just click on the Run button to start the execution of the program.

When you run a program that uses Accept or Display statements, a *text window* like the one at the top of this figure is displayed. Then, whenever an Accept statement is executed, the program waits for your entry. After you enter a value and press the Enter key, the program continues.

As you will soon see, the text window that's used for an Accept or Display statement is small, dark, and hard to read. But if the program is executed on its own (not within the Animator), it will use the full display screen. As you learned earlier in this chapter, though, one of the limitations of Personal COBOL is that it doesn't let you create executables that can be run on their own. To do that, you have to use a more full-featured compiler like the ones you learned about in chapter 1.

When a program runs until the Stop Run statement is executed, it is a *normal program termination*. In that case, a dialog box like the one in this figure is displayed with a *return code* of zero. But that doesn't mean the program is correct. You still have to study the output of the program to make sure that it worked correctly. If it didn't, you need to debug the program.

As you debug a program, you may need to run it two or more times to determine why it isn't working correctly. To re-run a program, though, you can't simply click on the Run button again. That's because when a program ends, whether it terminates normally or with a run-time error, the last statement that was executed is highlighted. If you click on the Run button at this point, the Animator will attempt to execute this statement again, which isn't what you want. Instead, you have to restart the program as described in this figure.

This figure also presents two techniques for cancelling the execution of a program. The first technique (pressing the Ctrl and the Break keys at the same time) is particularly useful for cancelling a program that's "caught in a loop." That can happen if a Perform Until statement is executing and the condition in the Until clause is never met. Unless you cancel out of the program, it will run indefinitely. The only time you can't use the Ctrl+Break key combination is if an Accept statement is being executed. Then, you have to use Ctrl+K.

Due to some bugs in Personal COBOL, cancelling a program doesn't always work the way you want it to. In some cases, you have to shut down Personal COBOL and restart it. In the worst cases, you have to shut down your entire system and restart it. Whenever possible, then, you should try to avoid logic errors that require cancelling a program.

The text window that's displayed when you run an interactive program

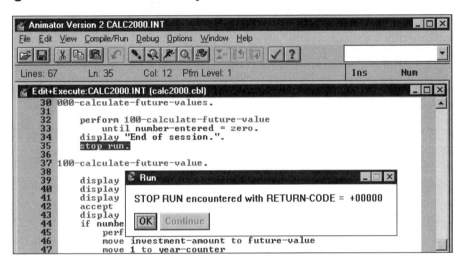

The document window and the dialog box that's displayed when a program terminates normally

How to start the execution of a program

- To run a program, open the compiled program (*int* extension) in execute mode. Then, click on the Run button.

How to cancel the execution of a program

- You can press Ctrl+Break to cancel the execution of a program that's stuck in a loop or a program that displays a text window like the one shown above, unless an Accept statement is being executed. In that case, you can press Ctrl+K to cancel execution.

How to restart the execution of a program

- When a program terminates normally, the Stop Run statement is highlighted, indicating that it was the last statement executed. To run the program again, use the Restart Application command in the Compile/Run menu to move the current execution point to the first executable statement. Then, click on the Run button.

Figure 2-11   How to test a program

How to correct run-time errors

If a run-time error occurs during a test run, a dialog box like the one at the top of figure 2-12 is displayed. Then, when you click on the OK button in that box, you are returned to the Animator and the statement that caused the error is highlighted.

In the example in this figure, the Perform statement is highlighted. Because the message in the dialog box says that the problem is an illegal character in a numeric field, though, you can assume that the problem is with one of the variables in the Until clause of that statement. There, the values in the two variables are being compared numerically to see whether the first is greater than the second.

If you study the example, you can see that the statement before the high-lighted one has an asterisk in column 7, so it's treated as a comment and ignored by the compiler. But this is the statement that sets the year-counter variable to 1. If this isn't done and a Value clause hasn't given it a starting value, the data will usually be invalid because it has the value of whatever was left in those storage positions by the last program.

Invalid data in a numeric field is the most common cause of run-time errors in Personal COBOL. To help you figure out what caused the problem, you can display the current values of the variables. You can also set breakpoints and step through a program to see exactly what's happening as the program executes. You'll learn those debugging skills in the next topics.

When you know what the cause of the run-time error is, you can correct the error, recompile the program, and rerun it. When you recompile the program, it's automatically restarted so the first executable statement is highlighted. Then, you can just click on the Run button to execute it.

This figure also describes how Personal COBOL handles two conditions that usually cause run-time errors with other compilers. The first condition occurs when the result of an arithmetic operation is too large for the receiving field. In that case, Personal COBOL truncates the result. The second condition occurs when a Divide or Compute statement attempts to divide by zero. In that case, Personal COBOL treats the zero as a one.

Keep in mind that the results will be incorrect even though run-time errors won't occur for these conditions. That's why you need to check the results to make sure that neither one of these conditions led to an error. In contrast, if these conditions do cause run-time errors as they do on most other compilers, you don't have to worry that truncated or altered results will sneak into your program. Either way, though, you need to check the results to make sure they're accurate.

A dialog box for a run-time error

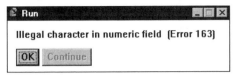

The Animator with the error statement highlighted

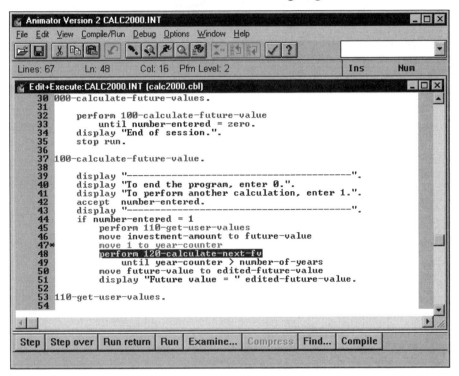

Description

- When a run-time error occurs, the program is interrupted and a dialog box that contains an error message is displayed.

- When you click on the OK button in the dialog box, you are returned to the code in the Animator with the statement that caused the error highlighted. You then can correct the error, recompile the program, and test it again.

- The most common cause of a run-time error is invalid numeric data.

How Personal COBOL handles two other types of run-time errors

- If an arithmetic operation has a result that is too large for the receiving field and the On Size Error clause hasn't been coded, the result is truncated instead of causing a run-time error.

- If a divide operation tries to divide by zero, the zero is treated as one instead of causing a run-time error.

Figure 2-12   How to correct run-time errors

Exercise 2-2   Test the sales tax program

This exercise will guide you through the process of compiling and running the sales tax program that's presented in chapter 1. This assumes that you've done exercise 2-1 so your default folder is set right and so the button bar is displayed.

Open the sales tax program for editing and compile it

1. Start Personal COBOL, and close the window for the new file.

2. Choose the Open for Edit command in the File menu or on the toolbar, and open the file named calc1000 that's in the c:\cobol folder. If your defaults are set right, you shouldn't have to change the folder before you open the file.

3. Click on the Compile button. This should result in a clean compile.

Open the program for execution and test it

4. Choose the Open for Execution command from the File menu, and open the file named calc1000.int. This is the intermediate version of the program that you just compiled. Note that you don't have to close the windows that are open for editing before you start this command.

5. Click on the Run button in the button bar to run the program in a text window.

6. For the first test run, enter zero and press the Enter key. A dialog box is then displayed that tells you that the program ended with a return code of zero. That means the program ended normally, so click on the OK button.

7. To run the program again, choose the Restart Application command from the Compile/Run menu. Then, click on the Run button again. For this test run, enter several values that will show you whether this program works correctly. When you're satisfied that it does, enter a zero to end the program.

Close the program

8. Close the sales tax program by clicking on the Close button in the upper right corner of the document window.

Exercise 2-3   Correct compile-time and run-time errors

This exercise forces you to correct some compile-time errors and fix a bug in the sales tax program. This will give you an appreciation for what you have to do when you compile and test your own programs.

Correct the compile-time errors

1. Open the program named calc100x for editing. Then, compile the program. When the Checking dialog box is displayed, click on the Zoom button to stop the compiler from displaying any more error messages.

2. Oops! There are several compile-time errors. These are the ones shown in figure 2-10. If you want more information about an error, right-click on the statement and choose the Error Help command.

3. Can you correct these errors on your own? You should be able to. At the least, try to correct them on your own before you read on.

4. The first error message says that the operand Y is not declared, which normally means that the variable isn't defined in the Data Division. In this case, though, Y is supposed to be a literal, so it should be coded as "Y".

5. The second message says that an Else phrase doesn't have a matching If. The problem, though, is that there's a period at the end of the line before the Else. Since a period ends a statement, the compiler thinks the word Else is the first word in the next statement.

6. The third and fourth messages say that the variable named SALES-TAX isn't declared, and this time the messages are right. If you look in the Data Division, you can see that a variable named TAX-AMOUNT is defined, but there's no variable named SALES-TAX.

7. Correct these errors and recompile the program. This time, there shouldn't be any errors. But if you did something wrong, fix it and recompile until you get a clean compile.

Test the program

8. Open the calc100x.int program for execution, and run it. Oops again! The program ends without calculating the sales tax.

9. To fix this problem, think about what must be happening. Somehow the program thinks that the condition in the first Perform statement is true when the program starts. When you figure out what the problem is, fix it, recompile the program, and rerun it. This time, the program should work correctly.

Close the program

10. Close the program.

How to use the debugging features

When you test a program and a run-time error occurs or the output isn't what you expect it to be, it can be difficult to locate the source of the errors just by looking at the code. That's why Personal COBOL supplies you with debugging tools that save you time and frustration as you test your programs. The topics that follow present the best of these tools.

How to display and modify the values of variables

When a program is interrupted by a run-time error, the Animator window is displayed in *break mode* and you can display the value of any variable by double-clicking on it. This opens a dialog box that shows the variable name and its value. In figure 2-13, for example, you can see that the value of the future-value variable at the time of the run-time error is 1000. You can also open a dialog box like this by clicking on the Examine button and entering the name of the variable you want to display in the resulting dialog box.

Another way to view the values of variables is to set up a *monitor/watch list* like the one shown in this figure. One way to do that is to click on the Add to List button in the dialog box for a single variable. In this example, two variables have been added to the Monitor/Watch List dialog box. In contrast to the dialog boxes for individual variables, this dialog box stays open from one execution of the program to another.

If you study the values in the monitor/watch list in this figure, you can see that the number-of-years variable has a valid value of 10, but year-counter has a value of:

    x"20 20 20"

Here, the *x* means that the value that follows is represented in *hexadecimal* (or *hex*) *code* with two hex digits for each byte of storage. If you know hex code, you know that hex 20 is the ASCII code for a blank, so the value in this numeric field is three blanks, which is an invalid numeric value.

In general, when you display the value of a numeric field, the Animator displays it in decimal if it is a valid numeric value. If it is invalid, though, the Animator displays it in hex. As a result, you don't need to know what the hex codes are to know when a field is invalid. Note, however, that you can display any characters in hex code by clicking on the Hex button in the display box. To learn more about hex codes, please refer to chapter 6.

If you want to change the value of a variable while a program is in break mode, you can do that from the dialog box that displays the variable's value. Just type over the value that's displayed and click on the Apply button. Or, if you're using a monitor/watch list, you can click on the Change button with the old value highlighted and then enter a new value. After you change the value to the one the one you want, you can click on the Run button to continue the test run with the new value.

The Animator while the program is in break mode

Two ways to display the value of any variable

- Double-click on the variable name. This opens a dialog box that displays the current value of that variable.

- Click on the Examine button. Then, enter the name of the variable whose value you want to display in the Examine dialog box, and click on OK.

How to set up a monitor/watch list

- The easiest way to set up a *monitor/watch list* is to display the value of a variable and then click on the Add to List button. If the Monitor/Watch List dialog box isn't already displayed, it's opened and the variable is added to it. Otherwise, the variable is added to the existing list.

How to change the value of a variable

- Display the value of the variable, then type the new value over the current value in the dialog box that's displayed and click on the Apply button.

- If the variable is displayed in the monitor/watch list, select the variable, click on the Change button, and enter the new value in the dialog box that follows.

Why hexadecimal code is used for some values

- If a numeric field contains invalid data, the Animator displays it in *hexadecimal* (or *hex*) *code* as shown for the year-counter field above. This code is preceded by an *x*. Then, each pair of hex characters that follows represents the data for one byte of storage. One of the most common forms of invalid numeric data is hex 20, which represents one space. For more information about hex code, please refer to chapter 6.

Figure 2-13   How to display and modify the values of variables

How to use breakpoints

Another valuable debugging feature is the ability to set breakpoints. This is illustrated in figure 2-14. When you set a *breakpoint* on a statement, the program enters break mode each time it comes to that statement. In this figure, for example, a breakpoint has been set on the Perform Until statement, as you can see by the BrkPt> tag in the left margin.

While in break mode, you can display and change the values of variables. In this figure, the monitor/watch list is used to display the values of the five variables used by the program. This lets you analyze the way this program works so you can tell for sure whether it's working correctly. If necessary, you can set two or more breakpoints in a program so you can monitor the operation of a program at all of its critical points.

The Animator when it reaches a breakpoint

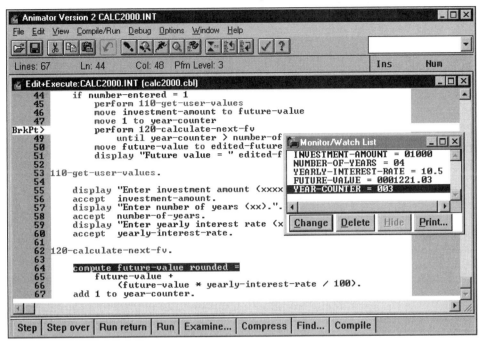

Description

- You can set a *breakpoint* on any executable COBOL statement or paragraph heading in the Procedure Division. Program execution stops when it reaches the statement you marked or the first statement in the paragraph you marked.

- When a program reaches a breakpoint, a dialog box is displayed. Then, you can click on Continue to continue program execution or on OK to display the document window in break mode so you can debug the program.

- In break mode, you can display and change the values of variables.

How to set and remove breakpoints

- The easiest way to set or remove a breakpoint is to double-click in the margin to the left of a statement. Another way to do that is to right-click on the statement to display the shortcut menu and then select the Breakpoint or Unset command.

- To remove all breakpoints, choose the Clear all Breakpoints command from the Debug menu.

Figure 2-14   How to use breakpoints

How to step through a program

From break mode or when you start a program, you can *step through the program* instead of running all the statements without intervention. Then, you can see how the values of the variables change as each statement or group of statements is executed. Figure 2-15 describes some of the techniques you can use to step through a program.

At the top of this figure, for example, you can see the result of clicking on the Step Over button after the program has reached the breakpoint on the Perform Until statement. This command causes the program to execute the performed procedure (in this case, procedure 120) without stopping. Then, it enters break mode again before the statement after the Perform Until statement is executed. In this case, the next statement is Move.

The simplest step technique is to step through the program one statement at a time. If, for example, you click on the Step button when the Move statement is highlighted, the Move statement is executed and the program enters break mode before the next statement is executed. This is illustrated by the examples in this figure. If you click on the Step button again, the program executes the next statement and enters break mode again. You can continue in this way until you're sure you understand how the program works. Whenever you want to run the rest of the program without stopping, you just click on the Run button.

Another step technique is to run the rest of the statements in the procedure that's currently executing without stopping. To do that, you use the Run Return command. You may want to do that if you enter a procedure that you already know works. Then, the program enters break mode again at the statement after the Perform statement that called the procedure.

The breakpoint and step features in combination with the features for displaying the values of variables can save you many hours of debugging time. In addition, these features are wonderful learning tools. By stepping through code that you don't understand and displaying the values of related variables, you can see exactly how a program works.

The Animator after the Step Over command is executed from the breakpoint

```
       37 100-calculate-future-value.
       38
       39     display "----------------------------------".
       40     display "To end the program, enter 0.".
       41     display "To perform another calculation, enter 1.".
       42     accept  number-entered.
       43     display "----------------------------------".
       44     if number-entered = 1
       45         perform 110-get-user-values
       46         move investment-amount to future-value
       47         move 1 to year-counter
BrkPt>         perform 120-calculate-next-fv
       49             until year-counter > number-of-years
       50         move future-value to edited-future-value
       51         display "Future value = " edited-future-value.
```

The Animator after the Step command is executed from the screen above

```
       37 100-calculate-future-value.
       38
       39     display "----------------------------------".
       40     display "To end the program, enter 0.".
       41     display "To perform another calculation, enter 1.".
       42     accept  number-entered.
       43     display "----------------------------------".
       44     if number-entered = 1
       45         perform 110-get-user-values
       46         move investment-amount to future-value
       47         move 1 to year-counter
BrkPt>         perform 120-calculate-next-fv
       49             until year-counter > number-of-years
       50         move future-value to edited-future-value
       51         display "Future value = " edited-future-value.
```

How to step through a program

- To execute the current statement, click on the Step button. After the statement is executed, the program enters break mode at the next statement.

- To execute the statements in a performed procedure without stopping, click on the Step Over button. After the performed statements are executed, the program enters break mode at the next statement after the Perform statement.

- To execute the rest of the statements in the current procedure without stopping, click on the Run Return button. Then, the program enters break mode at the statement after the Perform statement that called the procedure.

- To execute the statements up to the statement that contains the cursor without stopping, choose the Run to Cursor command from the Compile/Run menu.

- To execute all the remaining statements in the program without stopping, click on the Run button.

Figure 2-15   How to step through a program

A summary of the other debugging features

Figure 2-16 summarizes some of the other debugging features that are available with the Animator. Although you may never need to use any of these features, you may want to know what they are. If so, you can study this figure and the text that follows. Otherwise, you can skip to the next page.

In addition to the Step commands presented in figure 2-15, you can also use the Step All command. This command steps through all the statements in the program one at a time at the speed you specify. Note that the program doesn't enter break mode before it executes each statement. Instead, it executes at a reduced speed so you can see the values of the variables in the monitor/watch list as the program executes. You can also use the Step All dialog box that's displayed while the program is executing to change the execution speed or enter break mode.

The four Skip commands in this figure let you skip the execution of one or more statements. For example, you can use the Skip Statement command to skip the current statement, and you can use the Skip to Cursor command to skip all the statements between the current statement and the statement that contains the cursor.

The Set Advanced command lets you use some advanced features for setting breakpoints. For example, you can cause a program to enter break mode when the value of a variable changes or when a certain condition is met. These features can be useful for pinpointing the source of a logical error.

The Do Statement command lets you execute any valid COBOL statement while in break mode. After changing the value of a variable, for example, you may want to re-execute a statement that uses that variable. To do that, you just enter the statement into the dialog box that's displayed when you select the Do Statement command from the Debug menu.

You can use the last statement in this figure, Backtrack, to trace the execution of a program. To use this feature, you must turn backtracking on as described in this figure. Then, the Animator keeps a record of each statement that's executed, and you can use the Backtrack command to trace backwards through the program from the current statement. As you backtrack, the Animator simply highlights the previously executed statement.

Some of the other debugging features you can use with the Animator

Menu	Command	Description
Compile/Run	Step All	Displays a dialog box that lets you step through all the statements in a program at a selected speed. You can use the Step All dialog box to select the speed, stop program execution, and continue execution without stepping.
	Skip Statement	Skips execution of the current statement. The current execution point moves to the next physical statement in the program.
	Skip Return	Skips execution of the remaining statements in the procedure currently being performed.
	Skip to Cursor	Moves the current execution point to the statement that contains the cursor, skipping the execution of any statements prior to that statement.
	Skip to Start	Moves the current execution point to the first executable statement of the program without initializing the data in working storage.
Debug	Set Advanced	Displays a dialog box that lets you set advanced breakpoints. These breakpoints can (1) cause program execution to stop when the value of a specified variable changes; (2) cause program execution to stop at the specified line when a condition is met; (3) cause program execution to stop at any line when a condition is met; (4) cause program execution to stop when a specified program is entered; and (5) cause a specified COBOL statement to be executed when the line containing the breakpoint is reached.
	Do Statement	Displays a dialog box that lets you execute any valid COBOL statement.
	Backtrack	Displays a dialog box that lets you trace the execution of the statements in a program. Before you can use this command, you must select the Backtrack On option from the dialog box that's displayed when you choose the Execute Options command from the Options menu.

Additional help

- For more information on using these commands, see the online help for the Animator.

Figure 2-16   A summary of the other debugging features

Exercise 2-4   Test the future value program

This exercise will guide you through the process of compiling and testing the future value program that's presented in chapter 1. It will also show you how to use a breakpoint, step through the program, and display the values of variables.

Compile and test the program

1. Open the program named calc2000 for editing. Then, compile the program. This should result in a clean compile.

2. Open the program for execution. Then, run the program. When the text window is displayed, enter a value of zero for this first test run. This should end the program.

3. Restart the program, and run it again. This time, enter 100, 1, and 10 as the values for the investment amount, number of years, and interest rate. Does the program display the correct future value (110.00)?

4. Continue testing the program by entering values that test the minimum and maximum values. Note that you can test the minimum values easily, but if you enter large values, you'll start to get inconsistent results. That's because the future-value field isn't large enough to hold the calculated results, so Personal COBOL truncates them. When you're through experimenting, end the program.

Set a breakpoint and step through the program

5. Set a breakpoint on the Perform Until statement in procedure 100 as shown in figure 2-14. Next, set up a Monitor/Watch List dialog box so it displays the values for the five variables shown in that figure. Now, you can watch these variables change as you step through the program.

6. Restart the program and run it. When the Accept statements are executed, enter a 1 to perform another calculation, and enter 100, 3, and 10 for investment amount, number of years, and interest rate. When the breakpoint is reached, step through the program to see how the variable values change after each statement is executed and to see the sequence in which the statements are executed. When you're past the portion of the code that you're interested in, click on the Run button to continue without stopping.

7. If you want to try that again, enter another set of variable values and step through the program when the breakpoint is reached. This should clear up any questions that you have about how this program works. When you're satisfied that you understand it completely, end the program.

Close the program and end the Animator

8. Close the program. Then, exit from the Animator by clicking on the close button it the upper right corner of its window.

Perspective

Now that you know how to compile and test a program using Micro Focus Personal COBOL, you should be able write simple interactive programs of your own. Then, in the next chapter, you will learn how to write programs that read files and prepare reports.

As you work with Personal COBOL, you should know that many mainframe programmers do most of their development work on PCs using the Animator for Micro Focus Workbench or Micro Focus Mainframe Express. After they compile and test their programs on PCs, they use the Workbench or Mainframe Express tools to upload their programs and data to the mainframe for final testing. Because Workbench and Mainframe Express on a PC provide a friendlier environment and better debugging tools than a mainframe, developing programs in this way can be much more efficient than developing them directly on the mainframe.

Summary

- You use the Animator to develop programs for Micro Focus Personal COBOL on a PC. This is the same type of Animator that is used with the Micro Focus products for developing UNIX and mainframe programs.

- To enter and compile the initial code for a program, you open the program in *edit mode*. When the program compiles without errors, called a *clean compile*, you open the program in *execute mode* so you can *test* and *debug* it.

- A *compile-time error* occurs when the compiler can't convert a statement into machine language because its syntax is incorrect. A *run-time error* occurs when the Animator is unable to execute a statement. And a *logical error* occurs when the program runs successfully, but the results aren't what you expected.

- To help you debug a program, the Animator provides debugging tools. These tools let you set *breakpoints*, display and change the values of variables while the program is in *break mode*, and *step through a program* one statement at a time.

Terms

Integrated Development Environment (IDE)
document window
information line
status line
key status area
edit mode
execute mode
source code
source program
source file
intermediate file
testing
debugging
compile-time error
run-time error
logical error
production program
executable
object module
object program

diagnostics
linkage editor
link edit
link
COBOL profile
button bar
tagged line
compressing lines
expanding lines
tag
clean compile
text window
normal program termination
return code
break mode
monitor/watch list
hexadecimal code
hex code
breakpoint
stepping through a program

Objectives

- Given the specifications for a simple interactive program like the ones in chapter 1, use Micro Focus Personal COBOL to enter, compile, test, and debug the program.

- Describe the differences between testing and debugging.

- Describe the differences between compile-time, run-time, and logical errors.

- Explain why you should start your new programs from old programs.

- Explain how the debugging features can help you debug a program.

3

How to write a program that prepares a report

In this chapter, you'll learn how to write a program that gets data from a disk file, prepares a report, and prints the report on a printer. This is a realistic use of COBOL in business. In fact, COBOL was designed for working with the data in files and for preparing printed reports from that data. Today, tens of thousands of COBOL report-preparation programs are in use throughout this country.

A simple report-preparation program

To start, this chapter is going to present a simple report-preparation program. This program reads the data from the customer records in a sequential disk file, processes the data into the form of a sales report, and prints the report. The file and report specifications follow.

The file specifications

The input to the program is a *sequential file* on disk that consists of customer master *records*. When data is stored in a sequential file, the program reads the records in sequence starting with the first record. As a result, the report that's prepared from the file is in the same sequence as the records in the file.

Each customer record in the sequential file consists of the *fields* shown in figure 3-1. If you look at the record layout at the top of this figure, you can see that the branch number field is stored in bytes 1 and 2; the salesrep number field is in bytes 3 and 4; and so on. You also can see that COBOL picture notation is used to indicate the format of each field. For instance, the customer number is an unsigned five-digit number; the customer name field consists of 20 characters; and the sales last year-to-date field is a signed seven-digit number with two decimal places.

Right after the record layout for this file, you can see how the record description will be coded in COBOL. Here, the 01 level is a group item that represents the entire record; the 05 levels represent the fields within that record. Notice in the field definitions that the prefix CM (short for Customer Master) is used as the start of each data name. This isn't required by COBOL, but it shows that the field is part of the customer master record. When a program consists of two or more record descriptions, this naming technique helps you keep the fields straight. As a result, you'll see this technique used in all of the record descriptions in this book.

This figure also presents the test data you can use for the first test run of this program. If you looked at the actual data in this file, you would see that there's nothing in each record to mark the start or end of each field. For example, the first record really looks like this:

```
121211111INFORMATION BUILDERS01234560111111
```

In other words, the data from one field is followed immediately by the data from the next field. In this figure, though, the fields are presented in a table so you can easily identify the contents of each field.

Notice that the data for the two sales fields doesn't include decimal points, even though the Pic clauses in the record descriptions for these fields indicate that they contain two decimal places. As you learned in chapter 1, that's because the V in the Pic clause just shows where the decimal point should be. When each record is read, it is the field definitions that determine how the data is interpreted.

The record layout

Bytes 1-2	Bytes 3-4	Bytes 5-9	Bytes 10-29		Bytes 30-36	Bytes 37-43
Branch number	Salesrep number	Customer number	Customer name		Sales this year-to-date	Sales last year-to-date
9(2)	9(2)	9(5)	X(20)		S9(5)V99	S9(5)V99

The record description in COBOL

```
01  CUSTOMER-MASTER-RECORD.
    05  CM-BRANCH-NUMBER        PIC 9(2).
    05  CM-SALESREP-NUMBER      PIC 9(2).
    05  CM-CUSTOMER-NUMBER      PIC 9(5).
    05  CM-CUSTOMER-NAME        PIC X(20).
    05  CM-SALES-THIS-YTD       PIC S9(5)V9(2).
    05  CM-SALES-LAST-YTD       PIC S9(5)V9(2).
```

The test data for the first test run

Branch number	Salesrep number	Customer number	Customer name	Sales this year-to-date	Sales last year-to-date
12	12	11111	INFORMATION BUILDERS	0123456	0111111
12	12	12345	CAREER TRAINING CTR	1234567	2222222
22	10	22222	HOMELITE TEXTRON CO	3454500	0000000
22	14	34567	NEAS MEMBER BENEFITS	0011111	0000000
22	14	55555	PILOT LIFE INS. CO.	1000000	0100000
34	10	00111	DAUPHIN DEPOSIT BANK	1409900	1993000
34	10	54321	AIRCRAFT OWNERS ASSC	0542612	4042000
34	17	33333	NORFOLK CORP	0639635	0446288
47	11	12121	GENERAL SERVICES CO.	1144400	1105956
47	11	24680	INFO MANAGEMENT CO.	1748145	1189247
47	21	99999	DOLLAR SAVINGS BANK	0505900	0462195
47	21	76543	NATL MUSIC CORP.	0238346	0443526

Description

- This program reads a *sequential file* of customer *records* that are stored on disk. Each of these records consists of 43 bytes of data that is divided into six *fields*.

- Because the COBOL record description gives the same information as the record layout, COBOL record descriptions are often used to document the layout of the fields in a disk record.

- If you study the test data, you can see that the decimal points aren't in the data. Remember that the V indicates the position of an assumed decimal point.

- Although the Pictures for the year-to-date fields indicate that they can carry signs, the data doesn't include any negative values. We avoided the use of negative values because signs are stored differently on different types of computers (see chapter 6).

Figure 3-1   The file specifications for the program

The report specifications

Figure 3-2 presents the report specifications for this program. To plan a report, a *print chart* like the one at the top of this figure can be used. If you compare this chart with the printed output for the test run, you can see how the two are related.

Where you see words like YEAR-TO-DATE SALES REPORT in the print chart, the words are supposed to be printed in those print positions. And where you see COBOL notation like X(20) or ZZ,ZZZ.99-, data is supposed to be printed. The other areas of the report are supposed to be left blank.

When you use a line printer on a mainframe, the printer usually has a line that is 132 characters long and the standard report form provides for a maximum of 66 lines on each page (6 lines per inch on an 11-inch form). In that case, each print line that's defined by your program must be 132 characters. You usually leave a few lines at the top and bottom of each page, though, so you print on approximately 60 lines of each page. In contrast, when you use a laser printer, the line length and number of lines per page can be adjusted to whatever is appropriate for the report.

In this example, the report is just 80 characters wide. If you develop the report for a mainframe, though, you need to fill out the other 52 characters in each line with spaces. In the program that follows, you'll see that 132 characters are printed in each line with a maximum of 55 customer lines on each page. If you add the six heading lines to the 55 lines, that means a total of 61 lines will be printed on each page.

When you develop a COBOL program that prepares a report, you need to realize that a printed report is treated as a file, and each line in the report is treated as one record in the file. In addition, the printed report is usually saved to a disk file before it is printed. This type of file can be called a *print file*.

The print chart

The printed output for the first test run

```
DATE:   01/26/2000          YEAR-TO-DATE SALES REPORT          PAGE:    1
TIME:   16:34                                                  RPT1000


CUST                        SALES              SALES
NUM       CUSTOMER NAME      THIS YTD           LAST YTD


11111     INFORMATION BUILDERS     1,234.56         1,111.11
12345     CAREER TRAINING CTR     12,345.67        22,222.22
22222     HOMELITE TEXTRON CO     34,545.00             0.00
34567     NEAS MEMBER BENEFITS       111.11             0.00
55555     PILOT LIFE INS. CO.     10,000.00         1,000.00
00111     DAUPHIN DEPOSIT BANK    14,099.00        19,930.00
54321     AIRCRAFT OWNERS ASSC     5,426.12        40,420.00
33333     NORFOLK CORP             6,396.35         4,462.88
12121     GENERAL SERVICES CO.    11,444.00        11,059.56
24680     INFO MANAGEMENT CO.     17,481.45        11,892.47
99999     DOLLAR SAVINGS BANK      5,059.00         4,621.95
76543     NATL MUSIC CORP.         2,383.46         4,435.26


                             120,525.72       121,155.45
```

Description

- A *print chart* is used to plan the format of a report. If you compare the output of the first test run with the print chart, you can see how they are related.

- A report usually has one or more heading lines that identify the report and provide information such as the date, time, and page number. Heading lines are also used to identify the data in the columns of the report.

- On a line printer for a mainframe, each line typically consists of 132 characters. Also, the standard report form provides for a maximum of 66 lines on each page.

- On a laser printer, the line length and number of lines on each page can be adapted to the requirements of the report.

- In COBOL, a printed report is thought of as a file, and each line in the report is one record in the file. In addition, the report is usually saved in a disk file before it is printed. This type of file can be called a *print file*.

Figure 3-2   The report specifications for the program

The COBOL code

If you understand what this program is supposed to do, you're ready to preview the code, which is presented in the four parts of figure 3-3. Although this program requires six new statements and one function (which are shaded), you shouldn't have any trouble understanding what they do. As a result, you should be able to understand how this program works before you learn the coding details for the new statements and function.

The Input-Output Section in the Environment Division

When your program works with disk and print files, it must contain a File-Control paragraph in the Environment Division. This paragraph contains one Select statement for each disk and print file. Each Select statement identifies the file by giving it a filename.

The File Section in the Data Division

For each Select statement you code in the Environment Division, you must code an FD (File Description) statement in the File Section of the Data Division. This statement is followed immediately by the record description for the file.

In the program in this figure, the FD statement for the customer master file is followed by a record description that includes the definitions for the six fields that make up the record. In contrast, the FD statement for the print file is followed by a record description named PRINT-AREA that is 132 characters long (the length of the print line). No fields are defined within this record, because the various lines that will be printed to this file are defined in the Working-Storage Section. You'll soon see how this works.

The end-of-file switch

In the Working-Storage Section of this program, you can see a SWITCHES group with one switch defined. It is named CUSTMAST-EOF-SWITCH, which is short for "customer master end-of-file switch." Notice that the Value clause for this switch initializes it to a value of N, which means the switch is off. Then, the switch is turned on when all of the records in the file have been read.

As you'll see as you progress through this book, all business programs require one or more switches. In programming jargon, a *switch* is a field that can have either a yes or no (or on or off) value. To simplify, we recommend that you define all switch fields as PIC X and that you treat a value of Y as Yes (or On) and a value of N as No (or Off).

The print-fields group

The four fields in the PRINT-FIELDS group are used to help control the printing of the report. Here, PAGE-COUNT keeps track of the current page number; LINES-ON-PAGE represents the number of customer lines that will be printed on each page (+55); LINE-COUNT is used to count the lines on each page; and SPACE-CONTROL is used to determine how many lines will be advanced before the next line is printed.

The report-preparation program   **Page 1**

```
 IDENTIFICATION DIVISION.
*
 PROGRAM-ID. RPT1000.
*
 ENVIRONMENT DIVISION.
*
 INPUT-OUTPUT SECTION.
*
 FILE-CONTROL.
*
     SELECT CUSTMAST ASSIGN TO CUSTMAST.
     SELECT SALESRPT ASSIGN TO SALESRPT.
*
 DATA DIVISION.
*
 FILE SECTION.
*
 FD  CUSTMAST.
*
 01  CUSTOMER-MASTER-RECORD.
     05  CM-BRANCH-NUMBER        PIC 9(2).
     05  CM-SALESREP-NUMBER      PIC 9(2).
     05  CM-CUSTOMER-NUMBER      PIC 9(5).
     05  CM-CUSTOMER-NAME        PIC X(20).
     05  CM-SALES-THIS-YTD       PIC S9(5)V9(2).
     05  CM-SALES-LAST-YTD       PIC S9(5)V9(2).
*
 FD  SALESRPT.
*
 01  PRINT-AREA      PIC X(132).
*
 WORKING-STORAGE SECTION.
*
 01  SWITCHES.
     05  CUSTMAST-EOF-SWITCH    PIC X    VALUE "N".
*
 01  PRINT-FIELDS.
     05  PAGE-COUNT      PIC S9(3)    VALUE ZERO.
     05  LINES-ON-PAGE   PIC S9(3)    VALUE +55.
     05  LINE-COUNT      PIC S9(3)    VALUE +99.
     05  SPACE-CONTROL   PIC S9.
*
 01  TOTAL-FIELDS.
     05  GRAND-TOTAL-THIS-YTD   PIC S9(7)V99    VALUE ZERO.
     05  GRAND-TOTAL-LAST-YTD   PIC S9(7)V99    VALUE ZERO.
*
 01  CURRENT-DATE-AND-TIME.
     05  CD-YEAR         PIC 9999.
     05  CD-MONTH        PIC 99.
     05  CD-DAY          PIC 99.
     05  CD-HOURS        PIC 99.
     05  CD-MINUTES      PIC 99.
     05  FILLER          PIC X(9).
*
```

Figure 3-3   The COBOL code for the program (part 1 of 4)

Note here that PAGE-COUNT has a starting value of zero because 1 will be added to it before the first page is printed. Note too that LINE-COUNT has a starting value of +99. Since that value is greater than the starting value of LINES-ON-PAGE, the program will start a new page before the first line of the report is printed. Although LINE-COUNT could be given any starting value greater than +55, +99 is used so it will work even if the starting value of LINES-ON-PAGE is increased later on.

The total-fields group

The TOTAL-FIELDS group on page 1 of the program defines two fields that are used for the grand totals of the report. They are given a starting value of zero. Then, as each record in the file is read, the last year-to-date and this year-to-date sales fields are added to the total fields. At the end of the program, these fields are moved to the grand total line and printed.

The current-date-and-time group

The last group on page 1 receives the current date and time fields when the program gets them from the computer system. These fields are then moved to the heading of the report.

The print-line groups

The six groups on page 2 of this program are the record descriptions for the six types of lines that are required by the sales report. The first four groups define the four heading lines. The next group defines the customer line. And the last group defines the grand total line. If you compare the definitions for the fields in these lines with the print chart, you'll see that they correspond directly to that layout.

Note that a prefix is used for each data name in these print lines to indicate which line the field belongs to. For instance, HL1 is the prefix for fields in the first heading line, and CL is the prefix for fields in the customer line. Later on, this makes it easier to code the statements in the Procedure Division that refer to those fields.

What's new here is the use of the word FILLER. When that reserved word is coded instead of a data name, it means that the field isn't going to be referred to by statements in the Procedure Division. Nevertheless, the field is required for a complete definition of the print line.

When you code a FILLER field, you need to give it a starting value of an alphanumeric literal or SPACE. Otherwise, leftover data from a previous program may be printed in the field. This is a common programming error, but one that's easy to fix.

Before you turn the page, you may want to take note of the definitions for the third and fourth heading lines. For each line, three 20-character FILLER fields are used to define the literals for the first 60 characters. This is a common programming technique for defining the literals that are needed in the heading of a report. Of course, you can code the literals for these lines in whatever style you prefer, but this style has some merit.

The report-preparation program   **Page 2**

```
01    HEADING-LINE-1.
      05    FILLER              PIC X(7)      VALUE "DATE:   ".
      05    HL1-MONTH           PIC 9(2).
      05    FILLER              PIC X(1)      VALUE "/".
      05    HL1-DAY             PIC 9(2).
      05    FILLER              PIC X(1)      VALUE "/".
      05    HL1-YEAR            PIC 9(4).
      05    FILLER              PIC X(11)     VALUE SPACE.
      05    FILLER              PIC X(20)     VALUE "YEAR-TO-DATE SALES R".
      05    FILLER              PIC X(20)     VALUE "EPORT              ".
      05    FILLER              PIC X(8)      VALUE "  PAGE: ".
      05    HL1-PAGE-NUMBER     PIC ZZZ9.
      05    FILLER              PIC X(52)     VALUE SPACE.
*
 01   HEADING-LINE-2.
      05    FILLER              PIC X(7)      VALUE "TIME:   ".
      05    HL2-HOURS           PIC 9(2).
      05    FILLER              PIC X(1)      VALUE ":".
      05    HL2-MINUTES         PIC 9(2).
      05    FILLER              PIC X(58)     VALUE SPACE.
      05    FILLER              PIC X(10)     VALUE "RPT1000".
      05    FILLER              PIC X(52)     VALUE SPACE.
*
 01   HEADING-LINE-3.
      05    FILLER              PIC X(20)     VALUE "CUST              ".
      05    FILLER              PIC X(20)     VALUE "          SALES   ".
      05    FILLER              PIC X(20)     VALUE "      SALES       ".
      05    FILLER              PIC X(72)     VALUE SPACE.
*
 01   HEADING-LINE-4.
      05    FILLER              PIC X(20)     VALUE "NUM    CUSTOMER NAME".
      05    FILLER              PIC X(20)     VALUE "           THIS YTD ".
      05    FILLER              PIC X(20)     VALUE "     LAST YTD       ".
      05    FILLER              PIC X(72)     VALUE SPACE.
*
 01   CUSTOMER-LINE.
      05    CL-CUSTOMER-NUMBER  PIC 9(5).
      05    FILLER              PIC X(2)       VALUE SPACE.
      05    CL-CUSTOMER-NAME    PIC X(20).
      05    FILLER              PIC X(3)       VALUE SPACE.
      05    CL-SALES-THIS-YTD   PIC ZZ,ZZ9.99-.
      05    FILLER              PIC X(4)       VALUE SPACE.
      05    CL-SALES-LAST-YTD   PIC ZZ,ZZ9.99-.
      05    FILLER              PIC X(78)      VALUE SPACE.
*
 01   GRAND-TOTAL-LINE.
      05    FILLER              PIC X(27)      VALUE SPACE.
      05    GTL-SALES-THIS-YTD  PIC Z,ZZZ,ZZ9.99-.
      05    FILLER              PIC X(1)       VALUE SPACE.
      05    GTL-SALES-LAST-YTD  PIC Z,ZZZ,ZZ9.99-.
      05    FILLER              PIC X(78)      VALUE SPACE.
*
```

Figure 3-3   The COBOL code for the program (part 2 of 4)

The Procedure Division

Now that you're familiar with the records and fields defined in the Data Division, you should be able to follow the code in the Procedure Division. Yes, it contains a few new statements, but it's not hard to tell what these statements do. As in all programs, the real trick is following the logic of the program.

As you can see, procedure 000 starts with an Open statement that opens the two files used by a program. Then, after it prepares the report, this procedure issues a Close statement that closes the files. You'll learn how and why you code these statements in just a moment.

Between these statements, though, this procedure issues three Perform statements that drive the logic of the program. The first one performs procedure 100 to get the current date and time and move those fields into the report heading. The second Perform statement repeatedly performs procedure 200 to prepare the lines of the report until all of the records in the customer file have been read. And the third Perform statement performs procedure 300 to print the grand totals at the end of the report.

In procedure 200, the first Perform statement performs procedure 210 to read the next customer record. Then, if the customer end-of-file switch hasn't been turned on, this procedure performs procedure 220 to print a customer line.

To make this logic work, procedure 210 contains a Read statement that reads the next record in the file. However, if there are no more records in the file (AT END), this statement moves Y to the end-of-file switch. That's the switch that's tested by the Perform Until statement in procedure 000 and the If statement in procedure 200.

The report-preparation program   **Page 3**

```
PROCEDURE DIVISION.
*
 000-PREPARE-SALES-REPORT.
*
     OPEN INPUT  CUSTMAST
          OUTPUT SALESRPT.
     PERFORM 100-FORMAT-REPORT-HEADING.
     PERFORM 200-PREPARE-SALES-LINES
         UNTIL CUSTMAST-EOF-SWITCH = "Y".
     PERFORM 300-PRINT-GRAND-TOTALS.
     CLOSE CUSTMAST
           SALESRPT.
     STOP RUN.
*
 100-FORMAT-REPORT-HEADING.
*
     MOVE FUNCTION CURRENT-DATE TO CURRENT-DATE-AND-TIME.
     MOVE CD-MONTH   TO HL1-MONTH.
     MOVE CD-DAY     TO HL1-DAY.
     MOVE CD-YEAR    TO HL1-YEAR.
     MOVE CD-HOURS   TO HL2-HOURS.
     MOVE CD-MINUTES TO HL2-MINUTES.
*
 200-PREPARE-SALES-LINES.
*
     PERFORM 210-READ-CUSTOMER-RECORD.
     IF CUSTMAST-EOF-SWITCH = "N"
         PERFORM 220-PRINT-CUSTOMER-LINE.
*
 210-READ-CUSTOMER-RECORD.
*
     READ CUSTMAST
         AT END
             MOVE "Y" TO CUSTMAST-EOF-SWITCH.
*
```

Figure 3-3   The COBOL code for the program (part 3 of 4)

The last three procedures of the program print the customer line, the heading lines, and the grand-total lines of the report. They make use of Write statements that print a line after advancing to the next page of the report or to a later line in the report.

Procedure 220 starts with an If statement that tests whether the value of LINE-COUNT is greater than or equal to LINES-ON-PAGE. Since this condition is true when the program starts (+99 is greater than +55), procedure 220 performs procedure 230 to skip to the top of the next page and print the four heading lines.

In procedure 230, you can see that 1 is added to PAGE-COUNT (which had a starting value of zero) and that value is moved to the first heading line before any lines are printed. Then, each of the heading lines is moved to the record area named PRINT-AREA and a Write statement writes the line from that area to the print file. The first of these Write statements advances to the next page before printing its line; the second one advances one line before printing; the third one advances two lines before printing; and the fourth one advances one line before printing. That is consistent with the vertical spacing shown on the print chart.

After all four lines have been printed, procedure 230 moves zero to LINE-COUNT, which will be used in procedure 220 to count the customer lines printed on each page. Then, procedure 230 moves 2 to SPACE-CONTROL, which is used by procedure 220 to determine how many lines to advance before printing the next customer line.

Back in procedure 220, you can see that four fields in the customer master record are moved to the customer line. Then, the customer line is moved to PRINT-AREA, and the Write statement writes the line from that area...after advancing the number of lines that are specified by the SPACE-CONTROL field. After that, one is added to LINE-COUNT, and the sales fields in the customer record are added to the grand total fields. Then, one is moved to SPACE-CONTROL, which means that the next customer line will be printed after advancing only one line.

If you follow this code, procedure 300 is just more of the same. After the two grand total fields are moved to the grand total line, that line is moved to PRINT-AREA. Then, the Write statement writes that line after advancing 2 lines.

At this point, you should understand how this program works. But if you still have some questions about it, you'll get a chance to step through the program when you do exercise 3-1 at the end of this chapter. Before that, though, you'll learn the coding specifics for the new statements and the function that this program uses.

The report-preparation program   **Page 4**

```
 220-PRINT-CUSTOMER-LINE.
*
     IF LINE-COUNT >= LINES-ON-PAGE
         PERFORM 230-PRINT-HEADING-LINES.
     MOVE CM-CUSTOMER-NUMBER    TO CL-CUSTOMER-NUMBER.
     MOVE CM-CUSTOMER-NAME      TO CL-CUSTOMER-NAME.
     MOVE CM-SALES-THIS-YTD     TO CL-SALES-THIS-YTD.
     MOVE CM-SALES-LAST-YTD     TO CL-SALES-LAST-YTD.
     MOVE CUSTOMER-LINE TO PRINT-AREA.
     WRITE PRINT-AREA AFTER ADVANCING SPACE-CONTROL LINES.
     ADD 1 TO LINE-COUNT.
     ADD CM-SALES-THIS-YTD TO GRAND-TOTAL-THIS-YTD.
     ADD CM-SALES-LAST-YTD TO GRAND-TOTAL-LAST-YTD.
     MOVE 1 TO SPACE-CONTROL.
*
 230-PRINT-HEADING-LINES.
*
     ADD 1 TO PAGE-COUNT.
     MOVE PAGE-COUNT       TO HL1-PAGE-NUMBER.
     MOVE HEADING-LINE-1 TO PRINT-AREA.
     WRITE PRINT-AREA AFTER ADVANCING PAGE.
     MOVE HEADING-LINE-2 TO PRINT-AREA.
     WRITE PRINT-AREA AFTER ADVANCING 1 LINES.
     MOVE HEADING-LINE-3 TO PRINT-AREA.
     WRITE PRINT-AREA AFTER ADVANCING 2 LINES.
     MOVE HEADING-LINE-4 TO PRINT-AREA.
     WRITE PRINT-AREA AFTER ADVANCING 1 LINES.
     MOVE ZERO TO LINE-COUNT.
     MOVE 2 TO SPACE-CONTROL.
*
 300-PRINT-GRAND-TOTALS.
*
     MOVE GRAND-TOTAL-THIS-YTD TO GTL-SALES-THIS-YTD.
     MOVE GRAND-TOTAL-LAST-YTD TO GTL-SALES-LAST-YTD.
     MOVE GRAND-TOTAL-LINE TO PRINT-AREA.
     WRITE PRINT-AREA AFTER ADVANCING 2 LINES.
```

Figure 3-3   The COBOL code for the program (part 4 of 4)

How to code Select statements and FD statements

For each file that a program reads or writes, you need to code one Select statement in the Environment Division and one FD statement in the Data Division. Because you code a Select statement for Personal COBOL differently than you do for mainframe COBOL, the syntax you use for each platform is presented separately.

How to code Select statements for Personal COBOL

Figure 3-4 shows how to code Select statements for sequential files when using Micro Focus Personal COBOL. This statement gives a *filename* to each file that can be used to refer to the file within the program. It also includes a *system name* that identifies the specific file on disk.

In the first example, you can see the Select statement for the customer master file. Here, CUSTMAST is the filename that will be used to refer to this file throughout the program. The name of the file on disk is custmast.dat, which should be located in the folder that's identified by this path:

```
c:\cobol\data
```

If the file isn't there when the program tries to open it, a run-time error occurs.

Similarly, the Select statement for the print file gives it a name of SALESRPT. When it is saved on disk, it will receive the name salesrpt.prn and it will be stored in the same folder as the customer file.

How do you print a report that's stored in a print file? You can use your word processing program or a text editor like NotePad. You'll learn more about that in figure 3-15.

The syntax of the Select statement for a sequential file on a PC

```
SELECT filename ASSIGN TO system-name
```

Typical Select statements for Micro Focus Personal COBOL

```
SELECT CUSTMAST ASSIGN TO "c:\cobol\data\custmast.dat".
SELECT SALESRPT ASSIGN TO "c:\cobol\data\salesrpt.prn".
```

The rules for forming a filename in standard COBOL

- Use letters, digits, and hyphens only.
- Don't start or end the name with a hyphen.
- Use a maximum of 30 characters.
- Use at least one letter in the name.

Description

- A Select statement identifies a disk file or a print file used by the program.
- The system name for a disk file or print file consists of the path and filename for the file.
- Because Personal COBOL uses the Windows 3.1 interface, you need to keep the file name in the system name to a maximum of 8 characters. You should also use *dat* as the extension for data files and *prn* as the extension for print files.
- Although you can also code the system name for a print file so the output goes directly to a printer, it's better to code the system name so it is saved in a disk file. Then, you can use your word processor or NotePad to print the output or to review the output on your monitor without ever printing it.

Figure 3-4   How to code Select statements for Micro Focus Personal COBOL

How to code Select statements on a mainframe

Figure 3-5 shows you how to code Select statements for sequential files when you're using COBOL on an IBM mainframe. In this case, the system name doesn't point to a specific file. Instead, the system name includes a *ddname* that gets associated with a specific file or printer when the program is run. This association is done by job control language, which you'll learn how to use in chapter 18.

When you code a Select statement for a mainframe, we recommend that the filename and the ddname in each statement be the same. That way, you won't have any trouble remembering which is which. By keeping the filename short, you also make it easier to code switch names like CUSTMAST-EOF-SWITCH that relate to the file. That's why all of the programs in this book use filenames that are eight or fewer characters.

As you can see in this figure, a mainframe provides for two types of sequential files: *VSAM* (*Virtual Storage Access Method*) files and non-VSAM files. Today, most sequential files are non-VSAM files, even though VSAM is the newer file organization method.

When a print file is prepared on a mainframe, it is stored in a queue (waiting list) with other print files. Then, the jobs in the print queue are printed one at a time as the printer becomes available. This is done automatically in a process called *spooling*. Alternately, you can hold the print file in the queue so it isn't printed until you release it. Then, you can review the print file on your screen and decide whether you want to print it. You can learn more about that in chapter 18.

The syntax of the Select statement for a sequential file

```
SELECT filename ASSIGN TO system-name
```

Typical Select statements for an IBM mainframe compiler

```
SELECT CUSTMAST ASSIGN TO AS-CUSTMAST.
SELECT SALESRPT ASSIGN TO SALESRPT.
```

The rules for forming a filename in standard COBOL

- Use letters, digits, and hyphens only.
- Don't start or end the name with a hyphen.
- Use a maximum of 30 characters.
- Use at least one letter in the name.

The syntax for a system name on an IBM mainframe

For a non-VSAM sequential disk file or a print file

```
ddname
```

For a VSAM sequential disk file

```
AS-ddname
```

Rules for forming a ddname

Use eight or fewer letters or digits, starting with a letter. For consistency, this should be the same as the filename.

Description

- The Select statement identifies a disk file or a print file used by the program.
- The ddname that's coded as part of the system name for a disk file is used in job control language when the program is run to assign the file in the COBOL program to a specific file on disk.
- IBM mainframes use two types of sequential disk files: VSAM and non-VSAM. Although VSAM is the newer file organization, non-VSAM sequential files are commonly used because they're easier to work with.
- The ddname that's coded for a print file is used in job control language when the program is run to assign the printed output to a specific printer or group of printers. Before the output is actually printed, though, it's written to a temporary disk file that's printed when a printer becomes available. This is called *spooling*.

Figure 3-5   How to code Select statements on a mainframe

How to code FD statements and record descriptions for disk files

Figure 3-6 shows how to write FD (File Description) statements for sequential disk files. In the FD statement itself, you identify the file using the filename from the Select statement for the file. After the FD statement, you code a record description for the file.

You also can code a RECORD CONTAINS clause in an FD statement. This clause specifies the number of characters (or bytes) in each record in the file. If you omit this clause, though, the compiler determines the number of characters in each record from the record description that follows. As a result, most programmers don't code this clause.

Because there's nothing in a disk file to indicate where one field in a record starts and ends, it's essential that the record description correspond with the records on the disk. If, for example, the record description calls for a two-digit branch number and the branch number on the disk is three digits, the branch number field in the program won't receive the right data when a record is read. Worse, none of the fields that follow that field in the disk record will receive the right data either. This usually leads to a run-time error.

How to code FD statements and record descriptions for print files

Figure 3-6 also shows how to code an FD statement and record description for a print file. In contrast to the FD statement for a disk file, individual fields aren't usually defined in the record description for a print file. That's because records of varying formats will be written to the print file, one for each type of line in the report. In programmer jargon, this record description area is often referred to as the *print area* so that's the name we use in all of our report-preparation programs.

The syntax of the FD statement for a sequential file

```
FD  filename
    [RECORD CONTAINS integer CHARACTERS]
```

A typical FD statement and record description for a disk file

```
FD   CUSTMAST.
*
01   CUSTOMER-MASTER-RECORD.
     05   CM-BRANCH-NUMBER        PIC 9(2).
     05   CM-SALESREP-NUMBER      PIC 9(2).
     05   CM-CUSTOMER-NUMBER      PIC 9(5).
     05   CM-CUSTOMER-NAME        PIC X(20).
     05   CM-SALES-THIS-YTD       PIC S9(5)V9(2).
     05   CM-SALES-LAST-YTD       PIC S9(5)V9(2).
```

An FD statement that indicates the number of characters in each record

```
FD   CUSTMAST
     RECORD CONTAINS 43 CHARACTERS.
```

A typical FD statement and record description for a print file

```
FD   SALESRPT.
*
01   PRINT-AREA       PIC X(132).
```

Description

- The FD statement provides a File Description. The filename used in this statement must be the same as the one coded in the Select statement in the Environment Division.

- Right after the FD statement for a file, you code a record description for the file. For a disk file, you often code a record description with a group item at the 01 level and all of the fields defined at the lower levels. For a print file, you usually code a one-line record description that gives the number of characters in the record.

- If you code the Record Contains clause, the number of characters you specify must be the same as the number of bytes in the record description for the file. If you omit this clause, the compiler determines the number of characters from the record description.

Figure 3-6   How to code FD statements and record descriptions for disk and print files

How to code the Procedure Division

To code the Procedure Division of a report-preparation program, you need to learn how to code just four new statements that work with files: Open, Close, Read, and Write. The figures that follow show you how to code these statements. After that, you'll learn how to use the Current-Date function so you can include the current date and time in your report headings. You'll also learn how to use the Accept statement to get the current date and time in case you're using a compiler that doesn't support the Current-Date function.

How to code Open and Close statements

Figure 3-7 shows how to code the Open and Close statements. Within these statements, you code the filenames that you defined in the Select statements. As you can see, you can open both disk files and print files with a single statement, and you can close them with a single statement.

What exactly do the Open and Close statements do? That varies from one platform to another. For an *input file* (a file the program reads), the Open statement at least checks to see whether the file is available. If it isn't, a run-time error occurs and the program ends. For an *output file* (a file the program writes to), the Open statement at least checks to make sure that there's enough available space for the file on the disk before opening it. In contrast, the Close statement releases the files so they can be used by other programs.

When you code a program that uses files, you have to make sure the files are opened before your program tries to read or write them. And you have to make sure they're closed before the program issues a Stop Run statement. Otherwise, run-time errors will occur.

You can, however, open and close a file more than once in a single program. You can do that when you want to read through the records in a file more than once. When you open a file the second time, you can read it again starting with the first record.

The syntax of the Open statement

```
OPEN INPUT  filename-1 ...
     OUTPUT filename-2 ...
```

The syntax of the Close statement

```
CLOSE filename ...
```

The Open and Close statements in the report-preparation program

```
OPEN INPUT  CUSTMAST
     OUTPUT SALESRPT.

CLOSE CUSTMAST
      SALESRPT.
```

An Open statement with two input files

```
OPEN INPUT  CUSTMAST
            BRCHMAST
     OUTPUT SALESRPT.
```

Description

- The filenames that you use in the Open and Close statements have to be the ones that you defined in the Select statements in the Environment Division.

- An Open statement has to be issued for a file before a program can issue a Read or Write statement for that file.

- A Close statement has to be issued for all open files before a program can issue a Stop Run statement.

- After you close a file, it is no longer available for processing. However, if you open an input file again, you can read the records again starting with the first record.

Figure 3-7   How to code Open and Close statements

How to code Read statements for sequential disk files

Figure 3-8 shows how to code Read statements. When a program issues a Read statement, it reads the next record in the file starting with the first record in the file. When there are no more records in the file, though, no record is read and the At End clause of the statement is executed. In this clause, you normally turn an EOF switch on to indicate that there are no more records in the file.

You can also code a Not At End clause on a Read statement. This is illustrated by the second example in this figure. Here, the Not At End clause contains a statement that adds 1 to a field named RECORD-COUNT.

How to code Write statements for print files

Figure 3-8 also summarizes the information you need for coding Write statements. The first thing you should notice here is that you code the name used in the record description for the file on this statement, not the filename as you do for a Read statement. The three Write statements shown in this figure all write the record description named PRINT-AREA.

The After Advancing clause of the Write statement determines how many lines are skipped before the next line is printed on the report. As you can see in the examples, you can code the reserved word PAGE in this clause to skip to the top of the next page before printing. You can code a literal value with or without the reserved word LINES (or LINE) to skip one or more lines before printing. And you can code a variable name with or without the reserved word LINES (or LINE) to skip the number of lines indicated by the variable value before printing.

If you're used to working with PC programs that print full pages at a time on a laser printer, you may have trouble imagining the paper skipping one or more lines before a line is printed. Remember, then, that COBOL was developed when all printers worked that way, and many printers today still do. That's why that type of printer is called a line printer. So even if you're using a laser printer, it helps to imagine the program printing one line at a time after the paper has been advanced one or more lines.

The syntax of the Read statement for a sequential disk file

```
READ filename [RECORD]
    AT END
        imperative-statement-1 ...
    [NOT AT END
        imperative-statement-2 ...]
```

Some typical Read statements for sequential disk files

```
READ CUSTMAST RECORD
    AT END
        MOVE "Y" TO CUSTMAST-EOF-SWITCH.
READ CUSTMAST
    AT END
        MOVE "Y" TO CUSTMAST-EOF-SWITCH
    NOT AT END
        ADD 1 TO RECORD-COUNT.
```

The syntax of the Write statement for a print file

```
WRITE record-name
```
$$
\text{AFTER ADVANCING}
\begin{cases}
\text{PAGE} \\
\text{integer} \left[\, \text{LINE} \mid \text{LINES} \,\right] \\
\text{data-name} \left[\, \text{LINE} \mid \text{LINES} \,\right]
\end{cases}
$$

Some typical Write statements for print files

```
WRITE PRINT-AREA
    AFTER ADVANCING PAGE.
WRITE PRINT-AREA
    AFTER ADVANCING 1 LINE.
WRITE PRINT-AREA
    AFTER ADVANCING SPACE-CONTROL LINES.
```

Description

- When the Read statement is executed for a sequential disk file, it reads the next record in sequence into the record description for the file. If there are no more records in the file, the At End clause is executed; otherwise, the Not At End clause is executed.

- Note that you can use only imperative statements in the At End and Not At End clauses. This means you can't code If statements in these clauses.

- When the Write statement is executed for a print file, one record is printed from the print area for the file and the paper is advanced the number of lines indicated by the After Advancing clause or to the top of the next page (PAGE).

- Note that you code the filename in a Read statement and the record name in a Write statement.

Figure 3-8   How to code Read and Write statements

How to use the Current-Date function to get the current date and time

If you're using a COBOL-85 compiler that supports the 1989 addendum to the standards, you can use the Current-Date function to get the current date and time from your computer. Although most COBOL-85 compilers support the 1989 functions, VS COBOL II and COBOL for MVS on IBM mainframes don't. So if you're using one of these compilers, you have to use the Accept statement to get the date and time as shown in the next figure.

Figure 3-9 presents the Current-Date function. You can use this function as if it's a variable in any statement where it makes sense. When you use it in a Move statement, for example, the current date and time are moved to the receiving field.

In the data description in this figure, you can see the eight fields that you get from this function. Normally, though, you use only the first five or six fields in a program. The program in this chapter, for example, uses only the first five fields in the heading lines of the report. As a result, the last three fields are defined as FILLER.

The syntax of the Current-Date function

```
FUNCTION CURRENT-DATE
```

The data description for the data returned by the Current-Date function

```
01  CURRENT-DATE-AND-TIME.
    05  CD-YEAR                       PIC 9(4).
    05  CD-MONTH                      PIC 9(2).
    05  CD-DAY                        PIC 9(2).
    05  CD-HOURS                      PIC 9(2).
    05  CD-MINUTES                    PIC 9(2).
    05  CD-SECONDS                    PIC 9(2).
    05  CD-HUNDREDTH-SECONDS          PIC 9(2).
    05  CD-GREENWICH-MEAN-TIME-SHHMM  PIC X(5).
```

Two statements that use the Current-Date function

```
DISPLAY FUNCTION CURRENT-DATE.

MOVE FUNCTION CURRENT-DATE TO CURRENT-DATE-AND-TIME.
```

Description

- In 1989, an addendum was added to the COBOL-85 standards that provided for *intrinsic functions*. Although they were treated as an optional feature, most modern COBOL-85 compilers include these functions. You'll learn more about intrinsic functions in chapter 7.

- The Current-Date function gets the current date and time. The four-digit year that's returned by this function makes it easy to display years like 2000 in a form that makes sense.

- The Current-Date function can be used to represent a single variable in any statement where that makes sense.

- Before the Current-Date function became available, you had to use the Accept Date and Accept Time statements to get the date and time. You can learn more about these statements in the next figure.

- The five-character Greenwich Mean Time that is returned by this function indicates the number of hours and minutes that the current time is ahead or behind Greenwich Mean Time (+hhmm or –hhmm). If this information isn't available, this function puts zeros in this field.

Figure 3-9   How to use the Current-Date function

How to use Accept statements to get the current date and time

Figure 3-10 shows how to get the current date and time if your compiler doesn't support the Current-Date function. To get the current date, you use the Accept Date statement. To get the current time, you use the Accept Time statement. Once you get the date and time, you can move the components of these data items to the heading lines of a report just as you do when you use the Current-Date function.

In the syntax for the Accept Date statement, the shaded portion is an IBM extension that became available with the COBOL for MVS compiler. When this is coded (YYYYMMDD), the Accept Date statement gets the date with a four-digit year. Without that extension, the Accept Date statement gets the date with a two-digit year.

Since the VS COBOL II compiler doesn't provide for the YYYYMMDD extension, you can't get the current date with a four-digit year when using that compiler. That means you have to use special coding to determine what century a year belongs to now that we've reached the year 2000. Because of that limitation, most IBM mainframe shops upgraded to the COBOL for MVS or COBOL for OS/390 compiler during the last few years. That made it easier for them to upgrade their old programs so they are Y2K-compliant.

The syntax of the Accept statement for getting the date and time

```
ACCEPT data-name FROM  { DATE [ YYYYMMDD ] }
                       { TIME            }
```

VS COBOL II code that gets the date with a two-digit year

```
01  CURRENT-DATE-AND-TIME.
    05  CD-CURRENT-DATE.
        10  CD-CURRENT-YEAR     PIC 99.
        10  CD-CURRENT-MONTH    PIC 99.
        10  CD-CURRENT-DAY      PIC 99.
    .
    .
    .
    ACCEPT CD-CURRENT-DATE FROM DATE.
```

COBOL for MVS or OS/390 code that gets the date with a four-digit year

```
01  CURRENT-DATE-AND-TIME.
    05  CD-CURRENT-DATE.
        10  CD-CURRENT-YEAR     PIC 9999.
        10  CD-CURRENT-MONTH    PIC 99.
        10  CD-CURRENT-DAY      PIC 99.
    .
    .
    .
    ACCEPT CD-CURRENT-DATE FROM DATE YYYYMMDD.
```

IBM mainframe code that gets the time

```
01  CURRENT-DATE-AND-TIME.
    05  CD-CURRENT-TIME.
        10  CD-CURRENT-HOURS       PIC 99.
        10  CD-CURRENT-MINUTES     PIC 99.
        10  CD-CURRENT-SECONDS     PIC 99.
        10  CD-CURRENT-HUNDREDTHS  PIC 99.
    .
    .
    .
    ACCEPT CD-CURRENT-TIME FROM TIME.
```

Description

- If your compiler doesn't support the Current-Date function, you need to use the Accept Date and Accept Time statements to get the date and time.

- With the VS COBOL II compiler, you can't get the date with a four-digit year because the YYYYMMDD option isn't available. With the COBOL for MVS compiler, you can use the YYYYMMDD option to get the date with a four-digit year. With the COBOL for OS/390 compiler, you can use either the YYYYMMDD option or the Current-Date function to get the date with a four-digit year.

Figure 3-10   How to use Accept statements to get the current date and time

An enhanced version of the report-preparation program

If you study the program in figure 3-3, you should now be able to figure out how every statement in it works and why every statement is needed. Of course, there are other ways in which this program can be coded so it gets the same results, and you'll see some of these variations in the next chapter.

Now, if you feel confident that you understand the first version of the report-preparation program, it's time to make some enhancements to this program. These enhancements will make the program more realistic. They will also demonstrate some new coding techniques.

The enhanced report specifications

Figure 3-11 presents the report specifications for the enhanced program. Here, you can see that two columns have been added to the report. The first shows the change in sales from this year to last year; the second shows the change as a percent. Both of these are calculated from the input fields. In addition, this report should print a customer line only when the current year-to-date sales for the customer are greater than or equal to $10,000.

Before you turn the page, try to visualize the changes that need to be made to the original program. What needs to be added to the Data Division? What needs to be added to the Procedure Division?

The print chart for the enhanced report

```
     1234567 8901234567890 1234567890123456789012345678901234567890123456789012345678901234567890
 1  DATE:     99/99/9999              YEAR-TO-DATE  SALES  REPORT                          PAGE:    ZZZ9
 2  TIME:     99:99                                                                        RPT1000
 3
 4  CUST                                      SALES          SALES          CHANGE         CHANGE
 5  NUM        CUSTOMER  NAME                 THIS  YTD       LAST  YTD      AMOUNT         PERCENT
 6
 7  99999      XXXXXXXXXXXXXXXXXXXXX     ZZ,ZZZ.99-      ZZ,ZZZ.99-     ZZ,ZZZ.99-     ZZZ.9-
 8
 9                                   Z,ZZZ,ZZZ.99-   Z,ZZZ,ZZZ.99-  Z,ZZZ,ZZZ.99-   ZZZ.9-
10
```

The printed output for the test run

```
DATE:   01/27/2000            YEAR-TO-DATE SALES REPORT              PAGE:    1
TIME:   13:52                                                        RPT1000

CUST                        SALES          SALES          CHANGE       CHANGE
NUM     CUSTOMER NAME       THIS YTD       LAST YTD        AMOUNT       PERCENT

12345   CAREER TRAINING CTR  12,345.67      22,222.22       9,876.55-      44.4-
22222   HOMELITE TEXTRON CO  34,545.00           0.00      34,545.00      999.9
55555   PILOT LIFE INS. CO.  10,000.00       1,000.00       9,000.00      900.0
00111   DAUPHIN DEPOSIT BANK 14,099.00      19,930.00       5,831.00-      29.3-
12121   GENERAL SERVICES CO. 11,444.00      11,059.56         384.44       3.5
24680   INFO MANAGEMENT CO.  17,481.45      11,892.47       5,588.98      47.0

                            99,915.12      66,104.25      33,810.87      51.1
```

Description

- Two columns of data have been added to the print chart. Both of these are calculated from the data in the input records.

- Instead of printing one line for each record in the file, this report lists only those customers with this year-to-date sales that are $10,000 or greater.

- If the last year-to-date field for a customer is zero, the program should print 999.9 in the change percent column. The program should also print 999.9 in this column if the result of the calculation is too large for the calculated field.

Figure 3-11   The report specifications for the enhanced program

The changes to the Data Division code

Figure 3-12 presents just the code that illustrates the changes that need to be made to the Data Division of the program. Here, the lines that have been added to the program are shaded along with any changes to the original lines.

In the Working-Storage Section, you can see a new group item called CALCULATED-FIELDS. It consists of an elementary item called CHANGE-AMOUNT that will receive the result of a calculation that's done for each customer line in the report. Because most programs require more than one calculated field, a group like this makes it easier to find those fields.

Then, in the print line descriptions, you can see that the required headings and fields have been added to the code. The locations of those headings and fields, of course, are based on the specifications in the print chart. To complete the program, the statements in the Procedure Division have to make the right calculations and move the right data to the new fields before the lines are printed.

The Data Division changes

```
01  CALCULATED-FIELDS.
    05  CHANGE-AMOUNT            PIC S9(7)V99.
*
        .
        .
*
01  HEADING-LINE-3.
    05  FILLER          PIC X(20)    VALUE "CUST                ".
    05  FILLER          PIC X(20)    VALUE "             SALES   ".
    05  FILLER          PIC X(20)    VALUE "       SALES         ".
    05  FILLER          PIC X(20)    VALUE "CHANGE      CHANGE   ".
    05  FILLER          PIC X(52)    VALUE SPACE.
*
01  HEADING-LINE-4.
    05  FILLER          PIC X(20)    VALUE "NUM    CUSTOMER NAME".
    05  FILLER          PIC X(20)    VALUE "             THIS YTD ".
    05  FILLER          PIC X(20)    VALUE "      LAST YTD       ".
    05  FILLER          PIC X(20)    VALUE "AMOUNT      PERCENT  ".
    05  FILLER          PIC X(52)    VALUE SPACE.
*
01  CUSTOMER-LINE.
    05  CL-CUSTOMER-NUMBER  PIC X(5).
    05  FILLER              PIC X(2)      VALUE SPACE.
    05  CL-CUSTOMER-NAME    PIC X(20).
    05  FILLER              PIC X(3)      VALUE SPACE.
    05  CL-SALES-THIS-YTD   PIC ZZ,ZZ9.99-.
    05  FILLER              PIC X(4)      VALUE SPACE.
    05  CL-SALES-LAST-YTD   PIC ZZ,ZZ9.99-.
    05  FILLER              PIC X(4)      VALUE SPACE.
    05  CL-CHANGE-AMOUNT    PIC ZZ,ZZ9.99-.
    05  FILLER              PIC X(3)      VALUE SPACE.
    05  CL-CHANGE-PERCENT   PIC ZZ9.9-.
    05  FILLER              PIC X(55)     VALUE SPACE.
*
01  GRAND-TOTAL-LINE.
    05  FILLER              PIC X(27)     VALUE SPACE.
    05  GTL-SALES-THIS-YTD  PIC Z,ZZZ,ZZ9.99-.
    05  FILLER              PIC X(1)      VALUE SPACE.
    05  GTL-SALES-LAST-YTD  PIC Z,ZZZ,ZZ9.99-.
    05  FILLER              PIC X(1)      VALUE SPACE.
    05  GTL-CHANGE-AMOUNT   PIC Z,ZZZ,ZZ9.99-.
    05  FILLER              PIC X(3)      VALUE SPACE.
    05  GTL-CHANGE-PERCENT  PIC ZZ9.9-.
    05  FILLER              PIC X(55)     VALUE SPACE.
*
```

Figure 3-12   The Data Division changes for the enhanced program

The changes to the Procedure Division code

In figure 3-13, you can see the additions and changes that need to be made to the Procedure Division. In procedure 200, you can see that the If statement has been changed to a nested If statement. If the EOF switch is off, the nested If statement checks to see whether the value of sales this YTD (year-to-date) in the current customer record is greater than or equal to 10000. If it is, procedure 220 is performed to print a customer line on the report.

Once you've got this program logic coded, it's relatively easy to add the statements that the other enhancements require. In procedure 220, for example, the first Compute statement calculates the change amount for each line, and a Move statement moves it to the print line. Then, an If statement checks whether the last YTD value is zero. If it is, the program moves 999.9 to the change percent field. If it isn't, the Compute statement calculates the change percent. Notice that this statement includes an On Size Error clause that sets the change percent field to 999.9 if the result is too large for the field. That could happen if last YTD sales are small compared to this YTD sales. After the If statement, the procedure continues as before and prints the customer line, which now includes the new fields.

Before you go on, you should understand why the Compute statement in this figure is coded the way it is. When we first wrote this program in Personal COBOL, we coded the Compute statement like this because that seemed to be the logical way to code it:

```
COMPUTE CL-CHANGE-PERCENT ROUNDED =
       CHANGE-AMOUNT / CM-SALES-LAST-YTD * 100
```

Although this worked right with Personal COBOL, this didn't get the right result when using the mainframe compilers. The problem has to do with the intermediate result field that the mainframe compilers use to hold the result of the divide operation. By switching the sequence of operations as shown in this figure, though, this Compute statement gets the right result for both PC and mainframe compilers. In chapter 7, you can learn how the intermediate result fields are defined by the mainframe compilers so you'll be better able to handle this type of problem.

Since procedure 300 requires similar calculations and coding, the best way to add those statements to procedure 300 is to copy them from procedure 220. Then, you can modify the statements so they use the appropriate data names.

Note that the CHANGE-AMOUNT field is used in both procedure 220 and procedure 300. It is also used with the Compute statement that calculates the change percent. That's why CHANGE-AMOUNT can't be defined within a print line as a numeric edited item like the change percent fields are.

The Procedure Division changes

```
200-PREPARE-SALES-LINES.
*
     PERFORM 210-READ-CUSTOMER-RECORD.
     IF CUSTMAST-EOF-SWITCH = "N"
         IF CM-SALES-THIS-YTD >= 10000
             PERFORM 220-PRINT-CUSTOMER-LINE.
*


 220-PRINT-CUSTOMER-LINE.
*
     IF LINE-COUNT GREATER LINES-ON-PAGE
         PERFORM 230-PRINT-HEADING-LINES.
     MOVE CM-CUSTOMER-NUMBER   TO CL-CUSTOMER-NUMBER.
     MOVE CM-CUSTOMER-NAME     TO CL-CUSTOMER-NAME.
     MOVE CM-SALES-THIS-YTD    TO CL-SALES-THIS-YTD.
     MOVE CM-SALES-LAST-YTD    TO CL-SALES-LAST-YTD.
     COMPUTE CHANGE-AMOUNT =
         CM-SALES-THIS-YTD - CM-SALES-LAST-YTD.
     MOVE CHANGE-AMOUNT TO CL-CHANGE-AMOUNT.
     IF CM-SALES-LAST-YTD = ZERO
         MOVE 999.9 TO CL-CHANGE-PERCENT
     ELSE
         COMPUTE CL-CHANGE-PERCENT ROUNDED =
             CHANGE-AMOUNT * 100 / CM-SALES-LAST-YTD
             ON SIZE ERROR
                 MOVE 999.9 TO CL-CHANGE-PERCENT.
     MOVE CUSTOMER-LINE TO PRINT-AREA.
     WRITE PRINT-AREA AFTER ADVANCING SPACE-CONTROL LINES.
     ADD 1 TO LINE-COUNT.
     ADD CM-SALES-THIS-YTD TO GRAND-TOTAL-THIS-YTD.
     ADD CM-SALES-LAST-YTD TO GRAND-TOTAL-LAST-YTD.
     MOVE 1 TO SPACE-CONTROL.
*


 300-PRINT-GRAND-TOTALS.
*
     MOVE GRAND-TOTAL-THIS-YTD TO GTL-SALES-THIS-YTD.
     MOVE GRAND-TOTAL-LAST-YTD TO GTL-SALES-LAST-YTD.
     COMPUTE CHANGE-AMOUNT =
         GRAND-TOTAL-THIS-YTD - GRAND-TOTAL-LAST-YTD.
     MOVE CHANGE-AMOUNT TO GTL-CHANGE-AMOUNT.
     IF GRAND-TOTAL-LAST-YTD = ZERO
         MOVE 999.9 TO GTL-CHANGE-PERCENT
     ELSE
         COMPUTE GTL-CHANGE-PERCENT ROUNDED =
             CHANGE-AMOUNT * 100 / GRAND-TOTAL-LAST-YTD
             ON SIZE ERROR
                 MOVE 999.9 TO GTL-CHANGE-PERCENT.
     MOVE GRAND-TOTAL-LINE TO PRINT-AREA.
     WRITE PRINT-AREA AFTER ADVANCING 2 LINES.
```

Figure 3-13   The Procedure Division changes for the enhanced program

How to test a report-preparation program

When you develop a report-preparation program, testing is more difficult than when you test a simple interactive program for several reasons. First, you often have to prepare your own test files. Second, it's more difficult to review the data in input files and print files. Third, run-time errors are more likely. The topics that follow present some information that should help you do a better job of testing.

How to prepare a test plan and test data

When you develop a report-preparation program, it often makes sense to develop a plan for testing the program. This *test plan* normally divides the testing into three or more phases as shown in figure 3-14. In phase 1 of this plan, just the main logic of the program is tested with "clean" data. That means that the data doesn't test for exceptional conditions like zero values in the last year-to-date field. As a result, the program should run to completion and print the report without any serious problems.

In phase 2 of this test plan, the limits of the input data are tested, including the maximum values that the fields can store, zero values, and negative values. When that testing is complete, the program should work correctly for all combinations of input data. Then, in phase 3, page overflow is tested.

Note that you don't need many records for the early phases of testing. For instance, the first phase in the plan calls for just three records with year-to-date values that test to make sure the right records are printed (those with values greater than or equal to $10,000). Similarly, it takes just a few more records to test the limits of the input data in a program like this. By keeping the number of records low, you make it easier to tell whether the program has worked correctly after each test run. Then, in the last phase, you can add as many records as you need for testing volume conditions like page overflow.

As you create your test plan, you should decide where the test run data will come from. Will you create the test files yourself using a word processor, a text editor, or the utility programs that are available on your system? Does another program in the system create test data that you can use? Can you copy some production data for your test files? For the early phases of testing, it's often best to create your own data. That way, you can be sure that you've tested all the conditions that the program should provide for.

For the exercises and projects in this book, you can get the test data from the CD ROM so you won't have to create a test plan or test data. When you develop your own programs, though, you should take the time to do a thorough job of testing. The test plan is a critical tool for making sure you do that right.

A test plan for the enhanced report-preparation program

Phase	Description	Data
1	Test main logic with clean data	Three records: one with this YTD sales < $10,000; one with it equal to $10,000; and one with it > $10,000
2	Limit test the calculations	Phase 1 data plus records that test the maximum and minimum values of the input fields, including at least one record with last YTD sales equal to zero
3	Page overflow	Phase 2 data plus enough records to cause page overflow

Sources of test data

- Enter your own data into a sequential file by using a text editor like NotePad, a word processor, or a utility program that's available on your system.

- If test data is available for other programs that use the same file, you can get a copy of that data.

- If other programs that use the same file are already in production, you can get a copy of that "live" data.

Description

- When you're ready to test a program, it often makes sense to develop a *test plan* for it. The test plan should describe the phases of testing as well as the data that should be used in each of the phases.

- For a large program, it makes sense to do the testing in at least three phases. These phases should test (1) the main logic of the program, (2) the maximum and minimum values that the program provides for, and (3) volume or overflow conditions like page overflow.

- For the first phase of testing, you usually need just a few records. For each later phase, you can add the records you need.

- When you prepare your own data, you have complete control of the data so you can test every input possibility. When you use live data or test data that's prepared by others, you need to list it or display it on your screen so you know for sure what the input data is.

Figure 3-14   How to prepare a test plan and test data

How to review input files and print files when using Personal COBOL

When you use a test file that has been prepared by someone else or by another program, you need to review the data so you know what the test results should be. To do that on a mainframe or mid-range system, you can use a utility program to display or print the data. To do that on a PC, you can use your word processing program or a text editor like NotePad.

In figure 3-15, for example, you can see how the test file for the enhanced report-preparation program looks when it's opened in Word. As you can see, nothing separates one field from another or one record from another. Instead, the entire file is one string of characters that is rolled over into lines due to the margin settings. When you open this file with NotePad, it is even harder to interpret because the entire file is displayed on one line.

Nevertheless, you can review the disk data when you open it this way. Then, to make it more readable, you can move the cursor to the end of each record and press the Enter key. If you do that for all of the records in the file, the data will be displayed with one line for each record. At that point, you can print the data if you want to refer to it later. *But don't save the data in this form*, because your program won't be able to open the file if you do. Instead, you must close the file without saving the changes.

When your program writes a report to a print file on disk, you have to use a similar process to review the report. On a mainframe or mid-range system, utility programs are available for displaying or printing the report. But on a PC, you need to use your word processing program or a text editor. In this figure, for example, you can see the enhanced sales report after it has been opened by Word.

If the print file has long lines, you may need to format the report before it looks the way you want it to. For instance, you may want to change the layout from Portrait to Landscape or reduce the size of the font. Once you've got it the way you want it, you can review it on the screen or print it.

In this figure, you can see that the report starts with a page break, because the program skips to the next page before it prints the first line. To save paper, then, you can delete the page break before you print the report. For many of your unsuccessful test runs, though, you won't need to print the report at all.

The disk file when it's opened in Word

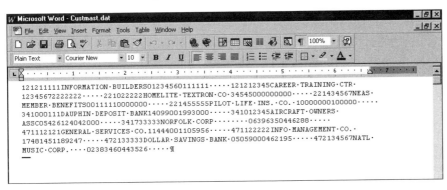

The print file when it's opened in Word

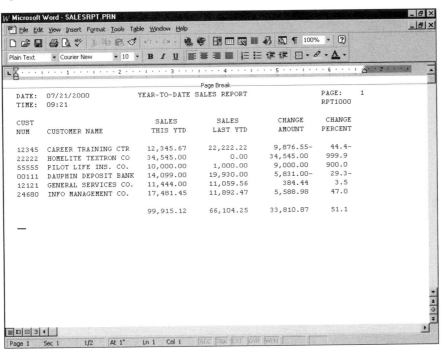

Description

- To review the data in an input file, you can open the file with your word processing program or NotePad. Note, however, that the data isn't neatly aligned so it is difficult to read.

- To review or print the data in a print file, you can open the file with your word processor or with NotePad. To make the data more readable, you may want to change the page layout to landscape, change the margins, or change the font or font size. Then, you can review the output without printing it, or you can print it.

Figure 3-15   How to review input files and print files when using Personal COBOL

Common run-time errors

When you develop a report-preparation program, you're likely to encounter some common run-time errors. Since you'll be better able to avoid these errors by knowing what they are and what causes them, figure 3-16 presents a brief overview.

The first group of errors are file handling errors. These occur when a serious error occurs while the program tries to open or close a file or read or write a record in a file. On a mainframe, this type of error is called an *operation exception*. If, for example, a program tries to open a file that it can't find on the disk, an operation exception occurs. This figure also lists three other common causes of operation exceptions, and there are others that you'll learn about in section 3.

The second group of errors are data errors, and you should already be familiar with them. If, for example, a Compute statement tries to operate upon a field that contains invalid data, a run-time error occurs. On a mainframe, this is known as a *data exception*.

Although there are many causes of data exceptions, this type of error commonly occurs when the COBOL description for a disk record doesn't match the data. If, for example, you define one of the input fields in your program as S9(4) and the field is actually S9(3), that can lead to a data exception later on. So if a data exception occurs during the first test run for a report-preparation program, be sure to check this possibility.

The other two data errors aren't specifically related to report-preparation programs, but they often occur when you're not familiar enough with the input data to provide for all possible data conditions in your program. That happens when you don't take the time to review the test data or live data that you have been given.

The first of these errors occurs when the result of an arithmetic operation is too large for the receiving field and On Size Error hasn't been coded. On a mainframe, this is called an *overflow exception*. The best prevention for this is to know the data and define the receiving fields so they are large enough to handle the results.

The second one occurs when an arithmetic operation tries to divide by zero. On a mainframe, this is called a *divide exception*. Here again, the best prevention is to know the data so you won't be surprised when one of the fields turns up with a value of zero.

Note that the last two conditions don't cause run-time errors with Personal COBOL. Instead, Personal COBOL makes adjustments so the statements can execute successfully. In this case, though, the results are incorrect so this is still a programming error.

File handling errors

- The file can't be opened.

- A Read or Write statement is executed before the file is opened.

- The program refers to a field in the record description area for a file after the At End clause has been executed or before the first Read statement has been executed.

- A Stop Run statement is executed before all opened files are closed.

- On a mainframe, errors like these are called *operation exceptions*.

Data errors

- A statement tries to perform an arithmetic operation or a numeric comparison on invalid numeric data. This type of error can occur when the data in an input record doesn't match the record description. This causes a run-time error on a mainframe and with Personal COBOL. On a mainframe, this type of run-time error is called a *data exception*.

- An arithmetic operation gives a result that is too large for the receiving field. On a mainframe, this causes a run-time error called an *overflow exception*. With Personal COBOL, the result is truncated instead of causing a run-time error.

- A divide operation tries to divide by zero. On a mainframe, this causes a run-time error called a *divide exception*. With Personal COBOL, the zero is treated as a one instead of causing a run-time error.

Figure 3-16   Common run-time errors when developing report-preparation programs

Perspective

The program in this chapter has many of the characteristics of a production program in business. In the real world, a report will have more columns and require more calculations. And many reports will require summary information, which will increase the logical complexity of the program. But the program in this chapter gives you a good idea of how a report-preparation program is developed in business.

Curiously, the enhanced version of the program requires only 11 different statements in the Procedure Division. So the difficulty in writing this kind of program isn't mastering the syntax of the COBOL statements. Instead, the difficulty is controlling the logic of the program.

If you had any trouble understanding the logic in this program, consider that the program is only 211 lines long and requires only seven procedures. Now imagine a program that gets data from two or more files, prints totals at two or more levels, and consists of 1500 lines or more, which is typical of a report-preparation program. To handle the logical complexity of a program of that size, you need to take a highly structured approach to its development. And that's what you'll learn how to do in the next chapter.

Summary

- A *sequential file* on disk consists of *records* that are read in sequence. Each record consists of *fields*.

- To plan a report, you create a *print chart* that shows the content and format of each line to be printed.

- A *switch* is a field that can have a value of either yes or no (or on or off). All business programs require one or more switches.

- An *input file* is a file that is read by a program, and an *output file* is a file that is written to. A *print file* is an output file that contains a report that can be printed.

- Each file that's used by a program must be identified with a Select statement in the File-Control paragraph of the Environment Division. In addition, the File Section of the Data Division must contain an FD statement and record description for each file.

- Before you can read from or write to a file, you must open it. Before a program ends, you must close all open files.

- A Read statement for a sequential disk file reads the next record in a file, starting with the first record. A Write statement for a print file writes one record for each line of the report.

- If you're using a compiler that supports the *intrinsic functions*, you can use the Current-Date function to get the current date and time from the system. Otherwise, you can use the Accept Date and Accept Time statements.

- A *test plan* lists the test phases and describes the test data that will be used in each phase.

- Four common types of run-time errors on a mainframe are *operation exceptions*, *data exceptions*, *overflow exceptions*, and *divide exceptions*.

Terms

sequential file	system name	intrinsic function
record	ddname	test plan
field	spooling	operation exception
print chart	print area	data exception
print file	input file	overflow exception
switch	output file	divide exception
filename		

Objectives

- Given the specifications for a report-preparation program like the ones in this chapter, develop a program that prepares the report.

- Given the specifications for a report-preparation program, prepare a test plan for it.

- Describe the characteristics of a sequential file on disk.

- Describe the use of a print chart.

- Describe the use of a switch.

- List two ways that you can get the current date and time into a program.

- Describe each of these types of errors: operation exception, data exception, overflow exception, and divide exception.

- If you're using Micro Focus Personal COBOL, use your word processing program to open, display, and print an input file or a print file.

Exercise 3-1   Test the sales report program

This exercise will guide you through the process of testing the sales report program in this chapter when you're using Micro Focus Personal COBOL. It will also show you how to use your word processor to review the input data and the report that's prepared from it.

Compile and test the program

1. Start Personal COBOL, and open for edit the program named rpt1000.cbl that's in the c:\cobol folder. Then, compile the program (it should have a clean compile).

2. Close the document window, and open the program for execution. Then, run the program (it should end with a return code of zero).

Review the sales report and the test data

3. Start your word processor and open the print file named salesrpt.prn that's in the c:\cobol\data folder. If it looks like the one in figure 3-15, it means the program worked correctly. If you want to print the file, delete the page break at the start of the file, adjust the font size and page setup (if necessary), and print. Then, close the file.

4. If necessary, you can also use your word processor or NotePad to review the test data for the program. To do that, open the file named custmast.dat that's in the c:\cobol\data folder. If you're using Word, the data should look the way it does in figure 3-15. Then, you can move the cursor to the end of the first record and press the Enter key to display that record on one line by itself. If you repeat that process for the next record, you get a better view of what the input data looks like. When you're through experimenting, close the file…*but don't save it or your program won't be able to open it.*

5. To test whether page overflow works, change the LINES-ON-PAGE field in your program to a value of 10, recompile, and rerun. Then, open the print file in your word processor to see whether the report prints with 10 lines per page. If it does, close the print file, reset the LINES-ON-PAGE value to 55, and recompile.

Step through the program to see how it works, then close the program

6. If you have any doubts about how this program works, use the skills you learned in chapter 2 to step through the program from the start. Or use a breakpoint to step through any parts of the program that you don't understand. As you step, display the contents of the fields that are being operated upon.

7. When you're satisfied that you understand exactly how this program works, close the document window for the program.

Exercise 3-2   Compile and test a flawed program

To give you some practice with compiling and testing a report-preparation program, this exercise forces you to correct some compile-time errors and debug some run-time errors.

Correct the compile-time errors

1. Open the program named rpt1000x for edit, and compile it. Since we put a few errors in it, it doesn't compile cleanly.

2. Correct the errors and recompile until you get a clean compile. You should be able to do that without much trouble.

Test the program

3. Close the document window and open the same program for execution. Then, run it. The first time, you should see a message box for a run-time error like this:

   Then, when you click on the OK button, you return to the Animator with the Open statement highlighted. This indicates that there's either a problem with the Select statement or the file isn't where it's supposed to be.

4. Fix the problem, recompile, and rerun the program. This time, another run-time error message is displayed: "Illegal character in numeric field." Then, when you click on the OK button, a Move statement in procedure 220 is highlighted. The clue here is that the statement moves a field from the customer master record to a numeric edited field. This indicates that there's either a problem with the data or with the FD statement or record description that defines the data, but you already know that the data is okay.

5. To fix the problem, you need to make sure that the FD and record description match up with the input specifications. When you find the problem, correct it, recompile, and rerun the program. This time the program should run to a normal termination.

6. Use your word processor to check the report that was printed. At a glance, you can see that the report is double-spaced when it should be single-spaced. Don't stop there, though; do a thorough review of the report to make sure it works correctly. Check that the data values in each column are what you expected. Then, close the word processing document and return to the Animator. Fix the problems, recompile, and retest until you've got everything working right.

Close the program

7. Close the word processing document and the program. Now, you've got two programs that work the same: rpt1000 and rpt1000x.

Exercise 3-3 Enhance the sales report program

To show you how easy it is to enhance a well-written program, this exercise guides you through the process of enhancing the sales report program.

Enhance the original program

1. Open the program named rpt1000 for edit, change the Program-ID to RPT2000, and save the program as rpt2000. Then, close and re-open the program.

2. Make the enhancements to the program that are specified in figure 3-11. To learn the most from this exercise, try to make these enhancements without referring to the code in figures 3-12 and 3-13.

3. Compile and test the enhanced program until it works correctly.

Modify the enhanced program

4. Change the Program-ID to RPT2100, save the program as rpt2100, and close and re-open it.

5. Instead of printing a customer line on the report only when this year's YTD sales are greater than or equal to $10,000, modify this version of the report so it prints a customer line when the change amount is greater than or equal to $5,000. Then, compile and test the program until that works right.

6. If that was easy enough to do, modify the report again so it prints a customer line only when the change percent is positive and greater than or equal to 25.0%. Then, compile and test the program until it works right.

Close the program

7. Close the program, and exit from Micro Focus Personal COBOL.

4

How to design, code, and test a structured program

Today, a typical COBOL program in business contains 1500 or more lines of code. When you write a program of that size, you need to use structured techniques as you design, code, and test the program. These techniques will help you work more productively and develop programs that are easier to test, debug, and maintain. In this chapter, you'll learn the structured techniques for designing a program and for coding and testing a program from the top down.

The specifications for a summary report-preparation program

Figure 4-2 presents the specifications for a program that can be used to illustrate the use of structured design, pseudocode, and top-down testing. This program reads a file of customer records that are in sequence by customer number within branch number. As the file is read, one line is printed on the sales report for each customer record. In addition, a branch total line is printed whenever the records for one branch end and those for another branch begin. At the end of the report, a grand total line is printed.

A report like this is called a *summary report* because it summarizes the data for a group of records. In contrast, a report like the one in chapter 3 is called a *detail report* because it shows just the data that's in the input records without any summary data. In this figure, the report shows both detail and summary data, but some summary reports show only the summary data (see exercise 4-3).

The trick to writing a program that prepares a summary report is determining when a summary line should be printed. This should happen whenever the value in the *control field* changes. This is referred to as a *control break*. In this case, the control field is the branch number, and the program should print a branch total line whenever the value of the branch number field changes. You'll see how this works when you review the code for this program.

As simple as this program is, it's the type of program that gave unstructured programmers fits. And it's the type of program that can give structured programmers fits too … unless they use effective methods for designing and coding the program. That's why this is a good program for illustrating some basic design principles.

When you get the specifications for a program like this, you want to make sure that you understand exactly what the program is supposed to do and how it's supposed to work. In this case, because the figure presents sample input data and printed output, you should have a clear idea of what the program is supposed to do. In practice, though, you may not get any sample data so you'll have to create your own test data.

Worse, you usually won't get a sample of the printed output. Often, in fact, you'll get just a description of what the report is supposed to look like ("a summary report by customer with group totals by branch and grand totals at the end of the report"). In that case, you'll have to design the layout of the report yourself. No matter how sketchy the initial specifications are, though, be sure that you have complete specifications and a complete understanding of what the program is supposed to do before you start to design it.

The COBOL description for the customer master record

```
01  CUSTOMER-MASTER-RECORD.
    05  CM-BRANCH-NUMBER        PIC 9(2).
    05  CM-SALESREP-NUMBER      PIC 9(2).
    05  CM-CUSTOMER-NUMBER      PIC 9(5).
    05  CM-CUSTOMER-NAME        PIC X(20).
    05  CM-SALES-THIS-YTD       PIC S9(5)V9(2).
    05  CM-SALES-LAST-YTD       PIC S9(5)V9(2).
```

The data for five customer master records

Branch Number (1-2)	Salesrep Number (3-4)	Customer Number (5-9)	Customer Name (10-29)	Sales This YTD (30-36)	Sales Last YTD (37-43)	
12	12	11111	INFORMATION BUILDERS	0123456	0111111	
12	12	12345	CAREER TRAINING CTR	1234567	2222222	**Control break**
22	10	22222	HOMELIGHT TEXTRON CO	3454500	0000000	**(branch number)**
22	14	34567	NEAS MEMBER BENEFITS	0011111	0000000	
22	14	55555	PILOT LIFE INS. CO.	1000000	0100000	

How the printed report should look

```
DATE:  02/12/2000           YEAR-TO-DATE SALES REPORT              PAGE:    1
TIME:  12:52                                                       RPT3000

BRANCH  CUST                     SALES         SALES        CHANGE      CHANGE
 NUM    NUM    CUSTOMER NAME    THIS YTD      LAST  YTD     AMOUNT      PERCENT

  12   11111  INFORMATION BUILDERS  1,234.56    1,111.11      123.45      11.1
       12345  CAREER TRAINING CTR  12,345.67   22,222.22    9,876.55-    44.4-
                     BRANCH TOTAL  13,580.23   23,333.33    9,753.10-    41.8- *

  22   22222  HOMELITE TEXTRON CO  34,545.00        0.00   34,545.00    999.9
       34567  NEAS MEMBER BENEFITS    111.11        0.00      111.11    999.9
       55555  PILOT LIFE INS. CO.  10,000.00    1,000.00    9,000.00    900.0
                     BRANCH TOTAL  44,656.11    1,000.00   43,656.11    999.9  *

  34   00111  DAUPHIN DEPOSIT BANK 14,099.00   19,930.00    5,831.00-    29.3-
       54321  AIRCRAFT OWNERS ASSC  5,426.12   40,420.00   34,993.88-    86.6-
       33333  NORFOLK CORP          6,396.35    4,462.88    1,933.47     43.3
                     BRANCH TOTAL  25,921.47   64,812.88   38,891.41-    60.0- *

  47   12121  GENERAL SERVICES CO. 11,444.00   11,059.56      384.44      3.5
       24680  INFO MANAGEMENT CO.  17,481.45   11,892.47    5,588.98     47.0
       99999  DOLLAR SAVINGS BANK   5,059.00    4,621.95      437.05      9.5
       76543  NATL MUSIC CORP.      2,383.46    4,435.26    2,051.80-    46.3-
                     BRANCH TOTAL  36,367.91   32,009.24    4,358.67     13.6  *

                      GRAND TOTAL 120,525.72  121,155.45      629.73-     0.5- **
```

The processing specifications

* This program reads the same file of customer records that the programs in chapter 3 read. These records are in sequence by customer number within branch number.
* This program prepares a report that is like the enhanced report in chapter 3, but with one additional enhancement. This time, the report includes a summary line for each branch that summarizes the sales for that branch.

Figure 4-2   The specifications for a summary report-preparation program

How to design a structured program

Once you've got the specifications for a program, you design it from the top down using the principles of *structured design*. This is a critical step in the development process. If you don't do it right, it will have a negative effect on all the steps that follow.

As you design a program, you create a *structure chart* (or *hierarchy chart*) like the one in figure 4-3 to represent all the modules of a program. To start, you draw the top-level module, which represents the entire program. Beneath that module, you draw the modules that represent the functions that the top module needs to do. You continue this process until the entire program is divided into modules that represent independent functions that can be coded in single COBOL paragraphs.

In the topics that follow, you'll go step by step through the process of designing the report-preparation program. Before you start, though, you need to learn the terms for working with a structure chart.

The terms for working with a structure chart

If a module is connected to one or more modules below it in a structure chart, the top module is a *calling module* and the lower level modules are *called modules*. Because a calling module controls the execution of the modules that it calls, it also can be referred to as a *control module*. Since a called module is subordinate to a calling module, it also can be referred to as a *subordinate module*. The lowest-level called modules also can be called *work modules* because they do their work without calling any subordinate modules.

A *common module* is a module that is called by more than one calling module, so it's shown in more than one place on the chart. Wherever a common module appears, though, it has the same module number and name. To indicate that a module is used in more than one place, you can place a black triangle in the upper right corner of the box, but other graphic conventions like an asterisk after the module number can serve the same purpose.

A *chart leg* (or a *leg of a chart*) is just programmer jargon that helps you talk about a chart. For instance, the print-customer-line leg starts with module 320 and continues through module 350. And the print-branch-line leg consists of modules 360 and 350. Simply stated, a leg is just a group of modules that consists of a calling module and all of the modules that are subordinate to it.

How to name the modules in a chart

When you design a program, each module should represent only one function, and the name for each module should indicate what that function is. To make sure that each name represents just one function, you create names that consist of a verb, an adjective, and a noun. These, for example, are acceptable module names: prepare sales report, print customer line, and write report line.

The complete structure chart for the program

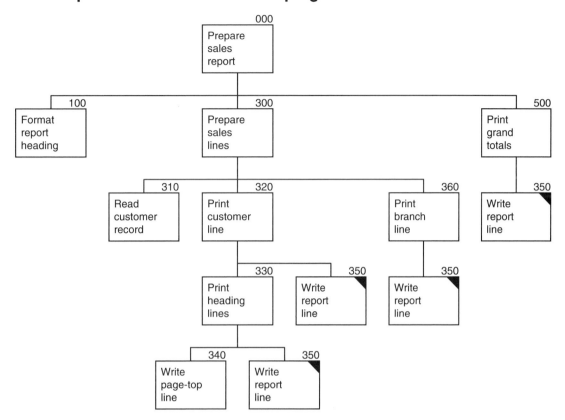

Terms for working with a structure chart

Calling module or control module	A module that connects to modules below it (like module 000, 300, or 320). A calling module *calls* subordinate modules.
Called module	A module that is connected to a module above it (like module 300, 310, or 320).
Common module	A module that is used in more than one place in a chart (like module 350). These modules are identified by a black triangle in the upper right corner of the module box.
Work module	A module that doesn't have any subordinate modules (like module 310, 340, or 350).
Chart leg	A group of modules that are subordinate to a control module, including the control module. For instance, modules 320 through 350 make up the print-customer-line leg, and modules 330 through 350 make up the print-heading-lines leg.

Figure 4-3   The structure chart for the summary report-preparation program

When you name the higher-level control modules, your names tend to be more general. As a result, "prepare" and "process" are acceptable verbs in these modules. As you get to the lower levels of your charts, however, your names should be more specific.

Within a programming group or department, you should try to agree on the verbs that you use in module names. You should also try to agree on the meanings of those verbs. For instance, you can agree that the verb *print* means "do everything associated with preparing a line for printing." If you can get all of the programmers in a COBOL shop to agree on a verb list with extended meanings like that, you go a long way toward improving program consistency throughout a shop.

Naming is important because the module names and numbers in the structure chart get converted to the procedure names in the COBOL program. For instance, module 000 in this chart becomes the procedure named 000-PREPARE-SALES-REPORT in the program, and module 320 becomes the procedure named 320-PRINT-CUSTOMER-LINE.

How to design the first two levels of a chart

Figure 4-4 shows the first two levels of the structure chart in figure 4-3 and gives some ideas for designing these levels. In all programs, the top module represents the entire program, and it becomes the first paragraph in the COBOL program. Usually, this module calls one primary module at the next level using a Perform Until statement until all of the records have been processed. In this example, the top-level module is named "prepare sales report."

The primary module that's called by the top module usually represents the processing for one set of input records. For this program, the primary module represents the processing that's done for one customer record, which includes the printing of both customer lines and branch total lines. The name of this module is "prepare sales lines," which isn't much different from the name for the top-level module.

Once you've established the top module and the primary module that it calls, you can add modules for functions that need to be done before the primary module starts doing its work and modules for functions that need to be done after the primary module finishes its work. In this figure, you can see that one module is added before the primary module and one after it. The first module formats the heading lines needed by the report. The last module prints the grand total lines for the report.

When you design the modules that are done before and after the primary control module, remember that each module should do one and only one function. So if two or more functions need to be done before or after the primary control module, add two or more modules to the chart. In particular, avoid the use of general-purpose modules with names like "program initialization" or "end-of-file processing" that do all of the functions that need to be done before or after the primary control module.

The primary control modules of the report-preparation program

All the modules in the first two levels of the report-preparation program

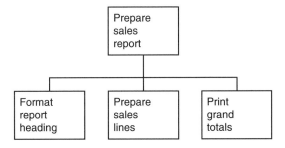

A general procedure for designing the first two levels of a structure chart

1. Draw the top-level module and give it a name that represents the entire program (like "prepare sales report").

2. Draw the primary control module that's subordinate to the top-level module. The primary control module is the one that is performed repeatedly from the top-level module with a Perform Until statement. The name for this module should represent the processing for one input record or one set of input records (like "prepare sales lines").

3. Draw one module in the second level for each function that has to be done *before* any of the input records can be processed. In the example above, the format-report-heading module should be performed before the sales lines are prepared.

4. Draw one module in the second level for each function that has to be done *after* all the input records have been processed. In the example above, this is the print-grand-totals module.

Note

*   Each module on the chart should represent a single function. As a result, you shouldn't have one module for all the functions that have to be done before the main processing of the program and another one for all the functions that have to be done after the main processing. Instead, you should have one module for each individual function.

Figure 4-4   How to design the first two levels of a chart

How to design the legs of a chart

Figure 4-5 presents the primary leg of the chart in figure 4-3 along with some ideas for designing the legs of a chart. The idea is to create one subordinate module for each function that a higher-level module needs to do. To prepare the sales lines for a set of input records, for example, you need at least three subordinate modules. One module must read the next customer record. Another must print the customer line for that record. The third must print a branch total line whenever the customer number changes.

After you create the subordinate modules for one calling module, you continue the process for the next level of the chart. To print the customer line, for example, the print-customer-line module needs to call a module that prints the heading lines whenever page overflow occurs.

If necessary, you continue this process for subsequent levels of the chart. You stop when all of the lowest-level functions are work modules that don't require any subordinate functions. In this figure, for example, the chart could be considered complete. As you'll learn in the next topic, however, we recommend that you include a separate module for each Read and Write function the program requires. After you design and code a few programs of your own, you'll find that this is a manageable process that you can do with relative ease.

The prepare-sales-lines leg of the report-preparation program

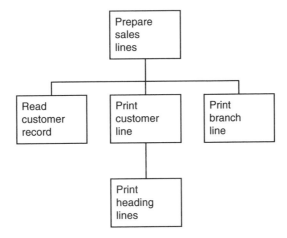

A general procedure for designing one leg of a structure chart

1. Draw one subordinate module for each function that the control module at the top of the leg needs to do. To prepare the sales lines, for example, the prepare-sales-lines module must read a customer record, print one customer line for each record, and, if necessary, print a total line for the branch.

2. Use the same thought process for the next level of modules. If any of them require more than one function, draw one subordinate module for each function. To print a customer line, for example, the print-customer-line module must print heading lines after skipping to the top of the next page when page overflow occurs.

3. If necessary, continue this process until each of the lowest-level modules consists of just one function.

Notes

*   Here again, each module should represent a single function.
*   When you're new to structured design, you may have a hard time deciding what the subordinate modules for a higher-level module should be or when the design process should end. You'll get better at that, though, as you get more experience coding the modules of a structure chart.

Figure 4-5 How to design the legs of a chart

How to add the Read and Write modules to a chart

When you design a program, you should include a separate module for each Read and Write statement required by the program. Figure 4-6 explains why and illustrates the additional modules that are required by the report-preparation program. One of these modules then can be called whenever a record needs to be read or written. By isolating the Read and Write statements in this way, you end up with a more efficient program and one that is easier to debug.

To write the lines on a report, a program requires two Write modules. The write-page-top-line module writes a line after advancing to the top of the next page. The write-report-line module writes a line after advancing one or more lines. Two modules are necessary because you can't use one Write After Advancing statement for both purposes.

In some cases, it's obvious that a Read or Write function should be included as a separate module. For instance, the read-customer-record module in figure 4-5 was included as a logical part of the design process. In other cases, you have to deliberately isolate the Read and Write statements in their own modules.

When you code a Read or Write module, the primary code is the Read or Write statement itself. In addition, a Read module is a good place to count the number of records read (a common practice), and a Write module is a good place to count the number of lines printed on each page of a report.

If you look at the note in this figure, you can see that the design of the print-branch-line and print-grand-totals legs implies that heading lines won't be printed before the branch and grand total lines, even if it's time for page over-flow. That way, the branch totals and grand totals will be printed at the bottom of the current page rather than at the top of a new page. If you want to provide for page overflow before printing a branch or grand total line, the print-heading-lines module has to be a common module that's subordinate to the print-branch-line and print-grand-totals modules as well as to the print-customer-line module.

The legs of the report-preparation program after the Read and Write modules have been added

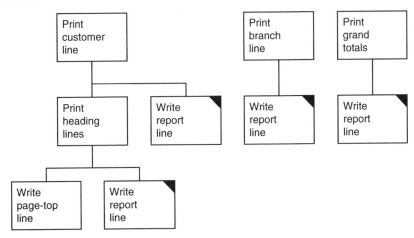

Why you should create a separate module for each Read or Write statement

- Read and Write statements are often the source of testing and debugging problems. That's why we recommend that each Read or Write statement for a file be coded in a separate module. Then, it's easy to locate and modify the Read and Write statements when problems occur.
- When each Read and Write statement is in its own module, there is usually just one Read statement for each input disk file, one Write statement for each output disk file, and two Write statements for each print file. This can improve both compile-time and run-time efficiency.

A general procedure for adding the Read and Write modules

- If necessary, add one Read module for each Read statement required by the program.
- If necessary, add one Write module for each Write statement required for an output disk file.
- If necessary, add two Write modules for each print file required by the program. The first module will skip to the top of the next page and print the first line on that page. The second module will print all the other lines of the document.

Note

- The print-branch-line leg and the print-grand-totals leg don't provide for page overflow. That way, these lines will be printed at the bottom of the current page instead of at the top of a new page. A typical report-preparation program usually allows enough space at the bottom of a page for these additional lines.

Figure 4-6   How to add Read and Write modules to a chart

How to number the modules in a chart

Figure 4-7 illustrates a practical system for numbering the modules in a chart. Just start with the top module, number the second level across in large increments, and number down the legs from the third level on. As you number, leave gaps so you can add modules to the program later on without renumbering.

In the resulting COBOL program, the module numbers become part of the paragraph names in the Procedure Division, and the paragraphs are kept in module number sequence. This means that most of the called paragraphs will be found right after the calling paragraph. This reduces the amount of page flipping or screen paging that you have to do when you read a program.

Note that the numbers do *not* indicate at what level a module can be found. This means that changes can be made to the structure chart without changing module numbers. In contrast, when more complex numbering systems are used, a change to the structure chart usually means a change to the module number, which in turn means a change in the COBOL source code.

Although this is the numbering system we recommend, you should realize that other systems can be used. In some shops, for example, a letter is used to indicate the type of module, so the number E420 may indicate that the module is a Read or Write module. In other shops, a letter indicates the module's level, such as C600 for the third level. Because the level might change, though, this numbering system is not recommended.

Frankly, numbering variations like those have only a minimal effect on program quality or programmer productivity. What's important is that the modules are numbered and that they are coded in the Procedure Division in sequence by module number. That way, they're easy to find.

How to draw charts that won't fit on one page

If you draw a chart that doesn't fit on one page, you can easily spread it over two or more pages. To do that, you put the number of the continuation page below a module that starts a leg that you want to continue on a later page. Then, you repeat this module on the continuation page and design its leg.

To illustrate, suppose the chart is large and you want to put the prepare-sales-lines leg of the chart on a second page. To do that, you put "Page 2" beneath module 300 on page 1. Then, you repeat module 300 on a second page, and design the leg on that page. As simple as this method is, it provides for charts of many pages with little chance for confusion.

The numbering sequence for the report-preparation program

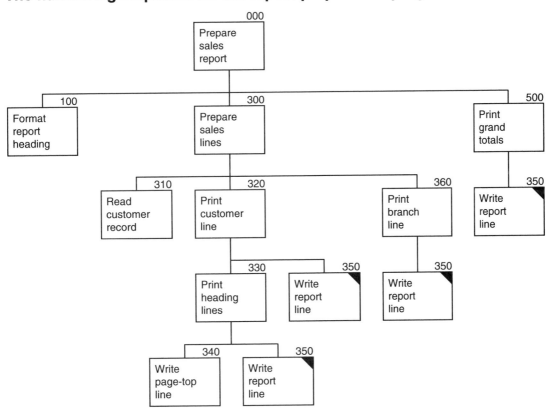

Numbering guidelines

- Use 000 or 0000 for the top-level module.
- Number the modules in the second level of the chart from left to right leaving large enough gaps for subordinate modules. If a chart is small, you can use hundreds at this level (like 100, 300, and 500). If a chart is large, you can use thousands (1000, 3000, and 5000). The goal is to leave number gaps large enough to provide for any subordinate modules.
- After the first two levels, number the modules down each leg in appropriate increments like tens or hundreds. That way, you can add modules to the chart later on without changing the numbers.

Notes

- When you code one COBOL paragraph for each module later on, the paragraph name will be the module number followed by the module name as in this example: 300-PREPARE-SALES-LINES.
- In the Procedure Division, you should keep the paragraphs in the sequence of the module numbers. That way, the called modules in each leg closely follow the calling modules, and it's easier to find specific modules.

Figure 4-7   How to number the modules in a chart

Alternatives to the structure chart

Although we've used the structure chart to illustrate the design process, you should be aware that there are graphical alternatives to the structure chart. These include tree charts, Warnier-Orr diagrams, and Nassi-Schneiderman diagrams. No matter what you use, though, you must design from the top down with one function in each module if you want to develop an effective structured program. In other words, the graphical differences shouldn't have any effect on the design and naming principles.

The trouble with all design documents including the structure chart is that it takes so long to create and modify them. That's true whether you draw them by hand or use PC software to create them. That's why most programmers today don't take the time to design their programs. Instead, they "compose" their programs as they enter the COBOL code, which means they're designing their programs as they code. As we see it, that's a major mistake that seriously degrades the quality of a COBOL program.

With that in mind, we suggest the simple alternative to the structure chart that's presented in figure 4-8. This is an outline called a *structure listing* that can be created in just a few minutes by using the outline feature of any modern word processor. Once created, you can easily make changes to the structure; you can analyze the structure with one or more of the lower levels hidden; and you no longer have an excuse for skipping the design phase of programming.

Then, when you finish a program, you can easily update the structure listing so it corresponds to the COBOL code and include it as part of the documentation for the program. An even better alternative, though, is to generate a structure listing from the COBOL code itself. That way, you're sure that the structure listing corresponds to the finished program.

In our shop, we developed a COBOL program called LISTMODS that generates a structure listing from another COBOL program. This program works as long as you adhere to the coding standards that are presented in this book. Then, the final documentation for a program is the COBOL code and the structure listing generated from the code. In exercise 4-4 at the end of this chapter, you'll use LISTMODS to generate a structure listing from your own program.

A structure listing for the report-preparation program

```
000-prepare-sales-report
    100-format-report-heading
    300-prepare-sales-lines
        310-read-customer-record
        320-print-customer-line
            330-print-heading-lines
                340-write-page-top-line
                350-write-report-line (c)
            350-write-report-line (c)
        360-print-branch-line
            350-write-report-line (c)
    500-print-grand-totals
        350-write-report-line (c)
```

A structure listing with only the first three levels shown

```
000-prepare-sales-report
    100-format-report-heading
    300-prepare-sales-lines
        310-read-customer-record
        320-print-customer-line
        360-print-branch-line
    500-print-grand-totals
        350-write-report-line (c)
```

Description

- A *structure listing* is an outline that uses indentation to show the levels of the modules. The letter c in parentheses can be used to identify common modules.

- A structure listing can be used to plan the modules of a program, and it also can be used as documentation when the program is finished.

How to create a structure listing

- When you're designing a program, you can use the outline feature of any modern word processor to prepare a structure listing. This feature lets you hide the lower levels of the outline so you can analyze the structure of the higher levels. This feature also makes it easy to reorganize the listing.

- When a program is finished, you can use a structure listing program to generate a structure listing from the COBOL code for the finished program. That way, you can be sure that the structure listing is accurate.

Figure 4-8   A simple alternative to the structure chart

When and how to use pseudocode

When you're new to structured program design or COBOL programming, you may have difficulty visualizing how some of the modules of the structure chart are going to be coded. That's particularly true for some of the higher-level control modules. You also may wonder whether a module can be coded in a single COBOL paragraph. In cases like those, you can remove any doubts by using *pseudocode* to plan the code for the modules in question.

The basics of using pseudocode

Figure 4-9 presents two examples of pseudocode and gives some guidelines for using it. As you can see, pseudocode is just a programmer's shorthand that lets you concentrate on the logic of the program instead of the programming details. When you use pseudocode, it's for your own use so you don't have to follow any rigid rules. Just use what works best for you.

In the past, programmers have used flowcharts to plan the coding of modules. But drawing flowcharts is a time-consuming process that clearly reduces programmer productivity. Besides that, studies have shown that it's easier to read and understand the logic of pseudocode (or COBOL code) than it is to interpret flowcharts. That's why flowcharts are no longer used as planning or documentation tools and pseudocode is the preferred tool for planning what you're going to code.

Simple pseudocode

```
Module 000:
    Open files.
    DO 100.
    DO 300
        UNTIL no more customer master records.
    DO 500.
    Close files.
    Stop run.
```

Pseudocode plus COBOL

```
000-prepare-sales-report.
    Open files.
    PERFORM 100-format-report-heading.
    PERFORM 300-prepare-sales-lines
        UNTIL custmast-eof-switch = "Y".
    PERFORM 500-print-grand-totals.
    Close files.
    Stop run.
```

How to use pseudocode

- Pseudocode is programmers' shorthand for the coding that a module is going to require in COBOL. As a result, you don't have to follow any rigid rules when coding it.

- In the simple form of pseudocode shown above, you code the structured programming verbs in capital letters with DO used as shorthand for PERFORM. You use just the module numbers (not the names too) when you need to refer to a module. And you use whatever shorthand you prefer for all other functions.

- If you prefer to prepare more directly for COBOL coding, you can use COBOL verbs and language that's closer to COBOL as shown in the second example above. Pseudocode is your own shorthand, so do it the way that works best for you.

When to use pseudocode

- Pseudocode is most useful when you're not sure whether the program design represented by the structure chart is going to work. Then, you can use pseudocode to plan the critical modules. Sometimes, this leads to a change in the structure chart. Other times, it assures you that your design is going to work.

- Pseudocode is also useful when you're not sure how a module on a structure chart is going to be coded or whether it can be coded in a single COBOL paragraph.

Figure 4-9   When and how to use pseudocode to plan the modules of a program

How to use pseudocode for the critical modules of a program

To show the value of pseudocode, figure 4-10 presents the pseudocode for the three critical modules of figure 4-7's structure chart. As you can see, module 000 repeatedly performs module 300, which represents the processing for one set of input records (in this case, one customer master record). This continues until there are no more records in the customer master file.

Module 300 is the most difficult in the entire program. It uses two switches to control its processing. One switch is used to tell whether the last record in the customer file has been read; the other switch is used to control the processing for the first record in the master file. Here, you can assume that custmast-eof-switch is set to N and first-record-switch is set to Y in working storage.

As its primary task, module 300 determines when to print customer lines and branch total lines. To accomplish this, module 300 uses a nested If statement that varies the processing based on three different conditions. If the custmast-eof switch is off (condition 1), the next If statement in the nest is executed. Then, if the first-record switch is on (condition 2), the program prints a customer line, turns the first-record switch off, and sets the old-branch-number control field to the branch number in the first record. After the first record has been processed, if the branch number in the next record is greater than the old branch number (condition 3), the program prints a branch total line for the old branch followed by a customer line for the current customer and then sets the old branch number equal to the current branch number. But if the branch number hasn't changed, the program just prints another customer line. Last, after all the records have been processed and the eof switch has been turned on (the last Else clause), the program prints a branch total line for the final branch.

Module 320 is the last control module of any difficulty. It starts by checking the line count to determine if it's time to start a new page. If it is, module 320 calls module 330. Then, it uses a nested If statement to determine if the branch number should be included in the customer line. As you can see, the branch number is included for the first record and whenever the branch number changes. Otherwise, module 320 just computes and moves the other fields that are going to be printed into the customer line. After that, it calls module 350 to actually print the assembled customer line. Last, it adds the customer totals to the branch totals for the next branch total line.

By writing the pseudocode for the critical modules, you can test the design of your program before you actually code the program. In some cases, you'll find that you have to restructure, add, or delete modules. When you're done, though, you'll have confidence that your design is going to work.

Why then do most COBOL programmers avoid pseudocode? Because once you get experience, it's usually more efficient to enter COBOL code directly into a source program. That way, you still can focus on the code for the critical modules, but you don't have to first code a module in pseudocode and then enter the code into the source program. When you're learning, though, pseudocode is a valuable planning tool that you should use whenever you think it will help you.

Pseudocode for the critical modules

```
000-prepare-sales-report.
    Open files.
    DO 100-format-report-heading.
    DO 300-prepare-sales-lines
        UNTIL custmast-eof-switch = "Y".
    DO 500-print-grand-totals.
    Close files.
    Stop run.


300-prepare-sales-lines.
    DO 310-read-customer-record.
    IF custmast-eof-switch = "N"————————————————————— Condition 1
        IF first-record-switch = "Y"————————————————— Condition 2
            DO 320-print-customer-line
            move "N" to first-record-switch
            move cm-branch-number to old-branch-number
        ELSE
            IF cm-branch-number > old-branch-number——————— Condition 3
                DO 360-print-branch-line
                DO 320-print-customer-line
                move cm-branch-number to old-branch-number
            ELSE
                DO 320-print-customer-line
    ELSE
        DO 360-print-branch-line.

320-print-customer-line.
    IF line-count > lines-on-page
        DO 330-print-heading-lines.
    IF first-record-switch = "Y"
        move cm-branch-number to customer line
    ELSE
        IF cm-branch-number > old-branch-number
            move cm-branch-number to branch number in customer line
        ELSE
            move spaces to branch number in customer line.
    Move the other required fields to the customer line.
    Compute the required fields for the customer line.
    DO 350-write-report-line.
    Add customer totals to branch totals.
```

Note

- The processing represented by the last line in module 320, adding the customer totals to the branch totals, could be coded in module 300 since it isn't technically a part of printing a customer line. In our shop, however, we have agreed to add line totals to group totals in the module that prints the line.

Figure 4-10   Pseudocode for the critical modules of the report-preparation program

How to code each module so it is independent

Perhaps the most important principle of structured programming is that each module should be coded so it's as independent as possible. That way, you should be able to read the code in a paragraph without referring to other paragraphs in the program. This in turn makes a program easier to read, test, and debug.

To help you achieve module independence in your programs, figure 4-11 presents some useful guidelines. The most important of these is the first one, which says that the code for each module should contain *all* of the code for the function that the module represents and *only* the code for that function. If you obey that principle, your modules will be largely independent, which will make your program easier to code, test, debug, and maintain.

Even if you follow all of the guidelines in this figure, though, you can't ever achieve the goal of complete module independence. That's because all modules are somewhat dependent on the processing done by other modules. If, for example, one module tests the value of a switch set by another module, the first module depends on the processing done by the second module. In practice, then, you just do the best you can to keep each module as independent as possible.

Because passing switch values can easily get out of control in a structured program, you should try to pass them in a predictable way. That's why the fourth guideline in this figure recommends that you pass switch values up the legs of a chart, but not down or across. This means that a calling module can refer to a switch value that has been set by one of its subordinates and adjust its processing accordingly. However, a calling module shouldn't refer to a switch value that's set in another leg or in a higher level module of the structure chart. This simple guideline will help insure that you don't use switches in a way that makes programs harder to read, test, and debug.

One common mistake that reduces module independence is illustrated by the first example in this figure. Here, the programmer has created a module called 200-initialize-sales-report that does the processing for the first customer master record. The trouble is that this processing should be part of module 300, which is supposed to prepare all of the sales lines in the report. By dividing the code over two modules, neither module is independent. Although this seems innocent enough in this simple program, this can lead to serious debugging and maintenance programs in more complicated programs.

Another common mistake is illustrated by the second example in this figure. Here, module 320 contains the control code that decides whether or not it does its own function: to print a customer line. But this makes it impossible to read and understand the module that calls it without looking at the code in this subordinate module. To solve this problem, the first If statement should be moved up into the calling module. Although that will make the code in the calling module more complicated, you'll be able to read it without checking the code in module 320, and the code in module 320 will be simplified.

Guidelines for keeping each module independent

- The code for each module should contain *all* of the code for the function of the module and *only* the code for the function of the module.
- In general, you should be able to code a module without checking the code for other modules, and you should be able to read and understand the code for a module without checking the code for other modules.
- Each control module should determine when each of its subordinate modules is called. As a result, a module should *not* contain the code that decides whether its own processing is done.
- Switches should be passed up the legs of a chart, not down or across.

Two modules that aren't independent because module 200 does work that should be done in module 300

```
000-prepare-sales-report.
    Open files.
    DO 100-format-report-heading.
    DO 200-initialize-sales-report.
    DO 300-prepare-sales-lines
        until custmast-eof-switch = "Y".
    DO 500-print-grand-totals.
    Close files.
    Stop run.

200-initialize-sales-report.
    DO 310-read-customer-record.
    IF custmast-eof-switch = "N"
        DO 320-print-customer-line
        move cm-branch-number to old-branch-number.

300-prepare-sales-lines.
    DO 310-read-customer-record.
    IF custmast-eof-switch = "N"
        IF cm-branch-number = old-branch-number
            DO 320-print-customer-line
        ELSE
            DO 360-print-branch-line
            DO 320-print-customer-line
            move cm-branch-number to old-branch-number
    ELSE
        DO 360-print-branch-line.
```

A module that decides whether its own function is done

```
320-print-customer-line.
    IF cm-sales-this-ytd >= 10000
        IF line-count > lines-on-page
            DO 330-print-heading-lines
        END-IF
        move required fields to customer line
        compute the required fields for the customer line
        DO 350-write-report-line
        add customer totals to grand totals.
```

Figure 4-11   How to code each module so it is independent

How to code and test a program from the top down

When you take the time to design a program, you then can code and test the program from the top down. This is called *top-down coding and testing*, or just *top-down testing*.

When you use top-down testing, you start by coding and testing the top module of the program along with a few subordinate modules. Once these modules work correctly, you code and test a few more modules. When these modules plus the earlier modules work correctly, you code and test a few more modules, and you continue like this until all of the modules are coded and tested.

Two obvious benefits of top-down testing are (1) that it's relatively easy to find and correct bugs when you test only a few modules at a time, and (2) that it's easier to make sure that you test all of the conditions in each module. From management's point of view, this translates into improved programmer productivity and fewer bugs in the programs that are put into production. From a programmer's point of view, this is a more enjoyable way to develop programs. The alternative is to code the entire program and then try to find and correct the dozens of bugs that a large program is likely to contain … a potential nightmare!

How to plan the coding and testing sequence

To plan the coding and testing sequence you're going to use, we recommend that you develop a *test plan* using the guidelines presented in figure 4-12. This figure also presents two acceptable test plans for the summary report-preparation program to show that there isn't just one right sequence for testing the modules. In the test plans in this figure, the module numbers correspond to the structure chart in figure 4-7.

In phase 1 of the first test plan, the input data consists of just three records, and only customer lines are printed on the report. In phase 2, the modules for printing the heading lines are added. And in phase 3, the module for printing the branch lines is added. These three phases test the critical logic of the program. After that, the module for printing grand totals is added.

In contrast, the second test sequence in this figure tests the critical logic of the program in the first two phases and doesn't even use test data until phase 3. Then, phase 3 can determine whether there are any bugs related to the data (a common problem), and phase 4 can test the modules that format the report heading and print the grand totals.

Which sequence of testing is better? That depends on the programmer. Yes, you should try to test the critical modules early in the plan. But otherwise, you can use the testing sequence that suits you best. What's most important is that you take the time to make a plan.

Guidelines for preparing a top-down test plan

- Test just a few modules at a time, but test all of the processing in each module.
- Test the critical modules of the program early in the plan.
- Test the remaining modules in whatever sequence you prefer.
- Keep the test data to a minimum in the early test phases.

A top-down test plan for the report preparation program

Phase	Modules	Test data
1	000, 300, 310, 320, 350	Three customer records: 2 for one branch and 1 for the second branch
2	Add 100, 330, and 340	Same as above
3	Add 360	Same as above
4	Add 500	Same as above
5	All modules	Enough customer records to test page overflow

Another acceptable sequence of modules to be tested

Phase	Modules	Test data
1	000, 300, 320-350	Simulate one input record for module 310
2	Add 360	Same as above
3	Add 310	Three customer records: 2 for one branch and 1 for the second branch
4	Add 100 and 500	Same as above
5	All modules	Enough customer records to test page overflow

Figure 4-12   How to plan the coding and testing sequence

How to code the new modules for each phase of testing

Figure 4-13 presents some basic guidelines for coding the new modules for each phase of testing. In particular, you should note that you don't have to code the complete Environment or Data Division before you start testing the program. Instead, you need to code only the entries that are required by the Procedure Division modules that are going to be tested.

In phase 1 of the first sequence in figure 4-12, for example, only customer lines are going to be printed. As a result, you don't have to code the Data Division entries for the heading, branch, or total lines. Instead, you can add these entries when you test the modules that print the heading, branch, and total lines.

When you add a module to the Procedure Division, it's usually best to code it in its entirety. Then, if you want to exclude the processing of one or more lines, you can add an asterisk to column 7 of the line so it's treated as a comment. This is referred to as *commenting a line*. In this figure, the statements that perform module 360 are commented. Later on, when you're ready for a commented line to be tested, you can remove the asterisk, which is referred to as *uncommenting a line*.

Another way to handle this is to code a program stub for each paragraph that isn't going to be coded and tested until a later testing phase. You'll learn how to code program stubs next.

Guidelines for coding and testing from the top down

- To start, code the Identification Division and as much of the Environment and Data Divisions as are needed for the first phase of testing. Then, code the Procedure Division modules that are going to be tested.

- When you add new modules to the Procedure Division for the next phase of testing, add any code in the Environment or Data Division required to support those modules.

- If necessary, put an asterisk (*) in column 7 of any Procedure Division statement that you don't want executed during a test run. This, however, may force you to make some other programming adjustments.

How Perform statements can be treated as comments

```
300-PREPARE-SALES-LINES.
*
    PERFORM 310-READ-CUSTOMER-RECORD.
    IF CUSTMAST-EOF-SWITCH = "N"
        IF FIRST-RECORD-SWITCH = "Y"
            PERFORM 320-PRINT-CUSTOMER-LINE
            MOVE "N" TO FIRST-RECORD-SWITCH
            MOVE CM-BRANCH-NUMBER TO OLD-BRANCH-NUMBER
        ELSE
            IF CM-BRANCH-NUMBER > OLD-BRANCH-NUMBER
*               PERFORM 360-PRINT-BRANCH-LINE
                PERFORM 320-PRINT-CUSTOMER-LINE
                MOVE CM-BRANCH-NUMBER TO OLD-BRANCH-NUMBER
            ELSE
                PERFORM 320-PRINT-CUSTOMER-LINE
*   ELSE
*       PERFORM 360-PRINT-BRANCH-LINE.
    .
```

Note

- Because the last two lines in the nested If statement are commented out, you have to add a period to end the If statement. Otherwise, you'll get a compile-time error. In the code above, the period is added after the Else clause on a new line.

Figure 4-13   How to code the new modules for each phase of testing

How to code program stubs

Figure 4-14 presents the guidelines for coding the *program stubs* (or *dummy modules*) required for a test run. These are the modules that are called by other modules, but aren't fully coded yet. In conversation, the process of writing a program stub for a module is often referred to as "stubbing off" a module.

If a program stub doesn't have to do anything for the test run to work properly, the stub can consist of just the paragraph name. This is illustrated by the first example in this figure. Then, when the paragraph is performed, nothing is done and the program continues.

A step above this is to include a Display statement in the stub that displays the name of the module on the screen to show that it has been executed. This is illustrated by the second example in this figure.

For a program stub that represents an input module, it sometimes makes sense to simulate the reading of one or more records in the file. If, for example, the test data for a program isn't ready yet, this lets you start testing the program without waiting for the data. In the third example in this figure, the read stub just indicates that all the records in the file have been read. In the fourth example, the read stub simulates the reading of one record the first time it's executed and indicates that all the records in the file have been read the second time it's executed.

Similarly, an output stub can display a record on the screen instead of writing the record to a file or printing it. This is illustrated by the last example in this figure.

As you create your program stubs, the goal is to get the testing done right with a minimum of extra work. In most cases, you can do that with simple stubs that cause little extra work. When a program stub starts getting too elaborate, you're usually better off coding the entire module and adding it to that test phase.

Guidelines for coding a program stub

- If a program stub doesn't have to do anything for the successful completion of a test run, the module can consist of the paragraph name only.
- If you want to see whether a program stub gets executed during a test run, you can include a statement that displays the module name.
- If necessary, an input stub can simulate the reading of one or more records; a table-loading stub can simulate the loading of one or more table entries; a search stub can simulate the searching of a table; and so on.

A processing stub that consists of only the paragraph name

```
360-PRINT-BRANCH-LINE.
*
```

A processing stub that displays its module name to show that it has been executed

```
360-PRINT-BRANCH-LINE.
*
    DISPLAY "360-PRINT-BRANCH-LINE".
```

An input stub that displays its module name and sets the end-of-file switch

```
310-READ-CUSTOMER-RECORD.
*
    DISPLAY "310-READ-CUSTOMER-RECORD".
    MOVE "Y" TO CUSTMAST-EOF-SWITCH.
```

An input stub that simulates the reading of one input record, then sets the end-of-file switch

```
310-READ-CUSTOMER-RECORD.
*
    IF FIRST-RECORD-SWITCH = "Y"
        MOVE "019912345ORIGINAL SYSTEMS     01000000010000"
            TO CUSTOMER-MASTER-RECORD
    ELSE
        MOVE "Y" TO CUSTMAST-EOF-SWITCH.
```

An output stub that displays a record instead of writing it

```
350-WRITE-REPORT-LINE.
*
    DISPLAY "350-WRITE-REPORT-LINE".
    DISPLAY PRINT-AREA.
```

Figure 4-14   How to code program stubs

The code for the summary report-preparation program

Now that you've learned the basics of structured design, you should study the code for the summary report-preparation program that was introduced in figure 4-2. That way, you can see how each module in the structure chart is coded.

As you review this code, keep in mind that you have been using structured code from the start of this book. As a result, you already know how to code a structured program. That's the only type of coding that's illustrated in this book.

The Data Division code

Instead of presenting the complete Data Division for this program, figure 4-15 presents the primary additions and changes to the code for the detail report-preparation program that was presented in chapter 3. Besides these changes, spaces have been added within the first two heading lines so they are the same width as the customer, branch, and total lines, and the program name in the second heading line has been changed to RPT3000.

In this figure, you can see that a first-record switch has been added to the switches group. This switch, which has a starting value of Y, is used to control the processing for the first record in the customer master file.

After the switches, you can see a new group for control fields. For this program, this group requires only one field, but a more complicated report often requires two or more control fields. If, for example, summary lines were to be printed for salesreps as well as for branches, the program would require two control fields. As a result, this is a group that you'll use in many report-preparation programs.

After that, you can see that branch total fields have been added to the total-fields group. You can see how the heading and customer lines have been changed to accommodate the branch number column in the report. And you can see the complete description for the branch total line. Finally, you can see that the words GRAND TOTAL have been added to the beginning of the grand total line and two asterisks have been added to the end of that line.

Data Division code

```
01   SWITCHES.
     05   CUSTMAST-EOF-SWITCH      PIC X    VALUE "N".
     05   FIRST-RECORD-SWITCH      PIC X    VALUE "Y".
*
01   CONTROL-FIELDS.
     05   OLD-BRANCH-NUMBER        PIC 99.
     .
     .
01   TOTAL-FIELDS.
     05   BRANCH-TOTAL-THIS-YTD    PIC S9(6)V99    VALUE ZERO.
     05   BRANCH-TOTAL-LAST-YTD    PIC S9(6)V99    VALUE ZERO.
     05   GRAND-TOTAL-THIS-YTD     PIC S9(7)V99    VALUE ZERO.
     05   GRAND-TOTAL-LAST-YTD     PIC S9(7)V99    VALUE ZERO.
*
01   HEADING-LINE-3.
     05   FILLER      PIC X(8)     VALUE "BRANCH  ".
     .
     .
     05   FILLER      PIC X(44)    VALUE SPACE.
*
01   HEADING-LINE-4.
     05   FILLER      PIC X(8)     VALUE " NUM    ".
     .
     .
     05   FILLER      PIC X(44)    VALUE SPACE.
*
01   CUSTOMER-LINE.
     05   FILLER               PIC X(2)        VALUE SPACE.
     05   CL-BRANCH-NUMBER     PIC X(2).
     05   FILLER               PIC X(4)        VALUE SPACE.
     .
     .
     05   FILLER               PIC X(47)       VALUE SPACE.
*
01   BRANCH-TOTAL-LINE.
     05   FILLER               PIC X(23)       VALUE SPACE.
     05   FILLER               PIC X(14)       VALUE "BRANCH TOTAL".
     05   BTL-SALES-THIS-YTD   PIC ZZZ,ZZ9.99-.
     05   FILLER               PIC X(3)        VALUE SPACE.
     05   BTL-SALES-LAST-YTD   PIC ZZZ,ZZ9.99-.
     05   FILLER               PIC X(3)        VALUE SPACE.
     05   BTL-CHANGE-AMOUNT    PIC ZZZ,ZZ9.99-.
     05   FILLER               PIC X(3)        VALUE SPACE.
     05   BTL-CHANGE-PERCENT   PIC ZZ9.9-.
     05   FILLER               PIC X(47)       VALUE " *".
*
01   GRAND-TOTAL-LINE.
     05   FILLER               PIC X(23)       VALUE SPACE.
     05   FILLER               PIC X(12)       VALUE "GRAND TOTAL".
     .
     .
     05   FILLER               PIC X(47)       VALUE " **".
```

Figure 4-15   The changes to the Data Division code for the summary report-preparation program

The Procedure Division code

Figure 4-16 presents the entire Procedure Division for the summary report-preparation program. Because you've already seen the pseudocode for its critical modules, you should be able to follow this code with few problems. But here are some explanatory notes.

Although this program is similar to the programs you saw in chapter 3, the numbers of some of the procedures have been changed to correspond with the structure chart in figure 4-7. In particular, modules 200, 210, 220, 230, and 300 have been renumbered to 300, 310, 320, 330, and 500, respectively.

Procedure 300 starts by calling procedure 310 to read the first (or next) customer record. If the first-record switch is on, procedure 300 calls procedure 320 to print the first customer line on the report. After that, it turns off the switch and moves the branch number of the first record into the control field (OLD-BRANCH-NUMBER). That sets up the processing for the records that follow.

The next time procedure 300 is performed, the first-record switch is off and the nested If statements test to see whether the branch number in the record that has just been read is greater than the old branch number. If it is, a control break has occurred so procedure 300 calls procedure 360 to print a branch line for the previous branch, calls procedure 320 to print the first customer line for the next branch, and moves the new branch number to the old branch number. But if a control break hasn't occurred, procedure 300 calls procedure 320 to print another customer line within the same branch.

This is the critical logic of the program. Once you understand it, you won't have much trouble coding summary report-preparation programs.

Procedure Division code   **Page 1**

```
PROCEDURE DIVISION.
*
 000-PREPARE-SALES-REPORT.
*
     OPEN INPUT  CUSTMAST
          OUTPUT SALESRPT.
     PERFORM 100-FORMAT-REPORT-HEADING.
     PERFORM 300-PREPARE-SALES-LINES
         UNTIL CUSTMAST-EOF-SWITCH = "Y".
     PERFORM 500-PRINT-GRAND-TOTALS.
     CLOSE CUSTMAST
           SALESRPT.
     STOP RUN.
*
 100-FORMAT-REPORT-HEADING.
*
     MOVE FUNCTION CURRENT-DATE TO CURRENT-DATE-AND-TIME.
     MOVE CD-MONTH   TO HL1-MONTH.
     MOVE CD-DAY     TO HL1-DAY.
     MOVE CD-YEAR    TO HL1-YEAR.
     MOVE CD-HOURS   TO HL2-HOURS.
     MOVE CD-MINUTES TO HL2-MINUTES.
*
 300-PREPARE-SALES-LINES.
*
     PERFORM 310-READ-CUSTOMER-RECORD.
     IF CUSTMAST-EOF-SWITCH = "N"
         IF FIRST-RECORD-SWITCH = "Y"
             PERFORM 320-PRINT-CUSTOMER-LINE
             MOVE "N" TO FIRST-RECORD-SWITCH
             MOVE CM-BRANCH-NUMBER TO OLD-BRANCH-NUMBER
         ELSE
             IF CM-BRANCH-NUMBER > OLD-BRANCH-NUMBER
                 PERFORM 360-PRINT-BRANCH-LINE
                 PERFORM 320-PRINT-CUSTOMER-LINE
                 MOVE CM-BRANCH-NUMBER TO OLD-BRANCH-NUMBER
             ELSE
                 PERFORM 320-PRINT-CUSTOMER-LINE
     ELSE
         PERFORM 360-PRINT-BRANCH-LINE.
*
 310-READ-CUSTOMER-RECORD.
*
     READ CUSTMAST
         AT END
             MOVE "Y" TO CUSTMAST-EOF-SWITCH.
*
```

Figure 4-16   The Procedure Division for the summary report-preparation program
              (part 1 of 3)

On page 2 of figure 4-16, procedure 320 starts by checking whether the report has reached the bottom of the page. If so, procedure 320 performs procedure 330 to print the heading lines at the top of the next page.

Next, the first-record switch is used to determine when the branch number is printed. Since it should be printed only in the first line of a branch-number group, spaces are moved to the branch number field when the new branch number is the same as the old branch number. At the end of this procedure, you can see that the sales for this and last year are added to the branch totals, but not the grand totals, after each line is printed. Then, procedure 360 adds the branch totals to the grand totals. All other processing for printing the customer line is the same as you saw in chapter 3.

In procedure 330, you can see how procedures 340 and 350 are called to print the heading lines, and how the space-control field is used to control the spacing. In procedure 340, the line-count field is set to 1 after the first line of the page is printed. Then, in procedure 350, the value in the space-control field is added to the line-count field after each line is printed. As a result, the line-count field accurately counts the lines that are printed on each page.

Procedure Division code

```
320-PRINT-CUSTOMER-LINE.
*
    IF LINE-COUNT > LINES-ON-PAGE
        PERFORM 330-PRINT-HEADING-LINES.
    IF FIRST-RECORD-SWITCH = "Y"
        MOVE CM-BRANCH-NUMBER TO CL-BRANCH-NUMBER
    ELSE
        IF CM-BRANCH-NUMBER > OLD-BRANCH-NUMBER
            MOVE CM-BRANCH-NUMBER TO CL-BRANCH-NUMBER
        ELSE
            MOVE SPACE TO CL-BRANCH-NUMBER.
    MOVE CM-CUSTOMER-NUMBER   TO CL-CUSTOMER-NUMBER.
    MOVE CM-CUSTOMER-NAME     TO CL-CUSTOMER-NAME.
    MOVE CM-SALES-THIS-YTD    TO CL-SALES-THIS-YTD.
    MOVE CM-SALES-LAST-YTD    TO CL-SALES-LAST-YTD.
    COMPUTE CHANGE-AMOUNT =
        CM-SALES-THIS-YTD - CM-SALES-LAST-YTD.
    MOVE CHANGE-AMOUNT TO CL-CHANGE-AMOUNT.
    IF CM-SALES-LAST-YTD = ZERO
        MOVE 999.9 TO CL-CHANGE-PERCENT
    ELSE
        COMPUTE CL-CHANGE-PERCENT ROUNDED =
            CHANGE-AMOUNT * 100 / CM-SALES-LAST-YTD
            ON SIZE ERROR
                MOVE 999.9 TO CL-CHANGE-PERCENT.
    MOVE CUSTOMER-LINE TO PRINT-AREA.
    PERFORM 350-WRITE-REPORT-LINE.
    MOVE 1 TO SPACE-CONTROL.
    ADD CM-SALES-THIS-YTD TO BRANCH-TOTAL-THIS-YTD.
    ADD CM-SALES-LAST-YTD TO BRANCH-TOTAL-LAST-YTD.
*
 330-PRINT-HEADING-LINES.
*
    ADD 1 TO PAGE-COUNT.
    MOVE PAGE-COUNT      TO HL1-PAGE-NUMBER.
    MOVE HEADING-LINE-1 TO PRINT-AREA.
    PERFORM 340-WRITE-PAGE-TOP-LINE.
    MOVE HEADING-LINE-2 TO PRINT-AREA.
    MOVE 1 TO SPACE-CONTROL.
    PERFORM 350-WRITE-REPORT-LINE.
    MOVE HEADING-LINE-3 TO PRINT-AREA.
    MOVE 2 TO SPACE-CONTROL.
    PERFORM 350-WRITE-REPORT-LINE.
    MOVE HEADING-LINE-4 TO PRINT-AREA.
    MOVE 1 TO SPACE-CONTROL.
    PERFORM 350-WRITE-REPORT-LINE.
    MOVE 2 TO SPACE-CONTROL.
*
 340-WRITE-PAGE-TOP-LINE.
*
    WRITE PRINT-AREA AFTER ADVANCING PAGE.
    MOVE 1 TO LINE-COUNT.
*
```

Figure 4-16   The Procedure Division for the summary report-preparation program
(part 2 of 3)

Finally, on page 3 of figure 4-16, procedure 360 prints the branch lines. After it calls procedure 350 to print the line, it moves 2 to the space-control field so a space will be skipped before the next customer line is printed. Then, it adds the branch totals to the grand totals. Last, it moves zero to the branch totals so they can be used to accumulate the totals for the next branch line.

As you review the code for procedures 320, 360, and 500, please note that these print procedures include all the code that is related to printing a line. This includes doing the calculations for any fields that are printed in these lines, setting the space-control field for the printing of subsequent lines, adding the line totals to the next level of totals, and resetting any total fields that need to be reset. That's the way we code print procedures in our shop.

In other shops, though, you may find some of this code in the calling module. And if the calculations are complex, you may find them in a subordinate module that is called by the print module. These are reasonable variations that don't detract from the quality of the program.

Procedure Division code   **Page 3**

```
350-WRITE-REPORT-LINE.
*
    WRITE PRINT-AREA AFTER ADVANCING SPACE-CONTROL LINES.
    ADD SPACE-CONTROL TO LINE-COUNT.
*
360-PRINT-BRANCH-LINE.
*
    MOVE BRANCH-TOTAL-THIS-YTD TO BTL-SALES-THIS-YTD.
    MOVE BRANCH-TOTAL-LAST-YTD TO BTL-SALES-LAST-YTD.
    COMPUTE CHANGE-AMOUNT =
        BRANCH-TOTAL-THIS-YTD - BRANCH-TOTAL-LAST-YTD.
    MOVE CHANGE-AMOUNT TO BTL-CHANGE-AMOUNT.
    IF BRANCH-TOTAL-LAST-YTD = ZERO
        MOVE 999.9 TO BTL-CHANGE-PERCENT
    ELSE
        COMPUTE BTL-CHANGE-PERCENT ROUNDED =
            CHANGE-AMOUNT * 100 / BRANCH-TOTAL-LAST-YTD
            ON SIZE ERROR
                MOVE 999.9 TO BTL-CHANGE-PERCENT.
    MOVE BRANCH-TOTAL-LINE TO PRINT-AREA.
    MOVE 1 TO SPACE-CONTROL.
    PERFORM 350-WRITE-REPORT-LINE.
    MOVE 2 TO SPACE-CONTROL.
    ADD BRANCH-TOTAL-THIS-YTD TO GRAND-TOTAL-THIS-YTD.
    ADD BRANCH-TOTAL-LAST-YTD TO GRAND-TOTAL-LAST-YTD.
    MOVE ZERO TO BRANCH-TOTAL-THIS-YTD.
    MOVE ZERO TO BRANCH-TOTAL-LAST-YTD.
*
500-PRINT-GRAND-TOTALS.
*
    MOVE GRAND-TOTAL-THIS-YTD TO GTL-SALES-THIS-YTD.
    MOVE GRAND-TOTAL-LAST-YTD TO GTL-SALES-LAST-YTD.
    COMPUTE CHANGE-AMOUNT =
        GRAND-TOTAL-THIS-YTD - GRAND-TOTAL-LAST-YTD.
    MOVE CHANGE-AMOUNT TO GTL-CHANGE-AMOUNT.
    IF GRAND-TOTAL-LAST-YTD = ZERO
        MOVE 999.9 TO GTL-CHANGE-PERCENT
    ELSE
        COMPUTE GTL-CHANGE-PERCENT ROUNDED =
            CHANGE-AMOUNT * 100 / GRAND-TOTAL-LAST-YTD
            ON SIZE ERROR
                MOVE 999.9 TO GTL-CHANGE-PERCENT.
    MOVE GRAND-TOTAL-LINE TO PRINT-AREA.
    MOVE 2 TO SPACE-CONTROL.
    PERFORM 350-WRITE-REPORT-LINE.
```

Figure 4-16   The Procedure Division for the summary report-preparation program
(part 3 of 3)

Perspective

Although there is general agreement today that all COBOL programs should be structured, there are still major disagreements about what a structured program should look like. In addition, the managers in most COBOL shops don't enforce the shop standards for structured programming that are in place.

As a result, many programs today are "composed" at the screen without ever being designed. The coding in most programs is hard to understand, which makes maintaining them difficult. Testing and debugging still takes 60 percent or more of the development time for a program. And most programs contain bugs long after they've been put into production.

In this chapter, though, you've been introduced to the best methods for designing, coding, and testing a structured program. If you design each program using the structured design methods, you'll improve productivity and program quality. And if you code and test each program from the top down, you'll make significant reductions in the time it takes to debug a program.

To complete your knowledge of structured programming, the next chapter presents the best techniques for writing structured code. There, you'll learn how to use all of the structured programming language in the COBOL-85 standards. And that will make your structured programs even better.

Summary

- *Structured programming* refers to the development techniques that include *structured design, structured coding,* and *top-down coding and testing.*

- A report that includes totals for groups of records is called a *summary report.* The summary lines in a report like this are printed whenever the value in a *control field* changes, which is referred to as a *control break.*

- With *structured design,* you design a program from the top down. To do that, we recommend you create a structure chart.

- A *structure chart* is a design document that shows all the *modules* of a program and their hierarchy. A *calling module* connects to the modules below it, and a *called module* is subordinate to the module above it. Each module should represent a single function.

- *Pseudocode* is a programmer's shorthand you can use to plan the logic for the critical modules of your program or to plan the coding of any module.

- Each module in a program should be as independent as possible. To accomplish this, a module should contain *all* of the code for the function represented by the module and *only* the code for that function.

- With *top-down coding and testing,* you begin by coding and testing the top module of the program along with a few subordinate modules. When these work correctly, you code and test a few more modules, and you continue until all modules are coded and tested.

- A *test plan* shows the sequence in which modules will be coded and tested. It lists the modules to be tested and the test data to be used in each phase.

- When a module calls a subordinate module that isn't required for a testing phase, you can code a *program stub* in place of the subordinate module. The stub can contain just enough code to complete the testing phase.

Terms

structured programming	calling module	pseudocode
structured program	called module	top-down coding and
summary report	control module	testing
detail report	subordinate module	top-down testing
control field	work module	test plan
control break	common module	commenting a line
structured design	chart leg	uncommenting a line
structure chart	leg of a chart	program stub
hierarchy chart	structure listing	dummy module

Objectives

- Given input file specifications and report specifications like the ones in this chapter, create a structure chart or structure listing for the program.

- Given program specifications and a structure chart or a structure listing for a program, write pseudocode for the critical modules.

- Given program specifications and a structure chart or structure listing for a program, create a test plan for testing all the modules. This plan should include a description of the test data to be used for each phase.

- Given program specifications, a structure chart or structure listing, and a top-down test plan, code and test all the modules of the program.

- Explain how control fields and control breaks are used in programs that prepare summary reports.

- Given a structure chart for a program, identify the calling modules, called modules, common modules, and work modules in each chart leg.

- Describe the differences between a structure chart and a structure listing.

- List three guidelines for coding program modules so they're independent from one another.

- Describe the process of top-down coding and testing.

- Explain what is meant by "commenting" a line of code or "stubbing off" a module.

Exercise 4-1   Restructure the detail report program

This exercise guides you through the process of restructuring the enhanced version of the sales report program in figure 3-3 of the last chapter. In particular, you need to add two Write modules to that program.

Design the detail report-preparation program of chapter 3

1. Start Personal COBOL, and open the program named rpt2000 in the c:\cobol folder. If you study this program, you can see that it consists of seven procedures (modules).

2. Create a structure chart for the rpt2000 program using its code as a guide.

3. Compare the structure chart you just created with the structure chart in figure 4-7. Then, modify the structure chart in figure 4-7 so it will create the rpt2000 report. To do that, you'll see that you just need to delete one leg from the structure chart.

Modify the code for this program

4. Modify the code for rpt2000 so it conforms to the structure chart that you created in step 3. Be sure to rename or renumber procedures wherever appropriate. The code for the Write modules should be the same as it is in figure 4-16, which means that you need to add procedures 340 and 350 to the code and make some changes to procedures 320, 330, and 500. For example, since module 350 counts the number of lines that are printed, you need to remove the line of code that counts customer lines from procedure 320. You also need to remove the Write statements from these procedures and perform procedures 340 and 350 instead.

5. Compile and test rpt2000 to make sure that it gives the same results as the original program. (The output should look like the output in figure 3-11, except it should include a line for every customer.)

Close the program

6. Close the program.

Exercise 4-2   Develop the summary report program

This exercise guides you through the development of the summary report program presented in figures 4-15 and 4-16. You'll start this program from the code for the report program that you created in exercise 4-1, and you'll create the new program in three phases. That should give you a better appreciation for top-down coding and testing.

Add the branch number to the heading and customer lines

1. Open the program named rpt2000 for edit, and change the Program-ID in the Identification Division to RPT3000. Then, save the program as rpt3000 and close it.

2. Open the rpt3000 program, and modify the code in the Data Division and Procedure Division so the heading lines and customer line provide for the branch number. For this phase of testing, the program should print the branch number in every customer line. Also, be sure to change the report number in the second heading line to RPT3000.

3. Test and debug. To view the printed report properly with your word processor, you may need to change the page orientation to landscape. Note that the columns in the grand total line won't align properly at this point.

Print the branch summary lines

4. Add the Data Division and Procedure Division code for printing the branch summary lines. For this phase of testing, the program can still print the branch number in every customer line, so you don't have to add the code in module 320 that checks whether the branch number has changed. Also, modify the grand total line so the words GRAND TOTAL appear at the beginning of the line and two asterisks appear at the end of the line, as shown in figure 4-2.

5. Test and debug.

Print the branch number in just the first line of each group

6. Add the code to module 320 that checks for a new branch number and prints the branch number in just the first customer line of each group, not in every customer line.

7. Test and debug.

Close the program

8. Close the program.

Exercise 4-3   Modify the summary report

In this exercise, you'll modify the summary report program that you created in exercise 4-2 so it prints only the branch summary lines, not the customer detail lines. The resulting report should look like this:

```
DATE:  03/24/2000              YEAR-TO-DATE SALES REPORT              PAGE:    1
TIME:  16:44                                                         RPT4000

BRANCH      SALES          SALES         CHANGE        CHANGE
  NUM      THIS YTD      LAST YTD        AMOUNT        PERCENT

   12     13,580.23     23,333.33       9,753.10-      41.8- *
   22     44,656.11      1,000.00      43,656.11      999.9  *
   34     25,921.47     64,812.88      38,891.41-      60.0- *
   47     36,367.91     32,009.24       4,358.67       13.6  *

TOTAL   120,525.72    121,155.45         629.73-       0.5- **
```

Modify the structure chart for the program

1. Review the structure chart in figure 4-7. Then, modify this structure chart so it's a proper design for a program that prepares the report shown above.

2. Open the program named rpt3000 for edit, and change the Program-ID to RPT4000. Then, save the program as rpt4000 and close it.

Code and test the changes

3. Open the rpt4000 program, then code and test the required changes using the modified structure chart as a guide. Be sure to change the report number in the second heading line to RPT4000.

4. When your program works the way it's supposed to, close the program.

Exercise 4-4   Generate a structure listing

In this exercise, you'll use our LISTMODS program to generate a structure listing from the program that you developed in exercise 4-2.

Run LISTMODS

1. Open the program named LISTMODS.

2. Modify the system name in the Select statement in the Environment Division for the file named SRCEFILE so it points to the program that you developed for exercise 4-2. The system name should be c:\cobol\rpt3000.cb1.

3. Compile and run the program. Then, use your word processing program to print the program's output. The first page is the structure listing for rpt3000; the second page presents statistics that were derived from the program.

Close the program

4. Close the program and exit from Micro Focus Personal COBOL.

5

How to use the features for structured coding

In the first four chapters of this book, you learned how to code structured programs using simple If and Perform Until statements. Now, in this chapter, you'll learn how to use all of the COBOL features for coding structured programs. To start, though, you'll be introduced to the principles of structured programming.

Introduction to structured programming

In the mid-1970s, a typical COBOL program contained dozens or hundreds of Go To statements that branched from one paragraph to another ... but never returned. The result was often referred to as "spaghetti code" or "rat's nest code" because it was so difficult to follow. This type of coding limited the productivity of the average programmer to less than 100 lines of tested code per week, and it made testing and debugging a nightmare.

Way back in 1965, though, Professor Edsger W. Dijkstra of the University of Eindhoven, Netherlands, recommended that the Go To statement be removed from all programming languages. He was convinced that a program was easiest to read, code, and debug when it contained no Go To statements at all. This led Professor Dijkstra and other computer scientists to give rigid definitions for the structures that are acceptable in a program. These efforts led to the theory of *structured programming*.

The three valid structures

The basic theory of structured programming is that any program can be written using only three logical structures. These control structures are summarized in figure 5-1. They are called the sequence, selection, and iteration structures.

A *sequence structure* (or *Do structure*) consists of one or more functions executed in sequence. Each function consists of one or more imperative statements like Move, Accept, or Display statements. You also can think of a Perform statement as a sequence structure because it performs a procedure and returns to the statement that follows it.

The *selection structure* (or *If-Then-Else structure*) provides a choice between two functions based on a condition. In COBOL, this structure is implemented by an If statement. If the condition is true, one function is done; if it's false (Else), the other function is done. If one of the functions is omitted (null), the structure is still valid. In that case, the Else clause can be omitted.

The *iteration structure* performs a function repeatedly as long as a condition is true (the *DO While structure*) or until a condition becomes true (the *Do Until structure*). In COBOL, though, the DO Until structure is usually implemented by the *Perform Until structure*, which is slightly different than the Do Until structure. The difference is that the condition is tested after the function is performed in the Do Until structure and before the function is performed in the Perform Until structure. Later in this chapter, though, you'll learn that the Perform Until statement can be coded with a With Test After clause that makes the statement equivalent to the Do Until structure.

Notice that all the structures in this figure have only one *entry point* and one *exit point*. As a result, a program that's made up of only these structures will have just one entry and one exit point. A program like that can be called a *proper program*.

The sequence structure (Do)

The selection structure (If-Then-Else)

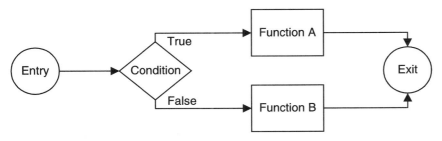

Three variations of the iteration structure

The Do While structure

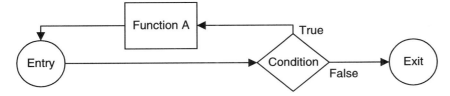

The Do Until structure

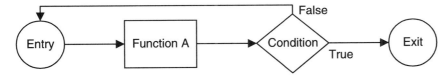

The COBOL Perform Until structure

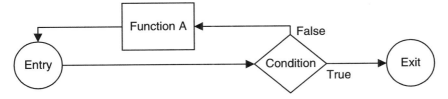

Theory

- You can code any structured program using three basic structures: the *sequence*, *selection*, and *iteration structures*. Each structure has just one entry point and one exit point, and a program composed of these structures is a *proper program*.

Figure 5-1   The three valid structures of structured programming

The principles of substitution and combination

To create a program, the theory of structured programming says that you can substitute one valid structure for the function of another valid structure. It also says you can combine two or more valid structures in sequence and treat them as a single structure. The result is still a proper program.

These principles are illustrated by the code in figure 5-2. In procedure 300, for example, you can see that the second If statement is substituted for the function in the first If statement. The result is still a valid structure with one entry and one exit point.

Similarly, procedure 000 combines a sequence structure (the Open statement), another sequence structure (the first Perform statement), an iteration structure (the Perform Until statement), another sequence structure (the last Perform statement), and two more sequence structures (the Close and Stop Run statements). As a result, the entire procedure is still a valid structure with one entry point (the Open statement) and one exit point (the Stop Run statement).

From theory to practice

What a simple but elegant theory! By adhering to its principles, you can create complex structures with the assurance that they will have only one entry and exit point so they will be executed in a controlled manner from start to finish. That should make it easier to read, write, test, and debug a program.

Like most theories, though, this one left many questions unanswered like: How do you design a large program? How do you code a program in a way that makes it easier to test, debug, and maintain? And how do you get the programmers in a shop to adhere to the principles of structured programming when the language includes Go To statements? These questions were especially tough for COBOL programmers because COBOL wasn't designed for structured programming and it did provide for Go To statements.

By the mid-1970s, though, most COBOL shops had developed methods for applying the theory of structured programming to COBOL programs. These methods included structured design and top-down coding and testing, which you learned about in the last chapter, and they focussed on *structured coding*, which this book has presented from the start. Now, in this chapter, you'll learn how to use all of the COBOL features for structured coding.

Before you continue, though, please note that COBOL provides for valid structures other than the sequence, selection, and iteration structures. For instance, the Read statement with an At End clause and the Compute statement with an On Size Error clause aren't sequence structures, and they aren't selection or iteration structures either. However, they are structures with just one entry and one exit point so they are valid structures. For the same reason, the Evaluate statement is a valid structure, but you'll soon see that it is far more complex than a selection or an iteration structure.

Iteration and selection structures within COBOL procedures

```
000-PREPARE-SALES-REPORT.
*
     OPEN INPUT   CUSTMAST
         OUTPUT SALESRPT.
     PERFORM 100-FORMAT-REPORT-HEADING.
     PERFORM 300-PREPARE-SALES-LINES
         UNTIL CUSTMAST-EOF-SWITCH = "Y".
     PERFORM 500-PRINT-GRAND-TOTALS.
     CLOSE CUSTMAST
           SALESRPT.
     STOP RUN.
     .
     .
     .
300-PREPARE-SALES-LINES.
*
     PERFORM 310-READ-CUSTOMER-MASTER.
     IF NOT CUSMAST-EOF
         IF CM-SALES-THIS-YTD >= 1000
             PERFORM 320-PRINT-CUSTOMER-LINE.
```

Theory

- One valid structure can be substituted for a function in another valid structure. The result is still a proper program.

- Two or more valid structures can be combined so they are treated as a single function. The result is still a proper program.

Notes

- Although the original theory of structured programming dealt with only the sequence, selection, and iteration structures, any structure that has only one entry and one exit point is a valid structure.

- COBOL provides several valid structures besides the sequence, selection, and iteration structures. For instance, the Compute statement with an On Size Error clause and the Read statement with an At End clause are valid structures that aren't sequence, selection, or iteration structures. Without the clauses, though, these statements are sequence structures.

- The Evaluate statement is another valid structure that you'll learn about in figures 5-12 through 5-14.

Figure 5-2   The principles of substitution and combination

Shop standards for structured coding

To promote and enforce the theory of structured programming, most COBOL shops have a manual that presents their *shop standards* for program development. These standards present the coding rules and guidelines that the programmers in a COBOL shop are supposed to follow. In general, the standards go way beyond prohibiting the use of Go To statements.

In figure 5-3, for example, you can see some structured coding guidelines that are typical of those you'll find in a shop's standards. These are the guidelines that all of the programs in this book follow. Because these guidelines are so simple, they are easy to remember and follow if you're a programmer. And they're easy to review and enforce if you're a programming manager. Nevertheless, they can have a significant effect on programmer productivity and program quality.

In the Data Division, for example, you should group data items to show their relationships. You should code the groups in the same sequences in each program that you write, so you'll be able to find the data items more quickly. You should use meaningful data names. And you should use a two- or three-character prefix at the start of each field name that's within a record to show which record it belongs to.

Although guidelines like these have been recommended for years, you still find data names like BOB, X1, MTN, SUB1, and much worse in programs. The more meaningful your names are, of course, the easier it is to remember the names you've used when you code the Procedure Division, and the easier it is for someone else to read and maintain your program later on. As simple as this notion is, poor data names are a major weakness in most COBOL programs. So don't hesitate to use all 30 characters in a data name if that's what it takes to make a meaningful name.

In the Procedure Division, you obviously shouldn't use Go To statements. In addition, though, you should use indentation and spacing to make the code easier to read. You should code each module on the structure chart in a single COBOL paragraph. You should create the paragraph name from the number and name that you used on the structure chart. And, above all, you should do everything you can to keep each procedure independent.

Beyond that, a shop's standards may include recommendations on when and how to use nested Ifs, Performs, Evaluate statements, and so on. So when you start a new job, you should find out what the shop standards are. If the shop doesn't have any standards, though, just follow the recommendations in this book. If you do, you'll end up with structured programs that meet the standards of the best COBOL shops.

With that as background, you're ready to learn about all the COBOL features for structured coding. As you will see, many of these became available with the COBOL-85 standards.

Typical Data Division standards

- Use blank lines and indentation to improve readability. (If compile time matters, you should use blank comment lines, not completely blank lines.)

- Group related data items so it's easier to find the items you're looking for.

- Use a consistent sequence of entries in the Working-Storage Section of all of your programs. Suggested sequence:

    1. Switches
    2. Flags
    3. Control fields
    4. Print fields
    5. Date and time fields
    6. Count fields
    7. Calculated fields
    8. Total fields
    9. Tables
    10. Record descriptions for input and output files
    11. Heading line descriptions for print files
    12. Detail or body line descriptions for print files
    13. Total line descriptions for print files

- Use meaningful data names.

- Use a two- or three-character prefix for each field that's defined within a record to indicate which record the field belongs to.

Typical Procedure Division standards

- Don't use Go To statements.

- Use blank lines and indentation to improve readability. (If compile time matters, you should use blank comment lines, not completely blank lines.)

- Code each module on the structure chart with a single COBOL paragraph.

- Create the paragraph names from the structure chart by combining the module numbers with the module names as in 000-PREPARE-SALES-REPORT. If a resulting name is more than 30 characters, shorten one or more of the words in the module name.

- Keep the paragraphs in sequence by module number.

- Do everything you can to make each procedure as independent as possible with one function in each procedure.

Description

- *Shop standards* are set by the staff of a programming department. These standards are designed to ensure that the coding that's done within the shop is structured, consistent, and relatively easy to maintain by all programmers on the staff.

- Today, not all COBOL shops have standards. Worse, many shops that have standards don't enforce them. As a result, the quality of the coding that's done in most shops varies dramatically from one programmer to another.

Figure 5-3   Shop standards for structured coding

How to code conditions

In chapters 1 and 3, you learned how to code If and Perform Until statements that were based on simple *conditions*. In particular, you learned how to code conditions that compared the data in one field with the data in another field or with a literal value. In the next three figures, you'll learn more about coding that type of condition as well as other types of conditions for selection, iteration, and case structures.

How to code relation, sign, and class tests

Figure 5-4 shows how to code relation, sign, and class tests. Once you learn how to code these types of conditions, you can use them in If and Perform Until statements. You also can use them in other types of statements like the Evaluate statement.

In the syntax summaries in this figure, the underlined words are required, and the words that aren't underlined can be omitted. For example, you can omit the word IS in any of the tests. This underlining convention is standard COBOL notation, and it will be used from now on.

If you study the syntax for a *relation test*, you can see that you can use one to compare a field (identifier), a literal, or an arithmetic expression with another field, literal, or arithmetic expression. Since you've been coding this type of test since chapter 1, you shouldn't have any trouble with the first two examples in this figure. In the third example, though, you can see how an arithmetic expression can be used in this kind of test. This is useful when you don't need the result of the calculation for any other purpose.

With a *sign test*, you can find out whether a field or an expression is positive, zero, or negative. Although this is occasionally useful, you can get the same result with a relation test. For instance,

```
FIELD-A IS POSITIVE
```

is the same as

```
FIELD-A > ZERO
```

As a result, you don't ever have to code a sign test, although a sign test does make the purpose of the test more obvious. When you use a sign test, the field that you're testing has to be signed numeric, which means that its Picture must start with S.

The last type of test in this figure is a *class test*. You can use this test to determine whether a field is numeric, alphabetic, all uppercase letters, or all lowercase letters. This is useful when you need to test whether the data that has been entered into a field is valid numeric or alphabetic data.

The syntax of a relation test

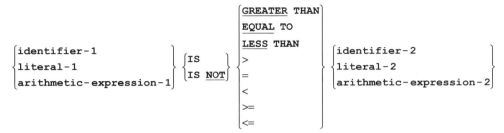

Examples

```
THIS-YTD-SALES >= 10000
CUSTMAST-EOF-SWITCH NOT = "Y"
ON-HAND-STOCK + ON-ORDER-STOCK <= REORDER-POINT
```

The syntax of a sign test

$$\left\{\begin{array}{l}\texttt{identifier}\\\texttt{arithmetic-expression}\end{array}\right\}\left\{\begin{array}{l}\texttt{IS}\\\texttt{IS NOT}\end{array}\right\}\left\{\begin{array}{l}\underline{\texttt{POSITIVE}}\\\texttt{ZERO}\\\underline{\texttt{NEGATIVE}}\end{array}\right\}$$

Examples

```
SALES-CHANGE IS POSITIVE
THIS-YTD-SALES - LAST-YTD-SALES IS NOT NEGATIVE
```

The syntax of a class test

$$\texttt{identifier}\left\{\begin{array}{l}\texttt{IS}\\\texttt{IS NOT}\end{array}\right\}\left\{\begin{array}{l}\texttt{NUMERIC}\\\texttt{ALPHABETIC}\\\texttt{ALPHABETIC-LOWER}\\\texttt{ALPHABETIC-UPPER}\end{array}\right\}$$

Examples

```
LAST-NAME IS ALPHABETIC
PURCHASE-AMOUNT IS NOT NUMERIC
```

Notes

- When you code a relation test, you should compare numeric items with numeric items and alphanumeric items with alphanumeric items.
- When you code a sign test, the field that's being tested has to be signed numeric.
- When you code a numeric class test, the field that's being tested can be alphanumeric or numeric (signed or unsigned). An unsigned numeric field is numeric if it contains only digits. A signed numeric field is numeric if it contains all digits with a valid sign.
- When you code an alphabetic class test, the field that's being tested has to be alphabetic (see chapter 6) or alphanumeric. The field is alphabetic if it contains just letters (uppercase or lowercase) and spaces. It is alphabetic-upper if it contains just uppercase letters and spaces, and it is alphabetic-lower if it contains just lowercase letters and spaces.

Figure 5-4   How to code relation, sign, and class tests

How to code compound conditions

Figure 5-5 shows how to code *compound conditions*. These are conditions that use *logical operators* to connect two or more conditions. When two conditions are connected by AND, both have to be true for the entire condition to be true. When two conditions are connected by OR, just one has to be true for the entire condition to be true.

When a compound condition is evaluated, the NOT conditions are evaluated first, then the AND conditions, and then the OR conditions. If you want to change this sequence or if there's any doubt about how a compound condition is going to be evaluated, you can code parentheses to clarify the sequence of evaluation. Then, the conditions within parentheses are evaluated first.

If you omit the subject or the operator in one part of a compound condition, the compiler assumes that it's the same as the previous subject or operator. In this case, you're using an *implied subject* or *implied operator*. In some cases, this makes the code easier to understand. But if there's any chance for confusion, you should avoid the use of implied subjects and operators.

Since compound conditions are frequently required as you develop programs, you'll use them often. To make these conditions easy to read and understand, you should align the parts of a condition as shown in the examples. And you should use parentheses whenever that clarifies how a condition should be interpreted.

The logical operators that can be used to create compound conditions

```
AND
OR
```

Examples of compound conditions

```
    EM-HOURS IS NUMERIC
AND EM-RATE IS NUMERIC

   AP-CODE > 18
OR AP-CODE = 1

   (CM-TIMES-OVERDUE < 4 AND CM-CUST-YEARS > 2)
 OR CM-OVER-60-BALANCE-DUE = ZERO
```

Examples of compound conditions with implied subjects and operators

```
AP-CODE > 18 OR = 1              (Implied subject)

AP-AGE > 18 AND > PREVIOUS-AGE   (Implied subject)

AP-AGE > 18 AND PREVIOUS-AGE     (Implied subject and operator)

AP-AGE NOT < 18 OR PREVIOUS-AGE  (Implied subject and operator)
```

Description

- When you use the AND operator, both conditions have to be true for the compound condition to be true.

- When you use the OR operator, just one condition has to be true for the compound condition to be true.

- When a compound condition is evaluated, the NOT conditions are evaluated first, followed by the AND conditions, and then by the OR conditions.

- When you use parentheses, the condition within the parentheses is interpreted first. If you code parentheses within parentheses, the condition in the innermost set of parentheses is interpreted first.

- When you omit the subject or operator in a compound condition, the previous subject or operator is assumed.

Structured coding recommendations

- When you code a compound condition in an If, Perform Until, or Evaluate statement, use indentation to align the parts of the condition that are connected by AND or OR whenever that will make the condition easier to interpret.

- Use parentheses to clarify how a compound condition should be interpreted.

- Avoid the use of implied subjects or operators whenever there's a chance for confusion.

Figure 5-5   How to code compound conditions

How to code and use condition names

A *condition name* is a name that refers to a condition. For instance, the name CUSTMAST-EOF can be a name for this condition:

```
CUSTMAST-EOF-SWITCH = "Y"
```

To define a condition name, you use an 88 level in the Data Division as shown in figure 5-6. Once defined, the condition name can be used as the condition in an If, Perform Until, or Evaluate statement.

Condition names are frequently used with switches and flags. As you should already know, a *switch* is a one-character field that has either a value of N for No or Y for Yes. When you code the condition name for a switch, we recommend that you use the name of the switch without SWITCH at the end. That way, it's easy to tell that a specific condition relates to a specific switch.

In contrast to a switch, a *flag* is a one-character field that can have values other than Y or N. In the example in this figure, a flag named TRAN-CODE can have values of 1, 2, 3, 4, D, E, or F, and three condition names are assigned to this flag. The TC-ISSUE condition is true when the flag has a value of 1; the TC-RECEIPT condition is true when it has a value of 2 or 3; and the TC-RETURN condition is true when it has a value of 4, D, E, or F. This shows how you can apply more than one value to a single condition name.

Once the condition names are defined, you can use them in statements that require conditions. This is illustrated by the If and Perform Until statements in this figure. You also can use condition names as parts of compound conditions, which is illustrated by the first If statement example in this figure.

If you compare the statements that use condition names with those that don't, you can see that the use of condition names simplifies the code. It also makes the statements easier to code because you don't have to remember the specific values that you used for flags once you've defined them in the Data Division. Last, the use of condition names makes a program easier to maintain when the values of flags change, because you only have to change the 88 levels, not the statements that use the condition names. For these reasons, we recommend that you use condition names whenever they apply.

The syntax for defining a condition name

```
88   condition-name VALUE IS {literal-1 [{THROUGH | THRU} literal-2]} ...
```

An example of code that defines a switch condition

```
01   SWITCHES.
     05   CUSTMAST-EOF-SWITCH     PIC X      VALUE "N".
          88   CUSTMAST-EOF                  VALUE "Y".
```

An example of code that defines three condition names

```
01   FLAGS.
     05   TRAN-CODE               PIC X.
          88   TC-ISSUE                      VALUE "1".
          88   TC-RECEIPT                    VALUE "2" "3".
          88   TC-RETURN                     VALUE "4" "D" THRU "F".
```

Statements that refer to the condition names

Code with condition names

```
PERFORM 300-PREPARE-SALES-LINES
    UNTIL CUSTMAST-EOF.

IF    NOT CUSTMAST-EOF
  AND TC-ISSUE
    ADD 1 TO ISSUE-COUNT.

IF TC-ISSUE
    PERFORM 410-PROCESS-ISSUE-TRAN.
IF TC-RECEIPT
    PERFORM 420-PROCESS-RECEIPT-TRAN.
IF TC-RETURN
    PERFORM 430-PROCESS-RETURN-TRAN.
```

Code without condition names

```
PERFORM 300-PREPARE-SALES-LINES
    UNTIL CUSTMAST-EOF-SWITCH = "Y".

IF    CUSTMAST-EOF-SWITCH NOT = "Y"
  AND TRAN-CODE = "1"
    ADD 1 TO ISSUE-COUNT.

IF TRAN-CODE = "1"
    PERFORM 410-PROCESS-ISSUE-TRAN.
IF TRAN-CODE = "2" OR "3"
    PERFORM 420-PROCESS-RECEIPT-TRAN.
IF TRAN-CODE = "4" OR "D" OR "E" OR "F"
    PERFORM 430-PROCESS-RETURN-TRAN.
```

Description

- When you code an 88 level that's subordinate to a data item, you define a *condition name* for that item. Then, that condition name can be used as a condition in an If, Perform, or Evaluate statement.

- Two or more values can be coded in the Value clause for a condition. Also, the word THRU can be coded to express a series of values.

- In general, a *switch* is a field with just two possible settings: Yes and No (or Off and On). In contrast, a *flag* is a field that can have two or more possible settings.

Structured coding recommendations

- Use condition names for all switches and flags because they make a program easier to understand.

- Use the Set to True statement shown in figure 5-15 to turn on switches and flag conditions.

Figure 5-6   How to code and use condition names

How to code selection and iteration structures

Now that you know how to code conditions, you can learn more about the selection and iteration structures that use those conditions. Since the If statement implements the selection structure and the Perform Until implements the iteration structure, you already know how to code the simple forms of these structures. In the topics that follow, you'll see some other coding options.

How to code If statements

Figure 5-7 shows you how to code If statements. If you study the syntax for this statement, you can see that you can use the word CONTINUE in either the If or Else clause when you don't want the program to do anything for that condition, which is occasionally useful. You also can use End-If to end a statement, which is most useful when you're coding nested Ifs, as shown in the next topic.

In the examples in this figure, you can see how CONTINUE can be used to do nothing when the condition is true. You also can see how indentation can be used to make compound conditions easier to read. In addition, you can see how to end an If statement with End-If. Since you've been using If statements since chapter 1, you shouldn't have any trouble using simple statements like these.

When you're maintaining someone else's program, you may see NEXT SENTENCE in either the If or Else clause of an If statement. Note, however, that this is not the same as CONTINUE. Instead of doing nothing, NEXT SENTENCE jumps out of the If statement so the program continues with the next statement. Since this has the effect of a Go To statement, we recommend that you avoid the use of NEXT SENTENCE in all of your programs.

The syntax of the If statement

```
IF condition-1 THEN
    {statement-1 ... | CONTINUE}
[ELSE
    {statement-2 ... | CONTINUE}]
[END-IF]
```

If statements without End-Ifs

```
IF NOT CUSTMAST-EOF
    ADD 1 TO RECORD-COUNT.

IF SALES-AMOUNT = ZERO
    CONTINUE
ELSE
    COMPUTE SALES-TAX ROUNDED =
        SALES-AMOUNT * .0785.
```

An If statement with an End-If

```
IF SALES-AMOUNT = ZERO
    MOVE "Y" TO END-OF-SESSION-SWITCH
ELSE
    COMPUTE SALES-TAX ROUNDED =
        SALES-AMOUNT * .0785
END-IF.
```

If statements with compound conditions and End-Ifs

```
IF      NOT CUSTMAST-EOF
    AND CM-SALES-THIS-YTD >= 10000
        PERFORM 210-PRINT-CUSTOMER-LINE
END-IF.
IF    (CM-TIMES-OVERDUE < 4 AND CM-CUST-YEARS > 2)
    OR CM-OVER-60-BALANCE-DUE = ZERO
        PERFORM 430-PROCESS-GOOD-CUSTOMER
END-IF.
IF      CM-TIMES-OVERDUE < 4
    OR CM-CUST-YEARS > 2
    OR CM-OVER-60-BALANCE-DUE = ZERO
        PERFORM 430-PROCESS-GOOD-CUSTOMER
END-IF.
```

Description

- You can code the word CONTINUE in the If or Else portion of an If statement when you don't want anything done for that condition.

- You also can code the words NEXT SENTENCE in the If or Else portion of an If statement, *but we don't recommend that.* When executed, NEXT SENTENCE causes the program to continue with the statement that starts after the period that ends the If statement, which is equivalent to a Go To statement that provides a second exit to the structure.

Figure 5-7   How to code If statements

How to code nested If statements

Although simple If statements shouldn't give you any trouble, *nested If statements* are hard to code and understand once they get three or more levels deep. That's why you should use indentation to show the levels of nesting and to align the clauses in each If statement. You can also use an End-If to end each of the nested Ifs whenever that improves the clarity of the statement. This is illustrated by the first example in figure 5-8.

No matter how the code is indented, please remember that the compiler pairs each Else clause and End-If clause with the first unpaired If clause that precedes it. That's why you should make sure that your indentation reflects this interpretation of the code. Otherwise, your code will be misleading, which will lead to debugging problems. In the second example in this figure, the clauses aren't properly aligned, which surely will cause problems later on. (The first End-If applies to the first If statement, and the Else clause applies to the second If statement.)

When you need to test a field for a series of values, you can code the nested If statements as a *linear nest*. This is illustrated by the third example in this figure. Here, a field is being tested for four different values. If the field doesn't contain any of these values, the last Else clause handles this error condition. If you compare the linear nest with the same code written in the normal way, you can see that the linear nest is easier to read. In this case, the linear nest is easy to read even though it's four levels deep.

Normally, though, nested If statements are hard to follow once they reach the third or fourth level. In that case, you can often improve the code by rewriting the nested If statements with an Evaluate statement. You'll learn how to do that in figure 5-12.

Nested If statements with End-Ifs

```
IF NOT CUSTMAST-EOF
    IF FIRST-RECORD
        PERFORM 320-PRINT-CUSTOMER-LINE
        MOVE "N" TO FIRST-RECORD-SWITCH
        MOVE CM-BRANCH-NUMBER TO OLD-BRANCH-NUMBER
    ELSE
        IF CM-BRANCH-NUMBER = OLD-BRANCH-NUMBER
            PERFORM 320-PRINT-CUSTOMER-LINE
        ELSE
            PERFORM 360-PRINT-BRANCH-LINE
            PERFORM 320-PRINT-CUSTOMER-LINE
            MOVE CM-BRANCH-NUMBER TO OLD-BRANCH-NUMBER
        END-IF
    END-IF
ELSE
    PERFORM 360-PRINT-BRANCH-LINE
END-IF.
```

— If-Else pair

Nested If statements with alignment problems

```
IF FIRST-RECORD
    MOVE CM-BRANCH-NUMBER     TO CL-BRANCH-NUMBER
    END-IF
    IF CM-BRANCH-NUMBER > OLD-BRANCH-NUMBER
        MOVE CM-BRANCH-NUMBER TO CL-BRANCH-NUMBER
ELSE
    MOVE SPACE TO CL-BRANCH-NUMBER
END-IF.
```

This End-If and Else aren't aligned with the related If.

A linear nest of If statements

```
IF TRAN-CODE = "1"
    PERFORM 410-PROCESS-TRAN-1
ELSE IF TRAN-CODE = "2"
    PERFORM 420-PROCESS-TRAN-2
ELSE IF TRAN-CODE = "D"
    PERFORM 430-PROCESS-TRAN-D
ELSE IF TRAN-CODE = "F"
    PERFORM 440-PROCESS-TRAN-F
ELSE
    MOVE "N" TO VALID-TRAN-SWITCH.
```

A regular nest of If statements

```
IF TRAN-CODE = "1"
    PERFORM 410-PROCESS-TRAN-1
ELSE
    IF TRAN-CODE = "2"
        PERFORM 420-PROCESS-TRAN-2
    ELSE
        IF TRAN-CODE = "D"
            PERFORM 430-PROCESS-TRAN-D
        ELSE
            IF TRAN-CODE = "F"
                PERFORM 440-PROCESS-TRAN-F
            ELSE
                MOVE "N" TO VALID-TRAN-SWITCH.
```

Structured coding recommendations

* In a regular nest, use indentation to align the Else and End-If with the related If. Remember that the compiler always pairs an Else clause and an End-If with the first unpaired If that precedes it, no matter how the code is indented.

* In a *linear nest*, code the Else and If clauses on the same line.

* Use End-Ifs to end each of the If statements in a nest whenever that improves the clarity of the code.

Figure 5-8   How to code nested If statements

How to code Perform Until statements with tests before and after

In chapters 1 and 3, you learned how to code simple Perform Until statements. In that type of statement, the condition is tested before the procedure is performed. Then, if the condition is false, the procedure is executed. If it's true, the procedure isn't executed, and the program proceeds with the next statement in sequence.

Figure 5-9 shows how to code Perform Until statements that test the condition *before* or *after* the procedure is executed. As you can see, if the With Test clause is omitted, the condition is tested before. But if you code the With Test After clause, the condition is tested after.

Normally, you can get the result you want with the test either before or after. This is illustrated by the first two examples in this figure, which get the same result, one with the test before and one with the test after. Note, however, that the condition has to be coded so it's appropriate for the type of test. Here, greater than (>) is used with the test before, and greater than or equals (>=) is used with the test after. (Although just equals should work with the test after, you normally code a test like this with greater than or equals so the program won't enter an infinite loop if the equals test doesn't work.)

In the third example in the figure, the Perform tests a compound condition before the procedure is performed. If either condition is true, then the entire condition is true. In that case, the Perform performs the procedure. When both conditions are false, the Perform ends.

The syntax of the Perform Until statement

```
PERFORM procedure-name
    [WITH TEST {BEFORE | AFTER}]
    UNTIL condition
[END-PERFORM]
```

A Perform Until with the test before

```
PERFORM 120-CALCULATE-NEXT-FV
    UNTIL YEAR-COUNTER > NUMBER-OF-YEARS
END-PERFORM.
```

A Perform Until with the test after

```
PERFORM 120-CALCULATE-NEXT-FV
    WITH TEST AFTER
    UNTIL YEAR-COUNTER >= NUMBER-OF-YEARS
END-PERFORM.
```

A Perform Until with a compound condition

```
PERFORM 100-CALCULATE-FUTURE-VALUE
    UNTIL NUMBER-ENTERED = ZERO
        OR END-OF-SESSION
END-PERFORM.
```

Description

- When you omit the With Test clause, the condition is tested before the procedure is performed.
- When you code With Test After, the condition is tested after the procedure is performed. As a result, the procedure is performed at least once.
- You can end the Perform Until with an End-Perform.

Structured coding recommendations

- Use indentation and parentheses to clarify the interpretation of a compound condition.
- Code the With Test After clause when it improves the clarity of the coding. Omit this clause when you want the test before.

Figure 5-9   How to code Perform Until statements with tests before and after

When and how to code inline Perform statements

When you code an *inline Perform statement*, the procedure that's performed is coded within the Perform statement. It isn't coded in a separate paragraph. This is shown by the syntax of the Perform Until statement in figure 5-10. As you can see, you code the sequence of statements that are performed right after the Until clause.

The benefit of an inline Perform is that it lets you put all of the code for a single function in a single paragraph. If you study the two examples in this figure, you can see that the first one uses an inline Perform; the second one performs a separate paragraph. Although both get the same result, the first example calculates the future value of an investment in a single paragraph. The second example divides this single function into two paragraphs, which is contrary to the principles of structured design.

The problem with the inline Perform statement is that it makes it relatively easy for you to code more than one function as a single COBOL paragraph. Since this makes a module more difficult to read, debug, and maintain, you should avoid the use of these statements for that purpose.

The syntax of the inline Perform statement

```
PERFORM
    [WITH TEST {BEFORE | AFTER}]
    UNTIL condition
        statement-1 ...
[END-PERFORM]
```

An iterative routine that uses an inline Perform

```
 100-CALCULATE-FUTURE-VALUE.
*
     MOVE INVESTMENT-AMOUNT TO FUTURE-VALUE.
     MOVE 1 TO YEAR-COUNTER.
     PERFORM
         WITH TEST AFTER
         UNTIL YEAR-COUNTER >= NUMBER-OF-YEARS
             COMPUTE FUTURE-VALUE ROUNDED =
                 FUTURE-VALUE +
                 (FUTURE-VALUE * YEARLY-INTEREST-RATE / 100)
             ADD 1 TO YEAR-COUNTER
     END-PERFORM.
```

The same routine without an inline Perform

```
 100-CALCULATE-FUTURE-VALUE.
*
     MOVE INVESTMENT-AMOUNT TO FUTURE-VALUE.
     MOVE 1 TO YEAR-COUNTER.
     PERFORM 120-CALCULATE-NEXT-FV
         WITH TEST AFTER
         UNTIL YEAR-COUNTER >= NUMBER-OF-YEARS
     END-PERFORM.
*
 120-CALCULATE-NEXT-FV.
*
     COMPUTE FUTURE-VALUE ROUNDED =
         FUTURE-VALUE +
             (FUTURE-VALUE * YEARLY-INTEREST-RATE / 100).
     ADD 1 TO YEAR-COUNTER.
```

Description

- When you code an inline Perform, the statements after the Until clause are performed until the condition is met. This group of statements can be ended by either a period or End-Perform.

Structured coding recommendations

- Use the inline Perform when it allows you to combine two parts of a single function in the same procedure.
- Don't use the inline Perform to combine two functions in a single procedure. Remember that the goal of structured design is to divide a large program up into manageable modules with one function in each module.

Figure 5-10   When and how to code inline Perform statements

How to code Perform statements
with Varying and Times clauses

Figure 5-11 shows you how to use the Varying and Times clauses with the Perform statement. You can use the Varying clause when you need to vary the value in a field each time a procedure is performed. You can use the Times clause when you want to perform a procedure a specific number of times. You can use either of these clauses to perform a procedure in a separate paragraph or to perform an inline procedure.

The first example in this figure shows how you can use the Varying clause to vary the value in the YEAR-COUNTER field each time the inline procedure is performed. If you compare this code with the code in the preceding figure, you can see how the use of the Varying clause can simplify the code. Specifically, this clause sets the starting value of YEAR-COUNTER to 1 and increases it by 1 each time the procedure is performed so you don't have to use separate state-ments to set and increase the starting value.

The second example in this figure shows how you can use the Times clause to get the same result. This Perform statement just says to perform the inline procedure the number of times that's indicated by the value in the NUMBER-OF-YEARS field.

In general, you should use the Varying and Times clauses whenever they improve the clarity of your code. In practice, though, you'll rarely use the Times clause so this is the only mention of it in this book. In contrast, you'll frequently use Varying clauses when you're processing tables. You'll learn how to do that in chapter 10.

The syntax of the Perform Varying statement

```
PERFORM [procedure-name]
    [WITH TEST {BEFORE | AFTER}]
    [VARYING identifier-1
        FROM {identifier-2 | integer-1} BY {identifier-3 | integer-2}
    UNTIL condition
        [statement-1 ...]
[END-PERFORM]
```

The syntax of the Perform Times statement

```
PERFORM [procedure-name]
    {identifier | literal} TIMES
        [statement-1 ...]
[END-PERFORM]
```

An inline iterative routine with a Perform Varying statement

```
100-CALCULATE-FUTURE-VALUE.
*
    MOVE INVESTMENT-AMOUNT TO FUTURE-VALUE.
    PERFORM
        WITH TEST AFTER
        VARYING YEAR-COUNTER FROM 1 BY 1
        UNTIL YEAR-COUNTER >= NUMBER-OF-YEARS
            COMPUTE FUTURE-VALUE ROUNDED =
                FUTURE-VALUE +
                (FUTURE-VALUE * YEARLY-INTEREST-RATE / 100)
    END-PERFORM.
```

An inline iterative routine with the Times option

```
100-CALCULATE-FUTURE-VALUE.
*
    MOVE INVESTMENT-AMOUNT TO FUTURE-VALUE.
    PERFORM NUMBER-OF-YEARS TIMES
        COMPUTE FUTURE-VALUE ROUNDED =
            FUTURE-VALUE +
            (FUTURE-VALUE * YEARLY-INTEREST-RATE / 100)
    END-PERFORM.
```

Description

- The Varying and Times clauses can be used with inline Performs or regular Performs.
- The Varying clause sets the starting value in the first field named to the value in the From clause. Then, after the Perform is executed, this value is incremented by the value in the By clause. Both the From and By fields must be defined as integers.
- The Varying clause is used most often when working with tables, as described in chapter 10. There, you'll see an expanded form of this clause.
- The Times clause is seldom used.

Figure 5-11   How to code Perform statements with Varying and Times clauses

How to use Evaluate statements

The Evaluate statement became available with COBOL-85. It has a complicated syntax that lets you use this statement for a variety of purposes. No matter how you code it, though, it always has one entry point and one exit point, so it is a valid structure for structured programming.

How to use an Evaluate statement instead of nested If statements

Figure 5-12 shows the syntax of the Evaluate statement when you use it to replace nested If statements. The example that follows shows how you can use this statement to replace nested If statements that are three levels deep. After that, you can see the nested Ifs that work the same as the Evaluate statement.

When you code the Evaluate statement, remember that the conditions in the When clauses are evaluated in sequence, starting with the first one. Then, if the condition in a When clause is true, the statements that follow are executed, and the Evaluate statement ends. This means that the sequence of the When clauses is critical. In the Evaluate statement in this example, the When clause for the CUSTMAST-EOF condition must be coded first. If it is coded last, it will never get executed since one of the preceding conditions will always be true.

Once you get used to the coding for Evaluate statements, you'll probably agree that it's usually better to use an Evaluate statement than nested If statements whenever you get three or more levels deep. If that isn't made obvious by the three-level example in this figure, it becomes more obvious as you get to the fourth level, which you'll see in figure 5-20.

The syntax of the Evaluate statement as an If-statement alternative

```
EVALUATE TRUE
    {WHEN condition-1 imperative-statement-1 ... } ...
    [WHEN OTHER imperative-statement-2 ...]
[END-EVALUATE]
```

An Evaluate statement that does the work of nested Ifs

```
EVALUATE TRUE
    WHEN CUSTMAST-EOF
        PERFORM 360-PRINT-BRANCH-LINE
    WHEN FIRST-RECORD
        PERFORM 320-PRINT-CUSTOMER-LINE
        MOVE "N" TO FIRST-RECORD-SWITCH
        MOVE CM-BRANCH-NUMBER TO OLD-BRANCH-NUMBER
    WHEN CM-BRANCH-NUMBER > OLD-BRANCH-NUMBER
        PERFORM 360-PRINT-BRANCH-LINE
        PERFORM 320-PRINT-CUSTOMER-LINE
        MOVE CM-BRANCH-NUMBER TO OLD-BRANCH-NUMBER
    WHEN CM-BRANCH-NUMBER = OLD-BRANCH-NUMBER
        PERFORM 320-PRINT-CUSTOMER-LINE
END-EVALUATE.
```

Nested If statements that work the same as the Evaluate statement

```
IF NOT CUSTMAST-EOF
    IF FIRST-RECORD
        PERFORM 320-PRINT-CUSTOMER-LINE
        MOVE "N" TO FIRST-RECORD-SWITCH
        MOVE CM-BRANCH-NUMBER TO OLD-BRANCH-NUMBER
    ELSE
        IF CM-BRANCH-NUMBER > OLD-BRANCH-NUMBER
            PERFORM 360-PRINT-BRANCH-LINE
            PERFORM 320-PRINT-CUSTOMER-LINE
            MOVE CM-BRANCH-NUMBER TO OLD-BRANCH-NUMBER
        ELSE
            PERFORM 320-PRINT-CUSTOMER-LINE
ELSE
        PERFORM 360-PRINT-BRANCH-LINE.
```

Description

- Each time an Evaluate statement is executed, the conditions in the When clauses are tested in sequence, starting with the first When clause. When a condition in a When clause is true, the statements in that clause are executed and the Evaluate statement ends without evaluating the other conditions.

- Although it isn't illustrated, you can code the reserved word Other in the last When clause. Then, that clause is executed when none of the conditions in the preceding clauses are true. You can also code compound conditions in When clauses.

Structured coding recommendation

- Use the Evaluate statement instead of nested If statements whenever it improves the clarity of your code.

Figure 5-12   How to use an Evaluate statement instead of nested If statements

How to use Evaluate statements to implement case structures

Figure 5-13 shows how you can use the Evaluate statement to implement a specific type of structure called a *case structure*. This structure is used to evaluate the values in one or more fields. Since a case structure has just one entry and exit point, it is another valid structure for structured programming.

In the first example in figure 5-13, you can see that When clauses are coded for each of the possible values in a field named RETURN-CODE. Here, the condition in the first When clause is true when the value in the return code is equal to 1; the condition in the second When clause is true when the value is equal to 2; and so on until the fourth When clause. In that clause, the word THRU is used to indicate that the condition is true when the value in the return code is equal to 4, 5, 6, 7, or 8. In the last When clause, the word OTHER is used to indicate that the condition is true for all other values.

In the example that follows, you can see that you can get the same result by coding a linear nest of If statements. Which code is easier to read and understand? Once you get used to Evaluate statements, you'll probably agree that the Evaluate statement is.

The third example in this figure illustrates the use of an Evaluate statement for a case structure that tests the values in three different fields. For instance, the condition in the first When clause is true when the value in FIELD-1 is 1, the value in FIELD-2 is B, and the value in FIELD-3 is 1. Similarly, the condition in the fifth When clause is true when the value in FIELD-1 is 3, the value in FIELD-2 is any value, and the value in FIELD-3 is 1. Note the use of the words ALSO and ANY in this statement. Also note the use of the comment line to separate the field names from the When clauses. Although this isn't required, it makes the code easier to understand.

Here again, you can get the same result by coding nested If statements with compound conditions. But this time, there's no question that the Evaluate statement will be easier to read and understand. Although you can't always align the fields as neatly as in this example, the Evaluate statement will be easier to read even if each When clause is coded over two or more lines.

An Evaluate statement that implements a one-level case structure

```
EVALUATE RETURN-CODE
    WHEN 1             PERFORM 240-PROCESS-CODE-1-RETURN
    WHEN 2             PERFORM 250-PROCESS-CODE-2-RETURN
    WHEN 3             PERFORM 260-PROCESS-CODE-3-RETURN
    WHEN 4 THRU 8  PERFORM 270-PROCESS-OTHER-CODE-RETURN
    WHEN OTHER         MOVE "N" TO VALID-RETURN-CODE-SWITCH
END-EVALUATE.
```

An If statement that works the same as the Evaluate statement

```
IF RETURN-CODE = 1
    PERFORM 240-PROCESS-CODE-1-RETURN
ELSE IF RETURN-CODE = 2
    PERFORM 250-PROCESS-CODE-2-RETURN
ELSE IF RETURN-CODE = 3
    PERFORM 260-PROCESS-CODE-3-RETURN
ELSE IF RETURN-CODE => 4 AND <= 8
    PERFORM 270-PROCESS-OTHER-CODE-RETURN
ELSE
    MOVE "N" TO VALID-RETURN-CODE-SWITCH.
```

An Evaluate statement that implements a three-level case structure

```
EVALUATE FIELD-1 ALSO FIELD-2 ALSO FIELD-3
*        -------       -------      -------
    WHEN    1    ALSO   "B"   ALSO   1    PERFORM 310-ACTION-1
    WHEN    1    ALSO   "M"   ALSO   2    PERFORM 320-ACTION-2
    WHEN    2    ALSO   "P"   ALSO   1    PERFORM 330-ACTION-3
    WHEN    2    ALSO NOT "P" ALSO   2    PERFORM 340-ACTION-4
    WHEN    3    ALSO   ANY   ALSO   1    PERFORM 350-ACTION-5
    WHEN    3    ALSO   ANY   ALSO   2    PERFORM 360-ACTION-6
    WHEN OTHER                            PERFORM 370-DEFAULT
END-EVALUATE.
```

Description

- A *case structure* tests the values in one or more fields and performs one or more statements for the one condition that is true. Since this structure has just one entry and one exit point, it is a valid structured programming structure.

- The Evaluate statement can be used to implement a case structure for one or more fields. When you work with more than one field, you use the word ALSO before each additional field. Then, in the When clauses, you use the word ALSO before each additional value.

- To test for a series of values in a field, you can use the word THRU or THROUGH as in 1 THRU 3 or "A" THRU "C". To indicate that any value in a field satisfies the condition, you use the word ANY.

- If the When clauses don't provide for all possible conditions, you can add a final When clause containing the word OTHER. This clause is executed when none of the conditions in the preceding When clauses is true.

Figure 5-13   How to use Evaluate statements to implement case structures

The complete syntax of the Evaluate statement

Now that you've seen the two common uses of the Evaluate statement, you may be interested in the complete syntax for this statement, which is shown in figure 5-14. As you can see, there's a lot more to this statement than the examples so far have illustrated. And to make it even more complicated, you can nest Evaluate statements within Evaluate statements.

The examples in this figure show two more ways that you can use this statement, but there are many more. In the first example, two logical expressions are evaluated, and the When clauses provide for the four combinations of True and False evaluations. In the second example, each When clause contains two conditions, and the processing depends on whether both conditions are true. If neither condition is true, the When Other clause is performed.

Although this is a powerful statement that provides for a wide variety of processing options, it is also a statement that can get impossibly complicated. As a programmer, then, you should use indentation and comments to make your statements easier to read. You should also avoid nesting Evaluate or If statements within Evaluate statements. Whenever you use an Evaluate statement, your goal should be to write code that's easier to read and understand than the comparable code when using nested If statements.

The complete syntax of the Evaluate statement

$$\text{EVALUATE} \left\{ \begin{array}{l} \text{identifier-1} \\ \text{literal-1} \\ \text{expression-1} \\ \underline{\text{TRUE}} \\ \underline{\text{FALSE}} \end{array} \right\} \quad \left[\underline{\text{ALSO}} \left\{ \begin{array}{l} \text{identifier-2} \\ \text{literal-2} \\ \text{expression-2} \\ \underline{\text{TRUE}} \\ \underline{\text{FALSE}} \end{array} \right\} \right] \dots$$

```
{{WHEN

  ANY
  condition-1
  TRUE
  FALSE
  [NOT] { identifier-3    } [ THROUGH { identifier-4            } ]
        { literal-3       }   THRU    { literal-4               }
        { arithmetic-expression-1 }   { arithmetic-expression-2 }

[ALSO

  ANY
  condition-2
  TRUE
  FALSE
  [NOT] { identifier-5    } [ THROUGH { identifier-6            } ]  ] ... } ...
        { literal-5       }   THRU    { literal-6               }
        { arithmetic-expression-3 }   { arithmetic-expression-4 }

imperative-statement-1 ... } ...
[WHEN OTHER imperative-statement-2 ...]
[END-EVALUATE]
```

Examples

```
EVALUATE FIELD-1 > FIELD-2 ALSO FIELD-3 > FIELD-4
*        -----------------      -----------------
    WHEN TRUE            ALSO TRUE      PERFORM 310-ACTION-1
    WHEN TRUE            ALSO FALSE     PERFORM 320-ACTION-2
    WHEN FALSE           ALSO TRUE      PERFORM 330-ACTION-3
    WHEN FALSE           ALSO FALSE     PERFORM 340-ACTION-4
END-EVALUATE.
EVALUATE TRUE       ALSO TRUE
*        --------        --------
    WHEN F1 > F2  ALSO F3 > F4   PERFORM 310-ACTION-1
    WHEN F1 = F2  ALSO F3 > F4   PERFORM 320-ACTION-2
    WHEN F1 < F2  ALSO F3 = F4   PERFORM 330-ACTION-3
    WHEN OTHER               PERFORM 340-ACTION-4
END-EVALUATE.
```

Structured coding recommendation

- Use indentation and comments to make your Evaluate statements as readable as possible.
- Avoid nesting Evaluate or If statements within Evaluate statements.

Figure 5-14   The complete syntax of the Evaluate statement

Other features for improved coding

Three more features for structured programming that became available with COBOL-85 are the Set to True statement, structured delimiters, and Not clauses. You'll learn more about these features in the topics that follow.

How to use Set to True statements

Figure 5-15 shows how to use the Set to True statement to turn on the condition represented by a condition name. As you can see in the examples, these statements are easier to code than Move statements because you don't have to remember the values for the conditions. They also make your code easier to modify if the values are changed later on because you only have to modify the 88 levels, not the Set to True statements. For those reasons, you should routinely use Set to True statements for turning on conditions.

The syntax of the Set to True statement

```
SET condition-name-1 ... TO TRUE
```

Code that defines condition names

```
01   SWITCHES.
     05   CUSTMAST-EOF-SWITCH      PIC X     VALUE "N".
          88   CUSTMAST-EOF                  VALUE "Y".
*
01   FLAGS.
     05   TRAN-CODE            PIC X.
          88   TC-ISSUE                      VALUE "1".
          88   TC-RECEIPT                    VALUE "2" "3".
          88   TC-RETURN                     VALUE "4" "D" THRU "F".
```

Code that turns conditions on

With Set to True statements

```
SET CUSTMAST-EOF TO TRUE.

SET TC-ISSUE TO TRUE.

SET TC-RETURN TO TRUE.
```

Without Set to True statements

```
MOVE "Y" TO CUSTMAST-EOF-SWITCH.

MOVE "1" TO TRAN-CODE.

MOVE "4" TO TRAN-CODE.
```

Description

- The Set to True statement turns on the condition specified by a condition name. In other words, it sets the related field to the value specified by an 88-level description.

- If a condition has more than one value, the Set to True statement sets the condition to the first value given by the Value clause. If TC-RETURN in the third example is set to true, it receives the value 4.

Structured coding recommendations

- Use the Set to True statement to turn on all conditions that are represented by condition names.

Figure 5-15   How to use Set to True statements

When and how to use structured delimiters

A *structured delimiter* is simply the word End- followed by the verb name, as in End-If. You have already seen these delimiters used with If, Perform, and Evaluate statements. However, delimiters can be used with all the verbs listed in figure 5-16.

Structured delimiters are most useful when you're coding one statement within another one. For instance, the End-Compute delimiter is used in the example in this figure to end a Compute statement that's coded within an If statement. Without the delimiter, the statement after the delimiter would be treated as part of the On Size Error clause, so you couldn't code this calculation this way.

Once structured delimiters became available, some programmers started using delimiters instead of periods to end their statements. Since extra periods or missing periods are often the cause of programming problems, they reasoned that eliminating periods would improve their programs. You still need to end each paragraph with a period, though, and some programmers code each period on a separate line after the last statement in the paragraph to make the period obvious.

Although this is a relatively harmless coding practice, it's unnecessary. It also takes extra compile time. As a result, we recommend that you use a period to mark the end of each statement that isn't contained within another statement, and that you use structured delimiters whenever they improve the clarity of your code.

The verb list for structured delimiters

Input/output	Computation	Other
Read	Add	Perform
Write	Subtract	If
Rewrite	Multiply	Evaluate
Delete	Divide	Search
Return	Compute	Call

An If statement that requires the use of the End-Compute delimiter

```
IF CM-SALES-LAST-YTD NOT EQUAL ZERO
    COMPUTE CHANGE-PERCENT ROUNDED =
        CHANGE-AMOUNT * 100 / CM-SALES-LAST-YTD
            ON SIZE ERROR
                MOVE 999.9 TO CHANGE-PERCENT
    END-COMPUTE
    MOVE CHANGE-PERCENT TO CL-CHANGE-PERCENT
ELSE
    MOVE 999.9 TO CL-CHANGE-PERCENT
END-IF.
```

Description

- A structured delimiter consists of the word End, the hyphen, and the verb name. Thus, End-Compute is the delimiter for the Compute statement.
- Structured delimiters are useful when you need to end a statement but can't use a period to end it. This is illustrated by the Compute statement within the If statement in the example above.

Structured coding recommendation

- Use structured delimiters whenever they improve the clarity of your code.
- Don't use structured delimiters where periods work just as well.

Figure 5-16   When and how to use structured delimiters

When and how to use Not clauses

Figure 5-17 presents some statements that provide Not clauses. These clauses are counterparts to other clauses within a statement. For instance, the Not At End clause is a counterpart to the At End clause, and the Not On Size Error clause is a counterpart to the On Size Error clause. In the rest of this book, you will see Not clauses in the syntax summaries for all statements that provide for them.

If you look at the first example in this figure, you can see how the Not At End clause can be used with a Read statement. Here, the end-of-file switch is turned on if there are no more records in the file (At End). Otherwise, 1 is added to the record count (Not At End). If you compare this code with the code in the second example, you can see that using the Not At End clause makes the code somewhat easier to read.

In the third example in this figure, you can see how a Not On Size Error clause can be used in an arithmetic statement. Although this may be useful while you're debugging, you don't normally use Not clauses with arithmetic statements in production programs.

Statements that provide Not clauses

Clause	Statements
NOT AT END	Read
NOT ON SIZE ERROR	Add, Subtract, Multiply, Divide, Compute
NOT ON OVERFLOW	String, Unstring (see chapter 9)
NOT ON EXCEPTION	Call (see chapter 11)
NOT INVALID KEY	Read, Start, Write, Delete, Rewrite (see chapters 13 through 15)

A logical use of a Not clause

```
READ CUSTMAST
    AT END
        SET CUSTMAST-EOF TO TRUE
    NOT AT END
        ADD 1 TO RECORD-COUNT.
```

The coding without the Not clause

```
READ CUSTMAST
    AT END
        SET CUSTMAST-EOF TO TRUE.
IF NOT CUSTMAST-EOF
    ADD 1 TO RECORD-COUNT.
```

A Not clause used for debugging

```
ADD 1 TO RECORD-COUNT
    ON SIZE ERROR
        DISPLAY "THE RECORD-COUNT FIELD HAS OVERFLOWED"
    NOT ON SIZE ERROR
        DISPLAY "CURRENT RECORD COUNT IS " RECORD-COUNT
END-ADD.
```

Description

- Not clauses are most useful when coding input/output statements like Read and Write statements. You rarely need them for other types of statements.

Structured coding recommendation

- Use Not clauses whenever they help you improve the clarity of your code.

Figure 5-17   When and how to use Not clauses

A program that prepares a two-level summary report

This chapter concludes by presenting a program that prepares a two-level summary report. This program requires a procedure that can be coded with nested If statements that are four levels deep ... or an Evaluate statement with five When clauses. When you review these coding alternatives in figure 5-20, you can decide which code is easier to follow.

The program specifications

Figure 5-18 presents the specifications for this program. As you can see, this program reads the same file of customer master records that the programs in chapters 3 and 4 read. This time, however, the program uses the salesrep number field.

If you study the report that this program prepares, you can see that it has sales totals for each salesrep and sales totals for each branch. That's why it's called a *two-level summary report*. In contrast, a program with just one level of totals can be called a one-level summary report. (Note that the grand totals aren't considered to be a level.)

When you prepare a two-level report, the input records have to be in sequence by the levels of the report. In this case, the records have to be in sequence by salesrep number within branch number. If you study the data for the first five records that are shown in this figure, you can see that salesrep numbers 10 and 14 are in sequence within branch number 22. For this report, the records are also in sequence by customer number within salesrep number so the customer lines for each salesrep will be printed in sequence.

In the data for a production program, of course, there would be more than a few customer records for each salesrep, and more than a few salesreps for each branch. But the point of this limited data is just to show that the report requires one summary line for each salesrep and one for each branch.

The logic of this program is based on the control breaks that occur when a customer record is read. Whenever the branch number changes, both a salesrep and a branch total line have to be printed. And whenever the salesrep number changes but the branch number doesn't change, just a salesrep line has to be printed. For instance, both a salesrep and branch line are printed when the branch number changes from 12 to 22, and only a salesrep line is printed when the salesrep number changes from 10 to 14 but the branch number (22) doesn't change.

The COBOL description for the customer master record

```
01  CUSTOMER-MASTER-RECORD.
    05  CM-BRANCH-NUMBER       PIC 9(2).
    05  CM-SALESREP-NUMBER     PIC 9(2).
    05  CM-CUSTOMER-NUMBER     PIC 9(5).
    05  CM-CUSTOMER-NAME       PIC X(20).
    05  CM-SALES-THIS-YTD      PIC S9(5)V9(2).
    05  CM-SALES-LAST-YTD      PIC S9(5)V9(2).
```

The data for the first five customer master records in the file

Branch Number	Salesrep Number	Customer Number	Customer Name	Sales This YTD	Sales Last YTD
12	12	11111	INFORMATION BUILDERS	0123456	0111111
12	12	12345	CAREER TRAINING CTR	1234567	2222222
22	10	22222	HOMELITE TEXTRON CO	3454500	0000000
22	14	34567	NEAS MEMBER BENEFITS	0011111	0000000
22	14	55555	PILOT LIFE INS. CO.	1000000	0100000

How the two-level summary report should look

```
DATE:   04/17/2000              YEAR-TO-DATE SALES REPORT                    PAGE:    1
TIME:   16:04                                                                RPT5000

BRANCH  SLSREP  CUST                      SALES         SALES        CHANGE      CHANGE
NUM     NUM     NUM    CUSTOMER NAME       THIS YTD      LAST YTD     AMOUNT      PERCENT

 12      12     11111  INFORMATION BUILDERS  1,234.56     1,111.11      123.45       11.1
                12345  CAREER TRAINING CTR  12,345.67    22,222.22    9,876.55-      44.4-
                       SALESREP TOTAL       13,580.23    23,333.33    9,753.10-      41.8- *

                       BRANCH TOTAL         13,580.23    23,333.33    9,753.10-      41.8- **

 22      10     22222  HOMELITE TEXTRON CO  34,545.00         0.00   34,545.00      999.9
                       SALESREP TOTAL       34,545.00         0.00   34,545.00      999.9  *

         14     34567  NEAS MEMBER BENEFITS    111.11         0.00      111.11      999.9
                55555  PILOT LIFE INS. CO.  10,000.00     1,000.00    9,000.00      900.0
                       SALESREP TOTAL       10,111.11     1,000.00    9,111.11      911.1  *

                       BRANCH TOTAL         44,656.11     1,000.00   43,656.11      999.9  **
                          .
                          .
                          .
                       GRAND TOTAL         120,525.72   121,155.45      629.73-       0.5- ***
```

The processing specifications

- This program reads the same file of customer records that the programs in chapters 3 and 4 read. These records are in sequence by customer number within salesrep number within branch number.

- This program prepares a report that is like the summary report in chapter 4, but this report prints salesrep totals as well as branch totals. This means there's a control break when the branch number changes and also when the salesrep number changes.

Figure 5-18   The specifications for program that prepares a two-level summary report

The structure chart

Before you start the coding for a report like this, you should design a structure chart for it. In this case, since you're enhancing the summary report program in chapter 4, you can start by enhancing its structure chart as shown in figure 5-19.

To provide for the salesrep lines, you need to add just one new module that's subordinate to module 300. It should be named print-salesrep-line, and it should be given a number like 355, which is between 350 and 360. In addition, you need to draw common module 350 as a subordinate to module 355. Then, module 355 calls module 350 whenever it needs to write a line.

This shows how easy it is to adapt a well-designed structure chart to an enhanced version of the program or to a similar program. This also shows that all report-preparation programs have a similar structure.

The structure chart

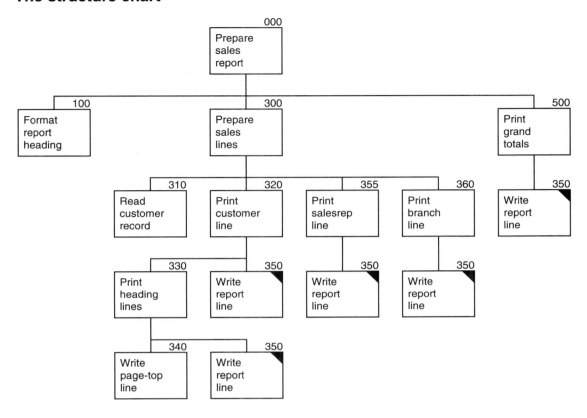

Description

- To create the structure chart for the two-level report program from the structure chart for the one-level report program in figure 4-7, you just need to add module 355 with common module 350 subordinate to it. Module 355 will print the salesrep summary lines.

- When you code this program, you only need to modify the code in three modules of the one-level report program. Module 300, the primary control module, has to provide the logic for calling module 355 and printing the salesrep lines. Module 320 has to provide for the salesrep fields in the customer line. And module 360 has to provide for a blank line before the branch line.

- When you code this program, you also have to add module 355. However, this module should be so similar to module 360 that you can start it from a copy of module 360.

Figure 5-19   The structure chart for the two-level report program

The COBOL code for the primary control module

When you code a program like this, the only module that you should have any trouble with is the primary control module. This is module 300 in the structure chart. In figure 5-20, you can see two ways that this module can be coded.

If you code this module with nested If statements, you need to nest them four levels deep. That way, you can provide for the five conditions that dictate the logic of this program. If you study the nested Ifs in this figure, you can see that they provide for (1) the end-of-file condition, (2) the first-record condition, (3) a branch number control break, (4) a salesrep number control break, and (5) no change in either branch or salesrep number (the second-to-last Else clause). In this case, End-Ifs aren't used so these examples will fit on one page, but the code is still easy to follow.

The alternative is to code this module with one Evaluate statement that contains five When clauses. Because these clauses are evaluated in sequence and only the first When clause that's true is executed, the sequence in which you code these clauses is critical. For a summary report, the proper sequence is the one shown in this figure. After the end-of-file and first record conditions are handled, you code the control break clauses in sequence from the top down starting with the highest level control break. The When Other clause at the end of the statement provides for the case when no break occurs.

Is the Evaluate statement easier to read and understand than the nested Ifs? Once you get used to working with Evaluate statements, I think you'll agree that it is. Then, when you need to add another level to a report, you just add another When clause to the Evaluate statement instead of another level to the nested Ifs.

Once you understand the code for this procedure, you should be able to develop the rest of the program with relative ease. In the Data Division, you need to add the control field for the old salesrep number, the total fields for the salesrep totals, and the line description for the salesrep line. You also need to modify the other print lines so they provide for the salesrep field. In the Procedure Division, you need to modify the code in procedures 300, 320, and 360, and you need to add the new procedure 355. It's that easy to convert a one-level report to a two-level report.

Procedure 300 when coded with nested If statements

```
300-PREPARE-SALES-LINES.
*
     PERFORM 310-READ-CUSTOMER-RECORD.
     IF NOT CUSTMAST-EOF
         IF FIRST-RECORD
             PERFORM 320-PRINT-CUSTOMER-LINE
             MOVE "N" TO FIRST-RECORD-SWITCH
             MOVE CM-SALESREP-NUMBER TO OLD-SALESREP-NUMBER
             MOVE CM-BRANCH-NUMBER TO OLD-BRANCH-NUMBER
         ELSE
             IF CM-BRANCH-NUMBER > OLD-BRANCH-NUMBER
                 PERFORM 355-PRINT-SALESREP-LINE
                 PERFORM 360-PRINT-BRANCH-LINE
                 PERFORM 320-PRINT-CUSTOMER-LINE
                 MOVE CM-SALESREP-NUMBER TO OLD-SALESREP-NUMBER
                 MOVE CM-BRANCH-NUMBER TO OLD-BRANCH-NUMBER
             ELSE
                 IF CM-SALESREP-NUMBER > OLD-SALESREP-NUMBER
                     PERFORM 355-PRINT-SALESREP-LINE
                     PERFORM 320-PRINT-CUSTOMER-LINE
                     MOVE CM-SALESREP-NUMBER
                         TO OLD-SALESREP-NUMBER
                 ELSE
                     PERFORM 320-PRINT-CUSTOMER-LINE
     ELSE
         PERFORM 355-PRINT-SALESREP-LINE
         PERFORM 360-PRINT-BRANCH-LINE.
```

Procedure 300 when coded with an Evaluate statement

```
300-PREPARE-SALES-LINES.
*
     PERFORM 310-READ-CUSTOMER-RECORD.
     EVALUATE TRUE
         WHEN CUSTMAST-EOF
             PERFORM 355-PRINT-SALESREP-LINE
             PERFORM 360-PRINT-BRANCH-LINE
         WHEN FIRST-RECORD
             PERFORM 320-PRINT-CUSTOMER-LINE
             MOVE "N" TO FIRST-RECORD-SWITCH
             MOVE CM-SALESREP-NUMBER TO OLD-SALESREP-NUMBER
             MOVE CM-BRANCH-NUMBER TO OLD-BRANCH-NUMBER
         WHEN CM-BRANCH-NUMBER > OLD-BRANCH-NUMBER
             PERFORM 355-PRINT-SALESREP-LINE
             PERFORM 360-PRINT-BRANCH-LINE
             PERFORM 320-PRINT-CUSTOMER-LINE
             MOVE CM-SALESREP-NUMBER TO OLD-SALESREP-NUMBER
             MOVE CM-BRANCH-NUMBER TO OLD-BRANCH-NUMBER
         WHEN CM-SALESREP-NUMBER > OLD-SALESREP-NUMBER
             PERFORM 355-PRINT-SALESREP-LINE
             PERFORM 320-PRINT-CUSTOMER-LINE
             MOVE CM-SALESREP-NUMBER TO OLD-SALESREP-NUMBER
         WHEN OTHER
             PERFORM 320-PRINT-CUSTOMER-LINE
     END-EVALUATE.
```

Figure 5-20   The code for the primary control module

Perspective

Now that you have completed this last chapter in the first section of this book, you should be able to design, code, and test structured programs of considerable complexity. In particular, you should be able to develop programs that prepare reports. And you should be able to code those programs with structured code that meets the standards of the best COBOL shops.

Of course, you still have a lot to learn. So in the next section, you can learn other COBOL essentials like how to work with functions, character strings, dates, and tables. In section 3, you can learn how to read and write disk files with sequential, indexed, and relative organizations. And in section 4, you can learn how to use COBOL on specific platforms like IBM mainframes.

Since you don't have to read the remaining chapters in sequence, you can now skip to any section that interests you. If, for example, you would like to learn more about working with files, you can skip directly to chapter 12 of section 3. Or, if you would like to learn how to work with tables, you can skip directly to chapter 10. If you don't have specific interests, though, we suggest that you continue with the next chapter so you'll better understand how data can be defined, moved, and initialized.

Summary

- In *structured programming* terms, a *proper program* is made up of *sequence*, *selection*, and *iteration structures*.

- In COBOL, statements that don't include conditions implement the sequence structure. The If statement implements the selection structure. The Perform Until statement implements the iteration structure.

- You should use your *shop standards* for structured programming if your COBOL shop has established them. Otherwise, you should follow the recommendations in this book.

- For the condition that's used in an If, Perform Until, or Evaluate statement, you can code a *relation*, *sign*, or *class test*. You also can code *compound conditions*.

- *Condition names* describe the conditions that are related to switches and flags. A *switch* is a one-character field that can have either a Yes or a No value. A *flag* is a one-character field that can have other values.

- In general, n*ested If statements* become difficult to read when they reach the third or fourth level. However, *linear nests* are easy to read no matter how many levels deep they go.

- *Inline Perform statements* are useful when they let you code a single function in a single paragraph. They shouldn't be used to combine two or more functions in a single paragraph.

- You can use the Evaluate statement to improve the clarity of nested If statements that are three or more levels deep. The Evaluate statement also can be used to implement a *case structure*.

- You can use Set to True statements to turn on all conditions that are defined as condition names.

- You can use *structured delimiters* to end statements that are coded within other statements.

- You use Not clauses primarily in input/output statements.

- A *two-level summary report* shows group totals at two different levels.

Terms

structured programming	proper program	implied operator
sequence structure	structured coding	condition name
Do structure	shop standards	switch
selection structure	condition	flag
If-Then-Else structure	relation test	nested If statements
iteration structure	sign test	linear nest
Do While structure	class test	inline Perform statement
Do Until structure	compound condition	case structure
Perform Until structure	logical operator	structured delimiter
entry point	implied subject	two-level summary report
exit point		

Objectives

- Given the specifications for a *two-level summary report* like the one in this chapter, develop a program that prepares the report.

- Use any of the features presented in this chapter as you develop programs of your own.

- Describe the three valid structures of structured programming.

- Explain how the principles of substitution and combination lead to a proper program.

- Explain what is meant by *shop standards*. Then, list three typical Data Division standards and three typical Procedure Division standards.

- Describe the characteristics of *relation*, *sign*, and *class tests*.

- Explain how the use of *condition names* can improve coding.

- Describe the proper use of an inline Perform statement.

- Describe the characteristics of a *case structure*.

- Explain how the use of Set to True statements can improve coding.

Exercise 5-1   Improve the future value program

In this exercise, you'll modify the future value program of chapter 1 so it uses an inline Perform statement.

1.   Open the program named calc2000.

2.   Modify this program so it uses an inline Perform Varying statement to do the future value calculation (see figure 5-11). Then, test the program to make sure that it still works correctly.

3.   Close the program.

Exercise 5-2   Improve the summary report program

In this exercise, you'll improve the summary report program that you developed in exercise 4-2 by using some of the language that you learned in this chapter.

1.   Open the program named rpt3000.

2.   Define condition names for the first-record and end-of-file switches in the Data Division. Then, use the condition names in the Procedure Division to refer to the conditions, and use a Set to True statement to turn the end-of-file condition on. After you've made these changes, test them. You should still get a report like the one in figure 4-2.

3.   Rewrite the nested If statements in procedures 300 and 320 so they use Evaluate statements. Then, test the program to make sure that it still works correctly.

4.   Close the program.

Exercise 5-3   Prepare a two-level summary report

In this exercise, you'll enhance the summary report program that you modified in exercise 5-2 so it prepares the two-level summary report shown in figure 5-18.

1.   Open the program named rpt3000, change the Program-ID to RPT5000, and save it as rpt5000. Then, close the program and re-open it.

2.   Enhance the code in the Data Division of rpt5000 so it provides for the two-level report shown in figure 5-18.

3.   Modify procedures 300, 320, and 360 in the Procedure Division so they provide for the two-level report, and add procedure 355, which will print the salesrep lines. Then, test the program to make sure that it works correctly.

4.   Close the program.

Section 2

Other COBOL essentials

This section consists of six chapters that show you how to use specific types of
COBOL features. Since each chapter is treated as an independent unit, you
don't have to read these chapters in sequence. Instead, you can read them in
whatever sequence you prefer.

If, for example, you want to learn how to work with tables next, you can
skip to chapter 10. Or if you want to learn how to use the intrinsic functions,
you can skip to chapter 7. Unless you have a specific interest, though, we
recommend that you start by reading chapter 6 because it presents some skills
that apply to all types of programs.

6

How to define, move, and initialize fields

In section 1, you learned how to define fields in the Data Division with simple Picture and Value clauses. You also learned how to code Move statements that moved data from a field or a literal to another field. Now, in this chapter, you'll learn all of the COBOL language for defining, moving, and initializing fields.

How to define fields in the Data Division

Figure 6-1 presents the complete syntax for defining fields in the Data Division. In this chapter, you'll learn how to use all of the clauses that are shown. You'll also learn how to use the Usage extensions for IBM mainframes. As you read about the individual clauses in this chapter, you may want to refer back to this figure to see how they all fit together.

When to omit the word Filler

In figure 6-1, you should notice that the word Filler isn't underlined in the syntax summary, which means that it isn't required. So even though all the programs in section 1 use the word Filler for those fields that aren't referred to in the Procedure Division, it isn't required. In practice, the older programmers still tend to use Filler, while the younger ones omit it. Before you stop coding it, though, you ought to check your shop standards to see whether that's okay.

The basic syntax for data definitions

```
01-49  {data-name | FILLER }
       [{PICTURE | PIC} IS character-string]
       [VALUE IS literal]
       [BLANK WHEN ZERO]
       [            ⎧ DISPLAY         ⎫ ]
       [ [USAGE IS] ⎨ BINARY          ⎬ ]
       [            ⎩ PACKED-DECIMAL  ⎭ ]

88     condition-name VALUE IS {literal-1 [{THROUGH | THRU} literal-2]} ...
```

The syntax for redefining a field

```
01-49  data-name-1 REDEFINES data-name-2
```

Three other clauses that you can use in a data definition

```
[[SIGN IS] {LEADING | TRAILING} [SEPARATE CHARACTER]]
[{JUSTIFIED | JUST} RIGHT]
[{SYNCHRONIZED | SYNC} [LEFT | RIGHT]]
```

Data definitions with the word Filler omitted

```
01  HEADING-LINE-2.
    05                    PIC X(7)     VALUE "TIME:   ".
    05  HL2-HOURS         PIC 9(2).
    05                    PIC X(1)     VALUE ":".
    05  HL2-MINUTES       PIC 9(2).
    05                    PIC X(57)    VALUE SPACE.
    05                    PIC X(11)    VALUE "RPT1000".
    05                    PIC X(52)    VALUE SPACE.
```

Description

- When you define a field, you use 01 for the top level group items. Then, for the next levels, you can use the numbers 02 through 49. In practice, though, most programmers use 05 for the second level, 10 for the third level, and so on.

- All programmers should know how to define fields with Picture, Value, and Blank When Zero clauses (figure 6-3). They should also know when and how to use Usage clauses because these clauses can improve the efficiency of a program (figure 6-4).

- You can code a Redefines clause when you want to define the same field in storage in two different ways (figure 6-5).

- Although you may never need the Sign, Synchronized, or Justified clauses, you should at least know what they're for (figure 6-6).

- Notice that the word Filler isn't underlined in the basic syntax summary. That means that you don't have to code it for fields that you aren't going to refer to. This is illustrated by the example.

Figure 6-1   The syntax for defining fields in the Data Division

How to code literals and figurative constants

In chapter 1, you learned how to code literals and some of the figurative constants. Now, figure 6-2 lists all of the figurative constants. It also shows how to continue a long literal from one line to the next.

To keep your code simple and consistent, we recommend that you use the singular form of each figurative constant (Zero, Space, Quote, High-Value, and Low-Value). That works whether the field it applies to is singular or plural. When you read section 3 of this book, you'll see that High-Value and Low-Value are often used with programs that work with files.

To continue a literal from one line to the next, you need to put a hyphen (-) in column 7 of the second coding line. You also need to start the second line with a quotation mark, although you don't end the first line with a quotation mark.

The allowable characters in literals

Type	Characters	Examples
Nonnumeric	Any	`"Y"` `"End of Session"`

Numeric	0-9 + - .	`1.23`
		`-100`
		`+55.1`

The complete list of figurative constants

Constant	Meaning

`ZERO`
`ZEROS`
`ZEROES`
	One or more zeros

`SPACE` `SPACES`	One or more spaces
`ALL "literal"`	One or more occurrences of the literal within the quotation marks
`QUOTE` `QUOTES`	One or more occurrences of the quotation mark
`HIGH-VALUE` `HIGH-VALUES`	One or more occurrences of the highest value that can be stored in a byte
`LOW-VALUE` `LOW-VALUES`	One or more occurrences of the lowest value that can be stored in a byte

A data definition that defines a variable that contains 40 asterisks

```
05  LINE-SEPARATOR    PIC X(40)    VALUE ALL "*".
```

An alphanumeric literal that's continued from one line to the next

```
01  ERROR MESSAGES.
*
    05  MESSAGE-1     PIC X(80)    VALUE "ARITHMETIC OVERFLOW HA
-   "S OCCURRED SO THE RESULT THAT'S SHOWN IS INACCURATE.".
```

Description

- Literals and figurative constants can be used in Value clauses in the Data Division and in some statements in the Procedure Division. When a figurative constant is used in a Value clause, it fills the entire field.

- To continue a literal from one line to the next, start the literal on the first line and continue coding until you reach column 72. Then, code a hyphen (-) in column 7 of the line that follows, code a quotation mark in the B margin (usually, column 12), and code the rest of the literal. If necessary, you can repeat this on subsequent lines.

Figure 6-2   How to code literals and figurative constants

How to code Picture, Value, and Blank When Zero clauses

Figure 6-3 shows the five types of data items you can define and the characters that you use in the Pictures for those items. Since you already know how to code Picture and Value clauses for three types of data items, you shouldn't have any trouble coding the two new types. Later, in figures 6-7 and 6-8, you can learn which moves are legal and how data is edited when you move it into an alphanumeric edited or numeric edited item.

When you code the Blank When Zero clause, a numeric field that contains a value of zero is changed to spaces. If, for example, a field is defined with a Picture of ZZZ.99, it will look like .00 if a value of zero is moved to it. If you use the Blank When Zero clause with it, though, the field will be converted to spaces.

Data types and the allowable characters in Picture clauses

Type	Characters	Examples
Alphabetic	A	`A(20)`
Alphanumeric	X	`X(20)`
Numeric	9 S V	`S9(3)V99`
Alphanumeric edited	X B /	`XXBXX`
		`XX/XX/XX`
Numeric edited	B / Z 9 , . * + - $ CR DB	`99B99`
		`99/99/99`
		`ZZZ.99CR`
		`ZZ,ZZZ.99DB`
		`**,***.99`
		`--,---,---`
		`+++,+++.99`
		`$$$,$$$,$$$.99CR`

The syntax of the Value and Blank When Zero clauses

```
[VALUE IS literal]
[BLANK WHEN ZERO]
```

Examples of Picture, Value, and Blank When Zero clauses

```
05   HL1-EDITED-DATE          PIC 99/99/99.
05   THIS-YTD-SALES-TOTAL     PIC S9(7)V99        VALUE ZERO.
05   GTL-THIS-YTD-SALES-TOTAL PIC Z,ZZZ,ZZZ.99CR  BLANK WHEN ZERO.
```

Description

- So far, you've been introduced to three of the COBOL data types: *alphanumeric*, *numeric*, and *numeric edited*. In the table above, though, you can see that there are two other data types: *alphabetic* and *alphanumeric edited*. You can also see the full range of characters that are allowed in numeric edited items.

- Alphabetic data types can contain only alphabetic characters and spaces. Because this is limiting, you normally use alphanumeric instead of alphabetic data types.

- In general, alphanumeric edited items are used to edit alphanumeric items, and numeric edited items are used to edit numeric items. This happens when one item is moved to the other (see figure 6-8).

- The Blank When Zero clause turns a numeric field to spaces when its value is zero.

Figure 6-3   How to code Picture, Value, and Blank When Zero clauses

How to code Usage clauses

In the first section of this book, Usage clauses weren't used. In practice, though, you need to code Usage clauses to tell the compiler what formats to use for specific fields. In particular, you should specify numeric usages for fields that are going to be used for computations or numeric comparisons. If you don't, your program will run less efficiently than it ought to.

Figure 6-4 shows you how to code Usage clauses for the three standard data formats. Since Display is the default if you omit this clause, all of the numeric fields used in the programs in the first section of this book have Display usage. In that format, one character is stored in one byte of storage. So a field with a Picture of 9(5) or 9(3)V99 requires five bytes of storage.

When you use Packed-Decimal usage for a numeric field, two digits are stored in each byte of a field with the exception of the rightmost byte, which stores one digit and the sign for the field. As a result, this is a more efficient form of storage than Display usage. For instance, a field with a Picture of S9(5) or S9(3)V99 requires just three bytes of storage.

When you use Binary usage for a numeric field, a field of from 1 through 4 digits is usually stored in two bytes. A field of from 5 through 9 digits is usually stored in four bytes. And a field of from 10 through 18 digits is usually stored in eight bytes. Again, this is a more efficient form of storage than Display usage.

Besides storage efficiency, though, Packed-Decimal and Binary usage lead to improved compile-time and run-time efficiency. That's because a computer has to convert fields with Display usage to Packed-Decimal or Binary usage before it can use them in computations or in numeric comparisons. So if you define these fields with the proper usage, the computer has less work to do when it compiles your statements and less work to do when it executes them.

In general, then, you should code Usage clauses for all numeric fields that are going to be used in computations or numeric comparisons. As you can see in this figure, you can code these clauses at the elementary or group level. Note, however, that you need to find out what usages your computer provides for and what the preferred usages are for different types of fields. If your computer provides for Packed-Decimal usage, though, you normally use that usage for all numeric fields.

Because a field with Packed-Decimal usage is always stored with a sign and an odd number of digits, you should code the pictures for these fields with a leading S and an odd number of digits. That improves both compile-time and run-time efficiency. Similarly, a field with Binary usage always includes a sign, so you should also code the pictures for those fields with a leading S.

When a field is defined with Packed-Decimal or Binary usage, you should realize that its data will be unintelligible if you display or print it. Before it will make sense, you need to move it to a numeric edited field that changes it to a readable form.

Incidentally, data can also be stored on tape or disk files with Packed-Decimal or Binary usage. This makes better use of the storage media and also improves program efficiency when the files are used.

The syntax of the Usage clause

$$[\underline{USAGE}\ IS\ ] \left\{ \begin{array}{l} \underline{DISPLAY} \\ \underline{PACKED-DECIMAL} \\ \underline{BINARY} \end{array} \right\}$$

Usage clauses for elementary items

```
05   YTD-SALES-TOTAL PIC S9(7)V99  VALUE ZERO   PACKED-DECIMAL.
05   CONTROL-FIELD    PIC S999      VALUE +99    BINARY.
```

Usage clauses at the group level

```
01   TOTAL-FIELDS         PACKED-DECIMAL.
     05   MONTHLY TOTAL    PIC S9(5)V99.
     05   YEARLY-TOTAL     PIC S9(7)V99.
01   PRINT-FIELDS         BINARY.
     05   LINE-COUNT       PIC S9(3)        VALUE +99.
     05   LINES-ON-PAGE    PIC S9(3)        VALUE +60.
```

Description

- Most computers can store data in two or more formats, and the Usage clause lets you specify the format that you want to use for a numeric field. Although you don't ever have to code Usage clauses, they can improve the storage and run-time efficiency of a program.

- When you specify Display usage, one character of data is stored in one byte of storage. If the field is numeric, the sign of the field is usually carried in the rightmost byte along with the rightmost digit of the field.

- Display usage is appropriate for all alphabetic and alphanumeric fields and for numeric fields that aren't going to be involved in computations or numeric comparisons. Since this is the default, you don't need to code Usage clauses for Display usage.

- When you specify Packed-Decimal usage for a numeric field, the rightmost byte in the field contains one digit and the sign, and all other bytes in the field contain two digits. Thus, a 5-digit field can be stored in three bytes of storage.

- When you specify Binary usage, a field of 1 to 4 digits is usually stored in two bytes; a field of 5 to 9 digits is usually stored in four bytes; and a field of 10 to 18 digits is usually stored in eight bytes. The sign is always included in a binary field.

- Although all computers provide for Binary usage, not all provide for Packed-Decimal usage. If both are available, packed-decimal is usually the preferred format for numeric fields in business programs, but you need to find out what's right for your computer.

- When you code a Usage clause, the words Usage Is are optional so they are usually omitted. If you decide to include them, the word Usage is required, but the word Is is optional.

- If you code the Usage clause at the group level, it applies to all the fields in the group. If you code it at the elementary level, it applies to just that item.

Figure 6-4   How to code Usage clauses

How to code Redefines clauses

Occasionally, you will need to define a field in more than one way. To do that, you use the Redefines clause as shown in figure 6-5.

In the first example, you can see that a field that's going to be printed is defined as both a numeric field and an alphanumeric field. Then, the numeric field name is used as the receiving field in a Compute statement so it will receive a valid computed value, but the alphanumeric field name is used if a message like OVRFLW or N/A (not applicable) needs to be moved into the field. By redefining the field, you get around the COBOL limitation that doesn't allow you to move alphanumeric data to a numeric edited field. Remember, though, that both CL-CHANGE-PERCENT and CL-CHANGE-PERCENT-X refer to the same six bytes of storage.

In the second example, you can see how the Redefines clause lets you define a data field as both an elementary and a group item. That way, you can refer to the entire date as a numeric field, and you can also refer to the month, day, and year fields within the date.

The syntax of the Redefines clause

```
01-49  data-name-1 REDEFINES data-name-2
```

A Redefines clause that redefines a print field

```
05  CL-CHANGE-PERCENT     PIC ZZ9.9-.
05  CL-CHANGE-PERCENT-X   REDEFINES CL-CHANGE-PERCENT
                          PIC X(6).
.
.
IF CM-SALES-LAST-YTD EQUAL ZERO
    MOVE "  N/A " TO CL-CHANGE-PERCENT-X
ELSE
    COMPUTE CL-CHANGE-PERCENT ROUNDED =
        CHANGE-AMOUNT * 100 / CM-SALES-LAST-YTD
        ON SIZE ERROR
            MOVE "OVRFLW" TO CL-CHANGE-PERCENT-X.
```

A Redefines clause that redefines a date field

```
05  CD-CURRENT-DATE       PIC 9(8).
05  CD-CURRENT-DATE-X     REDEFINES CD-CURRENT-DATE.
    10  CD-YEAR           PIC 9(4).
    10  CD-MONTH          PIC 9(2).
    10  CD-DAY            PIC 9(2).
```

Description

- The Redefines clause lets you define a field in storage in two or more ways. When used, this clause must have the same level number as the data item it is redefining and it must come right after that item.

- Because the definition and the redefinition both refer to the same bytes of storage, you can code a Value clause only on the original definition.

Figure 6-5   How to code Redefines clauses

How to code Sign, Justified, and Synchronized clauses

Since signs are usually embedded in numeric fields, you usually don't need to use the Sign clause. Since alphanumeric fields are usually left justified (which is the default), you usually don't need to use the Justified clause. And since most systems don't require any synchronization, you usually don't need to use the Synchronized clause. But just in case you do need to use one of these clauses, figure 6-6 shows how.

The syntax of the Sign, Justified, and Synchronized clauses

```
[[SIGN IS] {LEADING | TRAILING} [SEPARATE CHARACTER]]
[{JUSTIFIED | JUST} RIGHT]
[{SYNCHRONIZED | SYNC} [LEFT | RIGHT]]
```

Examples of data definitions

```
05   NUMBER-ENTERED    PIC S9(5)      SIGN LEADING SEPARATE.
05   GROUP-TOTAL-NAME  PIC X(20)      JUSTIFIED RIGHT.
05   CM-YTD-SALES      PIC S9(7)V99   BINARY  SYNC.
```

A Move statement that moves data to a right-justified field

```
MOVE "BRANCH TOTAL" TO GROUP-TOTAL-NAME.
```

Description

- On most systems, you won't ever need to use the Sign, Justified, or Synchronized clauses.

- In general, the sign of a number is embedded in the number so it doesn't require an extra storage position. This is true whether the usage is Display, Binary, or Packed-Decimal. To override this, though, you can use the Sign clause to specify whether the sign should be leading or trailing and whether it should require a separate byte of storage.

- When data is stored in or moved to an alphanumeric field, it is left justified. To override this, though, you can use the Justified clause.

- On some computers, some usages are processed more efficiently if they are aligned on storage boundaries. To make sure that a field is aligned properly, you can code the Synchronized clause.

Figure 6-6   How to code Sign, Justified, and Synchronized clauses

How to use Move and Initialize statements

In chapter 1, you learned how to use simple Move statements. Now, you'll learn how to use the complete Move syntax with all five data types. You'll also learn how to use Initialize statements to give initial values to fields.

How to code Move statements

Figure 6-7 summarizes what you need to know for using Move statements. In the syntax and examples, you can see that you can use one Move statement for moving a literal or field to two or more other fields. This is particularly useful when you want to move spaces or zeros to two or more fields.

This figure also shows which data types can be moved to other data types. Note, however, that the usage of numeric fields doesn't have any effect on whether a move is legal. If necessary, the usage of the data that's being moved is changed to the usage of the receiving field.

When you move a field to an alphanumeric edited or numeric edited field, the data is *edited* as it is moved. In the next figure, you can see how all of the legal Picture characters can be used for editing.

If you move a numeric edited field to a numeric field, the data can be *de-edited*. This is useful in interactive programs that get edited input data from the user, but need to use that data in computations.

In general, when you code a Move statement, you should coordinate the size of the sending and receiving fields. Although it's okay to move a smaller field to a larger one, you usually want to avoid moving a larger field to a smaller one.

The syntax of the Move statement

```
MOVE {identifier-1 | literal-1} TO identifier-2 ...
```

Examples

```
MOVE "Y" TO CUSTMAST-EOF-SWITCH.
MOVE CM-CUSTOMER-NAME TO CL-CUSTOMER-NAME.
MOVE ZERO TO SALESREP-LAST-YTD-TOTAL
             SALESREP-THIS-YTD-TOTAL.
```

Legal moves

Type of move	Legal?
Alphabetic to alphabetic	Yes
Alphabetic to alphanumeric	Yes
Alphabetic to alphanumeric edited	Yes
Alphanumeric to alphabetic	Only if the sending field is alphabetic
Alphanumeric to alphanumeric	Yes
Alphanumeric to alphanumeric edited	Yes
Alphanumeric to numeric	Only if the sending field is an integer
Alphanumeric to numeric edited	Only if the sending field is an integer
Numeric to alphanumeric	Only if the sending field is an integer
Numeric to alphanumeric edited	Only if the sending field is an integer
Numeric to numeric	Yes
Numeric to numeric edited	Yes
Numeric edited to numeric	Yes, to de-edit a field
Alphanumeric edited to alphanumeric	Yes, but this doesn't de-edit a field

Description

- The Move statement moves data from a literal or *sending field* to one or more *receiving fields*, but the original data is retained in the sending field. If necessary, the data that's moved is converted to the usage of the receiving field.

- When a field is moved to an alphanumeric edited or numeric edited field, the field is *edited*. That means that the data is converted to a more readable form.

- When a field is moved from a numeric edited field to a numeric field, the field is *de-edited*.

- If the receiving field is larger than the sending field, the receiving field is filled out with trailing spaces in an alphanumeric move or leading zeros in a numeric move. If the receiving field is smaller than the sending field, the data that's moved may be truncated.

Figure 6-7   How to code Move statements

How to code Pictures for alphanumeric and numeric editing

Figure 6-8 presents a table that shows how a variety of Pictures for alphanumeric edited and numeric edited fields work when data is moved to them. By using these examples as guides, you should be able to code the Pictures that you need for any editing requirements.

In groups 1 and 2, you can see how spaces and slashes can be inserted into fields. This is useful for editing fields that contain data like dates and social security numbers. You can also see how zeros can be inserted into fields so, for example, a number representing hundreds or thousands can be expanded into its full value.

In group 3, you can see how leading zeros can be converted to spaces. This is referred to as *zero suppression*. You can also see how commas and decimal points can be inserted into fields. Notice that there's one Z in the Picture of the receiving field for each digit in the sending field.

In group 4, you can see how the symbols CR, DB, plus (+), and minus (-) can be used to show the sign of a number. Without one of these symbols in the Picture of the receiving field, a negative value appears to be positive as shown by the third example in the third group. Although you usually use the minus sign to mark negative values, CR (credit) and DB (debit) are appropriate for some applications.

In group 5, you can see how the *fixed dollar sign* is coded in the Picture of a receiving field. Here, one dollar sign is coded to the left of the field. When data is edited in this field, the dollar sign appears in its original position.

In contrast, group 6 shows how to code the Picture for a *floating dollar sign*. Here, the dollar signs replace the Z's that would be used for zero suppression, and an extra dollar sign is coded at the left. In other words, you need to code one more dollar sign than there are digits to the left of the decimal point. When numeric data is moved to a field that's coded like this, the dollar sign is placed to the left of the edited value.

Check protection, shown in group 7, is often used when printing checks to make sure that no one changes the amount to a larger amount. Here, you need to code at least one asterisk for each digit to the left of the decimal point, but extra asterisks are okay.

In the last two groups in this figure, you can see how *floating plus signs* and *floating minus signs* can be used to show the sign for an edited field. In either case, you must code one more sign than the number of digits to the left of the decimal point in the sending item.

Editing examples

Group		Value of sending field	Picture of receiving field	Edited result
1	Insertion characters (Alphanumeric editing)	392380401 03212000	XXXBXXBXXXX XX/XX/XXXX	392 38 0401 03/21/2000
2	Insertion characters (Numeric editing)	392380401 03212000 125	999B99B9999 99/99/9999 999000	392 38 0401 03/21/2000 125000
3	Zero suppression	12345 00123 00123- 142090 001242 000009	ZZZ.99 ZZZ.99 ZZZ.99 Z,ZZZ.99 Z,ZZZ.99 Z,ZZZ.99	123.45 1.23 1.23 1,420.90 12.42 .09
4	Sign control	001234 001234- 001234 001234- 001234 001234- 001234 001234-	ZZZ,ZZZCR ZZZ,ZZZCR ZZZ,ZZZDB ZZZ,ZZZDB ZZZ,ZZZ- ZZZ,ZZZ- ZZZ,ZZZ+ ZZZ,ZZZ+	1,234 1,234CR 1,234 1,234DB 1,234 1,234- 1,234+ 1,234-
5	Fixed dollar sign	001234 123456 000012-	$ZZZ,ZZZ $ZZZZ.99 $ZZZZ.99BCR	$ 1,234 $1234.56 $ .12 CR
6	Floating dollar sign	142090 001242 000009-	$$,$$$.99 $$,$$$.99 $$,$$$.99BCR	$1,420.90 $12.42 $.09 CR
7	Check protection	142090 001242 123456	$*,***.99 $*,***.99 **,***.99	$1,420.90 $***12.42 *1,234.56
8	Floating plus sign	142090 142090- 001242 001242-	++,+++.99 ++,+++.99 ++,+++.99 ++,+++.99	+1,420.90 -1,420.90 +12.42 -12.42
9	Floating minus sign	142090 142090- 001242 001242-	--,---.99 --,---.99 --,---.99 --,---.99	1,420.90 -1,420.90 12.42 -12.42

Coding recommendations

- Make sure that the Picture of the receiving field has the same number of decimal positions as the sending field.
- For the Pictures of floating dollar signs, plus signs, and minus signs, make sure there's one more floating character than there are digits to the left of the decimal point in the sending field.

Figure 6-8   How to code Pictures for alphanumeric and numeric editing

How to code Initialize statements

The Initialize statement, which became available with COBOL-85, can be used to set the initial values for fields. Figure 6-9 shows how.

As you can see in the first example in this figure, the easiest way to use this statement is to code it without the Replacing clause and to refer to a group item. Then, all the numeric fields in the group are set to zeros, and all the alphabetic and alphanumeric fields are set to spaces. In contrast, if you code the Replacing clause, you can specify which types of fields you want to change, and you can specify the characters that you want those fields to be initialized with.

Note, however, that it's usually better to initialize fields in working storage by coding Value clauses for them. That way, your program doesn't require any run time for initializing them. As a result, you should use the Initialize statement only when you need to re-initialize fields after the program has started.

One of the benefits—and dangers—of using the Initialize statement is that you can initialize large record descriptions and tables with a single statement. Because this is so easy to do, though, you may do it even when it isn't necessary. If, for example, you carelessly initialize a 50,000-byte table that doesn't need to be initialized, you slow the performance of the program for no reason.

The syntax of the Initialize statement

```
INITIALIZE identifier-1 ...

    ⎡            ⎧ ALPHABETIC           ⎫                    ⎧ identifier-2 ⎫    ⎤
    ⎢            ⎪ ALPHANUMERIC         ⎪                    ⎪              ⎪    ⎥
    ⎢ REPLACING  ⎨ NUMERIC              ⎬  DATA BY           ⎨              ⎬... ⎥
    ⎢            ⎪ ALPHANUMERIC-EDITED  ⎪                    ⎩ literal-1    ⎭    ⎥
    ⎣            ⎩ NUMERIC-EDITED       ⎭                                        ⎦
```

A record description

```
01  CUSTOMER-MASTER-RECORD.
    05  CM-BRANCH-NUMBER        PIC 9(2).
    05  CM-SALESREP-NUMBER      PIC 9(2).
    05  CM-CUSTOMER-NUMBER      PIC 9(5).
    05  CM-CUSTOMER-NAME        PIC X(20).
    05  CM-SALES-THIS-YTD       PIC S9(5)V9(2)      PACKED-DECIMAL.
    05  CM-SALES-LAST-YTD       PIC S9(5)V9(2)      PACKED-DECIMAL.
```

Initialize statements that apply to the record description

```
INITIALIZE CUSTOMER-MASTER-RECORD.

INITIALIZE CM-SALES-THIS-YTD CM-SALES-LAST-YTD.

INITIALIZE CUSTOMER-MASTER-RECORD
    REPLACING ALPHANUMERIC DATA BY SPACE
              NUMERIC DATA BY ZERO.
```

Description

- If an Initialize statement without a Replacing clause is used to initialize a group item, all numeric and numeric edited fields are set to zero, and all alphabetic, alphanumeric, and alphanumeric edited fields are set to spaces.
- If an Initialize statement without a Replacing clause is used to initialize an elementary item, it is set to spaces or zeros depending on how it's defined.
- When you code a Replacing clause for a group item, only the data types that are specified in the clause are initialized. The other data types are ignored.
- The Initialize clause always ignores fields that are defined as Filler, fields that are redefined, and index data items (see chapter 10).

Coding recommendations

- Use Value clauses to initialize fields in working storage whenever that's possible.
- Use Move or Initialize statements to re-initialize fields whenever that's necessary.
- Don't use Initialize statements to initialize large tables or record descriptions that don't need to be initialized.

Figure 6-9   How to code Initialize statements

Usages and data formats on an IBM mainframe

To give you a better understanding of why you need to define fields with usages and signs, this chapter now presents more information on the IBM usage extensions and the formats that are used for storing those usages on an IBM mainframe.

IBM mainframe extensions to the standard usages

Figure 6-10 presents the three standard usages, plus the several extensions to these usages that are available on the compilers for IBM mainframes. For most new programs, you should need only the standard usages. In old programs, though, you are likely to see Comp-3 usage, which is the same as Packed-Decimal, as well as Comp or Comp-4 usage, which is the same as Binary.

Beyond those usages, mainframe compilers provide for both short and long floating-point usage (Comp-1 and Comp-2). They also provide Display-1 usage, which lets your programs use the Double Byte Character Set (DBCS). For most business programs, though, you won't need to use any of these usages.

If you look at the coding recommendations at the bottom of this figure, you can see that you should code S in the Pictures for all numeric fields, and you should specify an odd number of digits in the Pictures for all packed-decimal fields. After you study the next two figures, you should understand why.

COBOL-85 usages

```
DISPLAY
PACKED-DECIMAL
BINARY
```

IBM mainframe extensions to the COBOL-85 usages

`COMPUTATIONAL or COMP`	Binary
`COMPUTATIONAL-1 or COMP-1`	Short floating-point
`COMPUTATIONAL-2 or COMP-2`	Long floating-point
`COMPUTATIONAL-3 or COMP-3`	Packed-decimal
`COMPUTATIONAL-4 or COMP-4`	Binary
`DISPLAY-1`	Double Byte Character Set

Description

- In new programs, you should use the standard usages. In practice, though, most mainframe programmers use Comp-3 for Packed-Decimal usage and Comp or Comp-4 for Binary usage in both new and old programs.

- You usually don't need Comp-1 or Comp-2 usage in business programs because these formats are designed for very large and very small numbers. In addition, these formats aren't as precise as the binary or packed-decimal formats.

- Display-1 usage is used with the Double Byte Character Set (DBCS). In this format, two bytes are used for each character. This format is used for special purposes like storing text in non-Western languages (like Japanese) or representing chemical structures.

Coding recommendations

- Use S in the Picture for all numeric fields of all usages unless you want the sign to be stripped from the number.

- Use an odd number of digits in all fields with Packed-Decimal usage.

Figure 6-10   IBM mainframe extensions to the standard usages

Binary, hex, and EBCDIC notation

On tape, on disk, or in internal storage, the *byte* is the measuring unit. For instance, we say that a disk drive holds one gigabyte of data (one billion bytes) or a computer has 128 megabytes (128 million bytes) of RAM (internal storage). But what can a byte hold?

As figure 6-11 explains, a byte consists of eight *binary digits*, or *bits*, that can be turned on or off (1 or 0). Since there can be 256 different combinations of on and off bits, a single byte can represent up to 256 different characters. These can include both uppercase and lowercase letters, the digits 0-9, and special characters.

Because binary codes are difficult to work with, you usually use *hexadecimal*, or *hex*, *codes* as shorthand for binary codes. For instance, as this figure shows, D4 is the hex code for binary 11010100. Here, one hex digit replaces four binary digits as shown by the conversion chart in this figure.

On an IBM mainframe, *EBCDIC* (pronounced ee'-bee-dick or ib'-si-dick) is used to represent the 256 characters that can be stored in a byte. In this figure, you can see the hexadecimal codes for some of the common characters in the EBCDIC *character set*. For instance, hex 40 is a space, hex C1 is the letter A, and hex F3 is the digit 3.

Because the debugging features for a COBOL compiler often show the hex codes for a field, you should be familiar with some of the common hex codes. For instance, it helps to know that hex 40 is one space, that the digits 0-9 are represented by the hex codes F0 through F9, and that the uppercase letters are represented by hex codes C1 through C9, D1 through D9, and E2 through E9.

The EBCDIC codes for the character set also represent the *collating sequence* for the computer. This is the sequence in which the characters will be sorted. As you would guess, the characters are sorted in sequence by their hex codes. Thus, the space (hex 40) comes before the letter S (hex E2), which comes before the number 1 (hex F1).

Although EBCDIC code is used on IBM mainframes, PCs and most midrange computers use *ASCII* (pronounced as'-key) code to represent the characters that can be stored in a byte. This means that COBOL programs and data that are used on a PC or mid-range have to be converted to EBCDIC before they can be used on a mainframe. Fortunately, software is available that makes this conversion easy.

However, since the collating sequences for EBCDIC and ASCII are slightly different, the sort sequence of a file is changed during a conversion if the field that determines the sequence contains both letters and digits. This sometimes means that a file needs to be sorted after its data has been converted.

The eight bits in the binary code for the letter M

```
1101 0100
```

The hex code for the letter M

```
D4
```

A binary-to-hexadecimal conversion chart

Binary	Hex	Binary	Hex	Binary	Hex	Binary	Hex
0000	0	0100	4	1000	8	1100	C
0001	1	0101	5	1001	9	1101	D
0010	2	0110	6	1010	A	1110	E
0011	3	0111	7	1011	B	1111	F

The EBCDIC codes for some common alphanumeric characters

Character	Hex	Character	Hex	Character	Hex	Character	Hex	Character	Hex
space	40							0	F0
.	4B	A	C1	J	D1			1	F1
(	4D	B	C2	K	D2	S	E2	2	F2
+	4E	C	C3	L	D3	T	E3	3	F3
&	50	D	C4	M	D4	U	E4	4	F4
$	5B	E	C5	N	D5	V	E5	5	F5
*	5C	F	C6	O	D6	W	E6	6	F6
)	5D	G	C7	P	D7	X	E7	7	F7
;	5E	H	C8	Q	D8	Y	E8	8	F8
-	60	I	C9	R	D9	Z	E9	9	F9

Description

- A *byte* of internal or disk storage consists of eight *binary digits*, or *bits*, that can be either on (1) or off (0). The first four bits are the *zone bits*; the last four are the *digit bits*.

- The *hexadecimal*, or *hex*, numbering system has 16 digits: 0, 1, 2, 3, 4, 5, 6, 7, 8, 9, A, B, C, D, E, and F. With this notation, you can use one hex digit to represent the zone bits in a byte, and one to represent the digit bits. This notation is often used by the debugging features of a system when the contents of fields are displayed.

- Because eight bits can be turned on or off in 256 different combinations, one byte of storage can be used to represent 256 different characters. On an IBM mainframe, the code that's used to represent these characters is EBCDIC (Extended Binary Coded Decimal Interchange Code). The 256 characters make up the *character set* for the computer.

- Although IBM mainframes use EBCDIC, most other computers use ASCII (American Standard Code for Information Interchange). So when data is transferred to or from an IBM mainframe, the code has to be converted from ASCII to EBCDIC or vice versa.

- The codes that are used for a character set also represent the *collating sequence* for the computer. In the EBCDIC codes, the special characters come before the letters, which come before the numbers. But in the ASCII codes, the numbers come after the special characters but before the letters.

Figure 6-11   Binary, hex, and EBCDIC notation

The primary formats for numeric data

Now that you know how character data is stored on an IBM mainframe, you can learn how numeric data is stored in the three primary formats. These are summarized in figure 6-12.

Zoned-decimal is the numeric format used for Display usage. For an unsigned field, the digits in the field are represented by the EBCDIC codes shown in the previous figure (F0 through F9). In a signed number, though, the zone bits in the rightmost byte of the field are either hex C for positive or hex D for negative.

When a zoned-decimal field carries a sign, it has to be moved into a numeric edited field with sign control before it can be displayed or printed properly. Otherwise, the rightmost byte in the field will be displayed or printed as a letter. For instance, hex C4 (a positive 4) is the code for the letter D. So a positive 224 will be displayed or printed as 22D if it isn't edited.

Packed-decimal is the format used for Packed-Decimal or Comp-3 usage. In this format, the sign for the field (hex C or hex D) is carried in the digit bits of the rightmost byte in the field. Thus, hex 2C represents +2, and hex 123D represents –123. For debugging purposes, you may need to convert the hex code for a field to its decimal value, and you should be able to do that with relative ease.

Binary is the format used for Binary, Comp, or Comp-4 usage. This type of field consists of two, four, or eight bytes, depending on the number of digits in the Picture for the field. Although there's no easy way to convert the hex code for a binary field to its decimal equivalent, you should know that the decimal values 0 through 15 are represented by the 16 hex digits. Thus, hex 0002 in a two-byte field is decimal 2, and hex 0000000A in a four-byte field is decimal 10. If you need to convert larger numbers than that, the best way to do it is to use a calculator that provides for hex-to-decimal conversions.

If you study the formats in this figure, you can see that all three provide for a sign. That's why you should start the picture for every numeric field with an S, unless you want the sign of the number to be stripped from the field. By coding the S, you improve both compile-time and run-time efficiency. Similarly, you should now see how packed-decimal and binary usage can improve storage efficiency. You should also see why the Picture for a packed-decimal field should contain an odd number of digits.

Zoned-decimal format (Display usage)

F0	F0	F1	F2	F3	Unsigned number with a value of 123
F0	F0	F1	F2	C3	Positive number with a value of +123
F0	F0	F1	F2	D3	Negative number with a value of –123

Description

In an unsigned zoned-decimal number, the zone bits in all the bytes are hex F. In a signed zoned-decimal number, the zone bits in the rightmost byte are set to hex C if the number is positive or hex D if the number is negative.

Packed-decimal format (Packed-Decimal or Comp-3 usage)

00	12	3F	Unsigned number with a value of 123
00	12	3C	Positive number with a value of +123
00	12	3D	Negative number with a value of -123

Description

In this format, the digit bits in the rightmost byte hold the sign of the number and the zone bits in that byte hold the rightmost digit in the number. All other bytes hold two digits each. As a result, each packed-decimal number has an odd number of digits and a sign.

Binary format (Binary, Comp, or Comp-4 usage)

00	0B			Positive number with a value of +11
0C	41	2B	22	Positive number with a value of +205,597,474

Description

In this format, each bit has a place value. Starting from the right, these values are 1, 2, 4, 8, 16, and so on. To find the value of a binary number, you can add up the place values of the on bits. Thus, hex 0B (binary 1011) has a value of 11 (the on bits are the 8, 2, and 1 bits, which add up to 11). Binary numbers are two, four, or eight bytes, depending on the number of digits that the Picture clause provides for. The leftmost bit of the number indicates whether the value is positive or negative.

What the COBOL programmer should be able to do

- Determine the decimal value of a zoned-decimal or packed-decimal field when it's displayed in hex.

- Determine the decimal value of a positive binary field that's less than or equal to 15 when it's displayed in hex. For the numbers 0–9, the hex value is the same as the decimal value. For the numbers 10–15, the hex values are A–F.

- Use a calculator with a hex-to-decimal conversion feature when you need to determine the value of a positive binary field with a decimal value that's greater than 15.

Figure 6-12   The primary formats for numeric data on an IBM mainframe

Perspective

Now that you've completed this chapter, you should be able to define fields in the Data Division so they do what you want and so they work as efficiently as possible. You should also be able to use Move and Initialize statements to edit and initialize fields.

With one exception, this is all you need to know about data definitions. That one exception is the use of the Occurs clause for defining tables, which you'll learn about in chapter 10.

Summary

- The Picture clause lets you define five different data types. Of these, you'll use *alphanumeric*, *numeric*, and *numeric edited* fields most of the time.

- The Usage clause lets you specify the way that you want numeric fields to be stored. Because this improves the efficiency of a program, you should code either Packed-Decimal or Binary usage for all numeric fields that are going to be used in computations or numeric comparisons.

- The Redefines clause lets you define a field in two or more ways.

- When you use the Move statement to move data to a numeric edited field, the data is *edited*. When you move data from a numeric edited field, the data can be *de-edited*.

- The Initialize statement can be used to initialize fields in working storage. Most of the time, though, it's better to use Value clauses to initialize fields.

- On an IBM mainframe, EBCDIC is used to represent the characters in the *character set*. This code also determines the *collating sequence* of the computer.

- Two *hexadecimal* digits can be used to represent the data in one byte of storage. Decoding hex data is often useful when you're debugging.

- Numeric data can be stored in five different formats on an IBM mainframe. The three that you normally use with COBOL programs are *zoned-decimal*, *packed-decimal*, and *binary*.

Terms

alphabetic item	byte
alphanumeric item	binary digit
numeric item	bit
alphanumeric edited item	zone bits
numeric edited item	digit bits
sending field	hexadecimal code
receiving field	hex code
editing	character set
de-editing	EBCDIC
zero suppression	ASCII
fixed dollar sign	collating sequence
floating dollar sign	zoned-decimal format
check protection	packed-decimal format
floating plus sign	binary format
floating minus sign	

Objectives

- Apply the coding features and recommendations presented in this chapter to the programs that you develop.

- Given EBCDIC hex codes for a zoned-decimal or packed-decimal field, tell what value is stored in the field.

- Explain how Usage clauses improve the efficiency of a program.

- List three ways you can initialize fields in working storage, and name the preferred way.

- Explain why you should code an S in the Picture clause for a numeric field and why you should code an odd number of digits in the Picture clause for a packed-decimal field.

Exercise 6-1   Modify the summary report program

In this exercise, you'll apply some of the skills that you learned in this chapter as you modify the summary report program that you prepared for chapter 4.

Open the program

1. Open the program named rpt3000 that you prepared for chapter 4 and modified in chapter 5.

Modify the program

2. Apply Packed-Decimal usage to these groups: PRINT-FIELDS, CALCULATED-FIELDS, and TOTAL-FIELDS. Then, check to make sure that the Pictures for all of the fields in these groups have signs and an odd number of digits, which will improve both compile-time and run-time efficiency. If some don't, modify their pictures.

3. Delete the word Filler from the fields in the first two heading lines.

4. Change the Pictures for the dollar amount fields in the branch total and grand total lines so they have floating dollar signs. Change the Pictures for the change percents in these lines so they have floating plus signs. If necessary, adjust the spacing in the lines so the data will still be aligned properly.

5. Redefine the change percent fields in the customer, branch total, and grand total lines as six-byte alphanumeric fields. Then, modify the code in procedures 320, 360, and 500 so N/A is moved to these fields if the last year-to-date sales are zero and OVRFLW is moved to these fields if overflow occurs during the percent computation.

6. Near the end of procedure 360, use just one Move statement to move zeros to the two year-to-date total fields.

Compile and test the program

7. Compile and test the program until you're sure that it works correctly.

8. Close the program.

7

How to use intrinsic functions and arithmetic statements

In section 1, you learned how to use the Compute and Add statements. Now, in this chapter, you can learn more about those statements. You can also learn how to use the 42 functions that come with most versions of COBOL as well as three other arithmetic statements (Subtract, Multiply, and Divide).

How to use intrinsic functions

In 1989, an addendum was published for the 1985 COBOL standards. This addendum provided for 42 *instrinsic functions*, or just *functions*, that can be used to perform useful operations that are difficult or impossible to do otherwise. Today, most COBOL-85 compilers provide for all 42 functions.

A summary of the six types of functions

Figure 7-1 presents 25 of the 42 functions that became available through the 1989 addendum. As you can see, they are divided into six types.

If you study these functions, you can see that they provide a number of useful functions. For instance, the Current-Date function, which you learned how to use in chapter 3, gets the current date and time from the system. The Integer-Of-Date function converts a standard date to a number that can be used in calculations. The Lower-Case function converts the uppercase letters in an alphanumeric field to lowercase letters. The Sqrt function gets the square root of a value. And the Mean function gets the average of a series of values.

With that as an introduction, this chapter now shows you how to use all of the mathematical, statistical, and financial functions. Later, you can learn how to use all the functions for working with dates in chapter 8 and all the functions for working with characters in chapter 9. Note, however, that no more will be said about the trigonometric functions because you shouldn't need them in a business application.

25 of the 42 intrinsic functions

Function type	Function name	Function
Date	CURRENT-DATE	Get the current system date and time.
	DATE-OF-INTEGER	Convert a Gregorian date (the number of days after December 31, 1600) to a standard date (yyyymmdd).
	DAY-OF-INTEGER	Convert a Gregorian date to a Julian date (yyyyddd).
	INTEGER-OF-DATE	Convert a standard date to a Gregorian date.
	INTEGER-OF-DAY	Convert a Julian date to a Gregorian date.
Character	LENGTH	Get the length of the argument as an integer.
	REVERSE	Reverse the characters in the argument.
	UPPER-CASE	Convert all letters in the argument to uppercase.
	LOWER-CASE	Convert all letters in the argument to lowercase.
Mathematical	SUM	Get the sum of the arguments.
	SQRT	Get the square root of the argument.
	REM	Get the remainder of argument-1 divided by argument-2.
Statistical	MEAN	Get the mean of the arguments.
	MEDIAN	Get the median of the arguments.
	VARIANCE	Get the variance of the arguments.
	MAX	Get the maximum value in the arguments.
	MIN	Get the minimum value in the arguments.
Financial	ANNUITY	Return the ratio relative to 1 of an annuity paid for argument-2 periods at the interest rate of argument-1.
	PRESENT-VALUE	Return the present value of a series of argument-2 payments at the interest rate of argument-1.
Trigonometric	SIN	Get the sine of the argument.
	COS	Get the cosine of the argument.
	TAN	Get the tangent of the argument.
	ASIN	Get the arcsine of an argument expressed in radians.
	ACOS	Get the arccosine of an argument expressed in radians.
	ATAN	Get the arctangent of an argument expressed in radians.

Description

- In 1989, 42 *intrinsic functions* (or just *functions*) were added to COBOL as an addendum to the 1985 standards, and more functions are expected as part of the 2002 standards.

- In this chapter, you'll learn how to use the mathematical, statistical, and financial functions. Then, you can read chapter 8 to learn how to use all of the date functions and chapter 9 to learn how to use all of the character functions.

- The six trigonometric functions aren't presented in any more detail than what's shown above because you usually don't need that type of function in a business application.

Figure 7-1   A summary of the six types of intrinsic functions

How to code any function

Figure 7-2 presents the general guidelines for coding any function. As you can see in the examples, a function can require none, one, two, or more *arguments*. Although you can use commas to separate those arguments, that isn't required.

When you code a function, it's normally within a Move or a Compute statement. This is illustrated by the second set of examples in this figure. In a Move statement, you can move the result of a function to another field. In a Compute statement, you can use a function within the arithmetic expression.

When a function requires a series of arguments, you can code the arguments in sequence or you can use the values in a table for those arguments. In chapter 10, you can learn how to create and use tables and how to use the values in these tables as the arguments for functions. But for now, this figure gives a simple example of how the values in a table can be used as the arguments in three statistical functions. Here, a one-level table is defined that holds 50 test scores. Then, after the test score values have been loaded into the table, three Compute statements in procedure 200 use three functions to determine the average, median, and maximum scores. Note the use of the reserved word All to show that all the items in the table are to be used as the arguments for the functions.

Although the examples don't illustrate this, an argument can be coded as a literal, a variable name, an arithmetic expression, another function, or an arithmetic expression that contains other functions. No matter what you use, though, it has to be consistent with what the function requires. If, for example, the argument is supposed to be numeric, you need to supply a numeric value. And if the argument is supposed to be an integer, you need to supply a whole number value.

The syntax of a function

```
FUNCTION function-name [(argument-1 ...)]
```

Function examples

```
FUNCTION CURRENT-DATE        (No arguments)

FUNCTION UPPER-CASE (LAST-NAME)      (1 argument)

FUNCTION ANNUITY (INTEREST-RATE, NUMBER-OF-PAYMENTS)      (2 arguments)

FUNCTION MEAN (SALES-ATLANTA, SALES-BOSTON, SALES-CHICAGO)      (3 arguments)
```

Examples of functions in Move and Compute statements

```
MOVE FUNCTION CURRENT-DATE TO CURRENT-DATE-AND-TIME.

MOVE FUNCTION LOWER-CASE (LAST-NAME) TO EDITED-LAST-NAME.

COMPUTE PAYMENT-AMOUNT =
    LOAN-AMOUNT * FUNCTION ANNUITY (INTEREST-RATE, NUMBER-OF-PAYMENTS).
```

How the values in a table can be used as the arguments in a function

```
01  STUDENT-TEST-SCORE-TABLE.
    05  STUDENT-SCORE    PIC S9(3)    OCCURS 50 TIMES
                                      INDEXED BY SCORE-INDEX.
.
.
.
200-COMPUTE-SCORE-STATISTICS.
    COMPUTE AVERAGE-SCORE = FUNCTION MEAN (STUDENT-SCORE (ALL)).
    COMPUTE MEDIAN-SCORE  = FUNCTION MEDIAN (STUDENT-SCORE (ALL)).
    COMPUTE MAX-SCORE     = FUNCTION MAX (STUDENT-SCORE (ALL)).
```

Description

- Most functions require at least one *argument*, although the Current-Date function doesn't require any.

- The argument for a function can be a literal, a variable name, an arithmetic expression, another function, or an arithmetic expression that contains other functions. However, the resulting value has to be consistent with what that argument requires.

- A function will operate on all items in a one-level table when the word All is specified for the table's subscript or index. For more information on the use of table values as the arguments for functions, please see chapter 10.

- Although you can separate arguments with commas, that isn't required.

- Functions are usually used within Compute and Move statements. They can't be used within Add, Subtract, Multiply, or Divide statements as well as some other statements.

Figure 7-2   How to code any function

How to use the mathematical functions

Figure 7-3 summarizes the 12 mathematical functions and gives examples for using the first eight since these are the ones you're most likely to use in business applications. In the examples, literal values are used so you can easily understand the results. By studying the summary and the examples, you should be able to quickly see what each function does, but here is some additional information.

The Rem function returns the remainder of a division operation. Although you can also use the Divide statement to get the remainder, as you'll see in figure 7-9, using this function is easier. The Mod function works the same as the Rem function, except it only works with integer values.

The Integer and Integer-Part functions work the same for positive values. They both return the integer portion of a numeric value, like the integer 2 for the value +2.3. For a negative value, though, the Integer function returns the integer that's less than or equal to the argument (–4 for the value –3.2), and the Integer-Part function returns the integer (-3 for the value –3.2).

Last, the Numval and Numval-C functions can be used to get the numeric value from an edited numeric value. This is comparable to the de-editing that you can do by moving a numeric edited item to a numeric item. Although this varies somewhat from compiler to compiler, the Numval function can be used for simple de-editing and the Numval-C function for more complicated de-editing. If the edited value contains a non-standard currency sign, you can code the second argument of the Numval-C function with the symbol that's used for the currency sign.

Mathematical functions

Function name	Argument-1	Argument-2	Result
SUM	Numeric series		The sum of the arguments.
SQRT	Numeric		The square root of the argument.
REM	Numeric	Numeric	The remainder of argument-1 divided by argument-2.
MOD	Integer	Integer	Like the Rem function except the arguments have to be integers.
INTEGER	Numeric		The greatest integer less than or equal to the argument.
INTEGER-PART	Numeric		The integer part of the argument.
NUMVAL	Alphanumeric		The numeric value of an argument that contains leading spaces, decimal point, and sign symbol (-, CR, or DB).
NUMVAL-C	Alphanumeric	Symbol used as currency sign (optional)	The numeric value of an argument that contains leading spaces, commas, sign symbol, and currency sign.
RANDOM	Numeric		A random number expressed as a decimal fraction.
FACTORIAL	Integer		The factorial of the argument as an integer value. If the argument is zero, the factorial is 1.
LOG	Numeric		The natural logarithm.
LOG10	Numeric		The base-10 logarithm.

Examples

Function	Result
`FUNCTION SUM (85 65 75 85 95 100 75 75)`	720
`FUNCTION SQRT (81)`	9
`FUNCTION REM (9.5, 9)`	.5
`FUNCTION MOD (10, 9)`	1
`FUNCTION INTEGER (-3.2)`	-4
`FUNCTION INTEGER-PART (-3.2)`	-3
`FUNCTION NUMVAL (" 23.5-")`	-23.5
`FUNCTION NUMVAL-C ("$1,234.50CR")`	-1234.5

Description

- Although the examples are coded with literal values, you normally code field names for the arguments. For the Sum function, you normally code the name of a table item followed by the word All in parentheses.

Figure 7-3   How to use the mathematical functions

How to use the statistical functions

Figure 7-4 summarizes the 10 statistical functions and gives examples for using them all. In the examples, literal values are used so you can easily understand the results, but you normally code the arguments by specifying a table item with the word All. By studying the summary and the examples, you should be able to quickly see what each function does.

In case you need a quick reminder of what the common statistical terms mean, the description in this figure summarizes the main terms. In particular, you should know what the *mean* and *median* are since they are often used in business programs. In contrast, *standard deviation* and *variance* are more the province of statisticians so they aren't normally used in business programs.

Statistical functions

Function name	Arguments	Result
MEAN	Numeric series	The mean of the arguments.
MEDIAN	Numeric series	The median of the arguments.
STANDARD-DEVIATION	Numeric series	The standard deviation of the arguments.
VARIANCE	Numeric series	The variance of the arguments.
RANGE	Numeric series	The value of the maximum argument minus the value of the minimum argument.
MIDRANGE	Numeric series	The mean of the maximum and minimum arguments.
MAX	Alphanumeric series	The value of the largest argument.
MIN	Alphaumeric series	The value of the smallest argument.
ORD-MAX	Alphanumeric or numeric series	The ordinal position of the largest argument.
ORD-MIN	Alphanumeric or numeric series	The ordinal position of the smallest argument.

Examples

Function	Result
`FUNCTION MEAN (85 65 75 85 95 100 75 75 65)`	80
`FUNCTION MEDIAN (85 65 75 85 95 100 75 75 65)`	75
`FUNCTION STANDARD-DEVIATION (85 65 75 85 95 100 75 75 65)`	11.55
`FUNCTION VARIANCE (85 65 75 85 95 100 75 75 65)`	133.33
`FUNCTION RANGE (85 65 75 85 95 100 75 75 65)`	35
`FUNCTION MIDRANGE (85 65 75 85 95 100 75 75 65)`	82.5
`FUNCTION MAX (85 65 75 85 95 100 75 75 65)`	100
`FUNCTION MIN (85 65 75 85 95 100 75 75 65)`	65
`FUNCTION ORD-MAX (85 65 75 85 95 100 75 75 65)`	6
`FUNCTION ORD-MIN (85 65 75 85 95 100 75 75 65)`	2

Description

- The *mean* of a series of numbers is the same as the average of those numbers. In contrast, the *median* is the number that lies in the middle of the range of values.

- *Standard deviation* and *variance* are two measures of how much the items in the series vary from the mean.

- The Max and Min functions return the maximum and minimum values in a series, while the Ord-Max and Ord-Min functions return the position of those values in the series.

Figure 7-4   How to use the statistical functions

How to use the financial functions

Figure 7-5 presents the two financial functions that were included in the 1989 addendum. Frankly, these are quite limited when compared with the financial functions that are included with some languages. And you probably won't ever need to use either one.

In brief, the Annuity function lets you determine what the payments should be for repaying a one-dollar loan at the interest given by argument-1 for the number of periods given by argument-2. Then, you can multiply the function result by the amount of the loan to get the actual monthly payment. Note in the first example that an arithmetic expression is used for the first argument. This expression divides the yearly interest rate (.1) by 12 to get the monthly rate so that rate is consistent with the 36 monthly payments.

In contrast, the Present-Value function lets you determine the present value of a series of future payments when the interest rate is given by argument-1 and the payments are supplied by one or more arguments starting with argument-2. This is based on the theory that $1000 given to you a year from now has a discounted value that's based on the interest that you could have received during that year if you had the money right now. As the second example shows, that $1000 has a present value of $909.09 if the current interest rate is 10 percent. Similarly, as the third example shows, $1000 has a present value of $826.45 if it isn't paid until two years from now (zero payment the first year, $1000 the second year).

Financial functions

Function name	Argument-1	Argument-2	Result
ANNUITY	Interest rate as a decimal fraction	Number of periods as an integer	The ratio of an annuity paid for argument-2 periods at the interest rate of argument-1.
PRESENT-VALUE	Interest rate as a decimal fraction	Numeric series of future payments	The present value of a series of future payments (argument-2) discounted at the interest rate of argument-1.

Examples

Expression	Result
`10000 * FUNCTION ANNUITY (0.1 / 12, 36)`	322.67
`FUNCTION PRESENT-VALUE (0.1 1000)`	909.09
`FUNCTION PRESENT-VALUE (0.1 0 1000)`	826.45
`FUNCTION PRESENT-VALUE (0.1 1000 1000)`	1735.53
`FUNCTION PRESENT-VALUE (0.1 1000 1000 1000)`	2486.85

Description

- The Annuity function returns a decimal fraction that you can multiply by a loan amount to determine what the periodic payment amounts should be. To make this work properly, the interest rate must be consistent with the number of periods. If, for example, you want to determine the monthly payment amount, be sure that argument-1 provides the monthly interest rate and argument-2 provides the number of monthly payments.

- The Present-Value function gives the present value of a series of future payments that are discounted by the interest rate. To make this work properly, the interest rate must be consistent with the periods assumed for the future payments. If, for example, the future payments are yearly, the interest rate should be yearly, and each value in the argument-2 series should be a yearly payment.

Figure 7-5   How to use the financial functions

How to code arithmetic statements

The rest of this chapter summarizes the use of the five COBOL arithmetic statements: Compute, Add, Subtract, Multiply, and Divide. Since you already know how to use the Compute and Add statements, some of this is review so it should go quickly. Also, please keep in mind that you normally use the Compute statement instead of Multiply or Divide statements so you don't need to dwell on those statements.

How to code Compute statements

Figure 7-6 summarizes the use of the Compute statement. If you look at the syntax for this statement, you can see that it includes a Not On Size Error clause and an End-Compute delimiter. As chapter 5 pointed out, the delimiter is often useful, but you probably won't ever need the Not On Size Error clause.

You can also see an ellipsis (...) before the equals sign in the syntax. This means that the result of the arithmetic expression can be placed into more than one receiving field. This is illustrated by the fourth example of typical Compute statements, which saves the result without rounding in a field named MONTHLY-INTEREST and saves the result with rounding in a field named MONTHLY-INTEREST-ROUNDED.

The only other new technique that this figure illustrates is the use of functions within Compute statements. In the first example, the Annuity function is used to compute the monthly payment amount. In the second example, the Sqrt function is used to determine the economic order quantity when reordering an inventory item.

In general, you should avoid using the On Size Error clause with a Compute statement. Instead, you should define the result field so it provides for the maximum value that can occur based on your knowledge of the data. Although dividing by zero will always lead to a size error, you can avoid that possibility by using an If statement to test the divisor to make sure that it isn't zero before you issue the Compute statement.

The syntax of the Compute statement

```
COMPUTE {identifier-1 [ROUNDED]} ... = arithmetic-expression
    [ON SIZE ERROR imperative-statement-1]
    [NOT ON SIZE ERROR imperative-statement-2]
[END-COMPUTE]
```

Typical Compute statements

```
COMPUTE YEAR-COUNTER = YEAR-COUNTER + 1.

COMPUTE PERCENT-DIFFERENCE ROUNDED =
    (THIS-YEAR-SALES - LAST-YEAR-SALES) * 100 / LAST-YEAR-SALES.

COMPUTE FUTURE-VALUE ROUNDED =
    FUTURE-VALUE + (FUTURE-VALUE * YEARLY-INTEREST-RATE / 100)
    ON SIZE ERROR
        DISPLAY "FUTURE VALUE HAS BEEN TRUNCATED.".

COMPUTE MONTHLY-INTEREST MONTHLY-INTEREST-ROUNDED ROUNDED =
    LOAN-BALANCE * MONTHLY-INTEREST-RATE.
```

Compute statements that include functions

```
COMPUTE MONTHLY-PAYMENT ROUNDED =
    LOAN-AMOUNT * FUNCTION ANNUITY (INTEREST-RATE, NUMBER-OF-PERIODS).

COMPUTE ECONOMIC-ORDER-QUANTITY =
    FUNCTION SQRT ((2 * ANNUAL-USAGE * ORDER-PLACEMENT-COST)
        / (UNIT-COST * CARRYING-COST)).
```

Description

- The Compute statement calculates the arithmetic expression to the right of the equals sign and stores the result in the variable or variables to the left of the equals sign.

- All variables in the arithmetic expression must be numeric items.

- A variable that will receive the result of the arithmetic expression can be a numeric edited item if that variable isn't used in the arithmetic expression. Otherwise, it must be numeric.

- You can code the Rounded clause whenever the result of a calculation can have more decimal places than is specified in the picture of the result field. If you don't use the Rounded clause, the extra decimal places are truncated.

- You can code the On Size Error clause when there's a chance that the result may be larger than the receiving field. However, you shouldn't code this clause if there's no chance of overflow or if you can remove that chance by enlarging the Picture of the result field.

Figure 7-6   How to code Compute statements

How to code arithmetic expressions

Figure 7-7 summarizes the information that you need for coding the arithmetic expressions that are used within Compute statements. Except for the information on intermediate results, this repeats what you learned in chapter 1. So let's focus on intermediate results because they can have a serious effect on the accuracy of your calculations.

Whenever an expression consists of two or more operations, *intermediate result fields* are produced. In the expression, A * B / C, for example, the computer multiplies A times B to produce an intermediate result. Then, it divides that result by C.

How many digits does the intermediate result field provide for? That depends on the compiler and on the Pictures of the fields that are operated upon. And that's where a potential problem arises. Although the intermediate result fields should provide enough digits to prevent size errors, the intermediate result fields don't always provide as many decimal places as you need.

To illustrate, consider this example:

```
CHANGE-AMOUNT / LAST-YEAR-SALES * 100
```

If both CHANGE-AMOUNT and LAST-YEAR-SALES have Pictures of S9(5)V99, the intermediate result field also has that Picture so the intermediate result provides for just two decimal positions. Then, when that result is multiplied by 100, those decimal values become zeros, which means the decimal values in the final result have been lost.

One way to solve that problem is to rewrite the expression like this:

```
CHANGE-AMOUNT * 100 / LAST-YEAR-SALES
```

This time, CHANGE-AMOUNT is first multiplied by 100, so the intermediate result field has two decimal places. Then, when that result is divided by LAST-YEAR-SALES, the two decimal positions will be accurate.

Another way to solve this problem is to redefine CHANGE-AMOUNT so it forces more decimal positions in the intermediate result field. If, for example, the Picture for CHANGE-AMOUNT is S9(5)V9(4), the intermediate result field will have four decimal places when CHANGE-AMOUNT is divided by LAST-YEAR-SALES. Then, when that result is multiplied by 100, the decimal positions in the final result will be accurate.

This not only shows how intermediate result fields can affect the accuracy of your computations, but also illustrates the importance of testing. No matter how sure you are that you've defined your fields right and coded your Compute statements right, you need to test the results with a wide range of values.

Examples of arithmetic expressions

```
CHANGE-AMOUNT * 100 / LAST-YEAR-SALES
FUTURE-VALUE + (FUTURE-VALUE * YEARLY-INTEREST-RATE / 100)
LOAN-AMOUNT * FUNCTION ANNUITY (INTEREST-RATE, NUMBER-OF-PERIODS)
FUNCTION SQRT ((2 * ANNUAL-USAGE * ORDER-PLACEMENT-COST)
    / (UNIT-COST * CARRYING-COST))
```

The arithmetic operators

```
+   addition
-   subtraction
*   multiplication
/   division
**  exponentiation
```

The order of precedence for arithmetic operations

1. Exponentiation

2. Multiplication and division

3. Addition and subtraction

Use of parentheses

- To clarify or dictate the sequence in which the operations in an expression are done, you can use parentheses. Then, the operations in the inner sets of parentheses are done first, followed by the operations in the outer sets of parentheses.

- Otherwise, the sequence is from left to right based on the order of precedence.

The number of decimal places in an intermediate result field

Operation	Number of decimal places in the intermediate result field
Addition and subtraction	The maximum number of decimal places that the fields being operated upon provide for. For instance, S9(3)V99 plus S9(5) has an intermediate result field with two decimal places.
Multiplication	The sum of the decimal places in the Pictures of the fields that are multiplied. For instance, S9(3)V99 times S9(5)V99 has an intermediate result field with four decimal places.
Division	Usually, the same number of decimal places that the dividend has. For instance, S9(5)V99 (the dividend) divided by S9(3) has an intermediate result field with two decimal places.

How intermediate result fields can lead to errors

- When an expression consists of two or more operations, *intermediate result fields* are produced. A compiler determines the Picture of an intermediate result field based on the Pictures of the fields in the intermediate operation. This is compiler-dependent.

- In general, intermediate result fields provide for enough digits to the left of the decimal point, but they don't always provide for enough decimal places. That can lead to errors in the final result for the expression. To correct the errors, you can either redefine the fields used in the expression or re-sequence the operations in the expression.

Figure 7-7   How to code arithmetic expressions

How to code Add and Subtract statements

Figure 7-8 provides the syntax summaries for Add and Subtract statements. Although they may seem to be imposing at first, you normally code them in the simple forms shown by the examples. When you need to combine the operation of an Add or Subtract statement with other operations, you use the Compute statement.

When you use format 1 of the Add or Subtract statement, the value in one or more fields is added to or subtracted from the value in identifier-2. That means that the starting value in identifier-2 is changed. If, for example, 3 and 5 are added to identifier-2, which has a starting value of 5, its ending value is 13.

In contrast, when you use format 2 of the Add or Subtract statement, the value in one or more fields is added to or subtracted from the value in identifier-2 and the result is saved in identifier-3, which is coded in the Giving clause. In this case, the value in identifier-2 is unchanged, and identifier-3 can be either a numeric or numeric edited item.

In general, you should define the result fields for Add and Subtract statements so they provide for the maximum values that are going to occur. You do that based on your knowledge of the data. If, for example, a company's yearly sales are $50 million, a field of S9(9)V99 will provide for the grand sales total with no fear of a size error. As a result, you should rarely need to code the On Size Error clause for these statements.

The syntax of Add statements

Format 1

```
ADD {identifier-1 | literal-1} ... TO {identifier-2 [ROUNDED]} ...
    [ON SIZE ERROR imperative-statement-1]
    [NOT ON SIZE ERROR imperative-statement-2]
[END-ADD]
```

Format 2

```
ADD {identifier-1 | literal-1} ... TO {identifier-2 | literal-2}
    GIVING {identifier-3 [ROUNDED]} ...
    [ON SIZE ERROR imperative-statement-1]
    [NOT ON SIZE ERROR imperative-statement-2]
[END-ADD]
```

Examples

```
ADD 1 TO YEAR-COUNTER.

ADD THIS-MONTH-SALES TO THIS-YTD-SALES
                        CUMULATIVE-SALES.

ADD REGULAR-HOURS TO OVERTIME-HOURS GIVING TOTAL-HOURS.

ADD B1-SALES B2-SALES B3-SALES B4-SALES GIVING TOTAL-SALES.
```

The syntax of Subtract statements

Format 1

```
SUBTRACT {identifier-1 | literal-1} ... FROM {identifier-2 [ROUNDED]} ...
    [ON SIZE ERROR imperative-statement-1]
    [NOT ON SIZE ERROR imperative-statement-2]
[END-SUBTRACT]
```

Format 2

```
SUBTRACT {identifier-1 | literal-1} ... FROM {identifier-2 | literal-2}
    GIVING {identifier-3 [ROUNDED]} ...
    [ON SIZE ERROR imperative-statement-1]
    [NOT ON SIZE ERROR imperative-statement-2]
[END-SUBTRACT]
```

Examples

```
SUBTRACT 1 FROM YEAR-COUNTER.

SUBTRACT REGULAR-HOURS FROM TOTAL-HOURS GIVING OVERTIME-HOURS.

SUBTRACT FIT-AMOUNT SIT-AMOUNT FICA-AMOUNT
   FROM GROSS-PAY GIVING NET-PAY.
```

Description

- When you use format 1, the result is stored in identifier-2 so identifier-2 is changed. When you use format 2, the result is stored in identifier-3 in the Giving clause and identifier-2 isn't changed.

- This works the same way for the Multiply and Divide statements shown in the next figure.

Figure 7-8   How to code Add and Subtract statements

How to code Multiply and Divide statements

To complete this summary of the arithmetic statements, figure 7-9 presents the Multiply and Divide statements. You should rarely use these statements, though, because you can get the same results in a more readable form by using Compute statements. Nevertheless, you should be familiar with the Multiply and Divide statements because you may see them when you're maintaining old programs.

Here again, in format 1 for both statements, the result is stored in identifier-2 so that field is changed. In format 2, the result is stored in identifier-3, which is coded in the Giving clause, so identifier-2 isn't changed.

In format 3, which is similar to format 2, a Remainder clause is available, which means that the remainder of the division can be saved. Remember, though, that you can also get the remainder by using the Rem function.

The syntax of Multiply statements

Format 1

```
MULTIPLY {identifier-1 | literal-1} BY {identifier-2 [ROUNDED]} ...
    [ON SIZE ERROR imperative-statement-1]
    [NOT ON SIZE ERROR imperative-statement-2]
[END-MULTIPLY]
```

Format 2

```
MULTIPLY {identifier-1 | literal-1} BY {identifier-2 | literal-2}
    GIVING {identifier-3 [ROUNDED]} ...
    [ON SIZE ERROR imperative-statement-1]
    [NOT ON SIZE ERROR imperative-statement-2]
[END-MULTIPLY]
```

Examples

```
MULTIPLY 100 BY CHANGE-VALUE.

MULTIPLY FUTURE-VALUE BY INTEREST-RATE GIVING INTEREST-AMOUNT ROUNDED.
```

The syntax of Divide statements

Format 1

```
DIVIDE {identifier-1 | literal-1} INTO {identifier-2 [ROUNDED]} ...
    [ON SIZE ERROR imperative-statement-1]
    [NOT ON SIZE ERROR imperative-statement-2]
[END-DIVIDE]
```

Format 2

```
DIVIDE {identifier-1 | literal-1} {INTO | BY} {identifier-2 | literal-2}
    GIVING {identifier-3 [ROUNDED]} ...
    [ON SIZE ERROR imperative-statement-1]
    [NOT ON SIZE ERROR imperative-statement-2]
[END-DIVIDE]
```

Format 3

```
DIVIDE {identifier-1 | literal-1} {INTO | BY} {identifier-2 | literal-2}
    GIVING identifier-3 [ROUNDED]
    REMAINDER identifier-4
    [ON SIZE ERROR imperative-statement-1]
    [NOT ON SIZE ERROR imperative-statement-2]
[END-DIVIDE]
```

Examples

```
DIVIDE 100 INTO YEARLY-INTEREST-RATE.

DIVIDE CHANGE-AMOUNT BY LAST-YEAR-SALES GIVING CHANGE-PERCENT ROUNDED.

DIVIDE FIELD-A INTO FIELD-B GIVING FIELD-C ROUNDED
    REMAINDER FIELD-D.
```

Note

The On Size Error clause applies to both the quotient and the remainder fields.

Figure 7-9   How to code Multiply and Divide statements

Perspective

Now that you've completed this chapter, you should be able to use functions and arithmetic statements so they get the results you need in any programs you develop. This is not, however, all that you'll learn about functions. In chapter 8, you'll learn how to use the functions for working with dates. In chapter 9, you'll learn how to use the functions for working with characters. And in chapter 10, you'll learn more about using the functions that get arguments from a table.

Summary

- The 1989 addendum to the 1985 COBOL standards defined 42 *intrinsic functions*. Today, most COBOL-85 compilers include these functions.

- Most functions require one or more *arguments*. The functions themselves are normally coded within Move or Compute statements.

- When you code a Compute statement that requires two or more operations, *intermediate result fields* are produced. These fields can cause computational errors if they don't provide for enough decimal positions.

- Besides the Compute statement, COBOL provides Add, Subtract, Multiply, and Divide statements. You should use the Compute statement for most arithmetic operations, though, because it's easier to use and understand.

Terms

intrinsic function	mean	variance
function	median	intermediate result field
argument	standard deviation	

Objectives

- Apply any of the functions or arithmetic statements presented in this chapter to the requirements of the programs you develop.

- Explain how the intermediate result fields in Compute statements can lead to computational errors and what you can do to fix them.

Exercise 7-1   Calculate monthly payments

Write a program named calc3000 that calculates the monthly payment after the user enters the loan amount, interest rate, and number of months. The best way to do that is to open the program named calc2000, save it as calc3000, and modify its code until the program works the way you want it to.

8

How to work with dates

Dates are commonly used in business programs: report dates, purchase dates, payment dates, birth dates, hiring dates, and on and on. Dates are commonly stored as fields within disk records, and the current date is commonly printed on reports and displayed on screens. In this chapter, you'll learn everything you need to know for working with dates.

How to use Accept statements and the date functions

The 1985 COBOL standards provide four variations of the Accept statement that let you get the current date, time, day, and day of the week. In addition, the 1989 addendum to the 1985 standards provides for six functions that you can use for working with dates.

How to use Accept Date and Accept Time statements

In chapter 3, you learned how to use the Accept Date and Accept Time statements to get the current date and time. This information is repeated in figure 8-1. Remember, though, that you only need to use those statements if your compiler doesn't support the Current-Date function. If that function is available, you should use it.

The trouble with the standard Accept Date statement is that it gets the date with a two-digit year. Now that we're in the year 2000, though, this is no longer satisfactory. That's why the last two compilers for IBM mainframes offer a YYYYMMDD extension to this statement. When you code it, the Accept Date statement gets the date with a four-digit year. This extension is also promised by COBOL-2002, and Micro Focus Personal COBOL already supports it.

When you define date and time fields, it often makes sense to use the Redefines clause as shown in this figure. That way, you can refer to the entire date or time field as a numeric integer item. You can also refer to any of the component fields as numeric integer items.

Incidentally, when you use an IBM mainframe, you can't use CURRENT-DATE as the name of the current date field because it's a reserved word. That's why the examples in this figure use TODAYS-DATE as the name for the current date.

The syntax of the standard Accept Date statement

```
ACCEPT identifier FROM DATE
```

Example that gets a two-digit year

```
01  TODAYS-DATE          PIC 9(6).
01  TODAYS-DATE-R REDEFINES TODAYS-DATE.
    05  TD-YEAR          PIC 9(2).
    05  TD-MONTH         PIC 9(2).
    05  TD-DAY           PIC 9(2).
    .
    ACCEPT TODAYS-DATE FROM DATE.
```

The syntax of the Accept Date statement for IBM's COBOL for MVS or COBOL for OS/390

```
ACCEPT identifier FROM DATE [YYYYMMDD]
```

Example that gets a four-digit year

```
01  TODAYS-DATE          PIC 9(8).
01  TODAYS-DATE-R REDEFINES TODAYS-DATE.
    05  TD-YEAR          PIC 9(4).
    05  TD-MONTH         PIC 9(2).
    05  TD-DAY           PIC 9(2).
    .
    ACCEPT TODAYS-DATE FROM DATE YYYYMMDD.
```

The syntax of the standard Accept Time statement

```
ACCEPT identifier FROM TIME
```

Example that gets the time

```
01  TODAYS-TIME          PIC 9(8).
01  TODAYS-TIME-R REDEFINES TODAYS-TIME.
    05  TT-HOURS         PIC 9(2).
    05  TT-MINUTES       PIC 9(2).
    05  TT-SECONDS       PIC 9(2).
    05  TT-HUNDREDTHS    PIC 9(2).
    .
    ACCEPT TODAYS-TIME FROM TIME.
```

Description

- If your compiler doesn't support the Current-Date function (see figure 8-3), you have to use the Accept Date and Accept Time statements to get the system date and time.

- With the standard Accept Date statement, you get the date with a two-digit year. When you're using the MVS or OS/390 compiler on an IBM mainframe, though, you can code the YYYYMMDD option to get the date with a four-digit year.

- If you code a Redefines clause with the date or time, you can refer to the entire date or time or to any of their components as a numeric item.

Figure 8-1   How to use Accept Date and Accept Time statements

How to use Accept Day and Accept Day-Of-Week statements

Figure 8-2 shows you how to use two more variations of the Accept statement. The standard Accept Day statement gets the current day in *Julian date* format. This consists of a two-digit year followed by the day number starting with the first day of the year. For instance, day 1 refers to January 1, day 31 to January 31, and day 32 to February 1.

Here again, the trouble with the standard Accept Day statement is that the Julian date has a two-digit year. But here again, IBM has provided an extension for its last two compilers that lets you get the date with a four-digit year. This extension is also promised by COBOL-2002 and provided by Micro Focus Personal COBOL.

In contrast, the standard Accept Day-Of-Week statement gets a one-digit number that identifies the day of the week starting with Monday. In the example, you can see how an Evaluate statement can be used to convert this number to the full name of the day like Monday for day 1 and Tuesday for day 2.

The syntax of the standard Accept Day statement

```
ACCEPT identifier FROM DAY
```

Example that gets a two-digit year

```
05  CD-JULIAN-DATE        PIC 9(5).
05  CD-JULIAN-DATE-R      REDEFINES CD-JULIAN-DATE.
    10  CD-JULIAN-YEAR    PIC 9(2).
    10  CD-JULIAN-DAYS    PIC 9(3).
    .

ACCEPT CD-JULIAN-DATE FROM DAY.
```

The syntax of the Accept Day statement for COBOL for MVS or COBOL for OS/390

```
ACCEPT identifier FROM DAY [YYYYDDD]
```

Example that gets a four-digit year

```
05  CD-JULIAN-DATE        PIC 9(7).
05  CD-JULIAN-DATE-R      REDEFINES CD-JULIAN-DATE.
    10  CD-JULIAN-YEAR    PIC 9(4).
    10  CD-JULIAN-DAYS    PIC 9(3).
    .

ACCEPT CD-JULIAN-DATE FROM DAY YYYYDDD.
```

The syntax of the standard Accept Day-of-Week statement

```
ACCEPT identifier FROM DAY-OF-WEEK
```

Example that gets the day of the week

```
05  CD-DAY-OF-WEEK        PIC 9(1).
05  CD-DAY-NAME           PIC X(9).
    .
ACCEPT CD-DAY-OF-WEEK FROM DAY-OF-WEEK.
EVALUATE CD-DAY-OF-WEEK
    WHEN 1    MOVE "MONDAY"     TO CD-DAY-NAME
    WHEN 2    MOVE "TUESDAY"    TO CD-DAY-NAME
    WHEN 3    MOVE "WEDNESDAY"  TO CD-DAY-NAME
    WHEN 4    MOVE "THURSDAY"   TO CD-DAY-NAME
    WHEN 5    MOVE "FRIDAY"     TO CD-DAY-NAME
    WHEN 6    MOVE "SATURDAY"   TO CD-DAY-NAME
    WHEN 7    MOVE "SUNDAY"     TO CD-DAY-NAME
END-EVALUATE.
```

Description

- With the standard Accept Day statement, you get the *Julian date* with a two-digit year. When you're using the MVS or OS/390 compiler on an IBM mainframe, though, you can code the YYYYDDD option to get the Julian date with a four-digit year.

- The standard Accept Day-of-Week statement lets you retrieve a number from 1 to 7 that represents the day of the week.

- If you code a Redefines clause with the Julian date, you can refer to the entire date or either of its components as a numeric item.

Figure 8-2   How to use Accept Day and Accept Day-of-Week statements

How to use the functions for working with dates

Figure 8-3 presents six *functions* for working with dates. If you've read chapter 7, you should already know how to use functions. If not, you can just code them the way they're shown in the examples. After you code the word FUNCTION, you code the function name followed by the *argument* in parentheses. You usually use these functions in the expressions within Compute statements or as the sending fields in Move statements.

If you study the examples in this figure, you should be able to figure out what each function does. As you learned in chapter 3, the Current-Date function gets the current date and time in the format that's indicated by the data description in this figure. Since this function returns a four-digit year, this is the preferred way to get the date and time.

The next four functions let you convert dates to and from standard, Julian, and *Gregorian date* formats. The Gregorian format is useful because it is just a day number counting from December 31, 1600. So, January 1, 1601 is day 1; May 19, 2000 is day 145871; and May 21, 2000 is day 145873. Once you've converted two dates to this format, you can easily calculate the elapsed time between the dates by subtracting one date from the other. This is illustrated by the last example in this figure.

Besides the standard functions, your compiler may provide other functions for working with dates. For instance, the IBM COBOL for OS/390 compiler provides six more functions for use with its Millennium Language Extensions (see figures 8-6 and 8-7).

The standard functions for working with dates

Function name	Function
CURRENT-DATE	Get the current system date and time as yyyymmddhhmmddggggg, where ggggg is the number of hours and minutes that the current time is ahead or behind Greenwich Mean Time (+hhmm or –hhmm). If the system doesn't have the facility to get this differential, the last five characters are zeros.
INTEGER-OF-DATE	Convert a standard date (yyyymmdd) to a Gregorian date (the number of days after December 31, 1600).
INTEGER-OF-DAY	Convert a Julian date to a Gregorian date.
DATE-OF-INTEGER	Convert a Gregorian date to a standard date (yyyymmdd).
DAY-OF-INTEGER	Convert a Gregorian date to a Julian date (yyyyddd).
WHEN-COMPILED	Get the date and time of the compilation as yyyymmddhhmmddggggg.

Examples

Function	Result
`FUNCTION CURRENT-DATE`	20000519173617020000
`FUNCTION INTEGER-OF-DATE (20000519)`	0145871
`FUNCTION INTEGER-OF-DAY (2000140)`	0145871
`FUNCTION DATE-OF-INTEGER (0145871)`	20000519
`FUNCTION DAY-OF-INTEGER (0145871)`	2000140
`FUNCTION WHEN-COMPILED`	20000519173611220000

The data description for the data returned by the Current-Date function

```
01  CURRENT-DATE-AND-TIME.
    05  CD-YEAR                         PIC 9(4).
    05  CD-MONTH                        PIC 9(2).
    05  CD-DAY                          PIC 9(2).
    05  CD-HOURS                        PIC 9(2).
    05  CD-MINUTES                      PIC 9(2).
    05  CD-SECONDS                      PIC 9(2).
    05  CD-HUNDREDTH-SECONDS            PIC 9(2).
    05  CD-GREENWICH-MEAN-TIME-SHHMM    PIC X(5)
```

How to calculate the number of elapsed days between two dates

```
COMPUTE ELAPSED-DAYS =
    FUNCTION INTEGER-OF-DATE (DATE-1)
    - FUNCTION INTEGER-OF-DATE (DATE-2).
```

Description

- The 1989 addendum to the 1985 standards provided for 42 *intrinsic functions* (or just *functions*) including the six above. You normally use one of these functions in an expression within a Compute statement or as the sending field in a Move statement.

Figure 8-3 How to use the functions for working with dates

The Y2K problem and its solutions

You've probably heard about the "Y2K problem" because it received an extraordinary amount of publicity in the two or three years before January 1, 2000. Since this problem was based on the handling of dates within programs (especially, COBOL programs), you're now ready to understand it more thoroughly.

The Y2K problem

Prior to the late 1990s, dates were commonly stored with two-digit years and routines that worked with dates took that into consideration. When the century changed and the two-digit current year became 00, though, many of these routines weren't going to work. This became known as the *Y2K problem*, although it really was thousands of little Y2K problems, and businesses throughout the world spent billions of dollars fixing them.

To illustrate, the If statement in the first routine in figure 8-4 compares today's date with a due date, and both dates are stored with two-digit years. In this case, as long as the years in both dates are in the 1900s, the routine works. If, for example, today's date is 990404 (April 4, 1999) and the due date is 990403 (April 3, 1999), the condition is true so this routine works the way it's supposed to. However, if the century changes and today's date is 000110 (January 10, 2000) while the due date is 991227 (December 27, 1999), the condition isn't true and won't ever become true.

The second routine in this figure also illustrates the Y2K problem. This routine calculates the number of days that have elapsed between two Julian dates that are stored with two-digit years. It does this by calling procedure 130 to compute the total days since 1900 that each date represents. Then, it computes the elapsed days between the two dates by subtracting the total days for the first date from the total days for the second date. If procedure 130 looks more complicated than it ought to be, that's because it adjusts for the extra days that occur in leap years.

Here again, the second routine works correctly as long as the dates are in the 1900s. But as soon as one of the dates reaches the 2000s, the routine doesn't work, which means this is another Y2K problem.

In practice, of course, date routines are often more complicated than those in this figure are. For instance, the number of elapsed days are often computed from standard dates instead of Julian dates, which further complicates this problem. Nevertheless, these routines should give you an idea of how date routines were coded before the date functions became available. They also illustrate some typical Y2K problems.

A routine that compares two dates...with a Y2K problem

```
05   TODAYS-DATE              PIC 9(6).
05   DUE-DATE                 PIC 9(6).
     .
ACCEPT TODAYS-DATE FROM DATE.
     .
IF TODAYS-DATE >= DUE-DATE
     PERFORM 350-ISSUE-REMINDER-NOTICE.
```

A routine for calculating elapsed days...with a Y2K problem

```
01   DATE-1.
     05   D1-YEAR              PIC 9(2).
     05   D1-DAYS              PIC 9(3).
01   DATE-2.
     05   D2-YEAR              PIC 9(2).
     05   D2-DAYS              PIC 9(3).
01   WORK-DATE.
     05   WORK-YEAR            PIC 9(2).
     05   WORK-DAYS            PIC 9(3).
01   WORK-FIELDS.
     05   TOTAL-DAYS           PIC S9(5).
     05   TOTAL-DAYS-1         PIC S9(5).
     05   TOTAL-DAYS-2         PIC S9(5).
     05   ELAPSED-DAYS         PIC S9(3).
     05   YEAR-REMAINDER       PIC S9(3).
     05   LEAP-YEARS           PIC S9(3).
     .
     .
120-CALCULATE-ELAPSED-DAYS.
     MOVE DATE-1 TO WORK-DATE.
     PERFORM 130-COMPUTE-TOTAL-DAYS.
     MOVE TOTAL-DAYS TO TOTAL-DAYS-1.
     MOVE DATE-2 TO WORK-DATE.
     PERFORM 130-COMPUTE-TOTAL-DAYS.
     MOVE TOTAL-DAYS TO TOTAL-DAYS-2.
     COMPUTE ELAPSED-DAYS = TOTAL-DAYS-1 - TOTAL-DAYS-2.

130-COMPUTE-TOTAL-DAYS.
     DIVIDE WORK-YEAR BY 4 GIVING LEAP-YEARS
         REMAINDER YEAR-REMAINDER.
     COMPUTE TOTAL-DAYS = (WORK-YEAR * 365)
                     + WORK-DAYS + LEAP-YEARS.
     IF YEAR-REMAINDER = ZERO
         COMPUTE TOTAL-DAYS = TOTAL-DAYS - 1.
```

Description

*   The *Y2K problem* was caused by the use of two-digit years in date routines. For instance, neither of these routines will work right when one of the years is in the 2000s.

Figure 8-4   Two routines with Y2K problems

The Y2K solutions: date expansion and century windowing

The best solution for the Y2K problem is to expand all of the years in dates from two-digits to four-digits. This is referred to as *date expansion*. This includes dates used within programs like the current date as well as dates stored in disk files like receipt dates, due dates, and birth dates. Once that's done, all the routines that use the dates need to be checked and adjusted so they work correctly with the expanded dates.

The trouble is that it is often impractical to expand the dates in the millions of records that are stored on the disks of large companies. As a result, many date fields on disk files are still stored with two-digit years. Then, after a record is read, *century windowing* is commonly used to expand the year in each date so it will work with the other expanded dates.

Date expansion and century windowing are illustrated by the routine in figure 8-5. This routine is a Y2K-compliant version of the first routine in figure 8-4. As you can see, the YYYYMMDD option is used with the Accept Date field so the current date has a four-digit year. In addition, century windowing is used with the due date year to expand it from two to four digits. Once that's done, the If statement works correctly.

In a windowing routine, a *century window* is used to determine whether a year like 51 should be treated as 1951 or 2051. In this example, a year that's greater than 50 is treated as a year in the 1900s, and a year that's less than or equal to 50 is treated as a year in the 2000s. Thus, 51 is treated as 1951, and 50 is treated as 2050, so the century window is 1951-2050.

The trick to making a windowing routine work is to choose an appropriate century window. For instance, a 30-year mortgage that's issued in the year 2000 has an expiration date in the year 2030, and a 60-year old applicant has a birth year of 1940. So you can't just use the same century window for all expansions.

Remember, too, that century windowing is a short-term solution, because the problem recurs when the century window ends. As a result, the long-term solution is to convert all years to four digits. Until then, however, maintenance programmers have to deal with whatever date-handling routines they encounter, because most COBOL shops used a combination of date expansion and century windowing to solve their Y2K problems.

A routine that fixes the first Y2K problem in figure 8-4

```
05  TODAYS-DATE              PIC 9(8).
05  DUE-DATE                 PIC 9(6).
05  DUE-DATE-R REDEFINES DUE-DATE.
    10  DD-YEAR              PIC 9(2).
    10  DD-MONTH             PIC 9(2).
    10  DD-DAY               PIC 9(2).
05  DUE-DATE-EXPANDED        PIC 9(8).
05  DUE-DATE-EXPANDED-R REDEFINES DUE-DATE-EXPANDED.
    10  DDE-YEAR             PIC 9(4).
    10  DDE-MONTH            PIC 9(2).
    10  DDE-DAY              PIC 9(2).
    .
    .
    .
ACCEPT TODAYS-DATE FROM DATE YYYYMMDD.───────  Date expansion
    .
    .
MOVE DD-YEAR TO DDE-YEAR.
IF DD-YEAR > 50
    ADD 1900 TO DDE-YEAR
                                    ─────────  Century windowing
ELSE
    ADD 2000 TO DDE-YEAR.
MOVE DD-MONTH TO DDE-MONTH.
MOVE DD-DAY TO DDE-DAY.
IF TODAYS-DATE >= DUE-DATE-EXPANDED
    PERFORM 350-ISSUE-REMINDER-NOTICE.
```

Description

- The best solution to Y2K problems is to expand all dates so they include four-digit years, and then adjust any routines that use the dates accordingly. This is referred to as *date expansion*.

- Because it is sometimes impractical to expand the dates in the many thousands of records that are stored on disk, many files still contain date fields with two-digit years. Then, to work with these dates, a program needs to convert the two-digit years to four-digit years. This is usually done with a technique called *century windowing*.

- In most companies, a combination of date expansion and century windowing was used to solve the Y2K problem.

Figure 8-5   The Y2K solutions: date expansion and century windowing

How to use IBM's Millennium Language Extensions

To help companies solve their Y2K problems as quickly and easily as possible, IBM added some *Millennium Language Extensions* to the compilers for several platforms including the COBOL for OS/390 compiler for IBM mainframes. So if your job is to maintain mainframe programs that use these Extensions, you need to know how they work. Otherwise, you can skip to the Perspective at the end of this chapter.

How to define date fields with the Date Format clause

To tell the compiler what the format of each date field is, you code the Date Format clause. With this clause, you code a *date pattern* that tells the compiler where the year digits are in the field. Then, when you compile the program, you turn on the DATEPROC option and you set the YEARWINDOW option so the compiler knows what century window to use. This is summarized in figure 8-6.

For some programs, that's all you have to do to fix any Y2K problems. Later, when the program is run, the two-digit years in the date fields are automatically expanded to four digits whenever a statement in the Procedure Division uses the dates for computations or comparisons. You'll see how this works in the next figure.

To turn on the DATEPROC and YEARWINDOW compiler options, you code a JCL statement like this when you compile the program:

```
//STEP1    EXEC PROC=IGYWCLG,PARM.COBOL='DATEPROC(FLAG),
//         YEARWINDOW(1970)'
```

Here, IGYWCLG is the compile-link-and-go procedure for COBOL for OS/390; the DATEPROC option is turned on with diagnostic messages; and the century window is set to 1970-2069. For more information about using JCL, please refer to chapter 18.

When you code the DATEPROC option, you can code the FLAG parameter if you want all of the affected statements in the Procedure Division to be flagged by the diagnostic messages for the compilation. Then, you can check these statements to make sure that the adjusted routines are going to work.

When you code the YEARWINDOW option, you can either code a year or a negative number from –1 through –99. In the first case, the century window is 100 years starting with the year specified, so 1950 leads to a *fixed window* of 1950-2049. In the second case, the century window is a *sliding window* starting with the current year minus the number specified, so –50 leads to a window of 1951-2050 in the year 2001 and 1952-2051 in the year 2002. Thus, a sliding window leads to a permanent Y2K solution.

The syntax of the Date Format clause

```
DATE FORMAT date-pattern
```

Examples

```
05  WS-WINDOWED-DATE        PIC 9(6)   DATE FORMAT YYXXXX.
05  WS-EXPANDED-DATE        PIC 9(8)   DATE FORMAT YYYYXXXX.
05  WS-WINDOWED-JULIAN-DATE PIC 9(5)   DATE FORMAT YYXXX.
05  WS-EXPANDED-JULIAN-DATE PIC 9(7)   DATE FORMAT YYYYXXX.
```

The syntax of the DATEPROC compiler option

```
NODATEPROC | {DATEPROC({FLAG | NOFLAG}[,TRIG | ,NOTRIG])}
```

Examples	Meaning
NODATEPROC	The Date Format clauses compile but have no effect.
DATEPROC(NOFLAG)	The Date Format clauses affect program execution.
DATEPROC(FLAG)	The Date Format clauses affect program execution and the affected statements in the Procedure Division are flagged by the compiler.
DATEPROC(FLAG,TRIG)	The Procedure Division statements are flagged, and trigger values in date fields are expanded properly so they still work as triggers.

The syntax of the YEARWINDOW compiler option

```
YEARWINDOW(base-year)
```

Examples	Meaning
YEARWINDOW(1970)	Specifies a fixed century window from 1970-2069.
YEARWINDOW(-50)	Specifies a sliding century window from 50 years before the current date to 50 years after.

Description

- IBM's *Millennium Language Extensions* were designed to help companies solve their Y2K problems with a minimum of re-coding. These extensions are available with the compilers for several IBM platforms including COBOL for OS/390 mainframes.

- When you code a Date Format clause, you use Y's in the date pattern to indicate the location of the digits used for the year and X's to indicate the other characters in the field.

- To turn on the Millennium Language Extensions, you use the DATEPROC compiler option. Then, you use the YEARWINDOW option to specify the century window that's used for expanding dates with two-digit years to dates with four-digit years.

- If you use a four-digit year as the parameter in the YEARWINDOW option, you define a *fixed century window*. If you use a number from –1 through –99, you define a *sliding century window*.

- If zero, space, LOW-VALUE, HIGH-VALUE, or all 9's are used in date fields to trigger actions, you need to code the DATEPROC option with the TRIG parameter so these values will be expanded properly by the statements in the Procedure Division.

Figure 8-6   How to define date fields with the Date Format clause

How to work with date fields in the Procedure Division

Once you've defined the date fields with Date Format clauses and set the DATEPROC and YEARWINDOW options for the compilation, the rest should be automatic. Specifically, the compiler adds code that expands all two-digit years to four digits whenever they're involved in computations or comparisons. This is illustrated by the three routines in figure 8-7.

The first routine is the same one that's shown in figure 8-4 after the Millennium Language Extensions have been applied to it. In this case, the Y2K problem is solved because TODAYS-DATE and DUE-DATE are expanded to four-digit years when they are compared by the If statement. As a result, a date of 000110 is expanded to 20000110 so it is greater than 991227, which is expanded to 19991227.

The second routine shows how the Extensions can be used to expand date fields. Here, a date field is expanded with just two Date Format clauses and a Move statement. Without the Extensions, you need to code your own windowing routines like the one in figure 8-5.

The third routine shows how the Extensions can be used to fix the second routine in figure 8-4. This is the one that calculates the number of elapsed days between two dates. In this case, you also need to add a statement to procedure 130 so the total day computation will work the same as before. Or, you need to change the Picture for ELAPSED-DAYS from S9(3) to S9(5). This illustrates the need for checking the procedures that use the dates to make sure they're going to work correctly when the years are expanded, and that's why the FLAG parameter for the DATEPROC option is useful. In this case, though, a better solution is to use the functions for calculating the elapsed days as shown in figure 8-3. That would simplify the code dramatically.

If a program uses a value like zeros or all 9's in a date field to trigger an action, you need to code the TRIG parameter in the DATEPROC compiler option as shown in the previous figure. Then, a value like 999999 in a date field will be expanded to 99999999 instead 19999999 when it is used by a statement in the Procedure Division. But here again, you need to check the statements that use the field to make sure that they're still going to work correctly.

In addition to the Millennium Language Extensions that you've already seen, you should be aware that they provide for the six date functions that are summarized in figure 8-7. The Extensions also have some limitations that you should be aware of. For instance, you can't use date fields that are defined with Date Format clauses as arguments for intrinsic functions (except for the Undate function). You can't use these date fields in statements like the Inspect, String, and Unstring statements. And you can't use these date fields as the keys for indexed files.

Since the year 2000 has already passed, though, you shouldn't have to code new uses of the Millennium Language Extensions. They should already be implemented and working. As a maintenance programmer, then, this introduction to the Extensions should be all that you need.

A routine that fixes the first Y2K problem in figure 8-4

```
05   TODAYS-DATE              PIC 9(6)    DATE FORMAT YYXXXX.
05   DUE-DATE                 PIC 9(6)    DATE FORMAT YYXXXX.
     .
     ACCEPT TODAYS-DATE FROM DATE.
     .
     IF  TODAYS-DATE >= DUE-DATE
         PERFORM 350-ISSUE-REMINDER-NOTICE.
```

A routine that expands a date with a two-digit year to a date with a four-digit year

```
05   YYMMDD-DATE              PIC 9(6)    DATE FORMAT YYXXXX.
05   YYYYMMDD-DATE            PIC 9(8)    DATE FORMAT YYYYXXXX.
     .
     MOVE YYMMDD-DATE TO YYYYMMDD-DATE.
```

A routine that fixes the second Y2K problem in figure 8-4

```
01   DATE-1                   PIC 9(5)    DATE FORMAT YYXXX.
01   DATE-2                   PIC 9(5)    DATE FORMAT YYXXX.
01   WORK-DATE                PIC 9(7)    DATE FORMAT YYYYXXX.
01   WORK-DATE-R REDEFINES WORK-DATE.
     05   WORK-YEAR           PIC 9(4).
     05   WORK-DAYS           PIC 9(3).
     .
     .
120-CALCULATE-ELAPSED-DAYS.
     MOVE DATE-1 TO WORK-DATE.
     PERFORM 130-COMPUTE-TOTAL-DAYS.
     MOVE TOTAL-DAYS TO TOTAL-DAYS-1.
     MOVE DATE-2 TO WORK-DATE.
     PERFORM 130-COMPUTE-TOTAL-DAYS.
     MOVE TOTAL-DAYS TO TOTAL-DAYS-2.
     COMPUTE ELAPSED-DAYS = TOTAL-DAYS-1 - TOTAL-DAYS-2.

130-COMPUTE-TOTAL-DAYS.
     COMPUTE WORK-YEAR = WORK-YEAR - 1900.
     DIVIDE WORK-YEAR BY 4 GIVING LEAP-YEARS
         REMAINDER YEAR-REMAINDER.
     COMPUTE TOTAL-DAYS = (WORK-YEAR * 365)
                     + WORK-DAYS + LEAP-YEARS.
     IF YEAR-REMAINDER = ZERO
         COMPUTE TOTAL-DAYS = TOTAL-DAYS - 1.
```

Description

- When the DATEPROC option is on, a two-digit year in a field that's defined with a Date Format clause is automatically expanded into a four-digit year whenever it's involved in a computation or comparison in the Procedure Division.

- Six date functions are available with the Extensions: Dateval converts a numeric field to a date field; Undate converts a date field to a numeric field; Date-To-YYYYMMDD, Day-To-YYYYDDD, and Year-To-YYYY expand standard date, Julian date, and year fields; and Yearwindow returns the first year in the century window.

Figure 8-7   How to work with date fields in the Procedure Division

Perspective

If your compiler supports the intrinsic functions for working with dates, you should use them in new programs because they will help simplify your routines. If you maintain old programs, though, you're likely to run into complicated routines for what appear to be simple purposes like computing the number of elapsed days between two dates. In a well-run COBOL shop, routines like that are often treated as subprograms that can be used by any of the other programs, as shown in chapter 11.

Summary

- The 1985 COBOL standards provide for four variations of the Accept statement that get the standard date, time, Julian date, and day of the week. Both dates, however, are formatted with two-digit years.

- The 1989 extensions to the COBOL standards provide for six date functions that can simplify date-handling routines. These functions work with dates that have four-digit years.

- The *Y2K problem* was caused by the use of dates that contained two-digit years. Many of these routines would no longer work when the current year became 2000.

- *Date expansion* and *century windowing* are the two basic solutions to Y2K problems. Expansion of all dates is the long-term solution, while windowing is a short-term solution.

- To help solve the Y2K problem, IBM provided *Millennium Language Extensions* for some platforms. After you use the Date Format clause to tell the compiler where the years are located in date fields, the statements in the Procedure Division automatically expand two-digit years to four digits.

Terms

Julian date	century windowing
intrinsic function	century window
function	Millennium Language Extensions
argument	date pattern
Gregorian date	fixed century window
Y2K problem	sliding century window
date expansion	

Objectives

- Apply any of the features presented in this chapter to the requirements of the programs you develop.

- Describe the Y2K problem.

- Explain how date expansion and century windowing were used to solve the Y2K problem.

- Explain how IBM's Millennium Language Extensions were used to solve the Y2K problem.

Exercise 8-1   Fix the Y2K problem in an elapsed days routine

In this exercise, you'll fix a Y2K problem in a routine that calculates the number of elapsed days between two Julian dates that have two-digit years. Before you start, copy the programs for chapter 8 into the c:\cobol folder.

1. Open the program named date1000, change the Program-ID to DATE1100, and save the program as date1100. Then, close and re-open it.

2. Compile and run the program. For your first test, enter two Julian dates with years in the 90s (like 98100 and 99100). That should work. Then, enter one date with year 99 and another date with year 00 (like 99100 and 00100). That won't work correctly because there's a Y2K problem.

3. Modify the program so it gets Julian dates with four-digit years from the user. Then, make any other modifications that are necessary to fix the Y2K problem.

4. Test the program using the same data that you used in step 2. When you're sure that your modifications work correctly, close the program.

Exercise 8-2   Fix the elapsed days routine by using functions

In this exercise, you'll modify the program that you fixed in exercise 8-1 so it uses functions to calculate the number of elapsed days. As you will see, that's a better way to code this routine.

1. Open the program named date1100, change the Program-ID to DATE1200, and save the program as date1200. Then, close and re-open it.

2. Replace the routine that calculates the number of elapsed days with one statement that uses the intrinsic functions for working with dates. Then, delete any unnecessary fields in the Data Division.

3. Test the program using the same data that you used in exercise 8-1. When you're sure that the program works correctly, close the program.

Exercise 8-3 Calculate age from a birth date with two-digit years

In this exercise, you'll write a routine that calculates the user's age after the user enters a month, day, and two-digit year of birth. To save time, you'll start from a program that gets the user entries. (If you haven't already copied the programs for chapter 8 into the c:\cobol folder, do that now.)

1. Open the program named date2000, change the Program-ID to DATE2100, and save the program as date2100. Then, close and re-open it.

2. Compile and run the program. As you can see, this program uses the Accept Date statement to get the current date with a four-digit year. This program also gets the birth month, day, and two-digit year from the user. However, it doesn't calculate the user's age.

3. Write the routine that calculates the user's age using the two-digit year for birth date. To do that, you need to use a windowing technique.

4. Compile and test the program. As you test, be sure to try month entries that are equal to the current month along with day entries that are before, equal to, and after the current day. Also, test to see whether your routine works for this birth date: April 3, 1929.

5. When you're satisfied that the program works correctly, close the program.

Exercise 8-4 Calculate age from a birth date with four-digit years

In this exercise, you'll modify the routine that you developed for exercise 8-3 so it uses four-digit years.

1. Open the program named date2100, change its Program-ID to DATE2200, and save the program as date2200. Then, close and re-open it.

2. Modify the program so it gets the user entries with a four-digit year. Then, modify the routine that calculates the user's age so it uses the four-digit years for birth date.

3. Compile and test the program. As you test, be sure to try month entries that are equal to the current month along with day entries that are before, equal to, and after the current day.

4. When you're satisfied that the program works correctly, close the program.

9

How to work with characters

Most of the time, when you're working with fields, you work with complete fields. Sometimes, though, you need to work with the characters within a field. In this chapter, then, you'll learn the features, functions, and statements for working with characters. Specifically, you'll learn how to use reference modification, the intrinsic functions for working with characters, and the String, Unstring, and Inspect statements.

How to use reference modification and functions

Two quick and easy ways to work with characters are through reference modification and the intrinsic functions for working with characters. You'll learn how to use these features first.

How to use reference modification

Figure 9-1 shows how to use *reference modification*. This is just a coding technique that lets you refer to a portion of a field instead of the entire field. For instance, the first example in this figure is a Move statement that moves the characters in the fourth and fifth positions in the sending field to the third and fourth positions of the receiving field.

This figure also shows how you can do that move without using reference modification. In that case, you have to define the portions of each field that you want to work with as elementary items within group items. Since this requires considerably more code, reference modification is useful in a case like this.

As you will see later, reference modification can also be used in conjunction with the String, Unstring, and Inspect statements. These statements can help determine the *offset* and *length* that are required. If, for example, the Unstring statement puts the offset within a field named FULL-NAME in a field named POINTER-FIELD, you can code a reference to the three characters starting at that position like this:

```
FULL-NAME (POINTER-FIELD:3)
```

You'll see this illustrated later on.

Note that reference modification can also be used with the items in a table. In that case, the subscript or index for the table item comes before the offset and length for reference modification. For instance,

```
TABLE-ITEM (20) (5:1)
```

refers to the character at the fifth position in the 20th item in a table. You can learn more about this in chapter 10.

The syntax for reference modification

```
identifier (offset:length)
```

Examples of statements that use reference modification

```
MOVE SOCIAL-SECURITY-NUMBER (4:2) TO USER-PASSWORD (3:2).

MOVE "*" TO WORK-FIELD (20:1).

MOVE ZIP-CODE TO ADDRESS-LINE-3 (15:).

MOVE FULL-NAME (OFFSET-FIELD:LENGTH-FIELD) TO LAST-NAME.

MOVE WORK-FIELD (1:COUNT-2) TO EDITED-FIELD (6 - COUNT-2:).
```

How to refer to characters in a field without using reference modification

```
01  SOCIAL-SECURITY-NUMBER.
    05  SSN-FIRST-DIGITS              PIC X(3).
    05  SSN-MIDDLE-DIGITS            PIC X(2).
    05  SSN-LAST-DIGITS              PIC X(4).

01  USER-PASSWORD.
    05  UP-INITIALS                  PIC X(2).
    05  UP-LAST-DIGITS               PIC X(2).
    .
    .
    MOVE SSN-MIDDLE-DIGITS TO UP-LAST-DIGITS.
```

Description

* *Reference modification* lets you refer to a portion of a field within a field.
* To use reference modification, you code the field name followed by a set of parentheses. Within the parentheses, you code the starting position of the first character in the field that you want to work with (the *offset*), followed by a colon, followed by the number of characters that you want to work with (the *length*).
* Although the offset is required, the length is optional. If you omit the length, all of the remaining characters in the field are referred to.
* Either the offset or the length can be coded as a numeric literal, a data name, or an arithmetic expression.
* If you are referring to a field that requires an index or a subscript (see chapter 10), the parentheses for reference modification follow the parentheses for the index or subscript like this:

```
TABLE-ITEM (20) (5:1)
```

Figure 9-1   How to use reference modification

How to use the functions for working with characters

Figure 9-2 presents the eight *functions* for working with characters. If you've read chapter 7, you should already know how to use functions. If not, you can just code them the way they're shown in the examples. After you code the word FUNCTION, you code the function name followed by the *argument* or arguments in parentheses. You usually use these functions as the sending fields in Move statements.

If you study the examples in this figure, you should be able to figure out what each function does. Of the eight, Numval and Numval-C are likely to be the most useful because they convert data that contains signs, decimal points, and other editing characters into valid numeric data. You may also find an occasional need for the Lower-Case or Upper-Case functions.

In general, you use the Numval function when you need to do simple data conversions and the Numval-C function for more complicated conversions. For instance, if the data contains a non-standard currency sign, you can code the second argument of the Numval-C function with the symbol that's used for the currency sign.

Although the Length function is included in this figure, it is meant for working with tables that are defined with the Occurs Depending On clause. Then, this function gives the length of the table based on the value in that clause. Otherwise, this function just gives the length of a field or literal, which you should already know.

The functions for working with characters

Function name	Argument-1	Argument-2	Function
NUMVAL	Alphanumeric		Return the numeric value of an argument that contains leading spaces, decimal point, and sign symbol (-, CR, or DB).
NUMVAL-C	Alphanumeric	Symbol used as currency sign (optional)	Return the numeric value of an argument that contains leading spaces, commas, decimal point, sign symbol, and currency sign.
LOWER-CASE	Alphanumeric		Convert all letters in the argument to lowercase.
UPPER-CASE	Alphanumeric		Convert all letters in the argument to uppercase.
LENGTH	Nonnumeric literal or any data item		Get the length of the argument as an integer. This can be useful when you're working with a table that has an Occurs Depending On clause.
REVERSE	Alphanumeric		Reverse the order of the characters in the argument.
ORD	Alphanumeric character		Get the ordinal position of the alphanumeric character in the argument.
CHAR	Integer		Return the alphanumeric character that corresponds to the ordinal position given in the argument.

Examples

Statement	Result
`FUNCTION NUMVAL (" 23.5-")`	-23.5
`FUNCTION NUMVAL-C ("$1,234.50CR")`	-1234.5
`FUNCTION LOWER-CASE ("ANNE PRINCE")`	anne prince
`FUNCTION UPPER-CASE ("Anne Prince")`	ANNE PRINCE
`FUNCTION REVERSE ("prince     ")`	ecnirp
`FUNCTION LENGTH ("prince     ")`	10
`FUNCTION ORD ("&")`	39
`FUNCTION CHAR (39)`	&

Description

- The 1989 addendum to the 1985 standards provided for 42 *instrinsic functions* (or just *functions*) including the eight above. You normally use one of these functions as the sending field in a Move statement.

- Although the examples are coded with literal values, you normally code field names for the arguments.

Figure 9-2   How to use the functions for working with characters

How to use the String and Unstring statements

The String statement lets you combine two or more fields into one field, and the Unstring statement lets you extract two or more fields from a single field. These operations are often useful when you're working with data that's received from or sent to an interactive user.

How to use the String statement

Figure 9-3 shows how you can use the String statement to *string* together, or *concatenate*, two or more sending fields into a single receiving field. For each sending field, you use the Delimited By clause to specify the *delimiter* that marks the end of the characters that are to be sent.

In the example in this figure, three sending fields are concatenated in the receiving field. The first sending field (FIRST-NAME) is delimited by a literal that contains two spaces. The second sending field is a literal that contains one space, and it is delimited by Size so the entire field is sent. The third sending field (LAST-NAME) is delimited by SPACE, which is equivalent to one or more spaces. This statement results in a concatenated name field that can be used to display or print the full name in a readable form.

Why is the first sending field concatenated by two spaces instead of just one? So a first name that consists of two names like Anne Marie will be sent to the receiving field in its entirety. If the delimiter were just one space, only the first name would be sent.

If you code the With Pointer clause, the value in the Pointer field determines where the first character is stored in the receiving field. Then, when the statement is finished, the Pointer field indicates where the next position to be filled is located. This is sometimes useful as you'll see later in this chapter. In this example, the Pointer clause is included for illustration only.

If the receiving field isn't large enough to hold all of the characters that are sent to it or if the Pointer field doesn't point to a position within the receiving field, the On Overflow clause is executed. However, since you usually define the receiving field so it's large enough to receive all of the data that's sent to it, you usually don't need to code this clause.

The syntax of the String statement

$$\underline{\text{STRING}} \begin{Bmatrix} \text{identifier-1} \\ \text{literal-1} \end{Bmatrix} \dots \underline{\text{DELIMITED}} \text{ BY} \begin{Bmatrix} \text{identifier-2} \\ \text{literal-2} \\ \underline{\text{SIZE}} \end{Bmatrix} \dots \underline{\text{INTO}} \text{ identifier-3}$$

$\left[\text{WITH } \underline{\text{POINTER}} \text{ identifier-4}\right]$
$\left[\text{ON } \underline{\text{OVERFLOW}} \text{ imperative-statement-1}\right]$
$\left[\underline{\text{NOT}} \text{ ON } \underline{\text{OVERFLOW}} \text{ imperative statement-2}\right]$
$\left[\underline{\text{END-STRING}}\right]$

Example

```
MOVE 1 TO POINTER-FIELD.
MOVE SPACE TO FULL-NAME.
STRING  FIRST-NAME DELIMITED BY "   "
        " " DELIMITED BY SIZE
        LAST-NAME DELIMITED BY SPACE
    INTO FULL-NAME
    WITH POINTER POINTER-FIELD.
```

Field	FIRST-NAME	LAST-NAME	FULL-NAME	POINTER-FIELD
Picture	X(15)	X(15)	X(30)	S9(3)
Test 1	Anne Marie	Prince	Anne Marie Prince	+18
Test 2	Andi	Steelman	Andi Steelman	+14

Description

- The String statement *strings*, or *concatenates*, two or more sending fields into one receiving field.

- The Delimited By clause determines what part of a sending field is sent to the receiving field. If you delimit by Size, the entire field is sent. If you delimit by a literal, the characters up to the first occurrence of the characters in the literal are sent. If you delimit by what's in another field, the characters up to the first occurrence of the characters in that field are sent.

- Unlike the Move statement, if the sending fields don't completely fill the receiving field, the String statement doesn't replace the remaining positions with blanks.

- If the Pointer clause is coded, the first character that's moved to the receiving field is stored in the position indicated by the starting value of the Pointer field. Then, the value in the Pointer field is increased by one each time a character is moved into the receiving field. If this clause isn't coded, the operation starts with the first character in the receiving field.

- The On Overflow clause is executed when more characters are sent to the receiving field than it can hold or when the Pointer field has a value less than 1 or greater than the number of characters in the receiving field.

Figure 9-3   How to use the String statement

How to use the Unstring statement

Figure 9-4 shows how you can use the Unstring statement to *unstring* two or more fields from a single field. Here, you use the Delimited By clause to specify the delimiter that marks the end of each field that is to be unstrung. If you code the word All in this clause, two or more occurrences of the delimiter are treated as one.

If you study the example in this figure, you can see that the Delimited By clause says that the fields should be delimited by one or more spaces and that the unstrung values should be placed in fields named NAME-1, NAME-2, and NAME-3. In addition, the Tallying clause is coded so the number of unstrung fields is stored in the field named TALLY-FIELD. Note that this field is set to zero before the statement is executed.

In the test data after the example, you can see that the first full name gets unstrung into three fields and the Tally field contains a value of 3. In contrast, the second full name gets unstrung into two fields and the Tally field contains a value of 2. This illustrates that you can't easily unstring a full name into first-name and last-name fields if the first name is a combination of two names like Anne Marie.

If you need to do that, though, you can use the Tally field to tell which field contains the last name. Then, if the Tally field contains 2, you move NAME-2 to the last-name field and NAME-1 to the first-name field. But if the Tally field contains 3, you move NAME-3 to the last-name field, and you use the String statement to string the names in NAME-1 and NAME-2 into the first-name field. In the real world, of course, you have to deal with names like Alexander Byron Jackson III, which further complicates the problem.

If you need to unstring an address line that contains data like

```
Carson City, NV 98111
```

into city, state, and zip fields, you can use two Unstring statements like this:

```
MOVE 1 TO POINTER-FIELD.
UNSTRING ADDRESS-LINE DELIMITED BY ", "
    INTO CITY
    WITH POINTER POINTER-FIELD.
UNSTRING ADDRESS-LINE DELIMITED BY ALL " "
    INTO STATE ZIP-CODE
    WITH POINTER POINTER-FIELD.
```

Note that the Pointer field isn't reset to zero after the first Unstring statement so the second Unstring statement starts where the first leaves off.

If you need to unstring fields with two or more possible delimiters as in

```
UNSTRING ADDRESS-LINE DELIMITED BY ", " or ALL " "
```

you can code a Delimiter In clause for each unstrung field that receives the delimiter for that field. You can also code a Count clause for each field that receives the number of characters that are unstrung into that field. By combining these clauses with the Pointer and Tallying clauses, you can get all the information you need for coding complex unstringing routines.

The syntax of the Unstring statement

UNSTRING identifier-1 $\left[\underline{\text{DELIMITED}} \text{ BY } [\underline{\text{ALL}}] \left\{ \begin{array}{l} \text{identifier-2} \\ \text{literal-1} \end{array} \right\} \left[\text{OR } [\underline{\text{ALL}}] \left\{ \begin{array}{l} \text{identifier-3} \\ \text{literal-2} \end{array} \right\} \right] \dots \right]$

$\underline{\text{INTO}}$ {identifier-4 [$\underline{\text{DELIMITER}}$ IN identifier-5] [$\underline{\text{COUNT}}$ IN identifier-6]} ...

[WITH $\underline{\text{POINTER}}$ identifier-7]

[$\underline{\text{TALLYING}}$ IN identifier-8]

[ON $\underline{\text{OVERFLOW}}$ imperative-statement-1]

[NOT ON $\underline{\text{OVERFLOW}}$ imperative-statement-2]

[$\underline{\text{END-UNSTRING}}$]

Example

```
MOVE ZERO TO TALLY-FIELD.
UNSTRING FULL-NAME DELIMITED BY ALL " "
    INTO NAME-1 NAME-2 NAME-3
    TALLYING IN TALLY-FIELD.
```

Field	FULL-NAME	NAME-1	NAME-2	NAME-3	TALLY-FIELD
Picture	X(30)	X(10)	X(10)	X(10)	S9(3)
Test 1	Anne Marie Prince	Anne	Marie	Prince	+3
Test 2	Andi Steelman	Andi	Steelman		+2

Description

- The Unstring statement *unstrings* a field into the fields that are listed in the Into clause.

- The Delimited By phrase specifies one or more characters that indicate where each field ends. If All is specified for a delimiter, successive occurrences of that delimiter are treated as one.

- If you code the Delimiter In clause for a receiving field, the delimiter that marked the end of the field is stored in the Delimiter field. Using this clause only makes sense if you use the word Or in the Delimited By phrase to identify two or more delimiters.

- If you code the Count clause for a receiving field, the number of characters that are sent to that field is stored in its Count field.

- If you code the With Pointer clause, the unstring operation begins with the position in the sending field that's indicated by the Pointer field. Then, one is added to this field each time a character is processed in the sending field.

- If you code the Tallying clause, the number of receiving fields that receive data is stored in the Tallying field. This field should be set to zero before each use of the Unstring statement.

- If the end of the sending field is reached before one of the delimiters is found, the characters between the last delimiter and the end of the field are sent to the receiving field.

- The On Overflow clause is executed if there are no more receiving fields and there is still data in the sending field. Overflow also occurs when the Pointer field has a value of less than one or greater than the number of characters in the sending field.

Figure 9-4   How to use the Unstring statement

How to use the Inspect statement

The Inspect statement lets you count characters in a field or replace characters in a field. This statement has four different formats that vary based on the use of the Tallying, Replacing, and Converting clauses. You'll learn about each of these formats in the four figures that follow.

With the Tallying clause

Figure 9-5 shows how the Inspect statement with the Tallying clause works. This statement counts specific characters in the field that's being inspected. Although the syntax may seem formidable at first, you should be able to get the results that you need by using the examples as a guide.

When you code these statements, you need to remember that the count fields aren't automatically set to zero. As a result, you need to initialize these fields before your Inspect statements are executed. In the examples in this figure, the assumption is that all of the count fields have been set to zero before the Inspect statements are executed.

You also need to realize that each character in the field that's being inspected is only counted once. This is clearly illustrated by the third example. Here, COUNT-2 is used to count all of the characters, but its ending value is six instead of the eight characters that the field contains. That's because the comma and decimal point have already been counted in COUNT-1.

The syntax of the Inspect statement with the Tallying clause

```
INSPECT identifier-1 TALLYING

                  ⎡CHARACTERS ⎡⎧BEFORE⎫ INITIAL ⎧identifier-3⎫⎤ ...⎤
                  ⎢           ⎣⎩AFTER ⎭         ⎩literal-1   ⎭⎦    ⎥
⎧identifier-2 FOR ⎨                                                ⎬ ... ⎫ ...
                  ⎢⎧ALL    ⎫ ⎧identifier-4⎫ ⎧BEFORE⎫ INITIAL ⎧identifier-5⎫⎤ ...⎤ ...
                  ⎣⎩LEADING⎭ ⎩literal-2   ⎭ ⎩AFTER ⎭         ⎩literal-3   ⎭⎦
```

Examples

Statement	WORK-FIELD X(8)	COUNT-1 S9(3)	COUNT-2 S9(3)
INSPECT WORK-FIELD TALLYING COUNT-1 FOR CHARACTERS BEFORE SPACE.	ANNE	+4	N/A

INSPECT WORK-FIELD TALLYING
    COUNT-1 FOR CHARACTERS BEFORE ","
    COUNT-2 FOR CHARACTERS AFTER ".".
	1,234.56	+1	+2

INSPECT WORK-FIELD TALLYING
    COUNT-1 FOR ALL ","
           ALL "."
    COUNT-2 FOR CHARACTERS.
	1,234.56	+2	+6

INSPECT WORK-FIELD TALLYING
    COUNT-1 FOR LEADING "*"
    COUNT-2 FOR CHARACTERS.
	***12.**	+3	+5

INSPECT WORK-FIELD TALLYING
    COUNT-1 FOR ALL "*" BEFORE "."
    COUNT-2 FOR CHARACTERS AFTER "."
	***12.**	+3	+2

Description

- You can use the Inspect statement with the Tallying clause to count specific characters in the field that's inspected. That field can be alphabetic, alphanumeric, or numeric with Display usage.

- When you code CHARACTERS in the Tallying clause, it refers to all of the characters in the field that's being inspected. In contrast, ALL refers to all occurrences of the specified character or characters, and LEADING refers to all occurrences of the specified character or characters at the start of the field.

- Since the count fields aren't set to zero each time the Inspect statement is executed, you must set them to the starting values that you want before you issue this statement. The examples above assume that the count fields have been set to zero.

- If a character is identified by more than one phrase in the Tallying clause, it is only counted the first time it is encountered. A character isn't counted more than once.

- The nonnumeric literals that you use in the Tallying clause should be consistent with the data type of the field that's being inspected.

- The Before or After clause can only specify one character, although this restriction is supposed to be removed in COBOL-2002.

Figure 9-5   How to use the Inspect statement with the Tallying clause

With the Replacing clause

Figure 9-6 shows how the Inspect statement with the Replacing clause works. This statement replaces specific characters in the field that's being inspected. Here again, although the syntax may seem formidable, you should be able to get the results that you need by using the examples as a guide.

As you code the Replacing clause, you need to remember that this statement only replaces characters. It can't insert or delete characters. So when you code a phrase to replace a single character, you must replace it with just a single character. And if you code a phrase to replace two characters, like CR or DB in the third example in this figure, you must replace them with two characters, like two spaces.

The syntax of the Inspect statement with the Replacing clause

```
INSPECT identifier-1 REPLACING
```

$$\left\{ \begin{array}{l} \text{CHARACTERS } \underline{\text{BY}} \left\{ \begin{array}{l} \text{identifier-2} \\ \text{literal-1} \end{array} \right\} \left[\left\{ \begin{array}{l} \underline{\text{BEFORE}} \\ \underline{\text{AFTER}} \end{array} \right\} \text{INITIAL} \left\{ \begin{array}{l} \text{identifier-3} \\ \text{literal-2} \end{array} \right\} \right] \cdots \\ \left\{ \begin{array}{l} \underline{\text{ALL}} \\ \underline{\text{LEADING}} \\ \underline{\text{FIRST}} \end{array} \right\} \left\{ \left\{ \begin{array}{l} \text{identifier-4} \\ \text{literal-3} \end{array} \right\} \underline{\text{BY}} \left\{ \begin{array}{l} \text{identifier-5} \\ \text{literal-4} \end{array} \right\} \left[\left\{ \begin{array}{l} \underline{\text{BEFORE}} \\ \underline{\text{AFTER}} \end{array} \right\} \text{INITIAL} \left\{ \begin{array}{l} \text{identifier-6} \\ \text{literal-5} \end{array} \right\} \right] \cdots \right\} \cdots \end{array} \right\} \cdots$$

Examples

Statement	WORK-FIELD X(9) Before	WORK-FIELD X(9) After
`INSPECT WORK-FIELD REPLACING` `    CHARACTERS BY "0" AFTER ".".`	$1234.567	$1234.000
`INSPECT WORK-FIELD REPLACING` `    ALL "," BY SPACE.`	DAILY, CA	DAILY CA

`INSPECT WORK-FIELD REPLACING`
`    LEADING "*" BY ZERO`
`    ALL "CR" BY " "`
`    ALL "DB" BY " ".`
	***123 CR	000123

`INSPECT WORK-FIELD REPLACING`
`    ALL "A" BY "a" BEFORE "."`
`    FIRST "B" BY "b"`
`    ALL "C" BY "c" AFTER "."`
	BACK.BACK	baCK.BAcK

Description

- You can use the Inspect statement with the Replacing clause to replace specific characters in the field that's inspected. That field can be alphabetic, alphanumeric, or numeric with Display usage.

- When you code CHARACTERS in the Replacing clause, it refers to all of the characters in the field that's being inspected. In contrast, ALL refers to all occurrences of the specified character or characters, LEADING refers to all occurrences of the specified character or characters at the start of the field, and FIRST refers to just the first occurrence of the specified character or characters.

- The nonnumeric literals that you use in the Replacing clause should be consistent with the data type of the field that's being inspected.

- The Before or After clause can only specify one character, although this restriction is supposed to be removed in COBOL-2002.

Figure 9-6   How to use the Inspect statement with the Replacing clause

With the Tallying and Replacing clauses

The third format of the Inspect statement includes both the Tallying and Replacing clauses as shown in figure 9-7. So if you understand how these clauses are used in separate statements, you shouldn't have any trouble using them in a single statement because they work the same way.

To illustrate how the Inspect statement can be used for editing input data, this figure includes a routine that edits the data that has been entered into a five-character alphanumeric field. If the entry (USER-ENTRY) contains from one to five digits, this routine converts it to a valid numeric field (EDITED-RESULT), even if the data has spaces before or after the number.

To start, this routine moves zero to the count fields that are used by the Inspect statements. Then, it moves the five-character user entry field to a six-character work field. That way, the work field will have at least one space to the right of the user entry.

After this setup, the first Inspect statement counts the number of dollar signs, commas, and decimal points and replaces leading spaces by zeros. Then, if the count is equal to zero (which means the user didn't enter any invalid characters), the second Inspect statement counts the number of characters before the space or spaces at the end of the number. If, for example, the user entered 1234, COUNT-2 will contain a value of 4 when the Inspect statement ends.

At this point, the routine moves the valid digits in the work field to the edited result field with this statement:

```
MOVE WORK-FIELD (1:COUNT-2) TO EDITED-RESULT
```

Here, reference modification is used to move the digits that start at the left side of the work field to the result field. Since the picture of the result field is S9(5), the valid digits will be right justified in that field.

This routine should give you some idea of how Inspect statements can be used along with reference modification for checking the validity of fields as well as for converting fields to valid numeric forms. In this case, the entry is an integer, but the same logic can be applied to fields that include decimal points and decimal places. If, for example, the user enters 1.23, an editing routine can convert it to a valid numeric form with an assumed decimal point.

The good news is that you can use the Numval and Numval-C functions to get similar results with a single statement. As a result, you shouldn't need to use the Inspect statement as frequently in new programs. If you maintain old programs, though, you're likely to find routines like the one in this figure as well as others that are far more complicated.

The syntax of the Inspect statement with the Tallying and Replacing clauses

```
INSPECT identifier-1 TALLYING
```

```
REPLACING
```

A routine that uses the Inspect statement to edit a numeric input field

```
05   VALID-ENTRY-SWITCH      PIC X.
05   USER-ENTRY              PIC X(5).
05   WORK-FIELD              PIC X(6).
05   EDITED-RESULT           PIC S9(5).
05   COUNT-1                 PIC S9(3).
05   COUNT-2                 PIC S9(3).
.
.
.
MOVE ZERO TO COUNT-1 COUNT-2.
MOVE USER-ENTRY TO WORK-FIELD.
INSPECT WORK-FIELD
    TALLYING COUNT-1 FOR ALL "$" ALL "," ALL "."
    REPLACING LEADING " " BY "0".
IF COUNT-1 = 0
    INSPECT WORK-FIELD
        TALLYING COUNT-2 FOR CHARACTERS BEFORE " "
    MOVE WORK-FIELD (1:COUNT-2) TO EDITED-RESULT
    MOVE "Y" TO VALID-ENTRY-SWITCH
ELSE
    MOVE "N" TO VALID-ENTRY-SWITCH.
```

Description

- You can use the Inspect statement with the Tallying and Replacing clauses to both count and replace characters in a field. This is the same as first issuing an Inspect Tallying statement and then issuing an Inspect Replacing statement.

- The editing routine in this figure uses the Inspect statement to help convert an alphanumeric field of from one to five digits to a valid numeric field. The entered field may have leading or trailing spaces, but not a dollar sign, comma, or decimal point.

Figure 9-7   How to use the Inspect statement with the Tallying and Replacing clauses

With the Converting clause

If all you want to do is convert one or more characters in a field to other characters, you can do that with the Converting clause more easily than you can with the Replacing clause. Figure 9-8 shows how. Here, you use one literal to identify all of the characters you want to replace and another to identify the characters that you want to replace them with on a one-to-one basis.

One traditional use of the Inspect statement with the Converting clause has been to convert all the lowercase letters in a field to uppercase, or vice versa. That requires a simple statement like the one shown in this figure. If the Lower-Case and Upper-Case functions are available on your compiler, though, it's easier to use them.

The syntax of the Inspect statement with the Converting clause

```
INSPECT identifier-1 CONVERTING
{identifier-2}  TO  {identifier-3}  [{BEFORE}  INITIAL  {identifier-4}]  ...
{literal-1    }      {literal-2    }   [{AFTER }           {literal-3    }]
```

Examples

Statement	WORK-FIELD X(9) Before	WORK-FIELD X(9) After
INSPECT WORK-FIELD CONVERTING "*" TO "0".	**123.56*	00123.560
INSPECT WORK-FIELD CONVERTING "*" TO "0" BEFORE ".".	**123.56*	00123.56*
INSPECT WORK-FIELD CONVERTING "ABC" TO "abc".	BACK.BACK	bacK.bacK
INSPECT WORK-FIELD CONVERTING ".," TO ",.".	12.345,67	12,345.67

A routine that converts uppercase letters to lowercase

```
INSPECT WORK-FIELD CONVERTING
      "ABCDEFGHIJKLMNOPQRSTUVWXYZ"
   TO "abcdefghijklmnopqrstuvwxyz".
```

The same routine when using the Lower-Case function

```
MOVE FUNCTION LOWER-CASE (WORK-FIELD) TO NEW-WORK-FIELD.
```

Description

- The Inspect statement with the Converting clause became available with the 1985 COBOL standards. This statement simplifies the coding of a conversion function because you can specify all the characters you want to convert in a single literal.

Figure 9-8   How to use the Inspect statement with the Converting clause

Two illustrative routines

At this point, you have been introduced to all the features for working with characters (also known as *character strings*). To help you understand how these features can work together, this chapter ends by presenting two typical routines.

An editing routine

The first routine in figure 9-9 edits the data in a zip code field. It assumes that the data is valid if it consists of five digits, nine digits, or five digits followed by a hyphen. If the data is valid, this routine moves just the digits into a field that has a picture of X(9). If, for example, the user enters 11111-2222, the zip code will be stored in the result field as 111112222.

To start, this routine moves zeros to three count fields. Next, the first Inspect statement counts the number of hyphens and the characters before the first hyphen. Then, the second Inspect statement counts the number of characters before the first space. If there are no spaces in the field, this count is set to ten.

The nested If statements that follow move the digits from the input field to the edited field. If the first count is zero (no hyphens) and the third count is either 5 or 9 (characters before the first space), the input field is moved to the edited field as is. If the first count is one (one hyphen) and the second count is five (digits before the hyphen), reference modification is used to move the first five digits of the input field to the edited field. Then, if the third count is 10 (total characters in the field), reference modification is used to move the last four characters in the input field to the last four characters in the edited field. But if the third count isn't 10, which means the field has fewer than four digits after the hyphen, nothing else is moved, although the field is still considered valid.

A conversion routine

The second routine in this figure converts data that has been stored with all uppercase (or lowercase) letters to a more readable form. Specifically, this routine converts a name like ANNE PRINCE (or anne prince) to Anne Prince. The first statement in this routine uses the Lower-Case function to convert all of the characters in the FULL-NAME field to lowercase. Note that the field name in the function and the field name for the receiving field are the same.

The rest of the routine converts the first letter of each word from lowercase to uppercase. For simplification, though, this routine assumes a maximum of three words. The first letter in the first word is converted to uppercase by using the Upper-Case function and a simple reference modification (1:1). Then, to get the location of the first letters in the next two words, Unstring statements are used with Pointer fields, and the Pointer fields are used in the reference modifications. Note that the Pointer field isn't reset after the first Unstring statement so the second Unstring statement starts where the first left off, which is at the start of the next word to be unstrung.

An editing routine for a zip code entry

```
05  VALID-ENTRY-SWITCH        PIC X.
05  ZIP-CODE                  PIC X(10).
05  EDITED-ZIP-CODE           PIC X(9).
05  COUNT-1                   PIC S9(3).
05  COUNT-2                   PIC S9(3).
05  COUNT-3                   PIC S9(3).
    .
    .
MOVE ZERO TO COUNT-1 COUNT-2 COUNT-3.
INSPECT ZIP-CODE TALLYING
    COUNT-1 FOR ALL "-"
    COUNT-2 FOR CHARACTERS BEFORE "-".
INSPECT ZIP-CODE
    TALLYING COUNT-3 FOR CHARACTERS BEFORE " ".
IF COUNT-1 = 0 AND (COUNT-3 = 5 OR COUNT-3 = 9)
    MOVE ZIP-CODE TO EDITED-ZIP-CODE
    MOVE "Y" TO VALID-ENTRY-SWITCH
ELSE
    IF COUNT-1 = 1 AND COUNT-2 = 5
        MOVE ZIP-CODE (1:5) TO EDITED-ZIP-CODE
        MOVE "Y" TO VALID-ENTRY-SWITCH
        IF COUNT-3 = 10
            MOVE ZIP-CODE (7:4) TO EDITED-ZIP-CODE (6:)
        END-IF
    ELSE
        MOVE "N" TO VALID-ENTRY-SWITCH
    END-IF
END-IF.
```

A conversion routine that reformats a name to first caps

```
05  FULL-NAME                 PIC X(20).
05  NAME-1                    PIC X(20).
05  POINTER-FIELD             PIC S9(3).
    .
    .
MOVE FUNCTION LOWER-CASE (FULL-NAME) TO FULL-NAME.
MOVE FUNCTION UPPER-CASE (FULL-NAME (1:1))
    TO FULL-NAME (1:1).
MOVE 1 TO POINTER-FIELD.
UNSTRING FULL-NAME DELIMITED BY ALL " "
    INTO NAME-1
    WITH POINTER POINTER-FIELD.
MOVE FUNCTION UPPER-CASE (FULL-NAME (POINTER-FIELD:1))
    TO FULL-NAME (POINTER-FIELD:1).
UNSTRING FULL-NAME DELIMITED BY ALL " "
    INTO NAME-1
    WITH POINTER POINTER-FIELD.
IF POINTER-FIELD <= 20
    MOVE FUNCTION UPPER-CASE (FULL-NAME (POINTER-FIELD:1))
        TO FULL-NAME (POINTER-FIELD:1).
```

Figure 9-9   Two illustrative routines

Perspective

Now that you've completed this chapter, you should be able to use any of the features for working with characters in your programs. Since most business programs work with records and fields, not characters, you won't use these features that often. But every professional programmer needs to use them for special editing and conversion routines.

Summary

- *Reference modification* lets you refer to characters within a field by providing *offset* and *length* values.

- Eight functions for working with characters became available with the 1989 addendum to the 1985 standards. Of these, the Numval, Numval-C, Upper-Case, and Lower-Case functions are the most useful.

- The String statement lets you combine two or more fields into a single field, while the Unstring statement lets you extract two or more fields from a single field.

- The Inspect statement can be used to count or replace characters within a field.

Terms

reference modification	function	delimiter
offset	argument	unstring
length	string	character string
intrinsic function	concatenate	

Objectives

- Apply any of the features, functions, or statements presented in this chapter to the requirements of the programs you develop.

- Explain how reference modification can be used in conjunction with the String, Unstring, or Inspect statement.

Exercise 9-1   Edit numeric entries

In this exercise, you'll run a program that requires Inspect statements, and modify it so it uses the Numval function. Before you start, copy the chapter 9 programs into c:\cobol.

1. Open the program named char1000. This is the program that edits a numeric entry (see figure 9-7). Change the Program-ID to CHAR1500, and save the program as char1500. Then, close and re-open the program.

2. Compile and run the program. If you don't understand how it works, step through it and display the critical variables. Then, modify this program so it uses the Numval function to get the same result.

3. Change the picture of the user-entry field to X(10) and the picture of the edited-result field to S9(5)V99. Then, recompile and test again. This time, experiment with a variety of entries to see how well the Numval function works. When you're satisfied that you know what it can do, close the program.

Exercise 9-2   Unstring and string names

This exercise gives you a chance to use the Unstring and String statements. To start, you'll review the program named char2000, which converts a name to first cap format. Then, you'll modify this program so it unstrings a full name in one format and strings it back together in a new format. The interactive session for this program should look something like this (the user entries are shaded):

```
-------------------------------------------------
To end program, enter Y (or y).
n
-------------------------------------------------
Enter last name, first name.
Example: Prince, Anne Marie
Murphy, Michael Ray
Result: Michael Ray Murphy
-------------------------------------------------
To end program, enter Y (or y).
y
End of session.
```

Start the new program from an old program

1. If you haven't already copied the chapter 9 programs into c:\cobol, do that now. Then, open the program named char2000. This is the program that converts a name from all uppercase letters to first cap format (see the second routine in figure 9-9). Change the Program-ID to CHAR2500, save the program as char2500, and close and re-open the program.

2. Compile and run the program to see how it works. If you don't understand all of its code, step through it and display the critical variables.

Modify the program so it unstrings and strings names

3. Modify this program so it unstrings and strings names using an interactive session like the one shown above. Note that the last name that's entered by the user must be followed by a comma and a space for this to work. To start, assume that the last name will consist of just one word, but make this program work even if the user enters two or more names after the comma.

4. Modify the program so it works for last names that consist of two or more words like Van Erden. When you've got the program working the way you want it to, close the program.

Exercise 9-3   Edit phone numbers

This exercise gives you a chance to edit phone numbers that are entered with a variety of formats. To start, you'll review the program named char3000, which edits a zip code field. Then, you'll modify this program so it edits a phone number. The interactive session for this program should look something like this (the user entries are shaded):

```
-------------------------------------------------
To end program, enter Y (or y).
n
-------------------------------------------------
Enter phone number.
Acceptable formats: (999) 999-9999
                     999 999 9999
                     999-999-9999
 555 123 4567
Edited phone number = 5551234567
Formatted phone number = (555) 123-4567
-------------------------------------------------
To end program, enter Y (or y).
y
End of session.
```

Start the new program from an old program

1. If you haven't already copied the chapter 9 programs into c:\cobol, do that now. Then, open the program named char3000. This is the program that edits a zip code (see the first routine in figure 9-9). Change the Program-ID to CHAR3500, save the program as char3500, and close and re-open the program.

2. Compile and run the program to see how it works. If you don't understand all of its code, step through it and display the critical variables so you can see what's happening at each step.

Modify the program so it edits phone numbers

3. Modify this program so it edits the phone numbers that are entered by the user. These numbers can be entered with any of the formats shown above, but the edited phone number should have a picture of X(10) and this field should contain just ten digits when the editing is done. After the program edits each phone number, it should display it in its edited form as well as in the formatted style shown above. *Note that this program should work even if the user starts an entry with one or more spaces.*

4. Compile and test the program. When you've got the program working the way you want it to, close the program.

10

How to work with tables

Tables are used in many data-processing applications. For example, a tax table may be used to look up the amount of income tax to be withheld from payroll checks. And a rate table may be used to find the premium to be charged for an insurance policy. In this chapter, you'll learn the COBOL you need for working with tables like these.

How to use subscripts to work with one-level tables

The easiest way to work with tables is to use subscripts. So that's the technique this chapter presents first. As you'll learn later in this chapter, though, you can work more efficiently with tables by using indexes. Even so, you may want to use subscripts in some situations.

If you haven't read chapter 6 yet, you might want to look at figure 6-5 before you begin. It describes the Redefines clause, which is used in the table definitions in this chapter.

How to define a one-level table that uses subscripts

A *one-level table* is a table that contains data that's based on a single variable factor. The month table that's presented in figure 10-1, for example, contains data that varies depending on the month. And the price table that's presented in this figure contains data that varies depending on the item.

To define a one-level table, you code an Occurs clause that indicates how many occurrences the table will contain. For example, the month table in this figure will contain 12 occurrences of a single field named MONTH-NAME. Since this field is defined with a Picture of X(9), that means that the table will contain 108 bytes.

Although you can code the Occurs clause on an elementary item, it's more likely that you'll code it on a group item. Then, the entire group of fields will be repeated the indicated number of times. That's the case with the price table shown in this figure. Here, the field named PRICE-GROUP, which contains the elementary items named ITEM-NUMBER and ITEM-PRICE, occurs 16 times. As a result, the total size of this table is 112 bytes (three bytes for each item number plus four bytes for each price times 16 occurrences).

If a table contains data that changes frequently, it's usually loaded from a file at the beginning of the program. That's the case with the price table shown here. However, if a table contains data that doesn't change or changes infrequently, you can code the data as constant values within the table definition. This is illustrated by the month table in this figure. You'll learn more about how to define a table with constant values in just a minute.

The basic syntax of a table definition

```
level-number data-name OCCURS integer TIMES
```

The COBOL description for a one-level table that contains constant values

```
01    MONTH-TABLE-VALUES.
      05    FILLER            PIC X(9)    VALUE "JANUARY  ".
      05    FILLER            PIC X(9)    VALUE "FEBRUARY ".
      05    FILLER            PIC X(9)    VALUE "MARCH    ".
      05    FILLER            PIC X(9)    VALUE "APRIL    ".
      05    FILLER            PIC X(9)    VALUE "MAY      ".
      05    FILLER            PIC X(9)    VALUE "JUNE     ".
      05    FILLER            PIC X(9)    VALUE "JULY     ".
      05    FILLER            PIC X(9)    VALUE "AUGUST   ".
      05    FILLER            PIC X(9)    VALUE "SEPTEMBER".
      05    FILLER            PIC X(9)    VALUE "OCTOBER  ".
      05    FILLER            PIC X(9)    VALUE "NOVEMBER ".
      05    FILLER            PIC X(9)    VALUE "DECEMBER ".
*
01    MONTH-TABLE REDEFINES MONTH-TABLE-VALUES.
      05    MONTH-NAME        PIC X(9)
                              OCCURS 12 TIMES.
```

A one-level table that will be loaded from a file

The data for the table

Item number	Price	Item number	Price
101	12.50	277	1.11
107	50.00	297	7.77
111	7.70	305	.10
158	5.55	341	15.00
161	62.50	342	57.50
192	25.00	343	65.00
201	.40	347	22.50
213	6.66	351	.35

The COBOL description for the table

```
01    PRICE-TABLE.
      05    PRICE-GROUP       OCCURS 16 TIMES.
            10    ITEM-NUMBER PIC 9(3).
            10    ITEM-PRICE  PIC S99V99.
```

Description

- A *one-level table* contains data that depends on a single variable factor.
- The Occurs clause indicates how many times a field or a group of fields is repeated in storage and can be coded from level 02 through 49. Each occurrence holds one *table entry*.
- A table can contain constant values, which can be coded or copied directly into the program, or variable values, which can be loaded from a file.

Figure 10-1   How to define a one-level table that uses subscripts

How to initialize a table

In some cases, you may want to initialize the values in a table before you use the table. To do that, you can include Value clauses in the table definition as shown in the example at the top of figure 10-2. Here, the Value clause is coded on the elementary items in the table. Then, each occurrence of those items is initialized with the indicated value, in this case, zero.

Although you can initialize each field in a table separately, you can also initialize the entire table at once by coding a Value clause at the table level or at the group level (the level that contains the Occurs clause). However, that works only if all of the fields in the table are defined with the same usage and you want to initialize each field to the same value. Otherwise, you'll want to define each field separately.

You can also initialize a table as the program executes by using an Initialize statement like the one shown in the second example in this figure. Keep in mind, though, that initializing a large table in this way can reduce the efficiency of a program. So you'll want to initialize a table only when it makes sense. For more information on using the Initialize statement, please see chapter 6.

How to define a table with constant values

When the values in a table aren't likely to change, you may want to code them as constants in the Data Division. In figure 10-1, for example, you saw how the names of the months were defined as constants in the month table. When you define a table this way, you can save it in a copy member and then copy it into any program that needs it (see chapter 11).

Figure 10-2 shows two ways you can define a table with constant values. Both of the examples presented here use the price table you saw in figure 10-1. Since the values in this table would probably change periodically, it's not likely that it would be defined with constant values. However, you may come across tables that it would make sense to define this way.

The first technique for defining a table with constant values is to use the Redefines clause. With this technique, you start by defining the values for the table. Then, you code the Redefines clause on the table definition so the table redefines the area that contains the table values.

Because the price values contain signs, each value must be defined separately so the signs can be stored properly. If any of the fields in the table were defined with computational usage, the values for those fields would also need to be defined separately. If that's not the case, though, you may want to combine the values for each occurrence of the table data into a single alphanumeric item. In fact, you can even combine all of the values for the table into a single item. If you do that, you don't need to use the Redefines clause. Instead, you can just include the Value clause in the table definition as shown in the last example in this figure. In most cases, though, the table data will be easier to read if you code the values separately.

Code for initializing a table

In working storage

```
01  PRICE-TABLE.
    05  PRICE-GROUP           OCCURS 16 TIMES.
        10  ITEM-NUMBER   PIC 9(3)     VALUE ZERO.
        10  ITEM-PRICE    PIC S99V99   VALUE ZERO.
```

From the Procedure Division

```
INITIALIZE PRICE-TABLE.
```

Code for defining a table with constant values

Using the Redefines clause

```
01  PRICE-TABLE-VALUES.
    05  FILLER            PIC 9(3)       VALUE "101".
    05  FILLER            PIC S99V99     VALUE +12.50.
        .
        .
    05  FILLER            PIC 9(3)       VALUE "351".
    05  FILLER            PIC S99V99     VALUE +.35.
*
01  PRICE-TABLE REDEFINES PRICE-TABLE-VALUES.
    05  PRICE-GROUP           OCCURS 16 TIMES.
        10  ITEM-NUMBER   PIC 9(3).
        10  ITEM-PRICE    PIC S99V99.
```

Using the Value clause

```
01  PRICE-TABLE        VALUE "1011250107500011107701580555".
    05  PRICE-GROUP           OCCURS 4 TIMES.
        10  ITEM-NUMBER   PIC 9(3).
        10  ITEM-PRICE    PIC S99V99.
```

How to initialize a table

- To initialize a table at the start of a program, code a Value clause for each field in the table. That initializes each occurrence of that field to the specified value. You can also code the Value clause on a group field to initialize all the fields in that group to the same value.

- To re-initialize a table as the program executes, use the Initialize statement. See chapter 6 for more information on using this statement.

How to define a table with constant values

- One way to define the values for the fields in a table is to code each field as a separate data item as illustrated by the first example above. This is necessary if any of the fields require minus signs or are defined with a computational usage. Then, you can use the Redefines clause to define those fields as a table with an Occurs clause.

- If the constant values can be coded in a single Value clause, you can include that clause in the table definition as illustrated by the last example above. This Value clause must be coded at the level above the level that contains the Occurs clause.

Figure 10-2   How to initialize a table or define a table with constant values

How to refer to entries in a one-level table using subscripts

Each occurrence in a table represents one *table entry*. To refer to a specific table entry using subscripts, you indicate the *occurrence number* of the entry. The first entry in a table has an occurrence number of one, the second entry has an occurrence number of two, and so on. So, for example, if you want to refer to the sixth entry in the month table, you can code a statement like the first one shown in figure 10-3. Here, the field name is simply followed by the occurrence number enclosed in parentheses.

In most cases, you don't know the occurrence number of the entry you want to refer to when you code the program. In that case, you code the name of a *subscript* in place of the occurrence number as illustrated in the second example in this figure. Then, the program can set the subscript to the appropriate value as it executes.

Before you can use a subscript to refer to a table entry, you have to define the subscript in working storage. For example, you can define the subscript for the price table as shown in this figure. Notice that because the subscript will contain an occurrence number, it must be defined as an integer. For efficiency, it should also be defined with computational usage.

Another way to refer to an entry in a table is by using a *relative subscript*. When you use a relative subscript, you follow the name of the subscript with a plus or a minus sign followed by a literal value. This is illustrated in the third example in this figure. Here, one is subtracted from the field named MONTH-SUB, which is the subscript used for the month table. So if this field contains an occurrence number of 6 when this statement is executed, this statement will refer to the fifth entry in the table.

Regardless of the technique you use, keep in mind that the occurrence number you specify must fall between one and the number of occurrences in the table. If it doesn't, you're going to have a debugging problem.

The syntax for referring to a table entry in a one-level table

$$\text{data-name} \left[\left[\begin{matrix} \text{subscript-name} \ [\{+ \mid -\} \ \text{literal}] \\ \text{occurrence-number} \end{matrix}\right]\right]$$

Statements that refer to entries in a one-level table

```
MOVE MONTH-NAME (6) TO HDG3-MONTH-NAME.

COMPUTE LINE-ITEM-EXTENSION ROUNDED =
    TR-QUANTITY * ITEM-PRICE (PRICE-TABLE-SUB).

MOVE MONTH-NAME (MONTH-SUB - 1) TO HDG3-PRIOR-MONTH-NAME.
```

The definition of a subscript

```
05  PRICE-TABLE-SUB     PIC S99     COMP.
```

Description

- You can refer to table entries using subscripts, occurrence numbers, or relative subscripting. You can use these techniques to refer to a group field or an individual field.

- A *subscript* is a field that contains an *occurrence number*, which indicates the occurrence of the field you want to refer to. A subscript must be defined as an integer, and it should be defined with computational usage for efficiency.

- You can use *relative subscripts* to increase or decrease a subscript value by a literal value when you refer to a table entry.

- You can use the same subscript to refer to entries in two or more tables, and you can use two or more subscripts to refer to the entries in a single table.

Coding rules

- To refer to an entry in a one-level table, you code the name of the field you want to refer to followed by a space and the subscript name, an occurrence number, or a relative subscript enclosed in parentheses.

- If you code a relative subscript, the plus or minus sign must be preceded and followed by a space.

Figure 10-3   How to refer to entries in a one-level table using subscripts

How to load a one-level table using subscripts

When the values in a table are likely to change, you normally load the table into storage from a file at the start of any program that uses the table. To do that, you use code like that shown in figure 10-4. This code loads the data shown in figure 10-1 into the price table. It assumes that each table entry is stored in one record of a sequential file.

To load a table like this, you use the Perform Varying statement. In this example, an inline Perform statement is used. Each time this statement is executed, it performs module 110 to read a record from the price table file. Then, if the end of the file hasn't been reached, it loads the values from the current record into the price table.

For this to work, the Perform statement must vary the subscript for the price table so each record is loaded into the next table entry. This is accomplished by the Varying clause. The From phrase of this clause initializes the subscript, PRICE-TABLE-SUB, to a value of 1 so the first record will be loaded into the first table entry. Then, the By phrase causes the subscript to be increased by 1 each time the Perform statement is executed so it refers to the next table entry. This continues until the end of the file is reached (PTABLE-EOF) or the subscript is equal to 16, which is the maximum number of entries in the table.

Note that the With Test After clause is used in the Perform Varying statement so the conditions in the Until clause are tested after the processing is done for each subscript value. If you don't code this clause, the conditions are tested before the processing is done so the second condition in the Until clause has to be coded as:

```
PRICE-TABLE-SUB > 16
```

Otherwise, only 15 items will be loaded into the table. As you will see, the With Test After clause is used in many of the examples in this chapter because it makes the coding easier to understand.

You may have noticed that no special processing is done if the end of the price table is reached before all 16 table entries are loaded. If you look at the definition of the price table, though, you can see that it's initialized to a value of zero. That way, if values aren't loaded into an entry, it won't cause any problems when the table is processed later in the program.

Code for loading a one-level table using subscripts

```
WORKING-STORAGE SECTION.
    .
    .
01    SWITCHES.
    05    PTABLE-EOF-SWITCH    PIC X    VALUE "N".
        88    PTABLE-EOF               VALUE "Y".
*
01    SUBSCRIPTS            COMP.
    05    PRICE-TABLE-SUB    PIC S99.
*
01    PRICE-TABLE          VALUE ZERO.
    05    PRICE-GROUP       OCCURS 16 TIMES.
        10    ITEM-NUMBER   PIC 9(3).
        10    ITEM-PRICE    PIC S99V99.
*
01    PRICE-TABLE-RECORD.
    05    PT-ITEM-NUMBER    PIC 9(3).
    05    PT-ITEM-PRICE     PIC S99V99.
    .
    .

PROCEDURE DIVISION.
    .
    .
100-LOAD-PRICE-TABLE.
*
    PERFORM
        WITH TEST AFTER
        VARYING PRICE-TABLE-SUB FROM 1 BY 1
        UNTIL PTABLE-EOF
            OR PRICE-TABLE-SUB = 16
            PERFORM 110-READ-PRICE-TABLE-RECORD
            IF NOT PTABLE-EOF
                MOVE PT-ITEM-NUMBER
                    TO ITEM-NUMBER (PRICE-TABLE-SUB)
                MOVE PT-ITEM-PRICE
                    TO ITEM-PRICE (PRICE-TABLE-SUB).
*
110-READ-PRICE-TABLE-RECORD.
*
    READ PTABLE RECORD INTO PRICE-TABLE-RECORD
        AT END
            MOVE "Y" TO PTABLE-EOF-SWITCH.
    .
    .
```

Figure 10-4   How to load a one-level table using subscripts

How to search a one-level table using subscripts

Once a table has been loaded into storage, you can search it to find the entries your program requires. For a simple table like the month table, you can find the entry you want by setting the subscript to the appropriate value. If, for example, you want to move the name of the current month into a heading line, you can code statements like this:

```
MOVE CURRENT-MONTH TO MONTH-SUB.
MOVE MONTH-NAME (MONTH-SUB) TO HDG3-MONTH-NAME.
```

Here, the first Move statement moves the value of the CURRENT-MONTH field to the subscript used by the month table. Then, the second Move statement moves the month name for that month to a heading line. Technically, this isn't a search because the program gets the entry without searching through the other entries in the table.

Figure 10-5 illustrates a true search. Here, a Perform Varying statement is used to search through each entry in the price table in sequence until the requested item number is found. In this case, the item number must match the item number in the current transaction record. By the way, you can assume that this code is part of the same program that was used to load the table.

Like the Perform statement for loading the price table, the Perform statement for searching this table initializes the subscript to a value of 1 and increases it by 1 each time it's performed. The Perform statement ends when a matching entry is found or all of the entries have been searched. Then, if the item number is found, the price field in that entry is moved to a working-storage field for further processing.

At this point, if you would like to take a break and apply what you've learned, you can skip to exercise 10-1 at the end of this chapter. This exercise guides you through the process of loading and searching a one-level table.

Code for searching a one-level table using subscripts

```
WORKING-STORAGE SECTION.
    .
    .
01   SWITCHES.
     05   ITEM-FOUND-SWITCH    PIC X    VALUE "N".
          88   ITEM-FOUND               VALUE "Y".
*
01   SUBSCRIPTS              COMP.
     05   PRICE-TABLE-SUB    PIC S99.
*
01   PRICE-TABLE            VALUE ZERO.
     05   PRICE-GROUP        OCCURS 16 TIMES.
          10   ITEM-NUMBER   PIC 9(3).
          10   ITEM-PRICE    PIC S99V99.
*
01   WORK-FIELDS.
     05   UNIT-PRICE         PIC S99V99.
*
01   TRANSACTION-RECORD.
     05   TR-REFERENCE-CODE    PIC X(6).
     05   TR-REFERENCE-DATE    PIC X(8).
     05   TR-CUSTOMER-NUMBER   PIC 9(5).
     05   TR-ITEM-NUMBER       PIC 9(3).
     .
     .

PROCEDURE DIVISION.
    .
    .
    MOVE "N" TO ITEM-FOUND-SWITCH.
    PERFORM 350-SEARCH-PRICE-TABLE
        WITH TEST AFTER
        VARYING PRICE-TABLE-SUB FROM 1 BY 1
        UNTIL ITEM-FOUND
            OR PRICE-TABLE-SUB = 16.
    IF ITEM-FOUND
        MOVE ITEM-PRICE (PRICE-TABLE-SUB) TO UNIT-PRICE.
    .
    .
350-SEARCH-PRICE-TABLE.
*
    IF ITEM-NUMBER (PRICE-TABLE-SUB) = TR-ITEM-NUMBER
        MOVE "Y" TO ITEM-FOUND-SWITCH.
    .
    .
```

Figure 10-5   How to search a one-level table using subscripts

How to use subscripts to work with multi-level tables

One-level tables are appropriate only if the data in the table varies depending on a single factor. If the data varies depending on two or more factors, you'll want to use a *multi-level table*. Although you can define tables with up to seven levels, you're not likely to need tables with more than two or three levels. If you understand the code for working with two- and three-level tables, though, you shouldn't have any trouble extending it to tables with more than three levels if you ever need to.

How to define a multi-level table

To define a multi-level table, you code an Occurs clause within an Occurs clause. The definition of the two-level table in figure 10-6, for example, contains two Occurs clauses. To help you understand the definition of this table, take a look at the data for this table. As you can see, it contains insurance rates that are based on two factors: age and class. Because there are six possible age ranges, the table is defined with a field named AGE-GROUP that occurs six times. And because there are four possible classes within each age group, the AGE-GROUP field contains a field named CLASS-GROUP that occurs four times. Then, this group includes two fields that will contain the class number and the insurance rate for that class.

Notice that the AGE-GROUP field also contains a field named HIGH-AGE that will contain the highest age for that group. Although you could include fields for both the high age and the low age in the range, that may not be necessary. You'll see why when you see the search routine for this table.

This figure also presents a three-level table that contains data similar to the data in the two-level table. In this case, though, the four classes are divided into two classes for men and two classes for women. Because of that, the table that will contain this data is defined with three Occurs clauses. The AGE-GROUP field will occur six times just as in the two-level table. Within this group, though, the SEX-GROUP field occurs two times. And within that group, the field that contains the insurance rate occurs two times.

Notice that this table doesn't include a field for the class number. That's because the numbers are 1 and 2, so they can be referred to by their occurrence numbers. Similarly, if you assume that the first sex group contains the insurance rates for men and the second group contains the insurance rates for women, you don't need to include a field that indicates the sex. Also notice that the age group in this table includes fields for both the high and low age. That may or may not be necessary based on the requirements of the program.

A two-level table

Age range	Class 10	Class 20	Class 30	Class 40
18-34	23.50	27.05	35.25	52.90
35-39	24.00	27.55	35.75	53.40
40-44	24.60	28.15	36.35	54.00
45-49	25.30	28.85	37.05	54.70
50-54	26.30	29.85	38.05	55.70
55-59	28.00	31.55	39.75	57.40

The COBOL description for the table

```
01  RATE-TABLE.
    05  AGE-GROUP               OCCURS 6 TIMES.
        10  HIGH-AGE            PIC 99.
        10  CLASS-GROUP         OCCURS 4 TIMES.
            15  CLASS-NUMBER    PIC 99.
            15  INSURANCE-RATE  PIC S99V99.
```

A reference to the table

```
MOVE INSURANCE-RATE (AGE-SUB CLASS-SUB) TO POLICY-RATE.
```

A three-level table

Age range	Men		Women	
	Class 1	Class 2	Class 1	Class 2
18-34	23.50	27.05	24.75	28.45
35-39	24.00	27.55	25.80	29.50
40-44	24.60	28.15	27.10	30.80
45-49	25.30	28.85	29.10	32.80
50-54	26.30	29.85	31.55	35.25
55-59	28.00	31.55	35.00	38.70

The COBOL description for the table

```
01  RATE-TABLE.
    05  AGE-GROUP               OCCURS 6 TIMES.
        10  LOW-AGE             PIC 99.
        10  HIGH-AGE            PIC 99.
        10  SEX-GROUP           OCCURS 2 TIMES.
            15  INSURANCE-RATE  OCCURS 2 TIMES
                                PIC S99V99.
```

A reference to the table

```
MOVE INSURANCE-RATE (AGE-SUB SEX-SUB CLASS-SUB) TO POLICY-RATE.
```

Description

- A *multi-level table* contains data that depends on two or more factors. To define a multi-level table, you code an OCCURS clause within an OCCURS clause.

- To refer to an entry in a multi-level table, you code a subscript name, occurrence number, or relative subscript for each level.

Figure 10-6   How to define a multi-level table

How to refer to entries in a multi-level table using subscripts

Figure 10-6 also illustrates how to refer to entries in two- and three-level tables using subscript names. Just as you can with a one-level table, though, you can also refer to entries using relative subscripts or occurrence numbers. For example, you can refer to the insurance rate in the third class group of the first age group in the two-level table like this:

```
INSURANCE-RATE (1 3)
```

Notice that the occurrence numbers in this example and the subscript names used in this figure are specified in the same order that they're defined in the table. In other words, the occurrence of the highest level group must be specified first, followed by the other levels in order.

Also notice that the subscript names and occurrence numbers must be separated by at least one space. Although commas may be coded to separate the names or numbers, they're simply ignored by the compiler. As a result, you must be sure to include one or more spaces after each comma.

How to load a two-level table using subscripts

Figure 10-7 presents code for loading the two-level rate table you saw in figure 10-6. This table is loaded from the records in a rate table file. Each record in this file contains the data for a single age group. Because of that, the record description includes a class group that occurs four times.

To load the rate table from this file, the program uses two Perform Varying statements. The first one performs procedure 110 to load the entries in each age group. To do that, the Perform statement varies the subscript for the age group from a value of 1 to a value of 6. As a result, procedure 110 is executed six times.

Each time procedure 110 is executed, it performs procedure 120 to read a record from the rate table file. Next, if the end of the file hasn't been reached, it moves the high age field in the record to the high age field in the table entry indicated by the age subscript. Then, it executes the second Perform Varying statement, which is coded as an inline Perform. This Perform statement varies the subscript for the class group from 1 to 4 so it processes each of the four classes. Each time it's executed, it moves the current occurrence of the class number and insurance rate fields in the record to the related fields in the rate table.

Note that the program must use both the age subscript and the class subscript to refer to the fields in the rate table. Note too that the same class subscript is used for the class group in the rate table record. This shows that one subscript can be used to refer to the entries in two different tables.

Code for loading a two-level table using subscripts

```
WORKING-STORAGE SECTION.
    .
    .
 01   SUBSCRIPTS              COMP.
      05   AGE-SUB            PIC S9.
      05   CLASS-SUB          PIC S9.
*
 01   RATE-TABLE.
      05   AGE-GROUP                    OCCURS 6 TIMES.
           10   HIGH-AGE               PIC 99.
           10   CLASS-GROUP            OCCURS 4 TIMES.
                15   CLASS-NUMBER      PIC 99.
                15   INSURANCE-RATE    PIC S99V99.
*
 01   RATE-TABLE-RECORD.
      05   RT-HIGH-AGE        PIC 99.
      05   RT-CLASS-GROUP     OCCURS 4 TIMES.
           10   RT-CLASS-NUMBER    PIC 99.
           10   RT-INSURANCE-RATE  PIC S99V99.
    .
    .

PROCEDURE DIVISION.
    .
    .

 100-LOAD-RATE-TABLE.
*
     PERFORM 110-LOAD-RATE-TABLE-ENTRY
         WITH TEST AFTER
         VARYING AGE-SUB FROM 1 BY 1
         UNTIL AGE-SUB = 6
            OR RATE-TABLE-EOF.
*
 110-LOAD-RATE-TABLE-ENTRY.
*
     PERFORM 120-READ-RATE-TABLE-RECORD.
     IF NOT RATE-TABLE-EOF
         MOVE RT-HIGH-AGE TO HIGH-AGE (AGE-SUB)
         PERFORM
             WITH TEST AFTER
             VARYING CLASS-SUB FROM 1 BY 1
             UNTIL CLASS-SUB = 4
                 MOVE RT-CLASS-NUMBER (CLASS-SUB)
                     TO CLASS-NUMBER (AGE-SUB CLASS-SUB)
                 MOVE RT-INSURANCE-RATE (CLASS-SUB)
                     TO INSURANCE-RATE (AGE-SUB CLASS-SUB).
*
 120-READ-RATE-TABLE-RECORD.
*
     READ RTABLE RECORD INTO RATE-TABLE-RECORD
         AT END
             MOVE "Y" TO RATE-TABLE-EOF-SWITCH.
    .
    .
```

Figure 10-7   How to load a two-level table using subscripts

How to search a two-level table using subscripts

Figure 10-8 presents code for searching the two-level rate table. Like the code for loading this table, this code uses two Perform Varying statements. The first one performs procedure 360 as it varies the age subscript from 1 to 6. This procedure starts by checking if the age field in the current applicant record is less than or equal to the high age field in the current occurrence of the age group. If it is, it indicates that the appropriate age group has been found.

Before I go on, you should realize that this age search works only if you assume that the age entries are in the order that were shown in figure 10-6. In other words, they must be in order from the lowest to the highest. If they're not, you have to store both the high age and the low age in the table and then base the search on the range of ages. Alternatively, you could sort the records in the rate table file into age sequence before you load them into the rate table. Or, if your compiler provides a feature for sorting the entries in a table, you could use that feature to sort the entries into age sequence after they're loaded. You can learn about sorting the records in a file in chapter 16, and you can learn about sorting the entries in a table later in this chapter.

If the search for the age group in procedure 360 is successful, the second Perform Varying statement is executed. This statement performs procedure 370 as it varies the class subscript from 1 to 4. Procedure 370 simply checks if the class number in the table is equal to the class number in the record. If it is, it turns on the rate-found switch and the Perform statement ends. Then, back in module 350, the insurance rate for that entry is moved to a working-storage field so it can be used for further processing.

As you review this code, keep in mind that it illustrates just one way to search a multi-level table. Another way is to search each level independently of the other levels. Instead of nesting the second Perform statement in this figure within the first Perform statement, for example, you could code them both at the same level. Then, the first Perform statement would search the age group until the correct group was found or the end of the table was reached. If the correct age group was found, the second Perform statement could then be executed to search the class group. Although this is a minor variation from the code presented in this figure, you may find it easier to read. On the other hand, it requires the use of an additional switch. The point is that there is always more than one way to search the entries in a multi-level table.

Code for searching a two-level table using subscripts

```
WORKING-STORAGE SECTION.
    .
    .
01   SUBSCRIPTS              COMP.
     05  AGE-SUB            PIC S9.
     05  CLASS-SUB          PIC S9.
*
01   WORK-FIELDS.
     05  POLICY-RATE        PIC S99V99.
*
01   RATE-TABLE.
     05  AGE-GROUP                  OCCURS 6 TIMES.
         10   HIGH-AGE              PIC 99.
         10   CLASS-GROUP           OCCURS 4 TIMES.
             15   CLASS-NUMBER      PIC 99.
             15   INSURANCE-RATE    PIC S99V99.
*
01   APPLICANT-RECORD.
     05  AR-AGE          PIC 99.
     05  AR-CLASS        PIC 99.
         .
         .

PROCEDURE DIVISION.
    .
    .
350-SEARCH-RATE-TABLE.
*
    MOVE "N" TO RATE-FOUND-SWITCH.
    PERFORM 360-SEARCH-AGE-GROUP
        WITH TEST AFTER
        VARYING AGE-SUB FROM 1 BY 1
        UNTIL RATE-FOUND
           OR AGE-SUB = 6.
    IF RATE-FOUND
        MOVE INSURANCE-RATE (AGE-SUB CLASS-SUB) TO POLICY-RATE.
    .
    .
360-SEARCH-AGE-GROUP.
*
    IF AR-AGE <= HIGH-AGE (AGE-SUB)
        PERFORM 370-SEARCH-CLASS-GROUP
            WITH TEST AFTER
            VARYING CLASS-SUB FROM 1 BY 1
            UNTIL RATE-FOUND
               OR CLASS-SUB = 4.
*
370-SEARCH-CLASS-GROUP.
*
    IF CLASS-NUMBER (AGE-SUB CLASS-SUB) = AR-CLASS
        MOVE "Y" TO RATE-FOUND-SWITCH.
    .
    .
```

Figure 10-8   How to search a two-level table using subscripts

How to use indexes to work with tables

Although subscripts are easy to use, they're not as efficient as using *indexes*. That's because an index represents a *displacement value* that points directly to the location of a table entry. In contrast, a subscript represents an occurrence number that must be converted to a displacement value each time it's used. Because of that, you'll want to use indexes whenever possible.

How to define a table with an index

Figure 10-9 illustrates how you define a table that uses an index. To do that, you include an Indexed By clause in addition to the Occurs clause. The Indexed By clause names the index that will be used with the table. Although you can code more than one index name on this clause, you're not likely to do that.

The first example in this figure shows the definition of a one-level price table. This is the same table that was presented in figure 10-1. If you compare the table definitions in these two figures, you'll see that the only difference is that the one in this figure includes the Indexed By clause. Likewise, the example for the two-level rate table in this figure is the same as the one in figure 10-6 except that it includes two Indexed By clauses: one for each level of the table.

When you define a table with an index, you should know that the index is defined automatically. In other words, you don't need to define it in working storage. That way, it can be defined with the size and usage that's appropriate for your system. This is another benefit that you get from using indexes.

How to refer to table entries using an index

You use the same techniques to refer to table entries using an index that you use with subscripts. Instead of a subscript name, though, you use an index name. And instead of a relative subscript, you use a *relative index*. You can also use an occurrence number to refer to an entry. Then, the occurrence number is converted to a displacement value. Figure 10-9 presents some examples of these techniques for one- and two-level tables.

The syntax of a table definition with an index

```
level-number data-name OCCURS integer TIMES
                       INDEXED BY {index-name-1} ...
```

A one-level table that uses an index

Table definition

```
01  PRICE-TABLE.
    05   PRICE-GROUP          OCCURS 16 TIMES
                              INDEXED BY PRICE-TABLE-INDEX.
        10   ITEM-NUMBER      PIC 9(3).
        10   ITEM-PRICE       PIC S99V99.
```

Statements that refer to entries in the table

```
COMPUTE LINE-ITEM-EXTENSION ROUNDED =
    TR-QUANTITY * ITEM-PRICE (PRICE-TABLE-INDEX).

MOVE ITEM-PRICE (1) TO UNIT-PRICE.
```

A two-level table that uses indexes

Table definition

```
01  RATE-TABLE.
    05   AGE-GROUP                OCCURS 6 TIMES
                                  INDEXED BY AGE-INDEX.
        10   HIGH-AGE             PIC 99.
        10   CLASS-GROUP          OCCURS 4 TIMES
                                  INDEXED BY CLASS-INDEX.
            15   CLASS-NUMBER     PIC 99.
            15   INSURANCE-RATE   PIC S99V99.
```

Statements that refer to entries in the table

```
MOVE INSURANCE-RATE (AGE-INDEX CLASS-INDEX) TO POLICY-RATE.

MOVE INSURANCE-RATE (AGE-INDEX CLASS-INDEX + 2) TO POLICY-RATE.
```

Description

- An *index* represents a *displacement value* from the start of the table. Because of that, indexes are more efficient to use than subscripts, which have to be converted to displacement values.

- You define a table that uses an index the same way you define a table that uses a subscript except that you include the Indexed By clause. This clause names one or more indexes that will be used to refer to the table entries. The indexes you name are defined automatically.

- You can code constant values for a table that uses indexes just as you do for a table that uses subscripts. You can also initialize a table that uses indexes by including a Value clause in the table definition or by using the Initialize statement in the Procedure Division.

- You can refer to table entries using indexes, occurrence numbers, or *relative indexes*. You can use these techniques to refer to a group field or an individual field.

Figure 10-9   Basic skills for working with indexes

How to load a table using an index

You can load a table with indexes using the same techniques that you use for loading a table that uses subscripts. The only difference is that you have to vary an index instead of a subscript in the Perform Varying statement. To illustrate, figure 10-10 presents the code for loading the one-level price table. Here, you can see that the Perform Varying statement reads each record in the price table and loads it into an entry in the price table just as the code in figure 10-4 that uses subscripts did. The difference is that this Perform Varying statement varies the value of the index for the table instead of the subscript, and it refers to the table entries using the index.

To load a multi-level table into storage, you can use nested Perform Varying statements just as you do with subscripts. Then, the first Perform Varying statement varies the index defined for the first level of the table, the second Perform Varying statement varies the index defined for the second level of the table, and so on. You can refer back to figure 10-7 to see how this is done with subscripts. Then, if you're using indexes instead of subscripts, you simply vary the indexes defined for the table instead of the subscripts.

Code for loading a one-level table using an index

```
WORKING-STORAGE SECTION.
    .
    .
01   SWITCHES.
     05   PTABLE-EOF-SWITCH   PIC X    VALUE "N".
          88   PTABLE-EOF              VALUE "Y".
     .
     .
01   PRICE-TABLE              VALUE ZERO.
     05   PRICE-GROUP         OCCURS 16 TIMES
                              INDEXED BY PRICE-TABLE-INDEX.
          10   ITEM-NUMBER    PIC 9(3).
          10   ITEM-PRICE     PIC S99V99.
*
 01  PRICE-TABLE-RECORD.
     05   PT-ITEM-NUMBER      PIC 9(3).
     05   PT-ITEM-PRICE       PIC S99V99.
     .
     .
PROCEDURE DIVISION.
     .
     .
 100-LOAD-PRICE-TABLE.
*
     PERFORM
         WITH TEST AFTER
         VARYING PRICE-TABLE-INDEX FROM 1 BY 1
         UNTIL PTABLE-EOF
           OR PRICE-TABLE-INDEX = 16
            PERFORM 110-READ-PRICE-TABLE-RECORD
            IF NOT PTABLE-EOF
                MOVE PT-ITEM-NUMBER
                    TO ITEM-NUMBER (PRICE-TABLE-INDEX)
                MOVE PT-ITEM-PRICE
                    TO ITEM-PRICE (PRICE-TABLE-INDEX).
*
 110-READ-PRICE-TABLE-RECORD.
*
     READ PTABLE RECORD INTO PRICE-TABLE-RECORD
         AT END
             MOVE "Y" TO PTABLE-EOF-SWITCH.
     .
     .
```

Figure 10-10   How to load a one-level table using an index

How to code the Set statement

Because an index contains a displacement value and not an occurrence number, you can't use the standard COBOL statements to assign a value to an index or to change the value of an index. Instead, you have to use the Set statement to do that. This statement is described in figure 10-11.

To assign a value to an index, you use the first form of the Set statement. The first two examples in this figure illustrate how this works. In the first example, an index named MONTH-INDEX is assigned the value of an integer data item named CURRENT-MONTH. When this statement is executed, the value of the CURRENT-MONTH field is converted to a displacement value, which is then assigned to the index. Similarly, in the second example, a Set statement is used to convert an occurrence number of 1 to a displacement value and then assign it to the index.

To increase or decrease the value of an index, you use the second form of the Set statement. To increase the value of an index, you include the Up By clause followed by the number of occurrences you want to increase it by. And to decrease the value of an index, you include the Down By clause. The third example illustrates how this works. Here, the index is increased by one occurrence.

You can also use the Set statement with *index data items*. An index data item is just like an index except that it's defined explicitly in working storage. You may need to use an index data item from time to time to hold the value of an index.

To define an index data item, you include the Usage Is Index clause and you omit the Picture and Value clauses. For instance, the fourth example in this figure defines an index data item named WORK-INDEX. Then, the following Set statement assigns the value of MONTH-INDEX to that data item.

The syntax of the Set statement for setting index values

$$\underline{\text{SET}} \left\{ \begin{array}{l} \text{identifier-1} \\ \text{index-name-1} \end{array} \right\} \underline{\text{TO}} \left\{ \begin{array}{l} \text{identifier-2} \\ \text{index-name-2} \\ \text{literal} \end{array} \right\}$$

The syntax of the Set statement for adjusting an index value

$$\underline{\text{SET}} \text{ index-name} \left\{ \begin{array}{l} \underline{\text{UP BY}} \\ \underline{\text{DOWN BY}} \end{array} \right\} \left\{ \begin{array}{l} \text{identifier} \\ \text{literal} \end{array} \right\}$$

The syntax for defining an index data item

```
level-number data-name [USAGE IS] INDEX
```

Set statement examples

A Set statement that sets an index to the value of an integer data item

```
SET MONTH-INDEX TO CURRENT-MONTH.
```

A Set statement that sets an index to a literal value

```
IF MONTH-INDEX = 13
    SET MONTH-INDEX TO 1.
```

A Set statement that increases an index by one occurrence

```
SET MONTH-INDEX UP BY 1.
```

A Set statement that sets an index data item to the value of an index

```
05  WORK-INDEX    INDEX.
.
SET WORK-INDEX TO MONTH-INDEX.
```

Description

- The Set statement can be used with an index or an *index data item*. An index data item is a field that's defined with Index usage.

- An index data item contains a displacement value just like an index. The compiler determines the size of an index data item, so Picture and Value clauses aren't allowed.

- You can use the Set statement to set an index, an index data item, or an integer field to the value of another index or index data item. You can also use this statement to set an index or index data item to a literal value that represents an occurrence number or an integer data item that contains an occurrence number. Then, that occurrence number is converted to a displacement value.

- You can also use the Set statement to increase or decrease the value of an index or an index data item. The increment or decrement value you specify must represent an occurrence number, which is converted to a displacement value.

Figure 10-11   How to code the Set statement

How to perform a sequential search

To search a table with indexes, you can use a Perform Varying statement just as you do for a table that uses subscripts. However, COBOL provides a Search statement that's specifically for searching tables with indexes. Figure 10-12 presents the syntax of this statement and illustrates how you can use it.

After you name the table to be searched, you can code an At End clause that's executed if the end of the table is reached, indicating that the search was not successful. In addition, you can code one or more When clauses that test for various conditions. In most cases, you'll include a single When clause that tests for the condition that satisfies the search.

When the Search statement is executed, it searches the table entries in sequence starting with the current index value. This is called a *sequential* or *serial search*. Before you begin a sequential search, you usually code a Set statement to set the index used in the search to a value of 1. That way, the table will be searched starting with the first entry. You can see the Set statement at the beginning of the examples in this figure.

The first example searches the price table for a given item number. If the item number isn't found, the At End clause turns off the item-found switch. Otherwise, if the item number in the table entry matches the item number in the transaction record (TR-ITEM-NO), the When clause turns on the item-found switch.

If you study this Search statement example, you'll realize that it performs the same function as the code in figure 10-5 that uses a Perform Varying statement to search the price table. If you compare the code in these two examples, though, I think you'll agree that the Search statement simplifies the code considerably. In addition, the Search statement provides a way to code the entire search operation in a readable format within a single procedure. This is another benefit that you get from using indexes.

The second example in this figure shows a Search statement that searches the rate table that was presented in figure 10-9. This statement works just like the first Search statement in this figure, except that it tests for a less-than-or-equal-to condition. Notice, however, that although the rate table is a two-level table, this Search statement searches only one level. To search a two-level table, you have to use two Search statements. You'll soon see an example of this.

The third example in this figure illustrates a case where you might want to start a search at an entry other than the first. Here, the Search statement is executed repeatedly until the end of the price table is reached. This is done so that all of the items with a given price can be located. Notice that although the index for this search is initially set to a value of 1, the current value of the indexed is increased by 1 after each search operation. That way, the next time the Search statement is executed, it will start with the entry after the last one that was tested.

The syntax of the Search statement for a sequential search

$$\text{\underline{SEARCH}}\ identifier\text{-}1 \left[\text{\underline{VARYING}} \left\{ \begin{array}{l} identifier\text{-}2 \\ index\text{-}name \end{array} \right\} \right]$$

$$\left[\text{AT \underline{END}}\ imperative\text{-}statement\text{-}1 \right]$$

$$\left\{ \text{\underline{WHEN}}\ condition\text{-}1 \left\{ \begin{array}{l} imperative\text{-}statement\text{-}2 \\ \text{\underline{NEXT} \underline{SENTENCE}} \end{array} \right\} \right\}$$

$$\left[\text{\underline{END}\,-\,\underline{SEARCH}} \right]$$

A Search statement that tests for an equals condition

```
SET PRICE-TABLE-INDEX TO 1.
SEARCH PRICE-GROUP
    AT END
        MOVE "N" TO ITEM-FOUND-SWITCH
    WHEN ITEM-NUMBER (PRICE-TABLE-INDEX) = TR-ITEM-NO
        MOVE "Y" TO ITEM-FOUND-SWITCH.
```

A Search statement that tests for a less-than-or-equal-to condition

```
SET AGE-INDEX TO 1.
SEARCH AGE-GROUP
    AT END
        MOVE "N" TO AGE-GROUP-FOUND-SWITCH
    WHEN AR-AGE <= HIGH-AGE (AGE-INDEX)
        MOVE "Y" TO AGE-GROUP-FOUND-SWITCH.
```

Code that tests for multiple matching entries

```
SET PRICE-TABLE-INDEX TO 1.
MOVE "N" TO PTABLE-EOF-SWITCH.
PERFORM UNTIL PTABLE-EOF
    SEARCH PRICE-GROUP
        AT END
            MOVE "Y" TO PTABLE-EOF-SWITCH
        WHEN ITEM-PRICE (PRICE-TABLE-INDEX) = ITEM-PRICE
            DISPLAY "ITEM NUMBER: " ITEM-NUMBER (PRICE-TABLE-INDEX)
    END-SEARCH
    SET PRICE-TABLE-INDEX UP BY 1
END-PERFORM.
```

Description

- The Search statement performs a *sequential search* of the specified table starting with the entry identified by the current index value. When the end of the table is reached, the At End clause is executed.

- You can code one or more When clauses on a Search statement to test for specific conditions. When any of the conditions are satisfied, the Search statement ends.

- The Varying clause names the index you want to use for the search. You may want to use this clause if you associate more than one index with a table. If you omit this clause, the first index named on the Indexed By clause for the table is used.

Figure 10-12   How to perform a sequential search

Because the Search statement searches a table from its first entry to its last entry, the search will be more efficient if the entries that are used most often appear near the beginning of the table. Unfortunately, it can be difficult to store the entries so they're in the most efficient sequence for a sequential search. In that case, you may be able to improve the efficiency of the search by performing a binary search.

How to perform a binary search

If a table is in sequence by the field that will be used to search for values in that table, you may want to use a *binary search* rather than a sequential search. When you do a binary search, the search starts near the middle of the table rather than at the beginning of the table. Based on the search condition that's specified, the compiler can determine if the entry you're looking for is in the first half of the table or the second half of the table. Then, the next comparison is near the middle of the half that was just selected. The search continues by successively halving the remaining entries until the search condition is satisfied.

The advantage of a binary search is its speed. In a table with 16 entries, for example, any entry can be found with a maximum of just four comparisons. In contrast, a sequential search requires an average of eight comparisons to find an entry if the frequency of use is distributed evenly over the 16 entries. And the larger the table, the more efficient a binary search is likely to be.

To perform a binary search, you use the Search All statement as shown in figure 10-13. Before you can use this statement, though, you must identify the *key field* that the table is in sequence by. To do that, you include the Key clause in the table definition. In the example in this figure, for instance, the Key clause indicates that the price table is in ascending sequence by the item-number field.

The syntax of the Search All statement is similar to the Search statement. The main difference is that you can code only one When clause on the Search All statement, and that clause can test only for equal conditions. So, for example, you can't use this statement to test for a less-than-or-equal-to condition.

The example in this figure shows how you can use a binary search to search the price table. If you compare this statement with the first Search statement in figure 10-12, you'll see that they're identical except for the word ALL. Notice, however, that you don't have to set the starting value of the index for a binary search. That's because the search automatically starts in the middle of the table regardless of the index value. Also notice that the When clause tests the item-number field in the table, which must be the field that's specified on the Key clause for the table.

The syntax of a table definition for a binary search

```
level-number data-name-1 OCCURS integer TIMES
                         ┌ ASCENDING  ┐
                         │            │ KEY IS data-name-2
                         └ DESCENDING ┘
                         INDEXED BY {index-name-1} ...
```

The syntax of the Search statement for a binary search

```
SEARCH ALL identifier
    [AT END imperative-statement-1]
    WHEN equal-condition-1 [AND equal-condition-2] ...
        ┌ imperative-statement-2 ┐
        └ NEXT SENTENCE          ┘
[END-SEARCH]
```

Code for performing a binary search

```
01  PRICE-TABLE.
    05  PRICE-GROUP          OCCURS 16 TIMES
                             ASCENDING KEY IS ITEM-NUMBER
                             INDEXED BY PRICE-TABLE-INDEX.
        10  ITEM-NUMBER      PIC 9(3).
        10  ITEM-PRICE       PIC S99V99.
    .
    .
    .
SEARCH ALL PRICE-GROUP
    AT END
        MOVE "N" TO ITEM-FOUND-SWITCH
    WHEN ITEM-NUMBER (PRICE-TABLE-INDEX) = TR-ITEM-NO
        MOVE "Y" TO ITEM-FOUND-SWITCH.
```

Description

- When you use a *binary search*, an entry near the middle of the table is compared with the desired entry. Based on this comparison, the search continues in the first or second half of the table. Then, an entry near the middle of that half of the table is compared with the desired value. This continues until the entry is found or the entire table is searched.

- To perform a binary search, you use the Search All statement. The When clause of this statement specifies the condition that satisfies the search. When this condition is satisfied, the search ends.

- The condition that's specified in the When clause can consist of a condition name that's defined as a key field for the table or an equal condition between a key field and an identifier, a literal, or an arithmetic expression.

- If none of the entries in the table satisfy the search condition, the At End clause is executed.

- To use a binary search, the table entries must be in sequence by the field that will be used for the search, called the *key field*. The key field is identified by the Key clause for the table entry. The key field should be unique and can be in either ascending or descending sequence.

Figure 10-13   How to perform a binary search

How to search a two-level table using indexes

As you saw in the examples in the previous figures, the Search and Search All statements can search only one level of a table at a time. To search a multi-level table, then, you need to code one Search statement for each level. Figure 10-14 illustrates the easiest way to do that.

The code in this figure searches the two-level rate table. Here, procedure 350 performs procedure 360 to search the age group. This procedure starts by setting the age index to 1 so the search will start with the first entry in the table. Then, the Search statement that follows searches for an entry with the appropriate high-age value. If that entry is found, the When clause turns on the age-group-found switch. Otherwise, the At End clause turns off this switch.

If the age group is found, procedure 350 continues by performing procedure 370 to search the class group. Procedure 370 sets the class index to one, then executes a Search statement to search for a matching class within the current age group. If the class is found, module 350 moves the insurance-rate field for that class to a field in working storage.

Although it's not illustrated here, you should know that you can also use the Search All statement with multi-level tables. To do that, you use code similar to the code in this figure. Just be sure to include a Key clause on each level of the table to indicate the key field that will be used for the search of that level. Remember, though, that the When clause of a Search All statement can contain only an equals condition. So you couldn't replace the Search statement in procedure 360 of this code with a Search All statement.

At this point, if you would like to take another break and apply what you've learned, you can do exercises 10-2 and 10-3 at the end of this chapter. Assuming that you've already done exercise 10-1, these exercises guide you through the use of indexes and a binary search.

Code for searching a two-level table using indexes

```
WORKING-STORAGE SECTION.
       .
       .
 01   WORK-FIELDS.
      05   POLICY-RATE        PIC S99V99.
*
 01   RATE-TABLE.
      05   AGE-GROUP                OCCURS 6 TIMES
                                    INDEXED BY AGE-INDEX.
           10   HIGH-AGE            PIC 99.
           10   CLASS-GROUP         OCCURS 4 TIMES
                                    INDEXED BY CLASS-INDEX.
                15   CLASS-NUMBER   PIC 99.
                15   INSURANCE-RATE PIC S99V99.
*
 01   APPLICANT-RECORD.
      05   AR-AGE        PIC 99.
      05   AR-CLASS      PIC 99.
           .
           .
 PROCEDURE DIVISION.
       .
       .
 350-SEARCH-RATE-TABLE.
*
     PERFORM 360-SEARCH-AGE-GROUP.
     IF AGE-GROUP-FOUND
         PERFORM 370-SEARCH-CLASS-GROUP
         IF CLASS-FOUND
             MOVE INSURANCE-RATE (AGE-INDEX CLASS-INDEX)
                 TO POLICY-RATE.
*
 360-SEARCH-AGE-GROUP.
*
     SET AGE-INDEX TO 1.
     SEARCH AGE-GROUP
         AT END
             MOVE "N" TO AGE-GROUP-FOUND-SWITCH
         WHEN AR-AGE <= HIGH-AGE (AGE-INDEX)
             MOVE "Y" TO AGE-GROUP-FOUND-SWITCH.
*
 370-SEARCH-CLASS-GROUP.
*
     SET CLASS-INDEX TO 1.
     SEARCH CLASS-GROUP
         AT END
             MOVE "N" TO CLASS-FOUND-SWITCH
         WHEN CLASS-NUMBER (AGE-INDEX CLASS-INDEX) = AR-CLASS
             MOVE "Y" TO CLASS-FOUND-SWITCH.
           .
           .
```

Figure 10-14   How to search a two-level table using indexes

How to work with variable-length tables

All of the examples you've seen so far in this chapter work with tables that contain a fixed number of occurrences. If you don't know how many entries a table will hold, however, it usually makes sense to define it as a variable-length table so it can hold a variable number of entries. As you'll see in the following topics, variable-length tables are easy to use and can improve the efficiency of your programs.

How to define a variable-length table

Figure 10-15 shows you how to define a variable-length table. To start, you code the Occurs clause for the table so it indicates the minimum and maximum number of entries that it can contain. Then, you include the Depending On clause to name the field that will indicate the exact number of entries.

The table definition in this figure illustrates how this works. This definition is for the price table that you've seen throughout this chapter. In this case, the Occurs clause indicates that the table can hold anywhere from 1 to 100 entries. In addition, the Depending On clause indicates that the exact number of entries will be stored in a field named PT-ENTRY-COUNT. This field is defined in working storage as an integer that's large enough to hold a value up to 100. Note, however, that the value of this field isn't set automatically. As you'll see in a moment, you have to set this field to the appropriate value when you load the table.

Since indexes are more efficient than subscripts, all of the examples of variable-length tables in this chapter use indexes, including the one in this figure. If necessary, though, you shouldn't have any trouble applying what you learn here to variable-length tables that use subscripts.

The syntax of a table definition for a variable-length table

```
level-number data-name-1 OCCURS integer-1 TO integer-2 TIMES
                    DEPENDING ON data-name-2
          [[ ASCENDING  ]]
          [[ DESCENDING }] KEY IS data-name-3
          [ INDEXED BY {index-name-1}...]
```

A table definition for a variable-length table

```
01  PRICE-TABLE.
    05   PRICE-GROUP        OCCURS 1 TO 100 TIMES
                            DEPENDING ON PT-ENTRY-COUNT
                            ASCENDING KEY IS ITEM-NUMBER
                            INDEXED BY PRICE-TABLE-INDEX.
        10   ITEM-NUMBER    PIC 9(3).
        10   ITEM-PRICE     PIC S99V99.
```

The definition of the Depending On field

```
    05   PT-ENTRY-COUNT     PIC S9(3).
```

Description

- The Occurs clause for a variable-length table indicates the minimum and maximum number of times the group or field occurs in working storage. The minimum value is usually 1, but it can be any number from zero to the maximum value.

- The Depending On clause names a field that contains the actual number of occurrences. This field must be defined as an integer in working storage.

- Before you can refer to an entry in a variable-length table, the Depending On field must be set to a value that falls within the range specified by the Occurs clause.

- Although you can use either an index or a subscript with a variable-length table, indexes work better. That way, you can use the Search statements to search the table. When you use these statements with a variable-length table, only the number of entries specified by the Depending On clause are searched.

Figure 10-15   How to define a variable-length table

How to load a variable-length table

Figure 10-16 presents code for loading the variable-length price table. If you compare this with the code in figure 10-10 for loading the fixed-length price table, you'll notice only a few differences. The biggest difference is that after the table is loaded, a Set statement is used to decrease the value of the index for the table by one so it points to the last entry in the table. Then, another Set statement sets the value of the field named in the Depending On clause for the table to the value of that index. This converts the displacement value of the index to an integer value. As a result, the Depending On field indicates the occurrence number of the last entry in the table.

Earlier in this chapter, you learned that if you define a table with a fixed number of entries, you may want to initialize the table before you load it in case values aren't loaded into all of the entries. By doing that, you can avoid problems processing the table later on. When you define a variable-length table, though, you don't need to do that. That's because once you set the Depending On field, you can only refer to the number of entries indicated by that field. So if the Depending On field indicates that the table contains 59 entries, you can't refer to entry 60.

How to search a variable-length table

To search a variable-length table, you use the Search and Search All statements just as you do for fixed-length tables. In fact, you code these statements just as you would for fixed-length tables. The difference is that when you search a variable-length table, only the number of entries indicated by the Depending On clause are searched. In other words, the search is automatically limited to the occurrences that contain entries. Depending on the size of the table and the number of entries that it contains, this can dramatically improve the efficiency of a search operation.

Code for loading a variable-length table

```
WORKING-STORAGE SECTION.
    .
    .
    .
01  SWITCHES.
    05  PTABLE-EOF-SWITCH    PIC X    VALUE "N".
        88  PTABLE-EOF                VALUE "Y".
    .
    .
    .
01  COUNT-FIELDS.
    05  PT-ENTRY-COUNT       PIC S9(3).
*
01  PRICE-TABLE.
    05  PRICE-GROUP                 OCCURS 1 TO 100 TIMES
                                    DEPENDING ON PT-ENTRY-COUNT
                                    ASCENDING KEY IS ITEM-NUMBER
                                    INDEXED BY PRICE-TABLE-INDEX.
        10  ITEM-NUMBER     PIC 9(3).
        10  ITEM-PRICE      PIC S99V99.
*
01  PRICE-TABLE-RECORD.
    05  PT-ITEM-NUMBER      PIC 9(3).
    05  PT-ITEM-PRICE       PIC S99V99.
    .
    .
    .
PROCEDURE DIVISION.
    .
    .
    .
100-LOAD-PRICE-TABLE.
*
    PERFORM
        WITH TEST AFTER
        VARYING PRICE-TABLE-INDEX FROM 1 BY 1
        UNTIL PTABLE-EOF
            OR PRICE-TABLE-INDEX = 100
            PERFORM 110-READ-PRICE-TABLE-RECORD
            IF NOT PTABLE-EOF
                MOVE PT-ITEM-NUMBER
                    TO ITEM-NUMBER (PRICE-TABLE-INDEX)
                MOVE PT-ITEM-PRICE
                    TO ITEM-PRICE (PRICE-TABLE-INDEX)
            ELSE
                SET PRICE-TABLE-INDEX DOWN BY 1
                SET PT-ENTRY-COUNT TO PRICE-TABLE-INDEX.
*
110-READ-PRICE-TABLE-RECORD.
*
    READ PTABLE RECORD INTO PRICE-TABLE-RECORD
        AT END
            MOVE "Y" TO PTABLE-EOF-SWITCH.
    .
    .
```

Figure 10-16   How to load a variable-length table

Another technique for working with variable-length tables

Figure 10-17 illustrates another technique you can use to work with variable-length tables. Here, the table is defined with the maximum number of entries it contains. Then, when the table is loaded, the actual number of entries is stored in a count field that's defined in working storage. Notice that this field, PT-ENTRY-COUNT, is defined as an index data item. Because this field will be set to the value of the index for the table, this is the most efficient way to define it.

When you search a variable-length table that's not defined with the Occurs Depending On clause, you need to include an additional When clause that tests for the last entry in the table. This is illustrated in the second example in this figure. Here, the first When clause tests for an index value that's greater than the count field for the table. If this condition is true, it means that there are no more entries in the table and the Search statement ends.

One of the drawbacks to using this technique is that you have to include an additional When clause in the Search statement to limit the search. In contrast, if you use Occurs Depending On to define the table as variable-length, the search is automatically limited to the number of entries in the table.

Another drawback to this technique is that if you use the Search All statement to search the table, it will search all of the occurrences regardless of the actual number of entries. Because of that, you'll want to be sure to define any variable-length table that will be searched using the Search All statement with Occurs Depending On. Then, the search will be more efficient because only the occurrences that contain entries will be searched.

Of course, if you use subscripts with a table, you can't use the Search or the Search All statement. In that case, you need to include code that tests for the end of the table during a search, whether or not the table is defined with Occurs Depending On.

Code for loading a variable-length table

```
WORKING-STORAGE SECTION.
    .
01   COUNT-FIELDS.
     05   PT-ENTRY-COUNT        INDEX.
*
01   PRICE-TABLE.
     05   PRICE-GROUP           OCCURS 100 TIMES
                                INDEXED BY PRICE-TABLE-INDEX.
          10   ITEM-NUMBER      PIC 9(3).
          10   ITEM-PRICE       PIC S99V99.
*
01   PRICE-TABLE-RECORD.
     05   PT-ITEM-NUMBER        PIC 9(3).
     05   PT-ITEM-PRICE         PIC S99V99.
     .
PROCEDURE DIVISION.
    .
100-LOAD-PRICE-TABLE.
*
    PERFORM
        WITH TEST AFTER
        VARYING PRICE-TABLE-INDEX FROM 1 BY 1
        UNTIL PTABLE-EOF
          OR PRICE-TABLE-INDEX = 100
            PERFORM 110-READ-PRICE-TABLE-RECORD
            IF NOT PTABLE-EOF
                MOVE PT-ITEM-NUMBER
                    TO ITEM-NUMBER (PRICE-TABLE-INDEX)
                MOVE PT-ITEM-PRICE
                    TO ITEM-PRICE (PRICE-TABLE-INDEX)
            ELSE
                SET PRICE-TABLE-INDEX DOWN BY 1
                SET PT-ENTRY-COUNT TO PRICE-TABLE-INDEX.
*
110-READ-PRICE-TABLE-RECORD.
*
    READ PTABLE RECORD INTO PRICE-TABLE-RECORD
        AT END
            MOVE "Y" TO PTABLE-EOF-SWITCH.
```

A Search statement for the variable-length table

```
SET PRICE-TABLE-INDEX TO 1.
SEARCH PRICE-GROUP
    AT END
        MOVE "N" TO PRICE-FOUND-SWITCH
    WHEN PRICE-TABLE-INDEX > PT-ENTRY-COUNT
        MOVE "N" TO PRICE-FOUND-SWITCH
    WHEN ITEM-NUMBER (PRICE-TABLE-INDEX) = TR-ITEM-NO
        MOVE ITEM-PRICE (PRICE-TABLE-INDEX) TO UNIT-PRICE
        MOVE "Y" TO PRICE-FOUND-SWITCH.
```

Figure 10-17   Another technique for working with variable-length tables

Other features for working with tables

The features this chapter has presented so far are the ones you'll use most often for working with tables. But COBOL provides additional features for working with tables that you may want to use from time to time. You'll learn about these features in the remaining topics.

How to use the Perform Varying statement to vary more than one index or subscript

Typically, you'll search a multi-level table for a particular entry as shown earlier in this chapter. However, there are occasions when you need to manipulate all of the values in a table. In that case, you can use an expanded form of the Perform Varying statement that lets you vary two or more indexes or subscripts. The syntax of this statement is presented in figure 10-18.

To use this statement, you identify the first index or subscript to be varied on the Varying clause. Then, you identify the other indexes or subscripts to be varied on the After clauses that follow. Usually, the indexes or subscripts are specified in sequence from the highest to the lowest level for the table, but you can specify them in whatever sequence is appropriate for the situation.

To illustrate how to use this statement, this figure presents code you could use to add together all the rates in the two-level rate table. Here, the Perform statement varies the age index from one to six and the class index from one to four. As a result, it's executed 24 times: once for each of the four classes in each of the six age groups. Note that although this example uses the rate table with indexes, you can accomplish the same thing using subscripts.

Of course, you could also get the same result by using nested Perform Varying statements like the ones used to load the rate table in figure 10-7. In general, though, the use of the Perform Varying statement with one or more After clauses leads to code that is easier to follow. As a result, there's no reason to use nested Perform Varying statements when you can accomplish the same thing with a single statement.

The expanded syntax of the Perform statement

```
PERFORM [procedure-name]

    ⎡            ⎧ BEFORE ⎫⎤
    ⎢WITH TEST   ⎨        ⎬⎥
    ⎣            ⎩ AFTER  ⎭⎦

              ⎧ identifier-1 ⎫        ⎧ identifier-2  ⎫
    VARYING   ⎨              ⎬  FROM  ⎨ index-name-2  ⎬
              ⎩ index-name-1 ⎭        ⎩ integer-1     ⎭

            ⎧ identifier-3 ⎫
       BY   ⎨              ⎬  UNTIL  condition-1
            ⎩ integer-2    ⎭

    ⎡                                          ⎧ identifier-5 ⎫⎤
    ⎢AFTER {index-name-3} FROM                 ⎨ index-name-4 ⎬⎥ ...
    ⎢                                          ⎩ integer-3    ⎭⎥
    ⎢        ⎧ identifier-6 ⎫                                  ⎥
    ⎢   BY   ⎨              ⎬  UNTIL  condition-2              ⎥
    ⎣        ⎩ integer-4    ⎭                                  ⎦
            [statement-1]...
[END-PERFORM]
```

Code that uses a two-level Perform statement

```
WORKING-STORAGE SECTION.
    .
01  WORK-FIELDS.
    05  RATE-TOTAL          PIC S9(3)V99.
    .
01  RATE-TABLE.
    05  AGE-GROUP               OCCURS 6 TIMES
                                INDEXED BY AGE-INDEX.
        10  HIGH-AGE            PIC 99.
        10  CLASS-GROUP         OCCURS 4 TIMES
                                INDEXED BY CLASS-INDEX.
            15  CLASS-NUMBER    PIC 99.
            15  INSURANCE-RATE  PIC S99V99.
    .
PROCEDURE DIVISION.
    .
    PERFORM
        WITH TEST AFTER
        VARYING AGE-INDEX FROM 1 BY 1
        UNTIL AGE-INDEX = 6
            AFTER CLASS-INDEX FROM 1 BY 1
            UNTIL CLASS-INDEX = 4
                ADD INSURANCE-RATE (AGE-INDEX CLASS-INDEX)
                    TO RATE-TOTAL.
    .
    .
```

Description

- You can use the After clause of the Perform Varying statement to vary up to six indexes or subscripts in addition to the index or subscript varied by the Varying clause.

- In most cases, you'll specify the indexes or subscripts in sequence from the highest to the lowest level for the table.

Figure 10-18   How to use the Perform Varying statement to vary more than one index or subscript

How to use intrinsic functions with tables

In chapter 7, you learned about the intrinsic functions that are available with the COBOL-85 compilers. You also learned that if a function requires a series of arguments, the values of those arguments can be stored in a table. Figure 10-19 lists the functions you can use with tables and illustrates how you use them.

Both of the examples in this figure use the rate table you've seen throughout this chapter. The first example uses the Mean function to calculate the mean of all of the rates in the table. To do that, it uses the keyword ALL for both the age index and the class index. In contrast, the second example calculates the mean of all the rates in the first age group. In this case, the age index is specified with a literal value of 1.

Of course, you can also use an index name or a relative index to refer to a table entry. And you can use subscripts instead of indexes. If you understand the examples presented here, though, you should be able to figure out how to use tables with any of these functions.

Functions you can use with tables

Function name	Arguments	Result
MEAN	Numeric series	The mean of the arguments.
MEDIAN	Numeric series	The median of the arguments.
STANDARD-DEVIATION	Numeric series	The standard deviation of the arguments.
VARIANCE	Numeric series	The variance of the arguments.
RANGE	Numeric series	The value of the maximum argument minus the value of the minimum argument.
MIDRANGE	Numeric series	The mean of the maximum and minimum arguments.
MAX	Alphanumeric series	The value of the largest argument.
MIN	Alphanumeric series	The value of the smallest argument.
ORD-MAX	Alphanumeric or numeric series	The ordinal position of the largest argument.
ORD-MIN	Alphanumeric or numeric series	The ordinal position of the smallest argument.
SUM	Numeric series	The sum of the arguments.
PRESENT-VALUE	(1) Interest rate as a decimal fraction; (2) Numeric series of future payments	The present value of a series of future payments (argument-2) discounted at the interest rate of argument-1.

Examples

The table definition

```
01   RATE-TABLE.
     05   AGE-GROUP                OCCURS 6 TIMES
                                   INDEXED BY AGE-INDEX.
          10   HIGH-AGE            PIC 99.
          10   CLASS-GROUP         OCCURS 4 TIMES
                                   INDEXED-BY CLASS-INDEX.
               15   CLASS-NUMBER   PIC 99.
               15   INSURANCE-RATE PIC S99V99.
```

A function that calculates the mean of all the insurance rates

```
FUNCTION MEAN (INSURANCE-RATE (ALL ALL))
```

A function that calculates the mean of all the insurance rates in the first age group

```
FUNCTION MEAN (INSURANCE-RATE (1 ALL))
```

Description

- You can use a table with any intrinsic function that allows a series of values.
- To refer to all the entries in the table, use the keyword ALL. To refer to a specific entry, use an occurrence number for that entry or an index or subscript name.

Figure 10-19   How to use intrinsic functions with tables

How to sort a table

As they're currently written, the COBOL-2000 standards provide for a Sort statement that you can use to sort the entries in a table. Although this statement isn't included in the COBOL-85 standards, it has been implemented by the Micro Focus COBOL compiler. Figure 10-20 presents the syntax of this statement.

In its simplest form, the Sort statement can be coded with just the name of the table to be sorted. This is illustrated by the first example in this figure. In this case, the rate table is sorted by the high-age field in ascending sequence as specified by the key clause in the table definition. This is particularly useful for sorting a table that will be searched by using the Search All statement.

If the sort sequence isn't specified in the table definition, it can be specified on the Sort statement as illustrated by the second example in this figure. This Sort statement sorts the rate table by the high-age field in ascending sequence just as the first Sort statement does. Note that if a sort sequence is specified in the table definition as well as on the Sort statement, the sequence on the Sort statement takes precedence.

If a table contains two or more entries with the same key field value, you can include the With Duplicates clause on the Sort statement to keep the entries in their original order. Because that requires additional overhead, though, you should code this clause only if the order is important. If you omit this clause, the order of the duplicate entries will be unpredictable.

In chapter 6, you learned about the two most common *collating sequences*: EBCDIC and ASCII. In general, EBCDIC is used on all IBM mainframes, and ASCII is used on all other systems. When you sort a table, the exact sequence of the sorted entries depends on that collating sequence.

In most cases, you'll use the default collating sequence for your computer. If you want to use a collating sequence other than the default, you can code the Collating Sequence clause on the Sort statement. This clause refers to a name that's defined in the Special-Names paragraph of the program that identifies the collating sequence. Since you're not likely to change the collating sequence, though, you won't learn how to do that in this book.

The syntax of the Sort statement for sorting tables

$$\underline{\text{SORT}} \text{ data-name-1} \left[\text{ON} \left\{ \begin{array}{l} \underline{\text{ASCENDING}} \\ \underline{\text{DESCENDING}} \end{array} \right\} \text{KEY} \left[\text{data-name-2} \right] \dots \right] \dots$$

$$\left[\text{WITH } \underline{\text{DUPLICATES}} \text{ IN ORDER} \right]$$
$$\left[\text{COLLATING } \underline{\text{SEQUENCE}} \text{ IS alphabet-name} \right]$$

Code for sorting a table by its key field

The table definition

```
01   RATE-TABLE.
     05   AGE-GROUP              OCCURS 6 TIMES
                                 ASCENDING KEY IS HIGH-AGE
                                 INDEXED BY AGE-INDEX.
          10   HIGH-AGE          PIC 99.
          10   CLASS-GROUP       OCCURS 4 TIMES
                                 INDEXED BY CLASS-INDEX.
               15   CLASS-NUMBER     PIC 99.
               15   INSURANCE-RATE   PIC S99V99.
```

The Sort statement

```
SORT AGE-GROUP.
```

Code for sorting a table that's not defined with a key field

The table definition

```
01   RATE-TABLE.
     05   AGE-GROUP              OCCURS 6 TIMES
                                 INDEXED BY AGE-INDEX.
          10   HIGH-AGE          PIC 99.
          10   CLASS-GROUP       OCCURS 4 TIMES
                                 INDEXED-BY CLASS-INDEX.
               15   CLASS-NUMBER     PIC 99.
               15   INSURANCE-RATE   PIC S99V99.
```

The Sort statement

```
SORT AGE-GROUP
     ON ASCENDING KEY HIGH-AGE.
```

Description

- This format of the Sort statement is included in the COBOL-2000 standards and the current versions of Micro Focus COBOL.

- The Sort statement sorts a table based on the key fields defined in the table or the key fields specified on the Sort statement. The key fields specified on the Sort statement override key fields defined in the table.

- If the With Duplicates clause is coded, entries with duplicate keys are sorted in the same order as they initially appear in the table. If this clause is omitted, the order of entries with duplicate keys is unpredictable.

- The Collating Sequence clause lets you change the *collating sequence* for the sort by referring to a name defined in the Special-Names paragraph of the Configuration Section.

Figure 10-20   How to sort a table

Perspective

Since tables are commonly used in business programs, all COBOL programmers need to be adept at using them. Although you can use either subscripts or indexes to work with tables, the use of indexes generally leads to more efficient processing and code that's easier to understand. When you use indexes, you can also perform binary searches when the table entries are sorted by the key field. This can dramatically improve searching efficiency in a large table. For these reasons, you should use indexes for all but the simplest tables.

Summary

- When you work with a table, you can use either *indexes* or *subscripts*. An index represents a *displacement value*, and a subscript represents an *occurrence number* that must be converted to a displacement value. That's why using indexes is more efficient than using subscripts.

- A *one-level table* contains data that depends on a single variable factor. A *multi-level table* contains data that depends on two or more variable factors. A table can be defined with constant values or it can be loaded from a file at the beginning of any program that uses it.

- If you use subscripts to work with a table, you can refer to a table entry using the subscript name, an *occurrence number*, or a *relative subscript*. If you use indexes, you can refer to a table entry using the index name, an occurrence number, or a *relative index*.

- To load a table, you use a Perform Varying statement that varies the value of the subscript or index for the table. To search a table, you can use a Perform Varying statement for each level of the table.

- When you define a table with indexes, you can use the Search statement to perform a *sequential search* on the table. If the entries are in sequence by a *key field*, you can also use the Search All statement to perform a *binary search*.

- You use the Set statement to work with indexes or *index data items*. You can use this statement to assign an index value or to increase or decrease an index value.

- If you define a table as variable-length, the actual number of entries in the table must be stored in a working-storage field that's identified in the table definition. When you search a variable-length table using the Search or Search All statement, only the occurrences that contain entries are searched.

- You can use the Perform Varying statement to vary the indexes or subscripts for all the levels of a multi-level table at the same time.

- You can use the values in a table as the arguments for an intrinsic function that requires a series of values.

- With Micro Focus COBOL, you can use the Sort statement to sort the entries in a table. A statement like that will be included in the COBOL-2000 standards.

Terms

one-level table
table entry
subscript
occurrence number
relative subscript
multi-level table
index
displacement value

relative index
index data item
sequential search
serial search
binary search
key field
collating sequence

Objectives

- Given specifications for a program that uses a one-level or a multi-level table, develop the program using either subscripts or indexes. This may require loading a table, searching a table, or processing the entries in a table.

- Explain why using indexes is more efficient than using subscripts.

- List three ways that you can refer to a table entry using subscripts and three ways that you can refer to a table entry using indexes.

- Describe the difference between a sequential and a binary search.

- In general terms, describe the difference between working with a fixed-length table and a variable-length table.

- Explain how you can use the entries in a table with intrinsic functions.

Exercise 10-1 Use a branch table to add branch names to a sales report

In this exercise, you'll enhance the summary report program that you created in chapter 5 by adding branch names to it so it looks something like this:

```
BRCH                      CUST                         SALES        SALES
NUM   BRANCH NAME         NUM   CUSTOMER NAME        THIS YTD     LAST YTD

 12   FORT WAYNE          11111  INFORMATION BUILDERS   1,234.56     1,111.11
                          12345  CAREER TRAINING CTR   12,345.67    22,222.22
                                        BRANCH TOTAL   13,580.23    23,333.33
  .
  .
 47   KANSAS CITY NW      12121  GENERAL SERVICES CO.  11,444.00    11,059.56
                          24680  INFO MANAGEMENT CO.   17,481.45    11,892.47
                          99999  DOLLAR SAVINGS BANK    5,059.00     4,621.95
                          76543  NATL MUSIC CORP.       2,383.46     4,435.26
                                        BRANCH TOTAL   36,367.91    32,009.24


                                         GRAND TOTAL  120,525.72   121,155.45
```

Here, the first two heading lines and the last two columns of the report are deleted so the report will fit on this page, but your report should include them.

The branch names are stored in a file named brchmast.dat that's in sequence by branch number with this format:

```
01   BRANCH-MASTER-RECORD.
     05   BM-BRANCH-NUMBER    PIC 9(2).
     05   BM-BRANCH-NAME      PIC X(18).
```

This program should load the records in this file into a table at the beginning of the program. Then, it should use search logic to get the branch name for a given branch number whenever necessary. If a branch number isn't found, the program should print "NO BRANCH RECORD" in the branch name column.

Enhance the structure chart for the program

1. Enhance the structure chart for the report program that's shown in figure 4-7 so it includes modules for loading and searching the branch table.

Enhance the program

2. Open the program named rpt3000 for edit and change its Program-ID to RPT8000. Then, save the program as rpt8000 and close it.

3. Open the rpt8000 program you just created, and modify it so it loads the records in the branch master file into a branch table at the beginning of the program. The table should be defined so it uses subscripts and holds just the seven records in the branch master file.

4. Modify the remaining code so it prepares the report shown above. To make this manageable, you can do this in two parts. First, modify and test the program so it prints the branch name in each customer line. Then, modify and test the program so it prints the branch name in just the first line of each customer group.

5. When you've got the program working correctly, close it.

Exercise 10-2   Modify the branch table code so it uses indexes and a sequential search

In this exercise, you'll modify the sales report program you created in exercise 10-1 so the branch table uses indexes instead of subscripts and so it uses the Search statement.

1. Open the program named rpt8000 and change the Program-ID to RPT8100. Then, save the program as rpt8100 and close it.

2. Open the rpt8100 program, and modify the definition of the branch table so it includes an index. Next, modify the Procedure Division code so it uses the index instead of subscripts. Then, compile and test the program until it works correctly.

3. Change the code that searches the table so it uses a Search statement instead of a Perform Varying statement. Next, compile and test the program until this works correctly. Then, close the program.

Exercise 10-3   Change the sequential search to a binary search

In this exercise, you'll modify the sales report program you created in exercise 10-2 so it uses the Search All statement to search the branch table.

1. Open the program named rpt8100 and change the Program-ID to RPT8200. Then, save the program as rpt8200 and close it.

2. Open the rpt8200 program, and modify the definition of the branch table to indicate that its entries are in ascending sequence by the branch-number field. Then, modify the Procedure Division code for searching the table so it uses the Search All statement.

3. Compile and test the program. When you're sure it's correct, close the program.

Exercise 10-4   Change the branch table so it's variable-length

In this exercise, you'll modify the sales report program you created in exercise 10-3 so the branch table is defined as a variable-length table.

1. Open the program named rpt8200 and change the Program-ID to RPT8300. Then, save the program as rpt8300 and close it.

2. Open the rpt8300 program, and modify the definition of the branch table so it can hold from 1 to 20 entries. Then, modify the code that loads the table so it saves the actual number of entries in the count field that the table definition refers to.

3. Compile and test the program. When you're sure it's correct, close the program.

Exercise 10-5   Create a program that uses a two-level table

In this exercise, you'll create a program that loads, uses, and prints the two-level rate table that's presented in figure 10-6. Before you start, copy the chapter 10 program into c:\cobol.

Load the table

1. Open the program named tbl1000. To save you time, this program contains the beginning code for your program. This includes most of the data definitions you'll need. You may want to print this code now so you can refer to it as you code the required procedures.

2. Write the code for procedure 100 and its subordinates so it loads the rate table from the rate table file, which contains one record for each age group. Figure 10-7 presents code that you can use as a guide, but note that you need to load both the low age and the high age for each age group. Note too the class group in the record description for this file is not defined with an index, but the age group and the class group in the rate table are defined with indexes. This means you have to use the Set statement to convert the subscript to an index somewhere in your routine.

3. Compile and test the loading routine. To make sure it works, you can add Display statements to the code that display each table record after it has been read and the entire table after it has been loaded. When you're sure that the routine works, remove the Display statements.

Search the table

4. Write the code for procedure 200 and its subordinates so it displays the proper rate after the user enters an age and class number. Note that the code for getting the age and class number from the user is already there. But you need to add the Search statements and logic that get the proper rate. For this coding, you can use the code in figure 10-14 as a guide, but your routine should search for an age that is greater than or equal to the low age and less than or equal to the high age. If the age or class number can't be found in the table, your routine should print an appropriate error message.

5. Compile and test the search routine until you're sure it works correctly.

Print the table

6. Write the code for procedure 300 and its subordinates so it prints just the data (no headings) for the table that you've loaded. To give you a start on this, the data definitions for the print line are already in working storage so the first printed line should look like this:

```
18-34    23.50    27.05    35.25    52.90
```

7. Compile and test the printing routine so you're sure it works correctly.

Close the program

8. When you've got everything working right, close the program. You should now have a solid appreciation for how multi-level tables are used.

11

How to use copy members and subprograms

All professional programmers use copy members and subprograms. Copy members are portions of source code that you can copy into your programs by using the Copy statement. Subprograms are compiled and tested routines that you can call from your programs by using the Call statement.

How to use copy members

The Copy statement lets you copy portions of COBOL code that have been stored as copy members into your program. Since how you do this varies from one platform to another, the first figure in this chapter shows you how this works on a PC with Micro Focus Personal COBOL; the second figure shows you how this works on an IBM mainframe. Then, the third figure gives you some guidelines for using copy members that apply to all platforms and compilers.

How to use the Copy statement with Micro Focus Personal COBOL

When you use Micro Focus Personal COBOL, you can save COBOL source statements (like those for a record description) in a file that has *cpy* as the extension. This type of file can be referred to as a *copy member*. Then, you can use the Copy statement to copy the contents of the copy member into any of your programs. This is summarized in figure 11-1.

If you keep all of your copy members in a special folder, you can think of that folder as a *copy library*, or *source statement library*. However, that isn't necessary. Using a special folder for all copy members is just a way of keeping them organized.

When a program that uses Copy statements is compiled, the source statements in the copy members are copied into the program as shown in this figure. Here, stcpy> in columns 1-6 marks the first statement in each copy member and edcpy> marks the last statement. From that point on, you can see the copied statements in your source program so it's easy to work with them.

The basic syntax of the Copy statement

```
COPY "file-name"
```

A Personal COBOL example

```
COPY "c:\cobol\custmast.cpy".
```

A copy member that's stored in the file named c:\cobol\custmast.cpy

```
 01   CUSTOMER-MASTER-RECORD.
*
     05   CM-BRANCH-NUMBER       PIC 9(2).
     05   CM-SALESREP-NUMBER     PIC 9(2).
     05   CM-CUSTOMER-NUMBER     PIC 9(5).
     05   CM-CUSTOMER-NAME       PIC X(20).
     05   CM-SALES-THIS-YTD      PIC S9(5)V99.
     05   CM-SALES-LAST-YTD      PIC S9(5)V99.
```

How the member looks when it's copied into the source program

```
        copy "c:\cobol\custmast.cpy".
stcpy>  01   CUSTOMER-MASTER-RECORD.
     *
         05   CM-BRANCH-NUMBER       PIC 9(2).
         05   CM-SALESREP-NUMBER     PIC 9(2).
         05   CM-CUSTOMER-NUMBER     PIC 9(5).
         05   CM-CUSTOMER-NAME       PIC X(20).
         05   CM-SALES-THIS-YTD      PIC S9(5)V99.
edcpy>   05   CM-SALES-LAST-YTD      PIC S9(5)V99.
```

How to create a copy member

1. Start a new program and enter the code for the copy member just as you would if you were writing a complete program.

2. Save the program with cpy as the extension.

Description

- A *copy member* contains COBOL source statements that can be copied into a COBOL source program.

- With Micro Focus Personal COBOL, a *copy member* is just a file that has cpy as its extension.

- To keep copy members together on a PC, you can store them in a folder. Then, you can think of that folder as a *copy library*, or *source statement library*.

Figure 11-1   How to use the Copy statement with Micro Focus Personal COBOL

How to use the Copy statement with IBM mainframe COBOL

When you use COBOL on an IBM mainframe, you can save COBOL source statements (like those for a record description) in a member within a partitioned data set. In this case, the partitioned data set can be referred to as a *copy library*, or *source statement library*, and the member can be referred to as a *copy member*, or *copy book*. Then, you can use the Copy statement to copy the contents of the copy member into any of your programs. This is summarized in figure 11-2.

To tell the compiler which library it should use for the copy library, you use JCL to modify the procedure that you use for compiling the program. In this figure, you can see how the DD statement for the COBOL step in a procedure points to a library named MM01.TEST.COPYLIB. For more information about how this works, please refer to chapter 18.

As you edit a source program on a mainframe, only the Copy statements are shown, not the statements that are copied into the program. To see them, you have to compile the program and refer to the compiler listing that is prepared. As this figure shows, the copied statements are preceded by the letter C on the compiler listing. This makes it more difficult to create or edit a program because you have to refer to another document to get the data names that you need.

This inconvenience, though, is more than compensated for by the benefits that you get from using copy members. First, because most copy members contain many lines of COBOL code, using them saves coding time. Second, when all the programmers in a shop use the same copy members, you enforce the use of standard code and reduce the chance for errors. Third, if the statements in a copy member need to be modified, you only need to change the copy member and recompile all the programs that use it. You don't need to change the programs that use it.

The basic syntax of the Copy statement

```
COPY member-name
```

An IBM mainframe COBOL example

```
COPY CUSTMAST.
```

A copy member that's named CUSTMAST

```
01   CUSTOMER-MASTER-RECORD.
*
     05   CM-BRANCH-NUMBER        PIC 9(2).
     05   CM-SALESREP-NUMBER      PIC 9(2).
     05   CM-CUSTOMER-NUMBER      PIC 9(5).
     05   CM-CUSTOMER-NAME        PIC X(20).
     05   CM-SALES-THIS-YTD       PIC S9(5)V99.
     05   CM-SALES-LAST-YTD       PIC S9(5)V99.
```

How to identify the copy library in the JCL that compiles the program

```
//COBOL.SYSLIB  DD DSN=MM01.TEST.COPYLIB,DISP=SHR
```

How the member looks in the compiler listing

```
       COPY CUSTMAST.
C      01   CUSTOMER-MASTER-RECORD.
C      *
C           05   CM-BRANCH-NUMBER        PIC 9(2).
C           05   CM-SALESREP-NUMBER      PIC 9(2).
C           05   CM-CUSTOMER-NUMBER      PIC 9(5).
C           05   CM-CUSTOMER-NAME        PIC X(20).
C           05   CM-SALES-THIS-YTD       PIC S9(5)V99.
C           05   CM-SALES-LAST-YTD       PIC S9(5)V99.
```

How to create a copy member

1. Create a new member and enter the source code for it just as you would if you were writing a complete program.

2. Save the program as a member in a copy library.

Description

- A *copy member* contains COBOL source statements that can be copied into a COBOL source program.

- On a mainframe, a copy member is stored in a partitioned data set called a *copy library*, or *source statement library*.

- To identify the copy library when the program is compiled, you use JCL.

Figure 11-2   How to use the Copy statement with IBM mainframe COBOL

Guidelines for using copy members

Figure 11-3 presents the complete syntax of the Copy statement along with some guidelines for using copy members. In the syntax summary, you can see that you can use an Of or In clause to identify the library that a member is in. Although this works on many platforms, including Micro Focus Personal COBOL on a PC, that's not the way it works on a mainframe since the copy library or libraries are identified by the JCL.

You can also see a Replacing clause in the syntax summary. This clause lets you replace pseudo-text, data names, literals, or reserved words by other pseudo-text, data names, literals, or reserved words. Note, however, that the last guideline in this figure recommends that you avoid using the Replacing clause. Why? Because the Replacing clause lets different programs use different versions of the same copy member, which eliminates one of the benefits that you should get from using copy members.

What should you use copy members for? One use that everyone agrees on is for record descriptions because that clearly delivers the promised benefits. First, since record descriptions are often lengthy, this can save considerable coding time. Second, since the same record descriptions are used in all the programs that use the files, errors won't be introduced into the system by inconsistent descriptions. Third, if a record description has to be changed, which is often necessary, you just have to change one copy member and then recompile each program that uses it...you don't have to change the record description in each program.

You can also use copy members for Select statements in the Environment Division and FD statements in the File section of the Data Division. You can use them for common data descriptions like the current date and time fields that are returned by the Current-Date function. And you can use them for table descriptions that don't change (otherwise, you should keep the table data in files and load the data into tables whenever it's needed).

Some companies also use copy members for procedures like those for editing date, state, or zip-code fields. In that case, you often need to copy two members for each procedure: one for the data descriptions, and one for the Procedure Division statements. We don't recommend this use, though, because we think you can do that more efficiently by using subprograms.

If you look at the guidelines in this figure, you can see that all copy members need to be documented so the programmers in a shop know what's available to them. Then, as a programmer who's starting a new program, you need to check the documentation to find out what copy members are available to you. A common weakness in COBOL shops is that the documentation isn't kept up-to-date so the programmers don't know what's available.

Please remember that using copy members is just one way to copy source statements into your programs. The other way is to copy and paste portions of code from one program to another. Then, you can modify that code to suit the requirements of your programs. One of the keys to improved productivity is to avoid coding routines from scratch.

The complete syntax of the Copy statement

```
COPY member-name [{OF | IN} library-name]
    ⎡         ⎧⎡ ==pseudo-text-1== ⎤    ⎡ ==pseudo-text-2== ⎤⎫      ⎤
    ⎢         ⎪⎢ identifier-1      ⎥    ⎢ identifier-2      ⎥⎪      ⎥
    ⎢ REPLACING ⎨⎢ literal-1       ⎥ BY ⎢ literal-2         ⎥⎬ ...  ⎥
    ⎣         ⎩⎣ word-1            ⎦    ⎣ word-2            ⎦⎭      ⎦
```

A Copy statement that copies the source statements from the CUSTMAST member in the library named COPYLIB

```
COPY CUSTMAST IN COPYLIB.
```

A copy member that replaces all occurrences of the prefix CM with the prefix CMR and all 05 levels with 10s

```
COPY CUSTMAST
    REPLACING ==CM-== BY ==CMR-==
              ==05==  BY ==10==.
```

Description

- On some platforms, you can use the In or Of clause to identify the library that the copy member is in.

- You can use the Replacing clause to find and replace text within a copy member as it is copied into your program. If a pseudo-text entry that's going to be replaced contains more than one word, two or more spaces in the copy member are treated as a single space.

Typical copy members

- Record descriptions in the File Section or Working-Storage Section of the Data Division

- Data in the Working-Storage Section like the descriptions for the current time and date fields that are returned by the Current-Date function

- Table descriptions for tables that don't change like a state or zip-code table

- Processing routines that are used by more than one program like common calculating, printing, and editing routines

Recommended guidelines for using copy members

- Document all copy members so it's easy for programmers to find what they're looking for. For each member, the documentation should include the name and a description of the contents. It may also include a listing of the copy member.

- Before you start a new program, find out whether any copy members are available that will help you develop the program more efficiently.

- Avoid using the Replacing clause.

Figure 11-3   Guidelines for using copy members

How to use subprograms

A processing routine like one that edits a date or a zip code can be used by more than one program. In that case, you can create a subprogram for the routine. Then, any programs that need that routine can call the subprogram.

How to call a subprogram

Unlike a copy member, which contains source code that hasn't been compiled, a *subprogram* is source code that has been compiled into object code, or machine language. Then, to *call* this subprogram from one of your programs (the *calling program*), you code a Call statement as shown in figure 11-4.

In the Using clause of this statement, you list the fields that must be *passed* to the subprogram. In the examples, you can see that four fields are passed to the subprogram named CALCFV. You can refer to these as the *parameters*, or *arguments*, of the subprogram. This is analogous to coding the arguments for one of the intrinsic functions.

When you use a subprogram, you must make sure that the fields are passed to the subprogram in the sequence that the subprogram requires. You must also make sure that the passed fields are defined with the Pictures and Usages that the subprogram requires. To find out what these requirements are, you can refer to the documentation for the subprogram or to the code for the subprogram. Often, though, the code for the subprogram isn't available or the subprogram is written in another language like C or assembler language so you have to depend on the documentation for the subprogram.

When you're using COBOL on an IBM mainframe, the *object module* for the calling program and the object module for the subprogram need to be *link edited* into a *load module* before they can be executed. To make that work right, you need to identify the *subprogram library*, or *object library*, that the subprogram is stored in. To do that, you code a JCL statement like the one in this figure. This statement specifies that the library that's used for the link editing step in the procedure is MM01.TEST.OBJLIB. For more information about how this works, please refer to chapter 18.

In contrast, when you code the Call statement for Micro Focus Personal COBOL, you can code the path and file name for the compiled subprogram. With this compiler, the calling program and the subprogram don't have to be link edited before they can be run. Instead, you just compile the calling program and run it. Then, when a Call statement is executed, control passes from the calling program to the first statement in the subprogram, And when the subprogram is finished, control passes back to the first statement after the Call statement.

The basic syntax of the Call statement

```
CALL "subprogram-name" [USING identifier-1 ...]
```

A Personal COBOL example

```
call "c:\cobol\calcfv" using investment-amount      number-of-years
                              yearly-interest-rate  future-value.
```

An IBM mainframe COBOL example

```
CALL "CALCFV" USING INVESTMENT-AMOUNT      NUMBER-OF-YEARS
                    YEARLY-INTEREST-RATE   FUTURE-VALUE.
```

The data definitions for the fields passed by the calling program

```
01  USER-ENTRIES.
    05   INVESTMENT-AMOUNT        PIC 99999.
    05   NUMBER-OF-YEARS          PIC 99.
    05   YEARLY-INTEREST-RATE     PIC 99V9.
01  WORK-FIELDS.
    05   FUTURE-VALUE             PIC 9(7)V99.
```

How to identify the subprogram library in the JCL that compiles the program

```
//LKED.SYSLIB  DD
//             DD DSN=MM01.TEST.OBJLIB,DISP=SHR
```

Description

- A *subprogram* is a program that is *called* by a *calling program*. Before a subprogram can be called by another program, it must be compiled and ready for execution.

- The Using clause identifies the fields in the calling program that are *passed* to the subprogram. These can be referred to as *parameters* or *arguments*.

- The Using clause must list the passed fields in the sequence that the subprogram requires. These fields must be elementary items with Pictures and Usages that are equivalent to those used by the subprogram. However, the passed fields don't have to have the same names as those used in the subprogram.

- In a Call statement for Personal COBOL, you code the path and name of the subprogram file.

- In a Call statement for IBM mainframe COBOL, you code just the name of the subprogram, or *object module*. Later, when you compile and run the program, you use JCL to identify the *object library* that the subprogram is stored in. Then, the linkage editor *link edits* the calling program and the subprogram into a *load module* that can be run by the system. For more information about this process, please refer to chapter 18.

- A subprogram is often written by another programmer, and it may be written in another language.

Figure 11-4   How to call a subprogram

How to write a subprogram

Figure 11-5 shows how to write a subprogram. In brief, you need to code a Linkage Section that defines all of the fields that are passed to the subprogram. You need to code a Using clause on the Procedure Division header that lists the fields that are passed to the subprogram. And you need to end the subprogram with an Exit Program statement instead of a Stop Run statement.

When you look at the code in a subprogram, you can quickly see what the calling program has to do to use the subprogram. In brief, the Using clause in the Call statement in the calling program must list the passed fields in the same sequence as the Using clause in the Procedure Division statement of the subprogram. In addition, the passed fields must be defined with the same Pictures and Usages that are coded in the subprogram. Note, however, that the names of the fields in the calling program and the names in the subprogram don't have to be the same. In fact, the calling program and subprogram are linked after they have been converted to object modules so the names aren't even known when they're linked.

In this example, the calling program passes four fields to the subprogram. The first three fields are user entries, while the fourth field is used for the result of the calculation. In other words, the fourth field receives the data that is passed back to the calling program.

When you code a Call statement as shown in figure 11-4, the fields that are passed by the calling program and the fields that are received by the subprogram are actually the same fields in storage. As a result, any change that a subprogram makes to one of the fields is automatically made in the calling program too. To make this work on a mainframe, the linkage editor adjusts the storage addresses of the fields described in the Linkage Section of the subprogram so they're the same as the addresses of the passed fields in the calling program.

The syntax that you need for creating a subprogram

```
LINKAGE SECTION.

(Data definitions for fields that are passed by the calling program.)

PROCEDURE DIVISION USING identifier-1 ...
      .
      .
      EXIT PROGRAM.
```

The CALCFV subprogram that's called by the statement in figure 11-4

```
WORKING-STORAGE SECTION.
01  WORK-FIELDS.
    05  YEAR-COUNTER          PIC 999.

LINKAGE SECTION.
77  LS-INVESTMENT-AMOUNT      PIC 99999.
77  LS-NUMBER-OF-YEARS        PIC 99.
77  LS-YEARLY-INTEREST-RATE   PIC 99V9.
77  LS-FUTURE-VALUE           PIC 9(7)V99.

PROCEDURE DIVISION USING LS-INVESTMENT-AMOUNT      LS-NUMBER-OF-YEARS
                         LS-YEARLY-INTEREST-RATE   LS-FUTURE-VALUE.

000-CALCULATE-FUTURE-VALUE.
    MOVE LS-INVESTMENT-AMOUNT TO LS-FUTURE-VALUE.
    MOVE 1 TO YEAR-COUNTER.
    PERFORM
        UNTIL YEAR-COUNTER > LS-NUMBER-OF-YEARS
            COMPUTE LS-FUTURE-VALUE ROUNDED =
                LS-FUTURE-VALUE +
                (LS-FUTURE-VALUE * LS-YEARLY-INTEREST-RATE / 100)
            ADD 1 TO YEAR-COUNTER
    END-PERFORM.
    EXIT PROGRAM.
```

Description

- The Linkage Section defines the fields that must be passed to the subprogram from the calling program. As a result, you can't code Value clauses in the Linkage Section, except for 88 levels.

- The Using clause in the Procedure Division header lists the fields that must be passed to the subprogram.

- On some systems, the Program-ID paragraph in the Identification Division needs to give the name of the subprogram.

- The calling program must define the passed fields the same way they're defined in the Linkage Section, and the Call statement must list the passed fields in the same sequence that they're listed in the Using clause in the Procedure Division statement.

Figure 11-5   How to write a subprogram

Another example of a calling program and subprogram

Figure 11-6 presents another example of a subprogram along with the related code in the calling program. This subprogram loads a branch table from a file of branch master records. If you haven't read chapter 10 yet, you won't understand the code for working with the branch table, but you should still get a better idea of how subprograms work and what they can do.

As you can see, only one field is listed in the Using clause of the Call statement. However, this field is a group item that consists of other fields. To make this work, the Using clause in the Procedure Division of the subprogram also lists just one field, and this group item is defined just as it is in the calling program. This is an acceptable way to code the passed fields in the calling program and the subprogram. In this case, all of the data names are the same in both the calling program and the subprogram, but that isn't necessary.

If you study the code in the subprogram, you can see that it opens a file, loads the data from each record in the file into a table, and closes the file. This shows that a subprogram can work with files as well as process data. If necessary, a subprogram can also call another subprogram, which can be referred to as *nesting subprograms*. In some shops, some subprograms consist of hundreds of lines of code that perform complete system functions like printing reports.

Now, look again at the Call statement in the calling program. It consists of just four words. This illustrates the power of subprograms. With just a single statement, a calling program can execute dozens or hundreds of lines of tested COBOL code.

The data definitions and Call statement in the calling program

```
01  BRANCH-TABLE.
    05  BT-ENTRIES                 OCCURS 100 TIMES
                                   INDEXED BY BT-INDEX.
        10  BT-BRANCH-NUMBER       PIC XX.
        10  BT-BRANCH-NAME         PIC X(18).
    05  BT-ENTRY-COUNT             INDEX.
    .
    .
    .
    CALL "LDBRTBL" USING BRANCH-TABLE.
```

A subprogram named LDBRTBL that loads a branch table

```
ENVIRONMENT DIVISION.
INPUT-OUTPUT SECTION.
FILE-CONTROL.
    SELECT BRCHMAST ASSIGN TO BRCHMAST.

DATA DIVISION.
FILE SECTION.
FD  BRCHMAST.
01  BRANCH-MASTER-RECORD.
    05  BM-BRANCH-NUMBER       PIC XX.
    05  BM-BRANCH-NAME         PIC X(18).
    .
    .
LINKAGE SECTION.
01  BRANCH-TABLE.
    05  BT-ENTRIES       OCCURS 100 TIMES
                         INDEXED BY BT-INDEX.
        10  BT-BRANCH-NUMBER     PIC XX.
        10  BT-BRANCH-NAME       PIC X(18).
    05  BT-ENTRY-COUNT           INDEX.

PROCEDURE DIVISION USING BRANCH-TABLE.
000-LOAD-BRANCH-TABLE.
    OPEN INPUT BRCHMAST.
    PERFORM WITH TEST AFTER
        VARYING BT-INDEX FROM 1 BY 1
        UNTIL BRCHMAST-EOF OR BT-INDEX = 100
            PERFORM 100-READ-BRANCH-RECORD
            IF NOT BRCHMAST-EOF
                MOVE BM-BRANCH-NUMBER TO BT-BRANCH-NUMBER (BT-INDEX)
                MOVE BM-BRANCH-NAME   TO BT-BRANCH-NAME (BT-INDEX)
            ELSE
                SET BT-ENTRY-COUNT TO BT-INDEX
            END-IF
    END-PERFORM.
    CLOSE BRCHMAST.
    EXIT PROGRAM.

100-READ-BRANCH-RECORD.
    READ BRCHMAST RECORD
        AT END MOVE "Y" TO BRCHMAST-EOF-SWITCH.
```

Figure 11-6   Another example of a calling program and subprogram

Other language for working with subprograms

Figure 11-7 presents some other language that you can use for working with subprograms. Note, however, that you can use subprograms effectively with just the language that you've learned so far. Nevertheless, you should at least be aware that this other language exists.

When you code the Using clause in a Call statement, you can code By Reference or By Content to specify whether the fields should be passed *by reference* or *by content*. When you omit these words, By Reference is assumed so that's how the fields have been passed in the examples so far. In that case, the passed fields in the calling program are the same as those in the Linkage Section of the subprogram.

In contrast, when you pass a field By Content, a copy of the field is made by the subprogram. Then, when the subprogram changes the data in this field, the field in the calling program isn't changed. If, for example, you want to make sure that the subprogram doesn't change the data in some of the passed fields, you can code them as in this example. You shouldn't need to do that, though, because each subprogram should be written so it only changes the fields that are supposed to receive results.

If you code the On Exception clause with the Call statement, the clause is executed when the subprogram can't be executed. On a mainframe, though, you don't need this because any problems should be resolved when the calling program and subprogram are link edited. How this works on other systems varies from one platform to another, but you probably won't ever need this clause.

If you need to reinitialize the starting values in a subprogram, you can issue the Cancel statement in the calling program. But if the values need to be reinitialized each time the subprogram is executed, the subprogram should make sure that the values are reinitialized. That shouldn't be left to the calling program. As a result, you should only need this statement for special circumstances.

If you're maintaining programs on an IBM mainframe, you should definitely be familiar with the Goback statement because it is widely used on that platform. In a subprogram, this statement has the same effect as the Exit Program statement. In a main program, you will often see this statement used instead of the Stop Run statement. In either case, this statement means that the control of the system should go back to where it came from.

The complete syntax of the Call statement

```
CALL "subprogram-name"  [ USING  { [ BY REFERENCE ] identifier-1 ... }  ... ]
                                 { BY CONTENT identifier-2 ...         }
    [ ON EXCEPTION imperative-statement-1 ]
    [ NOT ON EXCEPTION imperative-statement-2 ]
[ END-CALL ]
```

Example

```
CALL "CALCFV" USING BY CONTENT    INVESTMENT-AMOUNT
                                  NUMBER-OF-YEARS
                                  YEARLY-INTEREST-RATE
                    BY REFERENCE  FUTURE-VALUE.
```

The syntax of the Cancel statement for a calling program

```
CANCEL "subprogram-name" ...
```

Example

```
CANCEL "LDBRTBL".
```

The syntax of the IBM Goback statement for a subprogram

```
GOBACK
```

Description

- When a calling program passes a field to a subprogram *by reference*, the address of the field in the calling program is passed. In this case, both the calling program and the subprogram refer to the same field in storage so any changes to the data in the subprogram also change the data in the calling program. Since this is the default, you don't have to code the words BY REFERENCE to pass fields in this way.

- When a calling program passes a field to a subprogram *by content*, the passed data is stored in a new field in the subprogram. Then, if the subprogram changes the data that's passed, it doesn't affect the data in the calling program. To pass data this way, you code the words BY CONTENT.

- The On Exception clause is executed when the subprogram can't be executed. This is an error condition that shouldn't occur on a mainframe because that type of problem should be resolved when the calling program and subprogram are link edited.

- The Cancel statement can be used to restore all of the variables in a subprogram to their initial state.

- The Goback statement is often used instead of the Exit Program statement in subprograms written for IBM mainframes. It just returns control to the calling program.

Figure 11-7   Other language for working with subprograms

Guidelines for using subprograms

What should you use subprograms for? Any routines that are relatively difficult to write that are likely to be used by several other programs. If, for example, it takes an hour to write a routine that is going to be used by 10 different programs, it probably makes sense to create a subprogram for the routine. And if it takes two hours to write a routine that's going to be used by 20 different programs, it surely makes sense to create a subprogram for the routine. In figure 11-8, you can see a list of some typical types of subprograms.

The alternative to using subprograms is to copy the source code for the routine into each program that requires it. But this clutters up a program with copied data definitions and routines, and that can make testing more difficult.

The trouble with using subprograms is that they can lead to some testing and debugging problems that you won't experience otherwise. If, for example, a subprogram ends abnormally or returns the wrong result, it's hard to tell whether the cause of the problem is in the calling program or the subprogram. If the subprograms have been thoroughly tested, though, the problem is usually in the "interface between the calling program and the subprogram." That means that the calling program didn't send the arguments in the right sequence or didn't define them in the way that's required by the subprogram.

To get the best results from using subprograms, the programmers in a COBOL shop should follow the guidelines given in this figure. First, if you're writing a subprogram, be sure to adhere to the principles of structured programming. This means that each subprogram should have only one entry and one exit point and it should do only one function. In practice, though, you'll often find that these principles are violated, which makes the subprograms more difficult to use.

Second, after you create a subprogram, you should make sure the documentation for it is adequate. This documentation should be specific about what the subprogram does, what each passed field is used for, how each field should be defined, and what sequence the fields should be passed in. A common weakness in COBOL shops is that the subprogram documentation is incomplete, which discourages the programmers from using the subprograms.

Third, if you're a programmer who's starting a new program, you need to check the subprogram documentation to find out what subprograms are available to you. If you don't do this, of course, the potential benefits of subprograms are never realized. But this is a common shortcoming in many COBOL shops.

Fourth, once you decide what subprograms you're going to use, you should add the subprogram modules to the structure chart for your program as shown in this figure. Later, you can use this chart as a guide to your coding. Whether you call a procedure or a subprogram, the principles are the same.

How to identify subprograms in a structure chart

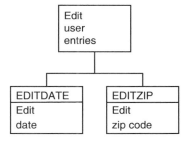

Typical subprograms

- Editing subprograms that check the validity in fields like date, state, and zip-code fields
- Calculation subprograms that do complex calculations
- Character-manipulation subprograms
- Date handling subprograms
- Table loading subprograms

Testing and debugging considerations

- When you're testing a program that uses a subprogram and the subprogram doesn't work correctly, it is usually because the calling program has passed the parameters to the subprogram in a different sequence or format than the subprogram requires.
- Sometimes, when you write a subprogram, none of the programs that use it have been developed yet. Then, you can write a simple calling program to test your subprogram.

Recommended guidelines for using subprograms

- Write each subprogram so it does a single function and has only one entry and one exit point. This is consistent with the principles of structured programming.
- Document all subprograms so it's easy for programmers to find what they're looking for. For each subprogram, the documentation should tell what the function is, what each passed field is used for, what the format of each passed field needs to be, and what the sequence of the passed fields must be.
- Before you start a new program, find out whether any subprograms are available that will help you develop the program more efficiently.
- When you create a structure chart for a new program, add one module to the chart for each subprogram as shown above. The striped area at the top of the module should give the subprogram name.

Figure 11-8   Guidelines for using subprograms

Perspective

Copy members and subprograms are used by all professional programmers because they help improve programmer productivity. In most COBOL shops, copy members are used primarily for data definitions, and subprograms are used for processing routines. In some shops, though, you can use either a copy member or a subprogram for a routine.

Summary

- *Copy members* contain source statements that can be copied into COBOL programs by using the Copy statement. On most platforms, each copy member is stored in a *copy library*.

- *Subprograms* are compiled programs that do commonly-used routines. To *call* a subprogram from a *calling program*, you use the Call statement.

- On a mainframe, subprograms are compiled into *object modules* that are stored in an *object library*. Then, the object modules for the calling program and the subprograms are *link edited* into a *load module* that is ready for execution.

Terms

copy member	argument
copy library	object module
source statement library	object library
copy book	subprogram library
subprogram	load module
calling a subprogram	link editing
calling program	nested subprograms
passing fields to a subprogram	passing by reference
parameter	passing by content

Objectives

- Given the documentation for available copy members, use them in your programs.

- Given the documentation for available subprograms, use them in your programs.

- Given the specifications that you need for creating a copy member on your system, create a new copy member.

- Given the specifications for a subprogram, write it in COBOL.

- Explain why it's usually better to implement a processing routine as a subprogram instead of a copy member.

Exercise 11-1   Create and use a copy member

In this exercise, you'll create and use a copy member for a customer master record.

1. Open the program named rpt1000, change its Program-ID to RPT1100, save it as rpt1100, and close and re-open it. Then, find the record description for the file named CUSTMAST, highlight it, and use the Copy command (Ctrl+C) to copy it to the clipboard.

2. Open a new program or switch to the one that's already open. Next, use the Paste command (Ctrl+V) to paste the contents of the clipboard into this file. Those should be the only entries in the file. Then, save this file as custmast.cpy, and close this file. You have just created a copy member.

3. Switch to the rpt1100 program, and delete the statements that you just copied to the copy member. In their place, code a Copy statement that refers to the copy member that you created in step 2.

4. Compile the program, and notice how the statements in the copy member are copied into the program. Then, run the program. It should work the same way that it did before.

5. When you're satisfied that the program works correctly, close the program.

Exercise 11-2   Create and use a subprogram

In this exercise, you'll create and use a subprogram that calculates the future value of an investment amount.

1. Open the program named calc2000, change its Program-ID to CALCFV, and save it as calcfv. Then, close and re-open the program.

2. Modify this program so it becomes a subprogram that gets four fields passed to it: investment amount, number-of-years, yearly-interest-rate, and future value. The first three fields contain data that's entered by the user. The last field should receive the result of the calculation.

3. When you've made the changes, compile the subprogram. After you get a clean compile, close the program. You have just created a subprogram.

4. Open the program named calc2000 again, change its Program-ID to CALC2100, save it as calc2100, and close and re-open it. Next, delete all the statements in the Procedure Division that are used to calculate future value, and replace them with a Call statement that calls the calcfv subprogram that you created in step 3. Then, delete all the statements in the Data Division that are no longer needed.

5. Compile, test, and debug the program. If something isn't working right, you can set a breakpoint and step through the statements that follow including the statements in the subprogram (even though the subprogram isn't open). This makes debugging easy on this platform.

6. When you've got this working correctly, close the program.

Exercise 11-3   Write a subprogram that edits a date field

In this exercise, you'll write a subprogram named EDITDATE that checks an eight-digit date field (YYYYMMDD) for validity. To be valid, the month should be a number from 1 through 12 and the day should be a valid number for the month (from 1 through 31 for January, from 1 through 29 for February, and so on).

If the date is valid, the subprogram should set a valid-date switch to Y; otherwise, it should set the switch to N. To use this program, the calling program should pass two fields to the subprogram in this sequence: (1) the eight-digit date field, and (2) the valid-date switch.

To test this program, you need to write a simple calling program that gets a date from the user and passes it to the subprogram. Then, if the valid-date switch is set to Y, this program should display a message like "Valid date." Otherwise, it should display a message like "Invalid date."

1. Open the subprogram named calcfv, change the Program-ID to EDITDATE, save the subprogram as editdate, and close and re-open the subprogram. Next, modify the code so the subprogram does the function that's described above. Then, compile the subprogram, and close it.

2. If necessary, copy the chapter 8 program named date2000 into c:\cobol. Next, open that program, change the Program-ID to TESTEDIT, save the program as testedit, and close and re-open the program. Then, modify this program so you can use it for testing the subprogram that you wrote in step 1.

3. Compile and test your calling program. Then, if necessary, debug either the calling program or the subprogram.

4. When you're satisfied that the program and subprogram work correctly, close the calling program.

Section 3

COBOL for programs that work with disk files

COBOL is a language that's designed for working with disk files, and almost all COBOL programs work with the data in one or more files. That's why an effective COBOL programmer needs to master the skills for working with files. In this section, you'll learn those skills.

In chapter 12, you'll be introduced to the concepts and terms that you need for working with files. There, you'll learn about the three types of file organization that COBOL supports. Then, in chapter 13, you'll learn how to work with files that have sequential organization. In chapter 14, you'll learn how to work with files that have indexed organization. And in chapter 15, you'll learn how to work with files that have relative organization.

The last chapter in this section shows you how to use the sort/merge feature of COBOL. This is an important feature that can improve the efficiency of a system.

This section works best if you read the chapters in sequence. If you prefer, though, you can read chapter 16 after you read chapters 12 and 13. You can also skip chapter 15 because relative files are rarely used. Later, if you ever have to use relative files you can refer back to that chapter. Remember, though, that file processing is the essence of COBOL programming, so you should definitely read chapters 12, 13, 14, and 16.

12

Concepts and terms for working with disk files

In chapters 3, 4, and 5, you learned how to write a report-preparation program that reads the data from a file with sequential organization. Now, in this chapter, you'll learn more about how data is stored on and accessed from a disk file. You'll learn about two other types of file organization. And you'll be introduced to other types of programs that work with files.

Disk concepts and terms

This chapter starts by presenting the concepts and terms that apply to the way files are stored on disk drives and the way data is accessed on disk drives. Although this may be more than you want to know about how a disk drive works, you need to have this conceptual background if you want to write efficient COBOL programs.

How data is stored on a disk drive

Figure 12-1 gives two views of how data is stored on a *disk drive*. As you can see, each disk drive consists of *disks* that are stacked on a *spindle* within the drive; each magnetic recording surface on a disk is divided into *tracks*; and each track is divided into *sectors*.

This is conceptually true whether the disk drive is for a PC, a mid-range system, or a mainframe. What differs from one disk drive to another is the number of disks, the number of tracks on each recording surface, the number of sectors in each track, and the number of bytes in each sector. If, for example, a drive has 10 recording surfaces with 10,000 tracks per surface, 25 sectors per track, and 4000 bytes in each sector, the storage capacity of the disk is one billion bytes of data (a *gigabyte*). Today, disk drives with that capacity or more are common on PCs, and the disk drives for mainframes have capacities that are many times larger.

When a disk drive reads or writes data, it reads or writes one or more complete sectors. Because each sector has a unique *disk address*, the disk drive can read any sector directly, or randomly, without reading any of the other sectors first. Alternatively, a disk drive can read the sectors in sequence.

Incidentally, a disk drive on an IBM mainframe is called a *DASD*, which is short for *direct access storage device*. You should also know that the term *sector* isn't used for the addressable storage units of DASDs. The concept, however, is the same. The tracks on DASDs are divided into fixed-length units with unique disk addresses. As a result, you can still think of the addressable units as sectors.

The disks within a disk drive

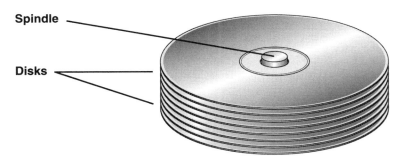

The tracks and sectors on one recording surface

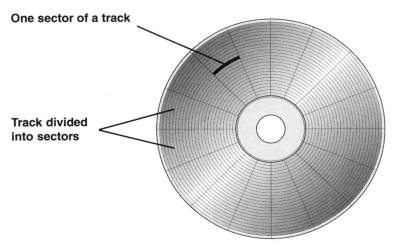

Description

- A *disk drive* contains a stack of metal platters (or *disks*) that are coated with a metal oxide. Data is recorded on one or both sides of each of the disks.

- Data is stored on each recording surface of a disk in concentric circles called *tracks*.

- Each track is divided into *sectors*, and each sector has a unique *disk address*. When the disk drive reads or writes data, it reads or writes one or more complete sectors.

- When the disk drive is in operation, the disks rotate around the *spindle* at high speeds. A common speed, for example, is 3600 rotations per minute.

Figure 12-1   How data is stored on a disk drive

How the data in a sector is read or written

When a disk drive is in operation, the disks on the spindle rotate at a high speed. To read or write the sectors on the disks, an *actuator* moves the *read/write heads* to the appropriate track. This is summarized in figure 12-2.

Note, here, that the actuator is a mechanism that consists of one read/write head for each track. When the actuator moves the heads from one track to another, all of the heads move in unison. If, for example, the actuator moves the heads from track 200 to track 300, all of the heads move to track 300.

The tracks that are positioned under the heads of the actuator at any one time can be thought of as a *cylinder*. As a result, there are as many cylinders in a disk drive as there are tracks on one of the recording surfaces. So a disk drive with 800 tracks per surface and 20 recording surfaces has 800 cylinders with 20 tracks in each. The notion of cylinders is important only because the disk areas that are assigned to files on some platforms are measured in cylinders. If, for example, you write COBOL programs for an IBM mainframe, you're likely to hear language like this: "We gave that file an initial allocation of 20 cylinders and a secondary allocation of 5 cylinders."

When a disk drive reads or writes a sector, it does the four steps that are shown in this figure. If, for example, the drive is supposed to read sector 5 on track 10 in cylinder 100, the sector is read using these steps. First, the actuator moves the read/write heads to cylinder 100 (called *actuator movement*). Second, read/write head 10 is turned on. Third, the disk drive waits for sector 5 to rotate to the read/write head (called *rotational delay*). Fourth, the read/write head reads the data in the sector.

The two steps that take the most time are the actuator movement and the rotational delay. Since actuator movement is mechanical, not electronic, it takes the most time. For instance, the average time for each actuator movement on some common mainframe disk drives is from 10 to 15 milliseconds (thousandths of a second). Similarly, if a disk drive is rotating at 3600 rotations per second, the average time for rotational delay is 8.3 milliseconds.

If those times seem fast, remember that the operations that are done once the data is in internal storage are measured in microseconds (millionths of a second) and nanoseconds (billionths of a second). Relatively speaking then, actuator movement and rotational delay are thousands of times slower than internal operations. As a result, the efficiency of most systems depends on the efficiency of its I/O operations, not its internal operations. That's why you normally design systems and write programs so they minimize actuator movement and rotational delay and thus maximize I/O efficiency.

The actuator and read/write heads for a disk drive

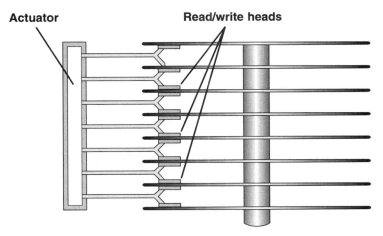

Description

- The *actuator* for a disk drive has one *read/write head* for each recording surface. This actuator can move to any track on the disk surfaces.
- When the actuator moves, all of the read/write heads move at the same time. As a result, the read/write heads are always positioned on the same track on the recording surfaces of the disk.
- The tracks that are positioned under the read/write heads can be referred to as a *cylinder*. As a result, a disk drive has as many cylinders as it has tracks on the recording surfaces.
- Only one read/write head can be turned on at one time. As a result, the data on only one track can be read or written at one time.

How a sector is read or written

1. The actuator moves to the cylinder that the sector is in. This is called *actuator movement*.
2. The read/write head for the disk surface that contains the sector is turned on.
3. The disk drive waits until the sector rotates around to the read/write head. This is called *rotational delay*.
4. The read/write head reads the sector into internal storage or writes the data from internal storage to the sector.

Why this matters

- Most business applications spend far more time reading and writing data than they spend processing it. As a result, the efficiency of a system or a program depends to a large extent on the efficiency of the I/O operations.
- When you design a system or write a new program, you should try to minimize actuator movement because that's the access step that takes the most time.

Figure 12-2   How the data in a sector is read or written

Blocked versus unblocked records

One way to reduce the time that's required for rotational delay is to *block* the records that are read. This means that two or more records are stored in a single sector. Then, when a sector is read, the entire block of records is read so there's only one rotational delay for all the records in the block. This is illustrated in figure 12-3.

In contrast, when records are *unblocked*, only one record is stored in a sector. That not only means more rotational delay as the records are read, but also wasted disk space in the unused portions of the sectors. If, for example, 300-byte records are stored in 512-byte sectors, 212 bytes are wasted in each sector.

To avoid wasted storage, an appropriate *blocking factor* should be chosen when a file is created. If, for example, 250-byte records are stored in 512-byte sectors with a blocking factor of 2, only 12 bytes in each sector are wasted. Similarly, 300-byte records can be stored in three 512-byte sectors with a blocking factor of 5. This wastes just 36 bytes in three sectors. In this case, a single block of records spans three sectors, and all three sectors for each block are read or written at once with just one rotational delay before they are accessed.

Because of these efficiencies, blocking is used for most files. Within the COBOL program, this usually doesn't require any extra code. Instead, the program is written as if it is reading or writing one unblocked record at a time. Behind the scenes, though, an entire block of records is read at one time, and one record is released to the program whenever a Read statement is executed. Similarly, an entire block of records is written only after the block has been filled by Write statements that write one record at a time to the block.

Fixed-length versus variable-length records

Most of the records in files are *fixed-length records*. That means that all of the records in an entire file have the same length. Occasionally, though, it makes sense to create a file that contains *variable-length records*. That means that a file contains records of different sizes. In most cases, the variable-length records are blocked for the same reasons that fixed-length records are blocked.

In figure 12-3, you can see an illustration of blocked, variable-length records. In sector 1, you can see three records of two different sizes and an unused portion of the sector. In sector 2, you can see two more records of different sizes. By using variable-length records for some applications, you can reduce the number of unused fields that you would have if you used fixed-length records.

When you use variable-length records in a COBOL program, you do have to provide some extra coding. When you write a variable-length record, for example, you have to tell the system how long the record is. Similarly, when you read a variable-length record, you have to determine how long the record is so you can process it correctly. In chapter 13, you can learn how to do both.

Unblocked records

Sector 1

Record 1	Unused

Sector 2

Record 2	Unused

Blocked records

Sector 1

Record 1	Record 2	Record 3	Record 4	Record 5

Sector 2

Record 6	Record 7	Record 8	Record 9	Record 10

Blocked versus unblocked records

- When records are *unblocked*, only one record is stored in each sector. When records are *blocked*, two or more records are stored in each sector. Since this makes better use of disk storage, most files contain blocked records.

- With blocked records, the disk drive reads or writes a block of records at a time. This means that there's only one rotational delay for each block of records, and that can improve the efficiency of a program that works with disk files.

- The *blocking factor* is the number of records that are stored in a block. To get the most from blocking, you use a blocking factor that wastes as little disk space as possible. If a block of records spans two or more sectors, all of the sectors are read or written at once.

- The COBOL programmer usually doesn't have to worry about blocking because this is handled automatically by the compiler and operating system. As a result, you write the program as if it were working with unblocked records.

Variable-length blocked records

Sector 1

Record 1	Record 2	Record 3	Unused

Sector 2

Record 4	Record 5

Fixed-length versus variable-length records

- Although most files contain *fixed-length records*, some files contain *variable-length records*. These records are usually blocked too.

- When a COBOL program reads a variable-length record, it needs to determine what the length of the record is. When a program writes a variable-length record, it must provide the length of the record.

Figure 12-3   Blocked and variable-length records

File organization concepts

Now that you know how data is stored and accessed on a disk drive, you need to learn how the records of a file can be organized. In particular, you need to know how the three types of file organizations that are supported by COBOL work. These are sequential file organization, indexed file organization, and relative file organization. Of the three, the first two are the ones you'll use all the time.

Sequential file organization

In chapter 3, you learned how to write a program that reads a file that has *sequential file organization* (a *sequential file*). In this type of file, the records are stored in consecutive disk locations. For efficiency, these files are usually blocked so a large block of records is read or written at one time.

When the records in a sequential file are processed, they usually need to be in sequence by one or more of the fields in the records. These fields are referred to as the *key fields*. Sometimes, a sequential file is created with the records in the proper key sequence. Sometimes, a sequential file needs to be sorted into the proper sequence before it can be processed.

Figure 12-4 summarizes the characteristics of a sequential file. There, you can see a file of employee records that's in sequence by employee number. When the records are read or written, they are always accessed in sequence by disk location, which can be referred to as *sequential access*.

The trouble with sequential files is that you have to read them in sequence. As a result, there's no way to read the 200th record in a file without first reading the first 199 records. But that means that sequential files can't take advantage of the disk drive's ability to read any sector on a direct, or random, basis. Nevertheless, sequential files are widely used in all COBOL shops.

A sequential employee file that's in sequence by employee number

Disk location	Employee number	Social security number	First name	Middle initial	Last name
1	00001	499-35-5079	Stanley	L	Abbott
2	00002	279-00-1210	William	J	Collins
3	00004	899-16-9235	Alice		Crawford
4	00005	703-47-5748	Paul	M	Collins
5	00008	558-12-6168	Marie	A	Littlejohn
6	00009	559-35-2479	E	R	Siebert
7	00010	334-96-8721	Constance	M	Harris
8	00012	213-64-9290	Thomas	T	Bluestone
9	00013	572-68-3100	Jean	B	Glenning
10	00015	498-27-6117	Ronald	W	Westbrook

Description

- In a file that has *sequential file organization*, the records are stored one after the other in consecutive disk locations. This type of file can also be called a *sequential file*.

- To retrieve records from a sequential file, you must read them sequentially by disk location. This type of record retrieval is referred to as *sequential access*.

- The records in a sequential file may be in ascending or descending sequence based on the values in one or more of the fields within the records. The field or fields that contain these values are called the *key fields*, or *keys*.

- Often, the records in a sequential file aren't in key sequence so they have to be sorted into a specific sequence before they can be processed.

- To improve I/O efficiency, the records in sequential files are usually blocked with a large blocking factor.

Figure 12-4   Sequential file organization

Indexed file organization

The records in a file with *indexed file organization* (an *indexed file*) can be read sequentially, and they can also be read randomly. To make that possible, an indexed file consists of two parts: a *data component* and an *index component* (or just *index*). The characteristics of this type of file are presented in figure 12-5.

The *primary index* for an indexed file contains the *primary key* values for the records in the file. For each key value, the index also contains the record's disk location in the data component of the file. Then, since the key values are in sequence in the index, the index can be used to read all of the records in the file in sequence. However, the index can also be used to read the record for any key value using *random access*.

To illustrate how random access works, suppose a program needs to read the record for employee number 00010. To start, the program looks up that key in the primary index for the file. Then, when it gets the disk location for the record, it reads the record in the data component of the file.

Because indexed organization provides for both sequential and random access, indexed files are commonly used for master files like inventory, customer, and employee master files. That way, the records in the file can be updated using random access, and reports can be prepared from the file using sequential access.

The trouble with indexed files is that they aren't as efficient as you might want them to be since all accessing is done through the index. As a result, reading a record on a random basis often means that one or more index records have to be read before the master record can be read. And adding a record to a file means that the index must be updated. This type of overhead isn't required when you use sequential files.

To make indexed files work as efficiently as possible, the records are usually stored in primary key sequence when a file is created. When you create an indexed file on an IBM mainframe, for example, the records have to be stored in primary key sequence. That way, there's less actuator movement when the file is read sequentially. When records are added to an indexed file, though, they may not be added in their sequential locations in the data component. That reduces the efficiency of sequential access.

To a large extent, though, the I/O efficiency of indexed files depends on how the indexes are implemented. On many systems, for example, an index is actually a separate file. This is true for the indexed files that are used with Micro Focus Personal COBOL. Then, to read a record randomly, a program first searches the index for the desired key. When it finds the key, it reads the master record randomly.

This method of implementation can be efficient if the entire index is read into internal storage when the file is opened. Then, the index is searched at electronic speeds with no actuator movement. Otherwise, the random access of a record requires two actuator movements, one for the index and one for the record. Although implementation details like these are beyond the scope of the COBOL programmer, they have a dramatic effect on the I/O efficiency of indexed files.

An employee file that's indexed by employee number

Index component

Employee number	Disk location
00001	1
00002	2
00004	3
00005	4
00008	5
00009	6
00010	10
00012	7
00013	8
00015	9

Data component

Disk location	Employee number	Social security number	First name	Middle initial	Last name
1	00001	499-35-5079	Stanley	L	Abbott
2	00002	279-00-1210	William	J	Collins
3	00004	899-16-9235	Alice		Crawford
4	00005	703-47-5748	Paul	M	Collins
5	00008	558-12-6168	Marie	A	Littlejohn
6	00009	559-35-2479	E	R	Siebert
7	00012	213-64-9290	Thomas	T	Bluestone
8	00013	572-68-3100	Jean	B	Glenning
9	00015	498-27-6117	Ronald	W	Westbrook
10	00010	334-96-8721	Constance	M	Harris

Description

- A file that has *indexed file organization* consists of two parts: an *index component* and a *data component*. Within the index component, each entry contains a key field value and the location of the corresponding record in the data component of the file. This type of file can be called an *indexed file*.

- An indexed file must have at least one index. The key for this index is called the *primary key*, and the index is called the *primary index*.

- Each key in the primary index must be *unique*. That means that there are no *duplicate keys* in the file.

- In the primary index, the primary keys are in sequence. That way, the index can be used to read the records in the data component sequentially by the key field. This is referred to as *sequential access*.

- The index can also be used to access a record directly by getting its disk location from the index component. This is referred to as *direct*, or *random*, *access*.

- When an indexed file is created, the records are usually written in their primary key sequence in the data component. That way, there's less access mechanism movement when the records are retrieved in sequence. When records are added to the file, however, they may not be added in their sequential locations in the data component. That reduces the efficiency of sequential access.

- How indexed files are implemented varies from one platform to another. One common way to implement these files is with one file for the index and another file for the data. On some platforms, though, the index and the data are implemented in a single file.

- To improve I/O efficiency, the records in indexed files are often blocked.

Figure 12-5   Indexed file organization

Indexed file organization with alternate indexes

Besides its primary index, an indexed file can have one or more *alternate indexes*. These indexes make it possible to access records sequentially or randomly based on the values in *alternate keys*. This is illustrated by the examples in figure 12-6.

In the first example, an alternate index is used for social security numbers. In this case, the keys are *unique* since there is only one social security number for each worker. This gives a program the ability to access the records in the file by either employee number (the primary key) or social security number.

In the second example, an alternate index is used for last names. These keys, however, are *non-unique*, which means that the index provides for *duplicate keys*. When a program accesses a record randomly by a duplicate key, only the first record with that key value is read. Then, to access the other records with that key, the program needs to read the records sequentially.

By using alternate keys, you can access the data in a file in whatever way is most logical. As you might guess, though, alternate keys add to the overhead that's associated with an indexed file. If, for example, a record is added to this employee file, three different indexes need to be updated. But here again, the efficiency of alternate keys depends to a large extent on how they're implemented, and that varies dramatically from one platform to another.

An employee file with unique alternate keys

Alternate index

Social security number	Disk location
213-64-9290	7
279-00-1210	2
334-96-8721	10
498-27-6117	9
499-35-5079	1
558-12-6168	5
559-35-2479	6
572-68-3100	8
703-47-5748	4
899-16-9235	3

Data component

Disk location	Employee number	Social security number	First name	Middle initial	Last name
1	00001	499-35-5079	Stanley	L	Abbott
2	00002	279-00-1210	William	J	Collins
3	00004	899-16-9235	Alice		Crawford
4	00005	703-47-5748	Paul	M	Collins
5	00008	558-12-6168	Marie	A	Littlejohn
6	00009	559-35-2479	E	R	Siebert
7	00012	213-64-9290	Thomas	T	Bluestone
8	00013	572-68-3100	Jean	B	Glenning
9	00015	498-27-6117	Ronald	W	Westbrook
10	00010	334-96-8721	Constance	M	Harris

An employee file with non-unique alternate keys

Alternate index

Last name	Disk location
Abbott	1
Bluestone	7
Collins	2
Collins	4
Crawford	3
Glenning	8
Harris	10
Littlejohn	5
Siebert	6
Westbrook	9

Data component

Disk location	Employee number	Social security number	First name	Middle initial	Last name
1	00001	499-35-5079	Stanley	L	Abbott
2	00002	279-00-1210	William	J	Collins
3	00004	899-16-9235	Alice		Crawford
4	00005	703-47-5748	Paul	M	Collins
5	00008	558-12-6168	Marie	A	Littlejohn
6	00009	559-35-2479	E	R	Siebert
7	00012	213-64-9290	Thomas	T	Bluestone
8	00013	572-68-3100	Jean	B	Glenning
9	00015	498-27-6117	Ronald	W	Westbrook
10	00010	334-96-8721	Constance	M	Harris

Description

- An indexed file can have one or more *alternate indexes*. The keys used in each alternate index are called *alternate keys*.

- The entries in an alternate index are maintained in alternate key sequence so the file can be read sequentially by the alternate key. The records can also be read randomly by alternate key. An alternate index can contain unique or *non-unique (duplicate) keys*.

- When a program accesses records randomly by an alternate index with duplicate keys, only the first record with the specified key is retrieved. To access all the records with that key, the subsequent records must be retrieved sequentially.

Figure 12-6   Indexed file organization with alternate indexes

Relative file organization

The records in a file with *relative file organization* (a *relative file*) can also be accessed both sequentially and randomly. The trouble is that not many files can be easily adapted to this type of organization. This is summarized in figure 12-7.

Each *record area* in a relative file is addressed by a *relative record number* from 1 through the number of record areas in the file. Since a relative record number can easily be converted to a sector address without using an index, the data in a record area can be efficiently accessed on a random basis. Similarly, since the record areas are read in sequence without using an index, sequential access is more efficient than it is with indexed organization.

The trick to using a relative file is converting a key field like employee number to a relative record number without creating duplicate record numbers and without wasting too many record areas. In the example in this figure, the employee numbers are unique keys that range from 1 through 15 so they can be used as the relative record numbers. Because 5 of the first 15 numbers aren't used, however, 5 of the first 15 record areas are wasted. This often happens as the records in a file are deleted, which is one reason why relative files are rarely used.

But what if a master file of 10,000 inventory records has item numbers that range from 100,000 to 2,000,000? How, for example, do you convert those item numbers to relative record numbers that range from 1 through 12,000 (that provides for 2,000 empty record areas)? Although you can try to develop a *randomizing routine* that does the conversion, it is likely to be impractical. That's the primary reason why relative files are rarely used.

VSAM file organizations

VSAM, which stands for *Virtual Storage Access Method*, is the set of IBM access methods that implement the three file organizations on an IBM mainframe. Within VSAM, though, different terms are used for the three file organizations. To start, a file is referred to as a *data set*. Then, a sequential file is an *entry-sequenced data set* (or *ESDS*). An indexed file is a *key-sequenced data set* (or *KSDS*). And a relative file is a *relative record data set* (or *RRDS*).

When VSAM became available way back in the mid-1970's, it provided major improvements in the efficiency with which indexed files could be processed. As a result, VSAM indexed files quickly replaced the previous implementation of indexed files, which were called ISAM files (Indexed Sequential Access Method). On the other hand, VSAM sequential files didn't work any better than the previous implementation of sequential files and VSAM sequential files were more difficult to work with. As a result, most sequential files that are in use today are non-VSAM files.

An employee file with relative organization

Relative record number	Employee number	Social security number	First name	Middle initial	Last name
1	00001	499-35-5079	Stanley	L	Abbott
2	00002	279-00-1210	William	J	Collins
3					
4	00004	899-16-9235	Alice		Crawford
5	00005	703-47-5748	Paul	M	Collins
6					
7					
8	00008	558-12-6168	Marie	A	Littlejohn
9	00009	559-35-2479	E	R	Siebert
10	00010	334-96-8721	Constance	M	Harris
11					
12	00012	213-64-9290	Thomas	T	Bluestone
13	00013	572-68-3100	Jean	B	Glenning
14					
15	00015	498-27-6117	Ronald	W	Westbrook

Concepts

- A file that has *relative file organization* consists of *record areas* that can contain one record each. Each of these areas is identified by a *relative record number* that indicates its relative position in the file. This type of file can be called a *relative file*.

- When the records in a relative file are accessed sequentially, the areas that don't contain records are skipped.

- To access a record randomly, a program must specify the relative record number of the area that contains the record. Then, the record is read or written directly without going through an index. This is more efficient than random access of an indexed file.

- The relative record number for a record is usually derived from a key field. In the simplest case, the key can be used as the relative record number as shown above. Usually, though, the key value has to be converted to a relative record number by using a *randomizing routine*.

- The purpose of a randomizing routine is to convert the values in a field to relative record numbers that fall between one and the number of record areas allocated to the file. If two or more records randomize to the same relative record number, additional routines must be used to put the record with the duplicate record number in an available area.

- When the keys in a file can be converted to relative record numbers with a minimum of duplicates and unused record areas, relative file organization is an efficient file organization. Relative files are used infrequently, though, because the keys in most files don't meet those qualifications.

Figure 12-7   Relative file organization

Typical programs that work with disk files

Now that you know how disk files can be organized, this chapter introduces you to typical programs that use disk files. Once you have a general idea of what these programs do, you can learn how to write the COBOL programs that do those types of processing.

Interactive programs

Figure 12-8 presents three types of *interactive programs*. This type of program gets data from the user's keyboard, and displays data on the user's screen based on the user entries. In other words, the program interacts with the user.

In this figure, *system flowcharts* are used to illustrate what each type of program does. In this type of flowchart, the symbol on the left represents user entries, the rectangle represents a program, and the symbol or symbols on the right represent disk files. Note the arrowheads on the lines that connect the symbols because they indicate whether data is input to a program, output from it, or both.

When an *inquiry program* runs, the user enters a request for data. Then, the program gets the data from one or more disk files and displays the data on the screen. If, for example, the user enters a customer number, the program randomly accesses the master record for that customer number and then displays some or all of its data on the screen. Note that the arrowhead on the line that connects the disk symbol with the program indicates that the disk file is input only. In other words, an inquiry program doesn't let the user change the data in the master record.

When a *maintenance program* runs, the user enters *transactions* that represent additions, deletions, and changes to a master file. This type of program usually *edits* the data for validity before trying to do the maintenance action. If the data for a transaction is invalid, the program displays an error so the user can correct the data and try the transaction again. If the data is valid, the program adds, deletes, or changes the record in the master file using random access. In this type of program, a transaction is invalid if it tries to delete or change a record that doesn't exist or if it tries to add a record that's already there (unless duplicate keys are allowed). Note that the arrowheads in the flowchart indicate that the master file is both input and output to the program.

When an *update program* runs, the user enters a transaction that affects the operational data in one or more files. A sales transaction, for example, should increase the sales data in a customer master file, increase the amount owed in an accounts receivable file, and decrease the on-hand balances of the items that have been sold in an inventory master file. Here again, each transaction is edited for validity before the files are updated, and a transaction is invalid if it tries to update a record that doesn't exist.

These are three of the most common types of interactive programs. Note that all three depend on the use of indexed files so the master records can be accessed randomly. And note that all three perform the requested actions right away.

A system flowchart for an interactive inquiry program

A system flowchart for an interactive maintenance program

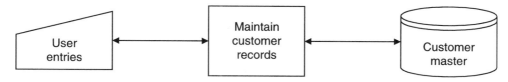

A system flowchart for an interactive update program

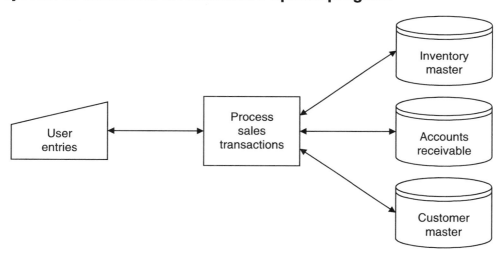

Description

- In an *inquiry program*, the terminal or PC user enters the key of the record to be displayed. Then, the program finds that record and displays some or all of its data, but it doesn't allow changes to that data.

- In a *maintenance program*, the terminal or PC user enters *transactions* that represent additions, deletions, and changes to the master file. As each transaction is entered, the program *edits* the data for validity. Then, if the data is valid, the program performs the maintenance action. Otherwise, the user is asked to correct the data.

- In an *update program*, the terminal or PC user enters transactions like customer orders, receipts to inventory, or course grades. For each valid transaction, the program updates all of the related master records, which can be in more than one file.

- Most interactive programs use indexed master files so they can access the records that the user wants to work with on a random basis.

Figure 12-8   Interactive programs

Batch programs

Unlike an interactive program, a *batch program* processes transactions in batches instead of one at a time. This is illustrated by the system flowchart in figure 12-9. It shows how an indexed inventory file can be updated by processing transactions that represent receipts to inventory. In this case, the master file is updated via random access.

This program starts with an interactive *edit program* that gets and edits user entries for the receipt transactions. Instead of updating the inventory master file as each transaction is entered, though, the program writes the transactions to a sequential transaction file. Then, sometime later on, the second program in this system (a *random update program*) reads the batch of transactions and updates the master records in the inventory transaction file. At that time, if a master record can't be found for a transaction, the transaction is invalid so it is written to an error transaction file for later correction.

In a system like this, the batches of transactions are often collected during the day and the files are updated during the off hours. The benefit of this type of processing is system efficiency because it results in fewer I/O operations overall. To improve that efficiency, the transactions are sometimes sorted into key sequence before they are used to update the master file. That reduces the total amount of actuator movement when the file is updated. Also, if more than one transaction can apply to the same master record, the program can be written so a master record is only rewritten to the file one time no matter how many transactions apply to it. That reduces the amount of rotational delay that's required.

In this example, the transactions are edited for validity, but that isn't always the case. Sometimes, the transactions are entered and written to a transaction file without editing. Then, the update program needs to edit the transactions as well as process them. Or, a separate edit program needs to read the transactions, edit them, write the valid transactions to a valid transaction file, and write the invalid transactions to an error transaction file. Then, the update program can process the file of valid transactions without editing them.

These are common variations that you'll run into when you work with a batch system. What differs, though, is just how the processing functions are divided into programs. In all batch systems, the transactions need to be entered and edited, and the related master files need to be updated.

A batch system for maintaining an indexed file on a random basis is similar to one for updating a file. The difference is that the transactions represent additions, deletions, and changes instead of just changes. After a batch of transactions has been edited, a *random maintenance program* processes the transactions and maintains the related records in the master file.

A system flowchart for randomly updating an indexed master file

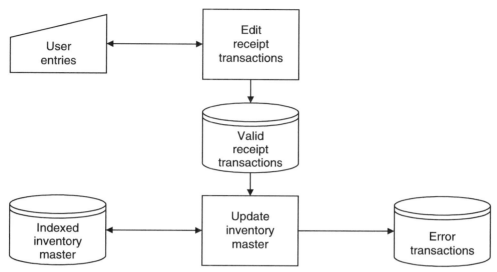

Description

- The first program in this system is an interactive *edit program* that gets the transactions from a terminal or PC user, edits them, and saves the valid transactions in a sequential disk file. If a transaction isn't valid, the user is asked to correct its data. A program like this doesn't update any master files; it just writes the valid transactions to a sequential disk file.

- The second program in this system is a *random update program*. It reads the records in the valid transaction file and then updates the records in the indexed master file on a random basis.

- The second program also writes a file of error transactions. Even though the transactions have been edited when the random update program starts, an error occurs when a master record can't be found with the key of the transaction record.

- A *random maintenance program* is like an update program. It reads transactions for records that are to be added, deleted, or changed. For each transaction, the maintenance program either adds, deletes, or changes a record on a random basis. Or, if an error is indicated, the program writes the transaction to the error file.

- To improve the efficiency of indexed file processing, an indexed file is periodically recreated. To do that, the indexed file is written to a sequential file in primary key sequence and the original indexed file is deleted. Then, the sequential file is used to recreate the indexed file with its original name in its original disk space. This removes the empty spaces for deleted records and puts the new records in their proper locations in the data component.

- A master file can also be updated or maintained sequentially as shown in the next figure. Often, this is more efficient than random processing because the I/O time is reduced.

Figure 12-9   Batch updating of an indexed file

Although the system in the last figure updates the master file on a random basis, it often makes sense to use sequential master files in a batch system. This is illustrated by the system in figure 12-10. Here, a sequential inventory file is updated by processing receipt transactions.

Here again, the first program in the system edits the data in the receipt transactions that are entered by the user. Then, the second program is a *sort program* that sorts the transactions into item number sequence. Once that's done, the transactions can be processed by a *sequential update program* that reads the transactions and updates the sequential master file.

Note, however, that the sequential update program doesn't just read an affected master record, update its data, and rewrite the master record in its original disk location. Instead, the program reads all of the records in the *old master file* and writes all of the records, including the updated records, to a *new master file*.

One benefit of this is that the old master file becomes a *backup file* that can be used to re-create the new master file if something goes wrong. In most production systems, for example, two or more generations of the backup files are kept along with the transaction files. Then, if the current master file is lost due to operator or hardware error, it can be re-created by re-running the sequential update program with the previous backup file and transaction file.

Another benefit of sequential update programs is that the programs tend to run faster than random update programs. Because the program processes all the records in one cylinder before moving on to the next one, actuator movement is reduced. Because large blocks of records are read and written at one time, rotational delay is reduced. Because of these benefits, sequential updates are still widely used in most COBOL shops.

A *sequential maintenance program* is similar to a sequential update program. Here again, the transactions need to be sorted in key sequence before the update program can be run. Then, the program reads the old master file and writes the new master file. As it writes the new master file, though, it doesn't write the records that have been deleted and it writes new records to the master file for those transactions that represent additions.

Although update and maintenance programs are central to all batch systems, other types of batch programs are also used. For instance, report-preparation programs are common to all systems. This type of program usually reads the records in the sequence that's required for preparing the report. To make that possible, a sequential file may need to be sorted before the report preparation program is run. Or, an indexed file may need to have an alternate index that allows the records to be read in the required sequence.

A system flowchart for updating a sequential master file

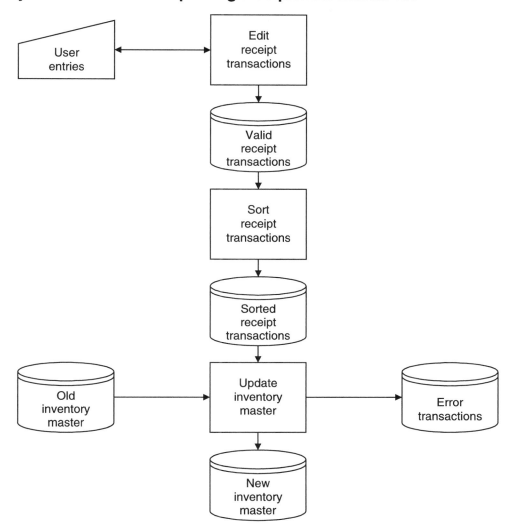

Description

- The first program in this system is an interactive edit program that gets the transactions from a terminal or PC user and saves the valid transactions in a sequential disk file. Note, however, that this interactive program doesn't update any master files.

- The second program in this system is a *sort program* that sorts the records into the key sequence of the master file that's going to be updated. A sort program is a utility program that's provided by the operating system.

- The third program in this system is a *sequential update program*. It reads the records in the valid transaction file and the records in the sequential master file (the *old master file*). It then updates the master records and writes all of the old records (not just the updated records) to a *new master file*.

Figure 12-10   Batch updating of a sequential file

Perspective

The goal of this chapter has been to introduce you to the concepts and terms that you need for writing COBOL programs that work with files. Now that you've finished this chapter, you can learn how to write those programs by reading the next four chapters.

In chapters 13 through 15, you can learn how to write programs that work with sequential, indexed, and relative files. Then, in chapter 16, you can learn how to use the sort/merge feature of COBOL so you can sort files within your COBOL programs.

Summary

- A *disk drive* consists of *disks* that have recording surfaces that consist of *tracks*. These tracks are divided into *sectors* that have unique *disk addresses* so they can be read and written on a random basis.

- To access a sector on a disk drive, the *actuator* moves the *read/write heads* to the *cylinder* that contains the requested sector. Then, the appropriate read/write head is turned on, the requested sector rotates to the head, and the sector is read or written. In this process, *actuator movement* and *rotational delay* take the most time.

- *Blocked records* make better use of disk storage and reduce rotational delay, so they are commonly used with all types of disk files. This includes files that have *fixed-length records* and files that have *variable-length records*.

- The records in a *sequential file* are read and written in sequence by a *key field*.

- The records in an *indexed file* are accessed through a *primary index* or an *alternate index*. Although the keys in the primary index have to be *unique*, *duplicate keys* are allowed in alternate indexes. Since the keys in an index are kept in key sequence, the records in an indexed file can be read with *sequential access* or *random access*.

- The records in a *relative file* can be accessed randomly by *relative record number*. Since this number can be converted to a disk location without using an index, this provides for efficient random access. Relative files are rarely used, though, because it's hard to convert the keys in a master file to relative record numbers with a minimum of duplicates and empty *record areas*.

- *VSAM* is the set of access methods on an IBM mainframe that provide for the use of sequential, indexed, and relative files. Because VSAM made major improvements to the efficiency of indexed file processing, VSAM files are used for almost all indexed files on a mainframe. However, non-VSAM sequential files are still in common use.

- Typical *interactive programs* include *inquiry*, *update*, and *maintenance programs*. Since these programs get data from a user and perform the requested file processing, random access of the master records is required.

- Typical *batch programs* include *random update*, *random maintenance*, *sequential update*, *sequential maintenance*, and *report-preparation programs*. Often, these programs are run in the off hours after the transactions have been collected during the day.

- Before sequential update or maintenance programs can be run, the transactions need to be sorted into the key sequence of the master file. This is done by a *sort program* that comes with the system. Then, the update or maintenance program reads the *old master file* and writes a *new master file* that has been updated by the transactions.

- Two benefits of sequential updating and maintenance are (1) the automatic creation of a backup file, and (2) improved efficiency due to reduced actuator movement and rotational delay.

Terms

disk drive	key	ESDS
disk	indexed file organization	key-sequenced data set
spindle	indexed file	KSDS
track	data component	relative record data set
sector	index component	RRDS
gigabyte	index	interactive program
disk address	primary key	system flowchart
DASD	primary index	inquiry program
direct access storage	unique key	maintenance program
device	duplicate keys	transaction
actuator	direct access	editing a transaction
read/write head	random access	update program
cylinder	alternate index	batch program
actuator movement	alternate key	edit program
rotational delay	non-unique key	random update program
unblocked records	relative file organization	random maintenance
blocked records	relative file	program
blocking factor	relative record number	sort program
fixed-length records	record area	sequential update
variable-length records	randomizing routine	program
sequential file	VSAM	old master file
organization	Virtual Storage Access	new master file
sequential file	Method	backup file
sequential access	data set	sequential maintenance
key field	entry-sequenced data set	program

Objectives

- Describe the way that data is stored on a disk drive.

- List the four steps that are taken when disk data is read or written.

- Explain how blocking improves the efficiency of I/O operations.

- Describe sequential file organization.

- Describe indexed file organization for a file that has only a primary index.

- Describe the use of alternate indexes with indexed files.

- Describe relative file organization.

- Describe the operation of an interactive update program.

- Describe the operation of a random update program in a batch system.

- Describe the operation of a sequential update program in a batch system.

13

How to work with sequential files

In chapter 3, you learned how to write programs that read sequential files of fixed-length records. Now, in this chapter, you'll learn how to update and maintain the records in sequential files. You'll also learn how to create and work with files that contain variable-length records.

COBOL for fixed-length records

Most of the sequential files that you work with contain *fixed-length records*. To work with these files, you need to know how to code proper Select and FD statements for them along with the Procedure Division statements for processing them. In addition, you need to know how to handle the I/O errors that can occur when you process sequential files.

How to code Select and FD statements

Figure 13-1 presents the syntax of the Select and FD statements for sequential files that contain fixed-length records. As you learned in chapter 3, the system name in a Select statement identifies a file on disk. On a PC, the system name is simply the path and file name for the file. On an IBM mainframe, though, the system name includes a *ddname*. Later on, this ddname is associated with a disk file through the JCL that's used to run the program (see chapter 18). Because most sequential files on a mainframe aren't VSAM files, you usually code just a ddname as the system name.

The Select statement format in this figure presents three new clauses. In most cases, you'll omit the Organization and Access clauses because the defaults are sequential organization and sequential access. However, you may want to include the File Status clause for some or all of the files that the program processes. The field named in this clause receives a code after each I/O operation for that file. This code indicates whether an error occurred during the operation. You'll learn more about this in figure 13-3.

This figure also presents the syntax of the FD statement for a sequential file with fixed-length records. As you learned in chapter 3, the Record Contains clause indicates the number of characters or bytes in each record. Although this clause is optional, you may want to code it for documentation. If you do, make sure that the number of characters you specify equals the number indicated by the record description for the file. If you don't, you'll get a compile-time error with some compilers. Worse, you're likely to get a run-time error even if you don't get a compile-time error.

If the records in the file are blocked, you can also code the Block Contains clause to indicate the number of records that are stored in each block. In most cases, though, the operating system keeps track of the block size so you don't have to code this clause.

The syntax of the Select statement

```
SELECT file-name ASSIGN TO system-name
    [ORGANIZATION IS SEQUENTIAL]
    [ACCESS MODE IS SEQUENTIAL]
    [FILE STATUS IS data-name]
```

The syntax for a system name on an IBM mainframe

For a non-VSAM sequential disk file or a print file

```
ddname
```

For a VSAM sequential disk file

```
AS-ddname
```

Rules for forming a ddname

Use eight or fewer letters or digits, starting with a letter.

The syntax for a system name on a PC

```
"path\filename"
```

The syntax of the FD statement

```
FD  file-name
    [BLOCK CONTAINS integer-1 RECORDS]
    [RECORD CONTAINS integer-2 CHARACTERS]
```

Select and FD statements for a non-VSAM file on an IBM mainframe

```
SELECT INVMAST  ASSIGN TO INVMAST
                FILE STATUS IS INVMAST-FILE-STATUS.

FD  INVMAST
    RECORD CONTAINS 70 CHARACTERS.
```

Description

- On a PC, the system name consists of the path and file name for the file. On an IBM mainframe, the system name includes a *ddname* that's used in the JCL for the program to assign the file in the program to a file on disk (see chapter 18).

- You can omit the Organization and Access clauses of the Select statement, since sequential organization and access are the defaults.

- The File Status clause identifies a field that is updated by the system as each I/O statement for the file is executed (see figure 13-3 for details).

- The Block Contains clause indicates how many records are stored or will be stored in each block. Since most systems keep track of the block size, you can usually omit this clause.

- The Record Contains clause specifies the number of bytes in each record. If you omit this clause, the length is determined from the record description for the file. If you include it, the number of bytes you specify should equal the number of bytes in the record description.

Figure 13-1   How to code Select and FD statements for fixed-length records

How to code Procedure Division statements

Figure 13-2 presents the five Procedure Division statements you can use with sequential files. As you can see, you use the Open statement to open a sequential file in one of four modes.

If you just want to read records from a file, you open it in *input mode*. If you just want to write records to the file, you open it in *output mode* or *extend mode*. If the file already exists, you use extend mode to add records to the end of the file. If the file doesn't exist, you use output mode to create it. Finally, if you want to read and change the records in the file, you can open the file in *I-O mode*.

If a file is opened in input or I-O mode, you can use the Read statement to retrieve records from the file. As you can see in this figure, you can code the optional word NEXT after the file name in this statement. However, since sequential access implies that the records are read in sequence, this word is usually omitted.

The Read statement also provides for the Into clause. Then, each record that's read is moved to the area in working storage that's specified by this clause. This is equivalent to a Read statement followed by a Move statement. You need to use this clause whenever you want to work with the last record in a file after the At End clause has been executed because the record is no longer available in the record area in the File Section. You'll see how this works in the program examples in this chapter.

If a file is opened in output or extend mode, you can use the Write statement to add records to the end of the file. If you include the From clause, the record is moved from the indicated area of working storage to the record area for the file before the record is written. If you omit this clause, the record is written directly from the record area in the File Section.

If you want to change the records in a sequential disk file without creating a new file, you can open the file in I-O mode and use the Rewrite statement. Before you issue a Rewrite statement, though, you need to issue a Read statement. Then, the Rewrite statement writes the record back into the location that the record has been read from.

Normally, though, you don't rewrite records on sequential files because that's not the most efficient way to work with them. In addition, a program doesn't create a backup file when it rewrites records. In contrast, when you read the records in an old master file, update them, and write the updated records in a new master file, you get both efficient processing and a backup file. You'll see how this works in a moment.

The last Procedure Division statement you can use with sequential files is the Close statement. This statement simply lists the names of the files to be closed.

The syntax of the Procedure Division statements for sequential files

The Open statement

OPEN { INPUT file-name-1 ...
OUTPUT file-name-2 ...
I-O file-name-3 ...
EXTEND file-name-4 ... } ...

The Read statement

```
READ file-name [NEXT] RECORD [INTO data-name]
    [AT END imperative-statement-1]
    [NOT AT END imperative-statement-2]
    [END-READ]
```

The Write statement

```
WRITE record-name [FROM data-name]
    [END-WRITE]
```

The Rewrite statement

```
REWRITE record-name [FROM data-name]
    [END-REWRITE]
```

The Close statement

```
CLOSE file-name-1 ...
```

Description

- You can use the Open statement to open files in one of four modes. *Input mode* means that the program will only read records from the file. *Output mode* means that the program will create the file and can then write records to it. *I-O mode* means that the program can read records from the file and can write them back to the file in the same locations. *Extend mode* means that the program can add records to the end of an existing file.

- The Read statement reads the next record into the record area for the file. If the Into clause is included, the record is then moved to the specified area in working storage.

- The Write statement writes the record in the record area for the file to the next available record location. If the From clause is included, the data in the specified area of working storage is moved to the record area for the file before the record is written.

- The Rewrite statement writes the record in the record area for the file back to the file. It can be used only for a record that already exists and only after executing a Read statement for that record. You can use the From clause to write the record from a specified area in working storage.

- The Close statement closes the specified files.

Note

- I-O mode and the Rewrite statement aren't normally used with sequential files (see text).

Figure 13-2   How to code Procedure Division statements for sequential files

How to work with file status codes

If you code the File Status clause for a file, the operating system places a *file status code* in the field you specify after each I/O operation for that file. These codes are summarized in figure 13-3. As you can see, each code consists of two digits.

The first digit of the file status code indicates the type of error that occurred. The second digit is more specific. In general, if the first digit of the file status code is a 0 or a 1, it indicates that the operation was successful or that the condition can be handled by the program. But if the first digit is a 3, 4, or 9, it indicates that a serious error has occurred so the program should be terminated.

If you study the codes in this figure, you can see that some are due to programming errors. For instance, code 41 means that the program tried to open a file that is already open, and code 46 means that the program tried to read a record after the end-of-file condition had occurred. When errors like this occur during testing, you need to debug them.

In contrast, some of the errors are operational errors. For instance, code 34 means that there's no more disk space for the file. To fix that on a PC, you need to delete some files so there's free space on the drive. To fix that on a main-frame, you need to assign more disk space to the file.

The technique you use to detect and handle errors depends on the operating system and file system you're using. For example, some systems provide default processing for error conditions, so you only need to use the File Status field if you want to use different routines for error processing. Note, however, that if you include the File Status clause for a file, the default error processing is usually bypassed. Because of that, you'll want to be sure to detect and handle all possible I/O errors for the file.

When you process sequential files on an IBM mainframe, the operating system assumes that the application program will handle I/O error conditions. As a result, most mainframe programs contain extensive error processing routines. You'll learn more about that later in this chapter.

File status categories

First digit	Meaning
0	The operation completed successfully.
1	An end-of-file condition occurred.
3	A permanent I/O error occurred.
4	A logic error occurred.
9	The operation was unsuccessful, and the condition is defined by the implementor.

File status codes

Code	Meaning
00	The I/O operation was successful.
04	The length of the record that was read doesn't conform to the attributes of the file.
10	The end-of-file condition occurred during a read operation (AT END condition).
30	The I/O operation was unsuccessful. No further information is available.
34	A write operation attempted to write a record beyond the externally defined boundaries of the file.
35	The program attempted to open a nonexistent file in I-O, input, or extend mode.
37	The program attempted to open a file that doesn't support the specified open mode.
39	A conflict occurred between the file attributes and the attributes specified in the program.
41	The program attempted to open a file that is already open.
42	The program attempted to close a file that is already closed.
43	A rewrite operation was attempted on a file, but the last successful operation on the file was not a Read statement.
44	The program attempted to rewrite a record that is not the same size as the record being replaced or is not within the allowed size range of a variable-length record.
46	A read operation was unsuccessful because the end-of-file condition already occurred or the previous read was unsuccessful.
47	The program attempted a read or start operation on a file that isn't opened in input or I-O mode.
48	The program attempted a write operation on a file that isn't opened in output, I-O, or extend mode.
49	The program attempted a delete or rewrite operation on a file that isn't opened in I-O mode.

Description

- If the File Status clause is specified, the File Status field must be defined in working storage as a two-byte alphanumeric field (XX).

- A file status code of 30 or greater indicates a serious error that a program typically can't recover from. If one of these errors occurs, the program should end.

Figure 13-3   File status codes for sequential files

A sequential update program

To show you how you can use the COBOL code for sequential files, this chapter now presents a complete program that updates a sequential file of inventory records. This type of program is still a workhorse in most large companies. As you review this program, you'll see that the difficulty in working with sequential files is in the program logic, not in the use of the COBOL statements.

The program specifications

Figure 13-4 presents the program specifications for a *sequential update program*. As the system flowchart at the top of this figure shows, the input files for this program are a receipt transaction file and the current (or old) master file. The output files are an updated (or new) master file and an error file of those receipt transactions that couldn't be processed.

To process the records in the transaction and master files, a program like this uses *matching record logic*. This means that after each transaction record is read, the program reads and writes the unaffected records in the master files until the *control field* (item number) in the transaction record *matches* (equals) the control field in the old master record. Then, the data in the transaction record is used to update the master record. On the other hand, if the transaction record is unmatched by a master record, an error is indicated. Then, the *unmatched transaction* is written to the file of error transactions.

For the matching record logic to work, both the transaction file and the old master file have to be in sequence by item number. Also, if a record in the old master file is unmatched by a transaction, it must still be written to the new master file. When the program ends, all of the records in the old master file have been written to the new master file...whether or not they were updated.

One of the benefits of this type of processing is that you end up with two generations of the master file, the old and the new. Then, if the new master file is damaged or its data is corrupted, you can rebuild that generation by rerunning the update program with the old transactions and the old master file. In some shops, three or more generations of each master file are kept along with all of the old transactions so the master files can be rebuilt if a disaster occurs.

The system flowchart for the sequential update program

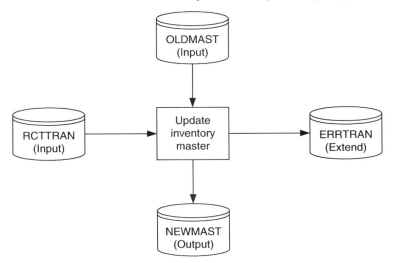

The record descriptions for the master and transaction files

```
01  INVENTORY-MASTER-RECORD.
    05  IM-ITEM-NO              PIC X(5).
    05  IM-DESCRIPTIVE-DATA.
        10  IM-ITEM-DESC        PIC X(40).
        10  IM-UNIT-COST        PIC S9(3)V99.
        10  IM-UNIT-PRICE       PIC S9(3)V99.
    05  IM-INVENTORY-DATA.
        10  IM-REORDER-POINT    PIC S9(5).
        10  IM-ON-HAND          PIC S9(5).
        10  IM-ON-ORDER         PIC S9(5).
```

```
01  RECEIPT-TRANSACTION.
    05  RT-ITEM-NO              PIC X(5).
    05  RT-VENDOR-NO            PIC X(5).
    05  RT-RECEIPT-DATE         PIC X(8).
    05  RT-RECEIPT-QUANTITY     PIC S9(5).
```

Processing specifications

- This program updates the data in an old master file (OLDMAST) based on the data in a file of receipt transactions (RCTTRAN). The output is a new master file (NEWMAST) that contains all the master records. It has the same record format as the old master file.

- If a transaction has the same item number as a master record, the transaction *matches* the master. Then, the transaction data should be used to update the master record.

- If a transaction has an item number that doesn't match any master record, the program should write the record to a file of error transactions (ERRTRAN). The records in this file should have the same format as the receipt transaction record.

- To update the master record, the receipt quantity in the transaction record should be added to the on hand quantity in the master file and subtracted from the on order quantity.

- This program assumes that the inventory master file and the receipt transaction file are in sequence by item number because that's the only way this sequential update program can work.

- This program also assumes that the receipt transactions have been previously edited so they contain valid data. But an *unmatched transaction* still represents an error condition.

Figure 13-4   The program specifications for the sequential update program

The test data and matching record logic

To help you understand how a sequential update program works, figure 13-5 shows test data for the receipt transaction and the old inventory master file. It also shows the test run output for the new master file and the error transaction file. As you can see, the records in all four files are in sequence by item number, and the old master file has the same number of records as the new master file.

If you study the data for the transaction file, you'll see that it contains three matched transactions: one for record number 10002, and two for record number 10011. For each of these transactions, the on hand quantity in the matching master record is increased by the receipt quantity and the on order quantity is reduced by the receipt quantity. The shaded fields in the master files show the fields that are updated.

The transaction file also contains one unmatched transaction. That of course indicates an error. In the test run output, you can see that this record has been written in the error transaction file.

Once you understand how the test data relates to the program specifications, you can consider the matching record logic that the program must follow. To start, the program reads the first transaction. Then, it reads and writes master records until the control field in the old master record is greater than or equal to the control field in the transaction record. Since the first transaction is for item number 10002, the program reads and writes master record 10001 and reads master record 10002 before this condition is met. Then, since the transaction matches the master record, the program *applies* the transaction data to the master. This means that the receipt quantity is used to update the fields in the master record, but the new master record isn't written to the file until later.

After the transaction has been applied, the program reads the next transaction, the one for item number 10006. Next, since the item number in the current master record isn't greater than or equal to 10006, the program writes that current master record (the updated record for item number 10002) and reads and writes the master records that follow until the one for item number 10011 is read. But this means that the transaction for item number 10006 is unmatched. As a result, the program writes the unmatched transaction to the error file.

After that, the program reads the next transaction record, the one for item number 10011. Since it matches the current master record, the receipt quantity is applied to the master record and the program reads another transaction. It too matches the current master record, so the receipt quantity is applied to the master record and the program reads another transaction. But this time, the end-of-file condition is turned on, which means that there are no more transactions.

At that point, the program must continue to write and read the master records until the end of the old master file is reached. That way, all of the records in the old master file are written to the new master file. When the end-of-file condition is turned on for both the transaction and old master files, the program ends.

If you understand this matching record logic, you're now ready to see how it can be implemented in the design and code for a sequential update program. As you will see, that's not quite as easy as this figure may make it seem.

Test data for the receipt transaction file

Item no.	Vendor no.	Receipt date	Receipt quantity	
10002	00235	05172000	05000	
10006	00194	05172000	00500	(Unmatched transaction)
10011	00235	05172000	05000	
10011	00235	05172000	05000	

Test data for the old master file

Item no.	Description	Unit cost	Unit price	Reorder point	On hand	On order
10001	CICS, Part 1	01250	04500	01000	05432	00000
10002	CICS, Part 2	01500	04500	05000	00390	05000
10004	DB2, Part 1	01095	04750	01000	06259	00000
10005	DB2, Part 2	01375	04750	00500	04765	00000
10011	Visual Basic 6	01435	04500	01500	00543	10000
10015	Structured COBOL	02210	06250	01000	02981	00000

Test run output for the new master file

Item no.	Description	Unit cost	Unit price	Reorder point	On hand	On order
10001	CICS, Part 1	01250	04500	01000	05432	00000
10002	CICS, Part 2	01500	04500	05000	05390	00000
10004	DB2, Part 1	01095	04750	01000	06259	00000
10005	DB2, Part 2	01375	04750	00500	04765	00000
10011	Visual Basic 6	01435	04500	01500	10543	00000
10015	Structured COBOL	02210	06250	01000	02981	00000

Test run output for the error transaction file

Item no.	Vendor no.	Receipt date	Receipt quantity
10006	00194	05172000	00500

The matching record logic

Read transaction 10002	Read old master 10001
	Write new master 10001
	Read old master 10002
	Apply transaction 10002
Read transaction 10006	Write new master 10002
	Read old master 10004
	Write new master 10004
	Read old master 10005
	Write new master 10005
	Read old master 10011
	Write unmatched error transaction 10006
Read transaction 10011	Apply transaction 10011
Read transaction 10011	Apply transaction 10011
Read transaction end-of-file	Write new master 10011
	Read old master 10015
	Write new master 10015
	Read old master end-of-file

Figure 13-5   The test data and matching record logic for the update program

The structure chart

Figure 13-6 presents the structure chart for this program. Here, module 000 performs module 300 until all of the transactions have been processed. Then, module 300 controls the processing that's done by the other modules.

To start, module 300 performs module 310 to read the first transaction record and module 320 to read and write the old master records until the item number in the master record is equal to or greater than the item number in the transaction record. Then, if the control fields are equal, module 300 performs module 350 to apply the receipt data to the master record. If they aren't, module 300 performs module 360 to write the transaction record to the error file. This logic is repeated until all of the old master records have been written to the new master file.

Please note that module 350 doesn't write a new master record to the file. It just applies the transaction data to the master record in storage. As a result, this program can process more than one transaction for a single master record. Then, when all of the transactions have been processed, module 340 writes the new master record.

The structure chart for the sequential update program

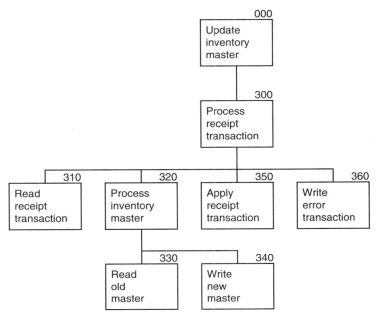

Description

- Module 000 of this program calls module 300 until all the records in the receipt transaction file have been processed and all of the old master records have been written to the new master file (whether or not they have been updated).

- Module 300 starts by calling module 310 to read a transaction record. Then, it calls module 320 until the item number in the old master record is equal to or greater than the item number in the current transaction.

- The first time module 320 is called, it calls module 330 to read the first old master record. After that, it calls module 340 to write a new master record and module 330 to read an old master record each time that it is called.

- When the item number in the transaction record and old master record are equal, module 300 calls module 350 to apply the transaction to the old master record. This just updates the fields in the matched master record; it doesn't write the new master record.

- When a transaction record is unmatched, module 300 calls module 360 to write a record on the error file.

Figure 13-6   The structure chart for the sequential update program

The COBOL code

Figure 13-7 presents the COBOL code for this sequential update program. If you look at the Select statements for the four files, you can see that they are coded for non-VSAM files on an IBM mainframe. For Micro Focus Personal COBOL, though, you just change the system names to the paths and file names for your files.

You can also see that the Select statements for the two output files are defined with File Status fields. Note that the field names consist of the file names followed by the words File Status as in NEWMAST-FILE-STATUS. This is an effective naming technique. Here, only the output files are defined with File Status fields because input errors aren't as critical as output errors.

In the File Section, you can see the FD statements and the record descriptions. In this case, though, none of the record descriptions include the fields that make them up. That's because the complete record descriptions are defined in the Working-Storage Section. To make this work, the program uses Read Into and Write From statements.

In the Working-Storage Section, you can see the two switches that are used by this program. You can also see the way the File Status fields are defined. Note that condition names have been defined for file status codes that have a value of zero. This means that the I/O operation was performed successfully.

The sequential update program   **Page 1**

```
IDENTIFICATION DIVISION.
*
PROGRAM-ID.  SEQ1000.
*
ENVIRONMENT DIVISION.
*
INPUT-OUTPUT SECTION.
*
FILE-CONTROL.
    SELECT RCTTRAN   ASSIGN TO RCTTRAN.
    SELECT OLDMAST   ASSIGN TO OLDMAST.
    SELECT NEWMAST   ASSIGN TO NEWMAST
                     FILE STATUS IS NEWMAST-FILE-STATUS.
    SELECT ERRTRAN   ASSIGN TO ERRTRAN
                     FILE STATUS IS ERRTRAN-FILE-STATUS.
*
DATA DIVISION.
*
FILE SECTION.
*
FD  RCTTRAN.
01  TRANSACTION-RECORD       PIC X(23).
*
FD  OLDMAST.
01  OLD-MASTER-RECORD        PIC X(70).
*
FD  NEWMAST.
01  NEW-MASTER-RECORD        PIC X(70).
*
FD  ERRTRAN.
01  ERROR-TRANSACTION        PIC X(23).
*
WORKING-STORAGE SECTION.
*
01  SWITCHES.
    05  FIRST-EXECUTION-SWITCH          PIC X    VALUE "Y".
        88  FIRST-EXECUTION                      VALUE "Y".
    05  ALL-RECORDS-PROCESSED-SWITCH    PIC X    VALUE "N".
        88  ALL-RECORDS-PROCESSED                VALUE "Y".
*
01  FILE-STATUS-FIELDS.
    05  NEWMAST-FILE-STATUS     PIC XX.
        88  NEWMAST-SUCCESSFUL              VALUE "00".
    05  ERRTRAN-FILE-STATUS     PIC XX.
        88  ERRTRAN-SUCCESSFUL              VALUE "00".
*
```

Figure 13-7   The COBOL code for the sequential update program (part 1 of 3)

On page 2 of this program, you can see the record descriptions for the receipt transaction and inventory master records. In this case, the transaction record will receive each record that's read, but it will also be used for writing error transactions. Similarly, the master record will receive each old record that's read, but it will also be used for writing each new record.

In procedure 000, you can see the Open statement for the four files. Here, the error transaction file is opened in extend mode. This means that any records that are written to the file will be written after those that have already been saved in the file by another program. Although a file like this is normally opened in output mode, this illustrates the use of extend mode.

Next, procedure 000 moves LOW-VALUE to the item number field in the inventory master record area in working storage. This makes the logic in procedure 300 work correctly. Then, procedure 000 performs procedure 300 until all of the records have been processed.

Procedure 300 holds the matching record logic of the program. After it performs procedure 310 to read a transaction record, it performs module 320 to read and write inventory master records until the old master record has an item number that is greater than or equal to the item number in the transaction record. Because the master item number was set to LOW-VALUE in procedure 000, its value will be lower than the transaction item number, so this Perform Until statement will work right the first time it's executed. Otherwise, the starting value of the master item number can't be predicted, so this may not work correctly.

The nested If statements in procedure 300 complete the matching record logic of this program. First, if the item number fields for both the transaction and master files have been set to HIGH-VALUE by procedures 310 and 330, the all-records-processed switch is turned on and no processing is done. Otherwise, if the item numbers in the transaction and master records match, procedure 350 is performed to apply the transaction data. If they don't match, procedure 360 is performed to write an error transaction.

In procedure 310, you can see a Read Into statement that sets the transaction item number to HIGH-VALUE when the end-of-file condition is reached. On the next page, you can see that procedure 330 also uses a Read Into statement that sets the master item number to HIGH-VALUE when its end-of-file condition is met. That way, the If statement in module 300 will continue to work after the end-of-file condition has occurred for either file. If, for example, there are no more transactions, but there are more old master records, the program will continue to read and write the master records until all have been processed. On the other hand, if there are more transactions but no more master records, those transactions will be read and written on the error file.

The sequential update program   **Page 2**

```
01  RECEIPT-TRANSACTION.
    05  RT-ITEM-NO              PIC X(5).
    05  RT-VENDOR-NO            PIC X(5).
    05  RT-RECEIPT-DATE         PIC X(8).
    05  RT-RECEIPT-QUANTITY     PIC S9(5).
*
01  INVENTORY-MASTER-RECORD.
    05  IM-ITEM-NO              PIC X(5).
    05  IM-DESCRIPTIVE-DATA.
        10  IM-ITEM-DESC        PIC X(40).
        10  IM-UNIT-COST        PIC S9(3)V99.
        10  IM-UNIT-PRICE       PIC S9(3)V99.
    05  IM-INVENTORY-DATA.
        10  IM-REORDER-POINT    PIC S9(5).
        10  IM-ON-HAND          PIC S9(5).
        10  IM-ON-ORDER         PIC S9(5).
*
 PROCEDURE DIVISION.
*
 000-UPDATE-INVENTORY-MASTER.
*
    OPEN INPUT   RCTTRAN
                 OLDMAST
         OUTPUT  NEWMAST
         EXTEND  ERRTRAN.
    MOVE LOW-VALUE TO IM-ITEM-NO.
    PERFORM 300-PROCESS-RECEIPT-TRAN
        UNTIL ALL-RECORDS-PROCESSED.
    CLOSE RCTTRAN
          OLDMAST
          NEWMAST
          ERRTRAN.
    STOP RUN.
*
 300-PROCESS-RECEIPT-TRAN.
*
    PERFORM 310-READ-RECEIPT-TRANSACTION.
    PERFORM 320-PROCESS-INVENTORY-MASTER
        UNTIL IM-ITEM-NO >= RT-ITEM-NO.
    IF     IM-ITEM-NO = HIGH-VALUE
       AND RT-ITEM-NO = HIGH-VALUE
           MOVE "Y" TO ALL-RECORDS-PROCESSED-SWITCH
    ELSE
        IF IM-ITEM-NO = RT-ITEM-NO
            PERFORM 350-APPLY-RECEIPT-TRANSACTION
        ELSE
            PERFORM 360-WRITE-ERROR-TRANSACTION.
*
 310-READ-RECEIPT-TRANSACTION.
*
    READ RCTTRAN INTO RECEIPT-TRANSACTION
        AT END
            MOVE HIGH-VALUE TO RT-ITEM-NO.
*
```

Figure 13-7   The COBOL code for the sequential update program (part 2 of 3)

On page 3 in procedure 320, you can see the processing for the old and new master files. The first time this procedure is executed (FIRST-EXECUTION), it performs procedure 330 to read an old master record and turns off the first-execution switch. All of the other times this procedure is executed, it performs procedure 340 to write a new master record before it performs procedure 330 to read the next old master record. As a result, all of the records that are read from the old master file are also written to the new master file.

That completes the critical logic of this program. After that, procedure 330 reads the old master records. Procedures 340 and 360 write the new master and error transaction records. And procedure 350 applies the transaction data to the master record. In this case, this procedure just adds the receipt quantity to the on hand quantity and subtracts it from the on order quantity, but an update program in the real world may update many fields.

In procedures 340 and 360, you can see that Write From statements are used to write records from the same areas in working storage that are used by the Read Into statements in procedures 310 and 330. You can also see how the file status codes are used. In both cases, if the file status code isn't zero, a message is displayed and the all-records-processed switch is turned on so the program will end.

If you now understand how this program works, you're well on your way to successful use of sequential files. On the other hand, if you're having some difficulty understanding its logic, you can step through this program when you do exercise 13-1. That should give you a solid understanding of how it works.

The sequential update program   **Page 3**

```
320-PROCESS-INVENTORY-MASTER.
*
      IF FIRST-EXECUTION
          PERFORM 330-READ-OLD-MASTER
          MOVE "N" TO FIRST-EXECUTION-SWITCH
      ELSE
          PERFORM 340-WRITE-NEW-MASTER
          PERFORM 330-READ-OLD-MASTER.
*
 330-READ-OLD-MASTER.
*
      READ OLDMAST INTO INVENTORY-MASTER-RECORD
          AT END
              MOVE HIGH-VALUE TO IM-ITEM-NO.
*
 340-WRITE-NEW-MASTER.
*
      WRITE NEW-MASTER-RECORD FROM INVENTORY-MASTER-RECORD.
      IF NOT NEWMAST-SUCCESSFUL
          DISPLAY "WRITE ERROR ON NEWMAST FOR ITEM NUMBER "
              IM-ITEM-NO
          DISPLAY "FILE STATUS CODE IS " NEWMAST-FILE-STATUS
          MOVE "Y" TO ALL-RECORDS-PROCESSED-SWITCH.
*
 350-APPLY-RECEIPT-TRANSACTION.
*
      ADD RT-RECEIPT-QUANTITY TO IM-ON-HAND.
      SUBTRACT RT-RECEIPT-QUANTITY FROM IM-ON-ORDER.
*
 360-WRITE-ERROR-TRANSACTION.
*
      WRITE ERROR-TRANSACTION FROM RECEIPT-TRANSACTION.
      IF NOT ERRTRAN-SUCCESSFUL
          DISPLAY "WRITE ERROR ON ERRTRAN FOR ITEM NUMBER "
              RT-ITEM-NO
          DISPLAY "FILE STATUS CODE IS " ERRTRAN-FILE-STATUS
          MOVE "Y" TO ALL-RECORDS-PROCESSED-SWITCH.
```

Figure 13-7   The COBOL code for the sequential update program (part 3 of 3)

A sequential maintenance program

In contrast to an update program, a *sequential maintenance program* can add, delete, or change the records in a master file. As you will see, this complicates the logic of the program, but the essential logic is still matching record logic.

The program specifications

Figure 13-8 presents the program specifications for a sequential maintenance program. As the system flowchart at the top of this figure shows, the input files are a maintenance transaction file and the current (old) inventory master file. The output files are a new inventory master file and a file of error transactions. Here again, the record descriptions for the old and new master files are the same, and the record descriptions for the transaction and error files are the same.

As you can see, the first field in the transaction record contains a code that tells whether the transaction is a deletion, addition, or change. If a transaction is for a deletion, the record contains just the item number of the record to be deleted. If a transaction is for an addition, the record contains data for all the fields. And if the transaction is for a change, the record contains the item number and the data for any fields to be changed.

For the matching record logic to work, the records in both input files have to be in sequence by item number. In addition, because this program provides for more than one transaction for each master record, the transaction records have to be in sequence by transaction code within item number. That way, a deletion for an item comes before an addition, which comes before a change. As a result, you can delete a master record, add a new record with the same item number, and change the data in the new record. Although the possibility of all three for one item number is remote, a program has to provide for all possibilities.

Although this program assumes that the transactions contain valid data, three error conditions are still possible. These include an unmatched deletion, an unmatched change, or a matched addition. The transaction records for all three of these errors should be written to the error transaction file.

The system flowchart for the sequential maintenance program

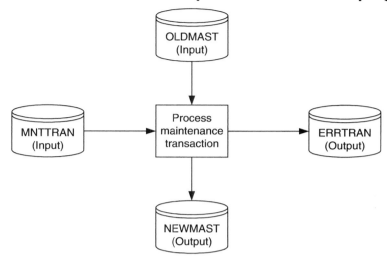

The record descriptions for the master and transaction files

```
01  INVENTORY-MASTER-RECORD.                    01  MAINTENANCE-TRANSACTION.
    05  IM-ITEM-NO          PIC X(5).               05  MT-TRANSACTION-CODE   PIC X.
    05  IM-DESCRIPTIVE-DATA.                             88  DELETE-RECORD     VALUE "1".
        10  IM-ITEM-DESC    PIC X(40).                   88  ADD-RECORD        VALUE "2".
        10  IM-UNIT-COST    PIC S9(3)V99.               88  CHANGE-RECORD     VALUE "3".
        10  IM-UNIT-PRICE   PIC S9(3)V99.           05  MT-MASTER-DATA.
    05  IM-INVENTORY-DATA.                               10  MT-ITEM-NO        PIC X(5).
        10  IM-REORDER-POINT PIC S9(5).                  10  MT-ITEM-DESC      PIC X(40).
        10  IM-ON-HAND      PIC S9(5).                   10  MT-UNIT-COST      PIC S9(3)V99.
        10  IM-ON-ORDER     PIC S9(5).                   10  MT-UNIT-PRICE     PIC S9(3)V99.
                                                         10  MT-REORDER-POINT  PIC S9(5).
```

Processing specifications

- This program adds, changes, and deletes records in an inventory master file (OLDMAST) based on the data in a file of maintenance transactions (MNTTRAN). The output is a new master file (NEWMAST) that reflects the additions, changes, and deletions.

- This program assumes that the maintenance transactions have been previously edited so they contain valid data. However, if MNTTRAN contains a change or delete transaction for a record that doesn't exist or an add transaction for an existing record, the program should write the record to a file of error transactions (ERRTRAN).

- This program also assumes that the records in the OLDMAST file are in sequence by item number and that the records in the MNTTRAN file are in sequence by transaction code within item number. That way, a single item can be deleted, added back, and then changed.

- A delete transaction contains data for just the transaction code and item number. An add transaction contains data for all the fields in the transaction record, and the program must set the on hand and on order fields to zeros. A change transaction contains data for the item number and any fields to be changed.

Figure 13-8   The program specifications for the sequential maintenance program

The test data and matching record logic

To help you understand how this program works, figure 13-9 shows test data for the maintenance transaction and the old inventory master files. As you can see, the records in the old master file are in sequence by item number, and the records in the transaction file are in sequence by transaction code within item number.

If you study the data for the transaction file, you'll see that it contains four valid transactions and three invalid transactions. The three invalid transactions are for an unmatched change, a matched addition, and an unmatched deletion. The descriptions for these test records indicate the error conditions so it's easier to tell how the program is supposed to handle each transaction during the test runs. The four valid transactions are for a change that changes the unit cost, unit price, and reorder point fields; a deletion; a change that changes the description field; and an addition.

Once you understand the test data, you can consider the matching record logic that the program must follow. Here again, the program starts by reading the first transaction. Then, it reads and writes master records until the control field in the old master record is greater than or equal to the control field in the transaction record. Since the first transaction is for item number 10004, the program reads and writes master records until old master record 10004 is read. Then, since the transaction is a change that matches the master record, the program applies the change transaction to the master. This means that the unit cost, unit price, and reorder point fields are changed, but the new master record isn't written to the file yet.

After the transaction has been applied, the program reads the next transaction, the one for item number 10007. Next, since the item number in the current master record isn't greater than or equal to 10007, the program writes the current master record (the changed record for item number 10004) and reads and writes the master records that follow until the one for item number 10007 is read. Then, since the transaction is a deletion that matches the current master record, the program applies the deletion. That means that it sets a switch so the old master record won't be written on the new master file.

After that, the program reads the next transaction record and the next old master record without writing the last old master. That concludes the deletion. Then, since the current transaction is a change for item number 10008, the program reads the next old master record, which is for item number 10009. Since that means the change transaction is unmatched, the transaction is written to the error file.

The program continues in this way until all the transactions have been read and processed. Note that when a valid addition transaction is processed, the added record is written to the new master, but the next old master record isn't read. That way, the last old record is still available for deletion or change. This, however, means that the new addition record and the old master record have to be stored in different storage areas. You should also note that the program doesn't stop until the end-of-file condition has been reached for both the transaction and old master files.

Test data for the maintenance transaction file

Tran code	Item no.	Description	Unit cost	Unit price	Reorder point
3	10004		01500	05000	00500
1	10007				
3	10008	Unmatched change	00000	00000	00000
2	10009	Matched addition	00000	00000	00000
3	10009	The CICS Desk Reference	00000	00000	00000
1	10013	Unmatched deletion			
2	10013	MVS JCL (3rd Edition)	01475	05000	01000

Test data for the old master file

Item no.	Description	Unit cost	Unit price	Reorder point	On hand	On order
10001	CICS, Part 1	01250	04500	01000	05432	00000
10002	CICS, Part 2	01500	04500	00500	00390	05000
10004	DB2, Part 1	01095	04750	01000	06259	00000
10005	DB2, Part 2	01375	04750	00500	04765	00000
10007	MVS JCL (Second Edition)	01185	05000	01000	11211	00000
10009	The CICS Programmer's Reference	01522	05000	00500	03191	00000
10011	Murach's Visual Basic 6	01435	04500	01500	00543	10000
10015	Murach's Structured COBOL	02210	06250	01000	02981	00000

The matching record logic

Read change transaction 10004

Read old master 10001
Write new master 10001
Read old master 10002
Write new master 10002
Read old master 10004
Apply change transaction 10004

Read delete transaction 10007
Write new master 10004
Read old master 10005
Write new master 10005
Read old master 10007
Apply delete transaction 10007

Read change transaction 10008
Read old master 10009 ———————————— **No write for deleted master record 10007**
Write unmatched change error transaction 10008

Read addition transaction 10009   Write matched addition error transaction 10009
Read change transaction 10009   Apply change transaction 10009
Read delete transaction 10013   Write new master 10009
Read old master 10011
Write new master 10011
Read old master 10015
Write unmatched delete error transaction 10013

Read addition transaction 10013   Apply add transaction
Read transaction end-of-file   Write new master 10013 ———————————— **No read of an old master after a write for added record 10013 so record 10015 is still available**
Write new master 10015
Read old master end-of-file

Figure 13-9   The test data and matching record logic for the maintenance program

The structure chart

Figure 13-10 presents the structure chart for the sequential maintenance program. This of course is just one design that will work for this type of program, but it's a design that has been used for many years in dozens of COBOL shops throughout the country. The benefit of this design is that it's relatively easy to understand and implement because the matching record logic is reflected by the chart.

After module 300 calls modules 310 and 320 to read a transaction and an old master, it calls module 330 to match the two. Next, based on the result of the comparison, module 330 calls module 350, module 360, or module 370. These modules do the processing for a master with a higher item number than the one in the transaction (an addition or an unmatched change or deletion), a master with a lower item number than the one in the transaction (no transaction), or a master with an item number that equals the one in the transaction (a change or deletion or a matched addition).

Then, modules 350, 360, and 370 call the modules that do the appropriate processing for the conditions that they represent. If, for example, the transaction is an addition, module 350 calls module 380 to apply the addition. Otherwise, it calls module 390 to write the unmatched transaction to the error file. Similarly, if the transaction is a deletion or change, module 370 calls module 400 or 410 to apply the transaction. Otherwise, it calls module 390 to write the matched transaction to the error file.

To implement this logic, modules 360, 380, 390, 400, and 410 need to set switches that indicate whether a transaction needs to be read, an old master needs to be read, or a new master needs to be written. For instance, module 360 turns the write-master and need-master switches on; module 380 turns the write-master and need-transaction switches on; and module 390 turns the need-transaction switch on. These switches are tested by module 300 as it decides whether to call module 310, 320, or 340. You'll see how this works when you review the code for this program.

Incidentally, we didn't number the modules down the legs of this chart the way we normally do because we wanted the related logic modules to be together in the COBOL code. That will make it easier for you to review the code.

The structure chart for the sequential maintenance program

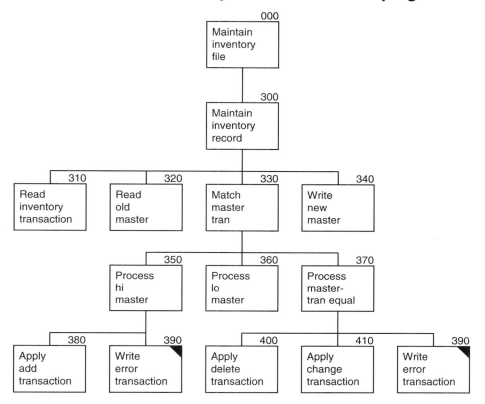

Description

- Module 000 of this program calls module 300 until all the records in the mainte-nance transaction file and the old master file have been processed.
- Module 300 calls modules 310, 320, and 340 based on the values of switches that are set by modules 360, 380, 390, 400, and 410.
- Module 330 compares (matches) the item number fields in the current transaction and master records. Based on that comparison, it calls module 350, 360, or 370.
- Module 350 checks the transaction code in the current record. If it's for an addition, it calls module 380 to apply the transaction. Otherwise, it calls module 390 to write the transaction on the error file.
- Module 370 checks the transaction code in the current record. If it's for a deletion or change, it calls module 400 or 410. Otherwise, it calls module 390 to write the transaction on the error file.

Figure 13-10   The structure chart for the sequential file maintenance program

The COBOL code

Figure 13-11 presents the COBOL code for the sequential maintenance program. On the first page, you can see the Select statements, FD statements, and record descriptions for the four files used by this program. Here, the record descriptions for three of the files consist of just one item that defines the entire record. For these files, the complete record descriptions are in working storage. In contrast, the record description for the new master record defines all of the fields in the record. You'll see why this is necessary later on.

In the switches for the program, you can see that the first one is the same as the first one for the sequential update program. It is turned on when all of the records in both the transaction and old master files have been read. In addition, there are three switches that indicate when the program needs to read the next transaction, read the next old master, or write the next new master. These switches are used to control the matching record logic of the program. Note that the need-transaction and need-master switches are turned on by these definitions so the program starts by reading a transaction and a master record.

The sequential maintenance program   **Page 1**

```
 IDENTIFICATION DIVISION.
*
 PROGRAM-ID.  SEQ2000.
*
 ENVIRONMENT DIVISION.
*
 INPUT-OUTPUT SECTION.
*
 FILE-CONTROL.
     SELECT MNTTRAN   ASSIGN TO MNTTRAN.
     SELECT OLDMAST   ASSIGN TO OLDMAST.
     SELECT NEWMAST   ASSIGN TO NEWMAST
                      FILE STATUS IS NEWMAST-FILE-STATUS.
     SELECT ERRTRAN   ASSIGN TO ERRTRAN
                      FILE STATUS IS ERRTRAN-FILE-STATUS.
*
 DATA DIVISION.
*
 FILE SECTION.
*
 FD  MNTTRAN.
 01  TRANSACTION-RECORD      PIC X(61).
*
 FD  OLDMAST.
 01  OLD-MASTER-RECORD       PIC X(70).
*
 FD  NEWMAST.
 01  NEW-MASTER-RECORD.
     05  NM-ITEM-NO             PIC X(5).
     05  NM-DESCRIPTIVE-DATA.
         10  NM-ITEM-DESC       PIC X(40).
         10  NM-UNIT-COST       PIC S9(3)V99.
         10  NM-UNIT-PRICE      PIC S9(3)V99.
     05  NM-INVENTORY-DATA.
         10  NM-REORDER-POINT   PIC S9(5).
         10  NM-ON-HAND         PIC S9(5).
         10  NM-ON-ORDER        PIC S9(5).
*
 FD  ERRTRAN.
 01  ERROR-TRANSACTION       PIC X(61).
*
 WORKING-STORAGE SECTION.
*
 01  SWITCHES.
     05  ALL-RECORDS-PROCESSED-SWITCH   PIC X   VALUE "N".
         88  ALL-RECORDS-PROCESSED              VALUE "Y".
     05  NEED-TRANSACTION-SWITCH        PIC X   VALUE "Y".
         88  NEED-TRANSACTION                   VALUE "Y".
     05  NEED-MASTER-SWITCH             PIC X   VALUE "Y".
         88  NEED-MASTER                        VALUE "Y".
     05  WRITE-MASTER-SWITCH            PIC X   VALUE "N".
         88  WRITE-MASTER                       VALUE "Y".
*
```

Figure 13-11   The COBOL code for the sequential maintenance program (part 1 of 4)

On page 2, you can see the way the File Status fields are defined. Here again, condition names have been defined for file status codes that have a value of zero. This means that the I/O operation was performed successfully.

After that, you can see the record descriptions for the transaction and master records and the first procedure of the Procedure Division. Because the code in the first procedure is like the code in the update program, you should already understand it.

The sequential maintenance program

Page 2

```
01  FILE-STATUS-FIELDS.
    05  NEWMAST-FILE-STATUS      PIC XX.
        88  NEWMAST-SUCCESSFUL            VALUE "00".
    05  ERRTRAN-FILE-STATUS      PIC XX.
        88  ERRTRAN-SUCCESSFUL            VALUE "00".
*
01  MAINTENANCE-TRANSACTION.
    05  MT-TRANSACTION-CODE      PIC X.
        88  DELETE-RECORD                VALUE "1".
        88  ADD-RECORD                   VALUE "2".
        88  CHANGE-RECORD                VALUE "3".
    05  MT-MASTER-DATA.
        10  MT-ITEM-NO          PIC X(5).
        10  MT-ITEM-DESC        PIC X(40).
        10  MT-UNIT-COST        PIC S9(3)V99.
        10  MT-UNIT-PRICE       PIC S9(3)V99.
        10  MT-REORDER-POINT    PIC S9(5).
*
01  INVENTORY-MASTER-RECORD.
    05  IM-ITEM-NO              PIC X(5).
    05  IM-DESCRIPTIVE-DATA.
        10  IM-ITEM-DESC        PIC X(40).
        10  IM-UNIT-COST        PIC S9(3)V99.
        10  IM-UNIT-PRICE       PIC S9(3)V99.
    05  IM-INVENTORY-DATA.
        10  IM-REORDER-POINT    PIC S9(5).
        10  IM-ON-HAND          PIC S9(5).
        10  IM-ON-ORDER         PIC S9(5).
*
 PROCEDURE DIVISION.
*
 000-MAINTAIN-INVENTORY-FILE.
*
    OPEN INPUT  OLDMAST
                MNTTRAN
         OUTPUT NEWMAST
                ERRTRAN.
    PERFORM 300-MAINTAIN-INVENTORY-RECORD
        UNTIL ALL-RECORDS-PROCESSED.
    CLOSE MNTTRAN
          OLDMAST
          NEWMAST
          ERRTRAN.
    STOP RUN.
*
```

Figure 13-11   The COBOL code for the sequential maintenance program (part 2 of 4)

On page 3, you can see most of the critical logic of the program. Each time procedure 300 is performed, it checks the appropriate switches to see whether it needs to perform procedure 310 or 320 to read a transaction or an old master. Then, it performs procedure 330 to match the current transaction and old master records. Last, it checks the appropriate switch to see whether it needs to perform procedure 340 to write a new master record. This logic is easy to follow and works the way you want it to…as long as the switches are set correctly by the lower-level modules.

In procedures 310 and 320, you can see that the Read statements use the Into clause to read the records into working storage. They also move HIGH-VALUE to the control fields when the At End clauses are executed. That way, the If statement in procedure 330 will continue to work after there are no more records in one of the files.

In procedure 340, you should note that the Write statement doesn't use the From clause. As a result, the data for the next master record has to be moved to NEW-MASTER-RECORD before this procedure is performed. For an addition, procedure 380 builds the record right in this area. Otherwise, the old master record in working storage is moved to this area by procedure 360.

In procedure 330, nested Ifs are used to compare the control fields in the transaction and old master records. Based on this comparison, procedure 350, 360, or 370 is performed. These represent the three possible results of the comparison: master control field is higher than the transaction control field; master is lower than the transaction; or master is equal to the transaction.

This simple logic continues in the procedures at the next level of the structure chart. For instance, when the master is high, procedure 350 performs procedure 380 if the transaction is an addition. Otherwise, it performs procedure 390 to write an unmatched change or deletion record to the error file. And when the master is low, procedure 360 moves the old master record from working storage to the record area for the new master file and turns on the write-master and need-master switches.

The sequential maintenance program   **Page 3**

```
300-MAINTAIN-INVENTORY-RECORD.
*
    IF NEED-TRANSACTION
        PERFORM 310-READ-INVENTORY-TRANSACTION
        MOVE "N" TO NEED-TRANSACTION-SWITCH.
    IF NEED-MASTER
        PERFORM 320-READ-OLD-MASTER
        MOVE "N" TO NEED-MASTER-SWITCH.
    PERFORM 330-MATCH-MASTER-TRAN.
    IF WRITE-MASTER
        PERFORM 340-WRITE-NEW-MASTER
        MOVE "N" TO WRITE-MASTER-SWITCH.
*
310-READ-INVENTORY-TRANSACTION.
*
    READ MNTTRAN INTO MAINTENANCE-TRANSACTION
        AT END
            MOVE HIGH-VALUE TO MT-ITEM-NO.
*
320-READ-OLD-MASTER.
*
    READ OLDMAST INTO INVENTORY-MASTER-RECORD
        AT END
            MOVE HIGH-VALUE TO IM-ITEM-NO.
*
330-MATCH-MASTER-TRAN.
*
    IF IM-ITEM-NO > MT-ITEM-NO
        PERFORM 350-PROCESS-HI-MASTER
    ELSE IF IM-ITEM-NO < MT-ITEM-NO
        PERFORM 360-PROCESS-LO-MASTER
    ELSE
        PERFORM 370-PROCESS-MAST-TRAN-EQUAL.
*
340-WRITE-NEW-MASTER.
*
    WRITE NEW-MASTER-RECORD.
    IF NOT NEWMAST-SUCCESSFUL
        DISPLAY "WRITE ERROR ON NEWMAST FOR ITEM NUMBER "
            IM-ITEM-NO
        DISPLAY "FILE STATUS CODE IS " NEWMAST-FILE-STATUS
        MOVE "Y" TO ALL-RECORDS-PROCESSED-SWITCH.
*
350-PROCESS-HI-MASTER.
*
    IF ADD-RECORD
        PERFORM 380-APPLY-ADD-TRANSACTION
    ELSE
        PERFORM 390-WRITE-ERROR-TRANSACTION.
*
360-PROCESS-LO-MASTER.
*
    MOVE INVENTORY-MASTER-RECORD TO NEW-MASTER-RECORD.
    MOVE "Y" TO WRITE-MASTER-SWITCH.
    MOVE "Y" TO NEED-MASTER-SWITCH.
```

Figure 13-11   The COBOL code for the sequential maintenance program (part 3 of 4)

Similarly, when the master and the transaction are equal, procedure 370 performs procedure 400 if the transaction is a deletion or procedure 410 if the transaction is a change. Otherwise, it performs procedure 390 to write a matched addition to the error file. If the master control field is HIGH-VALUE, though, which means that the transaction control field is also HIGH-VALUE, procedure 370 turns on the all-records-processed switch.

The last four procedures in this program apply the valid transactions and write error transactions. In procedure 380, for example, you can see the code for applying an addition transaction. Here, all the fields in the transaction record are moved to the new master fields that are defined in the File Section, not to the master fields in working storage. Next, zeros are moved to the on hand and on order fields to initialize them. Then, this procedure turns on the write-master and need-transaction switches, so the new master will be written and another transaction will be read, but another old master won't be read. Meanwhile, the last old master record is still in working storage ready for the comparison with the next transaction record.

In procedure 390, which writes an error transaction, you can see that the need-transaction switch is turned on if the transaction is written successfully. That means the next transaction will be read the next time procedure 300 is executed, but the master files won't be affected.

In procedure 400, which applies a delete transaction, the need-master and need-transaction switches are turned on so procedure 300 will read both a master and a transaction record the next time it is executed. Note, however, that the old master record won't be written, which in effect deletes that record.

Finally, in procedure 410, which applies a change transaction, the changes are applied to the master record in working storage. Then, the need transaction switch is turned on so the next transaction record will be read. This keeps the master record in working storage so another change transaction can be applied to it. Later, when procedure 360 is executed, the master record in working storage is moved to the record area in the File Section so the record can be written to the new master file.

The sequential maintenance program   **Page 4**

```
370-PROCESS-MAST-TRAN-EQUAL.
*
    IF IM-ITEM-NO = HIGH-VALUE
        MOVE "Y" TO ALL-RECORDS-PROCESSED-SWITCH
    ELSE
        IF DELETE-RECORD
            PERFORM 400-APPLY-DELETE-TRANSACTION
        ELSE
            IF CHANGE-RECORD
                PERFORM 410-APPLY-CHANGE-TRANSACTION
            ELSE
                PERFORM 390-WRITE-ERROR-TRANSACTION.
*
380-APPLY-ADD-TRANSACTION.
*
    MOVE MT-ITEM-NO TO NM-ITEM-NO.
    MOVE MT-ITEM-DESC TO NM-ITEM-DESC.
    MOVE MT-UNIT-COST TO NM-UNIT-COST.
    MOVE MT-UNIT-PRICE TO NM-UNIT-PRICE.
    MOVE MT-REORDER-POINT TO NM-REORDER-POINT.
    MOVE ZERO TO NM-ON-HAND
                 NM-ON-ORDER.
    MOVE "Y" TO WRITE-MASTER-SWITCH.
    MOVE "Y" TO NEED-TRANSACTION-SWITCH.
*
390-WRITE-ERROR-TRANSACTION.
*
    WRITE ERROR-TRANSACTION FROM MAINTENANCE-TRANSACTION.
    IF NOT ERRTRAN-SUCCESSFUL
        DISPLAY "WRITE ERROR ON ERRTRAN FOR ITEM NUMBER "
            MT-ITEM-NO
        DISPLAY "FILE STATUS CODE IS " ERRTRAN-FILE-STATUS
        MOVE "Y" TO ALL-RECORDS-PROCESSED-SWITCH
    ELSE
        MOVE "Y" TO NEED-TRANSACTION-SWITCH.
*
400-APPLY-DELETE-TRANSACTION.
*
    MOVE "Y" TO NEED-MASTER-SWITCH.
    MOVE "Y" TO NEED-TRANSACTION-SWITCH.
*
410-APPLY-CHANGE-TRANSACTION.
*
    IF MT-ITEM-DESC NOT = SPACE
        MOVE MT-ITEM-DESC TO IM-ITEM-DESC.
    IF MT-UNIT-COST NOT = ZERO
        MOVE MT-UNIT-COST TO IM-UNIT-COST.
    IF MT-UNIT-PRICE NOT = ZERO
        MOVE MT-UNIT-PRICE TO IM-UNIT-PRICE.
    IF MT-REORDER-POINT NOT = ZERO
        MOVE MT-REORDER-POINT TO IM-REORDER-POINT.
    MOVE "Y" TO NEED-TRANSACTION-SWITCH.
```

Figure 13-11   The COBOL code for the sequential maintenance program (part 4 of 4)

Special considerations for sequential update and maintenance programs

When you write a program that updates or maintains sequential files, you need to make sure that your error processing routines meet the requirements of your shop. You also need to use some testing and debugging techniques that are unique to this type of program. Last, you should be aware that there are many ways to design and code programs like this.

Error processing for I/O operations

On some platforms, error processing for input and output operations is done by the system so you don't have to provide any error processing routines in your COBOL programs. On other platforms, you need to use file status codes for the critical files and Display statements that display those codes when serious errors occur. You've just seen that type of error processing in the update and maintenance programs.

When you process files on an IBM mainframe, though, the operating system assumes that the application program will handle I/O error conditions. As a result, you need to include complete error processing routines in your COBOL programs. In particular, you need to end a program abnormally when a serious error occurs as summarized in figure 13-12.

In the mainframe environment, it's usually not enough to display an error message and end the program normally via the Stop Run statement. Why? Because displayed messages are usually displayed on an operator's console, where they may be ignored. In addition, an update program is likely to be running in a series of related programs that will continue to run as long as each program ends normally. If the update program doesn't work correctly, though, this series of programs should be aborted.

The solution to this problem is for the COBOL program to end abnormally, or *abend*, when a serious error occurs. Since COBOL doesn't provide a direct way for doing that, you call a subprogram that's written in assembler language. In some cases, this subprogram will print a *storage dump* in addition to abending, so you need to provide for SYSUDUMP output in the JCL for running the program.

Since the error processing requirements vary from one COBOL shop to another, you need to find out what's required on your system. Do you need to provide error processing routines for Open, Read, and Close statements as well as for Write statements? How should the error messages be formatted? Does your shop have a special subprogram for displaying error messages and abending? Once you get the answers for questions like these, you shouldn't have any trouble coding these routines.

A Write procedure with enhanced error processing

```
340-WRITE-NEW-MASTER.
*
    WRITE NEW-MASTER-RECORD FROM INVENTORY-MASTER-RECORD.
    IF NOT NEWMAST-SUCCESSFUL
        DISPLAY "WRITE ERROR ON NEWMAST FOR ITEM NUMBER "
            IM-ITEM-NO
        DISPLAY "FILE STATUS CODE IS " NEWMAST-FILE-STATUS
        PERFORM 999-TERMINATE-PROGRAM.
*
        .
        .
        .
*
 999-TERMINATE-PROGRAM.
*
    CALL "ABEND100".
```

Two OS/390 subprograms that start an abend

A subprogram that starts an abend without a dump

```
ABEND100    START  0
            SAVE   (14,12)
            ABEND  100
            END
```

A subprogram that starts an abend with a dump

```
ABEND200    START  0
            SAVE   (14,12)
            ABEND  200,DUMP
            END
```

How to direct the output of a storage dump in the JCL that runs the program

```
//GO.SYSUDUMP  DD    SYSOUT=*
```

Description

- In most mainframe shops, a program that detects a serious I/O error shouldn't end normally. Instead, it should end abnormally, which is referred to as an *abend*.
- Because there's no COBOL statement that causes an abend, the COBOL program must call a subprogram that's written in assembler language to start the abend. This is done by a Call statement as described in chapter 11.
- If an abend prints the contents of storage, which is referred to as a *storage dump*, you need to include a DD statement for SYSUDUMP output in the JCL for running the program. (See chapter 18 for details on how to code JCL.)
- The procedures that you are supposed to follow when a serious I/O error is detected vary from one COBOL shop to another. So when you start a new job, find out what the shop requirements are.

Figure 13-12   Error processing on an IBM mainframe

Testing and debugging

When you develop a sequential update or maintenance program, testing is difficult because there's no easy way to review the updated records. Often, for example, you have to print or display the contents of the old master file as well as the contents of the new master file so you can compare the two. To do that, you can use the utilities that are available with your system.

When you're using Micro Focus Personal COBOL, you can use *line sequential organization* to make it easier to create, display, and list the records in sequential files. With this organization, each record ends with a paragraph mark. As a result, you can use a text editor like Notepad or your word processing program to display and print the records in these files.

In figure 13-13, you can see how you code a Select statement for a file with line sequential organization. You can also see how a file with this organization is displayed with Notepad. Otherwise, the records are displayed one after the other with no indication of where one record ends and the next begins. Once you've got your program working right with line sequential organization, you can convert the program to sequential organization for final testing.

In this figure, you can also see listings of simple old master and new master files. By comparing the two, you can see whether a master file has been updated or maintained correctly. When the records are long and the processing is complex, this can be a time-consuming process. In this example, the affected records are shaded to show how the transactions shown in Notepad have affected the master files.

One technique for simplifying that process is to code a Display statement in a Read or Write procedure that displays all of the data in each record that is read or written. Then, you can review the input or output data on your screen without using separate programs to display or print the data. This works as long as the records aren't too long, there aren't too many records in each file, and the messages are displayed on your PC or terminal. You'll see how this works when you do exercise 13-1.

To complicate the testing process, you can't use just one test file of transaction data to completely test a sequential update or maintenance program. Instead, you need to test the program with files that test different combinations of transactions. For instance, you need to test the sequential maintenance program with a transaction file like the one in this figure that ends with a record that has an item number that's less than the one in the last master record. However, you also need to test the program with a transaction file that ends with a record that has an item number that's greater than the one in the last master record. Since you want to make sure the program works no matter what combination of records it has to process, you often need to test a program like this with several test files that have been carefully planned.

A Personal COBOL file that's defined with line sequential organization

```
SELECT MNTTRAN ASSIGN TO "c:\cobol\data\mnttranl.dat"
                ORGANIZATION IS LINE SEQUENTIAL.
```

A transaction file with line sequential organization displayed in Notepad

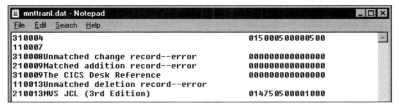

Old and new master file listings for the sequential maintenance program

Old master records

```
10001CICS for the COBOL Programmer, Part 1    01250045000010000543200000
10002CICS for the COBOL Programmer, Part 2    01500045000050000039005000
10004DB2 for the COBOL Programmer, Part 1     01095047500010000625900000
10005DB2 for the COBOL Programmer, Part 2     01375047500050000476500000
10007MVS JCL (Second Edition)                 01185050000010001121100000
10009The CICS Programmer's Desk Reference     01522050000050000319100000
10011Murach's Visual Basic 6                  01435045000150000054310000
10015Murach's Structured COBOL                02210062500010000298100000
```

New master records

```
10001CICS for the COBOL Programmer, Part 1    01250045000010000543200000
10002CICS for the COBOL Programmer, Part 2    01500045000050000039005000
10004DB2 for the COBOL Programmer, Part 1     01500050000050000625900000
10005DB2 for the COBOL Programmer, Part 2     01375047500050000476500000
10009The CICS Desk Reference                  01522050000050000319100000
10011Murach's Visual Basic 6                  01435045000150000054310000
10013MVS JCL (3rd Edition)                    01475050000010000000000000
10015Murach's Structured COBOL                02210062500010000298100000
```

A Write procedure that displays each output record

```
340-WRITE-NEW-MASTER.
*
    WRITE NEW-MASTER-RECORD.
    DISPLAY "NEWMAST = " NEW-MASTER-RECORD.
```

Description

- When you use *line sequential organization* with Micro Focus COBOL, each record ends with a paragraph mark. Then, you can use a text editor to create, display, and list test files.

- To make sure that a sequential update or maintenance program works correctly, you need to compare the old master records with the new ones. To do that, you can use a utility program or text editor to list the old and new master files.

- Instead of listing test files, you can use a Display statement in a Read or Write procedure to display the records that are read or written by that procedure.

Figure 13-13   Testing and debugging update and maintenance programs

Design alternatives

Sequential update and maintenance programs are difficult to design and code due to the need for matching record logic, which certainly isn't intuitive. As a result, many programmers have trouble developing this type of program.

In this chapter, though, you have been introduced to the best designs that we've ever seen for sequential update and maintenance programs. In particular, the sequential maintenance program uses an approach that is easy to learn and easy to convert to any sequential maintenance program that you have to develop. That approach was developed by Paul Noll way back in the 1970's, while he was working as a programming manager for Pacific Telephone. Since then, Paul has taught this approach to hundreds of programmers in dozens of companies. Now, some 25 years later, we still haven't seen a better approach to this type of program.

Obviously, though, that's not the only way to design a sequential maintenance program. For instance, the design in figure 13-14 will also work. In terms of structured design, in fact, this is a better design because each module represents an operational function. In contrast, the chart in figure 13-10 has modules like "process hi master" and "process lo master" that don't represent operational functions. Instead, they represent conditions that occur when the control fields are compared.

The trouble with the design in figure 13-14 is that it's more difficult to code. In fact, modules 320 and 350 are extremely difficult to code because the matching record logic is split between these modules. That means you have to go back and forth between the modules to make sure that all the records are being processed correctly.

With that as background, we recommend that you use the update and maintenance programs presented in this chapter as models for all the update and maintenance programs that you write. With minor adjustments, you'll be able to use all the logic in those programs for your new programs. You'll just need to change the details. That will save you many hours of design, coding, testing, and debugging time.

A design alternative for the sequential maintenance program

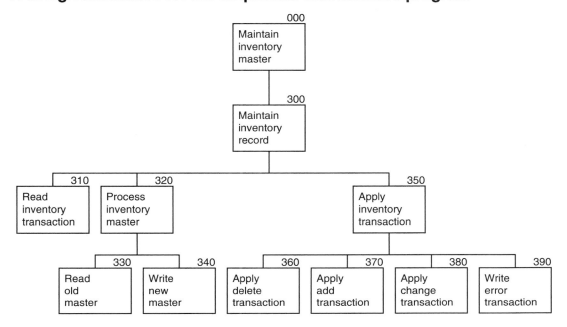

Description

- When you design a sequential update or maintenance program, you have many alternatives. For instance, the structure chart above is an alternative design for the maintenance program in figure 13-10 that extends the design of the sequential update program in figure 13-6.

- Although the design above is better than the design in figure 13-10 in terms of structured programming, it is more difficult to code.

- Once you're comfortable with the design and code for a sequential update or maintenance program, you should use that structure and code as a model for every update or maintenance program that you develop.

Figure 13-14   Design alternatives for update and maintenance programs

COBOL for variable-length records

Although most of the files that you'll work with will contain fixed-length records, you may occasionally need to work with a file that contains *variable-length records*. For example, you may need to work with a file that has two or more record types with different lengths or records that contain a segment that occurs a variable number of times. If so, the next five figures present what you'll need to know. If you don't think you'll ever work with variable-length records, though, you can skip to the Perspective at the end of this chapter and refer back to these figures if you ever need them.

How to code FD statements

Figure 13-15 presents the format of the FD statement for a file of variable-length records. However, you can usually omit the Block Contains clause because the system keeps track of the block size.

If you code the Block Contains clause, though, you'll want to indicate the maximum number of characters (bytes) that the block can contain rather than the number of records because that will lead to larger block sizes. If, for example, you code the Block Contains clause like this

BLOCK CONTAINS 4000 CHARACTERS

an output block of records isn't written until its size is greater than the maximum block size minus the maximum record size. In this case, if the file consists of records that are 50, 100, or 200 bytes long, a new block won't be written on the file until the block size is greater than 3800 bytes (4000 minus 200). This increases processing efficiency and saves disk space. In contrast, if you code the clause like this

BLOCK CONTAINS 20 RECORDS

the blocks will always receive 20 records regardless of their size. Then, if twenty 50-byte records are created in succession, the block will contain only 1000 bytes.

To indicate the number of bytes in each record, you can use either the Record Contains or the Record Is Varying In Size clause. Both clauses let you specify the minimum and maximum number of bytes that a record can contain. Although these clauses are optional, it's good to include them for documentation.

If you use the Record Is Varying In Size clause, you can also include the Depending On phrase. This phrase names a working-storage field that contains the length of the current record. This field is updated each time the program reads a record from the file. More importantly, before the program writes a record to the file, it must place the record length in this field. You'll see how this works in the programming examples that follow.

The syntax of the FD statement for a file of variable-length records

```
FD  file-name

    [ BLOCK CONTAINS integer-1 CHARACTERS ]

  ⎡⎧⎡ RECORD CONTAINS integer-2 TO integer-3 CHARACTERS ⎤⎫⎤
  ⎢⎪  RECORD IS VARYING IN SIZE                         ⎪⎥
  ⎢⎨      [[ FROM integer-4 ] [ TO integer-5 ] CHARACTERS ] ⎬⎥
  ⎣⎩      [ DEPENDING ON data-name ]                    ⎭⎦
```

Typical examples of the FD statement for a file of variable-length records

```
FD  VLTRAN
    RECORD CONTAINS 18 TO 128 CHARACTERS.


FD  VLCUST
    RECORD IS VARYING IN SIZE
        FROM 28 TO 408 CHARACTERS
        DEPENDING ON RECORD-LENGTH.
```

Description

- The Block Contains clause for a file of variable-length records gives the maximum number of bytes that a block can contain. Since most systems keep track of the block size, you usually don't need to code this clause.

- The Record Contains clause for a file of variable-length records gives the minimum and maximum number of bytes per record.

- You can also use the Record Is Varying In Size clause with the From and To phrases to specify the minimum and maximum number of bytes per record. Usually, the compiler treats From as documentation, but it compares the number you specify for To with the maximum size of the record description that follows to be sure they're the same.

- The Depending On clause names a field that receives the length of the record each time a record is read. Similarly, before a program writes a record, it must store the length of the record in this field.

Figure 13-15   How to code FD statements for variable-length records

How to write to a file that contains record types with different lengths

To write to a file that contains two or more record types of different lengths, you can describe each record type after the FD statement as shown in figure 13-16. Then, you must include one Write statement for each record type. In this example, since the file contains three different record types, the program must contain three Write statements. Then, since each Write statement gives the name of a record description, the system can determine the length of the record from that description. As a result, it isn't necessary to include the Depending On phrase of the Record Is Varying In Size clause.

When you define two or more record types for a file, you need to be sure to code the largest record description first. That's because the record descriptions that follow implicitly redefine the first record description, and an area that redefines another area can't be larger than the area it redefines.

General code for writing record types with different lengths

```
FD   VLTRAN
     RECORD IS VARYING IN SIZE
          FROM 18 TO 128 CHARACTERS.
*
01   HEADER-RECORD.
     05   HDR-RECORD-CODE    PIC X.
     05   HDR-FIELD-1        PIC X(30).
     05   HDR-FIELD-2        PIC X(30).
     05   HDR-FIELD-3        PIC X(30).
     05   HDR-FIELD-4        PIC X(30).
     05   HDR-FIELD-5        PIC S9(7).
01   DETAIL-RECORD.
     05   DET-RECORD-CODE    PIC X.
     05   DET-FIELD-1        PIC X(6).
     05   DET-FIELD-2        PIC X(6).
     05   DET-FIELD-3        PIC S9(5).
01   TRAILER-RECORD.
     05   TLR-RECORD-CODE    PIC X.
     05   TLR-FIELD-1        PIC X(50).
     05   TLR-FIELD-2        PIC S9(6).
     05   TLR-FIELD-3        PIC S9(7).
*
          .
          .
          .
     PROCEDURE DIVISION.
          .
          .
     WRITE HEADER-RECORD.
          .
     WRITE DETAIL-RECORD.
          .
     WRITE TRAILER-RECORD.
          .
          .
          .
```

Description

- If a file contains two or more record types, you can describe each record type after the FD statement. Although only one record area is used for all of the record types, different names are used to refer to the fields within each record description.

- The effect of defining two or more record types after the FD statement is the same as using a Redefines clause in the Working-Storage Section. Because of that, the record type with the largest record must be defined first.

- When you write to a file with different record types, you specify the name of the record type in the Write statement. In that case, you don't need to use the Depending On phrase of the Record is Varying In Size clause because the record length is defined by the record description.

Figure 13-16   How to write to a file that contains record types with different lengths

How to process a file that contains record types with different lengths

To read variable-length records, you can use one of two basic techniques. The first one is suggested by the code in figure 13-16. Here, all of the record types are completely defined in the File Section. Then, when a record is read, the program tests the record code to determine what type of record was read, and it adjusts its processing accordingly. In this case, the records are processed in the record area for the file.

If your program needs to process the records in working storage, though, you can use the technique that's illustrated in figure 13-17. Here, the record area for the file is defined in the File Section, but the record description for each record type is defined in the Working-Storage Section. In this case, the record area for the file includes the definition of the field that identifies the record type. Then, when a record is read, the program can test this field and move the record to the appropriate area in working storage. Note that these Move statements work properly when a larger area is moved to a smaller one because the number of characters that are moved depends on the length of the receiving field, not the length of the sending field.

Although the code in figures 13-16 and 13-17 illustrates the use of the Record Is Varying In Size clause, you can just as easily use the Record Contains clause. The only time you can't use that clause is if you're reading variable-length records that don't include a field that indicates the record type. Then, you have to use the Record Is Varying In Size clause with the Depending On phrase to determine the record type based on the size of each record.

General code for processing record types with different lengths

```
FD  VLTRAN
    RECORD IS VARYING IN SIZE
        FROM 18 TO 128 CHARACTERS.
*
01  TRANSACTION-AREA.
    05  TR-RECORD-CODE          PIC X.
        88  TR-HEADER-RECORD                VALUE "H".
        88  TR-DETAIL-RECORD                VALUE "D".
        88  TR-TRAILER-RECORD               VALUE "T".
    05  FILLER                  PIC X(127).
*
        .
        .

WORKING-STORAGE SECTION.
*
01  HEADER-RECORD.
        .
        .

01  DETAIL-RECORD.
        .
        .

01  TRAILER-RECORD.
        .
        .

PROCEDURE DIVISION.
        .
        .

    PERFORM 300-READ-TRANSACTION-RECORD.
    IF NOT VLTRAN-EOF
        IF TR-HEADER-RECORD
            MOVE TRANSACTION-AREA TO HEADER-RECORD
        ELSE IF TR-DETAIL-RECORD
            MOVE TRANSACTION-AREA TO DETAIL-RECORD
        ELSE IF TR-TRAILER-RECORD
            MOVE TRANSACTION-AREA TO TRAILER-RECORD.
        .
        .
```

Description

- When a file contains two or more record types, each record typically contains a field that indicates its type. Then, you can use that field to process the record accordingly.

- If you don't need to work with the records in working storage, you can define each record type in the File Section as shown in figure 13-16.

- If you need to work with the records in working storage, you can define a general record area in the File Section that can contain the longest record, and you can define the individual record types in working storage as shown above. Then, you can move the record area to the appropriate area in working storage.

Figure 13-17   How to process a file that contains record types with different lengths

How to write records with a varying number of segments

If you've read chapter 10, you already know how to define and work with tables. Although most tables are defined in working storage and contain constant values or data that's loaded from a file, you can also define a table within a record description. Then, each record can contain a varying number of occurrences of the table data, which are often referred to as *segments*. In fact, when a record is defined with a table, it is often divided into two segments: a *root segment* that contains data that applies to all the occurrences of the table data, and a *repeating segment* that contains the table data.

To write to a file that contains records with a varying number of segments, a program must indicate either the length of the record or the number of occurrences of the segment. To indicate the length of a record, you can use the Record Is Varying In Size clause along with the Depending On phrase in the FD statement for the file. This technique is illustrated in figure 13-18.

In this figure, you can see that the program writes a file of customer records that contain a root segment and a varying number of invoice segments. The length of each record is calculated and stored in the Depending On field as the record is formatted in the Procedure Division. In this case, the program sets the record length to the length of the root segment (8) each time it formats a root segment. Then, it adds the length of an invoice segment (20) to the record length each time it formats another invoice segment. As a result, when all the invoice segments have been formatted, the record-length field contains the correct length of the record.

The technique in this figure is the one we recommend for working with this type of variable-length record. However, you can also use the Record Contains clause instead of the Record Is Varying In Size clause. For that to work, though, you have to code the Occurs clause for the invoice segment of the record like this:

```
05  CR-INVOICE-SEGMENT      OCCURS 1 TO 20 TIMES
                            DEPENDING ON CR-INVOICE-COUNT
                            INDEXED BY SEGMENT-INDEX.
```

Here, the Occurs clause must give the range of times (1 to 20) that the segment can occur rather than the maximum number of times. In addition, the field that's named in the Depending On phrase of the Occurs clause must indicate the actual number of times that this segment occurs.

General code for writing records with a varying number of segments

```
FD  VLCUST
    RECORD IS VARYING IN SIZE
        FROM 28 TO 408 CHARACTERS
        DEPENDING ON RECORD-LENGTH.
*
01  CUSTOMER-RECORD.
    05  CR-ROOT-SEGMENT.
        10  CR-CUSTOMER-NO      PIC X(6).
        10  CR-INVOICE-COUNT    PIC S99.
    05  CR-INVOICE-SEGMENT      OCCURS 20 TIMES
                                INDEXED BY SEGMENT-INDEX.
        10  CR-INVOICE-DATE     PIC X(8).
        10  CR-INVOICE-NO       PIC X(5).
        10  CR-INVOICE-AMOUNT   PIC S9(5)V99.
        .
WORKING-STORAGE SECTION.
        .
    05  RECORD-LENGTH           PIC S9(3).
        .
PROCEDURE DIVISION.
        .
        .
320-FORMAT-ROOT-SEGMENT.
*
    MOVE IR-CUSTOMER-NO TO CR-CUSTOMER-NO.
    MOVE ZERO TO CR-INVOICE-COUNT.
    MOVE 8 TO RECORD-LENGTH.——————————— The length of the root segment
*
330-FORMAT-INVOICE-SEGMENT.
        .
    ADD 1 TO CR-INVOICE-COUNT.
    ADD 20 TO RECORD-LENGTH.——————————— The length of each invoice segment
        .
340-WRITE-CUSTOMER-RECORD
*
    WRITE CUSTOMER-RECORD.
```

Description

- When you use the Record Is Varying In Size clause with the Depending On phrase, you must place the length of the record in the specified field before you write the record.

- You can also use the Record Contains clause with records that contain a varying number of segments. To do that, you must give the minimum and maximum number of segments in the Occurs clause for the segment, and you must include the Depending On phrase of the Occurs clause to name a variable that will contain the actual number of occurrences.

Figure 13-18   How to write records with a varying number of segments

How to process records with a varying number of segments

To read and process a file that contains records with a varying number of segments, you can use code like that shown in figure 13-19. After each record is read, a Perform Varying statement is used to process each invoice segment in the record. Here, the value in the invoice-count field in the root segment of the record determines how many times procedure 320 is performed.

If the file you're processing doesn't contain a count field like this, though, you can use another technique to limit this statement. If, for example, you initialize the record area before each record is read, you can check a field in the invoice segment to see if it's empty. If it is, you know that there aren't any more occurrences of the invoice segment, and you can end the Perform Varying loop.

Unlike the code shown in figure 13-18, the Record Is Varying In Size clause of the FD statement for the customer file doesn't include the Depending On phrase. In this case, it isn't necessary because the program doesn't need to know the record length. Instead, it just needs to know how many occurrences of the invoice segment each record contains.

In a case like that, you can use the Record Contains clause instead of the Record Is Varying In Size clause. Be aware, though, that using one of these clauses to write records to a file and the other to read records from a file can cause problems. So you should choose one technique and stick with it.

General code for processing records with a varying number of segments

```
FD   VLCUST
     RECORD IS VARYING IN SIZE
          FROM 28 TO 408 CHARACTERS.
*
 01  CUSTOMER-RECORD.
     05   CR-ROOT-SEGMENT.
          10   CR-CUSTOMER-NO      PIC X(6).
          10   CR-INVOICE-COUNT    PIC S99.
     05   CR-INVOICE-SEGMENT       OCCURS 20 TIMES
                                   INDEXED BY SEGMENT-INDEX.
          10   CR-INVOICE-DATE     PIC X(8).
          10   CR-INVOICE-NO       PIC X(5).
          10   CR-INVOICE-AMOUNT   PIC S9(5)V99.
          .
          .
          .
 PROCEDURE DIVISION.
          .
          .

     PERFORM 310-READ-CUSTOMER-RECORD.
     IF NOT VLCUST-EOF
          MOVE ZERO TO AMOUNT-OWED
          PERFORM 320-ACCUMULATE-AMOUNT-OWED
               VARYING SEGMENT-INDEX FROM 1 BY 1
               UNTIL SEGMENT-INDEX > CR-INVOICE-COUNT
          .
          .
          .
 310-READ-CUSTOMER-RECORD.
*
     READ VLCUST
          AT END
               MOVE "Y" TO VLCUST-EOF-SWITCH.
*
 320-ACCUMULATE-AMOUNT-OWED.
*
     ADD CR-INVOICE-AMOUNT (SEGMENT-INDEX) TO AMOUNT-OWED.
          .
          .
          .
```

Description

- To process a record with a variable number of segments, you use a Perform Varying statement to vary the index associated with the segments.

- If the record contains a field that indicates the number of segments in the record, you can use that field to limit the Perform Varying statement as shown above. Otherwise, you can usually process the segments until you find an empty segment.

Figure 13-19   How to process records with a varying number of segments

Perspective

Although you might think that most update and maintenance programs are done with indexed files, sequential update and maintenance programs are still widely used, especially in large companies. Due to the need for matching record logic, though, sequential update and maintenance programs are more difficult to write than their indexed counterparts. That's why you should develop model programs that you use for the design and coding of all your sequential update and maintenance programs.

In the next chapter, you'll learn how to work with indexed files. In particular, you'll see how the maintenance program in this chapter works when it uses an indexed master file. You may be surprised to see how much easier the logic in that program is when it's compared with the logic in a sequential maintenance program.

Summary

- You can open a sequential file in *input mode*, *output mode*, *extend mode*, or *I-O mode*. The mode you use determines what I-O operations you can perform on the file.

- You can use the File Status clause in the Select statement for a sequential file to name a field that will receive a *file status code* after each I/O operation for the file. That value will indicate what the result of the operation was.

- A *sequential update program* creates a new master file from an old master file and a file of transactions that update fields in the old records. A *sequential maintenance program* creates a new master file from an old master file and a file of transactions that can add, delete, and change records in the master file.

- Sequential update and maintenance programs use *matching record logic* that's based on the comparison of *control fields* in the master and transaction records. This logic determines when records are read from the transaction and old master files and when records are written to the new master file.

- Error processing is usually a critical part of the coding in update and maintenance programs, especially on IBM mainframes. On those systems, you often need to *abend* a program when a serious error occurs.

- A file of *variable-length records* can have two or more record types with different lengths or a segment that occurs a varying number of times. You can process a file of variable-length records using either the Record Is Varying In Size or the Record Contains clause of the FD statement.

Terms

fixed-length records
ddname
input mode
output mode
extend mode
I-O mode
file status code
sequential update program
matching record logic
control field
matched transaction

unmatched transaction
apply a transaction
sequential maintenance program
abend
storage dump
line sequential organization
variable-length records
segment
root segment
repeating segment

Objectives

- Given the specifications for a sequential update or maintenance program, develop the program.

- Given the specifications for a program that processes a file of variable-length records, develop the program. The variable-length records can contain two or more record types or a varying number of segments.

- Explain how you use the File Status clause of the Select statement in a program.

- List the four Open modes you can use with a sequential file along with the I/O statements that you can use with each mode.

- In general terms, explain how matching record logic works in a sequential update or maintenance program.

- In general terms, describe the error processing that's done in the COBOL programs that are developed for IBM mainframes.

- Explain how you determine whether a test run for a sequential update or maintenance program has worked correctly.

- Describe two techniques that you can use to work with files that contain variable-length records.

Before you start the exercises for this section...

Before you start the exercises for any of the chapters in this section, we recommend that you do some housekeeping. First, copy all the programs in the c:\cobol folder to the c:\cobol\oldprogs folder. That will clean up your default folder. Then, copy the programs for chapters 13, 14, 15, and 16 from their folders to the c:\cobol folder. That will prepare you for the exercises in this section.

Exercise 13-1   Test the sequential update program

In this exercise, you'll test a version of the sequential update program that's presented in this chapter. That will give you a better idea of what testing this type of program involves.

Test the program with line sequential files

1. Open the program named seq1000, and review its Select statements. This is the program presented in figure 13-7, but all of the files have been changed to line sequential organization to make testing easier.

2. Before you test the program, use your word processing program to print listings of the records in the files named rcttranl.dat and oldmastl.dat. The letter *l* at the end of each name indicates that it contains line sequential data.

3. Compile and run the program.

4. Use your word processing program to print listings of the records in the output files named newmastl.dat and errtranl.dat. Then, check the listings of the four files to see whether the updating is correct (not an easy process).

5. If you have any trouble understanding how this program works, set a breakpoint at the first statement in module 300 and run this program again. When the breakpoint is reached, step through the statements that implement the matching record logic. As you step, display the values in the control fields so you can see how they change. When you're satisfied that you understand how this program works, go on to the next step.

Add a Display statement to improve the testing process

6. Add a Display statement in procedure 340 that displays the entire master record each time a new master record is written. Then, compile and run the program again. This time, you can review the updated records in the screen display.

7. Find the errtranl.dat file in your Windows Explorer, and double-click on it. That will display the file in Notepad. Note that this file contains the two error transactions two or more times, depending on how many times you ran the program. That's because this file is opened in extend mode, and the two error transactions are added to this file each time the program is tested.

Test the program with sequential files

8. Find the files named rcttran.dat and oldmast.dat in your Explorer, and double-click on them to open them in Notepad. These are the transaction and old master files in standard sequential format. As you can see, reviewing the data in this format is much more difficult.

9. If you want to test the program on standard sequential files, change the Select statements from line sequential to sequential files, and remove the letter *l* at the end of each file name. Then, compile and test the program.

10. When you're through experimenting, close the program.

Exercise 13-2   Add branch names to a sales report

To give you a chance to use matching record logic in another type of program, this program has you enhance the summary report program that you created in chapter 5 by adding branch names to it so it looks something like this:

```
BRCH                    CUST                           SALES        SALES
NUM   BRANCH NAME       NUM    CUSTOMER NAME          THIS YTD     LAST YTD

 12   FORT WAYNE        11111  INFORMATION BUILDERS    1,234.56     1,111.11
                        12345  CAREER TRAINING CTR    12,345.67    22,222.22
                                      BRANCH TOTAL    13,580.23    23,333.33
  .
  .
 47   KANSAS CITY NW    12121  GENERAL SERVICES CO.   11,444.00    11,059.56
                        24680  INFO MANAGEMENT CO.    17,481.45    11,892.47
                        99999  DOLLAR SAVINGS BANK     5,059.00     4,621.95
                        76543  NATL MUSIC CORP.        2,383.46     4,435.26
                                      BRANCH TOTAL    36,367.91    32,009.24

                                       GRAND TOTAL   120,525.72   121,155.45
```

Here, the first two heading lines and the last two columns of the report are deleted so the report will fit on this page. Your report, however, should include them.

To get the branch names that are printed by this program, the program needs to read a file named brchmast.dat that's in sequence by branch number with this format:

```
01   BRANCH-MASTER-RECORD.
     05   BM-BRANCH-NUMBER     PIC 9(2).
     05   BM-BRANCH-NAME       PIC X(18).
```

To make this program work, you need to use matching record logic like the logic in the sequential update program. If the branch number in the customer record is matched by a branch record, the program should print the branch name in the first line of each branch group. Otherwise, the program should print "NO BRANCH RECORD" in the branch name column.

Enhance the structure chart for the program

1. Enhance the structure chart for the report program that's shown in figure 4-7 so it includes a module for reading a record from the branch master file.

Enhance the program

2. Open the program named rpt3000, change its Program-ID to RPT6000, save it as rpt6000, then close the program and re-open it.

3. Modify the program so it prepares the report shown above. To make this manageable, you can do this in two parts. First, modify and test the program so it prints the branch name in each customer line. Then, modify and test the program so it prints the branch name in just the first line of each customer group.

4. When you've got the program working correctly, close the program.

Exercise 13-3   Modify the sequential update program

In this exercise, you'll modify the sequential update program in figure 13-7 so it uses the logic of the sequential maintenance program in figure 13-11. That will give you a better idea of your design and coding alternatives. It will also give you a better appreciation how the code in the sequential maintenance program works.

Design and modify the program

1. Open the program named seq1000, change its Program-ID to SEQ1100, save it as seq1100, then close it and re-open it.

2. Create a structure chart for this program based on the structure chart for the sequential maintenance program in figure 13-10.

3. Modify the code in this program so it corresponds to the design that you created in step 2. As you code, use the program in figure 13-11 as a guide. In particular, the logic in procedure 300 should be based on the settings of the need-transaction, need-master, and write-master switches.

4. Check the procedures that you've just created to make sure they turn the switches on and off in the same way that the program in figure 13-11 does. If you don't set the switches right, the program may get caught in a loop.

Compile and test the program

5. Compile and test the program.

6. When you're sure that it works the way the previous version of this program worked, close the program.

14

How to work with indexed files

Indexed files are commonly used in interactive programs because the random capabilities let you directly access the records in those files. Indexed files are also widely used in batch programs because the random capabilities let you update two or more files in a single program. In this chapter, you'll learn how to use indexed files in batch programs, but the same skills can also be applied to interactive programs.

COBOL for indexed files

An indexed file must be defined with at least one index, called the *primary index*. In the topics that follow, you'll learn the COBOL for processing an indexed file by its primary index. Later, you'll learn the COBOL for processing an indexed file by an alternate index.

How to code Select statements

Figure 14-1 presents the syntax of the Select statement for indexed files. Unlike the Select statement for a sequential file, the Organization clause is required to identify the file as an indexed file. If you omit this clause, the compiler assumes that the file is sequential.

The Access clause for an indexed file can specify one of three access modes. If it specifies *sequential access*, the file can only be accessed sequentially. If it specifies *random access*, the file can only be accessed randomly. But if it specifies *dynamic access*, the file can be accessed both sequentially and randomly. In most cases, though, you'll find that dynamic access isn't necessary.

By the way, if you omit the Access clause, sequential access is assumed. But even if the file will be accessed sequentially, it's a good idea to include this clause for documentation.

The Select statement for an indexed file must always contain a Record Key clause that identifies the primary index for the file. Note that the field this clause names must be coded as part of the record description for the file in the File Section. You'll see how that works in the programming examples presented later in this chapter.

You can also include a File Status clause on the Select statement for an indexed file just as you can for a sequential file. Then, each time an I/O operation is performed on the file, the File Status field is updated with a *file status code* that indicates the result of the operation. The program can test this field to determine whether error processing is necessary.

The syntax of the Select statement for indexed files

```
SELECT file-name ASSIGN to system-name
                ORGANIZATION IS INDEXED

                                  ⎡SEQUENTIAL⎤
                ACCESS MODE IS   ⎨ RANDOM    ⎬
                                  ⎣DYNAMIC   ⎦

                RECORD KEY IS data-name-1
              [ FILE STATUS IS data-name-2 ]
```

The syntax for a system name for a VSAM file on an IBM mainframe

```
ddname
```

The syntax for a system name on a PC

```
"path\filename"
```

A Select statement for a file that's accessed sequentially

```
SELECT INVMAST  ASSIGN TO INVMAST
                ORGANIZATION IS INDEXED
                ACCESS IS SEQUENTIAL
                RECORD KEY IS IM-ITEM-NO.
```

A Select statement for a file that's accessed randomly

```
SELECT INVMAST  ASSIGN TO INVMAST
                ORGANIZATION IS INDEXED
                ACCESS IS RANDOM
                RECORD KEY IS IM-ITEM-NO.
```

Description

- On a PC, the system name consists of the path and file name for the file.

- On an IBM mainframe, the system name consists of a *ddname* that's used in the JCL for the program to assign the file in the program to a VSAM file on disk. That ddname must consist of eight or fewer letters or digits, starting with a letter.

- You must code the Organization clause for an indexed file since the default is Sequential.

- You can specify three types of access for an indexed file. Sequential means that the records will be accessed sequentially by the key field. Random means that the records will be accessed randomly by the key field. And Dynamic means that the records will be accessed both sequentially and randomly.

- The Record Key clause identifies the primary key for the file. The field that's named on this clause must be included in the record description for the file in the File Section.

- You can use the File Status clause to name a field that will be updated by the system as each I/O statement for the file is executed. The File Status field must be defined in working storage as a two-byte alphanumeric field (XX).

Figure 14-1   How to code Select statements for indexed files

File status codes

Figure 14-2 presents the file status codes for indexed files. If you review these codes and their meanings, you'll see that many of them are the same as for sequential files. For example, a file status code of 10 indicates an end-of-file condition. That condition can occur when an indexed file is read sequentially.

Four file status codes that pertain only to indexed files are 21, 22, 23, and 24. Each of these codes indicates an invalid key condition. In a moment, you'll see how you can check for these errors without using the File Status field.

A file status of 21 indicates that a record key is out of sequence. This error can only occur if the file is being processed sequentially. Although it can occur for either a read or a write operation, it's most likely to occur for a write operation when the file is being created from a sequential file and the sequential file isn't in key sequence. If this error occurs, the program is usually terminated.

A file status of 22 indicates another common error. This error occurs when a program tries to write a record to the file with a key value that already exists in the file. Notice that this file status applies to alternate indexes that don't allow duplicates as well as to the primary index.

A file status of 23 simply indicates that a record with the specified key value wasn't found in the file. It can occur only when the file is being accessed randomly. In many cases, this is an expected error that can be handled by the program so the program can continue.

Finally, a file status of 24 indicates that the program tried to perform an operation on an area of storage that is beyond the space that's assigned to the file. This can happen during a write operation on a file that's being accessed either sequentially or randomly. This type of error doesn't occur often, but when it does, the program must usually terminate.

One of the file status codes presented here, 02, applies only to alternate indexes. It indicates that a duplicate key condition occurred on an alternate index that allows duplicates. You'll see how you can use this code to process alternate indexes later in this chapter.

File status categories

First digit	Meaning
0	The operation completed successfully.
1	An end-of-file condition occurred.
2	An invalid key condition occurred.
3	A permanent I/O error occurred.
4	A logic error occurred.
9	The operation was unsuccessful, and the condition is defined by the implementor.

File status codes

Code	Meaning
00	The I/O operation was successful.
02	A duplicate key condition occurred on an alternate index that allows duplicates.
04	The length of the record that was read doesn't conform to the attributes of the file.
10	The end-of-file condition occurred during a read operation (AT END condition).
21	A sequencing error occurred for an indexed file that is being accessed sequentially.
22	The program attempted to write or rewrite a record with a duplicate primary key or an alternate key that doesn't allow duplicates.
23	The program attempted to access a record randomly and the record didn't exist.
24	A write operation attempted to write a record beyond the externally defined boundaries of the file.
30	The I/O operation was unsuccessful. No further information is available.
35	The program attempted to open a nonexistent file in I-O, input, or extend mode.
37	The program attempted to open a file that doesn't support the specified open mode.
39	A conflict occurred between the file attributes and the attributes specified in the program.
41	The program attempted to open a file that is already open.
42	The program attempted to close a file that is already closed.
43	A delete or rewrite operation was attempted on a file with sequential access, but the last successful operation on the file was not a Read statement.
44	The program attempted to rewrite a record that is not the same size as the record being replaced or is not within the allowed size range of a variable-length record.
46	A read operation was unsuccessful because the end-of-file condition already occurred or the previous read was unsuccessful.
47	The program attempted a read or start operation on a file that isn't opened in input or I-O mode.
48	The program attempted a write operation on a file that isn't opened in output, I-O, or extend mode.
49	The program attempted a delete or rewrite operation on a file that isn't opened in I-O mode.

Figure 14-2   File status codes for indexed files

How to code the Open, Close, Read, Write, and Rewrite statements

In the last chapter, you learned how to code the Open, Close, Read, Write, and Rewrite statements for sequential files. Now, you'll learn how to code these same statements for indexed files. Then, in the next topics, you'll learn how to code two new statements for working with indexed files: Start and Delete.

Figure 14-3 presents the syntax of the Open, Close, Read, Write, and Rewrite statements for indexed files. If you review these statements, you'll see that the Open and Close statements have the same syntax as they do for sequential files. In addition, the syntax of the Read statement for accessing an indexed file sequentially is the same as for accessing a sequential file. Note, however, that if you specify dynamic access for the file, you must include the word Next on the Read statement. Otherwise, random access is assumed. If you specify sequential access for the file, though, you can omit the word Next.

To read a record from an indexed file using random access, you use the second Read statement syntax shown in this figure. Before the program issues this statement, though, it must place the key value of the record to be read in the field specified in the Record Key clause for the file. Then, if a record isn't found with that key, an invalid key condition (file status 23) occurs. To trap for this error, you can use the Invalid Key clause. You can also code the Not Invalid Key clause, which is executed when an invalid key condition doesn't occur.

You can also code the Invalid Key and Not Invalid Key clauses on the Write and Rewrite statements for an indexed file. That's true whether the file is being accessed sequentially, randomly, or dynamically. In any case, the record to be written or rewritten is specified by the value in the Record Key field.

For a Write statement, the Invalid Key clause is executed if a record with the same key value already exists (file status 22) or if a boundary violation occurs (file status 24). For a file being accessed sequentially, an invalid key condition can also occur if the key value for the record being written is out of sequence (file status 21).

For a Rewrite statement, the Invalid Key clause is executed if a record with the specified key doesn't exist on the file (file status 23). That shouldn't happen with sequential access because the key of the record being rewritten must be the same as the key of the last record read. Because of that, you usually don't need to code the Invalid Key clause on a Rewrite statement for a file with sequential access. With random access or dynamic access, though, you can issue a Rewrite statement without first issuing a Read statement, so an Invalid Key clause is usually required.

Notice that the Invalid Key clause is optional in the statements that provide for it. That's because you can also test for the invalid key condition by checking the File Status field. In the programs in this chapter, we'll use the Invalid Key clause exclusively. But you'll want to be sure to check if your shop has standards for how invalid key conditions are handled.

The syntax of the Open, Read, Write, Rewrite, and Close statements

The Open statement

```
        ⎧ INPUT  file-name-1 ... ⎫
        ⎪ OUTPUT file-name-2 ... ⎪
OPEN ⎨                        ⎬
        ⎪ I-O    file-name-3 ... ⎪
        ⎩ EXTEND file-name-4 ... ⎭
```

The Read statement for sequential access

```
READ file-name [NEXT] RECORD [INTO data-name]
    [AT END imperative-statement-1]
    [NOT AT END imperative-statement-2]
    [END-READ]
```

The Read statement for random access

```
READ file-name RECORD [INTO data-name]
    [INVALID KEY imperative-statement-1]
    [NOT INVALID KEY imperative-statement-2]
    [END-READ]
```

The Write statement

```
WRITE record-name [FROM data-name]
    [INVALID KEY imperative-statement-1]
    [NOT INVALID KEY imperative-statement-2]
    [END-WRITE]
```

The Rewrite statement

```
REWRITE record-name [FROM data-name]
    [INVALID KEY imperative-statement-1]
    [NOT INVALID KEY imperative-statement-2]
    [END-REWRITE]
```

The Close statement

```
CLOSE file-name-1 ...
```

Description

- You can open a file in extend mode only if sequential access is specified.
- If a file is opened for dynamic access, you must include the word NEXT on the Read statement to access the records sequentially. If not, random access is assumed. If the file is opened for sequential access, you can omit the word NEXT.
- If a file is being accessed sequentially, you can include the At End and Not At End clauses on the Read statement just as you do for sequential files. If the file is being accessed randomly, you can use the Invalid Key and Not Invalid Key clauses.
- If a file is opened for sequential access, the Rewrite statement can be used only after executing a Read statement for the record to be rewritten. If the file is opened for random or dynamic access, you can use Rewrite without a prior Read.
- The Invalid Key clause of the Read, Write, and Rewrite statements is executed whenever an invalid key condition occurs (file status 21, 22, 23, or 24). If an invalid key condition doesn't occur, the Not Invalid Key clause is executed.

Figure 14-3   How to code the Open, Read, Write, Rewrite, and Close statements

How to code the Start statement

When you read an indexed file sequentially, the default is to read it in key value sequence from the lowest to the highest value. Occasionally, though, you may want to start a sequential read operation with a key value other than the lowest one. To do that, you issue the Start statement before you issue the first Read statement for the file. This statement specifies the key where sequential processing should begin. Its syntax is shown in figure 14-4.

Before you issue a Start statement, you must place a key value in the Record Key field. Then, the Key clause of the Start statement establishes the first record to be processed. As you can see, that record can have a value that's either equal to, greater than, or greater than or equal to the value you specify. You can also omit the Key clause altogether. If you do, the file will be positioned at the first record whose key is equal to the value placed in the key field. For clarity, though, we recommend you always code the Key clause.

The Start statement shown in this figure illustrates how it can be used. Here, a value of 1000 is moved to the key field of the inventory master file. Then, a Start statement is issued that indicates that the file should be positioned at the first record with a key value that's greater than or equal to the value of the key field. That way, if the file contains a record with a key value of 1000, the file will be positioned at that record. Otherwise, it will be positioned at the next record with a higher key value. Then, when the program issues a Read statement, it will read that record. And successive Read statements will read the remaining records in the file in key sequence.

Notice that you can also code an Invalid Key clause on the Start statement. You might want to do that if the Key clause is omitted, which indicates an Equal To comparison, or if the Key clause explicitly indicates an Equal To comparison. Then, if a record doesn't exist with the specified key value (file status 23), the Invalid Key clause can handle the error.

How to code the Delete statement

Unlike sequential files, you can delete records from indexed files. To do that, you use the Delete statement, which is also shown in this figure. When you issue this statement, the record identified by the value in the key field is deleted from the file.

If you use the Delete statement for a file with sequential access, you must precede the Delete statement with a Read statement for the record you want to delete. In that case, it's not necessary to code the Invalid Key clause on the Delete statement because you know that the record exists. If the file is opened for random or dynamic processing, however, you can delete a record without first reading it. In that case, you'll want to include the Invalid Key clause to trap for an error caused by a record that doesn't exist (file status 23).

The syntax of the Start statement

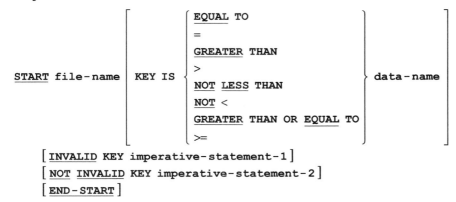

$$
\text{START file-name} \left[\text{KEY IS} \left\{ \begin{array}{l} \underline{\text{EQUAL}} \text{ TO} \\ = \\ \underline{\text{GREATER}} \text{ THAN} \\ > \\ \underline{\text{NOT}} \ \underline{\text{LESS}} \text{ THAN} \\ \underline{\text{NOT}} < \\ \underline{\text{GREATER}} \text{ THAN OR } \underline{\text{EQUAL}} \text{ TO} \\ >= \end{array} \right\} \text{data-name} \right]
$$

```
[INVALID KEY imperative-statement-1]
[NOT INVALID KEY imperative-statement-2]
[END-START]
```

A Start statement that positions the file at the record with a key value that's greater than or equal to a specified value

```
MOVE "1000" TO IM-ITEM-NO.
START INVMAST
    KEY IS >= IM-ITEM-NO.
```

Description

- You can use the Start statement to position an indexed file at a specific location based on a key value. Then, you can use the Read statement to access records sequentially starting with that record.
- You can use the Start statement with a file opened for sequential or dynamic access.

The syntax of the Delete statement

```
DELETE file-name RECORD
    [INVALID KEY imperative-statement-1]
    [NOT INVALID KEY imperative-statement-2]
    [END-DELETE]
```

A Delete statement that deletes a record read from a file with random access

```
DELETE INVMAST
    INVALID KEY
        DISPLAY "INVALID KEY ON READ FOR ITEM NUMBER "
            IM-ITEM-NO.
```

Description

- The Delete statement can be used only for a file that's opened in I-O mode.
- If a file is opened for sequential access, the Delete statement can be used only after executing a Read statement for the record to be deleted. In that case, the Invalid Key and Not Invalid Key clauses should not be specified.
- If a file is opened for random or dynamic access, the Delete statement can be used without first executing a Read statement for the record to be deleted. In that case, the Invalid Key clause should be specified.

Figure 14-4 How to code the Start and Delete statements

A sequential file creation program

To illustrate how to process an indexed file sequentially, the following topics present a program that creates an indexed file from a sequential file. Although the logic of this program is simple, it illustrates the basic requirements for processing indexed files sequentially.

The program specifications

Figure 14-5 presents the program specifications for the sequential file creation program. This program reads through a sequential file of inventory master records (INVMASTS) and creates an indexed file of those records (INVMASTI). To do that, the sequential file must be in sequence by the key value, which in this case is the item number. If it's not in sequence, an invalid key condition will occur when the Write statement is issued for the indexed file. An invalid key condition will also occur on the Write statement if two or more records in the sequential file have the same key value.

On most platforms, you have to create an indexed file sequentially, just as these specifications require. That way, the records are stored in sequence by primary key so they can be processed efficiently using sequential access. When records are added to the file, though, they usually aren't added in their sequential locations so sequential processing gets less and less efficient. Eventually, it makes sense to recreate the file so all of the records are in sequence by primary key again.

On some platforms, though, you don't have to write programs that create indexed files, because utilities are available for that purpose. On an IBM mainframe, for example, you can use one of the Access Method Services commands to create an indexed file from a sequential file. On the other hand, if file creation requires that you rearrange data in a record or combine data from several records, you may need to code a program like this one.

The structure chart

Figure 14-5 also presents the structure chart for the file creation program. Here, you can see that this program simply reads each record in the sequential input file and writes it to the indexed output file. Because both files have the same record layout, as indicated by the record description in this figure, no additional processing is required.

The system flowchart for a sequential file creation program

The record description for the inventory master file

```
01  INVENTORY-MASTER-RECORD.
    05  IM-ITEM-NO               PIC X(5).
    05  IM-DESCRIPTIVE-DATA.
        10  IM-ITEM-DESC         PIC X(40).
        10  IM-UNIT-COST         PIC S9(3)V99.
        10  IM-UNIT-PRICE        PIC S9(3)V99.
    05  IM-INVENTORY-DATA.
        10  IM-REORDER-POINT     PIC S9(5).
        10  IM-ON-HAND           PIC S9(5).
        10  IM-ON-ORDER          PIC S9(5).
```

The structure chart

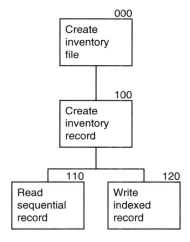

Processing specifications

- This program creates an indexed file of inventory master records (INVMASTI) from a sequential file of inventory master records (INVMASTS). The primary key for the indexed file is the item number.

- This program assumes that the records in the sequential file are in sequence by item number, which is the key of the indexed file. Then, as each record in the sequential file is read, it is written to the indexed file.

Figure 14-5   The program specifications and structure chart for a sequential file creation program

The COBOL code

The COBOL code for the sequential file creation program is presented in figure 14-6. The first thing you should notice is that the Select statement for the indexed file indicates that the file has indexed organization and that it will be accessed sequentially. It also specifies that the key field for the file is IR-ITEM-NO.

Now, look at the record description for this file in the File Section of the program. Notice that it includes the definition of the key field, and notice that this field has the same name as the key field specified on the Record Key clause of the Select statement.

In the Working-Storage Section of this program, you can see the record description that's used for both the files. Then, when a record is read from the sequential file, the Into clause on the Read statement places the record in this working-storage area. And when a record is written to the indexed file, the From clause on the Write statement writes the record from this area.

The sequential file creation program   **Page 1**

```
IDENTIFICATION DIVISION.
*
PROGRAM-ID. IND1000.
*
ENVIRONMENT DIVISION.
*
INPUT-OUTPUT SECTION.
*
FILE-CONTROL.
    SELECT INVMASTS  ASSIGN TO INVMASTS.
    SELECT INVMASTI  ASSIGN TO INVMASTI
                     ORGANIZATION IS INDEXED
                     ACCESS IS SEQUENTIAL
                     RECORD KEY IS IR-ITEM-NO.
*
DATA DIVISION.
*
FILE SECTION.
*
FD  INVMASTS.
*
01  SEQUENTIAL-RECORD-AREA  PIC X(70).
*
FD  INVMASTI.
*
01  INDEXED-RECORD-AREA.
    05  IR-ITEM-NO              PIC X(5).
    05  FILLER                  PIC X(65).
*
WORKING-STORAGE SECTION.
*
01  SWITCHES.
    05  INVMAST-EOF-SWITCH     PIC X     VALUE "N".
        88  INVMAST-EOF                  VALUE "Y".
*
01  INVENTORY-MASTER-RECORD.
    05  IM-ITEM-NO             PIC X(5).
    05  IM-DESCRIPTIVE-DATA.
        10  IM-ITEM-DESC       PIC X(40).
        10  IM-UNIT-COST       PIC S9(3)V99.
        10  IM-UNIT-PRICE      PIC S9(3)V99.
    05  IM-INVENTORY-DATA.
        10  IM-REORDER-POINT   PIC S9(5).
        10  IM-ON-HAND         PIC S9(5).
        10  IM-ON-ORDER        PIC S9(5).
*
```

Figure 14-6   The COBOL code for the sequential file creation program (part 1 of 2)

On page 2, you can see that the Write statement includes the Invalid Key clause. Then, if an invalid key condition occurs when this statement is executed, the program displays a message indicating that an error occurred. In addition, the program turns on the switch that indicates that the end of the input file has been reached so that no additional records are processed and the program ends.

An alternative to using the end-of-file switch would be to call a subprogram that causes the program to abend. That would make it obvious that the program did not complete its intended function. For more information on abend processing, please see figure 13-12 in the previous chapter.

Although the Invalid Key clause will trap and handle any invalid key condition, it doesn't reflect the cause of the error. In this case, for example, an invalid key condition could be caused by a record that's out of sequence, by a record that contains a duplicate key, or by a boundary violation. To determine the exact cause of the error, you need to include a File Status field for the file. Then, you can display the value of the File Status field when an invalid key condition occurs. For simplicity, that type of error processing has been omitted from the programs in this chapter.

You should also realize that the Invalid Key clause will trap only invalid key conditions. It won't trap any other error conditions that can occur on the file. For that reason, you may want to check the File Status field after an I/O operation and not use the Invalid Key clause at all. Or, you may want to use a combination of the Invalid Key and Not Invalid Key clauses and the File Status field. Be sure to check if your shop has standards for handling these types of errors.

The sequential file creation program   **Page 2**

```
PROCEDURE DIVISION.
*
 000-CREATE-INVENTORY-FILE.
*
     OPEN INPUT   INVMASTS
          OUTPUT INVMASTI.
     PERFORM 100-CREATE-INVENTORY-RECORD
         UNTIL INVMAST-EOF.
     CLOSE INVMASTS
           INVMASTI.
     STOP RUN.
*
 100-CREATE-INVENTORY-RECORD.
*
     PERFORM 110-READ-SEQUENTIAL-RECORD.
     IF NOT INVMAST-EOF
         PERFORM 120-WRITE-INDEXED-RECORD.
*
 110-READ-SEQUENTIAL-RECORD.
*
     READ INVMASTS INTO INVENTORY-MASTER-RECORD
         AT END
             MOVE "Y" TO INVMAST-EOF-SWITCH.
*
 120-WRITE-INDEXED-RECORD.
*
     WRITE INDEXED-RECORD-AREA FROM INVENTORY-MASTER-RECORD
         INVALID KEY
             DISPLAY "WRITE ERROR ON INVMASTI FOR ITEM NUMBER "
                 IR-ITEM-NO
             MOVE "Y" TO INVMAST-EOF-SWITCH.
*
```

Figure 14-6   The COBOL code for the sequential file creation program (part 2 of 2)

A random maintenance program

In chapter 13, you saw how to use matching record logic to perform file maintenance and update functions on a sequential file. When you use indexed files, though, you can access the records to be updated or maintained on a random basis, thus eliminating the need for matching record logic. Because of that, the logic of a random maintenance or update program is considerably simpler than the logic of a sequential maintenance or update program.

The program specifications

Figure 14-7 presents the specifications for a random maintenance program. This program reads through a sequential file of maintenance transactions that can add, change, or delete a record in the inventory master file. To do that, the item number field in each maintenance transaction is used to read a record in the inventory master file on a random basis. If the record is found, the transaction must be for a change or delete operation. If it isn't found, the transaction must be for an add operation. If a transaction is invalid, it's written to a file of error transactions.

Notice that this program assumes that the records in the transaction file are in sequence by the transaction code within the item number. Although this isn't a requirement for this type of application, it provides for the possibility that two or more transactions exist for the same item. For example, the first transaction can delete a record from the inventory master file, and the next transaction can add a record with the same item number back to the master file. Then, one or more transactions after that can change the record that was just added.

The system flowchart for a random maintenance program

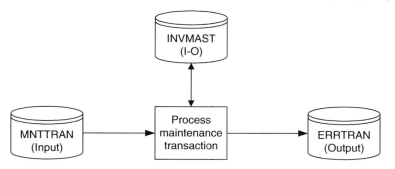

The record description for the maintenance transaction file

```
01    MAINTENANCE-TRANSACTION.
      05   MT-TRANSACTION-CODE     PIC X.
           88   DELETE-RECORD      VALUE "1".
           88   ADD-RECORD         VALUE "2".
           88   CHANGE-RECORD      VALUE "3".
      05   MT-MASTER-DATA.
           10   MT-ITEM-NO         PIC X(5).
           10   MT-ITEM-DESC       PIC X(40).
           10   MT-UNIT-COST       PIC S9(3)V99.
           10   MT-UNIT-PRICE      PIC S9(3)V99.
           10   MT-REORDER-POINT   PIC S9(5).
```

Processing specifications

- This program adds, changes, and deletes records in an inventory master file (INVMAST) based on the data in a file of maintenance transactions (MNTTRAN). The inventory master file is indexed by item number and should be updated randomly.

- This program assumes that the maintenance transactions have been previously edited so they contain valid data. For a delete transaction, the record contains just an item number. For an add transaction, all the fields in the record contain data. Since the transaction doesn't contain on-hand and on-order fields, the program should set these fields to zero in the new master record. For a change transaction, only the fields to be changed contain data.

- If MNTTRAN contains a change or delete transaction for a record that doesn't exist or an add transaction for an existing record, the program should write the record to a file of error transactions (ERRTRAN).

- This program also assumes that the records in the MNTTRAN file are in sequence by transaction code within item number. That way, a single item can be deleted, added back, and then changed.

Figure 14-7   The program specifications for a random maintenance program

The structure chart

Figure 14-8 presents the structure chart for the random maintenance program. Notice that module 300 controls most of the processing for this program. This module is executed for each record in the maintenance transaction file.

Module 300 starts by reading the next record in the maintenance transaction file (module 310). Then, it attempts to read a matching record in the inventory master file (module 320). If the transaction is for a change or delete operation and the master record is found, the master record is changed (module 360) or deleted (module 330). If the master record isn't found, a record is written to the error transaction file (module 380).

The processing for an add operation is similar. In this case, though, a record is written to the error transaction file if a matching master record is found. Otherwise, the new record is added to the master file (module 340).

The structure chart for the random maintenance program

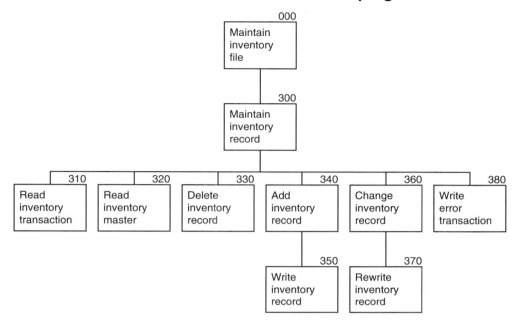

Description

- Module 000 of this program performs module 300 until all of the records in the maintenance transaction file have been processed.

- Module 300 performs module 310 to read a record from the maintenance transaction file. Then, it performs module 320 to read the inventory master file randomly to see if a record exists with the same item number.

- If the maintenance transaction is for a delete operation and a master record is found for the item, module 300 performs module 330 to delete the record. But if a master record isn't found, module 300 performs module 380 to write a record to the error transaction file.

- If the maintenance transaction is for an add operation and a matching master record isn't found, module 300 performs module 340 to add the record to the inventory master file. This module formats the record and then performs module 350 to write it to the file. If a matching master record is found, module 300 performs module 380 to write a record to the error transaction file.

- If the maintenance transaction is for a change operation and a matching master record is found, module 300 performs module 360 to change the inventory record. This module applies the change and then performs module 370 to rewrite the record. If a matching master record isn't found, module 300 performs module 380 to write a record to the error transaction file.

Figure 14-8   The structure chart for the random maintenance program

The COBOL code

Figure 14-9 presents the code for the random maintenance program. To start, notice that the Select statement for the inventory master file indicates that it's an indexed file and that the program will access it randomly. It also specifies that the key for each record accessed by the program can be found in the field named IR-ITEM-NO. This field is included in the record description for the file in the File Section of the program. The complete record description for this file, though, is coded in working storage.

The Working-Storage Section also includes the definitions of two switches used by the program. The program uses the transaction-eof switch to indicate when the end of the maintenance transaction file is reached. And it uses the master-found switch to indicate whether or not a record is found in the master file with the same item number as the current transaction.

The random maintenance program   **Page 1**

```
IDENTIFICATION DIVISION.
*
PROGRAM-ID.  IND2000.
*
ENVIRONMENT DIVISION.
*
INPUT-OUTPUT SECTION.
*
FILE-CONTROL.
    SELECT MNTTRAN  ASSIGN TO MNTTRAN.
    SELECT INVMAST  ASSIGN TO INVMAST
                    ORGANIZATION IS INDEXED
                    ACCESS IS RANDOM
                    RECORD KEY IS IR-ITEM-NO.
    SELECT ERRTRAN  ASSIGN TO ERRTRAN
                    FILE STATUS IS ERRTRAN-FILE-STATUS.
*
DATA DIVISION.
*
FILE SECTION.
*
FD  MNTTRAN.
*
01  TRANSACTION-RECORD      PIC X(61).
*
FD  INVMAST.
*
01  INVENTORY-RECORD-AREA.
    05  IR-ITEM-NO         PIC X(5).
    05  FILLER             PIC X(65).
*
FD  ERRTRAN.
*
01  ERROR-TRANSACTION      PIC X(61).
*
WORKING-STORAGE SECTION.
*
01  SWITCHES.
    05  TRANSACTION-EOF-SWITCH  PIC X    VALUE "N".
        88  TRANSACTION-EOF              VALUE "Y".
    05  MASTER-FOUND-SWITCH     PIC X    VALUE "Y".
        88  MASTER-FOUND                 VALUE "Y".
*
01  FILE-STATUS-FIELDS.
    05  ERRTRAN-FILE-STATUS     PIC XX.
        88  ERRTRAN-SUCCESSFUL           VALUE "00".
*
```

Figure 14-9   The COBOL code for the random maintenance program (part 1 of 4)

On page 2 of the program listing, you can see the complete record descriptions for the maintenance transaction file and the inventory master file. You can also see the top-level procedure for this program. This procedure controls the processing of procedure 300, which is performed until the last record in the maintenance transaction file has been read.

The random maintenance program

Page 2

```
01  MAINTENANCE-TRANSACTION.
    05  MT-TRANSACTION-CODE       PIC X.
        88  DELETE-RECORD                 VALUE "1".
        88  ADD-RECORD                    VALUE "2".
        88  CHANGE-RECORD                 VALUE "3".
    05  MT-MASTER-DATA.
        10  MT-ITEM-NO            PIC X(5).
        10  MT-ITEM-DESC          PIC X(40).
        10  MT-UNIT-COST          PIC S9(3)V99.
        10  MT-UNIT-PRICE         PIC S9(3)V99.
        10  MT-REORDER-POINT      PIC S9(5).
*
01  INVENTORY-MASTER-RECORD.
    05  IM-ITEM-NO               PIC X(5).
    05  IM-DESCRIPTIVE-DATA.
        10  IM-ITEM-DESC          PIC X(40).
        10  IM-UNIT-COST          PIC S9(3)V99.
        10  IM-UNIT-PRICE         PIC S9(3)V99.
    05  IM-INVENTORY-DATA.
        10  IM-REORDER-POINT      PIC S9(5).
        10  IM-ON-HAND            PIC S9(5).
        10  IM-ON-ORDER           PIC S9(5).
*
 PROCEDURE DIVISION.
*
 000-MAINTAIN-INVENTORY-FILE.
*
    OPEN INPUT   MNTTRAN
         I-O     INVMAST
         OUTPUT ERRTRAN.
    PERFORM 300-MAINTAIN-INVENTORY-RECORD
        UNTIL TRANSACTION-EOF.
    CLOSE MNTTRAN
          INVMAST
          ERRTRAN.
    STOP RUN.
*
```

Figure 14-9   The COBOL code for the random maintenance program (part 2 of 4)

Procedure 300 contains most of the logic for this program. Each time it's executed, it reads the next record in the maintenance transaction file. Then, if the end-of-file condition doesn't occur, it performs a random read operation on the inventory master file. Before the Read statement is executed in procedure 320, though, the item number in the transaction record is moved to the key field of the master file. If a record with that item number isn't found, the Invalid Key clause turns off the master-found switch. Otherwise, the Not Invalid Key clause turns on the master-found switch. This switch is used in procedure 300 in conjunction with the transaction code to determine the processing to be done.

If the transaction is for a delete operation and a matching master record is found, procedure 300 performs procedure 330 to delete the record. Notice that the Delete statement in this procedure doesn't include an Invalid Key clause. That's because the program has already checked that the record to be deleted exists, so an invalid key condition can't occur.

If the transaction is for an add operation and a matching master record isn't found, procedure 300 performs procedure 340 to add the new record. Procedure 340 moves the fields in the transaction record to the corresponding fields in the master record and moves zero to the on-hand and on-order fields. Then, it performs procedure 350 to write the new record. Unlike the Delete statement, the Write statement includes an Invalid Key clause. Although the program has already checked that a duplicate key condition doesn't exist, a write operation can also cause a boundary violation that can be trapped by the Invalid Key clause. If that error occurs, the program displays a message and turns on the transaction-eof switch so no more transactions are processed.

The random maintenance program   **Page 3**

```
300-MAINTAIN-INVENTORY-RECORD.
*
    PERFORM 310-READ-INVENTORY-TRANSACTION.
    IF NOT TRANSACTION-EOF
        PERFORM 320-READ-INVENTORY-MASTER
        IF DELETE-RECORD
            IF MASTER-FOUND
                PERFORM 330-DELETE-INVENTORY-RECORD
            ELSE
                PERFORM 380-WRITE-ERROR-TRANSACTION
        ELSE IF ADD-RECORD
            IF MASTER-FOUND
                PERFORM 380-WRITE-ERROR-TRANSACTION
            ELSE
                PERFORM 340-ADD-INVENTORY-RECORD
        ELSE IF CHANGE-RECORD
            IF MASTER-FOUND
                PERFORM 360-CHANGE-INVENTORY-RECORD
            ELSE
                PERFORM 380-WRITE-ERROR-TRANSACTION.
*
310-READ-INVENTORY-TRANSACTION.
*
    READ MNTTRAN INTO MAINTENANCE-TRANSACTION
        AT END
            MOVE "Y" TO TRANSACTION-EOF-SWITCH.
*
320-READ-INVENTORY-MASTER.
*
    MOVE MT-ITEM-NO TO IR-ITEM-NO.
    READ INVMAST INTO INVENTORY-MASTER-RECORD
        INVALID KEY
            MOVE "N" TO MASTER-FOUND-SWITCH
        NOT INVALID KEY
            MOVE "Y" TO MASTER-FOUND-SWITCH.
*
330-DELETE-INVENTORY-RECORD.
*
    DELETE INVMAST.
*
340-ADD-INVENTORY-RECORD.
*
    MOVE MT-ITEM-NO       TO IM-ITEM-NO.
    MOVE MT-ITEM-DESC     TO IM-ITEM-DESC.
    MOVE MT-UNIT-COST     TO IM-UNIT-COST.
    MOVE MT-UNIT-PRICE    TO IM-UNIT-PRICE.
    MOVE MT-REORDER-POINT TO IM-REORDER-POINT.
    MOVE ZERO             TO IM-ON-HAND.
    MOVE ZERO             TO IM-ON-ORDER.
    PERFORM 350-WRITE-INVENTORY-RECORD.
*
```

Figure 14-9   The COBOL code for the random maintenance program (part 3 of 4)

If the transaction is for a change operation and a matching master record is found, procedure 300 performs procedure 360 to change the inventory record. This procedure updates the fields in the master record with the data in the transaction record and then performs procedure 370 to rewrite the record. Like the Delete statement, the Rewrite statement doesn't include an Invalid Key clause because the program has already checked that the record to be rewritten exists. And this is the only invalid key condition that can occur on a rewrite operation.

If a matching master record isn't found for a delete or change operation or if a matching record is found for an add operation, procedure 300 performs procedure 380 to write a record to the error transaction file. The Write statement in this procedure is just like the one in the sequential maintenance program you saw in the last chapter. It uses the File Status field that's defined for this file to determine if the write operation is successful. If not, it displays an error message and turns on the transaction-eof switch so that no more transactions are processed.

After reviewing the code for this program, you might want to think about how else this program could be implemented. For example, you could simplify procedure 300 so it doesn't check for an existing master record before it processes the current transaction. Then, for a delete operation, you could include an Invalid Key clause on the Delete statement that writes a record to the error transaction file if an invalid key condition occurs. You could do the same thing for the Write statement for an add operation. For a change operation, though, the program would have to read the existing record first to get the current data since the transaction only includes data in the fields to be changed. As a result, it would require logic similar to what's shown here. The point is, you can use techniques other than the one presented here to get the same results.

The random maintenance program   **Page 4**

```
350-WRITE-INVENTORY-RECORD.
*
    WRITE INVENTORY-RECORD-AREA FROM INVENTORY-MASTER-RECORD
        INVALID KEY
            DISPLAY "WRITE ERROR ON INVMAST FOR ITEM NUMBER "
                IR-ITEM-NO
            MOVE "Y" TO TRANSACTION-EOF-SWITCH.
*
360-CHANGE-INVENTORY-RECORD.
*
    IF MT-ITEM-DESC NOT = SPACE
        MOVE MT-ITEM-DESC TO IM-ITEM-DESC.
    IF MT-UNIT-COST NOT = ZERO
        MOVE MT-UNIT-COST TO IM-UNIT-COST.
    IF MT-UNIT-PRICE NOT = ZERO
        MOVE MT-UNIT-PRICE TO IM-UNIT-PRICE.
    IF MT-REORDER-POINT NOT = ZERO
        MOVE MT-REORDER-POINT TO IM-REORDER-POINT.
    PERFORM 370-REWRITE-INVENTORY-RECORD.
*
370-REWRITE-INVENTORY-RECORD.
*
    REWRITE INVENTORY-RECORD-AREA FROM INVENTORY-MASTER-RECORD.
*
380-WRITE-ERROR-TRANSACTION.
*
    WRITE ERROR-TRANSACTION FROM MAINTENANCE-TRANSACTION.
    IF NOT ERRTRAN-SUCCESSFUL
        DISPLAY "WRITE ERROR ON ERRTRAN FOR ITEM NUMBER "
            MT-ITEM-NO
        DISPLAY "FILE STATUS CODE IS " ERRTRAN-FILE-STATUS
        MOVE "Y" TO TRANSACTION-EOF-SWITCH.
*
```

Figure 14-9   The COBOL code for the random maintenance program (part 4 of 4)

How to test and debug random update and maintenance programs

When you change a file using a sequential update or maintenance program as shown in the last chapter, you can check the old master, new master, and transaction files after the program is run to make sure that the program worked correctly. When you update a file on a random basis, though, you don't have an old master file and a new master file. Instead, the program updates the master file directly. Because of that, you have to be sure to check the data in the master file before you run the program so you can compare it to the data in the file after you run the program. You'll also want to be sure to save a copy of the original master file so you can restore it later if you need to.

If you're using an indexed file with Micro Focus Personal COBOL, you can display and work with the file using a text editor like Notepad. The first screen in figure 14-10, for example, shows how the inventory master file looks when displayed by Notepad. In addition to the record data, this display contains information related to the file's index, and the data isn't displayed one record per line as it is when you use line sequential files. Because of that, the data in an indexed file can be difficult to work with in Notepad.

Some compilers come with tools that let you work with the data in an indexed file in a more readable format. The second screen in this figure, for example, shows how the inventory master file looks when it's displayed by Micro Focus NetExpress. If your compiler doesn't have a tool like this, though, you may have to use Display statements in your program to display the data before and after it's updated.

If you're working with files on an IBM mainframe, you'll probably use a utility program called DITTO to work with the data in those files. This program lets you display, modify, print, and copy data in both VSAM and non-VSAM files. You'll use it frequently as you test and debug your programs.

Before you can test a program that changes the records in an indexed file, you have to create the indexed file. The only way to do that with Personal COBOL is to write a program like the one in figure 14-6. Some compilers or platforms, though, provide tools or utilities that let you create indexed files more easily. For instance, Micro Focus NetExpress provides an interactive tool that lets you enter the data for an indexed test file, and an IBM mainframe provides Access Method Services that let you create indexed files from sequential files.

The indexed inventory master file as displayed by Notepad

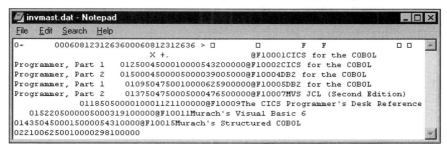

The indexed inventory master file as displayed by Micro Focus NetExpress

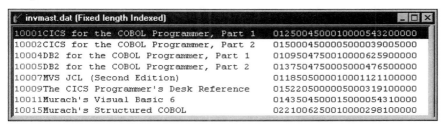

Description

- To make sure that a random update or maintenance program works correctly, you need to compare the data in the master file before the program is run with the data in the file after the program is run. Although you can use a text editor to work with indexed files, the files usually aren't presented in a form that's easy to read.

- Some compilers, like Micro Focus NetExpress, come with tools you can use to work with the data in an indexed file in a readable format.

- When you work with files on an IBM mainframe, you can use a utility program called DITTO to work with the data in a file.

- You can also use a Display statement in a Read, Write, or Rewrite procedure to display the records as they're processed by that procedure.

- Some compilers or platforms provide tools or utilities that make it easy for you to create the indexed files that you need for testing.

Figure 14-10   How to test and debug indexed update and maintenance programs

How to work with alternate indexes

Alternate indexes make it possible to access records in an indexed file by a field other than the primary key. Like a primary key, an alternate key can be accessed either sequentially or randomly. You'll see sample code for using both of these access modes in just a moment. But first, you need to learn some additional COBOL for working with alternate indexes.

How to code Select statements

At the top of figure 14-11, you can see the syntax of the Select statement for a file with one or more alternate indexes. To identify an alternate index, you use the Alternate Record Key clause. This clause names the alternate key field for the file. Like the primary key field, an alternate key field must be included in the record description for the file in the File Section.

If an alternate index allows *duplicate keys* (two or more records with the same key value), you include the With Duplicates phrase on the Alternate Record Key clause. If you omit this phrase, the program will assume that all of the records have *unique keys* (only one record for each key value). In that case, an invalid key condition will occur if the program tries to write a record with an alternate key value that already exists in the file.

If a file has more than one alternate index, you can code an Alternate Record Key clause for each one. Keep in mind, though, that you may not have to specify all of the alternate keys in every program that uses the file. In general, you only have to specify the alternate keys that your program is going to use to access records or that you want the program to update. Because alternate keys are implemented differently on different compilers, though, you'll want to find out what's required by the compiler you're using. With Personal COBOL, for example, you have to include the Alternate Record Key clause for each alternate index for a file even if the program doesn't use that index.

This figure also presents two file status codes that are particularly useful for working with alternate indexes. Both of them have to do with duplicate key conditions. If this condition occurs on an alternate index that doesn't allow duplicates, a file status code of 22 is returned. You can handle this file status using an Invalid Key clause just like you do for a primary key.

If a duplicate key condition occurs on an alternate index that allows duplicates, a file status of 02 is returned. In many cases, you don't need to take any special action when this condition occurs. If you use a File Status field to check for a successful operation, though, you'll want to check for a file status of 02 as well as 00.

The syntax of the Select statement for files with alternate indexes

```
SELECT file-name ASSIGN to system-name
            ORGANIZATION IS INDEXED
                        ⎧ SEQUENTIAL ⎫
            ACCESS MODE IS ⎨ RANDOM     ⎬
                        ⎩ DYNAMIC    ⎭
            RECORD KEY IS data-name-1
            [ALTERNATE RECORD KEY IS data-name-2 [WITH DUPLICATES]]...
            [FILE STATUS IS data-name-3]
```

File status codes for working with alternate indexes

Code	Meaning
02	A duplicate key condition occurred on an alternate index that allows duplicates.
22	The program attempted to write or rewrite a record with a duplicate primary key or an alternate key that doesn't allow duplicates.

Description

- The Alternate Record Key clause of the Select statement names an alternate key field for a file. The named field must be defined in the record description for the file in the File Section of the program along with the primary key.

- The With Duplicates phrase indicates that *duplicate keys* are allowed for the alternate index. If this phrase is omitted, the keys must be *unique*.

- You can code an Alternate Record Key clause for each alternate index that's defined for a file. In most cases, though, you only need to code this clause for the alternate keys that the program uses to access records and the alternate keys that you want to be updated by the program.

- If a duplicate key is detected during an I/O operation for an alternate key that allows duplicates, a file status code of 02 is returned. Your program can use this code during a retrieval operation to determine when all of the records with an alternate key value have been processed.

- If a duplicate key is detected during a write or rewrite operation and duplicate keys aren't allowed, a file status code of 22 is returned.

Figure 14-11   How to code Select statements for alternate indexes

If you're reading a file using an alternate index, you can use the File Status field to determine when there are no more records for a given key value. If you issue a random Read statement using an alternate key, for example, the record that's retrieved is the first record that was written to the file with the key value you specify. If the file contains additional records with the same alternate key value, you'll get an 02 file status code. Then, you can retrieve those additional records by issuing sequential Read statements. To do that, though, the Select statement for the file must specify dynamic access.

If you issue a sequential Read statement using an alternate key that allows duplicates, the 02 file status is returned if there is at least one more record in the file with the same key value. When you read the last, or only, record in the file with that alternate key value, though, a file status code of 00 is returned. In a minute, you'll see how you can use these codes to control the processing of an alternate index.

How to code Start and Read statements

Before you can access a file using an alternate index, you have to establish the key you want to use for retrieval operations. You can do that for sequential access by using the Start statement as shown in figure 14-12. The syntax of this statement is the same as it is for positioning a file based on a primary key. The difference is that the field you specify in the Key clause must be the name of an alternate key field. Then, any subsequent Read statements issued by the program will read the file sequentially by this key.

To establish the key for random retrieval, you use the Key clause of the Read statement as shown in this figure. This clause names the alternate key field you want to use to retrieve records. If this clause is omitted, the program assumes you want to retrieve records by the primary key.

The syntax of the Start statement for sequential access of a file by an alternate index

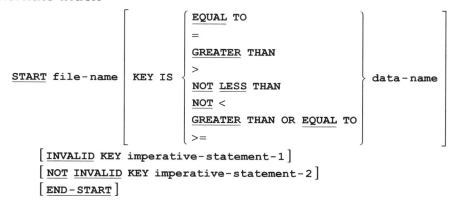

```
INVALID KEY imperative-statement-1
NOT INVALID KEY imperative-statement-2
END-START
```

The syntax of the Read statement for random access of a file by an alternate index

```
READ file-name RECORD [INTO identifier]
    KEY is data-name
    [INVALID KEY imperative-statement-1]
    [NOT INVALID KEY imperative-statement-2]
    [END-READ]
```

Description

- To position a file for sequential retrieval by an alternate index, you use the Start statement. On the Key clause of this statement, you name the alternate key field you want to use to access the file. Then, you can use the Read statement to access records sequentially by the alternate key.

- To read a record randomly based on an alternate key, you include the Key clause in the Read statement. This clause names the alternate key field you want to use to read the record.

Figure 14-12   How to code Start and Read statements for alternate indexes

How to process an alternate index sequentially

Figure 14-13 illustrates the use of the Start and Read statements for accessing a file sequentially by an alternate index. This code is from a program that prints a listing of a file of open item records. The primary index for this file is the invoice number, and the alternate index is the customer number. This listing is to be printed in customer number sequence, so it must be accessed sequentially by the alternate index. In addition, a total line is to be printed for each customer, so the program must know when it reads the last record for a customer.

The Select statement for the open item file names both the primary key and the alternate key. Because the file may contain two or more records for the same customer, the With Duplicates phrase is included on the Alternate Record Key clause. In addition, the alternate key field, OI-CUSTOMER-NUMBER, is included in the record description for the file in the File Section of the program. Finally, a File Status field is specified for this file.

Because the open item records are to be listed in customer number sequence, the program begins by issuing a Start statement that names the alternate key field. Before this statement is executed, though, Low-Value is moved to the key field. Then, the Key clause of the Start statement indicates that the file should be positioned at the first record in the file with a key value that's greater than or equal to the specified value. The result is that the file is positioned at the first record in the alternate index. Then, the subsequent Read statements will retrieve the records in alternate key sequence.

Notice in procedure 300 that the Last-Customer-Invoice condition is used to determine when customer totals are printed. If you look at the definition of the File Status field for this file, you'll see that this condition represents a file status of 00. Remember that when you work with alternate indexes, a file status of 02 indicates that there is at least one more record with the same key value as the record just read. In this case, that means that there's at least one more open item for the current customer. When a file status of 00 is returned, though, it indicates that there are no more records for the current customer. Then, the totals for that customer should be printed.

Instead of using a File Status field in this program, you could use a control field to determine when all the records for a customer have been read and a total line needs to be printed. You've seen logic like this in other report programs presented in this book. If you use File Status codes in your shop, though, you may want to code your programs using the method shown here.

Code for processing an indexed file sequentially by an alternate index

```
        SELECT OPENITEM ASSIGN TO OPENITEM
                       ORGANIZATION IS INDEXED
                       ACCESS IS SEQUENTIAL
                       RECORD KEY IS OI-INVOICE-NUMBER
                       ALTERNATE RECORD KEY IS OI-CUSTOMER-NUMBER
                            WITH DUPLICATES
                       FILE STATUS IS OPENITEM-FILE-STATUS.
         .
    FD  OPENITEM
        RECORD CONTAINS 69 CHARACTERS.
*
    01  OPEN-ITEM-RECORD.
        05  OI-INVOICE-NUMBER      PIC X(6).
        05  OI-INVOICE-DATE        PIC X(8).
        05  OI-CUSTOMER-NUMBER     PIC X(6).
         .
    WORKING-STORAGE SECTION.
         .
    01  FILE-STATUS-FIELDS.
        05  OPENITEM-FILE-STATUS   PIC XX.
            88  LAST-CUSTOMER-INVOICE       VALUE "00".
         .
    PROCEDURE DIVISION.
*
    000-PREPARE-OPEN-ITEM-LISTING.
        OPEN INPUT   OPENITEM
            OUTPUT OILIST.
        PERFORM 100-START-OPEN-ITEM-FILE.
        IF NOT OPENITEM-EOF
            PERFORM 300-PREPARE-OPEN-ITEM-LINES
                UNTIL OPENITEM-EOF
         .
    100-START-OPEN-ITEM-FILE.
        MOVE LOW-VALUE TO OI-CUSTOMER-NUMBER.
        START OPENITEM
            KEY IS >= OI-CUSTOMER-NUMBER
            INVALID KEY
                MOVE "Y" TO OPENITEM-EOF-SWITCH.
*
    300-PREPARE-OPEN-ITEM-LINES.
        PERFORM 310-READ-OPEN-ITEM-RECORD.
        IF NOT OPENITEM-EOF
         .
            IF LAST-CUSTOMER-INVOICE
                PERFORM 370-PRINT-TOTAL-LINE
         .
    310-READ-OPEN-ITEM-RECORD.
        READ OPENITEM
            AT END
                MOVE "Y" TO OPENITEM-EOF-SWITCH.
```

Figure 14-13   How to process an alternate index sequentially

How to process an alternate index randomly

The code in figure 14-14 shows how you can process a file randomly by an alternate index. This code is from a program that updates a file of employee master records based on the data in a file of employee transactions. Instead of using the primary index to access the records in the master file, this program uses an alternate index. In this case, the alternate index is the employee's social security number. As you can see in the Select statement for this file, no duplicate keys are allowed for this alternate index.

The basic logic of this program is to read a record in the employee transaction file, read a matching record in the employee master file, and update and rewrite the master record. Notice that the Key clause is included on the Read statement for the master file to establish the key that will be used to retrieve the records. Before this statement is executed, the social security number in the transaction record is moved to the alternate key field of the master record.

After a master record is read and updated, a Rewrite statement is issued to write the changes to the file. Although the syntax of this statement is the same as it is for working with a primary index, you should know about one difference for using this statement with an alternate index. That is, you can change the value of an alternate key by simply rewriting the record with a new key. In contrast, to change the primary key value of a record, you have to delete the existing record and write a new record with the new key. Although you probably won't need to change an alternate key value often, it's good to know you can do it if you need to.

Code for processing an indexed file randomly by an alternate index

```
        SELECT EMPMAST   ASSIGN TO EMPMAST
                         ORGANIZATION IS INDEXED
                         ACCESS IS RANDOM
                         RECORD KEY IS ER-EMPLOYEE-NUMBER
                         ALTERNATE RECORD KEY
                             IS ER-SOCIAL-SECURITY-NUMBER.
            .
            .
 FD   EMPMAST
      RECORD CONTAINS 103 CHARACTERS.
 *
 01   EMPLOYEE-RECORD-AREA.
      05   ER-EMPLOYEE-NUMBER         PIC X(5).
      05   FILLER                     PIC X(31).
      05   ER-SOCIAL-SECURITY-NUMBER  PIC X(9).
      05   FILLER                     PIC X(58).
            .
            .
 PROCEDURE DIVISION.
            .
            .
 300-UPDATE-EMPLOYEE-RECORD.
 *
      PERFORM 310-READ-EMPLOYEE-TRANSACTION.
      IF NOT TRANSACTION-EOF
          PERFORM 320-READ-EMPLOYEE-MASTER
          IF MASTER-FOUND
              PERFORM 330-UPDATE-EMPLOYEE-MASTER
              PERFORM 340-REWRITE-EMPLOYEE-MASTER
          ELSE
              PERFORM 350-WRITE-ERROR-TRANSACTION.
            .
            .
 320-READ-EMPLOYEE-MASTER.
 *
      MOVE EMT-SOCIAL-SECURITY-NUMBER TO ER-SOCIAL-SECURITY-NUMBER.
      READ EMPMAST INTO EMPLOYEE-MASTER-RECORD
          KEY IS ER-SOCIAL-SECURITY-NUMBER
          INVALID KEY
              MOVE "N" TO MASTER-FOUND-SWITCH
          NOT INVALID KEY
              MOVE "Y" TO MASTER-FOUND-SWITCH.
            .
            .
 340-REWRITE-EMPLOYEE-MASTER.
 *
      REWRITE EMPLOYEE-RECORD-AREA FROM EMPLOYEE-MASTER-RECORD
          INVALID KEY
              DISPLAY "REWRITE ERROR ON EMPMAST FOR SSN = "
                  ER-SOCIAL-SECURITY-NUMBER
              MOVE "Y" TO TRANSACTION-EOF-SWITCH.
            .
            .
```

Figure 14-14   How to process an alternate index randomly

Other processing techniques

If you specify dynamic access for an indexed file, the program can process the file using both sequential and random access. This type of processing can be referred to as *dynamic processing*. Although you probably won't need to use dynamic processing often, you should know how to use it in case you do. You should also know how to use a technique called *skip-sequential processing*. In many instances, you can use skip-sequential processing in place of dynamic processing.

How to use dynamic processing

In general, dynamic processing is most useful in interactive programs. For example, an interactive program might allow the user to get the data from one record in a file on a random basis and then let the user look over the next few records in the file on a sequential basis. Regardless of whether you use dynamic processing in an interactive or batch program, though, you use the same coding techniques to implement it.

Figure 14-15 presents code you can use to implement dynamic processing. This code is from a program that accesses a file of inventory location records. For each inventory item, there may be none, one, or more location records.

The key for the inventory location file consists of the item number followed by a two-digit sequence number. This is referred to as a *concatenated key* because it consists of more than one field. Dynamic processing is often used with files that have concatenated keys.

In this case, you can assume that the program will start by accepting an item number from the user. Then, the program will read and display the first record for the item. This is possible if you assume that the first record for an item always has a sequence number of 01. Then, the program can read and display the remaining records for the item in sequence.

In the Select statement for the inventory location file, you can see that dynamic access is specified so the program can use both random and sequential access. Then, before the random Read statement is executed, the program moves the item number entered by the user, which is stored in the ITEM-NUMBER field, into the item number field in the location record. It also moves 01 to the sequence number field of this record so the Read statement that follows will read the first record for the item.

If the random Read statement completes successfully, the program can then read the remaining records for the item sequentially. Notice that the Read statement that performs this function includes the Next Record clause to indicate that the next record in the file is to be read. To determine when the last record for an item has been read, the program checks the item number of the current location record to see if it's equal to the item number entered by the user. If it's not, the program sets a switch that ends the sequential retrieval operation.

Code for a program that uses dynamic processing

```
        SELECT INVLOC    ASSIGN TO INVLOC
                         ORGANIZATION IS INDEXED
                         ACCESS IS DYNAMIC
                         RECORD KEY IS IL-RECORD-KEY.
            .
            .
            .
    FD  INVLOC
        RECORD CONTAINS 30 CHARACTERS.
    *
    01  INVENTORY-LOCATION-RECORD.
        05  IL-RECORD-KEY.
            10   IL-ITEM-NO         PIC X(5).
            10   IL-SEQUENCE-NO     PIC XX.
        05  IL-LOCATION-DATA.
            .
            .
            .
    PROCEDURE DIVISION.
            .
            .
            .
    330-READ-FIRST-LOCATION-RECORD.
    *
        MOVE ITEM-NUMBER TO IL-ITEM-NO.
        MOVE "01"        TO IL-SEQUENCE-NO.
        READ INVLOC
            INVALID KEY
                MOVE "N" TO LOCATION-FOUND-SWITCH.
            .
            .
            .
    350-READ-NEXT-LOCATION-RECORD.
    *
        READ INVLOC NEXT RECORD
            AT END
                MOVE "N" TO LOCATION-FOUND-SWITCH.
        IF IL-ITEM-NO NOT = ITEM-NUMBER
            MOVE "N" TO LOCATION-FOUND-SWITCH.
    *
```

Random Read statement (braces around the READ INVLOC ... INVALID KEY ... MOVE "N" TO LOCATION-FOUND-SWITCH block)

Sequential Read statement (braces around the READ INVLOC NEXT RECORD ... AT END ... MOVE "N" TO LOCATION-FOUND-SWITCH block)

Description

- When you specify dynamic access mode for a file, you can read the file both randomly and sequentially. Usually, you'll use random access to read the first record in a group of records, and you'll use sequential access to read the rest of the records in the group.

- When you process a file dynamically, you must include the Next Record phrase on the Read statement that reads the file sequentially.

- You can use *dynamic processing* to access a file by its primary key or an alternate key. In either case, you must know the exact key value of the first record you want to read in a group so you can read it randomly. If you don't know the exact key value, you may want to use skip-sequential processing instead of dynamic processing.

Figure 14-15   How to use dynamic processing

How to use skip-sequential processing

To use dynamic processing, you have to know the exact key value of the first record to be retrieved so the program can retrieve it on a random basis. For example, the program presented in the previous figure assumed that the first record in a file of inventory location records could be identified by the item number and the sequence number 01. But what if the sequence number of the first record didn't have to be 01? In that case, you could use skip-sequential processing to retrieve the records for an item.

When you use skip-sequential processing, you use the Start statement to position the file at the first record you want to read. This is illustrated by the code in figure 14-16. Before the Start statement is executed, this program moves the item number entered by the user into the item number field in the inventory location record just like the program that uses dynamic processing did. Instead of moving the sequence number of the first record into the sequence number field, though, this program moves Low-Value to that field. Then, the Start statement that follows positions the file at the first record for the item regardless of its sequence number.

After the Start statement is executed, the program can read the records for the item sequentially just like the program that uses dynamic access. Notice, however, that the Next Record clause isn't included on the Read statement in this example. Since sequential access is specified for this file, the program reads the next record by default.

Code for a program that uses skip-sequential processing

```
        SELECT INVLOC    ASSIGN TO INVLOC
                         ORGANIZATION IS INDEXED
                         ACCESS IS SEQUENTIAL
                         RECORD KEY IS IL-RECORD-KEY.
          .
          .
 FD   INVLOC
      RECORD CONTAINS 30 CHARACTERS.
 *
  01   INVENTORY-LOCATION-RECORD.
       05   IL-RECORD-KEY.
            10   IL-ITEM-NO          PIC X(5).
            10   IL-SEQUENCE-NO      PIC XX.
       05   IL-LOCATION-DATA.
          .
          .
 PROCEDURE DIVISION.
          .
          .
 320-START-LOCATION-FILE.
 *
      MOVE ITEM-NUMBER TO IL-ITEM-NO.
      MOVE LOW-VALUE    TO IL-SEQUENCE-NO.
      START INVLOC
          KEY IS > IL-RECORD-KEY
              INVALID KEY
                  MOVE "N" TO LOCATION-FOUND-SWITCH.
          .
          .
 340-READ-LOCATION-RECORD.
 *
      READ INVLOC
          AT END
              MOVE "N" TO LOCATION-FOUND-SWITCH.
      IF IL-ITEM-NO NOT = ITEM-NUMBER
          MOVE "N" TO LOCATION-FOUND-SWITCH.
 *
```

Description

- To use *skip-sequential processing*, you use a Start statement to position the file at the first record to be read. Usually, you'll position the file at the first record with a specific key value or a key value that's greater than a given value.

- After you position the file, you use a Read statement to read the records that follow in sequence. Usually, you'll continue reading records until the key value or part of the key value changes. Then, you can use the Start statement again to position the file at the next group of records to be read.

- You can use skip-sequential processing to access a file by its primary key or an alternate key. In either case, you can specify sequential access mode for the file. If you specify dynamic access, be sure to include the Next Record phrase on the Read statement.

Figure 14-16   How to use skip-sequential processing

Perspective

Because you can access indexed files both randomly and sequentially, they provide flexibility that's not available with sequential files. In addition, the logic of a program that processes an indexed file is usually simpler than a comparable program that processes a sequential file. That is clearly illustrated by the random maintenance program in this chapter.

Remember, however, that the processing of an indexed file requires additional overhead. That's true even if you're just reading records from the file, but it's particularly true if you're updating the file. Then, the index must be updated as well as the data. And if the file contains one or more alternate indexes, the increase in overhead can be dramatic. That's why many large shops, particularly mainframe shops, continue to do a lot of their batch processing with sequential files.

On the other hand, indexed files are essential to interactive processing. In chapter 17, for example, you can see an interactive program that maintains an indexed master file. There, you can see that the processing of indexed files works the same whether it's in a batch or an interactive program.

Summary

- You can process an indexed file using *sequential access*, *random access*, or *dynamic access* that's based on its *primary index* or an *alternate index*.

- You can use *file status codes* to determine whether an I/O operation on an indexed file was successful. You can also use the Invalid Key clause of the Read, Write, Rewrite, Start, and Delete statements to catch the four file status codes that indicate an invalid key condition.

- You can use the Start statement to start sequential processing of an indexed file at a specific location.

- To process an indexed file by alternate keys, you code the Alternate Record Key clause on the Select statement for the file. If *duplicate keys* are allowed, you must also code the With Duplicates phrase.

- To read a record randomly using an alternate key, you must include the Key clause in the Read statement. To read records sequentially based on an alternate key, you can use the Start statement to position the file and then Read statements to read the records sequentially.

- You can use the File Status field to determine when all of the records with an alternate key value have been processed. A file status code of 02 indicates that the file contains at least one more record with the same key. A file status code of 00 indicates that there are no more records with the same key.

- You can use *dynamic processing* when you want to read the first record in a group randomly and then read the other records in the group sequentially. You can also use *skip-sequential processing* to process the records in a group.

Terms

primary index	dynamic access	unique keys
ddname	file status code	dynamic processing
sequential access	alternate index	concatenated key
random access	duplicate keys	skip-sequential processing

Objectives

- Given complete program specifications, develop a program that processes an indexed file sequentially, randomly, or dynamically. The program may use the primary key or an alternate key to access the records in the file.

- Name the three access modes you can use for an indexed file.

- Describe two ways that a program can detect I/O errors for indexed files.

- Describe the operation of the Read, Write, Rewrite, and Delete statements when used with random access of indexed files.

- Describe the operation of the Start statement and name the two types of access that it can be used with.

- Explain how you can use file status codes to determine when all of the records for a specific alternate key value have been processed.

- In general terms, describe dynamic processing.

- In general terms, describe skip-sequential processing.

Exercise 14-1   Run the indexed file creation program

In this exercise, you'll run the file creation program that's in figure 14-6. That will create an indexed inventory master file that you can use in exercise 14-2.

1. Open the program named ind1000. Then, compile and test the program. It should create an indexed inventory master file named invmasti.dat.

2. Use your Windows Explorer to find the file that you've just created in the c:\cobol\data folder. Then, note that two files have been created by this program. Invmasti.dat contains the data, while invmasti.idx contains the index that lets you use random access with the file. That's the way Micro Focus Personal COBOL implements an indexed file. On other systems, though, the data and index are stored in a single file.

3. Double-click on invmasti.dat to open the file in Notepad. There you can see that it's difficult to interpret the data because of the extra codes that the file contains for indexing. When you're done reviewing the data, close Notepad.

4. Close the file creation program, but note that you can rerun this program whenever you need to get a fresh copy of the inventory master file.

Exercise 14-2   Develop a random update program

In this exercise, you'll modify the sequential update program of chapter 13 so it updates the records in the inventory master file on a random basis. The logic is to read a receipt transaction record and update the master record with the same item number.

Create the program

1. Open the sequential update program named seq1000. Then, change the Program-ID to IND3000, save the program as ind3000, and close the program.

2. Create a structure chart for the random update program based on the structure chart for the random maintenance program in figure 14-8.

3. Open the program named ind3000 you created in step 1, and modify it so it randomly updates the indexed master file. As you work, use the chart you created in step 2 and the code for the random maintenance program in figure 14-9 as a guide. For simplicity, the program can read a transaction record, apply the transaction when the master record is found, and rewrite the updated master.

Compile and test the program

4. Compile and run the program. To review the transaction records, find the file named rcttranl.dat in the Explorer and double-click on it to open it in Notepad. There you can see that this line sequential file contains just four transactions. Then, to find out whether the master records have been updated correctly, open invmasti.dat in Notepad. But that doesn't help much, does it?

5. As an alternative, add Display statements to the program that display each master record right after it has been read and right after each updated master record has been rewritten. These statements should be placed in the Read and Rewrite procedures. Now, compile and test the program again.

6. The trouble now is that the master file has been updated at least twice in steps 4 and 5 so it's hard to tell whether the on hand and on order fields have been updated correctly. To get a fresh copy of the indexed master file, run the ind1000 program again. Then, test the random update program again. This time you can tell for sure whether the program has worked correctly.

7. When you've got the program working right, close it.

Exercise 14-3   Prepare a report from an indexed file

In this exercise, you'll modify the enhanced summary report program of chapter 5 so it reads an indexed file instead of a sequential file.

1. Open the program named rpt3000. Then, change the Program-ID to RPT3000I, save the program as rpt3000i, and close the program.

2. Open the program you created in step 1, and modify it so it reads the records in an indexed version of the customer master file that's named custmsti.dat. Here, the primary index is customer number, but branch number is an alternate index with duplicates. With Personal COBOL, you need to include the alternate index in the Select statement, even though the program isn't going to use the alternate index. Note, however, that other compilers don't require that.

3. Compile and test the program. When you're done, print a copy of the report so you can use it in the next exercise. Then, close the program.

Exercise 14-4 Retrieve records by primary key

In this exercise, you'll write an interactive program using Display and Accept statements that gets the data for customer records from the indexed customer master file that you used for exercise 14-3. For this program, the interactive session should look something like this (the user entries are shaded):

```
Enter a customer number.
Or, enter 99999 to end the program.
-----------------------------------------
11111
Number   Name                   YTD Sales
11111    INFORMATION BUILDERS     1,234.56
-----------------------------------------
Enter a customer number.
Or, enter 99999 to end the program.
-----------------------------------------
99999
```

1. Open the program named ind4000. This program contains code that will give you a good start on this program. Here again, the Select statement includes the Alternate Record Key clause for the branch index, but you won't need to use that index.

2. Change the Program-ID to IND4100, save the program as ind4100, and close the program.

3. Open the program you created in step 2, and modify it so it does what this program requires. If the user enters an invalid customer number, the program should print a message like: "No master record for customer number 00099."

4. Compile and test the program. Be sure to enter valid customer numbers that you can get from the report that you printed in exercise 14-3 as well as invalid customer numbers.

5. When you've got the program working right, close the program.

Exercise 14-5   Use alternate keys with duplicates

In this exercise, you'll modify the program that you created in exercise 14-4 so it displays the customer data for the branch number that the user enters. This time the interactive session should look something like this:

```
Enter a branch number.
Or, enter 99 to end the program.
----------------------------------------
12
Number   Name                  YTD Sales
11111    INFORMATION BUILDERS    1,234.56
12345    CAREER TRAINING CTR    12,345.67
----------------------------------------
Enter a branch number.
Or, enter 99 to end the program.
----------------------------------------
99
```

1. Open the program named ind4100 that you created in exercise 14-4. Then, change the Program-ID to IND4200, save the program as ind4200, and close the program.

2. Open the program you created in step 1, and modify it so it uses the branch number alternate key to get the data that the program requires. If the user enters an invalid branch number, the program should print a message like: "No customer records for branch 01." For a program like this, you can use either dynamic processing or skip-sequential processing, but use skip-sequential processing for this version of the program.

3. Compile and test until the program works correctly. Then, close the program.

Exercise 14-6   Use dynamic processing

In this exercise, you'll modify the program that you created in exercise 14-5 so it uses dynamic processing to get the same results.

1. Open the program named ind4200 that you created in the last exercise. Then, change the Program-ID to IND4300, save the program as ind4300, and close the program.

2. Open the program you created in step 1, and modify it so it uses dynamic processing instead of skip-sequential processing. Use the file status code for the file so the program only reads the customer records that apply to each branch number that the user enters. Otherwise, the program should work the same way it did before.

3. Compile and test until the program works correctly. Then, close the program.

15

How to work with relative files

Because relative files are used infrequently, you may never need to write a program that uses one. On the other hand, relative files can occasionally be useful for some applications, so you should at least know what you can do with them. In this chapter, then, you'll learn the COBOL for working with relative files.

COBOL for relative files

In chapter 12, you learned that a *relative file* consists of a specified number of areas. Each of these areas can contain a record, or it can be empty. To identify an area in a relative file, you use a *relative record number* that indicates the area's relative position in the file.

For the most part, the COBOL you use to work with relative files is the same as the COBOL you use to work with indexed files. The biggest difference is how you code the Select statement for a relative file.

How to code Select statements

Figure 15-1 presents the syntax of the Select statement for relative files. Here, you can see that you must code the Organization clause to indicate that the file has relative organization. Otherwise, the program will assume that it has sequential organization.

To specify the relative record number of a record you want to access, you code the Relative Key clause for the file. This clause names the field that will contain the relative record number. You'll need to specify a relative record number to access a record randomly using a Read, Write, Rewrite, or Delete statement or to position the file using the Start statement. However, you can omit this clause if the file is accessed sequentially and the Start statement isn't used to position the file. Then, the records are read sequentially by relative record number.

If you code the Relative Key clause, the field you name must be defined in working storage; it should not be a field in the record description for the file. That's because this field will contain a relative record number, which isn't typically stored in the record. The relative record number may be derived from a field in the record, though, as you'll see later in this chapter.

Like sequential and indexed files, you can include the File Status clause on the Select statement for a relative file. Then, you can use the File Status field to check for I/O errors. Because most of the *file status codes* for relative files are the same as for indexed files, they're not repeated in this chapter. For a list of the possible file status codes, please refer to figure 14-2. The only file status codes in that figure that don't apply to relative files are 02, which applies to alternate indexes, and 21, which applies specifically to indexed files.

The syntax of the Select statement for relative files

```
SELECT file-name ASSIGN to system-name
               ORGANIZATION IS RELATIVE
               ⎡                ⎧ SEQUENTIAL ⎫ ⎤
               ⎢ ACCESS MODE IS ⎨ RANDOM     ⎬ ⎥
               ⎣                ⎩ DYNAMIC    ⎭ ⎦
               [ RELATIVE KEY IS data-name-1 ]
               [ FILE STATUS IS data-name-2 ]
```

The syntax for a system name for a VSAM file on an IBM mainframe

```
ddname
```

The syntax for a system name on a PC

```
"path\filename"
```

A Select statement for a file that's accessed sequentially

```
SELECT INVMAST  ASSIGN TO INVMAST
                ORGANIZATION IS RELATIVE
                ACCESS IS SEQUENTIAL.
```

A Select statement for a file that's accessed randomly

```
SELECT INVMAST  ASSIGN TO INVMAST
                ORGANIZATION IS RELATIVE
                ACCESS IS RANDOM
                RELATIVE KEY IS INVMAST-RR-NUMBER.
```

Description

- On a PC, the system name consists of the path and file name for the file. On an IBM mainframe, the system name consists of a *ddname* that's used in the JCL for the program to assign the file in the program to a file on disk.

- You must code the Organization clause for a relative file since the default is Sequential.

- You can access the records in a relative file sequentially or randomly by relative record number or both sequentially and randomly. When a relative file is read sequentially, record areas that don't contain data are skipped.

- The Relative Key clause names the field that will contain the relative record number of the record to be accessed. This clause is required for random access, but is only required for sequential access if the Start statement will be used to position the file.

- The Relative Key field must be defined in working storage, and its definition must accommodate the full range of possible relative record numbers.

- You can use the File Status clause to name a working-storage field defined as XX that will be updated by the system as each I/O statement for the file is executed.

- The file status codes for relative files are the same as for indexed files, except that codes 02 and 21 do not apply to relative files. See figure 14-2 for a list of these codes.

Figure 15-1   How to code Select statements for relative files

How to code I/O statements

Figure 15-2 summarizes the I/O statements for working with relative files. If you compare the syntax of the statements presented in this figure with the syntax of the I/O statements for indexed files presented in figures 14-3 and 14-4, you'll see that they're identical. And, for the most part, these statements work the same way they do for indexed files. Because of that, you shouldn't have any trouble using them. However, you should be aware of two differences in the way you work with relative files.

First, remember from chapter 12 that some of the data areas in a relative file may be empty. When you read a relative file sequentially, then, the program must skip these empty areas. Fortunately, it does that automatically.

Second, before you can read a record in a relative file randomly, you have to place the relative record number of the record in the Relative Key field. Then, the Read statement will retrieve the record in that relative position in the file, if that area contains a record. If that area doesn't contain a record, an invalid key condition occurs, which can be handled by the Invalid Key clause of the Read statement.

Likewise, you have to specify a relative record number before you can write to a relative file. In that case, the Write statement will cause an invalid key condition if the area specified by the relative record number already contains a record. That can happen if the program uses a randomizing routine to calculate the relative record number, and the new record randomizes to the same relative record number as an existing record. In that case, the Invalid Key clause can call a routine that finds an empty record area where the record can be written.

Like indexed files, you can rewrite or delete a record in a relative file that's accessed randomly without first reading the record. To do that, you place the relative record number in the Relative Key field before you issue the Rewrite or Delete statement just like you do for a random Read or Write statement. Then, if that record exists, it is rewritten or deleted. If it doesn't exist, an invalid key condition occurs.

You can also use the Start statement with relative files. To do that, you place the relative record number in the Relative Key field. Then, you name that field in the Key clause of the Start statement. Alternatively, you can omit the Key clause. Then, the file will be positioned at the record with the relative record number specified in the Relative Key field if such a number exists. If it doesn't exist, an invalid key condition occurs.

The syntax of the Open statement

```
        ⎧ INPUT  file-name-1 ... ⎫
        ⎪ OUTPUT file-name-2 ... ⎪
OPEN  ⎨                          ⎬
        ⎪ I-O    file-name-3 ... ⎪
        ⎩ EXTEND file-name-4 ... ⎭
```

The syntax of the Read statement for sequential access

```
READ file-name [NEXT] RECORD [INTO data-name]
    [AT END imperative-statement-1]
    [NOT AT END imperative-statement-2]
    [END-READ]
```

The syntax of the Read statement for random access

```
READ file-name RECORD [INTO data-name]
    [INVALID KEY imperative-statement-1]
    [NOT INVALID KEY imperative-statement-2]
    [END-READ]
```

The syntax of the Write statement

```
WRITE record-name [FROM data-name]
    [INVALID KEY imperative-statement-1]
    [NOT INVALID KEY imperative-statement-2]
    [END-WRITE]
```

The syntax of the Rewrite statement

```
REWRITE record-name [FROM data-name]
    [INVALID KEY imperative-statement-1]
    [NOT INVALID KEY imperative-statement-2]
    [END-REWRITE]
```

The syntax of the Start statement

```
                        ⎧ EQUAL TO                  ⎫
                        ⎪ =                          ⎪
                        ⎪ GREATER THAN               ⎪
                        ⎪ >                          ⎪
START file-name  KEY IS ⎨                            ⎬ data-name
                        ⎪ NOT LESS THAN              ⎪
                        ⎪ NOT <                      ⎪
                        ⎪ GREATER THAN OR EQUAL TO   ⎪
                        ⎩ >=                         ⎭
    [INVALID KEY imperative-statement-1]
    [NOT INVALID KEY imperative-statement-2]
    [END-START]
```

The syntax of the Delete statement

```
DELETE file-name RECORD
    [INVALID KEY imperative-statement-1]
    [NOT INVALID KEY imperative-statement-2]
    [END-DELETE]
```

The syntax of the Close statement

```
CLOSE file-name-1 ...
```

Figure 15-2   How to code I/O statements for relative files

How to process relative files

To illustrate the COBOL for working with relative files, the next two topics present code from two programs. The first program processes a relative file sequentially to create a report, and the second program maintains a relative file randomly based on a sequential file of transactions.

Sequential processing

Figure 15-3 presents code from a program that reads a relative file of inventory master records sequentially and prints a listing of the records. Because the records are read sequentially from beginning to end, the Select statement doesn't include the Relative Key clause. Then, the Read statement reads the next record each time it's executed, skipping over any empty record areas in the file. When the end of the file is reached, the At End clause is used to set a switch that ends the program.

Remember that when you read a relative file sequentially, the records are read in sequence by their relative record numbers. Whether it makes sense to read a relative file sequentially, then, depends on how the relative record numbers are derived. If those numbers have a direct relationship with a unique field in the file, the records may be in a useful sequence for sequential retrieval. That's the case in the example in this figure, since the relative record numbers for the inventory master file are calculated by subtracting 10000 from the item number field. If a *randomizing routine* is used to calculate relative record numbers, though, the records would be stored in a random sequence. In that case, it probably wouldn't make sense to access them sequentially.

Like an indexed file, you typically create a relative file by writing a program that reads records from a sequential file and writes them to the new file. Unlike an indexed file, though, you usually write the records to a relative file on a random basis. That's because, depending on the routine you use to calculate the relative record numbers, those numbers may not be in sequence. But even if they are, it's common practice to create a relative file using random access.

Code for processing a relative file sequentially

```
        SELECT INVMAST  ASSIGN TO INVMAST
                        ORGANIZATION IS RELATIVE
                        ACCESS IS SEQUENTIAL.
*
 DATA DIVISION.
*
 FILE SECTION.
*
 FD   INVMAST.
*
 01   INVENTORY-MASTER-RECORD.
        .
        .
 PROCEDURE DIVISION.
*
 000-PREPARE-INVENTORY-LISTING.
*
     OPEN INPUT   INVMAST
          OUTPUT INVLST.
     PERFORM 100-FORMAT-DATE-AND-TIME.
     PERFORM 200-PREPARE-INVENTORY-LINES
         UNTIL INVMAST-EOF-SWITCH = "Y".
     CLOSE INVMAST
           INVLST.
     STOP RUN.
        .
        .
 200-PREPARE-INVENTORY-LINES.
*
     PERFORM 210-READ-INVMAST-RECORD.
     IF NOT INVMAST-EOF
         PERFORM 220-PRINT-INVENTORY-LINE.
*
 210-READ-INVMAST-RECORD.
*
     READ INVMAST
         AT END
             MOVE "Y" TO INVMAST-EOF-SWITCH.
        .
        .
```

Figure 15-3   How to process a relative file sequentially

Random processing

To process a relative file randomly, you use code like that shown in figure 15-4. This program adds, changes, and deletes records in a file of inventory master records based on the data in a file of maintenance transactions. This program is identical to the random maintenance program presented in chapter 14 except that it updates a relative file instead of an indexed file.

The Select statement for the inventory master file in this program specifies relative organization and random access. It also includes a Relative Key clause that names the field that will contain the relative record number of the record to be accessed. In this case, the relative record number is calculated by subtracting 10000 from the item number. Since the smallest item number is 10001 and the item number can contain a maximum of five digits, that means that the relative record numbers can range from 1 to 89999. Because of that, the Relative Key field is defined in working storage as a five-byte numeric field.

Procedure 320 contains the Read statement for the inventory master file. Before this statement is executed, a Compute statement is used to calculate the relative record number of the record to be retrieved. The Compute statement subtracts 10000 from the item number in the current transaction record and places the result in the Relative Key field. Notice that the Numval function is used to get the numeric value of the item number. That's necessary because the item number is defined as an alphanumeric field, which can't be used in a calculation.

After the relative record number is calculated, the Read statement reads the record in the area indicated by that number. If that area doesn't contain a record, the Invalid Key clause of the Read statement turns off the master-found switch. If the area does contain a record, though, the Not Invalid Key clause turns on the master-found switch.

Procedure 350 also contains the code to calculate a relative record number from an item number when a new master is being added to the file. Then, this procedure issues a Write statement to write the record in the area indicated by that relative record number. If that area already contains a record, though, the Invalid Key clause displays an error message and turns on the transaction-eof switch. That way, no more transactions are processed and the program ends.

The procedures that delete and rewrite records in the inventory master file (330 and 370) don't calculate the relative record number. That's because they're always preceded by a Read statement that reads the record to be rewritten or deleted and places the relative record number of the record in the Relative Key field. Then, the Delete or Rewrite statement just deletes or rewrites that record. Notice that because the Read statement establishes that the record to be deleted or rewritten already exists, the Delete and Rewrite statements don't include Invalid Key clauses. In contrast, the Write statement includes an Invalid Key clause because an error can occur if the relative record number leads to a disk address that's outside of the disk space that's allocated to the file.

Code for processing a relative file randomly

```
SELECT INVMAST   ASSIGN TO INVMAST
                 ORGANIZATION IS RELATIVE
                 ACCESS IS RANDOM
                 RELATIVE KEY IS INVMAST-RR-NUMBER.
     .
FD  INVMAST.
*
01  INVENTORY-RECORD-AREA   PIC X(70).
     .
WORKING-STORAGE SECTION.
*
01  KEY-FIELDS.
    05  INVMAST-RR-NUMBER        PIC 9(5).
     .
PROCEDURE DIVISION.
*
000-MAINTAIN-INVENTORY-FILE.
*
    OPEN INPUT   MNTTRAN
         I-O     INVMAST
          OUTPUT ERRTRAN.
    PERFORM 300-MAINTAIN-INVENTORY-RECORD
        UNTIL TRANSACTION-EOF.
     .
320-READ-INVENTORY-MASTER.
*
    COMPUTE INVMAST-RR-NUMBER =
        FUNCTION NUMVAL (MT-ITEM-NO) - 10000.
    READ INVMAST INTO INVENTORY-MASTER-RECORD
        INVALID KEY
            MOVE "N" TO MASTER-FOUND-SWITCH
        NOT INVALID KEY
            MOVE "Y" TO MASTER-FOUND-SWITCH.
*
330-DELETE-INVENTORY-RECORD.
*
    DELETE INVMAST.
     .
350-WRITE-INVENTORY-RECORD.
*
    COMPUTE INVMAST-RR-NUMBER =
        FUNCTION NUMVAL (MT-ITEM-NO) - 10000.
    WRITE INVENTORY-RECORD-AREA FROM INVENTORY-MASTER-RECORD
        INVALID KEY
            DISPLAY "WRITE ERROR ON INVMAST FOR ITEM NUMBER "
                IM-ITEM-NO
            MOVE "Y" TO TRANSACTION-EOF-SWITCH.
     .
370-REWRITE-INVENTORY-RECORD.
*
    REWRITE INVENTORY-RECORD-AREA FROM INVENTORY-MASTER-RECORD.
     .
```

Figure 15-4   How to process a relative file randomly

Perspective

Relative files have three main disadvantages when compared to indexed files. First, it's often difficult to convert a field in a master record to a unique relative record number. Second, a relative file is likely to use disk space inefficiently due to the number of empty records it contains. Third, a relative file can't use alternate keys. Because of that, relative files are used infrequently.

Remember, though, that relative files can be more efficient than indexed files for the right application because they don't require as much overhead. When you access a record in a relative file on a random basis, for example, the system goes directly to the record, not through an index. Similarly, when you add records to or delete records from a relative file, the system doesn't have to update any indexes.

In practice, then, relative files make sense when two conditions are met. First, the file should have keys that can be easily converted to relative record numbers with no duplicates and a minimum of empty records. Second, the file should have relatively few deletions so the number of empty records doesn't increase dramatically as the file is used. Unfortunately, few files meet these conditions, which is why you'll rarely use relative files.

Summary

- You can access a relative file sequentially, randomly, or dynamically. If you access the file randomly or if you use a Start statement to position the file, the Select statement for the file must identify the field that will contain the relative record number of the record to be accessed.

- The Relative Key field that's named in the Select statement for a relative file must be defined in working storage.

- You code the I/O statements for a relative file the same way you do for an indexed file. The difference is that the records are retrieved by their relative record numbers rather than by their key values.

- When you read a relative file sequentially, the program automatically skips over any record areas that don't contain data.

- When you process a relative file randomly, you can use the Invalid Key clause of the Read, Write, Rewrite, Delete, and Start statements to trap invalid key conditions just like you do for indexed files.

Terms

relative file
relative record number

file status codes
randomizing routine

Objectives

- Given complete program specifications, develop a program that processes a relative file.
- In general terms, describe how you process a relative file sequentially.
- In general terms, describe how you process a relative file randomly.

Exercise 15-1   Run the relative file creation program

In this exercise, you'll run a file creation program that will create a relative inventory master file that you can use in exercise 15-2.

1. Open the program named rel4000. Then, compile and test the program. It should create a relative inventory master file named invmastr.dat.

2. Use the Windows Explorer to find the file that you've just created in the c:\cobol\data folder. Then, double-click on it to open it in Notepad. There you can see that it's difficult to interpret the data because of the extra codes that the file contains for the relative record numbers. When you're done reviewing the data, close Notepad.

3. Close the file creation program, but note that you can rerun this program whenever you need to get a fresh copy of the inventory master file.

Exercise 15-2   Develop a random update program

In this exercise, you'll modify the random update program from chapter 14 so it works with the relative file you created in exercise 15-1.

1. Open the program named ind3000. Then, change the Program-ID to REL3000, save the program as rel3000, and close the program.

2. Open the program you created in step 1. Then, change the Select statement for the indexed inventory master file so it's appropriate for a relative file named invmastr.dat that will be accessed randomly.

3. Make the necessary changes to the File Section, the Working-Storage Section, and the Procedure Division of this program so it works with the relative file. The relative record number should be calculated by subtracting 10000 from the item number field in the input file.

4. Compile, test, and debug the program until it works correctly. Then, close the program.

16

How to use the sort/merge feature

Throughout this book, you've seen programs that require the input files to be in a certain sequence. To get the files in this sequence, they are usually sorted by using a utility program that comes with the compiler or the operating system. Although you can use this program to sort files before they're processed by a COBOL program, you can also use it from within a COBOL program. That's what you'll learn to do in this chapter. You'll also learn how to use this utility program to merge two or more sorted files into a single sorted file.

Concepts for sorting and merging

To arrange the records in a file into an appropriate sequence, the records can be *sorted*. Similarly, to combine the records in two or more sorted files into one sorted file, the records can be *merged*. To provide for these functions, your compiler or operating system typically provides a utility program called a *sort/merge program*. Because a sort/merge program is used for sorting far more frequently than it's used for merging, it's often referred to as just a *sort program*. In the topics that follow, you'll learn the concepts that you need for using the sort/merge program within your COBOL programs.

Sorting concepts

When you use the sort/merge program within a COBOL program, the sort function takes places in three steps as described in figure 16-1. First, the records to be sorted are released to the sort program by the COBOL program. Second, the records are sorted by the sort program. Third, the records are returned to the COBOL program.

Although it's not apparent in the illustration in this figure, the COBOL program doesn't have to release all of the records in the input file to the sort program. Instead, the COBOL program can select the records from the input file before passing them to the sort program. Then, only the selected records are sorted.

Before a COBOL program can perform a sort operation, it must tell the sort program how the records should be sorted. To do that, it identifies one or more *key fields* that contain the data that the file should be sorted on. It must also tell the sort program whether each key field should be sorted in ascending or descending sequence. Although most sort programs provide for eight or more key fields, it's common to use only one or two. All of the key fields for a sort operation are typically referred to as the *sort key*.

The exact sequence of the sorted file depends on the *collating sequence* of the computer. You learned about the two most common collating sequences in chapter 6: EBCDIC and ASCII. In general, EBCDIC is used on all IBM mainframes, and ASCII is used on all other systems.

With either the EBCDIC or ASCII collating sequence, alphabetic fields may not get sorted properly if they contain both lowercase and uppercase letters. With EBCDIC, for example, all lowercase letters come before all uppercase letters so *Murach* has a lower value than *MANNING*. With ASCII, all uppercase letters come before all lowercase letters so *MURACH* has a lower value than *Manning*. This isn't normally a problem, though, because standard entry formats (like all capital letters) are used. As a result, you shouldn't need to specify your own collating sequence when you use a sort program.

After the sort program sorts the records, they're returned to the COBOL program. Then, the COBOL program can write the records to an output file so it can be used as input to other programs. Or, it can perform further processing on the records.

How a COBOL program uses a sort/merge program to sort records

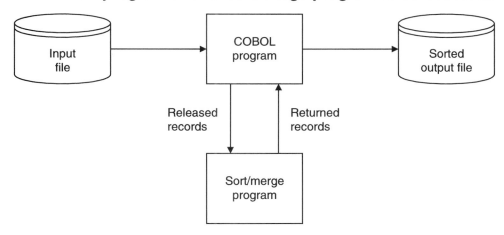

Three steps for sorting records using a sort/merge program

1. The COBOL program releases the records to be sorted to the sort/merge program.
2. The sort/merge program sorts the records.
3. The sorted records are returned to the COBOL program where they're written to an output file or processed further.

Description

- The COBOL program can release all of the records in a file to the *sort/merge program*, or it can select the records to be released from one or more input files.

- The sort/merge program sorts the records based on one or more *key fields*, which can be referred to collectively as the *sort key*. Each key field can be sorted in ascending or descending sequence.

- The exact sequence of the sorted records depends on the *collating sequence* of the computer. The EBCDIC collating sequence is used on all IBM mainframes, and the ASCII collating sequence is used on most other systems. See figure 6-11 in chapter 6 for more information on collating sequences.

- The input and output files used in a sort can have sequential, indexed, or relative organization. Records written to a relative file are written in relative record number sequence, beginning with 1. Records written to an indexed file are written in primary key sequence, so the file must be sorted into primary key sequence. Alternate keys can also be specified for an indexed output file.

- The records in an input or output file for a sort can be fixed-length or variable-length. In either case, the key fields must be in the same location in each record.

Figure 16-1   Sorting concepts

Although you'll typically use the sort program to sort the records in sequential files, you should know that you can also sort the records in indexed and relative files. And if the program creates an output file of the sorted records, that file can also have sequential, indexed, or relative organization. To create a indexed file, though, the records must be sorted in primary key sequence.

The input and output files used by a sort operation can have either fixed- or variable-length records. The only restriction is that the keys used to sort the records must be in the same location in each record. For more information on working with variable-length records, please see chapter 13.

Merging concepts

Figure 16-2 shows how a merge operation works. Like a sort operation, a merge operation is based on a sort key that indicates the sequence of the merged records. Unlike a sort operation, the input files must already be sorted into that sequence. Then, the merge operation just combines the input files into a single file with the same sort sequence.

To be sure you understand how this works, this figure shows the result of merging two sample files. Notice that both input files are sorted in ascending sequence by their key values. (The numbers and letters in parentheses indicate which file a record is from and the record's position in that file.) Then, when the files are merged, the merged file contains the records from both input files sorted in the same sequence.

Like the input file for a sort operation, the input files for a merge operation can have sequential, indexed, or relative organization. In addition, they can have fixed- or variable-length records, as long as the key values are in the same location in each record. However, the COBOL program can't select the records to be merged like it can for a sort operation. That means that all the records in the input files are merged into a single file. Then, when those records are returned to the COBOL program, they can be written to an output file or processed further by the program.

How a COBOL program uses a sort/merge program to merge records

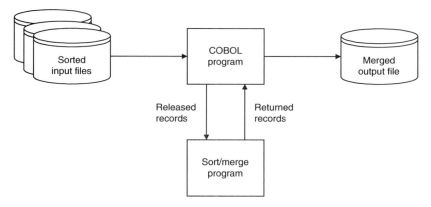

A sample merge operation

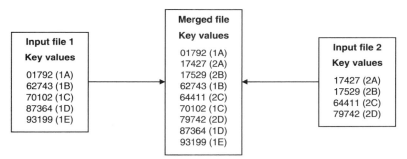

Three steps for merging records using a sort/merge program

1. The COBOL program releases the records in the files to be merged to the sort/merge program.
2. The sort/merge program merges the records.
3. The merged records are returned to the COBOL program where they can be written to an output file or processed further.

Description

- The COBOL program must release all of the records in the input files to the *sort/merge program*. It can't select the records to be processed for a merge operation.
- The sort/merge program merges the records based on one or more *key fields*. Each key field can be sorted in ascending or descending sequence.
- The exact sequence of the merged records depends on the *collating sequence* of the computer.
- The input and output files used in a merge can have sequential, indexed, or relative organization.
- The records in an input or output file for a merge can be fixed-length or variable-length. In either case, the key fields must be in the same location in each record of each file.

Figure 16-2   Merging concepts

Why COBOL sorts and merges improve efficiency

When you use a sort program from within a COBOL program, it is referred to as an *internal sort*. When you use a sort program by itself, it's referred to as a *standalone sort*. On most systems, a COBOL program with an internal sort is more efficient than a COBOL program plus a standalone sort.

To illustrate, figure 16-3 shows two ways that a report can be prepared from a file of invoice records. With a standalone sort, this process involves two steps. First, the invoice records are sorted to produce a sorted invoice file. Then, the sorted file is read and processed by a COBOL program to prepare the report. In contrast, when you use an internal sort, the COBOL program reads the invoice file, sorts it, and prepares the report.

On most systems, an internal sort will run more efficiently because the COBOL program doesn't have to take the time to write the file of sorted invoice records to disk. Instead, the sort program returns the sorted records directly to the COBOL program. As a result, the COBOL program with the internal sort doesn't require as many I/O operations as a standalone sort followed by a COBOL program. If, for example, the invoice file consists of 500 blocks of records, the first method in this figure will require 1000 more I/O operations than the program with the internal sort: 500 extra output operations for the sort program to produce the sorted invoice file, and 500 extra input operations for the COBOL program to read the sorted file.

For the same reason, *internal merges* can be more efficient than *standalone merges*. That is, the merged file isn't written to disk when an internal merge is used, so fewer I/O operations are required. Keep in mind, though, that before a merge can be run, the input files have to be in the appropriate sequence. Often, that means that they have to be sorted before they're merged. In that case, it's more efficient to sort all of the files in one sort operation than it is to first sort the files and then merge them. You'll see how to do that later in this chapter.

Although an internal sort or merge is usually more efficient than a standalone sort or merge, it may not make sense if the sorted or merged file will be used by two or more COBOL programs. For example, the sorted invoice records in this figure might be used to create a variety of reports. In that case, it would be more efficient to create a sorted file using a standalone sort. Then, the COBOL programs that prepared the reports wouldn't have to sort the records. Instead, they would just read the records from the sorted file.

How records are sorted with a standalone sort

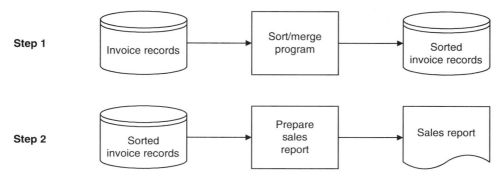

How records are sorted with an internal sort

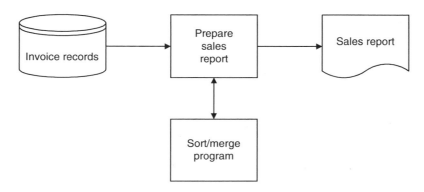

Description

- A sort that you do from within a COBOL program is called an *internal sort*. A sort that you do by invoking a sort/merge program directly is called a *standalone sort*.

- When you use a standalone sort, the sort/merge program reads the input file, sorts the records, and creates an output file of sorted records. Then, the sorted records can be read by the COBOL program that requires the records in that sequence.

- When you use an internal sort, the sort/merge program can return the sorted records to the COBOL program without creating an output file. That makes the sort more efficient by saving the time it takes to write the sorted file to disk and then read it from disk.

- An internal merge can also be more efficient than a standalone merge because the merged file is never created, so fewer I/O operations are required.

Figure 16-3   Why COBOL sorts and merges improve efficiency

COBOL for sorting

To perform a sort operation from a COBOL program, you have to define a *sort work file* that will hold the sorted records. Then, you refer to that file in the Sort statement that sorts the records. In addition to the Sort statement, you can use the Release statement to pass records to the sort program, and you can use the Return statement to retrieve the sorted records.

How to code Select and SD statements

The sort work file for a sort operation provides the work space that the sort program uses for sorting the records. Actually, a sort program usually uses more than one file for this work space. In COBOL, though, you only need to code a Select statement and file description for one sort work file no matter how many work files the sort program uses.

Figure 16-4 presents the format of the Select statement for a sort work file. Because it's treated as a sequential file, you can code the Select statement with just an Assign clause. If you're using Micro Focus COBOL, you can include the File Status clause, which can also be coded as Sort Status. Then, you can use the File Status field to check that the sort worked properly.

To code a file description for a sort work file, you use an SD statement as shown in this figure. The syntax of this statement is the same as the FD statement except that you can't code a Block Contains clause. That's because the blocking for this file is determined by the sort program.

After the SD statement for the sort work file, you code a record description just as you do for any other file. The only requirement is that the record description must contain the key fields that the sort will be based on. These fields will be named in the Sort statement, as you'll see in a moment.

If you're working on an IBM mainframe, you'll need to include two DD statements in the JCL that runs the program as shown in this figure. The SORTLIB DD statement identifies the library that contains the sort program, which is usually SYS1.SORTLIB. The SORTWK01 DD statement defines the space that will be used for the sort work file. Although only one file is shown here, be aware that a sort may require additional files. In that case, you should name the files sequentially with the names SORTWK01, SORTWK02, and so on. Even if the sort requires additional files, though, you only need to define one sort work file in your COBOL program. For more information on the JCL used to run COBOL programs, please see chapter 18.

Although it's not shown in this figure, you can also define a sort work file with variable-length records. Then, if you're sorting several types of variable-length records, you can code one record description for each format. In that case, you only have to define the key fields in one of the descriptions. However, the keys must be present in the same positions in all of the records. For more information on how to work with variable-length records, please see chapter 13.

The syntax of the Select statement for sort work files

```
SELECT sort/merge-file-name
    ASSIGN to system-name
```

The syntax of a system name for a VSAM file on an IBM mainframe

```
ddname
```

The syntax of a system name on a PC

```
"path\filename"
```

The syntax of the SD statement for sort work files

```
SD  sort/merge-file-name
    [RECORD CONTAINS integer RECORDS]
```

Select and SD statements for a sort work file on an IBM mainframe

```
SELECT SORTWORK ASSIGN TO SORTWK01.

SD  SORTWORK
    RECORD CONTAINS 70 CHARACTERS.
```

JCL that identifies the sort library and the sort work file

```
//SORTLIB   DD    DSNAME=SYS1.SORTLIB,DISP=SHR
//SORTWK01 DD    UNIT=SYSDA,SPACE=(CYL,(20,5))
```

Description

- A COBOL program that does an internal sort requires a *sort work file*. This file provides a work space that the sort/merge program uses to sort the records.

- To define a sort work file, you code a Select statement just as you do for any other file. The only clause required on this statement is the Assign clause.

- With Micro Focus Personal COBOL, you can also code the File Status or Sort Status clause. This works just like it does for other files. The possible status codes for a sort work file are 00 for a successful completion, 30 for a permanent I/O error, and 9x for various operating system errors.

- Instead of an FD statement, you code an SD statement for a sort work file. You code this statement just like an FD statement except that you can't code the Block Contains clause since blocking is controlled by the sort/merge program. You can also define a sort work file with variable-length records as described in chapter 13.

- After the SD statement, you code the record description for the sort work file. This description must include the key fields that will be used to sort the records.

- When you run a program that does an internal sort on an IBM mainframe, the JCL must include a DD statement that identifies the sort work library and a DD statement that allocates space to the sort work file. In most cases, you'll need to define more than one sort work file in the JCL. Then, you can number them consecutively as SORTWK01, SORTWK02, and so on. (See chapter 18 for more on the use of JCL.)

Figure 16-4   How to code Select and SD statements

How to code the Sort statement

The Sort statement controls the processing in a program that uses an internal sort. It specifies the name of the sort file, the sequence that the records are to be sorted into, the input file or input processing, and the output file or output processing. The syntax of this statement is presented in figure 16-5.

The Key clause of the Sort statement names the key fields that will be used for the sort and indicates whether each field should be sorted in ascending or descending sequence. In the first Sort statement in this figure, for example, the records will be sorted by customer number within salesrep number within branch number. Because all of the fields will be sorted in ascending sequence, only an On Ascending Key clause is required. Note, however, that you can include keys that are sorted in both ascending and descending sequence in the same sort by using both On Ascending Key and On Descending Key clauses.

The With Duplicate Keys clause tells the sort program to return records with duplicate key values in the same order that they were released for sorting. Because this requires additional processing time, you shouldn't use this clause unless you need to. If you omit this clause, the sort program will determine the order in which the records are returned.

If you want to use a collating sequence other than the default for your computer, you can code the Collating Sequence clause. This clause refers to a name that's defined in the Special-Names paragraph of the program that identifies the collating sequence. Since you're not likely to change the collating sequence, though, you won't learn how to do that in this book.

If you want to process the records in an input file before they're released for sorting, you code the Input Procedure clause as shown in the second example in this figure. This clause identifies the *input procedure* that will be used to process the records. The Sort statement passes control to this procedure before the sort function takes place. As you'll see in the program that's presented later in this chapter, you code an input procedure just like any other procedure.

Similarly, you can use the Output Procedure clause to name an *output procedure* that will process the records after they're sorted. The Sort statement passes control to this procedure after the sort function takes place. You can see how an output procedure is used in both examples in this figure.

If you don't need to process the input file before it's sorted, you can code the Using clause instead of the Input Procedure clause. This clause names the input file to be sorted as illustrated in the first example in this figure. Note that the Sort statement will open and close this file automatically, so it shouldn't be open when the Sort statement is executed. Also note that either sequential or dynamic access should be specified for the file so it can be accessed sequentially.

You can also code a Giving clause instead of an Output Procedure clause. Then, the Sort statement will write the sorted records directly to the output file you name. Like the input file in a Using clause, the output file in a Giving clause is opened and closed automatically by the Sort statement. In addition, sequential or dynamic access should be specified for the file so it can be accessed sequentially.

The syntax of the Sort statement

```
SORT sort-file-name
    { ON { ASCENDING  } KEY {data-name}... } ...
    {    { DESCENDING }                     }
    [ WITH DUPLICATES IN ORDER ]
    [ COLLATING SEQUENCE IS alphabet-name ]
    { INPUT PROCEDURE IS procedure-name-1 }
    { USING {file-name-1}...               }
    { OUTPUT PROCEDURE IS procedure-name-2 }
    { GIVING {file-name-2}...              }
```

A Sort statement that uses an input file and an output procedure

```
SORT SORTWORK
    ON ASCENDING KEY SW-BRANCH-NO
                     SW-SALESREP-NO
                     SW-CUSTOMER-NO
    USING CUSTMAST
    OUTPUT PROCEDURE IS 300-PRODUCE-SALES-REPORT.
```

A Sort statement that uses an input and an output procedure

```
SORT SORTWORK
    ON ASCENDING KEY SW-ITEM-NO
    INPUT PROCEDURE IS 100-EDIT-RECEIPT-TRANSACTIONS
    OUTPUT PROCEDURE IS 400-UPDATE-INVENTORY-RECORDS.
```

Description

* The file name you specify on the Sort statement is the name of the sort work file. This file must be defined with Select and SD statements as shown in figure 16-4.

* The Key clause specifies the names of the fields on which the records will be sorted and the sequence in which they will be sorted. These fields must be included in the record description for the sort work file.

* If the With Duplicates clause is coded, records with duplicate keys are returned from the sort/merge program in the same order that they were released to that program. If this clause is omitted, the order of records with duplicate keys is unpredictable.

* The Collating Sequence clause lets you specify the collating sequence to be used for the sort. The alphabet name within this clause refers to a name defined in the Special-Names paragraph of the Configuration Section.

* An *input procedure* is a procedure that processes one or more input files before the sort work file is sorted. An *output procedure* is a procedure that processes the data in a sort work file after the file has been sorted.

* If you don't need to process the records in the input file before they're sorted, you can code a Using clause instead of an input procedure. Then, the COBOL program automatically opens the input file, releases its records to the sort/merge program, and closes the file.

* If you don't need to process the sorted records, you can code a Giving clause instead of an output procedure. Then, the COBOL program automatically retrieves the sorted records, opens the output file, writes the sorted records to that file, and closes the file.

Figure 16-5   How to code the Sort statement

Notice in the syntax for the Sort statement that both the Using and the Giving clauses let you specify one or more files. If you specify two or more files on the Using clause, the records in the files are sorted into a single file. You'll see an example of that later in this chapter. If you specify two or more files on the Giving clause, the sorted records are written to each file. Because each file is identical to the others, though, it usually doesn't make sense to do that.

Incidentally, you'll probably never code both a Using and a Giving clause in the same Sort statement. That's because you can accomplish the same thing using a standalone sort. And, in this case, the standalone sort is more efficient.

You should also know that you can code more that one Sort statement in the same program, although you probably won't find many uses for that. If you need to code more than one Sort statement, though, keep in mind that only one can be executed at a time. In other words, you can't code a Sort statement in the input or output procedure of another Sort statement.

How to code the Release statement

When you code the Using clause on a Sort statement, the records in the input file are released to the sort program automatically. When you use an input procedure to process the records in the input file, though, you have to use the Release statement to release the selected records to the sort program. Figure 16-6 presents the syntax of this statement.

As you can see, the syntax of this statement is similar to the Write statement for a sequential file. Like the Write statement, you can code the From clause on the Release statement to move the data in an area of working storage to the sort work area before that area is released to the sort program. The Release statement in this figure, for example, will release the sort work area from the Maintenance-Transaction area that's defined in working storage. By the way, because the Release statement performs an output operation, we recommend you code it in its own module just like any other I/O statement.

How to code the Return statement

Figure 16-6 also presents the syntax of the Return statement. After the records in an input file are sorted, this statement makes the next sorted record available to the program. This statement must be included in the output procedure for a sort operation or another procedure that's performed by the output procedure. If the Giving clause is used instead of an output procedure, the records are returned to the program automatically so the Return statement isn't necessary.

The Return statement works much like the Read statement for a sequential file. On it, you can code the Into clause to move the returned record to another area. You must also code the At End clause so your program can tell when there aren't any more records in the sort work file. And you can code the Not At End clause that's processed for each record until the end of the file is reached.

The syntax of the Release statement

```
RELEASE sort-work-record-name
    [FROM data-name]
```

A Release statement with the From clause

```
RELEASE SORT-WORK-AREA
    FROM MAINTENANCE-TRANSACTION.
```

The syntax of the Return statement

```
RETURN sort/merge-file-name RECORD [INTO data-name]
    [AT END imperative-statement-1]
    [NOT AT END imperative-statement-2]
    [END-RETURN]
```

A Return statement with the Into clause

```
RETURN SORTWORK INTO MAINTENANCE-TRANSACTION
    AT END
        MOVE "Y" TO TRANSACTION-EOF-SWITCH.
```

Description

- The Release statement passes a record to the sort work area so it's ready for sorting. If you code the From clause, the data in the specified area of working storage is moved to the sort work area for the file before the record is released.

- The Return statement makes the next sorted record available to the program. If you code the Into clause, the record is moved to the specified area of working storage.

- You can use the At End clause of the Return statement to determine when there aren't any more records in the sort work file.

Figure 16-6   How to code the Release and Return statements

An edit-sort-and-update program

To help you understand the COBOL for performing an internal sort, the topics that follow present a complete COBOL program. This program reads through a file of transactions and edits them to be sure they contain valid data. Then, it sorts the valid transactions and uses them to update a master file. If you understand how this program works, you shouldn't have any trouble writing your own programs with internal sorts.

The program specifications

Figure 16-7 presents the specifications for the edit-sort-and-update program. This program is based on the sequential update program that was presented in chapter 13. That program updated an inventory master file based on the data in a receipt transaction file and created a new master file as output. For simplicity, it assumed that the receipt transactions had already been validated and sorted into item number sequence. The program in this chapter, though, doesn't make those assumptions. So it must include the necessary editing and sorting. However, it does assume that the inventory master file is already in sequence by item number, so it's not necessary to sort that file.

In the system flowchart in this figure, you can see that this program uses one file that wasn't required by the update program in chapter 13. This is the sort work file that will contain the sorted transaction records. Other than that, the input and output files are the same as the ones in the update program in chapter 13, and the updating that's done is the same as in that program.

In addition to the updating and sorting, this program edits the transactions before they're processed to be sure that they're valid. For this program, a transaction is valid if the item number, vendor number, and receipt quantity fields are numeric. Then, if a transaction isn't valid, it's written to the error transaction file. Later on, when the valid transactions are used to update the master file, an unmatched transaction is also written to the error file.

The system flowchart for the edit-sort-and-update program

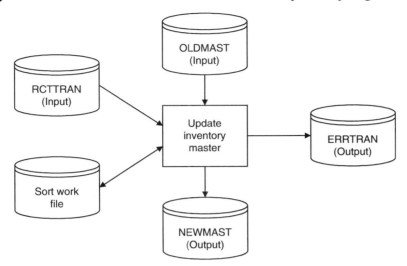

The record descriptions for the master and transaction files

```
01   INVENTORY-MASTER-RECORD.
     05   IM-ITEM-NO                 PIC X(5).
     05   IM-DESCRIPTIVE-DATA.
          10   IM-ITEM-DESC          PIC X(40).
          10   IM-UNIT-COST          PIC S9(3)V99.
          10   IM-UNIT-PRICE         PIC S9(3)V99.
     05   IM-INVENTORY-DATA.
          10   IM-REORDER-POINT      PIC S9(5).
          10   IM-ON-HAND            PIC S9(5).
          10   IM-ON-ORDER           PIC S9(5).
```

```
01   RECEIPT-TRANSACTION.
     05   RT-ITEM-NO            PIC X(5).
     05   RT-VENDOR-NO          PIC X(5).
     05   RT-RECEIPT-DATE       PIC X(8).
     05   RT-RECEIPT-QUANTITY   PIC S9(5).
```

Processing specifications

- This program edits the records in a file of receipt transactions (RCTTRAN), sorts the valid transactions, and then uses the sorted transactions to update data in an old master file (OLDMAST). The output is a new master file that contains the updated records (NEWMAST).

- For a transaction to be valid, the item number, vendor number, and receipt quantity must be numeric. If they're not, the transaction should be written to a file of error transactions (ERRTRAN).

- If a transaction is valid and has the same item number as a master record, the transaction data should be used to update the master record. If a transaction has an item number that doesn't match the item number in a master record, the transaction should be written to a file of error transactions (ERRTRAN).

- To update the master record, the receipt quantity in the transaction record should be added to the on-hand quantity in the master file and subtracted from the on-order quantity.

- This program assumes that the inventory master file is already in sequence by item number.

Figure 16-7   The program specifications for the edit-sort-and-update program

The structure chart

Figure 16-8 presents the structure chart for the edit-sort-and-update program. Here, you can see that the modules that are called by module 000 represent the three main functions that this program will perform. Module 100 will edit the file of receipt transactions and will serve as the input procedure for the sort; module 300 will sort the valid transactions; and module 400 will update the records in the inventory master file with the sorted transactions and will serve as the output procedure for the sort.

Actually, when you see the code for this program, you'll see that module 300 is coded as a comment. In other words, it doesn't really do anything. That's because the Sort statement takes care of the sorting, and that statement is coded in module 000 since it controls the processing that's done by the program. Although you don't have to include this module in the structure chart, we recommend you do. That way, it's clear that the program includes an internal sort.

If your program includes a Sort statement with a Using or a Giving clause instead of an input procedure or output procedure, you'll want to include a module that reflects the function of that clause too, even though that function will be performed by the Sort statement. That way, the structure chart will document all of the functions of the program. You'll see how that works when you develop the program for the exercise at the end of this chapter.

You shouldn't have any trouble understanding the two main legs of the chart in this figure. For each record in the receipt transaction file, module 100 calls module 200 to edit the transaction. Then, module 200 calls module 210 to read the next transaction and module 220 to edit the transaction. If the transaction is valid, module 200 calls module 230 to release it to the sort program. Otherwise, module 200 calls module 240 to write the transaction to the error file.

The leg of the program that's controlled by module 400 should look familiar to you. For the most part, it's the same as the structure chart for the sequential update program that's presented in figure 13-6 of chapter 13. The biggest difference is that instead of reading a record from the receipt transaction file, the program in this chapter will retrieve a record from the sorted file. Otherwise, it works the same as the update program in chapter 13.

You may have noticed in this structure chart that modules 200 and 500 are multiples of 100s instead of 10s as we recommend in chapter 4. That's because modules 100 and 400, the top-level modules in the input and output procedures, are roughly equivalent to 000 modules in other programs. As a result, the modules that they call should be numbered by 100s.

The structure chart for the edit-sort-and-update program

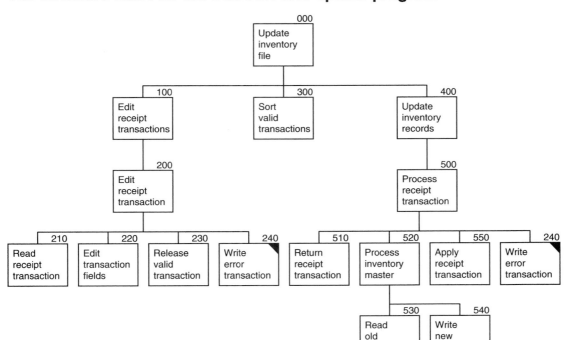

Description

- Modules 100, 300, and 400 reflect the three main functions of this program. The processing of these modules is controlled by the Sort statement that's coded in module 000.

- Module 100 calls module 200 for each record in the transaction file. Module 200 reads a receipt transaction (module 210) and then edits the transaction (module 220). If the transaction is valid, module 200 calls module 230 to release the transaction to the sort program. If the transaction is invalid, module 200 calls module 240 to write the transaction to an error file.

- Module 300 doesn't actually perform any processing. It's included in the structure chart to show the sort function, which is done by the sort/merge program.

- Module 400 is the top-level module for processing the sorted receipt transactions. It calls module 500 until all records have been processed.

- Module 500 starts by calling module 510 to retrieve a record from the file of sorted transactions. Then, it calls module 520 to read old master records (module 530) and write new master records (module 540) until it finds a record with a matching item number or an item number that's greater than the item number in the transaction record. If a matching record is found, module 500 calls module 550 to apply the transaction to that record. Otherwise, it calls module 240 to write the transaction to an error file.

Figure 16-8   The structure chart for the edit-sort-and-update program

The COBOL code

Figure 16-9 presents the COBOL code for this program. The first thing you should notice is that the Select statement for the sort work file is coded just like any other sequential file. In this case, the file is given the name SORTWORK, and it's assigned to the system name SORTWK01. If you look back to figure 16-4, you'll see that's the same as the ddname in the JCL to run a program with a sort on an IBM mainframe. Because this is the required ddname for a sort work file, you'll want to be sure you use this name in your COBOL programs if they'll be run on an IBM mainframe system.

In the File Section of this program, you can see that the entry for the sort work file is coded using an SD statement rather than an FD statement. Then, the record description that follows is defined so it can hold a receipt transaction record. Notice that the only field that's defined explicitly in this record description is the field that will be used to sort the valid transactions: SW-ITEM-NO.

The edit-sort-and-update program   **Page 1**

```
IDENTIFICATION DIVISION.
*
PROGRAM-ID.  SRT1000.
*
ENVIRONMENT DIVISION.
*
INPUT-OUTPUT SECTION.
*
FILE-CONTROL.
*
     SELECT RCTTRAN  ASSIGN TO RCTTRAN.
     SELECT OLDMAST  ASSIGN TO OLDMAST.
     SELECT NEWMAST  ASSIGN TO NEWMAST
                     FILE STATUS IS NEWMAST-FILE-STATUS.
     SELECT ERRTRAN  ASSIGN TO ERRTRAN
                     FILE STATUS IS ERRTRAN-FILE-STATUS.
     SELECT SORTWORK ASSIGN TO SORTWK01.
*
DATA DIVISION.
*
FILE SECTION.
*
FD  RCTTRAN.
01  TRANSACTION-RECORD       PIC X(23).
*
FD  OLDMAST.
01  OLD-MASTER-RECORD        PIC X(70).
*
FD  NEWMAST.
01  NEW-MASTER-RECORD        PIC X(70).
*
FD  ERRTRAN.
01  ERROR-TRANSACTION        PIC X(23).
*
SD  SORTWORK.
01  SORT-WORK-AREA.
    05  SW-ITEM-NO           PIC X(5).
    05  FILLER               PIC X(18).
*
WORKING-STORAGE SECTION.
*
01  SWITCHES.
    05  TRANSACTION-EOF-SWITCH          PIC X    VALUE "N".
        88  TRANSACTION-EOF                      VALUE "Y".
    05  VALID-TRANSACTION-SWITCH        PIC X    VALUE "Y".
        88  VALID-TRANSACTION                    VALUE "Y".
    05  FIRST-EXECUTION-SWITCH          PIC X    VALUE "Y".
        88  FIRST-EXECUTION                      VALUE "Y".
    05  ALL-RECORDS-PROCESSED-SWITCH    PIC X    VALUE "N".
        88  ALL-RECORDS-PROCESSED                VALUE "Y".
*
```

Figure 16-9   The COBOL code for the edit-sort-and-update program (part 1 of 4)

Now, take a look at the Procedure Division. Because the Sort statement will control all of the processing done by this program, it's coded in module 000. It specifies that the sort work file (SORTWORK) will be sorted by the key field (SW-ITEM-NO) in ascending sequence. Before the sort is executed, though, the input procedure named 100-Edit-Receipt-Transactions will be executed. And after the sort is executed, the output procedure named 400-Update-Inventory-Records will be executed.

Procedure 100 performs procedure 200 repeatedly until it reaches the end of the transaction file. Procedure 200 performs procedure 210 to read each transaction record and procedure 220 to edit each record. Then, if the transaction is valid, procedure 200 performs procedure 230 to release the record for sorting. If the transaction is invalid, though, procedure 200 performs module 240 to write the transaction to the error file.

After all the valid transactions are released to the sort program, the transactions are sorted. Because the actual sorting is done by the sort program, though, procedure 300 is coded as a comment. Although you don't have to include this comment, we think it clarifies the function of the program. It also makes the program code consistent with the structure chart for the program.

After the valid transactions are sorted, the output procedure, procedure 400, is executed. This procedure executes procedure 500 repeatedly until all of the records in the sorted transaction file and the old master file have been processed. Procedure 500, in turn, performs procedure 510, which returns a sorted record from the sort program. Then, it performs procedures 520 through 550 to update the master record that is affected by each transaction. If a transaction isn't matched by a master record, procedure 500 performs procedure 240 to write the record to the error file.

Efficiency considerations

When you develop a program that is going to sort hundreds or thousands of records, you have to consider the efficiency of the resulting program. Two of the most important factors for sorting efficiency are (1) the number of records to be sorted, and (2) the length of the records to be sorted. For maximum efficiency, you should write your programs so they sort as few records as possible and so the records to be sorted are as short as possible. This means that most programs with an internal sort should select and reformat records in the input procedure.

To illustrate, consider this edit-sort-and-update program. This program edits the receipt transactions before they're sorted so that only the valid transactions are included in the sort operation. However, it could also be written so the sorted records contain only the fields that are used by the output procedure: item number and receipt quantity. This would improve the efficiency of the program by reducing the sort work record from 23 to 10 bytes.

The edit-sort-and-update program   **Page 2**

```
01  FILE-STATUS-FIELDS.
    05  NEWMAST-FILE-STATUS      PIC XX.
        88  NEWMAST-SUCCESSFUL            VALUE "00".
    05  ERRTRAN-FILE-STATUS      PIC XX.
        88  ERRTRAN-SUCCESSFUL            VALUE "00".
*
01  RECEIPT-TRANSACTION.
    05  RT-ITEM-NO               PIC X(5).
    05  RT-VENDOR-NO             PIC X(5).
    05  RT-RECEIPT-DATE          PIC X(8).
    05  RT-RECEIPT-QUANTITY-X    PIC X(5).
    05  RT-RECEIPT-QUANTITY REDEFINES RT-RECEIPT-QUANTITY-X
                                 PIC 9(5).
*
01  INVENTORY-MASTER-RECORD.
    05  IM-ITEM-NO               PIC X(5).
    05  IM-DESCRIPTIVE-DATA.
        10  IM-ITEM-DESC         PIC X(40).
        10  IM-UNIT-COST         PIC S9(3)V99.
        10  IM-UNIT-PRICE        PIC S9(3)V99.
    05  IM-INVENTORY-DATA.
        10  IM-REORDER-POINT     PIC S9(5).
        10  IM-ON-HAND           PIC S9(5).
        10  IM-ON-ORDER          PIC S9(5).
*
 PROCEDURE DIVISION.
*
 000-UPDATE-INVENTORY-FILE.
*
    OPEN INPUT   OLDMAST
                 RCTTRAN
         OUTPUT  NEWMAST
                 ERRTRAN.
    SORT SORTWORK
        ON ASCENDING KEY SW-ITEM-NO
        INPUT PROCEDURE IS 100-EDIT-RECEIPT-TRANSACTIONS
        OUTPUT PROCEDURE IS 400-UPDATE-INVENTORY-RECORDS.
    CLOSE RCTTRAN
          OLDMAST
          NEWMAST
          ERRTRAN.
    STOP RUN.
*
 100-EDIT-RECEIPT-TRANSACTIONS.
*
    PERFORM 200-EDIT-RECEIPT-TRAN
        UNTIL TRANSACTION-EOF.
*
```

Figure 16-9   The COBOL code for the edit-sort-and-update program (part 2 of 4)

The edit-sort-and-update program

Page 3

```
200-EDIT-RECEIPT-TRAN.
*
     PERFORM 210-READ-RECEIPT-TRANSACTION.
     IF NOT TRANSACTION-EOF
         PERFORM 220-EDIT-TRANSACTION-FIELDS
         IF VALID-TRANSACTION
             PERFORM 230-RELEASE-VALID-TRANSACTION
         ELSE
             PERFORM 240-WRITE-ERROR-TRANSACTION.
*
210-READ-RECEIPT-TRANSACTION.
*
     READ RCTTRAN INTO RECEIPT-TRANSACTION
         AT END
             MOVE "Y" TO TRANSACTION-EOF-SWITCH.
*
220-EDIT-TRANSACTION-FIELDS.
*
     MOVE "Y" TO VALID-TRANSACTION-SWITCH.
     IF        RT-ITEM-NO NOT NUMERIC
         OR RT-VENDOR-NO NOT NUMERIC
         OR RT-RECEIPT-QUANTITY-X NOT NUMERIC
         MOVE "N" TO VALID-TRANSACTION-SWITCH.
*
230-RELEASE-VALID-TRANSACTION.
*
     RELEASE SORT-WORK-AREA FROM RECEIPT-TRANSACTION.
*
240-WRITE-ERROR-TRANSACTION.
*
     WRITE ERROR-TRANSACTION FROM RECEIPT-TRANSACTION.
     IF NOT ERRTRAN-SUCCESSFUL
         DISPLAY "WRITE ERROR ON ERRTRAN FOR ITEM NUMBER "
             RT-ITEM-NO
         DISPLAY "FILE STATUS CODE IS " ERRTRAN-FILE-STATUS.
*
*300-SORT-VALID-TRANSACTIONS.  DUMMY MODULE DONE BY SORT PROGRAM.
*
400-UPDATE-INVENTORY-RECORDS.
*
     MOVE LOW-VALUE TO IM-ITEM-NO.
     PERFORM 500-PROCESS-RECEIPT-TRAN
         UNTIL ALL-RECORDS-PROCESSED.
*
```

Figure 16-9   The COBOL code for the edit-sort-and-update program (part 3 of 4)

The edit-sort-and-update program   **Page 4**

```
500-PROCESS-RECEIPT-TRAN.
*
    PERFORM 510-RETURN-RECEIPT-TRANSACTION.
    PERFORM 520-PROCESS-INVENTORY-MASTER
        UNTIL IM-ITEM-NO >= RT-ITEM-NO.
    IF     IM-ITEM-NO = HIGH-VALUE
       AND RT-ITEM-NO = HIGH-VALUE
        MOVE "Y" TO ALL-RECORDS-PROCESSED-SWITCH
    ELSE
        IF IM-ITEM-NO = RT-ITEM-NO
            PERFORM 550-APPLY-RECEIPT-TRANSACTION
        ELSE
            PERFORM 240-WRITE-ERROR-TRANSACTION.
*
510-RETURN-RECEIPT-TRANSACTION.
*
    RETURN SORTWORK INTO RECEIPT-TRANSACTION
        AT END
            MOVE HIGH-VALUE TO RT-ITEM-NO.
*
520-PROCESS-INVENTORY-MASTER.
*
    IF FIRST-EXECUTION
        PERFORM 530-READ-OLD-MASTER
        MOVE "N" TO FIRST-EXECUTION-SWITCH
    ELSE
        PERFORM 540-WRITE-NEW-MASTER
        PERFORM 530-READ-OLD-MASTER.
*
530-READ-OLD-MASTER.
*
    READ OLDMAST INTO INVENTORY-MASTER-RECORD
        AT END
            MOVE HIGH-VALUE TO IM-ITEM-NO.
*
540-WRITE-NEW-MASTER.
*
    WRITE NEW-MASTER-RECORD FROM INVENTORY-MASTER-RECORD.
    IF NOT NEWMAST-SUCCESSFUL
        DISPLAY "WRITE ERROR ON NEWMAST FOR ITEM NUMBER "
            IM-ITEM-NO
        DISPLAY "FILE STATUS CODE IS " NEWMAST-FILE-STATUS
        MOVE "Y" TO ALL-RECORDS-PROCESSED-SWITCH.
*
550-APPLY-RECEIPT-TRANSACTION.
*
    ADD RT-RECEIPT-QUANTITY TO IM-ON-HAND.
    SUBTRACT RT-RECEIPT-QUANTITY FROM IM-ON-ORDER.
*
```

Figure 16-9   The COBOL code for the edit-sort-and-update program (part 4 of 4)

COBOL for merging

The COBOL for merging files is almost identical to the COBOL for sorting files. You must code a Select statement for the *merge work file*, and the file must be defined by an SD statement and a record description that includes the key fields for the merge. The only coding differences are in the Merge statement itself.

How to code the Merge statement

Figure 16-10 presents the syntax of the Merge statement. You should notice two differences between this statement and the Sort statement. First, the Merge statement doesn't provide for an input procedure. Instead, this statement must be coded with a Using clause that identifies the input files. Because the Merge statement will automatically open and close the input files, they must not be open when this statement is executed. In addition, the Merge statement will automatically make the records in these files available to the sort/merge program, so the Release statement isn't required.

The second difference between the Sort statement and the Merge statement is that the Merge statement doesn't include the With Duplicates clause. That's because the sort/merge program returns records with duplicate keys in order by default. So records with a duplicate key value in the first file are returned in their original order, followed by any records with the same value in the second file, and so on.

Like the Sort statement, the Merge statement includes a Key clause that names the fields that will determine the sequence of the merged records. Remember that all of the input files must already be sorted in this sequence before the Merge statement is executed. If they're not, the merge won't work.

The Merge statement must also include either an Output Procedure clause or a Giving clause. If it includes the Output Procedure clause, the output procedure must include a Return statement that retrieves records from the merged file. If it includes the Giving clause, the named files must not be open when the Merge statement is executed since this statement opens and closes the files automatically.

The syntax of the Merge statement

```
MERGE merge-file-name
     { ON { ASCENDING  } KEY {data-name}... } ...
     {    { DESCENDING }                     }
     [ COLLATING SEQUENCE IS alphabet-name ]
       USING file-name-1 {file-name-2}...
     { OUTPUT PROCEDURE IS procedure-name-1 }
     { GIVING {file-name-3}...              }
```

A Merge statement with an output procedure

```
MERGE MERGEWRK
     ON ASCENDING MW-ITEM-NO
     USING ITMTRAN1 ITMTRAN2 ITMTRAN3
     OUTPUT PROCEDURE IS 300-PROCESS-ITEM-TRANSACTIONS.
```

Description

- When you merge two or more files, you must define a merge work file in your program using Select and SD statements just as you do for a sort operation. Then, you name this file on the Merge statement.

- The Key clause specifies the name of the fields on which the records will be merged and the sequence in which they will be merged. These fields must be included in the record description for the merge work file.

- The Collating Sequence clause lets you specify the collating sequence to be used for the merge. The alphabet name within this clause refers to a name defined in the Special-Names paragraph of the Configuration Section.

- The Using clause names two or more files that you want to merge. The records in each of these files must be sorted as specified by the Key clause. The COBOL program automatically opens these files, releases their records to the sort/merge program, and closes the files.

- You can't use an input procedure to process the input files before they're merged. Because of that, you won't use the Release statement with a merge operation.

- You can write the merged records directly to an output file by coding a Giving clause that names the file. Then, the COBOL program automatically retrieves the merged records from the sort/merge program, opens the output file, writes the merged records to this file, and closes the file.

- You can use the Output Procedure clause instead of the Giving clause to process the records after they're merged. To retrieve the merged records for an output procedure, you use the Return statement as shown in figure 16-6.

Figure 16-10   How to code the Merge statement

How to use the Sort statement to merge files

When a Merge statement is executed, the input files must already be in the proper sequence. As a result, it's often more efficient to sort the records in more than one file into a single file than it is to sort the records in the files and then merge them. To sort the records from two or more files using the Sort statement, you can use one of the techniques illustrated in figure 16-11.

In the first example in this figure, three file names are listed on the Using clause of the Sort statement. When this statement is executed, the program will pass the records in each of these files to the sort program. Then, the sort program will sort the records and make them available to the program in a single sorted file.

In the second example, an input procedure is used to release records from three files to the sort program. Here, a separate procedure is performed to get the records from each file. Each of these procedures would call other procedures to read the records in the file and release them to the sort program. Of course, each procedure could also perform additional processing so that only selected records are released.

A Sort statement with a Using clause that merges and sorts the records in three files

```
SORT SORTWORK
    ON ASCENDING SW-ITEM-NO
    USING ITMTRAN1 ITMTRAN2 ITMTRAN3
    OUTPUT PROCEDURE IS 300-PROCESS-ITEM-TRANSACTIONS.
```

A Sort statement that merges and sorts selected records from three files

```
 000-PREPARE-SALES-REPORT.
*
    .
    .
    .
    SORT SORTWORK
        ON ASCENDING SW-ITEM-NO
        INPUT PROCEDURE IS 100-GET-VALID-TRANSACTIONS
        OUTPUT PROCEDURE IS 400-PROCESS-ITEM-TRANSACTIONS.
    .
    .
    .
 100-GET-VALID-TRANSACTIONS.
*
    PERFORM 200-GET-FIRST-TRAN-FILE
        UNTIL ITMTRAN1-EOF.
    PERFORM 230-GET-SECOND-TRAN-FILE
        UNTIL ITMTRAN2-EOF.
    PERFORM 260-GET-THIRD-TRAN-FILE
        UNTIL ITMTRAN3-EOF.
    .
    .
    .
```

Description

- You can use the Sort statement to merge and sort the records in two or more files. You'll want to do that to merge files that aren't already sorted.

- If you include the names of two or more files on the Using clause of the Sort statement, the sort/merge program sorts all of the records in all of the files together in the specified sequence.

- If you want to process the data in two or more files before they're merged and sorted, you can specify an input procedure on the Sort statement. Then, the input procedure can select the records to be included from each file and release them to the sort/merge program.

Figure 16-11   How to use the Sort statement to merge files

Special considerations for IBM mainframe programs

If you develop programs on an IBM mainframe, you'll want to know about three features that can affect the way you use the sort/merge program on that platform. You can use these features to simplify the coding of your programs that merge files using the Sort statement; to communicate with the sort/merge program; and to improve the efficiency of programs with internal sorts.

How to merge files using JCL

Instead of sorting and merging two or more files using one of the techniques in figure 16-11, you can use the technique illustrated at the top of figure 16-12. Here, the files to be sorted and merged are *concatenated* (or linked together) in the JCL that's used to run the program. When you use this technique, you code your COBOL program just as you would to sort a single file. Then, the program can read the records in the concatenated file as if they were all in one file.

The FASTSRT compiler option

By default, the COBOL compiler automatically performs the input and output operations on files that are specified on the Using or Giving clause of a Sort or Merge statement. If the Using or Giving clause names a single file, though, you can use the FASTSRT compiler option to improve the performance of the operation. When you use this option, the input and output is done by the sort/merge program rather than the COBOL compiler. That means that an input file doesn't have to be passed from the COBOL program to the sort/merge program for processing, and an output file doesn't have to be passed back to the COBOL program for processing.

IBM special registers

The IBM COBOL compilers provide special registers, called *sort registers*, that let your programs communicate with the sort/merge program during a sort or merge operation. The two sort registers you're most likely to use are presented in figure 16-12. Note that when you use these registers, you don't define them in working storage. That's because they're reserved words and have fixed meanings defined by the compiler.

The Sort-Return register contains a return code that indicates whether the sort program terminated normally or abnormally. If the program terminated normally, this register will contain a value of zero. If it terminated abnormally, this register will contain a value of 16. By the way, the Sort-Return register is also available with the Micro Focus COBOL compiler, so you can use it instead of the File Status or Sort Status clause.

How to concatenate input files

```
//CUSTMAST DD    DSN=MM01.ITMTRAN1.DAT,DISP=SHR
//         DD    DSN=MM01.ITMTRAN2.DAT,DISP=SHR
//         DD    DSN=MM01.ITMTRAN3.DAT,DISP=SHR
```

JCL for a compile job that specifies the FASTSRT compiler option

```
//STEP1    EXEC PROC=IGYWCLG,PARM.COBOL='FASTSRT'
```

IBM special registers for the sort/merge program

Sort register	Picture	Contents	Use
Sort-Return	S9(4)	The return code from the sort/merge program with zero indicating a normal termination.	You can test this register to make sure that the sort or merge operation worked properly. You can also cause the sort/merge program to end after the next Return or Release statement by moving a value of 16 to this register.
Sort-Control	X(8)	A ddname for the file that contains sort/merge control statements	You can use this register to give the ddname for a file that supplies sort/merge parameters that can improve the efficiency of the sort or merge.

Code that uses the Sort-Return register to test for errors

```
SORT SORTWORK
    ON ASCENDING KEY SW-ITEM-NO
    INPUT PROCEDURE IS 100-EDIT-RECEIPT-TRANSACTIONS
    OUTPUT PROCEDURE IS 400-UPDATE-INVENTORY-RECORDS.
IF SORT-RETURN NOT = ZERO
    DISPLAY "SORT OPERATION FAILED".
```

Code that uses the Sort-Return register to cancel the sort or merge operation

```
IF ERROR-CONDITION
    MOVE 16 TO SORT-RETURN.
```

Description

- When you use an internal sort on an IBM mainframe, you can specify two or more input files in the JCL for running the program. This *concatenates* the files so they're treated as a single file. Then, you code the COBOL program as if a single input file is being processed.

- By default, the COBOL program performs the input and output operations on files named in the Using and Giving clauses of the Sort and Merge statements. If you include the FASTSRT compiler option when you compile the program, though, the sort/merge program (not the COBOL program) will perform the I/O operations on these files. This can improve the performance of your program.

- IBM special registers, called *sort registers*, provide a way for your COBOL programs to communicate with the sort/merge program. Because the names of these registers are reserved words, you don't need to define them in your program.

Figure 16-12   Special considerations for sorting and merging on an IBM mainframe

The first example in this figure illustrates how you can check this register after a sort operation to perform error processing if an error occurs. In this case, the program simply displays an error message indicating that the sort failed.

The second example in this figure shows how you can use the Sort-Return register to cancel the sort/merge program if your COBOL program detects that something has gone wrong in the input or output procedure. To do that, you move 16 to the Sort-Return register. Then, when the program executes the next Return or Release statement, the sort/merge program will end and control will return to the statement following the Sort or Merge statement.

When you use the sort/merge program on an IBM mainframe, you can use sort control statements outside of the COBOL program to supply values like the size of the file to be sorted or the amount of internal storage to be used by the sort. Information like this can improve the efficiency of a sort or merge operation. To use sort control statements, you can put the ddname of the file that contains these statements in a register named Sort-Control. If you don't use this register, IGZSRTCD is used as the default ddname for the file of control statements.

Perspective

The main reason for using an internal sort is to improve processing efficiency. That's why many companies make frequent use of internal sorts. On the other hand, some companies never use internal sorts, either because its use doesn't lead to improved efficiency on their system or because it complicates the program code.

Internal merges are used much less frequently than internal sorts, because it's often more efficient to sort the data from several files into a single file than it is to sort the data in each of the files separately and then merge the separate files into one file. There are times, though, when the files to be merged are already in the appropriate sequence, so an internal merge makes sense. As a result, you should know how to use internal merges as well as internal sorts if you work for a company that uses them.

Summary

- When you *sort* a file, the records in the file are sequenced based on one or more *key fields*.

- When you *merge* two or more files, the records in the files are combined into a single file and are sequenced based on one or more key fields.

- Most systems or compilers provide a *sort/merge program* you can use to sort and merge the records in one or more files. When you execute this program directly, it's called a *standalone sort* or *standalone merge*. When you execute it from a COBOL program, it's called an *internal sort* or an *internal merge*.

- To perform an internal sort from a COBOL program, you use the Sort statement. To perform an internal merge, you use the Merge statement. In either case, you must define a work file that will provide a work space for the sort/merge program.

- For a sort operation, you can use an *input procedure* to select the records to be sorted from the input file. This procedure must include a Release statement to pass the selected records to the sort/merge program. If you don't use an input procedure, all of the records in the input file are sorted.

- After the records are sorted, you can use an *output procedure* to process the sorted records. This procedure must include a Return statement to retrieve the records from the sorted file. If you don't use an output procedure, the sorted records are written to an output file.

- You can't use an input procedure for a merge operation, which means that all of the records in the input files are merged. However, you can use an output procedure. If you don't, all of the merged records are written to an output file.

Terms

sort	internal merge
merge	standalone merge
sort/merge program	sort work file
sort program	input procedure
key field	output procedure
sort key	merge work file
collating sequence	concatenate
internal sort	sort register
standalone sort	

Objectives

- Given complete program specifications, develop a COBOL program that includes an internal sort or merge.

- In general terms, explain how you perform an internal sort or merge from a COBOL program.

- Explain why an internal sort or merge is typically more efficient than a standalone sort or merge.

Exercise 16-1   Modify the sales report program to include a sort

In this exercise, you'll modify the two-level sales report program you created in chapter 5 so it sorts the records in the customer file in customer number within salesrep number within branch number sequence before it prints the report. The specifications for this report are shown in figure 5-18.

Modify the structure chart

1. Modify the structure chart shown in figure 5-19 to include a sort function. To do that, you'll need to add another level that includes three modules that represent the main functions of this program: (1) get the input records; (2) sort the input records; and (3) print the report. To keep the changes to the code simple, number these modules 025, 050, and 075. Also, change the name of module 310 to indicate that it will perform a return function rather than a read function.

Modify the code

2. Open the program named rpt5000 and change the Program-ID to RPT7000. Then, save the program as rpt7000 and close the program.

3. Open the rpt7000 program you just created. Then, add a Select statement, an SD statement, and a record description for the sort work file. Also, change the system name in the Select statement for the customer file so it gets data from a file named custmstu.dat, which isn't in the right processing sequence.

4. Add a Sort statement to module 000. This statement should include a Using clause to get the records from the customer master file, a Key clause to sort the records in the appropriate sequence, and an Output Procedure clause that names the procedure that prints the report.

5. Add the code for the three modules you added to the structure chart in step 1. The Sort module should be coded as a comment since its function is performed by the Sort statement. The Get module should also be coded as a comment since its function is performed by the Using clause of the Sort statement. The third module, which represents the output procedure, should include the code for printing the report that was originally in module 000.

6. Modify the code in the output procedure so it retrieves records from the sorted customer file instead of from the customer master file.

Compile and test the program

7. Compile and test the program. When you run the program, you should get an error message indicating that the customer file is already open. Because the Sort statement includes a Using clause instead of an input procedure, this statement will open and close the file automatically. So you can delete the Open and Close statements for this file. Make this change, then compile and test the program again. When you're sure that it works the way the previous version of this program worked, close the program.

Section 4

COBOL for specific compilers and platforms

The first three sections in this book present the standard 1985 COBOL language. Now, in this section, you can learn the non-standard COBOL extensions for some common programming requirements as well as some other skills for working with specific compilers and platforms.

In chapter 17, for example, you can learn how to use the Micro Focus COBOL extensions for developing interactive programs. In chapter 18, you can learn how to compile and test COBOL programs on an IBM mainframe. In chapter 19, you can learn how to develop interactive programs on an IBM mainframe. And in chapter 20, you can learn how to develop database programs on an IBM mainframe.

Then, in chapter 21, you'll be introduced to the job of maintenance programming. There, you'll see some of the programming variations that are common in the real world. You'll also learn how to cope with these variations as you make the required changes to an old program.

Last, in chapter 22, you'll be introduced to object-oriented COBOL. This form of COBOL consist of features that are going to be part of the 2002 standards, and many of these features are already available on current compilers. Because learning to think in terms of objects instead of procedures is quite a change, no one knows how well object-oriented COBOL is going to be accepted. But this chapter will give you a good idea of what its potential is.

17

How to develop interactive programs with Micro Focus COBOL

In chapter 1, you learned how to use the standard Accept and Display statements to process screen input and output (I-O). Now, in this chapter, you'll learn how to use the non-standard Micro Focus extensions for processing screen I-O. These extensions let you accept and display single fields, groups of fields, and entire screens with a single statement. They also let you control various attributes of the screen fields, like color and position.

Even if you aren't using Micro Focus COBOL, you may want to read this chapter. That's because the Micro Focus extensions for screen I-O are similar to those that are used in some of the compilers for mid-range computers. They are also similar to the features for screen I-O that will be included in the COBOL-2002 standards.

How to use the enhanced Accept and Display statements

To accept and display data one field at a time with Micro Focus COBOL, you use enhanced versions of the Accept and Display statements. These statements let you specify a variety of attributes for each field as well as where the field will appear on the screen. They are most appropriate for low volume screen I-O with simple processing requirements. In the following topics, you'll learn about the options you're most likely to use with these statements. Keep in mind, though, that other options are available.

How to code the enhanced Display statement

Figure 17-1 presents the syntax of the enhanced Display statement. This statement lets you display the value of a variable or literal at the screen location specified by the Line and Column options of the At clause. Although you'll typically include both of these options to define the screen location explicitly, you can omit one or both of them. If you omit both, the field will appear in the next column of the line where the last field was displayed. If no other field was previously displayed, the field will appear in column 1 of line 1.

If only a column location is specified, the field will appear in that column on the line following the line where the last field was displayed. And if only a line location is specified, the field will appear in that line in the column following the column where the last field was displayed. If a field doesn't fit on the current line, it wraps to the next line. And if the next line is past the bottom of the screen, the screen will scroll up one line. By the way, the screen displayed by Micro Focus consists of 25 lines and 80 columns. Because the system displays messages in line 25, though, you usually don't use that line in your programs.

The With clause of the Display statement lets you specify a variety of screen attributes. Most of these attributes are self-explanatory. But a few of them have some special functionality you'll want to know about.

You can use the Foreground-Color and Background-Color options to set the default colors for the entire screen. For that to work, the With clause must also include the Blank Screen option. The first field you display on the screen, then, usually includes this option and the default colors as illustrated by the first example in this figure. Then, you can change the colors for individual fields by specifying the Foreground-Color and Background-Color options on the Display statements for those fields. Notice that you indicate the color you want to use by specifying an integer. You'll learn about the colors that are available and the integers that are associated with them later in this chapter.

The second example in this figure shows how to use the Control option of the With clause. This option lets you change the screen attributes of a field each time it's displayed by using a variable to specify the attributes. If the user enters invalid data into a field, for example, you might want to redisplay the field with the Highlight attribute as shown in this example so the field stands out on the

The syntax of the enhanced Display statement

```
DISPLAY  {identifier-1}
         {literal-1   }

    [AT [LINE NUMBER {identify-1}] [{COLUMN} NUMBER {identifier-3}]]
                     {integer-1 }   {COL   }        {integer-2   }

    [WITH [FOREGROUND-COLOR IS integer-3 ]
          [BACKGROUND-COLOR IS integer-4 ]
          [HIGHLIGHT ]
          [REVERSE-VIDEO ]
          [UNDERLINE ]
          [BLINK ]
          [BELL | BEEP ]
          [ERASE {EOL}]
                 {EOS}
          [CONTROL IS identifier-4]
          [BLANK {SCREEN}]]} ...
                 {LINE  }
```

A Display statement that clears the screen and sets the default colors

```
DISPLAY "Inventory inquiry"
    WITH BLANK SCREEN
    FOREGROUND-COLOR 7
    BACKGROUND-COLOR 1.
```

A Display statement that uses a variable to set the appearance of the screen item

```
MOVE "HIGHLIGHT" TO ITEM-NUMBER-CONTROL.
DISPLAY IM-ITEM-NUMBER AT LINE 5 COLUMN 22
    WITH CONTROL ITEM-NUMBER-CONTROL.
```

Description

- If the LINE and COLUMN options are omitted, the screen item is displayed in the next column on the same line as the last item displayed. If nothing is currently displayed on the screen, the item is displayed beginning in column 1 of line 1.

- The foreground and background colors apply to the entire screen if the BLANK SCREEN option is also included. Otherwise, they apply to all items displayed on the screen except those that have a WITH clause. See figure 17-3 for a list of the screen color values.

- You can erase the contents of a line or the entire screen starting with the position specified on the Display statement by including the ERASE EOL or ERASE EOS option. To clear an entire line or the entire screen, use the BLANK LINE or BLANK SCREEN option.

- You can use the CONTROL option to identify a variable that can contain any of the other WITH options. This lets you change the appearance of a screen item as the program executes.

- If you code the figurative constant SPACE (or SPACES) on a Display statement, the screen is cleared from the specified screen location. If you code the figurative constant LOW-VALUE (or LOW-VALUES), the cursor is moved to the specified screen location.

Figure 17-1   How to code the enhanced Display statement

screen. Note that you can code the Control option along with any of the other With options. That way, you can use Control to specify just the attributes that can change, and you can code the attributes that don't change explicitly.

How to code the enhanced Accept statement

Figure 17-2 presents the syntax of the enhanced Accept statement. As you can see, you use many of the same options with this statement as you do with the Display statement. A few options, though, are specific to the Accept statement.

By default, fields are displayed on the screen without any indication of how many characters they can contain. If you want the user to know how much data can be entered into a field, you can use the Prompt option to display a prompt character in each blank field position. If you include Prompt without specifying a character, an underline is used. Otherwise, the character you specify is used.

Another option you may want to use is Auto (or Auto-Skip). This option causes the Accept statement to end when the user enters a character into each position in a field. Then, the program continues automatically with the statement that follows the Accept statement. If you don't specify this option, the user has to press the Enter key to complete an Accept statement.

Two other options you can use with Accept are Required (or Empty-Check) and Secure (or No-Echo). If Required is specified for a field, an error message is displayed if the user doesn't enter a value for the field. And if Secure is specified, the value the user enters isn't displayed on the screen. This is useful for fields that contain passwords.

The syntax of the enhanced Accept statement

```
ACCEPT  identifier-1
    [ AT [ LINE NUMBER {identifier-2}] [{COLUMN} NUMBER {identifier-3}]]
                       {integer-1  }   {COL   }        {integer-2  }
    [ WITH  [FOREGROUND-COLOR IS integer-3]
            [BACKGROUND-COLOR IS integer-4]
            [ PROMPT [ CHARACTER IS {identifier-4}]]
                                    {literal-1  }
            [AUTO | AUTO-SKIP]
            [HIGHLIGHT]
            [REVERSE-VIDEO]
            [UNDERLINE]
            [BLINK]
            [BELL | BEEP]
            [UPPER | LOWER]
            [REQUIRED | EMPTY-CHECK]
            [SECURE | NO-ECHO]
            [CONTROL IS identifier-5]]
```

An Accept statement that accepts a required screen item

```
ACCEPT IM-ITEM-NO AT LINE 5 COLUMN 22
    WITH HIGHLIGHT PROMPT REQUIRED.
```

An Accept statement that lets the user enter only uppercase characters

```
ACCEPT SAVE-CHANGES-SWITCH AT LINE 24 COLUMN 15
    WITH UPPER HIGHLIGHT.
```

Description

- The LINE, COLUMN, FOREGROUND-COLOR, BACKGROUND-COLOR, and CONTROL options work the same as they do for the enhanced Display statement.

- If you include the PROMPT option without specifying a character, an underline is used.

- To end an Accept statement when the last character is entered into the screen item, include the AUTO or AUTO-SKIP option. Otherwise, the statement ends when the Enter key is pressed.

- If a screen item requires an entry, include the REQUIRED or EMPTY-CHECK option.

- If you don't want the characters entered by the user to appear on the screen, include the SECURE or NO-ECHO option.

Figure 17-2   How to code the enhanced Accept statement

How to specify screen colors

As you saw in figure 17-1, you can set foreground and background colors by specifying integers that represent the colors. Figure 17-3 lists all of the colors that are available along with their integer values. Note that the first eight colors, represented by the numbers 0 through 7, can be used for both foreground and background colors. However, the last eight colors, represented by the numbers 8 through 15, can be used only for foreground colors.

The problem with using integer values for the colors is that it's difficult to remember what color each integer represents. If you look back at the syntax of the Accept and Display statements, though, you'll see that you can only specify an integer for a color; you can't specify a data-name that contains the integer value for a color. In other words, you can't define a data item named RED that contains the value 4 and then refer to that data item in the Foreground-Color or Background-Color option.

To get around this problem, though, Micro Focus lets you specify a *constant* that contains an integer value. To define a constant, you use a 78 level data description entry as shown in this figure. Here, three constants are defined for the colors blue, white, and bright red. Then, the Display statement that follows uses the constant names in the Foreground-Color and Background-Color options instead of their integer values.

Screen color values

Foreground and background

Value	Color
0	Black
1	Blue
2	Green
3	Cyan
4	Red
5	Magenta
6	Brown
7	White

Foreground only

Value	Color
8	Bright black
9	Bright blue
10	Bright green
11	Bright cyan
12	Bright red
13	Bright magenta
14	Bright brown
15	Bright white

Data description entries for three screen color constants

```
78   BLUE              VALUE 1.
78   WHITE             VALUE 7.
78   BRIGHT-RED        VALUE 12.
```

A Display statement that uses screen color constants

```
DISPLAY "Inventory inquiry"
    WITH BLANK SCREEN
    FOREGROUND-COLOR WHITE
    BACKGROUND-COLOR BLUE.
```

Description

- You can use the values shown above to assign foreground and background colors to screen items. You can also use 78 level data description entries to define *constants* for the colors. Then, you can use the constants in place of the color numbers.

- Because the compiler allocates storage for a constant based on its value, you don't code a Picture clause for it.

- 78 level items are standalone entries and can't be included in a group item.

Figure 17-3   How to specify screen colors

A COBOL program that uses enhanced Accept and Display statements

Now that you know how to code enhanced Accept and Display statements, you'll see a program that uses these statements. This is a simple inquiry program that displays information from a file of inventory records.

The processing specifications

Figure 17-4 presents the basic processing specifications for the inquiry program. The two screens in this figure illustrate how the program works. To start, the program displays the information lines and prompts the user to enter the item number of the inventory item to be displayed.

If the user enters a valid item number, the related inventory record is retrieved and its information is displayed on the screen. Then, after reviewing the data, the user can press the Enter key to return to the initial display and enter another item number. Alternatively, the user can enter the letter N into the prompt at the bottom of the screen to end the program.

If the user enters an invalid item number, an error message is displayed on line 23 of the screen and the user can enter another item number. If the user enters 99999 for the item number, though, the program ends.

Screen 1

The program accepts an item number from the user.

```
■Animator V2 Text Window                                    _□×
Inventory inquiry

Type an item number. Then press Enter.

Item number. . . . . ____



















Enter 99999 to end.
```

Screen 2

When the user enters an item number and presses the Enter key, the program
retrieves the record for the inventory item and displays its data on the screen.

```
■Animator V2 Text Window                                    _□×
Inventory inquiry

Type an item number. Then press Enter.

Item number. . . . . 10001

Description:        Murach's Uisual Basic 6
Unit cost:             5.35
Unit price:           45.00
Reorder point:      1,500
On hand:              543
On order:          10,000














Do you want to display another item? Y
```

Processing specifications

- This program lets the user display data for any item in the inventory master file.
- If the user presses the Enter key without entering an item number or enters an item
  number for a record that doesn't exist, the program should display an error message
  on line 23. An error message should also be displayed if the user enters anything
  other than Y or N for the prompt on the second screen shown above.
- To end the program, the user can enter 99999 for the item number or N for the
  prompt on the second screen.

Figure 17-4   The processing specifications for the inquiry program

The structure chart

Figure 17-5 presents the structure chart for the inquiry program. You should be able to follow this chart without much trouble, so only the highlights are presented here. If you do have trouble understanding how any of this works, though, it should become clear after you review the code for this program.

Like most COBOL programs, module 000 performs module 100 repeatedly until the user ends the program. Module 100 starts by performing module 110 to display the heading lines. This is done before a new item number is accepted from the user so the data from the previous item is erased from the screen.

Next, module 100 performs module 120 to get an item number from the user. This module performs other modules that accept and edit the item number, display an error message when necessary, and erase any error message that's displayed after the user enters a valid value.

If the user enters a valid item number, module 100 continues by performing module 180 to display the data for that item. Then, it performs module 190 to determine whether the user wants to display another item or end the program. Like module 120, this module performs other modules that accept and edit the user's entry and display and erase error messages when necessary.

The structure chart

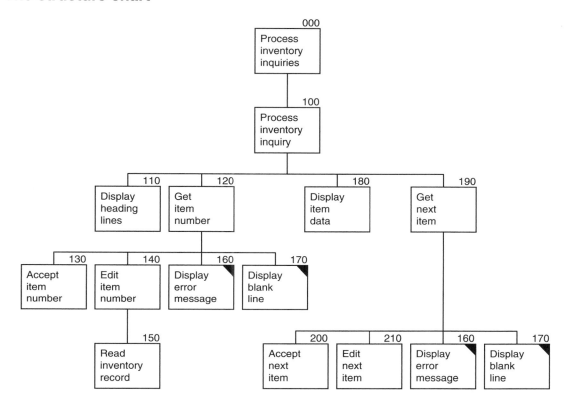

Description

- This program performs module 100 repeatedly until the user has no more inquiries. This module performs module 110 to display the heading lines and clear the screen before each entry. Then, it performs module 120 to get an item number from the user, module 180 to display the data for the item, and module 190 to determine if the user wants to display another item.

- Module 120 performs module 130 to accept an item number from the user. Then, it performs module 140 to edit the item number. This module performs module 150 to read the inventory record for the item.

- If the inventory record isn't found or if the user didn't enter an item number, module 120 performs module 160 to display an error message. Then, the user can enter another item number or end the program. If the inventory record is found, module 120 performs module 170 to clear any error message that was displayed.

- After the inventory data is displayed, module 190 performs module 200 to accept a response to the prompt that asks if the user wants to display another record. Then, module 190 performs module 210 to edit the response. If it's anything other than Y or N, module 160 is performed to display an error message. Otherwise, module 170 is performed to clear any error message that was displayed.

Figure 17-5   The structure chart for the inquiry program

The COBOL listing

The complete listing for the inquiry program is presented in figure 17-6 with the code for screen I-O shaded. Because the logic of this program is straightforward, you should be able to follow it without much trouble. But here are a few comments that may help.

In the Environment Division, you can see the Select statement for the inventory file. If you've already read chapter 14, you should know what this statement means. Otherwise, you can just accept the fact that this statement defines an indexed file that is read on a random basis using the item number field as the key field. In the record description for this file, you can see the descriptions for the seven fields that each record contains.

In the shaded areas on this page, you can see the definitions of the constants for the three colors used by this program. You can also see the definitions of six fields that will be displayed on the screen. The first field is used to display error messages. The other fields are used to display the numeric data that's retrieved from each inventory record in an edited format.

The inquiry program   **Page 1**

```
IDENTIFICATION DIVISION.
PROGRAM-ID. INQ1000.

ENVIRONMENT DIVISION.
INPUT-OUTPUT SECTION.
FILE-CONTROL.
    SELECT INVMAST  ASSIGN TO "c:\cobol\data\invmasti.dat"
                    ORGANIZATION IS INDEXED
                    ACCESS IS RANDOM
                    RECORD KEY IS IM-ITEM-NO.

DATA DIVISION.

FILE SECTION.

FD  INVMAST.

01  INVENTORY-MASTER-RECORD.
    05  IM-ITEM-NO              PIC X(5).
    05  IM-DESCRIPTIVE-DATA.
        10  IM-ITEM-DESC        PIC X(40).
        10  IM-UNIT-COST        PIC 999V99.
        10  IM-UNIT-PRICE       PIC 999V99.
    05  IM-INVENTORY-DATA.
        10  IM-REORDER-POINT    PIC S9(5).
        10  IM-ON-HAND          PIC S9(5).
        10  IM-ON-ORDER         PIC S9(5).

WORKING-STORAGE SECTION.

78  BLACK             VALUE 0.
78  WHITE             VALUE 7.
78  BRIGHT-WHITE      VALUE 15.

01  SWITCHES.

    05  END-OF-INQUIRIES-SWITCH     PIC X    VALUE "N".
        88  END-OF-INQUIRIES                 VALUE "Y".
    05  VALID-ENTRY-SWITCH          PIC X    VALUE "N".
        88  VALID-ENTRY                      VALUE "Y".
    05  ITEM-FOUND-SWITCH           PIC X    VALUE "Y".
        88  ITEM-FOUND                       VALUE "Y".
    05  NEXT-ITEM-SWITCH            PIC X    VALUE "Y".
        88  NEXT-ITEM                        VALUE "Y".

01  SCREEN-DISPLAY-FIELDS.

    05  ERROR-MESSAGE       PIC X(80)    VALUE SPACE.
    05  UNIT-COST           PIC ZZZ.ZZ.
    05  UNIT-PRICE          PIC ZZZ.ZZ.
    05  REORDER-POINT       PIC ZZ,ZZZ.
    05  ON-HAND             PIC ZZ,ZZZ.
    05  ON-ORDER            PIC ZZ,ZZZ.
```

Figure 17-6   The COBOL listing for the inquiry program (part 1 of 4)

On page 2 of this listing, you can see the code for the procedure that displays the heading lines (procedure 110). Notice that the first Display statement in this procedure includes the Blank Screen option to erase any data that was previously displayed on the screen. It also includes the Foreground-Color and Background-Color options to set the default colors for the screen.

In procedure 130, you can see the code that accepts an item number from the user. The first Display statement in this procedure displays the prompt for the item number entry. Then, the second Display statement displays the message in line 24 that instructs the user how to end the program. Finally, the Accept statement accepts the item number entry. This statement includes the Prompt option so the five character positions for the item number will be underlined.

On page 3 of the listing, you can see that procedure 150 reads the inventory record with the item number that has been stored in the key field, IM-ITEM-NO. If the record isn't found, though, the Invalid Key clause is executed and N is moved to the item found switch.

In procedure 160, you can see the Display statement that's executed when the user makes an invalid entry. This statement sets the foreground color for the message to bright white so it stands out on the screen. It also includes the Beep option so the alarm will sound to alert the user to the error.

In contrast, the Display statement in procedure 170 is executed when the user enters a valid entry. This statement erases any error message that may have been displayed previously. To do that, it uses the figurative constant Spaces. This causes the screen to be cleared from the specified location, in this case, from column 1 of line 23. Although this also erases line 24, a new message is displayed on that line in the next procedure that's executed. Another way to erase the error message would be to move Space to the error-message field, and then display that field.

If the user enters a valid item number, procedure 180 is performed to display the data in the inventory record for that item, which is retrieved by the Read statement in procedure 150. Procedure 180 starts by moving the data in the record to numeric edited fields in working storage. That way, the data is displayed in a more readable format. The Display statements that follow display a descriptive heading for each field followed by the field itself.

After the data for an item is displayed, procedure 200 on page 4 is performed. This procedure displays a message that asks if the user wants to display another item. Then, an Accept statement accepts the user's response into the next-item switch. Since this switch is set to Y before this procedure is performed, the user can simply press Enter to enter another item number.

Notice that the Accept statement in procedure 200 sets the foreground color for the entry to bright white. Also notice that the Upper option is included. That way, if the user enters a lowercase character, it's converted to uppercase. That's necessary because the definition of the next-item switch and the code in procedure 210 are written to work only with uppercase characters.

The inquiry program   **Page 2**

```
PROCEDURE DIVISION.

000-PROCESS-INVENTRY-INQUIRIES.

    OPEN INPUT INVMAST.
    PERFORM 100-PROCESS-INVENTORY-INQUIRY
        UNTIL END-OF-INQUIRIES.
    CLOSE INVMAST.
    STOP RUN.

100-PROCESS-INVENTORY-INQUIRY.

    PERFORM 110-DISPLAY-HEADING-LINES.
    MOVE "N" TO VALID-ENTRY-SWITCH.
    MOVE SPACE TO IM-ITEM-NO.
    PERFORM 120-GET-ITEM-NUMBER
        UNTIL VALID-ENTRY.
    IF NOT END-OF-INQUIRIES
        PERFORM 180-DISPLAY-ITEM-DATA
        MOVE "N" TO VALID-ENTRY-SWITCH
        PERFORM 190-GET-NEXT-ITEM
            UNTIL VALID-ENTRY.

110-DISPLAY-HEADING-LINES.

    DISPLAY "Inventory inquiry" AT LINE 1 COLUMN 1
        WITH BLANK SCREEN
        FOREGROUND-COLOR BLACK
        BACKGROUND-COLOR WHITE.
    DISPLAY "Type an item number. Then press Enter."
        AT LINE 3 COLUMN 1.

120-GET-ITEM-NUMBER.

    MOVE "Y" TO VALID-ENTRY-SWITCH.
    PERFORM 130-ACCEPT-ITEM-NUMBER.
    PERFORM 140-EDIT-ITEM-NUMBER.
    IF NOT VALID-ENTRY
        PERFORM 160-DISPLAY-ERROR-MESSAGE
    ELSE
        PERFORM 170-DISPLAY-BLANK-LINE.

130-ACCEPT-ITEM-NUMBER.

    DISPLAY "Item number. . . . . " AT LINE 5 COLUMN 1.
    DISPLAY "Enter 99999 to end." AT LINE 24 COLUMN 1.
    ACCEPT IM-ITEM-NO AT LINE 5 COLUMN 22
        WITH PROMPT.
```

Figure 17-6   The COBOL listing for the inquiry program (part 2 of 4)

The inquiry program   **Page 3**

```
140-EDIT-ITEM-NUMBER.

    IF IM-ITEM-NO = "99999"
        MOVE "Y" TO END-OF-INQUIRIES-SWITCH
    ELSE IF IM-ITEM-NO = SPACE
        MOVE "N" TO VALID-ENTRY-SWITCH
        MOVE "An item number is required." TO ERROR-MESSAGE
    ELSE
        MOVE "Y" TO ITEM-FOUND-SWITCH
        PERFORM 150-READ-INVENTORY-RECORD
        IF NOT ITEM-FOUND
            MOVE "N" TO VALID-ENTRY-SWITCH
            MOVE "Inventory record not found."
                TO ERROR-MESSAGE.

150-READ-INVENTORY-RECORD.

    READ INVMAST
        INVALID KEY
            MOVE "N" TO ITEM-FOUND-SWITCH.

160-DISPLAY-ERROR-MESSAGE.

    DISPLAY ERROR-MESSAGE AT LINE 23 COLUMN 1
        WITH FOREGROUND-COLOR BRIGHT-WHITE BEEP.

170-DISPLAY-BLANK-LINE.

    DISPLAY SPACES AT LINE 23 COLUMN 1.

180-DISPLAY-ITEM-DATA.

    MOVE IM-UNIT-COST TO UNIT-COST.
    MOVE IM-UNIT-PRICE TO UNIT-PRICE.
    MOVE IM-REORDER-POINT TO REORDER-POINT.
    MOVE IM-ON-HAND TO ON-HAND.
    MOVE IM-ON-ORDER TO ON-ORDER.
    DISPLAY "Description:"    LINE 7  COLUMN 1.
    DISPLAY IM-ITEM-DESC      LINE 7  COLUMN 22.
    DISPLAY "Unit cost:"      LINE 8  COLUMN 1.
    DISPLAY UNIT-COST         LINE 8  COLUMN 22.
    DISPLAY "Unit price:"     LINE 9  COLUMN 1.
    DISPLAY UNIT-PRICE        LINE 9  COLUMN 22.
    DISPLAY "Reorder point:"  LINE 10 COLUMN 1.
    DISPLAY REORDER-POINT     LINE 10 COLUMN 22.
    DISPLAY "On hand:"        LINE 11 COLUMN 1.
    DISPLAY ON-HAND           LINE 11 COLUMN 22.
    DISPLAY "On order:"       LINE 12 COLUMN 1.
    DISPLAY ON-ORDER          LINE 12 COLUMN 22.
```

Figure 17-6   The COBOL listing for the inquiry program (part 3 of 4)

The inquiry program   **Page 4**

```
190-GET-NEXT-ITEM.

    MOVE "Y" TO VALID-ENTRY-SWITCH.
    PERFORM 200-ACCEPT-NEXT-ITEM.
    PERFORM 210-EDIT-NEXT-ITEM.
    IF NOT VALID-ENTRY
        PERFORM 160-DISPLAY-ERROR-MESSAGE
    ELSE
        PERFORM 170-DISPLAY-BLANK-LINE.

200-ACCEPT-NEXT-ITEM.

    DISPLAY "Do you want to display another item?"
        LINE 24 COLUMN 1.
    ACCEPT NEXT-ITEM-SWITCH AT LINE 24 COLUMN 38
        WITH FOREGROUND-COLOR BRIGHT-WHITE UPPER.

210-EDIT-NEXT-ITEM.

    IF NOT NEXT-ITEM
        IF NEXT-ITEM-SWITCH = "N"
            MOVE "Y" TO END-OF-INQUIRIES-SWITCH
        ELSE
            MOVE "N" TO VALID-ENTRY-SWITCH
            MOVE "You must enter 'Y' or 'N'" TO ERROR-MESSAGE.
```

Figure 17-6   The COBOL listing for the inquiry program (part 4 of 4)

How to use screen definitions

Although the Accept and Display statements work fine for programs that work with a limited amount of data, they can become cumbersome for programs that perform more data-intensive operations. For those programs, you can define and work with entire screens of data rather than individual fields.

When you use screen definitions, you code them in a special section of the Data Division named the Screen Section. That way, the field definitions aren't spread throughout the Procedure Division like they are when you use Accept and Display statements. That's why a program that uses screen definitions is easier to modify and debug.

How to code screen definitions

Figure 17-7 shows you how to code screen definitions. To do that, you usually start by coding an 01 level entry that names the screen as shown in the screen definition in this figure. Then, you code subordinate entries that define individual fields or groups of fields on the screen.

In this example, seven 05 level entries are included. Notice that only one of these entries includes a screen name, which means that this is the only field you'll be able to refer to individually from the Procedure Division. In most cases, though, you won't need to refer to individual fields, so you can code the word Filler or omit the name altogether as shown here.

If you look at the syntax for a *screen description entry*, you'll see that it includes many of the same options that you can code on the Accept and Display statements presented earlier in this chapter. Since these options work the same way they do with those statements, this topic won't describe them again. Instead, it will focus on the options you haven't seen: Picture, Value, From, To, and Using.

The options you use for a screen description entry depend on the type of field you're defining. The four basic types of fields are *input fields*, *output fields*, *update fields*, and *literal fields*. To define a literal field, you simply code a Value clause that specifies the literal value. This is illustrated by three of the screen description entries in this figure. Notice in these examples that you do not code a Picture clause with the Value clause. Instead, Micro Focus determines the size of the field from the literal value.

To define a field that's used only for input, you use the To clause. Then, when the user enters a value into this field, it's stored in the specified variable. Because input fields don't display the current value of a field, they're not used very often. One use for an input field, though, is to accept a password from the user.

The syntax of a screen description entry

```
level-number  {screen-name}
              {FILLER     }

    [ LINE NUMBER IS {identifier-1}] [{COLUMN}  NUMBER IS {identifier-2}]
                     {integer-1   }   {COL   }            {integer-2   }

    [{PICTURE}  IS picture-string] [ FROM {identifier-3}] [ TO identifer-4 ]
     {PIC    }                            {literal-1   }
                                    [ USING identifier-5]

    [[ VALUE IS] literal-2]

    [ FOREGROUND-COLOR IS {integer-3    }]
                          {identifier-6 }

    [ BACKGROUND-COLOR IS {integer-4    }]
                          {identifier-7 }

    [ PROMPT [ CHARACTER IS {identifier-8}]]
                            {literal-3   }

    [ AUTO | AUTO-SKIP ] [ HIGHLIGHT ] [ REVERSE-VIDEO ] [ UNDERLINE ]
    [ BLINK ] [ BELL | BEEP ] [ SECURE | NO-ECHO ] [ REQUIRED | EMPTY-CHECK ]
    [ ERASE {EOL}] [ CONTROL IS identifier-9 ] [ BLANK {LINE  }]
            {EOS}                                      {SCREEN}
```

A screen description that includes two output fields, an update field, and three literal fields

```
01  ITEM-NUMBER-SCREEN.
    05  BLANK SCREEN
        BACKGROUND-COLOR BLUE FOREGROUND-COLOR WHITE.
    05  LINE 1   COLUMN 1   PIC X(80)
        FROM SCREEN-HEADING-LINE.
    05  LINE 3   COLUMN 1   VALUE "Type an item number. Then press "Enter.".
    05  LINE 5   COLUMN 1   VALUE "Item number. . . . . ".
    05  IN-ITEM-NUMBER    PIC X(5)
        LINE 5   COLUMN 22 USING IM-ITEM-NO
        CONTROL  ITEM-NUMBER-CONTROL.
    05  LINE 23 COLUMN 1   PIC X(80)
        FROM ERROR-MESSAGE HIGHLIGHT.
    05  LINE 24 COLUMN 1   VALUE "Enter 99999 to end.".
```

Description

- You code *screen description entries* in the Screen Section of a program. The Screen Section must be the last section in the Data Division.

- Many of the options you can code on a screen description entry are the same as the options you can code on Accept and Display statements. See figures 17-1 and 17-2 for details.

- To define a *literal field*, use the Value clause and omit the Picture clause.

- To define an *input field*, use the TO clause. Then, the data entered into the field is moved to the variable that's specified when the screen is accepted.

- To define an *output field*, use the FROM clause. Then, the data in the field is displayed when the screen is displayed.

- To define an *update field*, use both the TO and FROM clause or the USING clause.

Figure 17-7   How to code screen definitions

To define a field that's used only for output, you use the From clause along with the Picture clause. The From clause causes the data in the specified variable to be displayed, but it doesn't allow the user to change the data. The Picture clause specifies the size and contents of the field and can include editing characters. The screen definition in this figure, for example, includes two output fields. The first one displays the contents of the variable named Screen-Heading-Line on line 1 of the screen, and the second one displays the contents of a variable named Error-Message on line 23 of the screen.

If you want to both display the data in a field and let the user change it, you define it as an update field. To do that, you can code both the From and To clauses, or you can code the Using clause. This clause is used for the field in this figure that accepts an item number from the user. That way, the user will be able to see the current value of this field and will be able to change it.

If you look again at the screen description in figure 17-7, you'll see that the first 05 level entry doesn't include any of these options. Instead, it uses the Blank Screen option to clear the screen and the Foreground-Color and Background-Color options to set the default colors for the screen. This is typical of the first elementary item in the first screen that's displayed by a program.

How to use Accept and Display with screen description entries

To display the output, update, and literal fields defined by a screen definition, you use the Display statement format that's shown in figure 17-8. And to accept the input and update fields on a screen, you use the Accept statement format that's shown in this figure. In most cases, these statements simply identify the screen item you want to display, which can be an entire screen or a group or elementary item defined within the screen. However, these statements can also specify a screen location if it's not included in the screen definition.

The syntax of the Display statement for screen description entries

```
DISPLAY screen-name
    [ AT  [ LINE NUMBER {identifier-1}] [{COLUMN} NUMBER {identifier-2}]]
                        {integer-1   }  {COL   }        {integer-2   }
```

A Display statement that displays the screen defined in figure 17-7

```
DISPLAY ITEM-NUMBER-SCREEN
```

A Display statement that displays the screen item named IN-ITEM-NUMBER

```
MOVE SPACE TO ITEM-NUMBER-CONTROL.
DISPLAY IN-ITEM-NUMBER.
```

The syntax of the Accept statement for screen description entries

```
ACCEPT screen-name
    [ AT  [ LINE NUMBER {identifier-1}] [{COLUMN} NUMBER {identifier-2}]]
                        {integer-1   }  {COL   }        {integer-2   }
```

An Accept statement that accepts all the entries on a screen

```
ACCEPT ITEM-NUMBER-SCREEN.
```

An Accept statement that accepts the entry from a single field

```
ACCEPT IN-ITEM-NUMBER.
```

Description

- When used with screen definitions, the Accept and Display statements can display an entire screen, a group of fields on the screen, or an individual field.
- When a Display statement is executed, all literal fields, output fields, and update fields defined within the named screen item are displayed.
- When an Accept statement is executed, data is retrieved from all input and update fields defined within the named screen item.
- Line and column locations are typically defined within the screen definition. However, you can also specify the screen location on the Accept or Display statement for the screen.

Figure 17-8   How to use Accept and Display with screen description entries

How to position the cursor

When you use Accept statements to accept a single field from the user as shown earlier in this chapter, you usually don't need to worry about positioning the cursor. That's because it's automatically positioned at the beginning of the field specified in the Accept statement. When you use Accept with screen definitions, though, you may need to position the cursor. To do that, you include code like that shown in figure 17-9.

To start, you include the Special-Names paragraph in the Configuration Section of the Environment Division. Then, you code the Cursor clause as shown in this figure. This clause identifies a field in working storage that will be used to set the cursor position. In this case, the field is named Cursor-Position. This field must be defined as a four-byte, unsigned numeric field. The first two bytes identify the line where the cursor will be positioned, and the last two bytes identify the column where the cursor will be positioned.

To change the position of the cursor, you simply move the appropriate values to the line and column fields before an Accept or Display statement is executed. In the example in this figure, the cursor is moved to the beginning of the unit price field in column 22 of line 9 when the user enters an invalid value in this field. That way, the user can enter another value without having to move the cursor manually.

A Special-Names entry for positioning the cursor

```
SPECIAL-NAMES.
    CURSOR IS CURSOR-POSITION.
```

A Working-Storage entry for positioning the cursor

```
01  CURSOR-POSITION.
    05  CURSOR-LINE    PIC 99.
    05  CURSOR-COLUMN  PIC 99.
```

Procedure Division code that positions the cursor

```
IF IM-UNIT-PRICE NOT > IM-UNIT-COST
    MOVE "Unit price must be greater than unit cost."
        TO ERROR-MESSAGE
    MOVE 9  TO CURSOR-LINE
    MOVE 22 TO CURSOR-COLUMN
    MOVE "HIGHLIGHT" TO UNIT-PRICE-CONTROL
END-IF
```

Description

- The Special-Names paragraph is coded in the Configuration Section of the Environment Division.

- The data-name you specify on the CURSOR IS clause in the Special-Names paragraph must be defined in the Working-Storage Section of the program. This data-name must be defined as a four-byte number, where the first two bytes represent the line where the cursor will be positioned and the last two bytes represent the column where the cursor will be positioned.

- By default, the cursor is positioned at the first input or update field on the screen. If the screen doesn't contain any input or update fields, the cursor is positioned in column 1 of line 1.

Figure 17-9   How to position the cursor

A COBOL program that uses screen definitions

In the following topics, you'll see a complete program that uses screen definitions to process screen I-O. This program is similar to the program presented earlier in this chapter except that it lets the user modify the data in a selected inventory record. Because of the increased functionality of this program, it's much easier to code using screen definitions.

The processing specifications

Figure 17-10 presents the basic specifications for the inventory maintenance program. To start, this program displays a screen that accepts an item number from the user. Then, if the user enters a valid item number, the program displays the data for that item on the screen. Because the fields for the data are defined as update fields, the user can modify them and then press Enter to accept the changes.

If any of the values entered by the user are invalid, the program displays an error message on line 23. In addition, it highlights the invalid field and moves the cursor to the first position in that field. Then, the user can enter another value and try to save the changes again. Alternatively, the user can enter an N after the "Save changes?" prompt to cancel the changes.

Although it's difficult to tell from the screens shown here, this program uses different colors to identify the different types of fields. For example, literal fields and output fields are displayed in blue and update fields are displayed in green. That makes it easy for the user to tell which fields are modifiable. In addition, error messages are displayed in red. Because you can use a variety of colors, you'll want to find out if your shop has any color standards before you develop a program like this.

Item number screen

The program accepts an item number from the user.

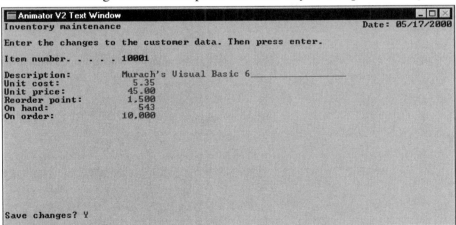

Item data screen

When the user enters an item number and presses the Enter key, the program retrieves the record for the inventory item and displays its data on the screen. Then, the user can change the data and press the Enter key to accept the changes.

Processing specifications

- This program works like the inquiry program presented in figure 17-4 except that it lets the user change the data for the selected item.
- The save-changes switch used on the second screen should default to Y so the changes are saved automatically when the user presses the Enter key.
- An entry is required for the description field, and the unit cost, unit price, and reorder point fields must be greater than zero. If one or more fields are in error, they should be highlighted and the cursor should be moved to the first field in error.

Figure 17-10   The processing specifications for the maintenance program

The structure chart

Figure 17-11 presents the structure chart for the maintenance program. The first thing you should notice about this structure chart is how simple it is. In fact, if you compare it to the structure chart for the inquiry program, you'll see that it's just as simple as that one, even though this program provides additional functionality.

Procedure 000 starts by performing module 100 to format the heading that will be displayed on the first line of the screen. Then, it performs module 200 to process each item number entered by the user. This module starts by performing module 210 repeatedly until the user enters a valid item number or ends the program. Module 210, in turn, performs module 220 to display the item number screen, module 230 to accept the item number screen, and module 240 to edit the item number entered by the user. To determine if the item number is valid, module 240 performs module 250 to read the inventory record for the item.

If the item number the user enters is valid, module 200 continues by performing module 260 to get the new data for the item. Like module 210, this module is performed repeatedly until the user enters valid data or cancels the modification. Module 260 starts by performing module 270 to display the current data on the screen. Then, it performs module 280 to accept any changes entered by the user and module 290 to edit the data. Finally, if the data entered by the user is valid, module 200 performs module 300 to rewrite the inventory record for the item.

The structure chart

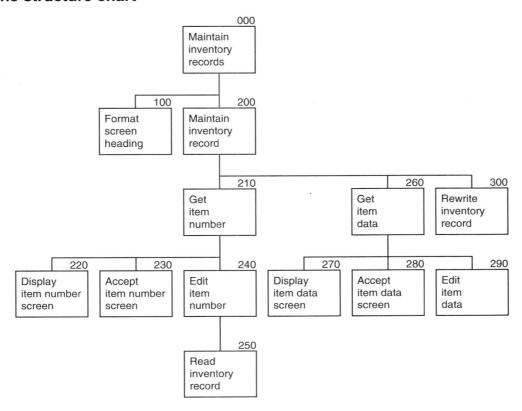

Description

- This program begins by performing module 100 to format the heading line that will be displayed on the screen. Then, it performs module 200 repeatedly until the user enters 99999 to end the program.

- Module 200 performs module 210 to get an item number from the user. If the item number is valid, module 200 performs module 260 to display the data for the inventory item and accept changes to the data. Then, if the changes are valid, module 200 performs module 300 to rewrite the record.

- Module 210 starts by performing module 220 to display the item number screen. Then, it performs module 230 to accept an item number from the user. Finally, it performs module 240 to edit the item number. This module performs module 250 to read the inventory record for the item.

- Module 260 performs module 270 to display the data for an inventory item, module 280 to accept changes to the data, and module 290 to edit the data.

Figure 17-11   The structure chart for the maintenance program

The COBOL listing

Figure 17-12 presents the complete COBOL listing for the inventory maintenance program. On the first page of this listing, you can see the Special-Names paragraph with the Cursor clause that will be used to implement cursor positioning. Then, in the Working-Storage Section, you can see the data description entry for the field this clause refers to.

The second page of this listing includes the definitions of the variables that will be used to control the attributes of some of the fields on the screen. These variables will be used to apply the Highlight attribute to a field that contains an invalid entry. Notice that each of these variables is defined with nine characters —just enough to hold the word "Highlight." If you want to be able to specify other attributes using these variables, though, you can make them as large as necessary.

Page 2 also includes the definitions for the four colors used by this program. Unlike the previous program, this program doesn't use constants for the color. That's because the Foreground-Color and Background-Color clauses of a screen description entry let you specify a data-name for the color. In contrast, the Accept and Display statements only let you specify an integer.

On page 3 of this listing, you can see the definitions of the two screens used by this program. These definitions correspond to the two screens in figure 17-10. When the program displays the first screen, it will clear the screen, set the default colors, and display the output and literal fields it defines. It will also display the current value of the IM-ITEM-NO field, since it's defined as an update field. Then, when the program accepts this screen, it will retrieve the value the user entered into the item number field.

When the program displays the second screen, it will display the current values in the inventory record for the selected item. When the program accepts this screen, it will retrieve the values of those fields. Notice that the definitions for most of these fields include a Control clause. That way, the program can change the attributes for these fields as needed. Also notice that all of the definitions for these fields include the Auto clause. That way, the cursor will move to the next update field automatically when the user completes the entry for the current field.

This screen overwrites the message in line 3 that was displayed by the first screen, and it redefines the item number field in line 5 so it's an output field rather than an update field. It also repeats the definition of the error message field in line 23 so its current value is retrieved from the error message variable when the screen is displayed. However, this screen doesn't repeat the definition of the screen heading field in line 1 since the value of this field doesn't change. Likewise, the literal in line 5 isn't repeated because it doesn't change.

The last two fields in this screen define the literal that's displayed to ask if the user wants to save the changes to the data and the switch that's used to accept the user's response. By default, this switch is set to Y so the user can just press the Enter key to accept the changes. The switch field also includes the Control clause so the program can highlight the entry if it's invalid.

The maintenance program   **Page 1**

```cobol
IDENTIFICATION DIVISION.

PROGRAM-ID. MNT1000.

ENVIRONMENT DIVISION.

CONFIGURATION SECTION.

SPECIAL-NAMES.

    CURSOR IS CURSOR-POSITION.

INPUT-OUTPUT SECTION.

FILE-CONTROL.

    SELECT INVMAST  ASSIGN TO "c:\cobol\data\invmasti.dat"
                    ORGANIZATION IS INDEXED
                    ACCESS IS RANDOM
                    RECORD KEY IS IR-ITEM-NO.

DATA DIVISION.

FILE SECTION.

FD  INVMAST.

01  INVENTORY-RECORD.

    05  IR-ITEM-NO      PIC X(5).
    05  FILLER          PIC X(65).

WORKING-STORAGE SECTION.

01  CURSOR-POSITION.

    05  CURSOR-LINE     PIC 99.
    05  CURSOR-COLUMN   PIC 99.

01  SWITCHES.

    05  END-OF-PROGRAM-SWITCH       PIC X   VALUE "N".
        88  END-OF-PROGRAM                  VALUE "Y".
    05  VALID-ENTRY-SWITCH          PIC X   VALUE "N".
        88  VALID-ENTRY                     VALUE "Y".
    05  ITEM-FOUND-SWITCH           PIC X   VALUE "Y".
        88  ITEM-FOUND                      VALUE "Y".
    05  SAVE-CHANGES-SWITCH         PIC X   VALUE "Y".
        88  SAVE-CHANGES                    VALUE "Y" "y".
```

Figure 17-12   The COBOL listing for the maintenance program (part 1 of 6)

The maintenance program

```
01   DATE-FIELDS.

     05   CURRENT-DATE-AND-TIME.
          10   CURRENT-YEAR          PIC 9999.
          10   CURRENT-MONTH         PIC 99.
          10   CURRENT-DAY           PIC 99.
          10   FILLER                PIC X(13).
     05   FORMATTED-DATE            PIC 9(8).
     05   FORMATTED-DATE-R          REDEFINES FORMATTED-DATE.
          10   FORMATTED-MONTH       PIC 99.
          10   FORMATTED-DAY         PIC 99.
          10   FORMATTED-YEAR        PIC 9999.

01   INVENTORY-MASTER-RECORD.

     05   IM-ITEM-NO               PIC X(5).
     05   IM-DESCRIPTIVE-DATA.
          10   IM-ITEM-DESC          PIC X(40).
          10   IM-UNIT-COST          PIC 999V99.
          10   IM-UNIT-PRICE         PIC 999V99.
     05   IM-INVENTORY-DATA.
          10   IM-REORDER-POINT      PIC S9(5).
          10   IM-ON-HAND            PIC S9(5).
          10   IM-ON-ORDER           PIC S9(5).

01   SCREEN-HEADING-LINE.

     05   SHL-PROGRAM-NAME     PIC X(50).
     05   FILLER               PIC X(14)    VALUE SPACE.
     05   FILLER               PIC X(6)     VALUE "Date: ".
     05   SHL-DATE             PIC 99/99/9999.

01   SCREEN-DISPLAY-FIELDS.

     05   ERROR-MESSAGE        PIC X(80)    VALUE SPACE.

01   ATTRIBUTE-CONTROL-FIELDS.

     05   ITEM-NUMBER-CONTROL       PIC X(9).
     05   ITEM-DESC-CONTROL         PIC X(9).
     05   UNIT-COST-CONTROL         PIC X(9).
     05   UNIT-PRICE-CONTROL        PIC X(9).
     05   REORDER-POINT-CONTROL     PIC X(9).
     05   SAVE-CHANGES-CONTROL      PIC X(9).

01   SCREEN-COLORS.

     05   BLUE       PIC S9(4)    VALUE 1.
     05   GREEN      PIC S9(4)    VALUE 2.
     05   RED        PIC S9(4)    VALUE 4.
     05   WHITE      PIC S9(4)    VALUE 7.
```

Figure 17-12   The COBOL listing for the maintenance program (part 2 of 6)

The maintenance program   **Page 3**

```
SCREEN SECTION.

01  ITEM-NUMBER-SCREEN.

    05   BLANK SCREEN
         BACKGROUND-COLOR WHITE
         FOREGROUND-COLOR BLUE.
    05   LINE 1   COLUMN 1  PIC X(80)    FROM SCREEN-HEADING-LINE.
    05   LINE 3   COLUMN 1  VALUE "Type an item number. Then press
-        "Enter.".
    05   LINE 5   COLUMN 1  VALUE "Item number. . . . . ".
    05   LINE 5   COLUMN 22 PIC X(5)     USING IM-ITEM-NO
         FOREGROUND-COLOR GREEN
         CONTROL ITEM-NUMBER-CONTROL.
    05   LINE 23 COLUMN 1   PIC X(80)    FROM ERROR-MESSAGE
         FOREGROUND-COLOR RED.
    05   LINE 24 COLUMN 1   VALUE "Enter 99999 to end.".

01  ITEM-DATA-SCREEN.

    05   LINE 3   COLUMN 1  VALUE "Enter the changes to the custome
-        "r data. Then press Enter.".
    05   LINE 5   COLUMN 22 PIC X(5)     FROM IM-ITEM-NO.
    05   LINE 7   COLUMN 1  VALUE "Description: ".
    05   LINE 7   COLUMN 22 PIC X(40)    USING IM-ITEM-DESC
         FOREGROUND-COLOR GREEN
         CONTROL ITEM-DESC-CONTROL AUTO.
    05   LINE 8   COLUMN 1  VALUE "Unit cost: ".
    05   LINE 8   COLUMN 22 PIC ZZZ.ZZ   USING IM-UNIT-COST
         FOREGROUND-COLOR GREEN
         CONTROL UNIT-COST-CONTROL AUTO.
    05   LINE 9   COLUMN 1  VALUE "Unit price: ".
    05   LINE 9   COLUMN 22 PIC ZZZ.ZZ   USING IM-UNIT-PRICE
         FOREGROUND-COLOR GREEN
         CONTROL UNIT-PRICE-CONTROL AUTO.
    05   LINE 10 COLUMN 1   VALUE "Reorder point: ".
    05   LINE 10 COLUMN 22 PIC ZZ,ZZZ    USING IM-REORDER-POINT
         FOREGROUND-COLOR GREEN
         CONTROL REORDER-POINT-CONTROL AUTO.
    05   LINE 11 COLUMN 1   VALUE "On hand: ".
    05   LINE 11 COLUMN 22 PIC ZZ,ZZZ    USING IM-ON-HAND
         FOREGROUND-COLOR GREEN AUTO.
    05   LINE 12 COLUMN 1   VALUE "On order: ".
    05   LINE 12 COLUMN 22 PIC ZZ,ZZZ    USING IM-ON-ORDER
         FOREGROUND-COLOR GREEN AUTO.
    05   LINE 23 COLUMN 1   PIC X(80)    FROM ERROR-MESSAGE
         FOREGROUND-COLOR RED.
    05   LINE 24 COLUMN 1   VALUE "Save changes?"
         BLANK LINE.
    05   LINE 24 COLUMN 15 PIC X         USING SAVE-CHANGES-SWITCH
         FOREGROUND-COLOR GREEN
         CONTROL SAVE-CHANGES-CONTROL.
```

Figure 17-12   The COBOL listing for the maintenance program (part 3 of 6)

Pages 4 through 6 of this listing show the Procedure Division code for this program. If you take a few minutes to review this code, you shouldn't have any trouble understanding how it works. But just to be sure, some highlights of the screen-handling code follow.

In procedure 200, you can see that Space is moved to the IM-Item-Number and Item-Number-Control fields before procedure 210 is performed to get an item number from the user. That way, the item number will be blank when the item number screen is first displayed, and it will be displayed with its default attributes. Likewise, Space is moved to the entire Attribute-Control-Fields group before procedure 260 is performed to get the data for an item so that all of the fields on the item data screen are displayed initially with their default attributes.

In procedures 220 and 230, you can see the Display and Accept statements for the item number screen. These statements just specify the name of the screen so the entire screen is displayed or accepted.

In procedure 240 on page 5, you can see the code that edits the item number entered by the user. Specifically, you can see that if the user doesn't enter an item number or enters an item number that's not found in the inventory file, an appropriate error message is moved to the error message field and the Highlight attribute is moved to the Item-Number-Control field. Then, when the item number screen is displayed again, the item number field is highlighted and the error message is displayed.

Procedures 270 and 280 contain the Display and Accept statements for the item data screen. Like the statements for the item number screen, these statements just specify the name of the screen.

Procedure 290 contains the code that checks the data entered on the item data screen to be sure it's valid. To start, it checks the value of the save-changes switch to be sure that it's an uppercase or lowercase N. If you look back at the definition of this switch on page 1 of this listing, you'll see that the value of the Save-Changes condition can be either an uppercase or a lowercase Y. That way, either of these values satisfies this condition. If the user doesn't enter one of these values, though, the program must check to be sure that an uppercase or lowercase N was entered. If not, the entry is invalid. In that case, an appropriate error message is moved to the error message field, the cursor is positioned so it will appear in that field, and the Highlight attribute is applied to the field.

If the user indicates that the changes should be saved, procedure 290 continues by checking the rest of the update fields on this screen. If an error is found, it sets the error message, cursor position, and field attributes accordingly. Notice that the fields are checked in reverse order from the order that they appear in on the screen. That way, if two or more fields are invalid, the error message will apply to the first field in error and the cursor will be positioned on that field. However, all of the fields in error will be highlighted.

The maintenance program   **Page 4**

```
PROCEDURE DIVISION.

000-MAINTAIN-INVENTORY-RECORDS.

    OPEN I-O INVMAST.
    PERFORM 100-FORMAT-SCREEN-HEADING.
    PERFORM 200-MAINTAIN-INVENTORY-RECORD
        UNTIL END-OF-PROGRAM.
    CLOSE INVMAST.
    STOP RUN.

100-FORMAT-SCREEN-HEADING.

    MOVE FUNCTION CURRENT-DATE TO CURRENT-DATE-AND-TIME.
    MOVE CURRENT-YEAR    TO FORMATTED-YEAR.
    MOVE CURRENT-MONTH   TO FORMATTED-MONTH.
    MOVE CURRENT-DAY     TO FORMATTED-DAY.
    MOVE FORMATTED-DATE TO SHL-DATE.
    MOVE "Inventory maintenance" TO SHL-PROGRAM-NAME.

200-MAINTAIN-INVENTORY-RECORD.

    MOVE "N" TO VALID-ENTRY-SWITCH.
    MOVE SPACE TO IM-ITEM-NO
                  ITEM-NUMBER-CONTROL.
    PERFORM 210-GET-ITEM-NUMBER
        UNTIL VALID-ENTRY.
    IF NOT END-OF-PROGRAM
        MOVE SPACE TO ATTRIBUTE-CONTROL-FIELDS
        MOVE "Y" TO SAVE-CHANGES-SWITCH
        MOVE "N" TO VALID-ENTRY-SWITCH
        PERFORM 260-GET-ITEM-DATA
            UNTIL VALID-ENTRY
        IF SAVE-CHANGES
            PERFORM 300-REWRITE-INVENTORY-RECORD.

210-GET-ITEM-NUMBER.

    MOVE "Y" TO VALID-ENTRY-SWITCH.
    PERFORM 220-DISPLAY-ITEM-NUMBER-SCREEN.
    PERFORM 230-ACCEPT-ITEM-NUMBER-SCREEN.
    PERFORM 240-EDIT-ITEM-NUMBER.

220-DISPLAY-ITEM-NUMBER-SCREEN.

    DISPLAY ITEM-NUMBER-SCREEN.

230-ACCEPT-ITEM-NUMBER-SCREEN.

    ACCEPT ITEM-NUMBER-SCREEN.
```

Figure 17-12   The COBOL listing for the maintenance program (part 4 of 6)

The maintenance program

```
240-EDIT-ITEM-NUMBER.

    MOVE SPACE TO ERROR-MESSAGE.
    IF IM-ITEM-NO = "99999"
        MOVE "Y" TO END-OF-PROGRAM-SWITCH
    ELSE IF IM-ITEM-NO = SPACE
        MOVE "N" TO VALID-ENTRY-SWITCH
        MOVE "An item number is required." TO ERROR-MESSAGE
        MOVE "HIGHLIGHT" TO ITEM-NUMBER-CONTROL
    ELSE
        MOVE "Y" TO ITEM-FOUND-SWITCH
        MOVE IM-ITEM-NO TO IR-ITEM-NO
        PERFORM 250-READ-INVENTORY-RECORD
        IF NOT ITEM-FOUND
            MOVE "N" TO VALID-ENTRY-SWITCH
            MOVE "Inventory record not found." TO ERROR-MESSAGE
            MOVE "HIGHLIGHT" TO ITEM-NUMBER-CONTROL.

250-READ-INVENTORY-RECORD.

    READ INVMAST INTO INVENTORY-MASTER-RECORD
        INVALID KEY
            MOVE "N" TO ITEM-FOUND-SWITCH.

260-GET-ITEM-DATA.

    MOVE "Y" TO VALID-ENTRY-SWITCH.
    PERFORM 270-DISPLAY-ITEM-DATA-SCREEN.
    PERFORM 280-ACCEPT-ITEM-DATA-SCREEN.
    PERFORM 290-EDIT-ITEM-DATA.

270-DISPLAY-ITEM-DATA-SCREEN.

    DISPLAY ITEM-DATA-SCREEN.

280-ACCEPT-ITEM-DATA-SCREEN.

    ACCEPT ITEM-DATA-SCREEN.

290-EDIT-ITEM-DATA.

    MOVE SPACE TO ERROR-MESSAGE.
    IF NOT SAVE-CHANGES
        IF SAVE-CHANGES-SWITCH NOT = "N" AND NOT = "n"
            MOVE "You must enter 'Y' or 'N'" TO ERROR-MESSAGE
            MOVE 24 TO CURSOR-LINE
            MOVE 15 TO CURSOR-COLUMN
            MOVE "HIGHLIGHT" TO SAVE-CHANGES-CONTROL
        END-IF
    ELSE
```

Figure 17-12   The COBOL listing for the maintenance program (part 5 of 6)

The maintenance program   **Page 6**

```
        IF IM-REORDER-POINT NOT > 0
            MOVE "Reorder point must be greater than zero."
                TO ERROR-MESSAGE
            MOVE 10 TO CURSOR-LINE
            MOVE 22 TO CURSOR-COLUMN
            MOVE "HIGHLIGHT" TO REORDER-POINT-CONTROL
        END-IF
        IF IM-UNIT-PRICE NOT > 0
            MOVE "Unit price must be greater than zero."
                TO ERROR-MESSAGE
            MOVE 9  TO CURSOR-LINE
            MOVE 22 TO CURSOR-COLUMN
            MOVE "HIGHLIGHT" TO UNIT-PRICE-CONTROL
        ELSE
            IF IM-UNIT-PRICE NOT > IM-UNIT-COST
                MOVE "Unit price must be greater than unit cost."
                    TO ERROR-MESSAGE
                MOVE 9  TO CURSOR-LINE
                MOVE 22 TO CURSOR-COLUMN
                MOVE "HIGHLIGHT" TO UNIT-PRICE-CONTROL
            END-IF
        END-IF
        IF IM-UNIT-COST NOT > 0
            MOVE "Unit cost must be greater than zero."
                TO ERROR-MESSAGE
            MOVE 8  TO CURSOR-LINE
            MOVE 22 TO CURSOR-COLUMN
            MOVE "HIGHLIGHT" TO UNIT-COST-CONTROL
        END-IF
        IF IM-ITEM-DESC = SPACE
            MOVE "Item description required." TO ERROR-MESSAGE
            MOVE 7  TO CURSOR-LINE
            MOVE 22 TO CURSOR-COLUMN
            MOVE "HIGHLIGHT" TO ITEM-DESC-CONTROL
        END-IF
    END-IF.
    IF ERROR-MESSAGE NOT = SPACE
        MOVE "N" TO VALID-ENTRY-SWITCH.

300-REWRITE-INVENTORY-RECORD.

    REWRITE INVENTORY-RECORD FROM INVENTORY-MASTER-RECORD
        INVALID KEY
            DISPLAY "Invalid REWRITE on item number "
                IR-ITEM-NO.
```

Figure 17-12   The COBOL listing for the maintenance program (part 6 of 6)

Perspective

Now that you've learned how to use both the enhanced Accept and Display statements and screen definitions for screen I-O, you may want to take a few minutes to compare the two techniques. If you do, I think you'll see that using the enhanced Accept and Display statements can quickly get out of control. As a result, you'll want to use screen definitions for all but the simplest applications.

Although this chapter has presented the major features for developing programs that use screen I-O, Micro Focus COBOL also provides other features that you should be aware of. In particular, you may want to know how to develop a program that provides for the use of the function keys and the mouse. For more information about other features for screen I-O, please refer to the Micro Focus *COBOL Reference Manual*.

Summary

- Micro Focus COBOL includes extensions to standard COBOL that let a program interact with the user using sophisticated screen I-O. These extensions are similar to the features for screen I-O that will be included in the 2002 standards.

- If you want to accept and display one field at a time, you can use the enhanced formats of the Accept and Display statements. These statements let you control screen attributes such as screen color and field positions.

- To use screen colors with the Accept and Display statement, you can use integers that represent the colors, or you can define *constants*. To define a constant, you code a level 78 data description entry.

- If you want to accept and display groups of fields or an entire screen at one time, you code screen definitions in the Screen Section of the Data Division. Each screen definition includes *screen description entries* that define the fields on the screen.

- A screen description entry can define a *literal field*, an *input field*, an *output field*, or an *update field*. Literal fields, output fields, and update fields are displayed using the Display statement. Input fields and update fields are retrieved using the Accept statement.

Terms

constant	input field	update field
screen description entry	output field	literal field

Objectives

- Given the specifications for a program that requires screen I-O, use the enhanced formats of the Accept and Display statements to develop it.

- Given the specifications for a program that requires screen I-O, use screen definitions to develop it.

- List four options that you can code on the With clause of an Accept or Display statement and explain what each one does.

- Explain the purpose of the Prompt and Auto options that you can code on the With clause of an Accept statement.

- List the four types of fields you can define with screen description entries, and name the clauses you use to define them.

- Explain how you use the Control clause of a screen description entry.

- Describe the code you must use to position the cursor when you use screen definitions for screen I-O.

Exercise 17-1   Use the enhanced Accept and Display statements

In this exercise, you'll modify the sales tax program presented in chapter 1 so it uses enhanced Accept and Display statements. When you run this program, the screen display should look something like this:

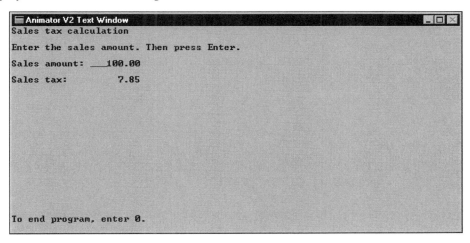

1. Start Personal COBOL, and open the calc1000 program. Then, change the Program-ID to INT1000, save the program as int1000, and close and re-open it.

2. Modify this program so it implements the screen layout shown above with enhanced Accept and Display statements. The default background color for the screen should be white (7), the default foreground color should be blue (1), and both colors should be defined as 78 levels.

3. When you've got the program working the way you want it to, close it.

Exercise 17-2 Use screen definitions

In this exercise, you'll modify the sales tax program you worked on in exercise 17-1 so it uses screen definitions.

1. Open the program named int1000 that you created in exercise set 17-1. Then, change the Program-ID to INT2000, save the program as int2000, and close and re-open it.

2. Modify the program so it implements the screen layout shown for exercise 17-1 with screen definitions in the Screen Section of the Data Division. Here again, the default background color should be white (7), and the default foreground color should be blue (1). In addition, the sales-amount field should be displayed in green (2). This time, the colors should be defined as normal field definitions, not 78 levels.

3. When you've got the program working the way you want it to, close it.

18

How to compile and test a program on an IBM mainframe

If you're working on an IBM mainframe system, you need to know how to use the facilities for developing COBOL programs on that system. That's what you'll learn in this chapter. Keep in mind, though, that this chapter presents only enough for you to get by. To learn more about any of the topics presented here, you can refer to some of our other books. For more information, see the perspective at the end of this chapter.

An introduction to mainframe program development

When you develop a COBOL program on an IBM mainframe system, you have to follow some specific steps to compile and test it. So this topic begins by describing those steps. Then, it describes some of the operating system facilities you'll use to perform these steps.

How a COBOL program is compiled, link-edited, and executed

In general, it takes three steps to compile and test a COBOL program on an IBM mainframe system as illustrated in figure 18-1. In the first step, the COBOL compiler reads the program you've written, called the *source program*, and converts it to an *object module* that is stored on disk. If the source program uses copy members, they're inserted into the program during this step.

Typically, the compiler produces printed output as part of this step. Among other things, this output can include a *compilation listing* that shows the COBOL statements in the program, including any copy members. The listing can also include a description of any *compile-time errors* that occurred during this step.

If the program compiles without any errors, the second step can be performed. In this step, a program called a *linkage editor* (or *link editor*) links the object module with any subprograms that it requires. These can be system subprograms or COBOL subprograms that you or another programmer has written. Note that if you include a COBOL subprogram, it must already be compiled into an object module.

The output of the link-edit step is a *load module* that is stored on disk. This is your program in a form that can be executed. The linkage editor can also create printed output that identifies the programs included in the load module.

In the third step, the executable program is run so you can see how it works. The input to this program is whatever the program calls for, and the output is whatever your program produces. In the programs in chapter 1 of this book, for example, the input is whatever the user enters through the keyboard, and the output is what's displayed on the user's screen. In the report programs in the other chapters in section 1, the input is a disk file that contains customer records, and the output is a printed report.

If a program runs until the Stop Run statement is executed, that's considered to be a normal completion, or *normal termination*. If an error occurs that causes the program to be interrupted or cancelled before it reaches the Stop Run statement, that's called an *abnormal termination* (or *abend*). This type of error, called a *run-time error*, occurs when a statement compiles cleanly but can't be executed.

A compile, link, and execute procedure

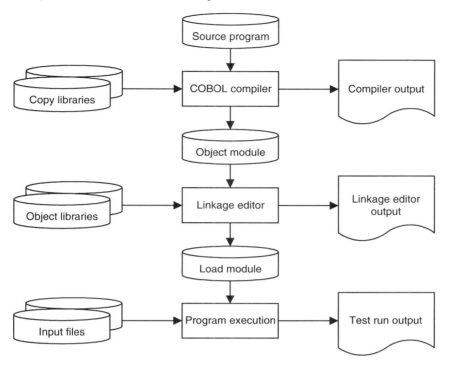

Step 1

- The COBOL compiler compiles the *source program* into an *object module*. If necessary, it gets the copy members it needs for the compilation from the specified copy libraries.
- During compilation, the compiler produces output that can be printed or displayed on the terminal or monitor.

Step 2

- The *linkage editor* links the object program with any subprograms it needs, thus creating an executable program called a *load module*.
- On most systems, the linkage editor links the object program with one or more system subprograms. However, it can also link it with COBOL subprograms.

Step 3

- The executable program runs so you can see whether it works correctly. This is the testing phase of program development.

Figure 18-1   How a COBOL program is compiled, link-edited, and executed

An introduction to the OS/390 program development environment

Figure 18-2 describes some of the program development facilities that are available with the current IBM mainframe operating system, called *OS/390*. This operating system provides a variety of facilities for developing COBOL programs. Before you learn the specifics for developing COBOL programs, then, you need to know about these facilities.

Like most operating systems, the OS/390 provides for both *batch processing* and *interactive processing*. With batch processing, a program is executed in the background without any user intervention. In contrast, an interactive program is executed in the foreground where the user can interact with it.

To perform batch processing under OS/390, you use *JCL* (*Job Control Language*). JCL processes work in units called *jobs*. A job causes one or more programs to be executed in sequence. Later in this chapter, for example, you'll see a job that compiles, link-edits, and executes a COBOL program.

To perform interactive processing under OS/390, you use *TSO* (*Time Sharing Option*). TSO is a subsystem that lets terminal users invoke MVS facilities interactively. TSO does this by treating each terminal user as a job.

ISPF (*Interactive System Productivity Facility*) runs as a part of TSO and takes advantage of the full-screen capabilities of IBM terminals. You'll most likely use a part of ISPF called *PDF* (*Program Development Facility*) as you develop programs and jobs. Although ISPF is an optional feature of OS/390, it's the interactive facility used in most mainframe shops.

This figure also describes the different *run-time environments* used by VS COBOL II and COBOL for MVS and COBOL for OS/390 programs. Programs written in COBOL for MVS and COBOL for OS/390 run in an environment called *Language Environment*. This environment provides essential run-time services, such as message handling, condition handling, and storage management, to all the high-level languages, including COBOL. In contrast, programs written in VS COBOL II execute in their own run-time environment.

Both the Language Environment and the VS COBOL II run-time environment provide debugging tools that you can use to help debug your programs. Because many shops don't use these tools, they aren't described in this chapter. If your shop uses them, though, or if it uses a third-party debugging tool, you'll want to find out how to use that tool.

A program development procedure

Figure 18-2 also presents a general procedure for developing COBOL programs using the OS/390 facilities. Note that instead of entering the source code directly onto the mainframe system, you can first enter and test it on a PC using a program like MicroFocus Personal COBOL (see chapter 2). Then, you can upload it to the mainframe for additional testing using one of several products that have been developed just for that purpose.

OS/390 program development facilities

- *OS/*390 is the operating system that runs on the current mainframe architecture called the *System/390*. This system provides many of the same features as a PC-based network, but can manage large volumes of data that those systems can't.

- OS/390 provides for both *batch processing* and *interactive processing*. Interactive processing is implemented using TSO, and batch processing is implemented using JCL.

- *TSO*, which stands for *Time Sharing Option*, is an OS/390 subsystem that lets terminal users invoke OS/390 facilities interactively. To use TSO, you issue TSO commands.

- *ISPF*, which stands for *Interactive System Productivity Facility*, provides a menu-driven, full-screen interface to most of TSO's features. You can use a part of ISPF called *PDF*, or *Program Development Facility*, to develop COBOL source programs and the JCL to compile, link-edit, and execute those programs.

- When batch processing is used, work is processed in units called *jobs*. *JCL*, or *Job Control Language*, describes a job by providing information that identifies the programs to be executed and the data to be processed.

COBOL run-time environments

- Before a COBOL program can be run, a *run-time environment* must be established. The run-time environment determines the facilities that are available to the program and how the program interacts with the operating system.

- VS COBOL II has its own run-time environment. This environment includes a debugging tool called VS COBOL II Debug that lets you debug a program in batch mode, interactive line mode, or interactive full-screen mode.

- COBOL for MVS and COBOL for OS/390 programs run in an environment called *Language Environment* that provides a common run-time environment for all the high-level languages, including COBOL, C, C++, Fortran, and PL/I. Language Environment includes a debugging tool called Debug Tool that lets you debug a program in batch mode, interactive line mode, or interactive full-screen mode.

A general procedure for developing COBOL programs

1. Enter the source code for the program using an editor like the one that comes with ISPF. Or, develop the program on a PC, then upload the source code to the mainframe and modify it as necessary.

2. Compile and link-edit the program using JCL. Correct any errors that are detected by the compiler, and compile and link-edit the program again. Repeat until all errors are corrected.

3. Run the program using JCL or TSO commands.

4. Review the output to make sure the program worked correctly. If necessary, use any available debugging tools to determine the cause of an abnormal termination or programming error. Then, correct the program and compile, link-edit, and test it again until it works as intended.

Figure 18-2   The OS/390 program development environment

How to create a source program using ISPF

In this topic, you'll learn how use the text editor that comes with ISPF to create your COBOL source programs. Before you can use this editor, though, you need to use another ISPF facility to create the data sets you'll need for your programs. So you'll learn how to do that right after you learn some basic skills for working with ISPF.

Basic skills for working with ISPF

To work with ISPF, you use its Primary Option Menu shown in figure 18-3. Since the exact procedure you use to access this menu varies from one installation to another, you need to find out how it's done at your installation. In general, though, you'll need to log on to TSO and then start ISPF by entering the ISPF command. By the way, most installations customize the Primary Option Menu, so the menu you see at your installation may not look like the one in this figure.

To use the Primary Option Menu, you simply enter the number or letter for the option you want in the *command area* at the top of the display screen, also called a *panel*. To edit the source code for a program, for example, you enter 2 in the command area and then press the Enter key. Then, ISPF displays a panel that lets you identify the file you want to edit.

Besides entering commands in the command area, you can control certain ISPF functions using the *program function (PF) keys*. This figure shows the default meanings of the more commonly used PF keys. These defaults may be changed at your installation, so be sure to find out what function each key performs on your system.

Most of the PF keys described in this figure are self-explanatory. However, you'll want to note the difference between the PF3/15 key, called the end key, and the PF4/16 key, called the return key. Although both keys terminate the current ISPF function, PF3/15 returns to the previous panel and PF4/16 returns directly to the Primary Option Menu.

The ISPF Primary Option Menu

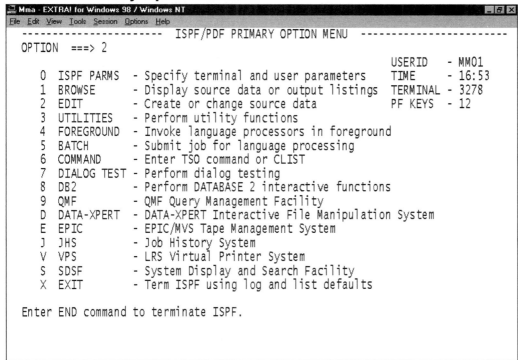

Commonly used PF keys

PF key	Command	Meaning
PF1/13	Help	Displays the online tutorial or additional information on an error message.
PF3/15	End	Returns to the previous panel.
PF4/16	Return	Returns directly to the Primary Option Menu.
PF7/19	Up	Scrolls the display up.
PF8/20	Down	Scrolls the display down.
PF10/22	Left	Scrolls the display to the left.
PF11/23	Right	Scrolls the display to the right.

Description

- If the Primary Option Menu isn't displayed when you log on to TSO, you can usually display it by entering ISPF at the TSO ready prompt. Check with your system administrator for the exact procedure at your shop.

- To select a menu option, enter it in the *command area* (Option ===>) and press the Enter key.

- You can control certain ISPF functions using *program function* (*PF*) *keys* like those shown above.

Figure 18-3   Basic skills for working with ISPF

How to create a partitioned data set

The files on a mainframe system are typically referred to as *data sets*. Although you can create several different types of data sets, you'll only learn about one here: the *partitioned data set*, also called a *PDS* or *library*. This is the type of data set you'll use to store your COBOL source programs as well as the object and load modules created from them and the JCL used to compile, link-edit, and execute them. Later in this chapter, you'll learn how to create a *sequential data set* that you can use to store the data used as input to a program.

A partitioned data set consists of a *directory* and one or more *members*. A directory is simply a list of the members in the library. And each member is functionally the same as a sequential data set. When you develop COBOL programs, for example, you'll store the source code for each program as a member of the same partitioned data set.

Figure 18-4 describes how you create, or *allocate*, a partitioned data set using the Data Set Utility panel. When you create a data set, you give it a name that follows a particular pattern. Specifically, each data set name must consist of one or more qualifiers separated by periods. Each qualifier can be a maximum of eight characters, and the entire data set name, including the periods, can be a maximum of 44 characters.

Under ISPF, a data set name typically consists of three qualifiers as shown in the panels in this figure. The first qualifier, also called the *high-level qualifier*, identifies the project and is typically your TSO user-id. In this example, the high-level qualifier is MM01. The second qualifier is the group name. This is usually a name you make up to identify the contents of the data set. In this example, the group name is TEST, which indicates that the data it contains is still under development. The third qualifier is the type, which indicates the type of data the data set contains. When you develop COBOL programs, you typically use some standard type qualifiers, like COBOL for COBOL source programs, OBJ or OBJLIB for object modules, LOAD or LOADLIB for load modules, and CNTL for JCL. In this example, the data set that's being created will contain COBOL source programs, so the type is COBOL.

When you create a partitioned data set as shown in this figure, the attributes for the data set default to the attributes for the last data set you created. If that's not what you want, you'll need to change them. In particular, you'll want to be sure that you specify the right amount of space for the data set. You'll also want to be sure that you specify the right number of directory blocks and that you enter PDS for the data set name type so that a partitioned data set is created rather than a sequential data set. For more information on the appropriate attributes, see your system administrator.

The panels for creating a partitioned data set

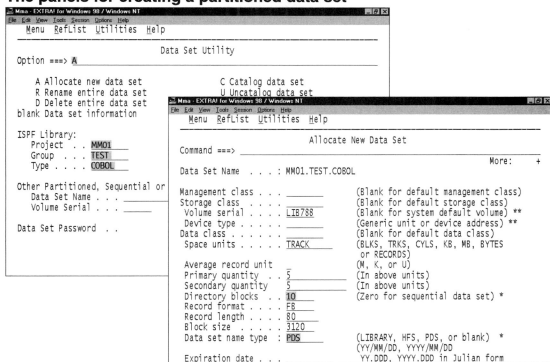

Concepts

- On a mainframe system, files are referred to as *data sets*. Each data set has a name that consists of one or more *qualifiers* separated by periods, like MM01.TEST.COBOL.

- Under ISPF, a data set name consists of a project-id, which is usually your TSO user-id; a library name or group name that can be any name you want; and a type that indicates the kind of data that's stored in the data set.

- You typically store program development data like source, object, and load files in *partitioned data sets*. A partitioned data set can contain one or more *members* that are functionally the same as sequential files.

Description

- Before you can use a new or existing data set, you must *allocate* it. To allocate a new data set, you can use the Data Set Utility panel shown above. To display this panel, select option 3 (Utilities) from the Primary Option Menu, then select option 2 (Data Set) from the Utility Selection panel that's displayed.

- To create a partitioned data set, or *library*, enter A in the command area; enter the Project, Group, and Type components of the data set name; and press Enter. Then, enter the appropriate information on the Allocate New Data Set panel, and press Enter.

Figure 18-4   How to create a partitioned data set

How to start an edit session

The ISPF editor lets you enter data and store it in a library member. It also lets you retrieve data from a library member and make changes to it. Figure 18-5 shows you how to start an edit session.

On the Edit Entry Panel, you enter the name of the library and member you want to edit. If you enter the name of a member that already exists, ISPF displays the data it contains in the edit data display shown in the next figure. If you enter the name of a new member, the edit data display will be empty so you can enter the data for that member.

In the last topic, you learned that the type you specify for a partitioned data set identifies the type of data the data set contains. When you edit a member of a partitioned data set, the editor uses the type to determine the *edit profile* it uses. If a partitioned data set has the type COBOL, for example, the editor will use the COBOL profile when you edit any of its members. This profile specifies, among other things, that the member contains 80-character, fixed-length records; that standard COBOL numbering should be used; and that tabs should be set at columns 7, 8, and every fourth column after that. Although the editor provides a number of commands that you can use to change the profile settings, you don't usually need to do that.

The Edit Entry panel

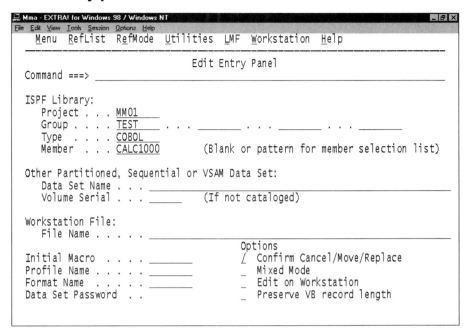

Description

- To display the Edit Entry panel, select option 2 (Edit) from the Primary Option Menu.

- To edit a member of a partitioned data set, enter the names of the data set and member and press Enter.

- If the member you specify already exists, its contents are displayed in the edit data display shown in the next figure. If the member doesn't exist, the edit data display is blank.

- ISPF uses the data set type to determine the *edit profile* it uses. The edit profile contains settings such as the number of columns in the editing area, the type of numbering that's used, the tab settings, and whether recovery mode is on or off.

Figure 18-5   How to start an edit session

How to work in the edit data display

Figure 18-6 shows the panel, called the *edit data display*, that's displayed when you create a new member. This panel consists of three distinct areas. The top two lines of the panel form the *heading area*. In this area, you can enter commands, called *primary commands*, that invoke various editing functions. The leftmost six columns of lines 3 through 24 form the *line command area*. In this area, you can enter *line commands* that affect specific lines. The rest of the panel is the *screen window*. In this area, you can enter the data for a new member or change the data for an existing member.

In this figure, a new member is displayed so the screen window is blank. To enter data in the screen window, you can just key in the characters you want in the positions you want. To move the cursor around the screen, you can use the terminal's cursor control keys. If you want to change the text displayed on the screen, you just type the new data over the old. When you're finished, you press the Enter key. Then, ISPF removes the lines you didn't key data into and re-places the apostrophes in the line command area of the other lines with line numbers.

Although you can start a COBOL program by typing code in the screen window, you probably won't want to do that. Instead, you'll want to start it from an existing program. To do that, you can use the COPY command to copy the existing program into the screen window. You'll learn more about the COPY commands and other commands you can use in the editor in the next topic.

If the member contains more data than can be displayed on a single screen, you'll need to use the PF7/19 and PF8/20 keys that were presented in figure 18-3 to scroll backwards and forwards through the source member. When you use these keys, the number of lines that are scrolled is determined by the scroll setting. You can see this setting at the right-hand side of the second line of the heading area. In this case, the setting is CSR, which means that the member will scroll so the line that contains the cursor is displayed at the top of the window. Three common scroll settings are listed in this figure.

The edit data display for a new data set

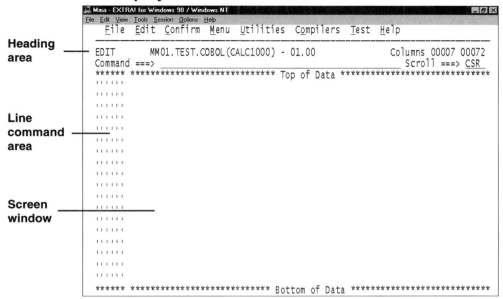

Heading area

Line command area

Screen window

Common scroll settings

Setting	Function
PAGE	Scrolls a whole page of data.
HALF	Scrolls half a page of data.
CSR	Scrolls to the line or column where the cursor is positioned.

Description

- The first line of the *heading area* identifies the file being edited and the leftmost and rightmost columns where editing is allowed.
- The second line of the heading area contains a command area where you can enter *primary commands* to invoke various editing functions. It also contains a scroll field where you can indicate the amount of data you want to scroll for each scroll operation.
- The leftmost six columns of lines 3 through 24 form the *line command area*. In this area, you can enter *line commands* that affect specific lines.
- The rest of the panel is the *screen window*. This is where the data for the member you're editing is displayed.

How to start a new member from an existing member

- Enter the COPY command in the command area and press the Enter key. Then, identify the existing member you want to copy in the panel that's displayed.

Figure 18-6   How to work in the edit data display

How to use line commands and primary commands

Figure 18-7 lists some of the most useful line and primary commands that you can use with the editor. As you can see, you can use line commands to delete lines, insert new lines, repeat lines, and move or copy lines. The commands shown in the edit data display in this figure, for example, will move (M) the line that contains the definition for the end-of-session switch before (B) the line that contains the definition for the sales-amount field.

Although the Move command shown in this figure operates on a single line, you can also enter commands that operate on a block of lines. To delete a block of lines, for example, you can enter DD in the first and last lines to be deleted. You can also specify the exact number of lines you want a command to affect by entering that number after the command. To insert 10 lines for example, you can enter I10. Then, 10 empty lines will be displayed after the line where you entered the command.

The primary commands let you perform functions like locating specific lines or text, changing all occurrences of a character string to another string, retrieving data from other members, and terminating the editor. One command you'll use frequently is CHANGE. For example, you could use this command to change all occurrences of the field named SALES-TAX to TAX-AMOUNT:

```
CHANGE SALES-TAX TAX-AMOUNT ALL
```

Another command you'll want to use is COPY. This command lets you copy data from another member. You'll want to do that when you start a new program so you don't have to code it from scratch. The easiest way to use the COPY command is to enter COPY in the command area and press the Enter key. Then, ISPF displays a panel that prompts you for the name of the member you want to copy. This panel also lets you specify the lines you want to copy if you don't want to copy the whole member.

Although none of the primary commands are illustrated here, you shouldn't have any trouble using them. Keep in mind, though, that most of the commands have more complicated formats than what's shown in this figure. So you may want to find out more about these and other commands.

How to terminate an edit session

In most cases, you'll end an edit session by pressing the end key (PF3/15). When you do that, ISPF saves the changes you made and returns you to the Edit Entry Panel where you can specify another member to edit. If you use PF4/16 instead, your changes are saved and you're returned to the Primary Option Menu. And if you enter the CANCEL primary command, ISPF ends the edit session without saving your changes.

The edit data display with M and B line commands

```
Mma - EXTRA! for Windows 98 / Windows NT                                      _ □ X
File  Edit  View  Tools  Session  Options  Help
   File   Edit  Confirm   Menu   Utilities   Compilers   Test   Help
─────────────────────────────────────────────────────────────────────────────
EDIT       MM01.TEST.COBOL(CALC1000) - 01.00          Columns 00007 00072
Command ===> _____ Scroll ===> CSR
000400  WORKING-STORAGE SECTION.
000500 *
B00700   77   SALES-AMOUNT              PIC S9(5)V99.
000800   77   SALES-TAX                 PIC Z,ZZZ.99.
M00900   77   END-OF-SESSION-SWITCH     PIC X        VALUE "N".
001000 *
001100  PROCEDURE DIVISION.
001200 *
```

Basic line commands

I/I*n*	Insert 1 or *n* lines following this line.
D/D*n*/DD	Delete this line, *n* lines beginning with this line, or the block of lines beginning and ending with DD.
R/R*n*/RR/RR*n*	Repeat this line or the block of lines beginning and ending with RR 1 or *n* times.
C/C*n*/CC	Copy this line 1 or *n* times, or copy the block of lines beginning and ending with CC.
M/M*n*/MM	Move this line 1 or *n* times, or move the block of lines beginning and ending with MM.
A/A*n*	Copy or move lines 1 or *n* times after this line.
B/B*n*	Copy or move lines 1 or *n* times before this line.

Useful primary commands

LOCATE *line-number*	Moves to the indicated line.
FIND *string*	Finds the first occurrence of *string*, starting from the current line. To find the next occurrence, press PF5.
CHANGE *string-1 string-2* [ALL]	Finds the first occurrence of *string-1*, starting from the current line, and changes it to *string-2*. To find the next occurrence, press PF5. To change the next occurrence, press PF6. To change all occurrences, include the ALL option.
COPY *member-name*	Retrieves data from the specified member; use an A or B line command to specify where the data should be placed. If you omit *member-name*, ISPF displays a panel that lets you enter a library and member name.
PROFILE	Displays the profile settings for the edit session.
RECOVERY [ON|OFF]	Determines whether edit recovery mode is on. Edit recovery mode lets you recover data after a system failure or power outage. It also lets you reverse editing changes using the UNDO command.
UNDO	Reverses the last editing change.
SAVE	Saves changes and continues the edit session.
END (PF3/15)	Saves changes and returns to the Edit Entry panel.
RETURN (PF4/16)	Saves changes and returns to the Primary Option Menu.
CANCEL	Returns to the edit entry panel without saving changes.

Figure 18-7   How to use line commands and primary commands

How to compile, link-edit, and execute a program

You can use several techniques to compile, link-edit, and execute a program under OS/390. One way to do that is to issue TSO commands. Another is to use the program development panels provided by ISPF. The most common way to compile, link-edit, and execute a program, though, is to use JCL along with the cataloged procedures provided by IBM. That's the technique you'll learn about in this topic. But first, you need to know the basics of creating jobs and using Job Control Language.

An introduction to jobs and Job Control Language

Figure 18-8 presents a simple job that contains JCL to print a member of a partitioned data set. I'll use this job to describe the basic format of a JCL statement and to describe the three JCL statements that you'll find in almost every job: JOB, EXEC, and DD.

A JCL statement consists of the four fields identified in this figure: the *identifier field*, the *name field*, the *operation field*, and the *parameters field*. Note that some of these fields must be coded in specific columns, so you'll want to follow the guidelines presented in this figure carefully. In addition, you'll want to align the fields as shown in this figure to make your JCL more readable.

Each job must begin with a JOB statement that identifies the job and supplies information related to the job and how it's processed. Because a variety of parameters and options are available for this statement, I won't describe them in detail. But you'll want to find out what's required for your installation.

Each job consists of one or more *job steps* identified by EXEC statements. The job in this figure consists of just one job step that executes a utility program named IEBGENER. The purpose of this program is to copy data from a file to a printer. It requires the four files defined by the DD statements in the job.

The first DD statement, named SYSPRINT, is for a printed listing of informational messages produced by the IEBGENER program. The specification SYSOUT=* tells MVS to direct the file to the default printer. The second DD statement, SYSUT1, identifies the input file to be copied to the printer. In this case, it's a member named CUSTMAST in a partitioned data set named MM01.COPYLIB.COBOL. The third DD statement, SYSUT2, is for the output file. As you can see, this output will be sent to the default printer along with the rest of the printed output. The last DD statement, SYSIN, isn't required for this job, so it's coded as a dummy data set.

To create a job like the one shown in this figure, you can use ISPF as described earlier in this chapter. Then, you can submit the job for processing by entering the SUBMIT primary command from the edit data display for the job.

JCL statements for a job that prints a library member

Identifier field

Name field	Operation field	Parameters field

```
//MM01P     JOB   (36512),'A PRINCE',NOTIFY=&SYSUID
//STEP1     EXEC  PGM=IEBGENER
//SYSPRINT  DD    SYSOUT=*
//SYSUT1    DD    DSN=MM01.COPYLIB.COBOL(CUSTMAST),DISP=SHR
//SYSUT2    DD    SYSOUT=*
//SYSIN     DD    DUMMY
```

Concepts

- A job consists of one or more *job steps*. Each job step executes a program or procedure.

- The *identifier field* identifies the statement as a JCL statement. For most statements, the identifier field consists of two slashes (//) in columns 1 and 2.

- The *name field* associates a name with the statement. The name consists of from one to eight characters and must begin in column 3.

- The *operation field* specifies the statement's function. It can be coded in any column, as long as it's separated from the name field by at least one blank.

- The *parameters field* begins at least one position after the end of the operation field and can extend into column 71. Within the parameters field, you can code one or more *parameters* that supply information that influences how the statement is processed.

- To continue a statement to another line, break the parameter field after a comma, code slashes in columns 1 and 2 of the following line, and code the next parameter beginning anywhere in columns 4 through 16.

Basic JCL statements

- The JOB statement must always be the first statement coded for a job. It identifies the job and supplies a *job name* (MM01P in the job shown above). It also supplies accounting information and various options that influence or limit how the job is processed.

- The EXEC statement identifies the program or procedure to be executed in the job step (a utility program named IEBGENER in the job shown above). To identify a job step, you can code a *step name* in the name field (STEP1 in the job shown above).

- The DD statement allocates the data sets required by the program or procedure specified in the preceding EXEC statement. The *ddname* you specify (SYSPRINT, SYSUT1, SYSUT2, and SYSIN in the job shown above) must be the same as the name that's used for the file in the program or procedure.

- If a program creates printed output, you typically code the DD statement for the printer file using the SYSOUT = * format. Then, the output is processed based on the output class you specify in the MSGCLASS parameter of the JOB statement.

- If a file that's used by a program or procedure isn't required, you can specify a dummy data set for it by coding the DUMMY parameter on the DD statement for the file.

Figure 18-8   An introduction to jobs and Job Control Language

The cataloged procedures for COBOL program development

To simplify the program development process, IBM provides *cataloged procedures* that contain most of the JCL you need to compile, link-edit, and execute your programs. Figure 18-9 presents the cataloged procedures that are provided for COBOL program development. As you can see, the procedures you use depend on whether you're using VS COBOL II or COBOL for MVS or OS/ 390.

This figure also shows the names of the job steps included in each procedure. The compile, link, and go procedure for VS COBOL II, for example, consists of three steps named COB2, LKED, and GO. The same procedure for COBOL for MVS and OS/390 consists of the same steps, but the compile step is named COBOL instead of COB2.

Each job step in these procedures requires one or more input files. These files are defined using the DD statements and ddnames indicated in this figure. The SYSIN data set that's defined on the COB2 or COBOL step, for example, identifies the source program you want to compile. And the SYSLMOD data set that's defined on the LKED step identifies the load module that's created as output by the linkage editor.

Although this figure identifies the files used by the cataloged procedures, the DD statements for these files aren't necessarily included in the cataloged procedures. Instead, you can supply these statements through the JCL you use to execute the procedure. And in other cases, you can use JCL to override or supplement the statement provided by the procedures. You'll see how to do that next.

Cataloged procedures

Procedure	VS COBOL II	COBOL for MVS or OS/390
Compile only	COB2UC	IGYWC
Compile and link	COB2UCL	IGYWCL
Compile, link, and go	COB2UCLG	IGYWCLG
Compile and go	COB2UCG	IGYWCG

Step names

Step	VS COBOL II	COBOL for MVS or OS/390
Compile	COB2	COBOL
Link	LKED	LKED
Go	GO	GO

DD statements used with the cataloged procedures

Step	ddname	Description
COB2/COBOL	SYSIN	Source program input for the COBOL compiler.
	SYSLIB	A library that's searched for members specified in Copy statements.
	SYSLIN	Object module output (supplied in all procedures except COB2UC and IGYWC).
LKED	SYSLIB	Subprogram library.
	SYSLIN	Object module input (supplied in all procedures that have a LKED step).
	SYSIN	Additional object module input.
	SYSLMOD	Load module output (supplied in all procedures that have a LKED step).
GO	SYSOUT	Output from DISPLAY statements.
	SYSIN	Input for ACCEPT statements.
	SYSDBOUT	Symbolic debugging output.
	SYSUDUMP SYSABEND	Abnormal termination dump output.

Description

- A *cataloged procedure* is a pre-written segment of JCL code. The cataloged procedures shown above are provided to simplify COBOL program development.
- To use a cataloged procedure, you invoke it using JCL as shown in the next figure. Within that JCL, you identify the required data sets using the ddnames shown above.
- The compile-and-go procedures use the *loader* rather than the linkage editor. The loader is similar in function to the linkage editor, but it doesn't create a load module.
- If you use a compile-and-go procedure, you include the data sets shown for the LKED step on the GO step instead.

Figure 18-9   The cataloged procedures for COBOL program development

How to use the compile-link-and-go procedure

Figure 18-10 presents JCL you can use to execute the compile, link, and go procedure for COBOL for OS/390. If you can understand the statements in this job, you should be able to use the other procedures without any problem. Note, however, that this JCL varies from one installation to another. So you'll want to find out what's required at your shop. In most cases, someone can probably provide you with the JCL you need.

After the JOB statement that identifies the job, an EXEC statement executes the cataloged procedure named IGYWCLG. If you look back to figure 18-9, you'll see that this is the name of the compile, link, and go procedure for COBOL for MVS and OS/390. Notice that the keyword PROC is used to identify it as a procedure rather than a program.

This EXEC statement also includes a PARM parameter that specifies compiler options for the COBOL step of the procedure. Note that when you include compiler options this way, they override any options that are included in the cataloged procedure. So you'll want to find out what these options are and include then on the PARM parameter if necessary.

Two DD statements are coded as input to the COBOL step of the procedure. Notice that the ddname identifies the job step as well as the ddname used in the procedure. That way, the same ddname can be used in more than one step of the procedure.

The SYSIN DD statement in this job step identifies the source program to be compiled (RPT1000 in the MM01.TEST.COBOL library). The SYSLIB DD statement identifies a copy library that contains copy members used by the program. If the program doesn't include any copy members, this statement can be omitted.

Two DD statements are also coded for the LKED step of the procedure. The first one, SYSLMOD, identifies the name of the member and the library where you want to store the load module that's produced as output by the linkage editor. The SYSLIB DD statement identifies a library that contains subprograms used by the program. Like the DD statement for the copy library, this DD statement can be omitted if the program doesn't call any subprograms.

Notice how the SYSLIB DD statement is coded in this job. This technique is used to *concatenate* a library with the library that's specified in the cataloged procedure. Because the SYSLIB DD statement in the cataloged procedure identifies a library that contains essential COBOL routines, you don't want to override this statement.

The last three DD statements in this job are used as input to the GO step of the procedure. The first two identify the input and output files used by the program. Note that the ddnames must be the same as the ddnames that you used in the Select statements for these files in the program. The last DD statement in this job indicates that any other printed output created by the job should be sent to the default printer.

JCL that invokes the compile-link-and-go procedure for COBOL for OS/390

```
//MM01CLG JOB (36512),'R MENENDEZ',MSGLEVEL=(1,1),REGION=4M,
//              MSGCLASS=X,CLASS=A,NOTIFY=&SYSUID
//*------------------------------------------------------------------*
//*  COMPILE, LINK, AND EXECUTE A COBOL FOR OS/390 PROGRAM
//*------------------------------------------------------------------*
//STEP1   EXEC PROC=IGYWCLG,PARM.COBOL='XREF,FLAG(I,E)'
//COBOL.SYSIN  DD DSN=MM01.TEST.COBOL(RPT1000),DISP=SHR
//COBOL.SYSLIB DD DSN=MM01.TEST.COPYLIB,DISP=SHR
//*------------------------------------------------------------------*
//LKED.SYSLMOD DD DSN=MM01.TEST.LOADLIB(RPT1000),DISP=SHR
//LKED.SYSLIB  DD
//              DD DSN=MM01.TEST.OBJLIB,DISP=SHR
//*------------------------------------------------------------------*
//GO.CUSTMAST  DD DSN=MM01.CUSTMAST.DATA,DISP=SHR
//GO.SALESRPT  DD SYSOUT=*
//GO.SYSOUT    DD SYSOUT=*
//
```

Description

- The job shown above will compile, link-edit, and execute the program named RPT1000 that's presented in chapter 3 using the IGYWCLG cataloged procedure. To process another program, change the program name in the DD statements for COBOL.SYSIN, LKED.SYSLMOD, and LKED.SYSLIB. Then, change the DD statements in the GO step so they're appropriate for the program.

- To change the options used by the compiler in the COBOL step of the procedure, code the PARM.COBOL parameter on the EXEC statement for the procedure. Then, include the compiler options you want to use in quotes as shown above.

- When you execute a procedure, the ddnames should include the appropriate step name. COBOL.SYSIN, for example, refers to the SYSIN data set in the COBOL step.

- If the program requires input or output files, you need to code DD statements in the GO step that identify those files. The names you use on the DD statements must be the same as the ddnames in the system names of the Select statements used in the program.

- You can use the ISPF editor to create jobs like the one shown above. To submit a job for processing, you can issue the SUBMIT primary command from the edit data display.

Figure 18-10   How to use the compile-link-and-go procedure for COBOL for OS/390

How to execute an existing program

In some cases, you'll use a compile and link procedure to process a COBOL program until it runs without any errors. Then, you can code a separate job to execute the load module created by that procedure. This is particularly useful during the testing phase of program development when you may want to execute a program two or more times without compiling and link-editing it. Alternatively, you can use TSO commands to execute the load module. You'll need to do that if the program includes Accept or Display statements that you want to process at the terminal.

At the top of figure 18-11, you can see a job for executing the RPT1000 program that was created by the job in figure 18-10. Notice that the EXEC statement identifies the program to be executed, and the STEPLIB DD statement identifies the library that contains the load module for the program. The remaining DD statements identify the input and output files used by the program and the output file created by the job.

This figure also shows the TSO commands for executing the same program. Here, ALLOCATE commands are used to identify the input and output files used by the program, and a CALL command is used to execute the program. Notice that the high-level qualifier is omitted from both the CUSTMAST data set and the data set that contains the load module. That's because TSO adds this qualifier by default. Alternatively, you can code a fully-qualified data set name by enclosing it in quotes. For example, you can code the name of the partitioned data set that contains the load module like this:

```
'MM01.TEST.LOADLIB(RPT1000)'
```

Then, TSO won't add the high-level qualifier to the name.

In chapter 1 of this book, you saw two programs that use Accept and Display statements to interact with the user at the terminal. To execute a program like this under TSO, you have to allocate the SYSIN and SYSOUT data sets to the terminal as shown in this figure. Keep in mind, though, that you don't typically use Accept and Display statements to implement interactive programs under OS/390. Instead, you use a subsystem called CICS. You'll learn more about CICS and how to code interactive programs in the next chapter.

JCL that executes a previously compiled and link-edited COBOL for OS/390 program

```
//MM01RN    JOB  (36512),'R MENENDEZ',MSGLEVEL=(1,1),REGION=4M,
//               MSGCLASS=X,CLASS=A,NOTIFY=&SYSUID
//STEP1     EXEC PGM=RPT1000
//STEPLIB   DD   DSN=MM01.TEST.LOADLIB,DISP=SHR
//CUSTMAST  DD   DSN=MM01.CUSTMAST.DATA,DISP=SHR
//SALESRPT  DD   SYSOUT=*
//SYSOUT    DD   SYSOUT=*
//
```

How to execute a program using JCL

- To execute a program using JCL, you code an EXEC statement that identifies the program. In addition, you need to include a STEPLIB DD statement to identify the library that contains the load module for the program.

- If the program requires input or output files, you need to code DD statements that identify those files. The names you use on the DD statements must be the same as the ddnames in the system names in the Select statements used in the program.

TSO commands for executing a COBOL program

```
ALLOCATE DDNAME(CUSTMAST) DSNAME(CUSTMAST.DATA)
ALLOCATE DDNAME(SALESRPT) DSNAME(*)
CALL TEST.LOADLIB(RPT1000)
```

Allocate commands for a program that includes Accept and Display statements

```
ALLOCATE DDNAME(SYSOUT) DSNAME(*)
ALLOCATE DDNAME(SYSIN) DSNAME(*)
```

How to execute a program using TSO commands

- To execute a program from TSO, you use the CALL command. On this command, you specify the name of the load module for the program.

- Before you can execute a program from TSO, you have to allocate the data sets the program requires using the ddnames in the Select statements in the program. In addition, if the program uses Accept and Display statements, you must allocate SYSIN and SYSOUT data sets. To allocate these data sets to the terminal, code an asterisk for the DSNAME option.

Note

- Because JCL is executed in the background, you can't use it to execute a program that accepts information from or displays information on a terminal. Instead, you can execute the program from TSO.

Figure 18-11   How to execute an existing program

How to create a sequential data set

Before you can execute a program like RPT1000, the input file the program uses must be available. If you need to, you can create a simple sequential data set like the one used by this program using ISPF. Keep in mind, though, that many of the programs you create will use VSAM files, and you can't create those using ISPF. If you need to create a VSAM file, then, you'll need to ask a colleague how to do that. Or, you can refer to one of our others books listed at the end of this chapter.

Figure 18-12 presents the ISPF panels you can use to create a sequential data set. Notice that these are the same panels you use to create a partitioned data set. The difference is that you enter the data set name for a sequential data set in the Data Set Name field on the Data Set Utility panel. Then, you enter 0 for the number of directory blocks on the Allocate New Data Set panel, and you leave the data set name type blank. Also, be sure to enter the appropriate record format (usually FB for fixed-blocked records) and record length.

After you create a sequential data set, you can use the ISPF editor to enter data into it. When you do that, be sure to turn numbering off so the editor doesn't add line numbers to the file. To turn numbering off, just enter the NUM OFF primary command.

The panels for creating a sequential data set

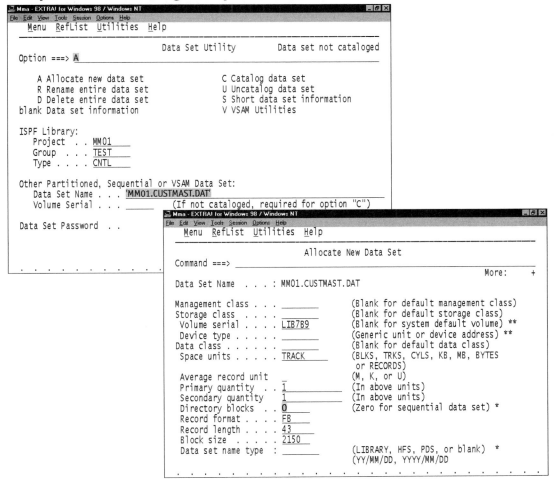

Description

- To allocate a new sequential data set, you use the Data Set Utility panel just as you do to create a partitioned data set. But instead of entering a project, group, and type, you enter the data set name.

- After you enter A in the command area and press the Enter key, the Allocate New Data Set panel is displayed. For a sequential data set, specify 0 for the directory blocks, and leave the data set name type blank.

- To enter the data for this file, you can use the ISPF editor as described earlier. When you open this file for the first time, be sure to enter the NUM OFF primary command so line numbers aren't added to the file.

Figure 18-12 How to create a sequential data set

How to use SDSF to work with jobs and job output

If you compile, link-edit, and execute programs using JCL, you need to know how to work with the jobs and the job output. To do that, you can use a facility called *SDSF*, or *System Display and Search Facility*. Note that because SDSF is a separately-licensed program, it may not be available on your system. In that case, though, it's likely that a similar product will be available.

Basic skills for working with SDSF

Figure 18-13 presents the SDSF Primary Option Menu. This menu contains four options that you can use to work with jobs and job output. If you select the I option, the *input queue* is displayed. This queue contains information about all the jobs that are executing or waiting to be executed. If you select the O option, the *output queue* is displayed. This queue contains job output that's waiting to be printed. In contrast, the *held output queue* contains job output that's being held or that has a reserved class that's not assigned to a printer. To display the held output queue, you select the H option. Finally, you can select the ST option to display a status panel that contains information from all three queues.

Since the status panel is the most flexible panel, you'll learn how to use it first. Then, you'll learn how to use the held output panel to work with job output. Finally, you'll learn how to display output data sets. Although I won't present the input and output queues here, you shouldn't have any trouble using them if you understand how to use the other panels.

The SDSF primary option menu

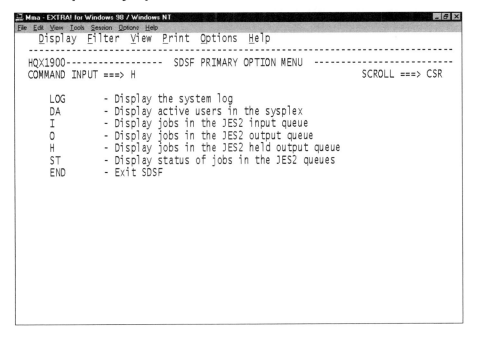

Description

- To start SDSF, enter SDSF at the TSO command prompt or select the SDSF option from the ISPF Primary Option Menu.
- To display any of the listed panels, enter the appropriate option in the command area and press Enter.
- The *input queue* contains jobs that are waiting for execution and jobs that are currently executing.
- The *output queue* contains jobs that have completed execution and are waiting to be printed.
- The *held output queue* contains jobs that have completed execution and are held or assigned to a reserved class.
- The status panel displays information from all of the queues.

Figure 18-13   Basic skills for working with SDSF

How to work with jobs

The easiest way to monitor a job is to use the status panel shown in figure 18-14. This panel lists all the jobs on the system, whether they are waiting to be executed, are currently executing, or have completed execution. The current disposition of a job is indicated by the value in the Queue column on this panel. In this figure, for example, you can see that the first job is executing and all the other jobs have completed execution and their output is waiting to be printed.

When a job is submitted for execution, it's assigned a unique *job-id*. In this figure, for example, seven jobs are listed with the name MM01CL and two are listed with the name MM01RN. The job-id for each is unique, though, so you can tell them apart. By the way, the first job listed on this panel is for the current TSO session. That's why the job-id starts with TSU instead of JOB, and that's why this panel shows that this job is executing.

In the NP column of the status panel, you can enter an action character to perform specific functions on the jobs. The action characters you're most likely to use with this panel are listed in the figure. If you enter a question mark as shown here, for example, SDSF will display a panel that lists the output data sets for the job. Then, you can use this panel to display the contents of each data set.

In addition to using the action characters, you can change the values of certain fields in this panel by typing over them. The two fields you're most likely to change from this panel are the job class (C) and priority (PRTY). Because job classes are set by each installation, you'll want to find out what classes are used in your shop. If two or more jobs have the same class, the one with the higher priority is executed first.

The status panel

```
Mma - EXTRA! for Windows 98 / Windows NT                              _ 回 区
File  Edit  View  Tools  Session  Options  Help
    Display  Filter  View  Print  Options  Help
--------------------------------------------------------------------------
SDSF STATUS DISPLAY ALL CLASSES                    LINE 1-10 (10)
COMMAND INPUT ===>                                 SCROLL ===> CSR
NP   JOBNAME  JOBID    OWNER   PRTY QUEUE    C  POS  SAFF  ASYS STATUS
     MM01     TSU04086 MM01      15 EXECUTION            DDC1  DDC1
     MM01CL   JOB03844 MM01       1 PRINT    C   85
     MM01CL   JOB06594 MM02       1 PRINT    A  256
     MM01CL   JOB06602 MM02       1 PRINT    C  257
     MM01CL   JOB00612 MM01       1 PRINT    A  486
     MM01CL   JOB00619 MM01       1 PRINT    A  492
     MM01RN   JOB01774 MM01       1 PRINT    A  571
     MM01CL   JOB02456 MM01       1 PRINT    A  661
 ?   MM01CL   JOB05828 MM01       1 PRINT    A  891
     MM01RN   JOB04096 MM01       1 PRINT    A 1775
```

Common action characters

Character	Function
S	Displays output data sets.
?	Displays a list of the output data sets for a job.
A	Releases a held job.
C	Cancels a job.
H	Holds a job.
O	Releases held output and makes it available for printing.
P	Purges a job and its output.

Description

- The status panel lists all of the jobs that are currently executing, that are waiting to be executed, or that have completed execution. The QUEUE column indicates a job's current status.

- You can enter an action character in the NP column to perform one of the functions shown above. You can also change some of a job's characteristics, such as its job class and priority, by typing over the appropriate fields.

Figure 18-14   How to work with jobs using SDSF

How to work with job output

Figure 18-15 shows the panel that displays the held output queue. It also lists the action characters you're most likely to use on this panel. To display the output data sets for a job, for example, you can enter S as shown in this figure.

If a job is listed in the held output queue, it means that output is on hold so that it isn't printed or the output is assigned to a reserved class that isn't associated with a printer. If the output is on hold, you can use the O action character to release it so it can be printed. If the job is assigned to a reserved class, you also have to change the job's class to route it to the appropriate printer. To do that, you can simply type over the current class with the new one.

In most cases, you won't print the output from a job. Instead you'll display it at your terminal. Then, when you're done with it, you can use the P action character to delete (purge) it from the system.

The held output queue display

```
🖳 Mma - EXTRA! for Windows 98 / Windows NT                                    _ ⦸ ✕
File  Edit  View  Tools  Session  Options  Help

    Display  Filter  View  Print  Options  Help
  --------------------------------------------------------------------
  SDSF HELD OUTPUT DISPLAY ALL CLASSES  LINES 611,105    LINE 19-28 (28)
  COMMAND INPUT ===>                                         SCROLL ===> CSR
  NP   JOBNAME JOBID   OWNER    PRTY C ODISP DEST              TOT-REC  TOT-
       MM01CL  JOB06341 MM02    144 X HOLD  LOCAL                 406
       MM01CL  JOB06397 MM02    144 X HOLD  LOCAL                 406
       MM01CL  JOB06428 MM02    144 X HOLD  LOCAL                 144
       MM01CL  JOB06431 MM02    144 X HOLD  LOCAL                 144
       MM01CL  JOB06590 MM02    144 X HOLD  LOCAL                 142
       MM01CL  JOB06593 MM02    144 X HOLD  LOCAL                 142
       MM01CL  JOB06594 MM02    144 X HOLD  LOCAL                 177
       MM01CL  JOB06602 MM02    144 X HOLD  LOCAL                 142
       MM02    TSU06178 MM02    128 Z HOLD  LOCAL               1,094
  S    MM01CL  JOB00612 MM01    144 X HOLD  LOCAL                 266
```

Common action characters

Character	Function
S	Displays output data sets.
?	Displays a list of the output data sets for a job.
O	Releases output and makes it available for printing.
P	Purges output data sets.

Description

- You can enter an action character in the NP column to perform one of the functions shown above. You can also change some of a job's characteristics, such as its job class and priority, by typing over the appropriate fields.

- To print output in the held output queue, use the O action character to release the output and make it available for printing. If the output is assigned to a reserved class, you must also change the class so it's routed to the appropriate printer.

Figure 18-15   How to work with job output using SDSF

How to display job output

Figure 18-16 shows the output that was produced by a job that compiles and link-edits a COBOL program. To display this data, you can use the S action character from any of the queue panels or the status panel. Alternatively, you can use the ? action character from any of these panels to list the individual data sets in the output, and then use the S action character to display a specific data set.

The first data set in a job's output is the *job log*, which shows the result of each job step. Note that if the job calls a cataloged procedure, the job log also shows the results of the steps within the procedure. In this figure, for example, you can see that the job consists of a single step named STEP1. The procedure that's called by this step, though, contains two job steps: COBOL and LKED. As you can see, the COBOL step completed with a return code (RC) of 12, which indicates a severe error. Then, because of the way the procedure is written, the LKED step wasn't executed. That's what the word FLUSH in the RC column for that step indicates.

In addition to the job log, job output typically includes a *JCL listing* and a *message log*. The JCL listing shows the JCL statements that were actually executed. This is particularly useful if the job executes a procedure because you can see how the statements in the job were combined with the statements in the procedure. The message log lists the system messages that were generated as the job executed.

The exact output that's produced by a job depends on the options you specify for the job and the functions that the job performs. If the job compiles a program, for example, the output will usually include a compilation listing. This listing includes all the statements in the source program, along with any statements that were copied into the program using Copy statements. If any errors occurred during the compilation, the compiler listing will also include a list of those errors. You'll learn more about that in the next topic.

When you display job output using SDSF, you can use standard ISPF commands and function keys to scroll through the data and locate particular entries. You can also move from one data set to the next using the NEXT and PREV commands. If you're familiar with ISPF, you won't have any trouble displaying job output.

The output for a compile-and-link job

```
Mma - EXTRA! for Windows 98 / Windows NT                                    _ 8 x
File Edit View Tools Session Options Help

   Display Filter View Print Options Help
--------------------------------------------------------------------------------
SDSF OUTPUT DISPLAY MM01CL   JOB00612  DSID      2 LINE 0       COLUMNS 02- 81
COMMAND INPUT ===> ■                                           SCROLL ===> CSR
******************************* TOP OF DATA *********************************
                 J E S 2   J O B   L O G  --  S Y S T E M   D D C 1  --  N O D E

18.12.53 JOB00612 ---- MONDAY,   10 APR 2000 ----
18.12.53 JOB00612 IRR010I  USERID MM01     IS ASSIGNED TO THIS JOB.
18.12.53 JOB00612 IEF677I WARNING MESSAGE(S) FOR JOB MM01CL   ISSUED
18.12.53 JOB00612 ICH70001I MM01    LAST ACCESS AT 18:10:20 ON MONDAY, APRIL 1
18.12.53 JOB00612 $HASP373 MM01CL   STARTED - INIT B   - CLASS A - SYS DDC1
18.12.53 JOB00612 IEF403I MM01CL - STARTED - TIME=18.12.53
18.12.56 JOB00612 -                                            --TIMINGS (M
18.12.56 JOB00612 -JOBNAME  STEPNAME PROCSTEP    RC    EXCP   CONN    TCB    SRB
18.12.56 JOB00612 -MM01CL   STEP1    COBOL       12    398    772    .00    .00
18.12.56 JOB00612 -MM01CL   STEP1    LKED     FLUSH     0      0    .00    .00
18.12.57 JOB00612 IEF404I MM01CL - ENDED - TIME=18.12.57
18.12.57 JOB00612 -MM01CL   ENDED.  NAME-A PRINCE          TOTAL TCB CPU TIM
18.12.57 JOB00612 $HASP395 MM01CL   ENDED
------ JES2 JOB STATISTICS ------
  10 APR 2000 JOB EXECUTION DATE
          12 CARDS READ
```

Description

- The output for a job includes a *job log* that shows the results of each job step. These results include a return code that indicates whether or not errors occurred and if so, how severe they were.

- The job output also includes a *JCL listing* that shows the JCL statements that were processed by the job. If the JCL executes a cataloged procedure, the JCL listing shows how the JCL in the job was combined with the JCL in the procedure.

- The job output also includes a *message log* that shows system messages concerning the execution of job steps and the allocation and deallocation of data sets.

- Additional information is included in the job output depending on the processing that's done. If the job compiles a program, for example, a compilation listing is usually included.

How to work with job output

- You can use the standard ISPF scrolling commands to browse the output for a job. You can also use the FIND and LOCATE commands presented in figure 18-7 to find a particular line of data in the output.

- If the output consists of more than one data set, you can use the NEXT and PREV commands to move to the next or previous data set.

Figure 18-16   How to display job output using SDSF

How to correct compile-time and run-time errors

When you compile a program, the compiler converts the source program into machine language that the computer can understand. If the syntax of a statement is incorrect, however, a compile-time error occurs. Then, you have to correct the error and compile the program again. Even if a statement compiles cleanly, though, a run-time error occurs if the statement can't be executed. In the next two topics, you'll see some examples of compile-time and run-time errors and learn how to correct them.

How to correct compile-time errors

When the COBOL compiler encounters an error in the syntax of a source statement, it generates an error message that's included in the compiler listing for that program. In the compiler listing shown in figure 18-17, for example, you can see that the compiler encountered three errors. For each error, the message includes the line number of the statement that was being executed when the error occurred as well as a description of the error. Most of the time, you can find the errors without much trouble by studying these error messages and the source code.

This figure also lists the types of error messages that can be generated during a compilation. The two most common types of errors are standard errors (E) and severe errors (S). In this figure, for example, one standard error and two severe errors were detected. Although the compiler tries to correct standard errors, the program usually won't work the way you want it to without modification. Severe errors always require modification for the program to execute correctly.

Each error type is associated with a return code that indicates the severity of the error. A return code of 8, for example, indicates a standard error, and a return code of 12 indicates a severe error. If you look back to figure 18-16, you can see that the highest return code for a job step is the one that's included in the job log for the job.

Job output that shows compile-time errors

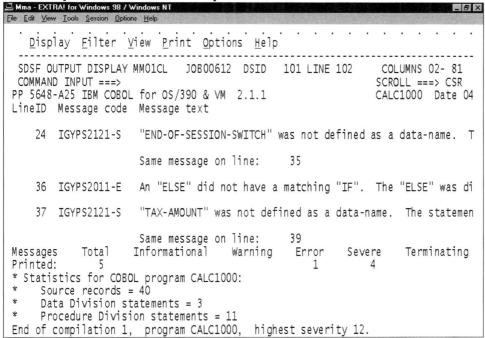

Types of compiler errors

Error type	Return code	Description
Informational (I)	0	Provides information only. The program will execute correctly without any modifications.
Warning (W)	4	Indicates a possible error. The program will most likely execute correctly without any modifications.
Error (E)	8	An error that the compiler has attempted to correct. The program will most likely require modification for it to execute correctly.
Severe (S)	12	A serious error that the compiler was unable to correct. The program will not execute correctly without modification.
Unrecoverable (U)	16	A serious error that caused the compilation to be terminated.

Description

- The compiler compiles a program into machine language that the computer can understand. If a statement can't be compiled into machine language, a *compile-time error* occurs.
- If compile-time errors are detected, the job output will contain a description of each error including the line number of the statement that was executing when the error occurred, the message code for the error, and a description of the error. You can use this information to locate and correct the error.
- The last character of the message code indicates the severity of the error as shown above.

Figure 18-17   How to correct compile-time errors

How to correct run-time errors

Figure 18-18 shows the output from the simple report-preparation program that's presented in chapter 3. Although the program compiled cleanly, a run-time error occurred when the program was executed. When a run-time error occurs, the system generates a message that indicates the type of error that occurred and the statement that was executing when it occurred. In this case, the error is a *data exception*, and it occurred at statement 151. If you use TSO commands to execute a program rather than JCL, this error message is displayed at your terminal.

In some instances, you'll be able to correct a run-time error by studying the statement and the data it operates on. In other instances, you'll need to use some debugging techniques to determine the cause of the error. Before you begin debugging a program, however, you'll want to find out what tools are available at your shop. Because a variety of tools are available, you won't learn about any specific tools here.

This figure also lists the most common types of run-time errors and their causes. The data exception shown in this figure, for example, was caused by invalid data in a numeric field. In other words, the field contained blanks or other nonnumeric data. After you deal with a few run-time errors, you'll get a better feel for what their common causes are.

Job output that shows a run-time error

```
Mma - EXTRA! for Windows 98 / Windows NT                          _ 8 X
File  Edit  View  Tools  Session  Options  Help

   Display  Filter  View  Print  Options  Help
  ------------------------------------------------------------------
  SDSF OUTPUT DISPLAY MM01RN    JOB01774  DSID    101 LINE 1       COLUMNS 02- 81
  COMMAND INPUT ===>                                              SCROLL ===> CSR
  DATE:  04/11/2000              YEAR-TO-DATE SALES REPORT              PAGE:    1
  TIME:  12:15                                                         RPT1000
  CUST                          SALES          SALES
  NUM    CUSTOMER NAME          THIS YTD       LAST YTD
  11111  INFORMATION BUILDERS   1,234.56       1,111.11
  12345  CAREER TRAINING CTR    12,345.67      22,222.22
  CEE3207S The system detected a data exception (System Completion Code=0C7).
          From compile unit RPT1000 at entry point RPT1000 at statement 151 at co
          00006912.
  ****************************** BOTTOM OF DATA *********************************
```

Common system completion codes

Code	Type	Description
OC1	Operation exception	Occurs when the system tries to perform an invalid operation like reading from or writing to an unopened file.
OC5	Addressing exception	Occurs when the system refers to a location in main storage that isn't available.
OC7	Data exception	Occurs when an operation is performed on a numeric field that has invalid data.
OCA	Decimal-overflow exception	Occurs when the result of an arithmetic operation can't be stored in a receiving field that's defined as a decimal number.
OCB	Decimal-divide exception	Occurs when the program tries to divide a number by zero.

Description

- If a statement compiles cleanly but can't be executed, a *run-time error* occurs when you run the program.

- If a run-time error occurs, the job output will contain a description of the error that includes a message code, a system completion code, and the number of the statement that was executing when the error occurred. You can use this information to locate and correct the error.

- The last character of the message code indicates the severity of the error: informational (I), warning (W), error (E), severe (S), or critical (C).

Figure 18-18   How to correct run-time errors

Perspective

Now that you've completed this chapter, you should be able to compile and test any of the programs presented in this book. The only thing you won't be able to do is create VSAM files. If you need to do that, you can ask a colleague for help, or you can refer to one of our VSAM books.

As you learned earlier in this chapter, you don't normally use Accept and Display statements in a COBOL program to interact with a mainframe user. Instead, you use a subsystem of OS/390 called *CICS*. To give you an understanding of how this works, chapter 19 presents an overview of CICS. Then, chapter 20 describes how you can use a database management system called DB2 to work with data that's stored in a database. These two chapters will give you a good foundation for developing CICS and DB2 programs of your own.

Although this chapter presented the basic program development facilities that are available on an OS/390 system, there's a lot more you need to know to develop programs efficiently and effectively. Fortunately, you can learn more about any of the topics presented in this chapter from other books published by Mike Murach & Associates. The three books you'll find most useful are *MVS JCL, Second Edition*; *MVS TSO Part 1: Concepts and ISPF*; and *MVS TSO Part 2: Commands and Procedures*. We also offer related books on VSAM, CICS, and DB2. For more information, see our web site at www.murach.com.

Summary

- The COBOL compiler converts a *source program* into an *object module*. If the source program uses copy members, they're included as input to the compiler.

- The *linkage editor* links the object module for a program with any subprograms it requires. The result is an executable module called a *load module*.

- To perform *batch processing* under the OS/390 operating system, you use *JCL*. To perform *interactive processing*, you use *TSO*.

- *ISPF* provides a menu-driven, full-screen interface to most of the features of TSO. You can use ISPF to develop your COBOL programs and the jobs that compile, link-edit, and execute them.

- The files on an IBM mainframe are called *data sets*. The two types of data sets you'll use most often are *partitioned data sets* and *sequential data sets*.

- A partitioned data set consists of a *directory* and one or more *members*. You use partitioned data sets to store your source programs, the object and load modules created from them, and the JCL to compile, link-edit, and execute them.

- Before you can use a data set, you must create, or *allocate*, it. You can do that using ISPF's Data Set utility.

- You can use the ISPF editor to create new members and edit existing members. You can also use the editor to enter data into a sequential data set.

- A *job* is identified by a JOB statement. Each job consists of one or more *job steps* that are identified by EXEC statements that execute programs or procedures. To allocate the data sets required by a program or procedure, you code DD statements.

- IBM provides *cataloged procedures* that include most of the JCL you need to compile, link-edit, and execute your COBOL programs. To use a cataloged procedure, you code a job that executes it and supplies the required input and output data sets.

- To execute an existing program, you can use JCL or TSO commands. You'll use TSO commands if you want to route input and output from Accept and Display statements to the terminal.

- You can use *SDSF* to work with jobs and their output. To do that, you use SDSF options to display the jobs in the *input queue* and the job output in the *output queue* and the *held output queue*.

- A *compile-time error* occurs when the compiler can't convert a source statement into machine language. Then, the compiler generates an error message that will help you correct the error.

- A *run-time error* occurs when a statement can't be executed. Then, the system generates an error message that will help you correct the error.

Terms

source program	ISPF
object module	Interactive System Productivity Facility
compilation listing	PDF
compile-time error	Program Development Facility
linkage editor	run-time environment
link editor	Language Environment
load module	command area
normal termination	panel
abnormal termination	program function key
abend	PF key
run-time error	data set
OS/390	partitioned data set
batch processing	PDS
interactive processing	library
JCL	sequential data set
Job Control Language	directory
job	member
TSO	allocating a data set
Time Sharing Option	qualifier

high-level qualifier	step name
edit profile	ddname
edit data display	cataloged procedure
heading area	loader
primary command	concatenating libraries
line command area	SDSF
line command	System Display and Search Facility
screen window	input queue
identifier field	output queue
name field	held output queue
operation field	job-id
parameters field	job log
job step	JCL listing
job name	message log

Objectives

- Describe the three steps involved in compiling and testing a program. Include a description of the input and output to each step.

- Use ISPF to create partitioned data sets for storing your COBOL source programs and the jobs for compiling, link-editing, and executing them.

- Use the ISPF editor to create a COBOL source program. Then, create and submit a job that uses a cataloged procedure to compile and link-edit the program.

- Use ISPF to create a sequential data set that will contain the data used as input to your program.

- Use SDSF to display the output from a compile and link job. If the job output contains compile-time errors, correct the errors and compile and link-edit the program again.

- Create and submit a job to execute your COBOL program, or use TSO commands to execute it. If a run-time error occurs, correct the problem and compile, link-edit, and execute the program again.

19

How to develop interactive programs on an IBM mainframe

On an IBM mainframe, most interactive programs are developed with *CICS* (*Customer Information Control System*). CICS can support dozens of terminal users at the same time who are running a wide range of application programs. CICS loads those programs, coordinates their execution, manages the data transmissions between the programs and terminals, controls the programs' access to stored data, and maintains the integrity of the stored data.

This chapter shows you how to write interactive COBOL programs that use CICS. As you read this chapter, you'll find that CICS programming involves concepts and COBOL features that are covered in detail in other chapters of this book. In particular, this chapter refers to the COBOL copy library, the Linkage Section, and subprogram linkage (chapter 11); indexed file handling (chapter 14); and the JCL for compiling and testing a mainframe program (chapter 18). So you may want to read those chapters before this one. You may also want to read chapter 17 to see how interactive COBOL programs are developed on other platforms before you read this chapter.

Keep in mind, though, that with or without the other chapters, this is only an introduction to this difficult subject. For a complete course on CICS programming, please refer to our two CICS books: *CICS for the COBOL Programmer, Part 1* and *Part 2*.

Program development concepts and techniques

This topic describes the concepts and techniques you need to know to develop CICS programs. To start, you'll learn how an application program uses CICS services. Then, you'll learn about a programming technique that's used by most CICS programs, called pseudo-conversational programming. Last, you'll be introduced to CICS commands, fields, and copy members.

How application programs use CICS services

Simply put, the job of CICS is to manage transactions. A *transaction* is a predefined unit of work, such as an inquiry or order processing program, that can be invoked by a terminal user. To manage transactions, CICS provides a variety of services. Some of the modules that provide those services are shown in figure 19-1.

To start a transaction, the user can enter a four-character code called a *transaction identifier* (or just *trans-id*) at the terminal. Then, CICS uses the trans-id to select the program to run. Alternatively, the user can invoke a program by selecting it from a menu displayed by another CICS program.

When a user invokes a transaction, CICS starts a *task* for the user. In other words, the application program actually executes within CICS. That means the storage that the program uses is CICS storage and the COBOL program has to contain code that will allow it interface with CICS.

In figure 19-1, the CICS subsystem is running programs for four users, and two of the users (1 and 4) are running the same transaction. As you can see, although several users may invoke the same transaction, CICS creates a separate task for each. However, for efficiency's sake, it loads only one copy of the program's executable code into storage, no matter how many tasks are using the program.

To support the application program related to a task, CICS provides a variety of functional modules. One of these is *Basic Mapping Support* (*BMS*), which lets you create a *mapset* that consists of one *map* for each screen that controls the format of the data that's displayed on and received from the terminal. The other is file control, which lets you access the data in VSAM files through CICS, not through the normal COBOL I/O statements.

CICS services

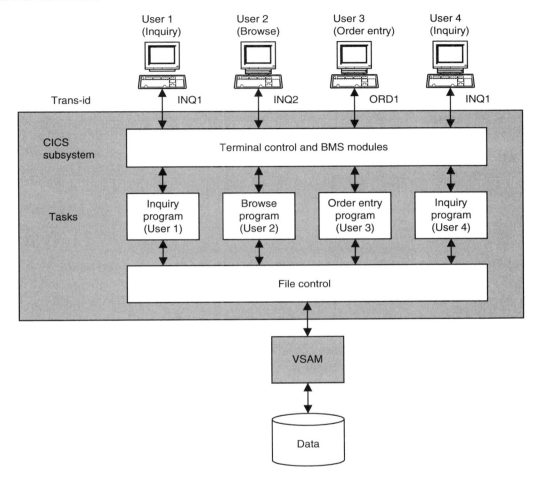

Concepts

- A *transaction* is a predefined unit of work that a terminal user can invoke by entering a *transaction identifier*, or *trans-id*. Each trans-id is associated with a program that CICS will load into storage and execute when the transaction is invoked.

- When a user invokes a transaction, CICS starts a *task* for that user. Although several users may invoke the same transaction, CICS creates a separate task for each.

- CICS provides functional modules that support application programs, including task control, terminal control, file control, and *Basic Mapping Support* (*BMS*).

- The terminal control and BMS modules control interactions with user terminals. These modules work together to provide an interface with the operating system's telecommunications access method, which provides support for the terminal devices.

- The file control module converts CICS file control statements to standard file processing statements and then passes them on to VSAM for processing.

Figure 19-1   How application programs use CICS services

How pseudo-conversational programming works

Although a single CICS system can support hundreds of terminals, it can't operate efficiently if the programs remain in storage while they wait for user input. As a result, most CICS programs use a style of programming called *pseudo-conversational programming*.

Figure 19-2 presents a flowchart that illustrates how pseudo-conversational programming works. As you can see, a program starts by sending its first map to the screen. Then, the program ends. That releases CICS resources while the user is entering input.

When the user indicates that the entry is complete, usually by pressing an *attention identifier (AID) key*, CICS restarts the program. Then, if the user didn't indicate that the program should end, the program retrieves the input data, processes it, sends its output data, and ends. This continues until the user ends the program.

If you compare this processing with the processing required for a *conversational program*, you'll see why most CICS installations require that programs be written in pseudo-conversational style. When a conversational program starts, it sends its initial map just like a pseudo-conversational program, but it remains in storage while it waits for input. Then, it retrieves the input data from the terminal, processes it, sends its output, and waits again. This means, however, that the program is waiting for the user most of the time that it is running, which is an unnecessary waste of valuable CICS resources. If you multiply this waste by hundreds of terminal users, you can see that this style of programming can seriously degrade the performance of the system.

Unfortunately, pseudo-conversational programming is more difficult than conversational programming because each program must be coded so it can figure out what it should do each time it's restarted. This requires a different type of design and logic than you've seen before. In a moment, you'll see how this works in a simple inquiry program.

Pseudo-conversational processing

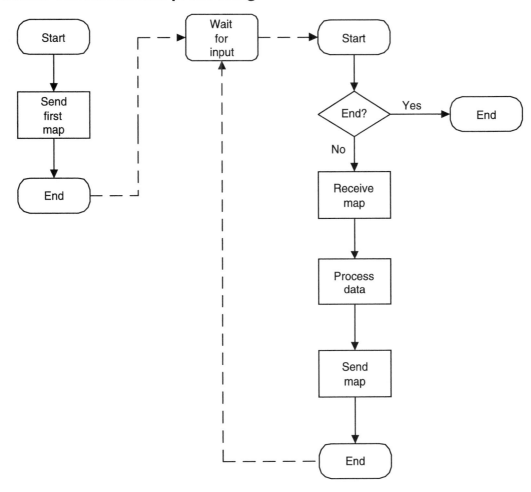

Description

- With *pseudo-conversational programming*, a program ends after it sends data to a terminal. This releases some of the resources that are used by the program. Then, CICS restarts the program when the terminal user completes an entry.

- When you develop a pseudo-conversational program, the program must be able to figure out what to do each time it's restarted. To do that, it uses information that's stored in the CICS communication area for the program.

Figure 19-2   How pseudo-conversational programming works

How to develop CICS programs

When you code a CICS program, you request CICS services by issuing CICS commands. To do that, you start each command with EXEC CICS, and you end each command with END-EXEC. Within these statements, you code the command and any options it requires. In figure 19-4, you can see a list of some of the common CICS commands for screen interactions, for passing control from one program to another, and for processing VSAM files.

In the example in this figure, you can see how the Receive Map command is coded. In accordance with standard CICS command syntax, the words outside the parentheses (MAP, MAPSET, and INTO) are all options of the command, while the values inside the parentheses are supplied by the programmer. As a result, this command tells CICS to receive data from a terminal using a mapset named INV1MS and a map within it named INV1MP1. The data in that mapset should be returned to a group item in working storage named INVlMP1I.

When you develop a CICS program in COBOL, you start by creating a BMS mapset. Once that's done, you can code the COBOL program using CICS commands that refer to the mapset. Your program can also refer to the fields in the maps within the mapset.

When you finish coding the COBOL program, you run a JCL procedure for compiling, linking, and running CICS programs. This procedure starts by running a *CICS translator* that converts the CICS commands in the program to Move and Call statements that can be compiled by the COBOL compiler. In this figure, for example, you can see the translated code for the RECEIVE MAP command. In addition, the CICS translator inserts some code into your program's Linkage Section.

When the translator is finished, the JCL procedure runs the COBOL compiler to compile the program and the linkage editor to link the program with the CICS subprograms that it has called. Then, the procedure runs your program so you can see whether it works correctly.

Incidentally, the code in the CICS statement in this figure uses single quotation marks (') instead of double quotation marks (") because that's the default on most mainframes. As you will see, single quotes are used in all of the other code in this chapter too.

CICS commands for doing BMS-controlled screen interactions

RECEIVE MAP	Retrieves input data from the terminal.
SEND MAP	Sends information to the terminal for display.

CICS commands for passing control from one program to another

LINK	Invokes a program at a lower level.
RETURN	Returns control to CICS.
XCTL	Transfers control to another program.

CICS commands for processing VSAM files

DELETE	Deletes a record from a VSAM file.
ENDBR	Terminates a browse operation.
READ	Retrieves a record from a VSAM keyed file.
READNEXT	Retrieves the next record during a browse operation.
READPREV	Retrieves the previous record during a browse operation.
RESETBR	Restarts a browse operation at a new position in the data set.
REWRITE	Updates a record in a file.
STARTBR	Initiates a browse operation, and identifies the location in the data set where the browse begins.
WRITE	Adds a record to a file.

A CICS command that receives data from the terminal screen

```
EXEC CICS
    RECEIVE MAP('INV1MP1')
            MAPSET('INV1MS')
            INTO(INV1MP1I)
END-EXEC.
```

Translated source code for the CICS command

```
MOVE '..}.............00061    ' TO DFHEIV0
MOVE 'INV1MP1' TO DFHC0070
MOVE 'INV1MS' TO DFHC0071
CALL 'DFHEI1' USING DFHEIV0 DFHC0070 DINMAP1I DFHDUMMY
DFHC0071.
```

Description

- To request CICS services, you code CICS commands within your COBOL program. Later, the *CICS translator* converts each CICS command into COBOL Move and Call statements. The translated program can then be compiled by the COBOL compiler.

- When you develop a CICS program, you use a three-step procedure. First, you create a BMS mapset that defines each screen that's going to be used by a program. Second, you code the COBOL program using CICS commands within the program. Third, you run a JCL procedure that translates, compiles, links, and runs the program.

Figure 19-3   How to develop CICS programs

The Execute Interface Block and the DFHAID copy member

One of the blocks of code that the CICS translator inserts into the Linkage Section of your program is called the *Execute Interface Block* (*EIB*). Its fields provide information about the current task. In figure 19-4, you can see the start of this block of fields. Curiously, this block doesn't appear in the source listing of your COBOL program, even though its fields have been inserted by the translator. As a result, you have to get the names of the fields that you want to use from other documentation.

The two EIB fields you'll use most often are EIBAID and EIBCALEN. The EIBCALEN field contains the length of the data that is passed to the program through its *communication area*. A program can use this area to store the data that it will need the next time it's executed. That's necessary because the contents of the working-storage fields are lost when a pseudo-conversational program ends. If the length of this area is zero, it means that no data is passed to the program.

In contrast, the EIBAID field gives the value of the last AID key that was pressed. You can use it to determine the processing the user has requested.

To make it easy to write the code that tests the values in the EIBAID field, IBM supplies a copy member named DFHAID. The first part of this member is shown in this figure. It gives a name to each of the values that represents an AID key. For instance, DFHENTER is the name for the value that represents the Enter key, and DFHPF3 is the name for the value that represents the PF3 key. As a result, you can code

```
IF EIBAID = DFHPF3
```

when you want to see if the AID key that was pressed was the PF3 key, instead of coding

```
IF EIBAID = '3'
```

Once you get used to the names in this copy member, you'll have no trouble using them.

The code for the Execute Interface Block

```
01    DFHEIBLK.
   02 EIBTIME      PIC S9(7) COMP-3.
   02 EIBDATE      PIC S9(7) COMP-3.
   02 EIBTRNID     PIC X(4).
   02 EIBTASKN     PIC S9(7) COMP-3.
   02 EIBTRMID     PIC X(4).
   02 DFHEIGDI     PIC S9(4) COMP.
   02 EIBCPOSN     PIC S9(4) COMP.
   02 EIBCALEN     PIC S9(4) COMP.
   02 EIBAID       PIC X(1).
   02 EIBFN        PIC X(2).
   .
   .
```

The code for the DFHAID copy member

```
01    DFHAID.
   02 DFHNULL     PIC  X   VALUE IS ' '.
   02 DFHENTER    PIC  X   VALUE IS ''''.
   02 DFHCLEAR    PIC  X   VALUE IS '_'.
   02 DFHCLRP     PIC  X   VALUE IS '('.
   02 DFHPEN      PIC  X   VALUE IS '='.
   02 DFHOPID     PIC  X   VALUE IS 'W'.
   02 DFHMSRE     PIC  X   VALUE IS 'X'.
   02 DFHSTRF     PIC  X   VALUE IS 'h'.
   02 DFHTRIG     PIC  X   VALUE IS '''.
   02 DFHPA1      PIC  X   VALUE IS '%'.
   02 DFHPA2      PIC  X   VALUE IS ''.
   02 DFHPA3      PIC  X   VALUE IS ','.
   02 DFHPF1      PIC  X   VALUE IS '1'.
   02 DFHPF2      PIC  X   VALUE IS '2'.
   02 DFHPF3      PIC  X   VALUE IS '3'.
   02 DFHPF4      PIC  X   VALUE IS '4'.
   .
   .
```

Description

- The CICS translator inserts code into the Linkage Section of the program that contains definitions for the *Execute Interface Block* (*EIB*). The EIB is a CICS area that contains information related to the current task, such as the date and time the task was started and the transaction-id that was used to start it.

- The EIBCALEN field contains the length of the data passed to the program through its *communication area* (DFHCOMMAREA). A length of zero indicates that no data was passed to the program, which means that it's the first execution of the program.

- The EIBAID field indicates the last *attention identifier (AID) key* that was pressed. You can use the value of this field to determine the processing the user has requested.

- The DFHAID copy member contains literal values that correspond to the AID keys that the user can press to communicate with the system. When the user presses a key, CICS passes a one-byte value to the program through the EIBAID field in the Execute Interface Block. This value indicates which key was pressed.

Figure 19-4   The Execute Interface Block and the DFHAID copy member

A CICS inquiry program

Now that you understand the basic logic and coding required for a CICS program, you're ready to see how an actual CICS program works. So the topics that follow present a complete inquiry program including its BMS mapset and its COBOL code. That should give you a solid appreciation for what CICS coding entails.

The program specifications

Figure 19-5 presents the program specifications for a simple CICS inquiry program that allows a user to check the status of any item in inventory. In brief, the user enters an item number, and the program retrieves the data for the item from a VSAM file with indexed organization. But if the record for the item number can't be found, the program displays an error message. The program should also display an error message if the user presses the Enter key without entering an item number.

If you study the first screen for this program, you can see that the first line shows the trans-id that's used to invoke the program (INV1) and the name of the program (Inventory Inquiry). The third line contains directions for the user. The fifth line includes the item number field that the user will enter. And the last line displays the two PF keys that the user can press to end the program: Exit (F3) or Cancel (F12). (By the way, we left this last line off the second screen to save space, but it would appear in the actual program output.)

In terms of pseudo-conversational programming, once the first screen is displayed, the program ends while it waits for the user to enter data. When the entry is finished, CICS restarts the program. The program then checks what was entered, and displays the appropriate screen in response. In this example, it displays data for the item, but the display would be different if the entry were invalid or if the user had pressed one of the other AID keys. Then, the program ends again and CICS waits for another entry before restarting it.

On the 3270-type display station that's common in mainframe installations, there are four other AID keys that are handled routinely in CICS programs. The first is the Clear key. When the user presses it, the program should erase any data on the screen, so it's displayed as if the program were being started for the first time. The other three are the *program attention (PA) keys*, PA1, PA2, and PA3. Although special functions are often assigned to these keys in other programs, this inquiry program shouldn't take any special action if the user presses one of them.

Incidentally, the screens in figure 9-5 show the mainframe output as it appears in a PC window when using a program called EXTRA! This program lets you attach your PC to an IBM mainframe via a direct, remote, or LAN connection. You can then use that window of your PC as a mainframe terminal. EXTRA! is just one of many third-party programs that provide this type of connectivity.

Screen 1

The program accepts an item number from the user.

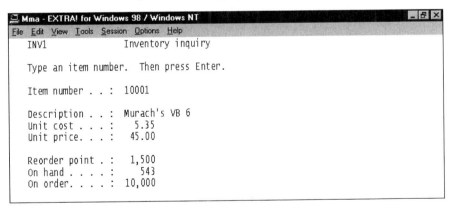

Screen 2

When the user enters a valid item number and presses the Enter key, the program retrieves the record for the inventory item and displays its data on the screen.

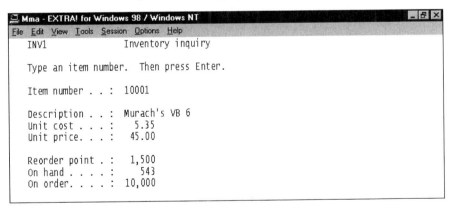

Processing specifications

- This program lets the user display data for any item in the inventory master file.
- If the user presses the Enter key without entering an item number or enters an item number for a record that doesn't exist, the program should display an error message.
- If the user presses the PF3 or PF12 key, the program should end.

Figure 19-5   The program specifications for an inquiry program

The BMS mapset

Figure 19-6 presents the BMS mapset for the screen in figure 19-5. This is a special type of *assembler language* program that defines the format of each screen, or map, that's used by a program. After you code the mapset, you run a program called an *assembler* that compiles (or assembles) the code into a *physical mapset* and a *symbolic mapset*. The physical mapset is used by CICS when the program that uses the mapset is run. The symbolic mapset is a copy member that can be copied into the COBOL program that uses the mapset.

When you code a mapset, you use three *macros*: DFHMSD to start the mapset; DFHMDI to start each map; and DFHMDF to define each field within a map. To end a mapset, you code another DFHMSD, as you can see on page 3 of this mapset.

In this mapset, the DFHMSD macro defines a mapset named INV1MS. Its parameters specify that the symbolic map that BMS generates from this mapset should be in COBOL (LANG=COBOL), that the symbolic map should include fields for both input and output (MODE=INOUT), that the mapset should work with a standard 3270-type display station (TERM=3270-2), and that it should support color (MAPPATTS=COLOR).

Then, the DFHMDI macro defines a map named INV1MP1 that represents the one screen that this program requires. This macro specifies that the size of the screen display is 24 lines of 80 characters each and that the map should be displayed starting in column 1 of line 1.

The other macros in this mapset are the DFHMDF macros that define the fields in the screen. For example, the fifth DFHMDF macro defines an item number field named ITEMNO. It says that this field should be positioned at column 14 in the fifth line. In fact, however, the POS parameter determines the location of the *attribute byte* for each field. This byte, which precedes each field, sets the attributes for the field. As a result, the item number field will actually start in column 15 of line 5.

The other parameters for a field give the length, attributes, color, initial value, and Picture for a field. Of these, the only entries that you may not understand are those for the ATTRB parameter. These entries are summarized at the bottom of page 2 of this listing.

With that as background, you should be able to understand how each field in the screen in figure 19-5 is defined. For instance, ITEMNO will be unprotected with the initial cursor on it; UCOST will be displayed with ZZ9.99 as its picture; and MESSAGE will be displayed in yellow with high intensity. All of these definitions follow IBM's *CUA (Common User Access)* standards, which are designed to insure that programs interact with users in consistent ways.

To enter the code for a BMS mapset, you use an editor like the ISPF editor that's presented in chapter 18. Another alternative, though, is to use a program called a *screen painter*. This lets you design the screen layout at your terminal interactively. Then, the screen painter generates the assembler language code that you need for the mapset. In this case, you still you need to understand the resulting assembler language code because you may need to refer to it later on.

The code for the BMS mapset   **Page 1**

```
          PRINT NOGEN
INV1MS    DFHMSD TYPE=&SYSPARM,                                   X
                 LANG=COBOL,                                      X
                 MODE=INOUT,                                      X
                 TERM=3270-2,                                     X
                 CTRL=FREEKB,                                     X
                 STORAGE=AUTO,                                    X
                 MAPATTS=(COLOR),                                 X
                 TIOAPFX=YES
*****************************************************************
INV1MP1   DFHMDI SIZE=(24,80),                                   X
                 LINE=1,                                          X
                 COLUMN=1
*****************************************************************
          DFHMDF POS=(1,1),                                      X
                 LENGTH=4,                                        X
                 ATTRB=(NORM,PROT),                               X
                 COLOR=BLUE,                                      X
                 INITIAL='INV1'
          DFHMDF POS=(1,20),                                     X
                 LENGTH=17,                                       X
                 ATTRB=(NORM,PROT),                               X
                 COLOR=BLUE,                                      X
                 INITIAL='INVENTORY INQUIRY'
*****************************************************************
          DFHMDF POS=(3,1),                                      X
                 LENGTH=79,                                       X
                 ATTRB=(NORM,PROT),                               X
                 COLOR=GREEN,                                     X
                 INITIAL='Type an item number.  Then press Enter.'
          DFHMDF POS=(5,1),                                      X
                 LENGTH=13,                                       X
                 ATTRB=(NORM,PROT),                               X
                 COLOR=GREEN,                                     X
                 INITIAL='ITEM NUMBER: '
ITEMNO    DFHMDF POS=(5,14),                                     X
                 LENGTH=5,                                        X
                 ATTRB=(NORM,UNPROT,IC),                          X
                 COLOR=TURQUOISE,                                 X
                 INITIAL='_____'
*****************************************************************
```

Description

- A BMS mapset is an *assembler language* program that defines the format of the maps that are used by a program. After you code a mapset, you run a program called an *assembler* that compiles (or assembles) the mapset. This produces a *physical map* that is used by CICS and a *symbolic map* that is used by the COBOL program.

- To code a mapset, you use three *macros*: a DFHMSD macro marks the start of each mapset; a DFHMDI macro marks the beginning of each map in the mapset; and a DFHMDF macro defines each field in a mapset.

Figure 19-6   The BMS mapset for the CICS inquiry program (part 1 of 3)

The code for the BMS mapset

```
            DFHMDF POS=(7,1),                              X
                   LENGTH=18,                              X
                   ATTRB=(NORM,PROT),                      X
                   COLOR=GREEN,                            X
                   INITIAL='DESCRIPTION . . : '
DESC        DFHMDF POS=(7,20),                             X
                   LENGTH=20,                              X
                   COLOR=TURQUOISE,                        X
                   ATTRB=(NORM,PROT)
            DFHMDF POS=(8,1),                              X
                   LENGTH=18,                              X
                   ATTRB=(NORM,PROT),                      X
                   COLOR=GREEN,                            X
                   INITIAL='UNIT COST . . . . : '
UCOST       DFHMDF POS=(8,20),                             X
                   LENGTH=06,                              X
                   COLOR=TURQUOISE,                        X
                   ATTRB=(NORM,PROT),                      X
                   PICOUT='ZZ9.99'
            DFHMDF POS=(9,1),                              X
                   LENGTH=18,                              X
                   ATTRB=(NORM,PROT),                      X
                   COLOR=GREEN,                            X
                   INITIAL='UNIT PRICE. . . : '
UPRICE      DFHMDF POS=(9,20),                             X
                   LENGTH=06,                              X
                   COLOR=TURQUOISE,                        X
                   ATTRB=(NORM,PROT),                      X
                   PICOUT='ZZ9.99'
            DFHMDF POS=(11,1),                             X
                   LENGTH=18,                              X
                   ATTRB=(NORM,PROT),                      X
                   COLOR=GREEN,                            X
                   INITIAL='REORDER POINT . : '
```

Description

- The parameters of a DMFHDF macro give the starting position of the field on the screen, the length of the field, its display attributes, its color, its initial value, and the Picture for how the data in a field should be formatted.

- The POS parameter gives the starting position of each field and the LENGTH parameter gives the length of each field. However, each field starts with an *attribute byte* that contains information about the attributes of the field. As a result, a field that starts in column 1 with a length of 4 actually appears in columns 2 through 5.

- The ATTRB parameter gives the attributes of a field. NORM means that the field should be displayed with normal intensity, while BRT means it should be displayed with high intensity. PROT means that a field can't be changed, while UNPROT means that a field can be changed. IC means that the initial cursor should be on the field when the screen is displayed.

Figure 19-6   The BMS mapset for the CICS inquiry program (part 2 of 3)

The code for the BMS mapset   **Page 3**

```
RPOINT     DFHMDF POS=(11,20),                                      X
                  LENGTH=06,                                        X
                  COLOR=TURQUOISE,                                  X
                  ATTRB=(NORM,PROT),                                X
                  PICOUT='ZZ,ZZ9'
           DFHMDF POS=(12,1),                                       X
                  LENGTH=18,                                        X
                  ATTRB=(NORM,PROT),                                X
                  COLOR=GREEN,                                      X
                  INITIAL='ON HAND . . . . : '
ONHAND     DFHMDF POS=(12,20),                                      X
                  LENGTH=06,                                        X
                  COLOR=TURQUOISE,                                  X
                  ATTRB=(NORM,PROT),                                X
                  PICOUT='ZZ,ZZ9'
           DFHMDF POS=(13,1),                                       X
                  LENGTH=18,                                        X
                  ATTRB=(NORM,PROT),                                X
                  COLOR=GREEN,                                      X
                  INITIAL='ON ORDER. . . . : '
ONORDER    DFHMDF POS=(13,20),                                      X
                  LENGTH=06,                                        X
                  COLOR=TURQUOISE,                                  X
                  ATTRB=(NORM,PROT),                                X
                  PICOUT='ZZ,ZZ9'
********************************************************************
MESSAGE    DFHMDF POS=(23,1),                                       X
                  LENGTH=79,                                        X
                  ATTRB=(BRT,PROT),                                 X
                  COLOR=YELLOW
           DFHMDF POS=(24,1),                                       X
                  LENGTH=20,                                        X
                  ATTRB=(NORM,PROT),                                X
                  COLOR=BLUE,                                       X
                  INITIAL='F3=Exit    F12=Cancel'
DUMMY      DFHMDF POS=(24,79),                                      X
                  LENGTH=1,                                         X
                  ATTRB=(DRK,PROT,FSET),                            X
                  INITIAL=' '
********************************************************************
           DFHMSD TYPE=FINAL
           END
```

Description

- A DFHMSD marks the end of each mapset as well as the start of each mapset. The ending macro has just one parameter: TYPE=FINAL.

- The PRINT NOGEN command at the start of the program tells the assembler not to print the statements that are generated by the assembly. This prevents the printing of hundreds of lines of assembled instructions that you'll never refer to.

- The END command tells the assembler that there are no more source statements. It must be the last command in the mapset.

Figure 19-6   The BMS mapset for the CICS inquiry program (part 3 of 3)

The symbolic map

Figure 19-7 presents the *symbolic mapset* that the assembler produces from the mapset in figure 19-6. This is a copy member that can be copied into your COBOL program. It represents the fields that are stored in the CICS area while a task is running so your COBOL program can access them. Because this symbolic mapset contains just one map, you can also refer to it as a *symbolic map*. Similarly, if a symbolic mapset contains more than one map, you can refer to each map as a symbolic map.

If you look at both pages of the symbolic map for the inquiry program, you can see that the group item named INV1MP1I is redefined by a group item INV1MP1O. In other words, the symbolic map defines each field as both input and output. As a result, different pictures can be used for input and output. In this example, you can see that the numeric fields in the output area are defined as numeric edited so they're displayed properly, while the same fields in the input area are defined as alphanumeric. That works because these fields aren't used for input.

For each screen field that's named in the mapset, the symbolic map contains a data field, a length field, an attribute field, and a field that indicates if the value of the field has changed. The names for these fields are created by adding a one-character suffix to the label that was coded on the DFHMDF macro in the mapset. So the name of the input field for the field labeled ITEMNO is ITEMNOI, the name of the length field is ITEMNOL, the name of the attribute field is ITEMNOA, and the name of the field that indicates a change is ITEMNOF.

The code for the symbolic map   Page 1

```
01  INV1MP1I.
    02  FILLER PIC X(12).
    02  ITEMNOL    COMP  PIC  S9(4).
    02  ITEMNOF    PICTURE X.
    02  FILLER REDEFINES ITEMNOF.
      03 ITEMNOA    PICTURE X.
    02  ITEMNOI  PIC X(5).
    02  DESCL     COMP  PIC  S9(4).
    02  DESCF     PICTURE X.
    02  FILLER REDEFINES DESCF.
      03 DESCA    PICTURE X.
    02  DESCI  PIC X(20).
    02  UCOSTL    COMP  PIC  S9(4).
    02  UCOSTF    PICTURE X.
    02  FILLER REDEFINES UCOSTF.
      03 UCOSTA    PICTURE X.
    02  UCOSTI  PIC X(6).
    02  UPRICEL    COMP  PIC  S9(4).
    02  UPRICEF    PICTURE X.
    02  FILLER REDEFINES UPRICEF.
      03 UPRICEA    PICTURE X.
    02  UPRICEI  PIC X(6).
    02  RPOINTL    COMP  PIC  S9(4).
    02  RPOINTF    PICTURE X.
    02  FILLER REDEFINES RPOINTF.
      03 RPOINTA    PICTURE X.
    02  RPOINTI  PIC X(6).
    02  ONHANDL    COMP  PIC  S9(4).
    02  ONHANDF    PICTURE X.
    02  FILLER REDEFINES ONHANDF.
      03 ONHANDA    PICTURE X.
    02  ONHANDI  PIC X(6).
```

Description

- A *symbolic map* is a COBOL copy member that's created when you assemble a mapset. The fields in a symbolic map represent the data that's sent to and received from a terminal by a COBOL program.

- You use a Copy statement to copy the symbolic map it into the Working-Storage Section of your program.

- A symbolic map includes two 01-level items: one for input and one for output. Because the second item contains a Redefines clause (see the next page), it occupies the same storage space as the first item. That way, different Picture clauses can be used for input to a field and output from it.

- For each input field in the mapset (I), the symbolic map contains a field that indicates the length of the data in the field (L), a field that indicates if the user made changes to the field (F), and a field that contains the attributes for output operations (A).

Figure 19-7   The symbolic map for the CICS inquiry program (part 1 of 2)

In the redefined area for the output fields, you'll notice that only the data fields are named, like ITEMNOO and DESCO. The length, attribute, and change indicator fields are coded as FILLER. To change the value of any of these fields for an output operation, then, you have to refer to the fields in the input area.

As you work with a symbolic map, remember that the map represents the screen data in CICS storage. As a result, you just need to know the names of the fields that you're going to use in your COBOL programs; you don't have to be concerned with the details of how they're defined. The fields you'll use the most are the length fields (with data names ending in *L*) and the fields that contain the data (with data names ending in *I* for input fields and *O* for output fields).

The code for the symbolic map   **Page 2**

```
02  ONORDERL     COMP  PIC  S9(4).
02  ONORDERF     PICTURE X.
02  FILLER REDEFINES ONORDERF.
   03 ONORDERA    PICTURE X.
02  ONORDERI  PIC X(6).
02  MESSAGEL     COMP  PIC  S9(4).
02  MESSAGEF     PICTURE X.
02  FILLER REDEFINES MESSAGEF.
   03 MESSAGEA    PICTURE X.
02  MESSAGEI  PIC X(79).
02  DUMMYL       COMP  PIC  S9(4).
02  DUMMYF       PICTURE X.
02  FILLER REDEFINES DUMMYF.
   03 DUMMYA     PICTURE X.
02  DUMMYI  PIC X(1).

01  INV1MP1O REDEFINES INV1MP1I.
02  FILLER PIC X(12).
02  FILLER PICTURE X(3).
02  ITEMNOO  PIC X(5).
02  FILLER PICTURE X(3).
02  DESCO  PIC X(20).
02  FILLER PICTURE X(3).
02  UCOSTO PIC ZZ9.99.
02  FILLER PICTURE X(3).
02  UPRICEO PIC ZZ9.99.
02  FILLER PICTURE X(3).
02  RPOINTO PIC ZZ,ZZ9.
02  FILLER PICTURE X(3).
02  ONHANDO PIC ZZ,ZZ9.
02  FILLER PICTURE X(3).
02  ONORDERO PIC ZZ,ZZ9.
02  FILLER PICTURE X(3).
02  MESSAGEO  PIC X(79).
02  FILLER PICTURE X(3).
02  DUMMYO  PIC X(1).
```

Description

- The definitions of the input fields are redefined by the definitions of the output fields. For each output field (O), the symbolic map contains a Picture for the output data.

Figure 19-7   The symbolic map for the CICS inquiry program (part 2 of 2)

The structure chart

Figure 19-8 presents the structure chart for the CICS inquiry program. Because it uses pseudo-conversational programming, its design is quite different from what you might expect. That's because each time CICS starts a program, the program has to determine if it should start from scratch or if it's in the middle of an interaction.

For now, assume that the user has entered an item number and pressed the Enter key, which is the normal condition. In that case, module 0000 invokes module 1000 to process the input map. Then, module 1000 calls module 1100 to retrieve the item-number from the screen and module 1200 to edit it. If module 1200 doesn't detect any problems with the item number, module 1000 calls module 1300 to issue a Read command that retrieves the requested record. If the record is read successfully, it's passed back to the program through CICS, and module 1000 calls module 1400 to send the output map to the screen with the data from the record. On the other hand, if either module 1200 or module 1300 detects an error condition, module 1000 calls module 1400 to send an error message to the terminal user.

If module 0000 detects a condition other than the "normal" condition, it can do one of three actions. First, it can call module 1400 to send an error message to the user. Second, it can call module 1400 to send a "fresh" data entry screen to the terminal to let the user start a new inquiry. Or third, it can call module 2000 to send a termination message by using a CICS statement that doesn't use the map.

Note, here, that module 1400 is called any time information is sent to the screen via the map. That's true whether the data from an inventory record is being displayed, an error message is being displayed, or the screen is being refreshed. To accomplish that, this module must be able to determine what information is to be sent to the screen. You'll see how that's done when you review the COBOL code for this program.

The structure chart for the CICS inquiry program

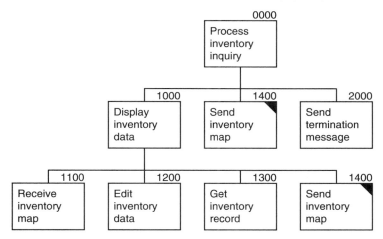

Description

- Because this program is pseudo-conversational, it must determine what processing needs to be done each time it's executed. Module 0000 makes that determination and calls module 1000, 1400, or 2000 based on the results.

- If the program is being executed for the first time, module 0000 calls module 1400 to display the inventory map on the screen. Module 0000 also calls module 1400 if the user requests that the screen be refreshed by pressing the Clear key.

- If the user presses the Enter key, module 0000 calls module 1000. This module begins by calling module 1100 to receive the inventory map. Then, it calls module 1200 to edit the item number entered by the user to make sure it's valid. If it is, module 1000 calls module 1300 to retrieve the record for that item from the inventory master file. If the record is found, module 1000 calls module 1400 to display the item information on the screen.

- If the user presses an invalid key, presses the Enter key without entering an item number, or enters an invalid item number, module 0000 calls module 1400 to display an error message on the screen.

- If the user presses the PF3 or PF12 key, module 0000 calls module 2000 to send a termination message. Then, module 0000 ends the transaction.

Figure 19-8   The structure chart for the CICS inquiry program

The COBOL listing

Figure 19-9 presents the source code for the CICS version of the customer inquiry program. The first thing you should notice is that the Environment Division and the File Section don't include any entries. That's because the inventory master file that's used by this program is defined in a CICS table called the *File Control Table*, or *FCT*. Because the FCT keeps track of the characteristics of the file, you don't have to code Select or FD statements for it.

In the Working-Storage Section of this program, you can see the one switch and the one flag used by this program. The three conditions that are defined for the flag will be used to determine which form of the SEND MAP command is used when the inventory map is sent to the screen.

The next field is for data related to the communication area. As you'll recall, this area can be used to store the data that's passed to and from the program. To use the communication area, you need to provide two definitions for it in your program: one in the Working-Storage Section and one in the Linkage Section. The working-storage definition in this program is named COMMUNICATION-AREA and the Linkage Section definition is named DFHCOMMAREA. Although you can use any name for the working-storage field, you must use the name DFHCOMMAREA for the Linkage Section field.

In a more complicated program, the communication area can contain many fields. In this program, however, the communication area is a simple one-byte field. You'll see how the inquiry program uses this communication area when you review the Procedure Division code.

The next working-storage entry is RESPONSE-CODE, which must be defined as Pic S9(8) Comp. This field is used to test the completion status of the CICS READ command that retrieves records from the inventory master file. This field is followed by a field that contains a message that's displayed when the user ends the program.

After the message field and the record description for the inventory file, there are two Copy statements. The first one copies the symbolic map for the mapset named INV1MS, while the second one copies the DFHAID member that is supplied by IBM.

The CICS inquiry program

Page 1

```
IDENTIFICATION DIVISION.
PROGRAM-ID.   INVS1I.
*
ENVIRONMENT DIVISION.
DATA DIVISION.
FILE SECTION.
*
WORKING-STORAGE SECTION.
*
01   SWITCHES.
     05   VALID-DATA-SWITCH        PIC X       VALUE 'Y'.
          88 VALID-DATA                        VALUE 'Y'.
*
01   FLAGS.
     05   SEND-FLAG                PIC X.
          88   SEND-ERASE                      VALUE '1'.
          88   SEND-DATAONLY                   VALUE '2'.
          88   SEND-DATAONLY-ALARM             VALUE '3'.
*
01   COMMUNICATION-AREA           PIC X.
01   RESPONSE-CODE                PIC S9(8)   COMP.
01   END-OF-SESSION-MESSAGE       PIC X(23)
                                  VALUE 'INVENTORY INQUIRY ENDED'.
*
01   INVENTORY-MASTER-RECORD.
     05   IM-ITEM-NO               PIC X(5).
     05   IM-DESCRIPTIVE-DATA.
          10   IM-ITEM-DESC        PIC X(40).
          10   IM-UNIT-COST        PIC S9(3)V99.
          10   IM-UNIT-PRICE       PIC S9(3)V99.
     05   IM-INVENTORY-DATA.
          10   IM-REORDER-POINT    PIC S9(5).
          10   IM-ON-HAND          PIC S9(5).
          10   IM-ON-ORDER         PIC S9(5).
*
COPY INV1MS.
*
COPY DFHAID.
*
LINKAGE SECTION.
01   DFHCOMMAREA                  PIC X.
```

Description

- The File Section in the Environment Division doesn't include any entries because the inventory master file is defined in a CICS table called the *File Control Table*, or *FCT*.

- The RESPONSE-CODE field is used to store the response code that's returned to the program when an I/O operation is requested.

- The first Copy statement is for the symbolic map. The second one is for the DFHAID copy member in figure 19-4.

- The DFHCOMMAREA field in the Linkage Section is a one-byte field that holds the data that's passed to the program through the CICS communication area.

Figure 19-9   The COBOL listing for the CICS inquiry program (part 1 of 4)

Page 2 of the COBOL listing presents the top-level procedure for this program. It contains the logic required to implement the pseudo-conversational design. To start, this procedure moves the data in the DFHCOMMAREA field in the Linkage Section to the Communication-Area field in the Working-Storage Section. Then, an Evaluate statement specifies the actions that are required for the several conditions the program may encounter when it's started.

The first When clause in this statement tests the value of EIBCALEN, which is the EIB field that contains the length of the data passed to the program through its communication area. If the length is zero, it means that no data was passed to the program, which indicates that there was no previous execution of the program. As a result, procedure 1400 is performed to send the inventory map to the screen. But first, the program initializes the map by moving Low-Value to the output area, and sets Send-Erase to True so procedure 1400 will know to clear the screen before displaying the map.

The next four When clauses test for values in the EIBAID field, which gives the value of the AID key that the user pressed to start this execution of the program. Each of these conditions uses a data name from the DFHAID copy member. The program checks the EIBAID field so it can avoid retrieving data from the terminal if the function it's about to perform doesn't call for it. That reduces network use and improves overall system performance.

If the user pressed the Clear key (DFHCLEAR), the program initializes the map, sets Send-Erase to True, and performs procedure 1400 to restart with a fresh screen. If the user pressed one of the program attention (PA) keys (DFHPA1 OR DFHPA2 OR DFHPA3), no special action is taken. Then, the Continue statement causes program execution to continue with the first statement after the Evaluate statement.

If the user pressed the PF3 or PF12 key (DFHPF3 OR DFHPF12), the program performs procedure 2000 to display a termination message and then issues a CICS RETURN command to end the program. Finally, if the user pressed the Enter key (DFHENTER), the program performs procedure 1000 to receive and process the item map.

If none of these conditions are true, the When Other clause performs procedure 1400 to display an error message that indicates that an invalid key was pressed. This time, Send-Dataonly-Alarm is set to True so procedure 1400 will use the right form of the SEND MAP command.

Unless the RETURN command was executed in response to PF3 or PF12, the program continues with the RETURN command that follows the Evaluate statement. It causes CICS to invoke the same trans-id (INV1) the next time the user presses one of the AID keys. It also says that the data in COMMUNICA-TION-AREA should be passed to the next execution of the program through the CICS communication area. Be aware that you can put a value in this field, if it's required by the program specifications. In this case, though, that's not necessary because the program never checks the value of COMMUNICATION-AREA, only its length.

The CICS inquiry program   **Page 2**

```
PROCEDURE DIVISION.
*
 0000-PROCESS-INVENTORY-INQUIRY.
*
     MOVE DFHCOMMAREA TO COMMUNICATION-AREA.

     EVALUATE TRUE
         WHEN EIBCALEN = ZERO
             MOVE LOW-VALUE TO INV1MP1O
             SET SEND-ERASE TO TRUE
             PERFORM 1400-SEND-INVENTORY-MAP
         WHEN EIBAID = DFHCLEAR
             MOVE LOW-VALUE TO INV1MP1O
             SET SEND-ERASE TO TRUE
             PERFORM 1400-SEND-INVENTORY-MAP
         WHEN EIBAID = DFHPA1 OR DFHPA2 OR DFHPA3
             CONTINUE
         WHEN EIBAID = DFHPF3 OR DFHPF12
             PERFORM 2000-SEND-TERMINATION-MESSAGE
             EXEC CICS
                 RETURN
             END-EXEC
         WHEN EIBAID = DFHENTER
             PERFORM 1000-DISPLAY-INVENTORY-DATA
         WHEN OTHER
             MOVE LOW-VALUE TO INV1MP1O
             MOVE 'Invalid key pressed.' TO MESSAGEO
             SET SEND-DATAONLY-ALARM TO TRUE
             PERFORM 1400-SEND-INVENTORY-MAP
     END-EVALUATE.

     EXEC CICS
         RETURN TRANSID('INV1')
                 COMMAREA(COMMUNICATION-AREA)
     END-EXEC.
```

Description

- To implement pseudo-conversational programming, the first procedure evaluates two fields in the Execute Interface Block in working storage. This block is inserted by the CICS translator although you can't see it in the source listing.

- This first When clause in the Evaluate statement tests to see whether EIBCALEN is equal to zero. If it is, it means that the DFHCOMMAREA has a length of zero, which means that this is the first execution of the program.

- The next four When clauses test the EIBAID field to see whether the user pressed one of the AID keys.

- The When Other clause is executed if the user pressed an invalid key.

- The CICS Return command after the Evaluate statement is executed unless the Return command has been executed in response to the PF3 or PF12 AID key.

Figure 19-9   The COBOL listing for the CICS inquiry program (part 2 of 4)

If the user pressed the Enter key, procedure 1000 is performed. This procedure performs procedure 1100 to get the item number the user entered on the screen and procedure 1200 to edit the number. If the number is valid, procedure 1000 performs procedure 1300 to retrieve the requested record from the inventory master file. Then, if the record is retrieved so the item number is still valid, the program displays the inventory data by performing procedure 1400 with Send-Dataonly set to True. Otherwise, procedure 1000 performs procedure 1400 with Send-Dataonly-Alarm set to True to alert the user that the item number isn't valid.

To get the user entry, procedure 1100 contains a single CICS RECEIVE MAP command. This command receives data from the terminal using the INV1MP1 map in the INV1MS mapset. After CICS processes this command, the item number the user entered is stored in the ITEMNOI field in the symbolic map.

The only editing requirement for this program is that the user must enter an item number. Procedure 1200 does this editing by checking the length and input fields of the item number in the symbolic map. If the length is zero, it means that the user didn't enter anything or pressed the Erase-EOF key. In either case, no data is transmitted back to CICS so the ITEMNOI field will contain low-values. Since low-values and spaces aren't the same, this routine also checks to see whether the input field contains spaces. If either of these error conditions is true, procedure 1200 turns the valid-data switch off so procedure 1000 can determine the processing it should do next. Procedure 1200 also moves an error message to the output MESSAGE field (MESSAGEO) in the symbolic map.

If procedure 1200 didn't turn the valid-data switch off, procedure 1000 performs procedure 1300 to issue the CICS command that retrieves the requested record from the inventory file. This procedure starts by issuing a CICS READ command that tells CICS to read a record from the file (dataset) named INVMAST into the working-storage field named INVENTORY-MASTER-RECORD. The RIDFLD specifies that the key value for the record is in ITEMNOI, which is in the symbolic map, and the RESP option specifies that the response code that indicates whether the operation was successful should be placed in the working-storage field named RESPONSE-CODE.

The code that follows the READ command tests the value of the response-code field. To do that, it uses the special keyword DFHRESP followed by the condition to be tested. Here, the program tests for a NORMAL response and the not-found condition (NOTFND). If the command completed normally, the program moves data from the inventory record to the corresponding fields in the output map. But if the NOTFND condition occurred, the program sets the valid-data switch to N, moves an appropriate error message to MESSAGEO, and clears the output fields in the symbolic map as shown on the next page of this listing.

The CICS inquiry program   **Page 3**

```
1000-DISPLAY-INVENTORY-DATA.
*
     PERFORM 1100-RECEIVE-INVENTORY-MAP.
     PERFORM 1200-EDIT-INVENTORY-DATA.
     IF VALID-DATA
         PERFORM 1300-GET-INVENTORY-RECORD
     END-IF.
     IF VALID-DATA
         SET SEND-DATAONLY TO TRUE
         PERFORM 1400-SEND-INVENTORY-MAP
     ELSE
         SET SEND-DATAONLY-ALARM TO TRUE
         PERFORM 1400-SEND-INVENTORY-MAP
     END-IF.
*
 1100-RECEIVE-INVENTORY-MAP.
*
     EXEC CICS
         RECEIVE MAP('INV1MP1')
                 MAPSET('INV1MS')
                 INTO(INV1MP1I)
     END-EXEC.
*
 1200-EDIT-INVENTORY-DATA.
*
     IF    ITEMNOL = ZERO
        OR ITEMNOI = SPACE
        MOVE 'N' TO VALID-DATA-SWITCH
        MOVE 'You must enter an item number.'
            TO MESSAGEO
     END-IF.
*
 1300-GET-INVENTORY-RECORD.
*
     EXEC CICS
         READ DATASET('INVMAST')
              INTO(INVENTORY-MASTER-RECORD)
              RIDFLD(ITEMNOI)
              RESP(RESPONSE-CODE)
     END-EXEC.
     EVALUATE RESPONSE-CODE
        WHEN DFHRESP(NORMAL)
            MOVE SPACE                TO MESSAGEO
            MOVE INV-ITEM-DESCRIPTION TO DESCO
            MOVE INV-UNIT-COST        TO UCOSTO
            MOVE INV-UNIT-PRICE       TO UPRICEO
            MOVE INV-REORDER-POINT    TO RPOINTO
            MOVE INV-ON-HAND          TO ONHANDO
            MOVE INV-ON-ORDER         TO ONORDERO
```

Figure 19-9   The COBOL listing for the CICS inquiry program (part 3 of 4)

If RESPONSE-CODE indicates any other condition, it means that a serious error occurred when the READ command was executed. In that case, the program handles the error by issuing a CICS ABEND command to terminate the program abnormally.

Unless procedure 1300 terminates the program, procedure 1000 continues by performing procedure 1400 to issue the appropriate SEND MAP command. In this procedure, one of three SEND MAP commands is issued depending on the setting of the Send-Flag field. Notice that all three commands specify the same mapset, map, and source of the data to be sent to the screen (the output area of the symbolic map). It's the other parameters that vary.

The first SEND MAP command is issued if the Send-Erase setting is turned on. That happens when the program is started for the first time or when the user presses the Clear key. This command includes the ERASE option, which causes the screen to be erased before the map is displayed. As a result, the screen will look like the first one in figure 9-5.

The second SEND MAP command is issued if the Send-Dataonly setting is turned on. That happens when the user enters a valid item number. Then, the SEND MAP command includes the DATAONLY option. That means that only the data in the symbolic map is sent to the terminal, because the literals that make up the headings, labels, and instructions are already there from the previous execution of the program. This improves the performance of the program.

The third SEND MAP command is issued if the Send-Dataonly-Alarm setting is turned on. That happens when the user presses an invalid key or enters an invalid item number. Then, the SEND MAP command includes the DATAONLY and ALARM options. The ALARM option causes an audio beep at the terminal to call the user's attention to the error.

The last procedure in this program, procedure 2000, is performed when the user presses the PF3 or PF12 key to end the program. This procedure issues a SEND TEXT command that displays the message that's stored in the working-storage field named END-OF-SESSION-MESSAGE. This command also includes the ERASE option to clear the screen before the message is displayed and the FREEKB option to unlock the keyboard after the message is sent. If FREEKB is omitted, the user has to press the Reset key to unlock the keyboard before continuing.

The CICS inquiry program   **Page 4**

```
        WHEN DFHRESP(NOTFND)
            MOVE 'N' TO VALID-DATA-SWITCH
            MOVE 'That inventory item does not exist.' TO MESSAGEO
            MOVE SPACE TO DESCO
            MOVE ZERO  TO UCOSTO
                          UPRICEO
                          RPOINTO
                          ONHANDO
                          ONORDERO
        WHEN OTHER
            EXEC CICS
                ABEND
            END-EXEC
    END-EVALUATE.
*
 1400-SEND-INVENTORY-MAP.
*
    EVALUATE TRUE
        WHEN SEND-ERASE
            EXEC CICS
                SEND MAP('INV1MP1')
                    MAPSET('INV1MS')
                    FROM(INV1MP1O)
                    ERASE
            END-EXEC
        WHEN SEND-DATAONLY
            EXEC CICS
                SEND MAP('INV1MP1')
                    MAPSET('INV1MS')
                    FROM(INV1MP1O)
                    DATAONLY
            END-EXEC
        WHEN SEND-DATAONLY-ALARM
            EXEC CICS
                SEND MAP('INV1MP1')
                    MAPSET('INV1MS')
                    FROM(INV1MP1O)
                    DATAONLY
                    ALARM
            END-EXEC
    END-EVALUATE.
*
 2000-SEND-TERMINATION-MESSAGE.
*
    EXEC CICS
        SEND TEXT FROM(END-OF-SESSION-MESSAGE)
                ERASE
                FREEKB
    END-EXEC.
```

Figure 19-9   The COBOL listing for the CICS inquiry program (part 4 of 4)

Perspective

The goal of this chapter has been to introduce you to the way that most interactive COBOL programs are developed on an IBM mainframe. To be an effective CICS programmer, though, there's much more to learn. In particular, you need to master all of the CICS commands and features as well as the pseudo-conversational programming style. For a complete course on CICS programming, we recommend our two *CICS for the COBOL Programmer* books.

If you've read chapter 17, you can now compare the two ways that interactive programs are developed. With a compiler like the one for Micro Focus COBOL, you use non-standard COBOL statements that are relatively easy to use. With CICS, you have to learn a completely new set of commands and features that are far more complicated than COBOL statements. That's why CICS programmers tend to be the highest paid COBOL programmers.

Summary

- Every CICS program is associated with a *transaction* that can be invoked by entering a *transaction-id*. When you invoke a transaction, CICS starts a *task* that runs within CICS and uses CICS storage.

- CICS provides functional modules that support CICS programs. The terminal control and *BMS* (*Basic Mapping Support*) modules control interactions with the display station, and the file control modules control interactions with the access methods like VSAM.

- To use BMS, you code an *assembler language* program called a *mapset* that contains the definitions of one or more *maps*. Then, you assemble the mapset to create a *physical map* that's used to determine the appearance of the data displayed on the screen and a *symbolic map* that's used by the COBOL program.

- CICS programs are typically implemented using *pseudo-conversational programming* to minimize the system resources they use. With this type of programming, a program ends after it sends data to a terminal. Then, CICS restarts the program when the user completes an entry.

- To use CICS services from a COBOL program, you code CICS commands. Then, before you compile the program, the *CICS translator* converts the commands to COBOL code that can be compiled by the COBOL compiler.

- The CICS translator also inserts the *Execute Interface Block* (*EIB*) into the Linkage Section of a COBOL program. The EIB includes an EIBAID field that contains the one-byte value that represents which key the user pressed and an EIBCALEN field that provides the length of the *communication area* that's passed to the program.

- Since the files that are used by a CICS program are defined in a CICS table called the *File Control Table*, you don't code Select or FD statements in the program. You also use CICS commands for all I/O operations.

Terms

CICS	EIB
Customer Information Control System	communication area
transaction	program attention key
transaction identifier	PA key
trans-id	assembler language
task	assembler
BMS	physical mapset
Basic Mapping Support	symbolic mapset
mapset	macro
map	attribute byte
pseudo-conversational programming	CUA
attention identifier key	Common User Access
AID key	screen painter
conversational program	symbolic map
CICS translator	File Control Table
Execute Interface Block	FCT

Objectives

- Describe the difference between a transaction and a task.

- Name two CICS modules that support application programming.

- Explain how pseudo-conversational programming works and why it's recommended for CICS programs.

- Describe two functions that the CICS translator performs.

- Describe the use of the Execute Interface Block and its EIBCALEN and EIBAID fields in a COBOL program.

- Describe the use of the DFHAID copy member in a COBOL program.

- In general terms, describe the three macros that you use when you code a BMS mapset.

- Explain how a symbolic map is used in a COBOL program.

- In general terms, describe the coding of the first procedure in a CICS program.

- In general terms, describe the coding of a CICS SEND MAP command.

- In general terms, describe the coding of a CICS READ command.

20

How to develop database programs on an IBM mainframe

In section 3 of this book, you learned how to work with data that's stored in standard sequential and indexed files. Some applications, though, require more complex data structures. For those applications, relational databases like DB2 are often used.

This chapter shows you how to write COBOL programs that process data that's stored in a DB2 database. However, it is only an introduction. For a complete course on DB2 programming, please refer to our two DB2 books: *DB2 for the COBOL Programmer, Part 1* and *Part 2*.

DB2 and the relational database model

In 1970, Dr. E. F. Codd developed a model for a new type of database called a *relational database*. This type of database eliminated some of the problems that were associated with standard files. By using the relational model, you can reduce data redundancy, which saves disk storage and leads to efficient data retrieval. You can also access and modify the data in a way that is both intuitive and efficient.

DB2, or *Database 2*, is a *relational database management system (RDBMS)* that runs on IBM mainframe computers. Because DB2 also runs on AS/400 mid-range computers and on PCs, DB2 can be used throughout an organization. In this chapter, you'll learn how to use DB2 through COBOL programs on an IBM mainframe.

How a relational database is organized

The model for a relational database states that data is stored in one or more *tables*. It also states that each table can be viewed as a two-dimensional array consisting of horizontal *rows* and vertical *columns*. This is illustrated by the relational database table in figure 20-1. In this table, each row contains information about a single customer.

At the intersection of each column and row is a *value*. In this figure, for example, the highlighted value is DENVILLE, which is the city for customer number 400002. The term *value* can be misleading, though, since it can be an alphanumeric (or *string*) value, a numeric value, or nothing (a *null* value).

In practice, the rows and columns of a relational database table are often referred to by the terms *records* and *fields*. This makes sense because each row is comparable to a record in a traditional file, and each column is comparable to a field. As a result, these terms can be used interchangeably.

If a table contains one or more columns that uniquely identify each row in the table, you can define these columns as the *primary key* of the table. For instance, the primary key of the customer table in this figure is the customer number, which has been given the name CUSTNO.

Indexes provide an efficient way to access the rows in a table based on the values in one or more columns. Because applications typically access table rows by referring to their key values, an index is automatically created for each primary key. But you can define indexes for other columns as well. Like a key, an index can include one or more columns.

A customer table

Primary Key		Columns			Value		
CUSTNO	FNAME	LNAME	ADDR	CITY	STATE	ZIPCODE	
400001	KEITH	MCDONALD	4501 W MOCKINGBIRD	DALLAS	TX	75209	
400002	KAREN	ANNELLI	40 FORD RD	DENVILLE	NJ	07834	
400003	SUSAN	HOWARD	1107 SECOND AVE	REDWOOD CITY	CA	94063	Rows
400004	CAROL ANN	EVANS	74 SUTTON CT	GREAT LAKES	IL	60088	
400005	ELAINE	ROBERTS	12914 BRACKNELL	CERRITOS	CA	90701	

Concepts

- A relational database uses *tables* to store and manipulate data. Each table consists of one or more *rows*, or records, that contain the data for a single entry. Each row contains one or more *columns*, or fields, with each column representing a single item of data.

- The data in a specific column of a specific row can be referred to as a *value*.

- Most tables contain a *primary key* that uniquely identifies each row in the table. The primary key often consists of a single column, but it can also consist of two or more columns. In the table above, the customer number (CUSTNO) is the primary key.

- An *index* can be applied to any column in a table to improve performance when rows are accessed based on the values in that column. At the least, each table requires a *unique index* for its primary key.

Figure 20-1   How a relational database table is organized

How the tables in a relational database are related

The tables in a relational database can be related to other tables by values in specific columns. The two tables shown in figure 20-2 illustrate this concept. Here, each row in the customer table is related to one or more rows in the invoice table. This is called a *one-to-many relationship*.

Typically, relationships exist between the primary key in one table and a *foreign key* in another table. The foreign key is one or more columns in a table that refer to a primary key in the other table.

Although one-to-many relationships are the most common, two tables can also have a one-to-one or many-to-many relationship. If a table has a *one-to-one relationship* with another table, the data in the two tables could be stored in a single table. Because of that, one-to-one relationships are used infrequently.

In contrast, a *many-to-many relationship* is usually implemented by using an intermediate table that has a one-to-many relationship with the two tables in the many-to-many relationship. In other words, a many-to-many relationship can usually be broken down into two one-to-many relationships.

The relationship between a customer table and an invoice table

CUSTNO	FNAME	LNAME	STREET	CITY	STATE	ZIPCODE
400001	KEITH	JONES	4501 W MOCKINGBIRD	DALLAS	TX	75209
400002	KAREN	ANNELLI	40 FORD RD	DENVILLE	NJ	07834
400003	SUSAN	HOWARD	1107 SECOND AVE	REDWOOD CITY	CA	94063
400004	CAROL ANN	EVANS	74 SUTTON CT	GREAT LAKES	IL	60088
400005	ELAINE	ROBERTS	12914 BRACKNELL	CERRITOS	CA	90701

Primary key   Foreign key

INVNO	INVCUST	INVDATE	INVTOTAL	PAYTOTAL	CRTOTAL
003584	400004	2000-04-28	51.75		
003585	400005	2000-04-28	292.83		
003586	400002	2000-04-28	68.87	68.87	
003587	400001	2000-04-28	22.09		
003588	400003	2000-04-28	57.63		
003589	400005	2000-04-28	711.05		150.00
003590	400001	2000-04-28	110.49	110.49	

Concepts

- The tables in a relational database are related to each other through their key columns. In the tables above, the customer number is used to relate the customer and invoice tables.

- In the customer table, the customer number column is the primary key. In the invoice table, the invoice number column is the primary key.

- In the invoice table, the customer number column is called a *foreign key* because it identifies a related row in the customer table.

- Three types of relationships can exist between tables. The most common type is *a one-to-many relationship* as illustrated above. A table can also have a *one-to-one relationship* or a *many-to-many relationship* with another table.

Figure 20-2   How the tables in a relational database are related

How to use SQL to work with a DB2 database

To work with the data in a relational database, you use *Structured Query Language*, or *SQL*. In the following topics, you'll learn about the SQL statements you're most likely to use in a COBOL program. Then, to give you a better understanding of how you use these statements, you'll see a complete COBOL program that includes many of them.

Introduction to Structured Query Language

Figure 20-3 summarizes some of the most common SQL statements used by DB2 application programmers. As you review the statements in this figure, keep in mind that they can have more complicated formats than what's shown here. These examples are intended only to give you a general idea of how you use these statements.

To retrieve data from a DB2 database, you use the SELECT statement as illustrated in the first example in this figure. This statement retrieves all the columns (*) from a table named MM01.CUSTOMER for the row whose customer number column (CUSTNO) has the value 400005. This data is then placed in a *result table*, which is a logical table that's created temporarily in the database. You'll learn more about working with result tables throughout the rest of this chapter.

The INSERT, UPDATE, and DELETE statements let you add, change, and delete rows from a table. The INSERT statement in this figure, for example, inserts a single row into the customer table with the indicated values. The UPDATE statement changes the value in the ZIPCODE column of the customer table to 93720 for all records that have a value of 93710 in that column. And the DELETE statement deletes the row from the customer table that has a value of 400005 in its CUSTNO column.

Incidentally, the execution of any of these first four statements can be referred to as a *query*. However, the term *query* is commonly used to refer to just the execution of SELECT statements, while the term *action query* is used to refer to INSERT, UPDATE, and DELETE statements. So that's the practice used in this chapter.

Although the SELECT statement shown in this figure creates a result table with a single row, a result table can contain many rows. To work with a multi-row result table from within a COBOL program, you use a *cursor*. You'll learn more about working with cursors later in this chapter. For now, just realize that to define and work with a cursor, you use the DECLARE CURSOR, OPEN, FETCH, and CLOSE statements listed in this figure.

The last statement listed in this figure, INCLUDE, works like the COBOL Copy statement. You use it to combine source code library members with your program code. You'll see how this works in the program that's presented later in this chapter.

SQL statements commonly used in COBOL programs

Statement	Description
SELECT	Retrieves data from one or more tables.
INSERT	Inserts one or more new rows into a table.
UPDATE	Updates one or more rows in a table.
DELETE	Deletes one or more rows from a table.
DECLARE CURSOR	Defines a cursor and the related cursor-controlled result table.
OPEN	Opens a cursor.
FETCH	Positions a cursor on the next row of its result table and assigns the values of that row to host variables.
CLOSE	Closes a cursor.
INCLUDE	Adds source code from library members into the program.

A SELECT statement that retrieves a single row from the customer table

```
SELECT  *
    FROM  MM01.CUSTOMER
        WHERE CUSTNO = '400005'
```

An INSERT statement that adds a single row to the customer table

```
INSERT INTO MM01.CUSTOMER
        (CUSTNO,    FNAME,    LNAME,    ADDR,
        CITY,      STATE,    ZIPCODE)
VALUES ('400006', 'CHUCK', 'GERARD', '811 E DECATUR',
        'FRESNO', 'CA',     '93720')
```

An UPDATE statement that changes the values in one column of selected rows of the customer table

```
UPDATE MM01.CUSTOMER
    SET ZIPCODE = '93720'
    WHERE ZIPCODE = '93710'
```

A DELETE statement that deletes one row from the customer table

```
DELETE FROM MM01.CUSTOMER
    WHERE CUSTNO = '400005'
```

Description

- The execution of a SELECT statement is commonly referred to as a *query*. In contrast, the execution of an INSERT, UPDATE, or DELETE statement can be referred to as an *action query*.

- The result of a SELECT statement is a *result table*. If a result table can contain more than one row, you must use a *cursor* to process it. See figure 20-6 for more information.

- In conversation, SQL is pronounced S-Q-L or *sequel*.

Figure 20-3   Introduction to Structured Query Language

How to retrieve data from a single table

Figure 20-4 presents another SELECT statement that illustrates how to get data from a single database table. This SELECT statement retrieves columns from a table named MM01.INVOICE. It selects a row from this invoice table only if it has a balance due that's greater than zero. And it sorts the returned rows by the balance due in descending sequence.

Please note in this SELECT statement that the last column in the query (BALANCE) is calculated by subtracting the payment total (PAYTOTAL) column and the credit total (CRTOTAL) column from the invoice total (INVTOTAL) column. In other words, the column named BALANCE doesn't actually exist in the database. This type of column is called a *calculated value*, and it exists only in the results of the query.

To help you understand how this SELECT statement works, this figure also shows the invoice table that this statement retrieves data from and the result table that's created as a result of this statement. As you can see, the result table contains only the columns specified in the SELECT statement. Three of those columns are taken directly from the invoice table, and the fourth is calculated from the other columns in this table. In addition, the result table contains rows only for those invoices that have a balance due that's greater than zero. Finally, the result table is sorted by the BALANCE column in descending sequence.

As you might guess, queries can have a significant effect on the performance of a program. In general, the more columns and rows that are returned by a query, the longer it takes to return the result table. When you design a query, then, you should try to keep the number of columns and rows to a minimum.

A SELECT statement that retrieves selected columns and rows from an invoice table

```
SELECT  INVNO, INVDATE, INVTOTAL,
        INVTOTAL - PAYTOTAL - CRTOTAL AS BALANCE
    FROM  MM01.INVOICE
        WHERE INVTOTAL - PAYTOTAL - CRTOTAL > 0
      ORDER BY BALANCE DESC
```

The INVOICE table

INVNO	INVCUST	INVDATE	INVTOTAL	PAYTOTAL	CRTOTAL
003584	400004	2000-04-28	51.75		
003585	400005	2000-04-28	292.83		
003586	400002	2000-04-28	68.87	68.87	
003587	400001	2000-04-28	22.09		
003588	400003	2000-04-28	57.63		
003589	400005	2000-04-28	711.05		150.00
003590	400001	2000-04-28	110.49	110.49	

The result table

INVNO	INVDATE	INVTOTAL	BALANCE
003589	2000-04-28	711.05	561.05
003585	2000-04-28	292.83	292.83
003588	2000-04-28	57.63	57.63
003584	2000-04-28	51.75	51.75
003587	2000-04-28	22.09	22.09

Explanation

Clause	Description
SELECT	Lists the columns to be included in the result table. Can include columns that are calculated from other columns in the table, called *calculated values*.
FROM	Specifies the name of the table that contains the columns you want to retrieve data from.
WHERE	Specifies a condition that must be met for a row to be included in the result table. The condition can refer to any of the columns in the table specified in the FROM clause.
ORDER BY	Lists one or more columns you want the result table sorted by. To sort a column in descending sequence, include the DESC keyword.

Figure 20-4   How to retrieve data from a single table

How to join data from two or more tables

Figure 20-5 presents a SELECT statement that retrieves data from two tables: a customer table and an invoice table. This type of operation is called a *join* because the data is joined together into a single result table. In this case, the result table includes one column from the customer table (LNAME) and three columns from the invoice table (INVNO, INVDATE, and INVTOTAL).

The SELECT statement in this figure illustrates the most common type of join, called an *inner join*, or *equi-join*. When you use an inner join, rows from the two tables in the join are included in the result table if their related columns match. These matching columns are specified in the SELECT statement. In the example in this figure, rows from the invoice and customer tables are included only if the value of the CUSTNO column in the customer table matches the value of the INVCUST column in one or more rows in the invoice table. If there aren't any invoices for a particular customer, that customer isn't included in the result table.

The second type of join is an *outer join*. These types of joins are distinguished by which unmatched rows they keep. In a *left outer join*, all of the rows in the first table are included in the result table. In a *right outer join*, all of the rows in the second table are included. And in a *full outer join*, the unmatched rows of both tables are included. If, for example, I had used a left outer join in this figure, all of the rows in the customer table would have been included in the result table, even if no matching rows were found in the invoice table.

Although this figure shows only how to join data from two tables, you should know that you can extend this syntax to join data from additional tables. If, for example, you also want to include line item data from a table named MM01.LINEITEM and the name of the invoice number column in that table is LIINV, you can code the FROM clause of the SELECT statement like this:

```
FROM MM01.CUSTOMER
    INNER JOIN MM01.INVOICE
        ON CUSTNO = INVCUST
    INNER JOIN MM01.LINEITEM
        ON INVNO = LIINV
```

Then, you can include any of the columns in the LINEITEM table in the column list of the SELECT statement.

A SELECT statement that joins data from a customer and an invoice table

```
SELECT LNAME, INVNO, INVDATE, INVTOTAL
    FROM MM01.CUSTOMER
        INNER JOIN MM01.INVOICE
            ON CUSTNO = INVCUST
            WHERE STATE = 'CA'
    ORDER BY LNAME, INVTOTAL DESC
```

The result table defined by the SELECT statement

LNAME	INVNO	INVDATE	INVTOTAL
HOWARD	003588	2000-04-28	57.63
ROBERTS	003589	2000-04-28	711.05
ROBERTS	003585	2000-04-28	292.83

Explanation

Clause	Description
SELECT	Lists the columns to be included in the result table. The columns can be from any of the tables specified on the FROM clause or can be calculated from any of the columns in those tables.
FROM	Specifies the names of the tables that contain the columns you want to retrieve data from and the relationship between them.
WHERE	Specifies a condition that must be met for a row to be included in the result table. The condition can refer to any of the columns in the tables specified on the FROM clause.
ORDER BY	Lists one or more columns you want the result table sorted by. To sort a column in descending sequence, include the DESC keyword.

Concepts

- A *join* lets you combine data from two or more tables into a single result table. The type of join you choose determines how the data is combined.

- An *inner join*, also called an *equi-join*, returns rows from both tables only if their related columns match. This is the join that's illustrated above.

- An *outer join* can return unmatched rows from one or both tables. A *left outer join* returns all of the rows from the first table and matching rows from the second table; a *right outer join* returns all of the rows from the second table and matching rows from the first table; and a *full outer join* returns all of the rows from both tables.

Figure 20-5   How to join data from two or more tables

How to create and work with result tables using embedded SQL

When you write a COBOL program that accesses data in a DB2 database, you code SQL statements within the COBOL program. These statements can be referred to as *embedded SQL statements*, or just *embedded SQL*. Figure 20-6 shows how to create and work with result tables using embedded SQL.

Notice that each of the statements presented in this figure starts with EXEC SQL and ends with END-EXEC. Also notice that most of the statements include references to one or more host variables. A *host variable* is a field that's defined within the COBOL program, and it's identified by a colon preceding the field name. The SELECT statement in this figure, for example, uses a host variable in its WHERE clause. That way, this statement can retrieve a different row each time it's executed depending on the value of this variable.

If you know that a result table will contain a single row, you can retrieve that row using a SELECT statement like the one shown in this figure. Unlike the SELECT statements presented earlier in this chapter, this statement includes an INTO clause. This clause specifies the names of the host variables where the data in the retrieved row will be placed.

If a result table can contain two or more rows, though, you have to use a cursor to work with it. A *cursor* is a pointer that identifies the current row in a result table. When you use a cursor, you work through a result table one row at a time, much as you read through a standard sequential file.

To define a cursor, you code a DECLARE CURSOR statement like the one shown in this figure. As you can see, this statement includes a SELECT statement. In this case, though, the SELECT statement doesn't include an INTO clause. That's because the DECLARE CURSOR statement just defines the cursor; it doesn't create the result table or process the data.

To create the result table that's defined by a cursor, you use an OPEN statement. This statement executes the SELECT statement within the DE-CLARE CURSOR statement to create a *cursor-controlled result table*. Then, DB2 positions the cursor just before the first row in the result table. Notice that the OPEN statement in this figure refers to the cursor by the name given on the DECLARE CURSOR statement, in this case, CUSTCURS.

To retrieve a row from a cursor-controlled result table, you use the FETCH statement. Notice that this statement includes an INTO clause that identifies the host variables where the data in the fetched row will be placed. Within a CO-BOL program, you can repeatedly execute FETCH statements until all the rows in the result table have been processed.

When you're done with a cursor, you can use the CLOSE statement to close it. Then, you can issue the OPEN statement to open it again and do further processing. You'll understand how that works when you see the program that's presented next. If you don't need to use the cursor again, though, you can omit the CLOSE statement and DB2 will automatically close the cursor when your program ends.

A SELECT statement that retrieves a single row

```
EXEC SQL
    SELECT CUSTNO, FNAME, LNAME, ADDR, CITY, STATE, ZIPCODE
    INTO :CUSTNO, :FNAME, :LNAME, :ADDR, :CITY, :STATE, :ZIPCODE
    FROM  MM01.CUSTOMER
        WHERE CUSTNO = :CUSTNO
END-EXEC.
```

A DECLARE CURSOR statement that defines a cursor named CUSTCURS

```
EXEC SQL
    DECLARE CUSTCURS CURSOR FOR
        SELECT CUSTNO, FNAME, LNAME, CITY, STATE, ZIPCODE
        FROM MM01.CUSTOMER
            WHERE STATE = :STATE
END-EXEC.
```

An OPEN statement that creates the result table defined by the CUSTCURS cursor

```
EXEC SQL
    OPEN CUSTCURS
END-EXEC
```

A FETCH statement that fetches the next row in the CUSTCURS result table

```
EXEC SQL
    FETCH CUSTCURS
        INTO :CUSTNO, :FNAME, :LNAME, :CITY, :STATE, :ZIPCODE
END-EXEC.
```

A CLOSE statement that closes the CUSTCURS cursor

```
EXEC SQL
    CLOSE CUSTCURS
END-EXEC.
```

Description

- SQL statements coded within a COBOL program are called *embedded SQL statements*, or just *embedded SQL*. These statements must be enclosed by EXEC SQL and END-EXEC as shown above.

- Embedded SQL statements can refer to fields defined within the COBOL program. These fields, called *host variables*, are identified by a colon preceding the field name.

- If a result table can contain more than one row, a *cursor* is used to identify the individual rows in the table and to scroll through those rows. To define the result table and the cursor that's used to process it, you use the DECLARE CURSOR statement. To process the result table, you use the OPEN, FETCH, and CLOSE statements.

- If a result table can contain a single row, you use the INTO clause in the SELECT statement to name the host variables where the column values from that row will be placed. You also use the INTO clause on a FETCH statement that retrieves a row from a cursor-controlled result table.

Figure 20-6   How to create and work with result tables using embedded SQL

A DB2 inquiry program

To help you understand how embedded SQL works, this chapter will now present an inquiry program that uses embedded SQL. This program retrieves data from the customer and invoice tables depending on the customer number entered by the user and then displays that data on a terminal. If you read the last chapter, you know that most mainframe shops use CICS to perform this type of interactive processing. To keep this program simple, though, it uses Accept and Display statements.

The interactive screen

Figure 20-7 illustrates how the inquiry program works. As you can see, this program accepts a series of customer numbers from the user. For each customer number, the program gets customer information from the customer table. It also gets the related invoice information for that customer from the invoice table. Because the invoice result table may contain more than one row for a customer, the inquiry program must use a cursor to process it.

In the first screen shown in this figure, you can see an inquiry for a customer who has made three purchases. The first line for this customer shows the data that's retrieved from the customer table; the next three lines show the data that's retrieved from the invoice table; and the last two lines show the summary data that's developed by the COBOL program. To end this session, the user has entered 999999.

In the second screen, you can see two more customer inquiries. The first inquiry shows customer and total data for a customer that didn't have any related rows in the invoice table. And the second inquiry shows the error message that's displayed when the user enters a customer number that can't be found in the customer table. This session also ends when the user enters 999999.

The screens in this figure show the mainframe output as it appears in a PC window when using a program called EXTRA! This program lets you attach your PC to an IBM mainframe via a direct, remote, or LAN connection. You can then use that window of your PC as a mainframe terminal. EXTRA! is just one of many third-party programs that provide this type of connectivity.

Screen 1

During the first inquiry session, the program displays information from three invoice rows for the customer number the user enters.

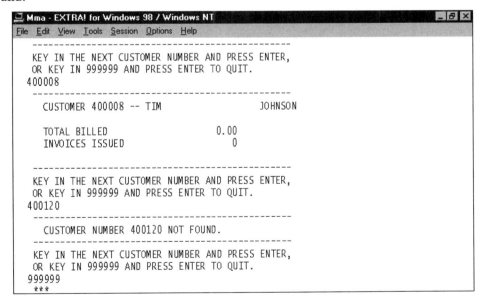

```
Mma - EXTRA! for Windows 98 / Windows NT                    _ 8 X
File  Edit  View  Tools  Session  Options  Help
     ------------------------------------------------
     KEY IN THE NEXT CUSTOMER NUMBER AND PRESS ENTER,
     OR KEY IN 999999 AND PRESS ENTER TO QUIT.
     400015
     ------------------------------------------------
       CUSTOMER 400015 -- VIVIAN            GEORGE

       INVOICE 062319 2000-05-17    181.42
       INVOICE 062320 2000-06-14   3405.00
       INVOICE 062333 2000-07-03    178.23
                                   -----------
       TOTAL BILLED                3764.65
       INVOICES ISSUED                   3


     ------------------------------------------------
     KEY IN THE NEXT CUSTOMER NUMBER AND PRESS ENTER,
     OR KEY IN 999999 AND PRESS ENTER TO QUIT.
     999999
       ***
```

Screen 2

During the second inquiry session, the user requests sales information for two customers. The first customer has no sales on file, and the second customer's number wasn't found.

```
Mma - EXTRA! for Windows 98 / Windows NT                    _ 8 X
File  Edit  View  Tools  Session  Options  Help
     ------------------------------------------------
     KEY IN THE NEXT CUSTOMER NUMBER AND PRESS ENTER,
     OR KEY IN 999999 AND PRESS ENTER TO QUIT.
     400008
     ------------------------------------------------
       CUSTOMER 400008 -- TIM              JOHNSON

       TOTAL BILLED                0.00
       INVOICES ISSUED                0


     ------------------------------------------------
     KEY IN THE NEXT CUSTOMER NUMBER AND PRESS ENTER,
     OR KEY IN 999999 AND PRESS ENTER TO QUIT.
     400120
     ------------------------------------------------
       CUSTOMER NUMBER 400120 NOT FOUND.
     ------------------------------------------------
     KEY IN THE NEXT CUSTOMER NUMBER AND PRESS ENTER,
     OR KEY IN 999999 AND PRESS ENTER TO QUIT.
     999999
       ***
```

Figure 20-7   The interactive screen for the inquiry program

The DCLGEN output

When you develop a COBOL program that gets data from a DB2 table, you include a description of the rows in the table called a *host structure*. Although you can code a host structure by yourself, it's easier to let DB2 develop it for you from the data definitions for the database. This is done by a utility that comes with DB2 called *DCLGEN*, which stands for *Declarations Generator*.

In the top of figure 20-8, you can see the DCLGEN output for the customer table. The first shaded block is an SQL DECLARE TABLE statement that names the table and defines each of its columns. This can be referred to as a *table declaration*, and it is taken right out of the DB2 catalog for the table.

The second shaded block in this figure is the host structure. It contains the COBOL definitions of the host variables you can use for a table. As you've already seen, you precede the name of a host variable with a colon when you use it in an SQL statement.

In the host variable declarations in this example, all of the fields contain character data. However, DB2 also supports other data types. DB2 uses these data types to determine the COBOL picture and usage for each field.

When you use DCLGEN to create the COBOL definitions for the host variables, you can be sure that the COBOL definitions correspond correctly to the DB2 data types. In addition, you supply the level-1 COBOL name for this host structure. In this example, I supplied the COBOL name CUSTOMER-ROW when I generated the declarations.

Normally, DCLGEN output is stored as a member of a partitioned data set so it can be included in the Working-Storage Section of a COBOL program using an INCLUDE statement. This is comparable to copying the copy member for the record description of a file into a COBOL program. You'll see an example of this in a moment.

This figure also shows the DCLGEN host structure for the invoice table. The first column in this table, INVCUST, contains the customer number that relates a row in this table to the customer table. In other words, INVCUST is a foreign key. Because a single customer can have more than one invoice, more than one invoice row can contain the same value in the INVCUST column. In contrast, the invoice number column, INVNO, is the primary key for the invoice table, and the value in this column uniquely identifies each row in the table.

Notice that four of the fields in this host structure, INVSUBT, INVSHIP, INVTAX, and INVTOTAL, are defined as numeric fields. That's because the corresponding columns in the invoice table are defined with the DECIMAL data type. The definition for the INVSUBT column, for example, looks like this:

```
INVSUBT    DECIMAL(9,2) NOT NULL
```

This indicates that the column should be defined with nine digits, two of which are to the right of the decimal point. So the host variable for this column is defined accordingly.

The DCLGEN output for the customer table

```
***********************************************************************
* DCLGEN TABLE(MM01.CUSTOMER)                                         *
*         LIBRARY(MM01.DB2.DCLGENS(CUSTOMER))                         *
*         ACTION(REPLACE)                                             *
*         LANGUAGE(COBOL)                                             *
*         STRUCTURE(CUSTOMER-ROW)                                     *
*         QUOTE                                                       *
* ... IS THE DCLGEN COMMAND THAT MADE THE FOLLOWING STATEMENTS        *
***********************************************************************
      EXEC SQL DECLARE MM01.CUSTOMER TABLE
      ( CUSTNO                    CHAR(6) NOT NULL,
        FNAME                     CHAR(20) NOT NULL,
        LNAME                     CHAR(30) NOT NULL,
        ADDR                      CHAR(30) NOT NULL,
        CITY                      CHAR(20) NOT NULL,
        STATE                     CHAR(2) NOT NULL,
        ZIPCODE                   CHAR(10) NOT NULL
      ) END-EXEC.
***********************************************************************
* COBOL DECLARATION FOR TABLE MM01.CUSTOMER                           *
***********************************************************************
  01  CUSTOMER-ROW.
      10 CUSTNO              PIC X(6).
      10 FNAME               PIC X(20).
      10 LNAME               PIC X(30).
      10 ADDR                PIC X(30).
      10 CITY                PIC X(20).
      10 STATE               PIC X(2).
      10 ZIPCODE             PIC X(10).
***********************************************************************
* THE NUMBER OF COLUMNS DESCRIBED BY THIS DECLARATION IS 7            *
***********************************************************************
```

— Table declaration

— Host structure

The host structure for the invoice table

```
01  INVOICE-ROW.
    10  INVCUST             PIC X(6).
    10  INVNO               PIC X(6).
    10  INVDATE             PIC X(10).
    10  INVSUBT             PIC S9999999V99 USAGE COMP-3.
    10  INVSHIP             PIC S99999V99 USAGE COMP-3.
    10  INVTAX              PIC S99999V99 USAGE COMP-3.
    10  INVTOTAL            PIC S9999999V99 USAGE COMP-3.
    10  INVPROM             PIC X(10).
```

Description

- When a COBOL program retrieves data from DB2 tables, it must include a *host structure* that defines the host variables where the data from a row in the result table will be stored.

- In most cases, you use a utility program that comes with DB2 called *DCLGEN* (*Declarations Generator*) to create a host structure from the table declaration. That way, you can be sure that the COBOL field definitions are compatible with the DB2 data.

- To include DCLGEN output in a COBOL program, you use the SQL INCLUDE statement.

Figure 20-8   The DCLGEN output for the customer and invoice tables

The structure chart

Figure 20-9 presents the structure chart for the DB2 inquiry program. To start, module 000 in this chart performs module 100 until the user signals the end of the program by entering 999999 as a customer number. Then, each time module 100 is performed, it performs module 110 to accept a customer number from the user, module 120 to get the related information from a row in the customer table, and module 130 to display that information. Next, it performs module 140 to get the invoices for the customer. Finally, it performs module 200 to display the sales totals for the customer.

Module 140 manages the functions that are needed to retrieve all the rows for the current customer from the invoice result table. To open the cursor-controlled result table, this module performs module 150. Then, it performs module 160 for each row in the result table. Module 160 performs module 170 to fetch the next row and module 180 to display the data in the row.

After all of the rows are processed, module 140 performs module 190 to close the cursor. That's necessary because if the user enters another customer number, module 150 will be executed again to open a new cursor-controlled result table that contains the invoice rows for that customer. If you have any trouble following how all this is going to work, it should become clear when you review the COBOL listing.

The structure chart

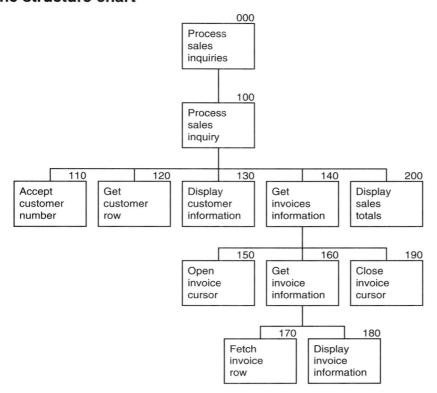

Description

- Module 000 in this structure chart performs module 100 once for each customer number that the user enters until the user ends the program by entering 999999 as the customer number.

- Module 100 performs module 110 to accept a customer number from the user; performs module 120 to get the row for that customer; and performs module 130 to display the information in that row. Then, module 100 performs module 140 to get the invoices related to the customer and module 200 to display the invoice totals for that customer.

- Each time module 140 is performed, it performs module 150 to open a cursor for an invoice result table that includes all the invoice rows for the customer that's being processed. Then, module 140 performs module 160 once for each invoice row. When all the invoices have been processed, module 140 performs module 190 to close the invoice cursor.

- Each time module 160 is performed, it performs module 170 to fetch the next invoice row in the cursor-controlled result table that has been opened. Then, module 160 performs module 180 to display the invoice information for that row.

Figure 20-9   The structure chart for the inquiry program

The COBOL listing

Figure 20-1 presents the source code for the DB2 inquiry program. The first thing you should notice is that you don't have to code anything for the database tables in the Input-Output Section of the Environment Division or in the File Section of the Data Division. Instead, you name the table you want to access when you code the SQL SELECT statement or DECLARE CURSOR statement. Then, DB2 gets the information it needs for that table from its DB2 catalogs. This simplifies the COBOL program.

In the Working-Storage Section of this program, you can see the definitions for four switches. These switches indicate (1) whether the user has entered 999999 to end the program; (2) whether a row matching the customer number entered by the user is found; (3) whether a valid cursor-controlled table has been created by the OPEN statement in module 150, the rows have been retrieved successfully from that table by the FETCH statement in module 170, and the cursor has been closed successfully by the CLOSE statement in module 190; and (4) whether the end of the invoice result table has been reached by the FETCH statement in module 170.

This program also includes two sets of fields for the totals the program accumulates as it processes the invoice rows for a customer. One group contains the INVOICES-COUNT and INVOICES-TOTAL fields that the program increments for each invoice row it processes. The other group contains the EDITED-COUNT and EDITED-TOTAL fields that are the edited versions of the total data that the program displays.

After these fields, you'll find three SQL INCLUDE statements. The first two statements include the DCLGEN output that defines the host variables for the rows in the customer and invoice tables. Then, you can refer to those variables in the Procedure Division of the program. The third statement includes the definition of the *SQL communication area*. DB2 uses this area to provide feedback about the success or failure of each operation. You'll see how to use one of the fields in this area in a moment.

The next SQL statement is the DECLARE CURSOR statement for the cursor-controlled result table that will hold the invoices for a customer. Within this DECLARE CURSOR statement, the SELECT statement defines the columns and rows that this table will contain. In this case, the result table will contain three columns from the invoice table and any rows whose INVCUST column have the same value as the CUSTNO host variable. This is the variable that will contain the customer number entered by the user.

Incidentally, this program uses single quotation marks (') instead of double quotation marks ("), which is common in mainframe programs. Also, this program uses SW in the switch names as an abbreviation for SWITCH. This too is a common practice.

The sales inquiry program   **Page 1**

```
IDENTIFICATION DIVISION.
*
PROGRAM-ID.     SALESINQ.
*
ENVIRONMENT DIVISION.
*
INPUT-OUTPUT SECTION.
*
FILE-CONTROL.
*
DATA DIVISION.
*
FILE SECTION.
*
WORKING-STORAGE SECTION.
*
01  SWITCHES.
*
    05  END-OF-INQUIRIES-SW     PIC X    VALUE 'N'.
        88  END-OF-INQUIRIES             VALUE 'Y'.
    05  CUSTOMER-FOUND-SW       PIC X    VALUE 'Y'.
        88  CUSTOMER-FOUND               VALUE 'Y'.
    05  VALID-CURSOR-SW         PIC X    VALUE 'Y'.
        88  VALID-CURSOR                 VALUE 'Y'.
    05  END-OF-INVOICES-SW      PIC X    VALUE 'N'.
        88  END-OF-INVOICES              VALUE 'Y'.
*
01  INVOICE-TOTAL-FIELDS    COMP-3.
*
    05  INVOICES-COUNT     PIC S9(5)    VALUE ZERO.
    05  INVOICES-TOTAL     PIC S9(7)V99 VALUE ZERO.
*
01  EDITED-TOTAL-FIELDS.
*
    05  EDITED-COUNT       PIC Z(4)9.
    05  EDITED-TOTAL       PIC Z(6)9.99.
*
    EXEC SQL
        INCLUDE CUSTOMER
    END-EXEC.
*
    EXEC SQL
        INCLUDE INVOICE
    END-EXEC.
*
    EXEC SQL
        INCLUDE SQLCA
    END-EXEC.
*
    EXEC SQL
        DECLARE INVCURS CURSOR FOR
            SELECT   INVNO, INVDATE, INVTOTAL
                FROM MM01.INVOICE
                WHERE INVCUST = :CUSTNO
    END-EXEC.
*
```

Figure 20-10   The COBOL listing for the inquiry program (part 1 of 3)

In the Procedure Division, module 000 performs module 100 until the end-of-inquiries switch is turned on. Module 100 starts by turning on the customer-found switch. Then, it performs module 110 to get the next customer number.

Module 110 uses Display statements to display the starting lines on the screen. Then, it issues an Accept statement to accept the customer number that the user enters into the host variable named CUSTNO. Last, it uses an If statement to turn on the end-of-inquiries switch if this customer number is 999999.

If the end-of-inquiries is turned on, module 100 doesn't perform any additional processing and the program ends. Otherwise, it continues by performing module 120 to get the customer row that corresponds to the customer number and module 130 to display the information for the customer.

Module 120 contains the SQL SELECT statement that retrieves a row from the customer table. Notice that the row that's retrieved is the one whose CUSTNO column has a value equal to the value of the CUSTNO host variable. If this row is found, DB2 moves the values of the two columns named in the SELECT clause into the host variables named in the INTO clause.

The If statement that follows this embedded SQL statement determines whether DB2 was able to find a customer row with a key that matched the value in the host variable. To determine that, the If statement tests the value of a variable named SQLCODE. This is one of the fields in the SQL communication area that was included in the Working-Storage Section of the program. This field gets set to zero if DB2 finds a matching row. If a matching row isn't found, this field gets set to a value other than zero and the If statement turns off the customer-found switch.

Module 130 contains a series of Display statements that display information on the screen. Note that this module is performed whether or not a matching customer row is found. If a row is found, this module displays the customer information on the screen. Otherwise, it displays a message indicating that the row wasn't found.

If a matching customer row is found, module 100 performs module 140 to get the invoices for that customer. This module starts by turning on the valid-cursor switch. Then, it performs module 150 to open the cursor-controlled result table that's defined by the DECLARE CURSOR statement in the Working-Storage Section. If the cursor is opened successfully, module 140 turns off the end-of-invoices switch and initializes the INVOICES-COUNT and INVOICES-TOTAL fields to zero. Then, it performs module 160 to get the information for each invoice in the result table and module 190 to close the cursor.

The sales inquiry program   **Page 2**

```
PROCEDURE DIVISION.
*
 000-PROCESS-SALES-INQUIRIES.
*
     PERFORM 100-PROCESS-SALES-INQUIRY
         UNTIL END-OF-INQUIRIES.
     STOP RUN.
*
 100-PROCESS-SALES-INQUIRY.
*
     MOVE 'Y' TO CUSTOMER-FOUND-SW.
     PERFORM 110-ACCEPT-CUSTOMER-NUMBER.
     IF NOT END-OF-INQUIRIES
         PERFORM 120-GET-CUSTOMER-ROW
         PERFORM 130-DISPLAY-CUSTOMER-INFO
         IF CUSTOMER-FOUND
             PERFORM 140-GET-INVOICES-INFORMATION
             PERFORM 200-DISPLAY-SALES-TOTALS.
*
 110-ACCEPT-CUSTOMER-NUMBER.
*
     DISPLAY '------------------------------------------------'.
     DISPLAY 'KEY IN THE NEXT CUSTOMER NUMBER AND PRESS ENTER,'.
     DISPLAY 'OR KEY IN 999999 AND PRESS ENTER TO QUIT.'.
     ACCEPT CUSTNO.
     IF CUSTNO = '999999'
         MOVE 'Y' TO END-OF-INQUIRIES-SW.
*
 120-GET-CUSTOMER-ROW.
*
     EXEC SQL
         SELECT     FNAME,    LNAME
             INTO :FNAME,  :LNAME
             FROM MM01.CUSTOMER
                 WHERE CUSTNO = :CUSTNO
     END-EXEC.
     IF SQLCODE NOT = 0
         MOVE 'N' TO CUSTOMER-FOUND-SW.
*
 130-DISPLAY-CUSTOMER-INFO.
*
     DISPLAY '-----------------------------------------'.
     IF CUSTOMER-FOUND
         DISPLAY ' CUSTOMER ' CUSTNO ' — ' FNAME ' ' LNAME
         DISPLAY ' '
     ELSE
         DISPLAY ' CUSTOMER NUMBER ' CUSTNO ' NOT FOUND.'.
*
 140-GET-INVOICES-INFORMATION.
*
     MOVE 'Y' TO VALID-CURSOR-SW.
     PERFORM 150-OPEN-INVOICE-CURSOR.
     IF VALID-CURSOR
         MOVE 'N' TO END-OF-INVOICES-SW
         MOVE ZERO TO INVOICES-COUNT
         MOVE ZERO TO INVOICES-TOTAL
         PERFORM 160-GET-INVOICE-INFORMATION
             UNTIL END-OF-INVOICES
         PERFORM 190-CLOSE-INVOICE-CURSOR.
```

Figure 20-10   The COBOL listing for the inquiry program (part 2 of 3)

In module 150, you can see the OPEN statement that actually creates the cursor-controlled result table that contains the invoice rows for the current customer. Notice that, like module 120, this module checks the value of the SQLCODE field to determine if the operation was successful. If it wasn't, this module turns off the valid-cursor switch so module 140 doesn't do any more processing for that customer number.

If the cursor is valid, module 160 is performed until there are no more rows in the result table. This module performs module 170 to fetch the data from the next invoice row. Then, if module 170 gets the next row, module 160 increments the total fields and performs module 180 to display the invoice data for that row.

In module 170, you can see the code that fetches the next row in the result table. After this statement is executed, an If statement turns on the end-of-invoices switch if the SQLCODE value is anything other than zero. Then, if this value isn't zero, another If statement checks to see if SQLCODE has a value other than 100. If the value is 100, it indicates that the end of the table has been reached. If the value is something other than 100, though, it indicates a serious error so this module turns off the valid-cursor switch.

In module 190, you can see that the valid-cursor switch is also turned off if the CLOSE statement for the cursor-controlled table doesn't return an SQLCODE value of zero to indicate that the close was successful. Then, in module 200, if the valid-cursor switch has been turned off because the OPEN, FETCH, or CLOSE statement for the invoice table was unsuccessful, the module prints an error message. Otherwise, it prints the invoice totals for the current customer.

Although this sales inquiry program uses only one cursor, you should realize that a program can use more than one cursor at the same time. If, for example, you want to display line item information for each invoice displayed by this program, you could use a second cursor to process a line item result table. To do that, you include a DECLARE CURSOR statement that defines the line item result table, and you code OPEN, FETCH, and CLOSE statements to process the rows in that table for each invoice that's displayed.

The sales inquiry program   **Page 3**

```
*
 150-OPEN-INVOICE-CURSOR.
*
     EXEC SQL
         OPEN INVCURS
     END-EXEC.
     IF SQLCODE NOT = 0
         MOVE 'N' TO VALID-CURSOR-SW.
*
 160-GET-INVOICE-INFORMATION.
*
     PERFORM 170-FETCH-INVOICE-ROW.
     IF NOT END-OF-INVOICES
         ADD 1        TO INVOICES-COUNT
         ADD INVTOTAL TO INVOICES-TOTAL
         PERFORM 180-DISPLAY-INVOICE-INFO.
*
 170-FETCH-INVOICE-ROW.
*
     EXEC SQL
         FETCH INVCURS
             INTO :INVNO, :INVDATE, :INVTOTAL
     END-EXEC.
     IF SQLCODE NOT = 0
         MOVE 'Y' TO END-OF-INVOICES-SW
         IF SQLCODE NOT = 100
             MOVE 'N' TO VALID-CURSOR-SW.
*
 180-DISPLAY-INVOICE-INFO.
*
     MOVE INVTOTAL TO EDITED-TOTAL.
     DISPLAY ' INVOICE ' INVNO ' ' INVDATE ' ' EDITED-TOTAL.
*
 190-CLOSE-INVOICE-CURSOR.
*
     EXEC SQL
         CLOSE INVCURS
     END-EXEC.
     IF SQLCODE NOT = 0
         MOVE 'N' TO VALID-CURSOR-SW.
*
 200-DISPLAY-SALES-TOTALS.
*
     IF VALID-CURSOR
         MOVE INVOICES-TOTAL            TO EDITED-TOTAL
         MOVE INVOICES-COUNT            TO EDITED-COUNT
         IF INVOICES-TOTAL > 0
             DISPLAY '                        ------------'
         END-IF
         DISPLAY ' TOTAL BILLED          '    EDITED-TOTAL
         DISPLAY ' INVOICES ISSUED       ' EDITED-COUNT
         DISPLAY ' '
     ELSE
         DISPLAY ' '
         DISPLAY '     *** INVOICE RETRIEVAL ERROR   ***'
         DISPLAY ' '.
```

Figure 20-10   The COBOL listing for the inquiry program (part 3 of 3)

How to develop a COBOL program that accesses DB2 data

When you develop a COBOL program that uses standard files on an IBM mainframe, the source program must be compiled and link edited before it can be tested. When you develop a COBOL program that uses a DB2 database, though, you have to perform some additional steps to prepare the program for execution. The complete process for developing a COBOL program that accesses DB2 data is illustrated in figure 20-11.

After you've entered the source code for the program, the first step is to run the *DB2 precompiler* on the source program. This produces two output files. The first is a *modified source program* in which each of the SQL statements has been translated into the COBOL statements that invoke the appropriate DB2 interface functions. Although the precompiler leaves the original SQL statements in the source program, it converts them to comments so they will be ignored by the COBOL compiler.

The second file produced by the precompiler is a *database request module*, or *DBRM*. It contains information about how your program will use DB2 and will be used as input in a later step of this development process.

After the precompiler is finished, the COBOL compiler compiles the modified source program into an object module. Then, the linkage editor links the object module with other required modules including DB2 interface modules. This produces a load module.

Before the load module can be executed, though, DB2 must *bind* the program. This bind procedure uses the DBRM that was created by the precompiler to check all the DB2 functions used in the program to make sure they are valid and that you are authorized to perform them. In addition, this procedure selects the most efficient way for DB2 to implement the functions your program requests.

You can bind a program directly into a plan or to a package and then to a plan. An *application plan* contains information about how DB2 will complete each database request made by your program. As you can see in this figure, the load module, DB2 catalog, and DB2 directory (which contains the application plan) are required when a program is executed. A *package* is a single DBRM with optimized access paths.

Although this may seem complicated, DB2 provides a program that you can use to prepare and run DB2 programs interactively through TSO. This program, called *DB2 Interactive*, or *DB2I*, makes it easy to prepare DCLGEN output as well as precompile, bind, compile, link, and run a COBOL program. DB2 also provides cataloged procedures that you can use to prepare a COBOL program. These procedures are similar to the ones you learned about in chapter 18, but they include a precompile step. Then, in the JCL that invokes one of these procedures, you can include the commands necessary to bind the program.

The steps required to prepare a DB2 COBOL program

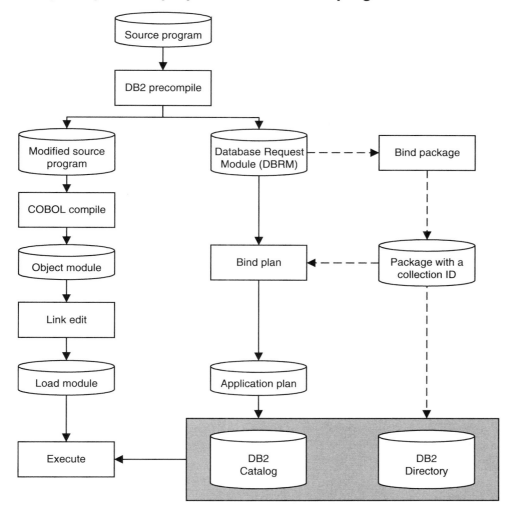

Notes

- The *DB2 catalog* stores information about the *plan* and *package*.
- The *DB2 directory* stores the actual plan and package.
- The load module, DB2 catalog, and DB2 directory must all be available when you execute a program.
- You can *bind* a program to a package or directly to a plan. However, you can't run a program that is bound to a package until that package is bound to a plan. Usually, a program is first bound to a package, and then the package is bound to a plan.

Figure 20-11   How to develop a COBOL program that accesses DB2 data

Perspective

The goal of this chapter has been to introduce you to the way that you work with the data in a DB2 database when you're writing COBOL programs. To be an effective DB2 programmer, though, there's much more to learn. In particular, you need to know how to code the SQL statements that access and update the DB2 data that your COBOL programs work with. For a complete course on DB2, we recommend our two *DB2 for the COBOL Programmer* books.

Summary

- A *relational database* consists of one or more *tables*. Each table contains one or more *rows*, or records, and each row contains one or more *columns*, or fields.

- Most tables contain a *primary key* that uniquely identifies each row in the table and one or more *indexes* that improve access to the rows in the table.

- Three types of relationships can exist between tables: a *one-to-one relationship*, a *one-to-many relationship*, and a *many-to-many relationship*. Tables are typically related by a *foreign key* in one table that refers to a primary key in another table.

- To work with the data in a relational database, you use *SQL (Structured Query Language)*.

- To retrieve data from a database, you use the SQL SELECT statement to create a *result table* that can consist of one or more rows. To modify the data in a database, you use the SQL INSERT, UPDATE, and DELETE statements.

- A SELECT statement can *join* data from two or more tables. The most common type of join is an *inner join* or *equi-join*. With this type of join, rows from the two tables are included in the result table only if their related columns match.

- To access DB2 data from a COBOL program, you use *embedded SQL*. Embedded SQL statements can refer to fields that are defined in the COBOL program, called *host variables*.

- If a result table will contain two or more rows, you have to use a *cursor* to process one row at a time. DB2 provides special SQL statements for defining and processing a *cursor-controlled result table* within a COBOL program.

- You can use a DB2 utility called *DCLGEN (Declarations Generator)* to generate a description of a DB2 table, called a *host structure*, from the table declaration for the table. You use a host structure within a COBOL program just as you use a record description for a sequential or indexed file.

- Before you can compile a program that accesses DB2 data, you have to run the *DB2 precompiler* to translate the SQL statements into COBOL statements that invoke DB2 functions. This produces a modified source program and a *database request module (DBRM)* that contains information about how your program will use DB2.

- After you compile and link edit a program to create a load module, DB2 must *bind* the program to check all the DB2 functions it uses. You can bind a program directly into an *application plan*, or into a *package* and then into a plan.

Terms

relational database	equi-join
DB2	outer join
Database 2	left outer join
relational database management system	right outer join
RDBMS	full outer join
table	embedded SQL statements
row	embedded SQL
column	host variable
value	cursor
string value	cursor-controlled result table
null value	host structure
primary key	DCLGEN
index	Declarations Generator
unique index	table declaration
one-to-many relationship	SQL communication area
foreign key	DB2 precompiler
one-to-one relationship	modified source program
many-to-many relationship	database request module
Structured Query Language	DBRM
SQL	binding a program
result table	application plan
query	package
action query	DB2 catalog
calculated value	DB2 directory
join	DB2 Interactive
inner join	DB2I

Objectives

- Describe how a table in a relational database is organized, and explain what a primary key and an index are.

- Explain how two tables in a relational database are related.

- List the three types of relationships that can exist between two tables in a relational database

- Name the SQL statement that you use to retrieve data from a relational database and describe the results of that statement.

- Name the three SQL statements you can use to modify the data in a relational database.

- Explain what a join is, and describe the most common type of join.

- In general terms, describe the syntax you use to include an SQL statement in a COBOL program.

- Explain what a cursor is and when you need to use one in a COBOL program.

- Name the four SQL statements you use to process a cursor-controlled result table within a COBOL program and explain the purpose of each statement.

- Explain what a host structure is and how you use it in a COBOL program.

- Describe the purpose of the DB2 precompiler and list its two types of output.

- In general terms, explain what binding a program means.

21

How to be an effective maintenance programmer

Your first job assignment as a COBOL programmer will more than likely involve the maintenance of existing programs. These programs may have been developed fairly recently. Or they may be *legacy programs* that have been in use for some time. In fact, many legacy programs have been around for so long that they're based on earlier versions of COBOL and wouldn't be written using the same coding or design techniques if they were being developed today. In any case, the job of the *maintenance programmer* is to update these programs with needed changes so they continue to do the processing required.

Although it may not be as exciting as designing new systems, maintenance programming can have its advantages. As a maintenance programmer, you will be exposed to a variety of programs written by different programmers in different ways. You will learn that there is more than just one way to solve a problem. And your analytical and debugging skills will greatly improve because of this experience.

Statements and features you should be aware of

The first 20 chapters of this book present what we believe to be the best techniques for designing and coding structured COBOL programs. When you maintain programs, though, you'll quickly discover that not everyone uses the best techniques. To help you adjust to that, this chapter begins by presenting statements and features that you're likely to encounter when you maintain old programs, even though you won't use them in new programs.

Perform Thru and Go To statements

So far in this book, each Perform statement has been written so it performs just one paragraph. As you can see in figure 21-1, though, you can also code the Perform statement so it performs more than one paragraph. In this case, the Perform statement names the first paragraph and the last paragraph that are to be performed by separating the names with the word THRU. Then, the statement performs all the paragraphs from the first statement in the first paragraph through the last statement in the last paragraph, including all intervening paragraphs.

This figure also shows you the syntax for the Go To statement, a statement that's common in legacy programs. When a Go To statement is executed, control passes (or *branches*) to the procedure it names and doesn't return. Go To statements are often used with Perform Thru statements as a way to skip over statements or paragraphs.

When you use Perform Thru statements, you usually code the last paragraph that is performed with an Exit statement that consists of just the word EXIT. The Exit statement doesn't have any real function other than to mark the end of the paragraphs that are performed by the Perform Thru. As a result, this paragraph provides a common exit point that the other paragraphs can branch to by using the Go To statement.

In the example in this figure, you can see how Perform Thru, Go To, and Exit statements work together. This is just another way to code the sales tax program that you were introduced to in chapter 1. Here, the Perform Thru statement in procedure 000 performs paragraphs 100 through 199. After paragraph 100 is performed, the program continues with the next statement in sequence, which is the first statement in paragraph 150. In other words, the logic *falls through* to the next paragraph. Then, in paragraph 150, if the sales amount is zero, a Go To statement causes the program to continue with paragraph 199, which is the exit paragraph. Otherwise, the program continues to execute the statements in paragraph 150 to compute and display the sales tax, and then the logic falls through to the exit paragraph.

Quite a difference from the way you've been writing programs, isn't it? Instead of performing single paragraphs and returning to the next statement in sequence, you can perform a series of paragraphs with a single statement, allow

The basic syntax of the Perform Thru statement

```
PERFORM procedure-name-1 {THRU | THROUGH} procedure-name-2
```

The syntax of the Go To statement

```
GO TO procedure-name
```

A routine that uses a Perform Thru statement

```
000-CALCULATE-SALES-TAX.
    PERFORM 100-DISPLAY-USER-PROMPT THRU 199-EXIT
        UNTIL END-OF-SESSION-SWITCH = "Y".
    DISPLAY "END OF SESSION.".
    STOP RUN.

100-DISPLAY-USER-PROMPT.
    DISPLAY "---------------------------------------------".
    DISPLAY "TO END PROGRAM, ENTER 0.".
    DISPLAY "TO CALCULATE SALES TAX, ENTER THE SALES AMOUNT.".
    ACCEPT SALES-AMOUNT.

150-CALCULATE-ONE-SALES-TAX.
    IF SALES-AMOUNT = ZERO
        MOVE "Y" TO END-OF-SESSION-SWITCH
        GO TO 199-EXIT.
    COMPUTE SALES-TAX ROUNDED =
        SALES-AMOUNT * .0785.
    DISPLAY "SALES TAX = " SALES-TAX.

199-EXIT.
    EXIT.
```

Description

- As the syntax above shows, you can name a second procedure in the Thru or Through clause of a Perform statement. This clause is followed by the other clauses of the statement, like the With Test After or Until clauses.

- When a Perform Thru statement is executed, control passes to the first statement in procedure-name-1 and returns after the last statement in procedure-name-2 is executed. There may be more than two procedures within that range, and the Perform Thru will execute them all.

- When a Go To statement is executed, control passes to the procedure named and doesn't return.

- The last procedure performed by a Perform Thru statement is usually a common exit point that is coded with the Exit statement. Since this statement doesn't do anything, it simply marks the end of the performed procedures.

- Perform Thru statements are commonly used in many COBOL shops, and Go To statements are allowed as long as they stay within the procedures performed by the Perform Thru statement. As we see it, though, the use of these statements makes a program harder to code, test, debug, and maintain.

Figure 21-1   Perform Thru and Go To statements

the logic to fall through from one paragraph to another, and use Go To statements to skip out of paragraphs. Unfortunately, though, this type of unstructured coding makes a program harder to code, test, debug, and maintain. In particular, it often leads to unintended logic problems.

Nevertheless, the COBOL standards in many shops allow this type of programming. Usually, they say that the last paragraph that's performed should be an exit paragraph and that any Go Tos within the paragraphs should go only to that exit paragraph. But even with that restriction, Perform Thrus can lead to some confusing code that's difficult to maintain.

Go To Depending statements

The Go To Depending statement can be thought of as a conditional Go To statement. As you can see in figure 21-2, this statement can branch to any number of procedures based on the numeric value in its identifier. The identifier must have a value that is consistent with the number of procedures listed. If the identifier's value is negative or zero or if it exceeds the number of procedures listed in the statement, the Go To Depending statement will be bypassed.

The example in this figure shows how a Go To Depending statement can be used. Based on the value in PT-TRAN-TYPE, the Go To Depending statement branches to one of the three transaction processing procedures. If the value is 1, the program will branch to procedure 300; if it's 2, to procedure 400; and if it's 3, to procedure 500. At the end of each of those procedures, a Go To statement branches back to the paragraph immediately following the Go To Depending statement.

In programs that predate COBOL-85, Go To Depending statements were often used to implement the case structure. However, the confusing nature of this statement and the fact that other Go To statements are needed to complete the structure make it vulnerable to logic errors. Today, you can use the Evaluate statement to implement case structures in a way that is consistent with the principles of structured programming as shown in chapter 5.

The syntax of the Go To Depending statement

```
GO TO procedure-name-1 {procedure-name-2} ...
    DEPENDING ON identifier
```

A routine that uses a Go To Depending statement

```
        05  PT-TRAN-TYPE          PIC 9.
            .
PROCEDURE DIVISION.
000-PROCESS-TRANS-RECORDS.
            .
100-READ-TRANS-FILE.
    READ PRCTRAN INTO PROCESS-TRANSACTION
        AT END GO TO 200-FINISH-UP.
    GO TO 300-ADD-NEW-MASTER
          400-UPDATE-OLD-MASTER
          500-DELETE-OLD-MASTER
        DEPENDING ON PT-TRAN-TYPE.
110-CONTINUE.
            .
    GO TO 100-READ-TRANS-FILE.
            .
200-FINISH-UP.
            .
    STOP RUN.

300-ADD-NEW-MASTER.
            .
    GO TO 110-CONTINUE.

400-UPDATE-OLD-MASTER.
            .
    GO TO 110-CONTINUE.

500-DELETE-OLD-MASTER.
            .
    GO TO 110-CONTINUE.
```

Description

- The Go To Depending statement is a conditional Go To statement. It goes to one of the procedures listed in the statement depending on the value in the identifier. That field must be numeric and have a value that's consistent with the number of procedures that are listed.

- If the value of the identifier is zero, negative, or exceeds the number of procedure names that are listed, the program executes the statement immediately after the Go To Depending statement.

- If you're a maintenance programmer, you're likely to find Go To Depending statements in some of the programs that you maintain. To further complicate the code, Go To statements are needed to return control to the proper place in the program.

- Prior to COBOL-85, the Go To Depending statement was often used to implement the case structure. Today, however, you can use the Evaluate statement to implement the case structure as shown in figure 5-13.

Figure 21-2   Go To Depending statements

Section names in the Procedure Division

All the programs you've seen so far in this book have used paragraphs for the procedures in the Procedure Division. But a Procedure Division can also be divided up into one or more *sections*, each made up of one or more paragraphs. A section is identified by a *section name* that consists of a procedure name followed by the word SECTION. The section ends when another section starts or when the end of the program is reached. This is summarized in figure 21-3.

When a section is performed, all of the paragraphs in that section are performed. This is illustrated by the example in this figure. When section 100 is performed by the Perform statement in section 000, paragraph 125 is executed first. Then, control falls through to paragraph 150. When the last statement in that paragraph is executed, control returns to the Perform statement in section 000.

Do you see a similarity between sections and Perform Thru statements? Like Perform Thru statements, you can perform more than one paragraph when you use sections. To complicate matters, though, you can perform sections in your Perform Thru statements. Then, multiple sections consisting of multiple paragraphs can be performed. Structures like that, however, can confuse even the most experienced of programmers!

Prior to COBOL-85, sections were necessary in certain coding situations like when you used the Sort statement. Today, sections are no longer needed, but you're still likely to run into programs that use them. In that case, you have to be aware of whether the Perform statements in the program are executing paragraphs or sections. If a section is performed when the intent is to perform a paragraph, the result may be the execution of unintended code...and a tough debugging problem.

The syntax for defining a section in the Procedure Division

```
procedure-name SECTION.
```

A routine that uses section names in the Procedure Division

```
    PROCEDURE DIVISION.
*
    000-CALCULATE-SALES-TAX SECTION.
*
        PERFORM 100-PROCESS-SALES-TAX-REQUEST
            UNTIL END-OF-SESSION-SWITCH = "Y".
        DISPLAY "END OF SESSION.".
        STOP RUN.
*
    100-PROCESS-SALES-TAX-REQUEST SECTION.
*
    125-DISPLAY-USER-PROMPT.
        DISPLAY "------------------------------------------------".
        DISPLAY "TO END PROGRAM, ENTER 0.".
        DISPLAY "TO CALCULATE SALES TAX, ENTER THE SALES AMOUNT.".
        ACCEPT SALES-AMOUNT.
*
    150-CALCULATE-ONE-SALES-TAX.
        IF SALES-AMOUNT = ZERO
            MOVE "Y" TO END-OF-SESSION-SWITCH
        ELSE
            COMPUTE SALES-TAX ROUNDED =
                SALES-AMOUNT * .0785.
            DISPLAY "SALES TAX = " SALES-TAX.
```

Description

- A program can be divided into two or more *sections*. Each starts with a *section name* and ends when the next section name or the end of the program is reached. Each section can contain one or more paragraphs.

- To define a section name, you code a procedure name followed by the word SECTION.

- When a section is performed, control is transferred to the first statement in the section. Then, all the paragraphs in the section are executed. Control returns when the last statement in the section is executed.

- When you code a Perform statement, the statement doesn't indicate whether you're performing a section or a paragraph. This can lead to an unintended error if you perform a section when you mean to perform a paragraph.

- The use of sections is still a common practice in many COBOL shops. Although sections were required when you used the sort/merge feature of COBOL-74, there is no advantage to using sections today. As a result, we recommend that each module of a new program be implemented as a single COBOL paragraph.

Figure 21-3   Section names in the Procedure Division

Qualification and the Move, Add, and Subtract Corresponding statements

From time to time, you may encounter programs that use the same data name for two or more data items. This is legal as long as the names are subordinate to unique group names. In figure 21-4, for example, AMOUNT-1, AMOUNT-2, and COUNT are repeated, but each name belongs to a group item with a unique name.

When two or more data items have the same name, you must *qualify* each non-unique item by its group name whenever you refer to it in your code. This is called *qualification*. In the examples in this figure, you can see how the AMOUNT-1 and COUNT fields are qualified in the Move and Add statements. Note in the second example that two levels of qualification are used for the COUNT field (although that isn't necessary).

You can also work with non-unique data items by using the Corresponding phrase of the Move, Add, or Subtract statement as shown in this figure. In this case, you don't need to qualify the data items because the statement refers to group names, not elementary names. When one of these statements is executed, the data items in the first group are moved to, added to, or subtracted from the data items with the same names in the second group.

This is illustrated by the examples in this figure. Here, the three fields in the first group are moved to, added to, or subtracted from the three fields in the second group. Note that the corresponding items don't have to be in the same order for the execution to be successful and they don't have to have matching pictures or usages.

The trouble with qualification is that it can make programs cumbersome and difficult to read. Also, an error occurs if a data item is qualified by the wrong group name. The trouble with the Corresponding phrase is that it's hard to tell which fields are operated upon. For these reasons, we don't recommend the use of these features in new programs, although you may have to struggle with them when you maintain some old programs.

A data structure with non-unique data items

```
01  REPORT-TOTALS.
    05  REPORT-SUB-TOTALS.
        10  AMOUNT-1          PIC S9(05)V99.
        10  AMOUNT-2          PIC S9(05)V99.
        10  COUNT             PIC 9(03).
    05  REPORT-GRAND-TOTALS.
        10  COUNT             PIC 9(05).
        10  AMOUNT-1          PIC S9(07)V99.
        10  AMOUNT-2          PIC S9(07)V99.
```

The syntax for qualifying non-unique data names

```
data-name {IN | OF} group-name
```

Examples of qualification

```
MOVE AMOUNT-1 IN REPORT-SUB-TOTALS
    TO AMOUNT-1 IN REPORT-GRAND-TOTALS.

ADD COUNT IN REPORT-SUB-TOTALS
    TO COUNT IN REPORT-GRAND-TOTALS OF REPORT-TOTALS.
```

The syntax of the three statements with Corresponding phrases

```
MOVE CORRESPONDING group-item-1 TO group-item-2
ADD CORRESPONDING group-item-1 TO group-item-2
SUBTRACT CORRESPONDING group-item-1 FROM group-item-2
```

Examples of the Move, Add, and Subtract Corresponding statements

```
MOVE CORRESPONDING REPORT-SUB-TOTALS
    TO REPORT-GRAND-TOTALS.

ADD CORRESPONDING REPORT-SUB-TOTALS
     TO REPORT-GRAND-TOTALS.

SUBTRACT CORRESPONDING REPORT-SUB-TOTALS
    FROM REPORT-GRAND-TOTALS.
```

Description

- When you use the same data name in two or more groups, the data names aren't unique. Then, you have to use *qualification* to refer to them.

- The Corresponding phrase in the Move, Add, and Subtract statements lets you move, add and subtract the data items in the first group to or from the data items with the same names in the second group. Since the items are matched by name, their order within the group data descriptions doesn't matter. However, subordinate items that contain Redefines, Renames, or Occurs clauses in their descriptions are ignored.

- Because the use of qualification and the Corresponding phrase tend to make the code in a program more cumbersome and difficult to read, we recommend that you avoid the use of these features.

Figure 21-4   Qualification and the Move, Add, and Subtract Corresponding statements

Declarative sections

Declarative sections are used in the Procedure Divisions of some programs as a way of "trapping" I/O errors. One or more of these sections can be coded at the start of the Procedure Division in a portion of the program that can be referred to as the *declaratives*. This is summarized in figure 21-5.

Within each declarative section, you code a Use statement that tells which file the errors should be trapped for. In the example in this figure, the Use statement traps the I/O errors for a file named INVMAST. Note, however, that errors aren't trapped for any I/O statements that include an At End or Invalid Key clause. As a result, only the I/O errors for the Open and Write statements in this example will be trapped.

Once an I/O error is trapped by a Use statement, all of the statements in that Declarative section are executed. Then, control returns to the first statement after the I/O statement that caused the error. In this example, though, the program calls a subprogram that abnormally terminates the program so the program ends.

Today, you can use the Invalid Key clause and the File Status field to test the error conditions after each I/O operation. Since this type of coding is consistent with the principles of structured coding, we recommend that you use it for handling all error conditions. Conversely, we don't recommend the use of declarative sections in new programs.

At one time, though, declarative sections were the primary means of trapping I/O errors so you'll find them in some old programs. In some shops, you may also find declarative sections in some new programs where they're used to trap the errors that aren't handled by Invalid Key clauses and File Status codes. In some programs, for example, you'll find declarative sections that are used to trap the errors for Open and Close statements, while the other errors are handled in the main section of the program.

The syntax for the declaratives

```
DECLARATIVES.
Section-name SECTION.
    USE AFTER STANDARD {EXCEPTION | ERROR} PROCEDURE
        ON file-name-1 ...
END DECLARATIVES.
```

A routine that uses a declarative section

```
SELECT INVMAST ...
    FILE-STATUS IS INVMAST-FILE-STATUS.
.
05  INVMAST-FILE-STATUS         PIC X(02).
.
PROCEDURE DIVISION.
DECLARATIVES.
D10-FILE-ERROR-HANDLING SECTION.
    USE AFTER ERROR PROCEDURE ON INVMAST.
D10-STATUS-CHECK.
    DISPLAY "AN ERROR WAS ENCOUNTERED ON INVMAST STATUS CODE: "
            INVMAST-FILE-STATUS.
    CALL "ABEND100".
END DECLARATIVES.
000-MAINTAIN-INVENTORY-FILE SECTION.
.
OPEN I-O INVMAST.
.
READ INVMAST INTO INVENTORY-MASTER-RECORD
    INVALID KEY ...
.
WRITE INVENTORY-RECORD-AREA FROM INVENTORY-MASTER-RECORD.
```

Description

- The *declaratives* portion of a program starts at the beginning of the Procedure Division with the word DECLARATIVES and ends with the words END DECLARATIVES.

- Within the declaratives, one or more *declarative sections* can be coded. Each section is performed when the Use statement within it is triggered by input or output errors that are produced by the specified file. When the last statement in a declarative section is executed, control returns to the first statement after the I/O statement that caused the error.

- If an I/O error occurs during the execution of an I/O statement that contains an At End or Invalid Key clause, the Use statement will *not* be executed.

- In the Use statement, the words Exception and Error are synonymous.

- Today, you can use the Invalid Key clause and the File Status field to handle the I/O errors for a file without using declarative sections. If you're a maintenance programmer, though, you're likely to find declarative sections in some old programs as well as some new ones.

Figure 21-5   Declarative sections

The basic skills for maintaining programs

Now that you've been introduced to some statements that you're likely to find in older programs, this chapter presents some procedures and guidelines that can help you with your first maintenance assignment. Keep in mind, though, that what we recommend here is not intended to replace any established procedures at your workplace. Our recommendations are simply designed to help you focus on the task at hand and not be overwhelmed by your first maintenance assignment.

A structured procedure for maintaining a program

To give you just a hint of what you're likely to run into when you maintain your first program, figure 21-6 presents the code for the first section in the Procedure Division of a program that's part of an expensive software package. There, you can see that the entire program is divided into sections, that the paragraph names within the sections don't indicate what the functions of the paragraphs are, that the data names don't clearly indicate what the data items represent, and so on. Technically, this is a structured program because it doesn't use Go To statements, but how do you even get started when you have to maintain it?

Because making changes to poorly-written or unstructured code is a reality of maintenance programming, you need to approach the job with a procedure like the one that's presented in this figure. We call it a "structured" procedure because it presents an organized approach to maintaining programs that are frequently unorganized.

In step 1, you need to get all of the documentation for the program. Although that can be substantial in some COBOL shops, the program's source code is always the primary documentation for a program because you know that it's accurate. All too often, though, it's the only documentation for the program.

In step 2, you study the documentation so you know in general terms what the program does and how it does it. If the source code is the only documentation, you may want to print the source listing so it's easier to review. If the program is structured, you may want to sketch out a structure chart that shows the structure of the program. Or, if the program adheres to the principles in this book, you can run our LISTMODS program to generate a structure listing for the program (see exercise 4-4). After you study the existing documentation, if you're still having trouble figuring out what the program is doing, you can try to get information from someone else who has worked on the program.

In step 3, you test the program the way it is. That provides a "baseline" that shows you what the program does and what its current output is. Then, in step 4, you make the modifications to the program. This, of course, is the critical step of the maintenance project, and the next figure presents two guidelines for doing it.

In step 5, you test the modified program to make sure that your changes work correctly. In this step, you compare the test results to the baseline results to make sure that the program still does everything that it used to do. That way, you can be

A coding sample from one program in an expensive software package

```
PROCEDURE DIVISION.
LEVEL-1 SECTION.
MAIN-LOGIC.
    PERFORM OPENING-PROCEDURE.
    IF OPENING-PROCEDURE-SUCCESSFUL
        IF PR-CTL-USE-JOB-NUMBER-FLAG IS = "N"
            PERFORM JOB-NOS-NOT-SELECTED-MESSAGE,
            MOVE UNSUCCESSFUL TO OPENING-PROCEDURE-STATUS,
        ELSE
            PERFORM ENTER-MENU-SELECTION,
            IF NOT END-KEY-PRESSED
                PERFORM JOB-FILE-MAINTENANCE UNTIL
                END-KEY-PRESSED.
    PERFORM CLOSING-PROCEDURE.
MAIN-LOGIC-EXIT.
    PERFORM WAIT-MESSAGE-ROUTINE.
    EXIT PROGRAM.
    STOP RUN.
LEVEL-2 SECTION.
OPENING-PROCEDURE.
    .
    .
```

A structured procedure for program maintenance

1. Get all the documentation you can find including the latest version of the source code.

2. Study the documentation so you know what the program does and how it does it. If necessary, print out the source listing, sketch out a structure chart for the program, generate a structure listing from the source code, or try to get more information from someone who's worked on the program.

3. Test the program before you make any changes to it to establish a baseline of how the program works.

4. Make the required changes to the program.

5. Test the modified program thoroughly, and compare your results to your baseline test.

6. Document your modifications.

Figure 21-6   A structured procedure for maintaining a program

sure that your modifications haven't affected other functions of the program (unless they were supposed to). When you've got the changes working correctly, you can forward your results to the person who requested the change so you can get the changes approved.

After the changes have been approved, step 6 is to document your modifications. Although most shops have standards for what that documentation should be, comments in the Identification Division of the source code should always be part of it. This is illustrated in figure 21-8.

What to change and where to change it

Step 4 in our structured procedure for program maintenance is making the required changes. Once you're familiar with the source code, you can identify the portions of code that will be affected by the changes. At that point, you need to decide what needs to be changed and where to make the changes. To help you make those decisions, figure 21-7 presents two guidelines.

If you look at the coding example in this figure, you can get an idea of how bad the coding in some production programs can be. Here, you can see procedure names and data names that are impossible to decipher; 8 Go To statements in just 14 lines of code; two statements written on one coding line; and no use of indentation to improve readability. In short, this is the type of unstructured mess that programmers refer to as "spaghetti code" or "rat's nest code."

When you have to modify code like this or code like the example in the previous figure, the hardest part of the job is figuring out what the code does and how it does it. Once you do that, it's relatively easy to make the program changes. Often, though, it's tempting to rewrite the portion of code that you have to modify (or the entire program) because that will surely make the program easier to modify the next time.

But that's where the first guideline in this figure comes in: Change only the portions of code that need modification. Don't try to improve other portions of the program because your job is to make the changes as quickly and as inexpensively as possible. Besides that, what appears to be a simple rewrite of a portion of poorly-structured code can have unintended results that lead you into many hours of debugging that you wouldn't have otherwise. As the saying goes, "If it ain't broke, don't fix it!"

The second guideline in this figure deals with the issue of where to make the program changes. If the changes are minor, you can usually make them within the existing code. In this case, you must make sure that your changes don't affect any of the surrounding logic. A carelessly placed period in an If statement, for example, can have a disastrous effect on the program.

If the changes are more complicated or you're adding a new function to a program, it often makes sense to create one or more new paragraphs for your changes. This is much less invasive to the logic of the program because all you need to insert in the existing code is a Perform statement. This is illustrated by the modified code in this figure. Then, the new paragraph is the top-level procedure for the program modifications.

A coding sample from an actual production program

```
AA43.   PERFORM KK.
        IF ITMSTS20 = " " GO TO AAA43.
        IF ITMSTS20 = "N" AND ITMSTS0 (A, SS) = "N"
        PERFORM A54G THRU X546 GO TO B43.
        IF ITMSTS20 = "N" PERFORM CC43 PERFORM A54J.
        MOVE "25" TO ACT40 MOVE ITMSTS20 TO ITMSTS40 GO TO B43.
        IF ITMSTS70 (A, SS) = "N" GO TO CC43.
AAA43.  PERFORM EQCHEC.
        IF EQWORK1 = EQWORK2 GO TO QQ43.
        IF EQWORK2 = SPACES GO TO QQ43.
        GO TO CC43.
QQ43.   PERFORM EE THRU KK.
B43.    PERFORM A54D THRU X54D GO TO D42.
CC43.   MOVE "40" TO ACT40.
        .
        .
```

The same program with the changes implemented in a new paragraph

```
AA43.   PERFORM KK.
        IF ITMSTS20 = " " GO TO AAA43.
        IF ITMSTS20 = "N" AND ITMSTS0 (A, SS) = "N"
        PERFORM A54G THRU X546 GO TO B43.
        IF ITMSTS20 = "Y" AND ITMSTSO (A, SS) = "Y"
            PERFORM M10A
        END-IF.
        IF ITMSTS20 = "N" PERFORM CC43 PERFORM A54J.
        MOVE "25" TO ACT40 MOVE ITMSTS20 TO ITMSTS40 GO TO B43.
        IF ITMSTS70 (A, SS) = "N" GO TO CC43.
AAA43.  PERFORM EQCHEC.
        IF EQWORK1 = EQWORK2 GO TO QQ43.
        IF EQWORK2 = SPACES GO TO QQ43.
        GO TO CC43.
QQ43.   PERFORM EE THRU KK.
B43.    PERFORM A54D THRU X54D GO TO D42.
CC43.   MOVE "40" TO ACT40.
        .
        .

M10A.
        .
        .
```

Guidelines

- Change only the portions of code that need modification. Don't change other portions of the program to make it more readable or logical. Your job is to make the changes as quickly as possible.

- Decide whether program modification should be made within the existing logic or if it is better to create one or more new paragraphs for your changes. Often, it makes sense to isolate the changes or enhancements in their own paragraphs.

Figure 21-7   What to change and where to change it

How to document the changes in the source code

Step 6 of our structured procedure for program maintenance is documenting the program changes after they have been approved. Often, your shop standards will detail what you need to do for this documentation. Some shops, for example, will require you to fill out change control forms. Others will require that you update a program change log or a projects database. Whatever the case, you should be as precise and thorough as possible.

As we said earlier, though, the main documentation in many COBOL shops is the source code itself. As a result, you should always document a program and its changes by putting comments in the Identification Division as shown in figure 21-8. Here, a "flower box" at the start of the program describes the program and lists the files that it uses. If you're the programmer who originates the program, you should include this flower box in your program. If you're a maintenance programmer and the program doesn't have this flower box, you should add one to the program.

After the program description, a *modification log* in the flower box lists all of the changes that have been made to the program. When you maintain a program, you should add your entry to the top of this log. In other words, the most recent modification is first in the log.

As you document your changes, remember that the more you comment now, the easier it will be to make changes later on. So if you had trouble figuring out what the program did when you started the assignment, it's worth taking the time to add a program description that will make it easier the next time or for the next maintenance programmer. This is different from rewriting portions of the code that don't need to be changed because this documentation should take only a few extra minutes and it won't have any effect on the operation of the program.

A sample flower box area in a program

```
IDENTIFICATION DIVISION.
PROGRAM-ID.      INV1100.
AUTHOR.          RAUL MENENDEZ.
*********************************************************************
* PROGRAM DESCRIPTION:                                             *
*                                                                  *
*    THIS PROGRAM EDITS A FILE OF INVENTORY TRANSACTIONS (INVTRAN).*
*    IF ALL OF THE FIELDS IN A TRANSACTION ARE VALID USING THE EDITING *
*    RULES, THE RECORD IS VALID.  ALL VALIDATED RECORDS WILL BE WRIT- *
*    TEN TO THE VALID TRANSACTION FILE (VALTRAN).  INVALID RECORDS ARE *
*    WRITTEN TO THE INVALID TRANSACTION FILE (ERRTRAN).  THE FORMAT *
*    OF THE RECORDS IN ALL THREE TRANSACTION FILES IS THE SAME.    *
*                                                                  *
* FILES USED:                                                      *
*                                                                  *
*    INVTRAN    INVENTORY TRANSACTION FILE           INPUT         *
*    VALTRAN    VALID INVENTORY TRANSACTION FILE     EXTEND        *
*    ERRTRAN    INVALID INVENTORY TRANSACTION FILE   OUTPUT        *
*                                                                  *
*********************************************************************
* MODIFICATION LOG:                                               *
*                                                                  *
*    06/19/2000 - RRM - THE ERRTRAN RECORD WAS EXPANDED TO INCLUDE AN *
*                       ERROR CODE TYPE AT THE BEGINNING OF THE RECORD.*
*                       THIS WILL ALLOW AN ERROR REPORT PROGRAM TO *
*                       IDENTIFY THE EXACT CAUSE OF THE TRANSACTION *
*                       ERROR.                                     *
*                                                                  *
*    02/22/1999 - AMP - THE DATE FIELDS IN ALL FILES HAVE BEEN CHANGED *
*                       TO ACCOMMODATE A 4-CHARACTER YEAR FIELD. THE *
*                       DATE VALIDATION ROUTINE HAS BEEN UPDATED TO *
*                       HANDLE THE 4-CHARACTER YEAR.               *
*                                                                  *
*********************************************************************
*
 ENVIRONMENT DIVISION.
 .
 .
```

Description

- If the program description isn't included in the Identification Division, create a "flower box" that describes what the program does, how it does it, and what files it uses.

- When you make changes to a program, always add your entry at the top of the *modification log*, which should be right after the program description. Your entry should give the date, your name or initials, and a description of what the modification was.

- Besides the source code documentation, your shop may have other documentation requirements. For instance, you may need to complete a change control form, update a program change log, or update a projects database.

Figure 21-8   How to document the changes in the source code

Perspective

If your first job as a programmer is maintenance programming, make the most of it. By maintaining the code of others, you'll learn a lot and hone your programming skills. Besides that, your study of old programs will be convincing proof of the need to develop programs by using the structured techniques that are presented in this book.

Summary

- Perform Thru statements let you execute more than one procedure in a single Perform statement. Within the performed procedures, Go To statements are commonly used to pass control to the exit procedure.

- Prior to COBOL-85, Go To Depending statements were often used to implement the case structure.

- A program can be divided into *sections* within the Procedure Division. Then, you can use Perform statements to perform sections.

- You use q*ualification* to identify non-unique data names. You can also use the Corresponding phrase in Move, Add, and Subtract statements to move, add, or subtract the non-unique data items in a group.

- A Use statement within a *declarative section* is executed when it is triggered by an I/O error produced by the specified file.

- To help you deal with the poorly-written or unstructured code that you're likely to encounter when you maintain a program, you should use a structured maintenance procedure.

- The primary documentation for any program is its source code. In the Identification Division of this code, you should include comments that provide a program description and a *modification log*.

Terms

legacy program	section	declarative section
maintenance programmer	section name	declaratives
branch	qualification	modification log
fall through		

Objectives

- Given the specifications for a program change, the source code for the program, and any other available documentation, make the required change.

- Describe the operation of any of the COBOL statements or features presented in this chapter.

- Explain how you should document a program within its source code.

22

Introduction to object-oriented COBOL

Throughout this book, you've used structured programming techniques to develop COBOL programs. Now, you'll be introduced to object-oriented programming. This type of programming is in common use with languages like Java and C++, and it will become available in COBOL with the 2002 standards. In the meantime, early versions of object-oriented COBOL are available with some COBOL compilers including Micro Focus Personal COBOL.

This chapter introduces you to object-oriented COBOL by presenting both concepts and a complete program that was developed in Personal COBOL. In chapter 17, you can see the structured version of that program so it's best if you read that chapter before this one. Since the program uses indexed files, you should also read chapter 14 before this one. When you complete this chapter, you should have a solid appreciation for what object-oriented COBOL is and how it may impact COBOL programming in the future.

Object-oriented COBOL concepts

Object-oriented programming (OOP) is built on the principles of encapsulation, inheritance, and polymorphism. To understand these principles, you have to understand what an object is and how it's created. So that's what you'll learn in the topics that follow. You'll also see how you can apply the principles of OOP to *object-oriented COBOL (OO COBOL)*.

An introduction to objects

The idea of object-oriented programming is that any program can be divided into two or more *objects* that interact with each other. But what exactly is an object? To illustrate, figure 22-1 presents a conceptual view of a book maintenance program that uses a book inventory object.

As you can see, the book inventory object includes the data related to a specific book. Because of that, the data doesn't need to be defined within the program. Instead, the program works with the data by invoking *methods* that are defined within the object. In other words, the object isolates the data so it's only available through the methods the object contains.

The methods that are defined within an object contain procedural code that performs predefined functions on the data. For example, the set-book-info method contains code that sets the values of the fields defined within the object. Then, the other methods are used to retrieve the data, get the book price, and adjust the on-hand amount for the book.

Note that a book inventory object might actually contain many more methods than are shown here. For example, it might contain a method to add a new book item or to delete an existing one. For simplicity, though, we've include only four methods in this example.

When a program invokes a method of an object, it can pass data to the method. When the book maintenance program invokes the set-book-info method, for example, it sends the data for the book to the object. As you'll see later, this method needs this data to perform its function.

A method can also return data to the program that invokes it. For example, the get-book-info method returns all the data for the book, and the get-book-price method returns just the price. The last method in this figure, adjust-on-hand, both sends and returns data.

The principle of combining data and the code that operates on it is called *encapsulation*. By encapsulating the data and the code, a program can perform functions on the data simply by invoking a method. The program—as well as the programmer—doesn't need to know how the method works. It just needs to know the name and function of the method, the information the method requires, and the information it returns.

A book maintenance program that uses a book inventory object

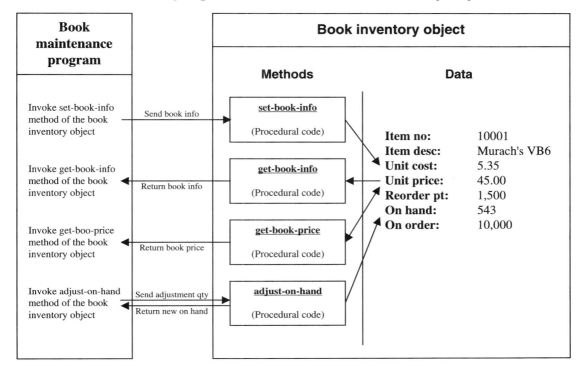

Concepts

- An *object* consists of two elements: data and methods. The data describes the state of the object at any given time. *Methods* consist of procedural code that perform functions on the object's data.

- Objects let you *encapsulate* the data and procedural code so that other objects and programs can't access the data directly. Instead, the data can be accessed only by invoking the object's methods.

- When you use an object, you don't need to know how it works. You just need to know what methods it contains, what functions those methods perform, what information you need to send to the methods, and what information the methods return.

Figure 22-1   An introduction to objects

An introduction to classes

Before a program can interact with an object, it must create the object. To do that, it creates an *instance* of a *class* that defines the object as shown in figure 22-2. This process is called *instantiation*.

A class can be thought of as a template that's used to create objects. Like an object, a class contains data definitions and methods. Unlike an object, a class doesn't contain data values. That way, each object that's created from the class can contain unique values.

In this figure, the book inventory class is used to create two book inventory objects. Both objects contain the methods that are defined by the class. However, each object contains different data. The first object contains data related to a book named *Murach's VB6*, and the second object contains data related to a book named *Murach's DB2*.

Although you can refer to a class by its name, objects don't have names. Instead, when you create an object, it's assigned a *handle*. A handle is an object reference that points to the location of the object in memory. Once you create an object, you use its handle to refer to it. You'll see how you do that in the next topic.

At this point, you may be wondering why you would want to use classes and objects. The main reason is that classes are reusable. In other words, once you create a class, any program can use the data and methods it contains. The trick is designing classes so they can be reused. You'll have a better idea of how to do that after you complete this chapter.

Two book inventory objects created from a book inventory class

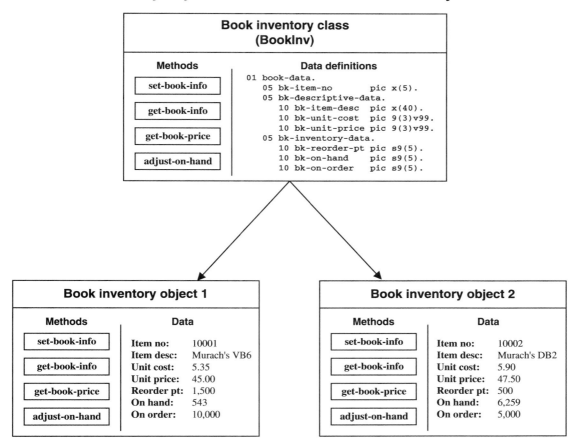

Concepts

- A *class* can be thought of as a template that's used to create objects. A class defines the data that an object will contain and the methods that can be used to interact with that data.

- An object is an *instance* of a class. Because of that, the objects that are created from a class all have the same methods and data definitions. However, the data values in each object are unique.

- To refer to a class from a program or another class, you use the class name (BookInv for the class shown above). To refer to an object, however, you use its *handle*. A handle contains a pointer to the object, which you assign to a field in the program that uses the object.

Figure 22-2   An introduction to classes

A program that uses the book inventory class

To help you understand how to use classes and objects in a COBOL program, figure 22-3 presents code from a book maintenance program. One of the functions of this program is to adjust the on-hand quantity for a book. To do that, this program uses the book inventory class described in the last topic.

To start, take a look at the first Invoke statement in the Procedure Division of this program. This statement is used to create an instance of the book inventory class named BookInv. Notice that this class is declared in the Environment Division of the program. In this case, it's declared in the Class-Control paragraph of the Object Section. However, this is unique to the Micro Focus COBOL compiler. Later in this chapter, you'll see the standard technique for declaring a class.

To create an instance of the BookInv class, this program invokes a method named New. You may recall that this was not one of the methods defined in the book inventory class. Instead, it's defined in a system class that the book inventory class has access too. You'll see how that works later in this chapter.

When the New method is invoked, it returns a handle that contains the location of the newly created object. This handle is then stored in the field that's named on the Returning clause of the Invoke statement, which in this case is bookInvObj. Notice that this field is defined in working storage with a usage of Object Reference.

After the program creates the book inventory object, it can use the Invoke statement to invoke any of its methods. For instance, the second Invoke statement invokes the set-book-info method. Notice that this statement refers to the object by its handle (bookInvObj). Also notice that a field named book-data is passed to the method on the Using clause of the statement. This field contains the data that will be stored in the object.

The last Invoke statement in this figure invokes the adjust-on-hand method of the book inventory object. This statement passes the adjustment quantity to the method. In return, the method passes back the new on-hand quantity.

Code from the book maintenance program

```
Identification Division.
Program-id. Bookmnt.
Environment Division.
       .
Object Section.
Class-Control.
   BookInv is class "bookinv".
       .
Data Division.
Working-Storage Section.
       .
01  work-fields.
    05  on-hand-adjustment      pic s9(03).
    05  on-hand-qty             pic s9(05).
01  book-data                   pic x(70).
01  object-handles.
    05  bookInvObj              usage is object reference.
       .
Procedure Division.
       .
    invoke BookInv "New" returning bookInvObj.
    invoke bookInvObj "set-book-info"
                  using book-data.
       .
300-adjust-on-hand-quantity.

    move "N" to valid-entry-sw.
    perform 310-get-adjustment-amount.
    if valid-entry
        invoke bookInvObj "adjust-on-hand"
                    using on-hand-adjustment
                    returning on-hand-qty
        perform 320-display-new-on-hand
       .
```

Description

- Before you can use an object from a program, you must declare the class that it's created from, and you must create an instance of that class.

- The technique you use to declare a class depends on the COBOL compiler you're using. For the Micro Focus compiler, you name the class in the Class-Control paragraph of the Object Section in the Environment Division. See figure 22-7 for details.

- To create an instance of a class, you use the Invoke statement with the New method. This method returns the handle you can use to refer to the object. The field that will contain the handle must be defined in working storage with Object Reference usage.

- After you create an object, you use the Invoke statement to invoke its methods. This statement must include any data to be sent to or returned from the method. See figure 22-10 for more information on coding the Invoke statement.

Figure 22-3   A program that uses the book inventory class

The book inventory class

Figure 22-4 presents some of the code from the book inventory class. If you review this code, you'll get a general feel for what's involved in defining a class. Later on, you'll learn the syntax for the code that's presented in this figure.

For now, you should focus on the code in the Object paragraph. This is the code that will be used to define the objects that are created from this class. It contains a Data Division that defines the data that can be used by any of the methods in the class. In this case, the Data Division contains a description of the fields for a book.

The Object paragraph also contains a Procedure Division. Within the Procedure Division are the definitions of the methods for the class. For simplicity, only the code for the adjust-on-hand method is presented here.

The definition of this method includes a Linkage Section that defines the field that's passed to the method from the program that invokes it and the field that the method returns to the invoking program. These fields are also listed on the Using and Returning clauses of the Procedure Division paragraph. Then, the procedural code simply adds the adjustment quantity that was passed to the method to the on-hand quantity for the book and moves the new on-hand quantity to the on-hand field that's returned to the program.

Although this class module and the program in figure 22-3 that uses it are somewhat simplistic, they illustrate the basic techniques for creating and using classes and objects. If you don't understand all the code in these figures, though, don't worry. It'll make more sense after you see the syntax and the expanded program example that are presented later in this chapter.

Code that defines the book inventory class

```
Identification Division.
Class-id.  BookInv
           inherits from Base.
Environment Division.
Object Section.
Class-Control.
    BookInv   is class "bookinv"
    Base      is class "Base".
Object.
    Data Division.
    Working-Storage Section.
    01  book-data.
        05  bk-item-no              pic x(05).
        05  bk-descriptive-data.
            10  bk-item-desc         pic x(40).
            10  bk-unit-cost         pic 9(03)v99.
            10  bk-unit-price        pic 9(03)v99.
        05  bk-inventory-data.
            10  bk-reorder-pt        pic s9(05).
            10  bk-on-hand           pic s9(05).
            10  bk-on-order          pic s9(05).
    Procedure Division.
************************************************************
    Method-ID. "set-book-info".
       .
    End Method "set-book-info
************************************************************
    Method-ID. "get-book-info".
       .
    End Method "get-book-info".
************************************************************
    Method-ID. "adjust-on-hand".
    Data Division.
    Linkage Section.
    01  ls-adjustment              pic s9(03).
    01  ls-on-hand                 pic s9(05).
    Procedure Division using ls-adjustment
                      returning ls-on-hand.
       add ls-adjustment to bk-on-hand.
       move bk-on-hand to ls-on-hand.
    End Method "adjust-on-hand".
************************************************************
    Method-ID. "get-book-price".
       .
    End Method "get-book-price".
************************************************************
End Object.
End Class BookInv.
```

Description

- The definition of a class includes the definitions of the data it will contain and the methods that will operate on that data.

- Data that's defined within the Data Division of a method can be accessed only by that method. Data that's defined within the Data Division of the Object paragraph can be accessed by any method in the class.

Figure 22-4   The book inventory class

An introduction to inheritance

If you look back at the class definition in figure 22-4, you'll notice that the Class-ID paragraph includes the name of the class along with the Inherits phrase. This phrase indicates that the class that's being defined should *inherit* the data definitions and methods of another class. In this case, the BookInv class inherits the data definitions and methods of the Base class. This is a system class that's provided by Micro Focus COBOL. It contains the New method you use to create an instance of an object.

Inheritance is an important aspect of object-oriented programming because it lets you base a new class on an existing class. To illustrate, consider the two classes shown in figure 22-5. The first class is the book inventory class you've seen throughout this chapter. The second class is a discount book inventory class. Because this class requires the same data definitions and methods as the book inventory class, it can be defined so that it inherits those definitions and methods. That way, they don't have to be defined again within the discount class, which significantly simplifies the code that's required to define the class.

In this case, the discount book inventory class is a *subclass*, and the book inventory class is a *superclass*. Then, the subclass inherits the data definitions and methods from the superclass. Besides that, though, the subclass can contain its own data definitions and methods. In this example, a data definition is added for a field that will hold the discount percent for a book. In addition, a method named update-discount is added that can be used to update the discount percent.

The other method that's unique to the discount book inventory class is the one named get-book-price. Notice, however, that the book inventory class contains a method by the same name, which means that method is inherited by the discount class. Whenever a subclass contains the definition of a method that's inherited from a superclass, the method in the subclass overrides the inherited method.

The book inventory class

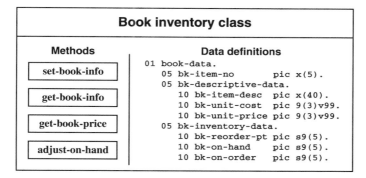

A class that inherits the book inventory class

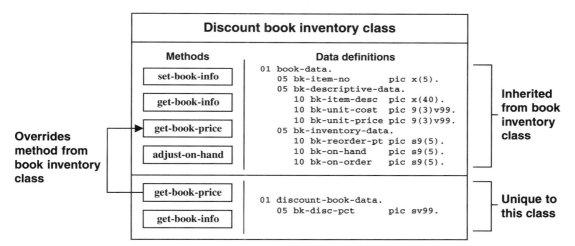

Concepts

- The principle of *inheritance* lets you base a new class you create on an existing class. Then, the new class *inherits* the data definitions and methods of the existing class.

- A class that inherits data definitions and methods from another class is called a *subclass*. The class it inherits from is called a *superclass*.

- A class can include data definitions and methods in addition to those it inherits from another class. Then, those data definitions and methods are unique to that class.

- If a subclass includes a method with the same name as a method in the superclass, the method in the subclass overrides the method in the superclass.

Figure 22-5   An introduction to inheritance

An introduction to polymorphism

The last principle of object-oriented programming you need to understand is *polymorphism*. Polymorphism simply means that multiple objects can have methods with the same name. For example, two objects that are created from the same class have methods with the same name. That's polymorphism. Polymorphism also results when two objects are created from two different classes that have methods with the same name.

Figure 22-6 illustrates the concept of polymorphism. This figure presents two objects. The first one was created from the book inventory class, and the second one was created from the discount book inventory class. Notice that both objects contain a method named get-book-price. However, each method contains different code. The method in the book inventory object simply moves the value of the bk-unit-price field to the ls-price field. In contrast, the method in the discount book inventory object calculates the value of the ls-price field using the bk-unit-price field and the bk-disc-pct field. In both cases, the method then returns the value of the ls-price field to the invoking program. (This code isn't shown in the figure).

One of the advantages of polymorphism is that the invoking program doesn't have to know what class an object was created from. The Invoke statement shown in this figure, for example, could be used to invoke the get-book-price method of either object as long as the same handle is assigned to the object regardless of the class it's created from. That's possible because even though these methods work differently, they return the same information. Of course, these methods could be defined so that they received or returned different information. If that was the case, though, they would probably have different names.

Two objects that have the get-book-price method

An object created from the book inventory class

abookInvObj	
Methods	**Data**

set-book-info

get-book-info

get-book-price
`move bk-unit-price to ls-price.`

adjust-on-hand

Data

Item no:	10001
Item desc:	Murach's VB6
Unit cost:	5.35
Unit price:	45.00
Reorder pt:	1,500
On hand:	543
On order:	10,000

An object created from the discount book inventory class

abookInvObj	
Methods	**Data**

set-book-info

get-book-info

get-book-price
`compute ls-price =` `    bk-unit-price * (1 - bk-disc-pct).`

adjust-on-hand

Data

Item no:	09500
Item desc:	Murach's VB5
Unit cost:	6.50
Unit price:	40.00
Reorder pt:	0
On hand:	300
On order:	0
Disc pct:	.20

An Invoke statement that invokes the get-book-price method

```
Invoke abookInvObj "get-book-price" returning book-price.
```

Concepts

- The principle of *polymorphism* lets you use the same name for a method in two or more objects. Although the methods have the same name, they can perform different functions.

- Two objects created from the same class always have the same methods that perform the same function. Two objects created from different classes can have the same methods and the same or different functions.

- When you invoke a method of an object, you do not need to know what class the object was created from. You just identify the handle for the object, and the code for the specified method in that object will be executed.

Figure 22-6   An introduction to polymorphism

How to work with classes and objects

Now that you've been introduced to the basic principles of object-oriented programming, you're ready to learn the syntax for defining classes and invoking methods with object-oriented COBOL. To make this syntax easier to understand, I'll illustrate it by using code from the book inventory class and the book maintenance program you saw earlier in this chapter. As you read the following topics, keep in mind that only the basic syntax is presented here.

How to define a class

Classes are the building blocks of object-oriented programming. To develop an object-oriented program, then, you need to know how to define a class. In this topic, you'll see the basic structure of a class. Then, the topics that follow will expand on that structure by presenting more of its details.

Figure 22-7 presents the syntax of a class definition. To start, the Identification Division contains a Class-ID paragraph that names the class. This is analogous to the Program-ID paragraph that you include in a traditional program. In the example in this figure, the class-id is BookInv.

The Class-ID paragraph can also include an Inherits clause. This clause indicates whether or not the class inherits data definitions and methods from another class. The BookInv class, for example, inherits a class named Base. This is a system class that's provided by Micro Focus COBOL that you can include in any of the classes you create. It contains methods for creating and maintaining objects. You learned about one of those methods, New, earlier in this chapter. Another method of the Base class is Finalize. You can use this method to remove an object from memory when you're done with it.

In the Environment Division of a class definition, you declare other classes the will be used by this class. In Micro Focus COBOL, you do that by coding entries in the Class-Control paragraph of the Object Section. In the proposed COBOL-2002 standards, however, you declare classes within the Repository paragraph of the Configuration Section.

Regardless of which technique you use, each class declaration assigns a name to the class that will be used within the program, and it associates that name with an external reference that identifies the file that contains the compiled code for the class. Note that although the external reference and the name that you use to refer to the class from within the program are usually the same, they don't have to be.

In the example in this figure, two classes are declared. The first one is the book inventory class itself. In Micro Focus COBOL, you have to make this declaration in certain situations. In the proposed standards, though, you don't. The second class is the Base class that's inherited by the book inventory class. If the book inventory class created instances of other classes or invoked methods of other classes, they would have to be declared as well. You'll see an example of that in the enhanced book inventory application that's presented later in this topic.

The syntax of a class definition

```
IDENTIFICATION DIVISION.
CLASS-ID. class-name-1
         [INHERITS [FROM] class-name-2].


ENVIRONMENT DIVISION.
```

```
OBJECT-SECTION.                                          │─ Micro
CLASS-CONTROL.                                           │  Focus
    [[class-name-3 IS CLASS "external-name-3"] ...]
```

```
CONFIGURATION SECTION.                                   │  Proposed
REPOSITORY.                                              │─ 2002
    [[ CLASS class-name-3 IS "external-class-name-3"] ...]│  standard
```

```
    [{factory definition}]
    {object definition}
    .
END CLASS class-name-1.
```

Code that defines the BookInv class

```
Identification Division.
Class-id.  BookInv
           inherits from Base.
Environment Division.
Object Section.
Class-Control.
    BookInv    is class "bookinv"
    Base       is class "Base".
    .
    .
    .
    Object definition
    .
    .
    .
End Class BookInv.
```

Description

- The Class-ID paragraph specifies the name of the class. It can also include an Inherits clause that names a class that data definitions and methods are inherited from.

- If the class will refer to another class, it must declare that class in the Environment Division. With Micro Focus COBOL, you declare the class in the Class-Control paragraph of the Object Section. With the proposed COBOL-2002 standards, you declare it in the Repository paragraph of the Configuration Section.

- To declare a class, you specify the class name to be used by the program along with an external file name that identifies the class.

- After the class declarations, you code the object definition and the optional factory definition as shown in figure 22-8. Then, you code the End Class marker to end the class definition.

Figure 22-7   How to define a class

After you declare the classes that will be used by the class you're defining, you define the object that will be created from the class and, optionally, a factory for the class. You'll see how to do that in the next two topics. To end the definition of a class, you code the End Class marker.

How to define an object

Figure 22-8 presents the syntax for the Object paragraph, which contains the definition of an object. Notice that this paragraph can include an Environment Division, a Data Division, and a Procedure Division. Within the Data Division, you define data that can be used by any of the object's methods. You define the methods for the object within the Procedure Division of the object definition. To end the object definition, you code the End Object marker.

The example in this figure shows the code that defines the book inventory object. Here, the Working-Storage Section of the Data Division contains the data definitions for a book. (With Micro Focus COBOL, you can also use the header Object-Storage Section instead of Working-Storage Section.) Then, the Procedure Division contains the methods that will interact with the book data in an object that's created from the book inventory class. You'll see the complete definition of one of these methods in just a moment.

How to define a factory

In addition to defining an object, a class can also define a *factory*. A factory contains data definitions and methods that can be used without creating an object. For example, the New method that you use to create an instance of a class is a factory method that's defined in the Base class. Although you probably won't define factory methods often, they can be useful in some situations. For example, you could use a factory method in any class to keep a count of how many objects are created from the class.

The syntax for defining a factory is similar to the syntax for defining an object. The only difference is that you start the definition with a Factory header instead of an Object header, and you end it with an End Factory marker. This syntax is also presented in figure 22-8.

The syntax of an object definition

```
OBJECT.
[ENVIRONMENT DIVISION.]
[DATA DIVISION.
    {data shared by object methods}]
[PROCEDURE DIVISION.
    {method} ...]
END OBJECT.
```

Code that defines the BookInv object

```
Object.
    Data Division.
    Working-Storage Section.
    01  book-data.
        05  bk-item-no                pic x(05).
        05  bk-descriptive-data.
            10  bk-item-desc          pic x(40).
            10  bk-unit-cost          pic 9(03)v99.
            10  bk-unit-price         pic 9(03)v99.
        05  bk-inventory-data.
            10  bk-reorder-pt         pic s9(05).
            10  bk-on-hand            pic s9(05).
            10  bk-on-order           pic s9(05).
    Procedure Division.
        .
        .
        Methods
        .
        .
End Object.
```

The syntax of a factory definition

```
FACTORY.
[ENVIRONMENT DIVISION.]
[DATA DIVISION.
    {data shared by factory methods}]
[PROCEDURE DIVISION.
    {method} ...]
END FACTORY.
```

Description

- The Object paragraph defines the data and methods that will be included in any object that's created from the class. This paragraph can include an Environment Division, a Data Division that contains data that can be shared by all the object's methods, and a Procedure Division that contains the method definitions.

- The Factory paragraph contains data and methods that are available through the class rather than through an object created from the class. Like the Object paragraph, it can include an Environment Division, a Data Division that contains data that can be shared by all the factory's methods, and a Procedure Division that contains the method definitions.

Figure 22-8   How to define an object or factory

How to define a method

To define a method, you use the syntax that's presented in figure 22-9. To start, you name the method by coding a literal that contains the name you want to use on the Method-ID header. The code in this figure, for example, shows the definition of the method named adjust-on-hand.

Within the Method-ID paragraph, you can code an Environment Division, a Data Division, and a Procedure Division. To end the definition of a method, you code the End Method marker with the name of the method.

Within the Data Division, you can code a File Section, a Working-Storage Section, a Local-Storage Section, and a Linkage Section. Any data that's defined in the File or Working-Storage Section is maintained between invocations of the method. If the method reads a record from a file, for example, that record will be available from the File Section each time the method is invoked. Data that's defined in the Local-Storage Section, however, is not maintained between invocations of the method. Each time the method is invoked, the data items in this section are assigned a different area of storage that can contain different values.

The Linkage Section of a method contains the data definitions for the data that will be received from or returned to the invoking program. To receive and send these fields, they must also be named in the Using or Returning clause of the Procedure Division header for the method. The Using clause names the fields where the data that's received from the invoking program will be stored, and the Returning clause names the fields where the data that's returned to the invoking program will be stored.

Within the Procedure Division of a method, you include the procedural code that performs the function of the method. In most cases, that code will work with the data that's defined within the method or the object that contains it. The method that's shown in this figure, for example, adjusts the on-hand amount for the book whose data is stored in the object's Working-Storage Section (see figure 22-8). To do that, it uses an adjustment value that's passed to it from the invoking program and stored in the Linkage Section of the object. Then, it returns the new on-hand amount to the invoking program by moving that value from the object's Working-Storage Section to the Linkage Section of the method.

The syntax of a method

```
METHOD-ID. "method-name-1".
[ENVIRONMENT DIVISION.]
[DATA DIVISION.
[FILE SECTION.
    {data that is maintained between invocations of the method}]
[WORKING-STORAGE SECTION.
    {data that is maintained between invocations of the method}]
[LOCAL-STORAGE SECTION.
    {data that is unique to each invocation of the method}]
[LINKAGE SECTION.
    {data that's used to pass parameters to and from the method}]]
[PROCEDURE DIVISION [USING data-name-1 ...]
                    [RETURNING data-name-2 ...].
    {procedural code}]
END METHOD "method-name-1".
```

Code that defines the adjust-on-hand method

```
Method-ID. "adjust-on-hand".

Data Division.

Linkage Section.

01  ls-adjustment           pic s9(03).
01  ls-on-hand              pic s9(05).

Procedure Division using ls-adjustment
                   returning ls-on-hand.

    add ls-adjustment to bk-on-hand.
    move bk-on-hand to ls-on-hand.

End Method "adjust-on-hand".
```

Description

- The definition of a method begins with a Method-ID header that names the method and ends with an End Method marker that also includes the method name.

- The data that's defined within a method can be accessed only by that method. Data that's defined within the File Section or Working-Storage Section of a method is maintained between invocations of the method. Data that's defined within the Local-Storage Section of a method is unique to each invocation of the method.

- Data that's received from or returned to the invoking program must be defined within the Linkage Section of the method. The fields used to store data that's received from the invoking program must be named on the Using clause of the Procedure Division header. The fields used to return data to the invoking program must be named on the Returning clause of the Procedure Division header.

Figure 22-9   How to define a method

How to invoke a method

After you create and compile the code that defines a class, you can invoke it from another program or class. To do that, you use the Invoke statement. Its syntax is presented in figure 22-10.

To start, you should notice that you can specify either an object reference (a handle), a class name, or the word SELF on this statement. You specify a class name when you want to invoke a factory method such as the New method you use to create a new object. This is illustrated in the first example in this figure. You specify an object reference when you want to invoke an object method as illustrated in the second example. And you specify SELF when you want to invoke a method from within the object that contains the method. You'll see an example of that later in this chapter.

After the class name or object reference, you code a literal that contains the name of the method you want to invoke. The two Invoke statements shown in this figure, for example, invoke the New and adjust-on-hand methods. Instead of a literal, you can code the name of a field that contains the name of the method. If you do that, you can invoke different methods using the same statement. In most cases, though, you won't need to do that.

If you need to send data to the invoked method, you can do that by coding a Using clause with the names of the fields that contain that data. Similarly, if the method will return any data to the invoking program, you can code a Returning clause with the names of the fields where the returned data will be stored. When you use either of these clauses, you should make sure that the fields they name are defined with the same pictures and usages as they are in the method. You should also make sure that they're coded in the same sequence as in the method. If you don't, the method won't work as intended, or, worse yet, a run-time error may occur.

Because the New method that's invoked in the first example doesn't require any data, the Using clause is omitted from the Invoke statement. However, this statement does include a Returning clause that names the field where the handle for the newly created object will be stored. As you can see, that field is defined in working storage with a usage of Object Reference.

The Invoke statement for the adjust-on-hand method includes both a Using and a Returning clause. The Using clause names the field that contains the adjustment quantity that will be passed to the method. Then, the method returns the new on-hand amount, which is stored in the field that's named in the Returning clause.

You should also notice in the first example in this figure that the program includes a Class-Control paragraph. This paragraph declares the book inventory class that's used by this program. You code this paragraph the same way you do within a class definition. You can refer back to figure 22-7 to see the actual syntax for this paragraph.

The syntax of the Invoke statement

```
INVOKE  ⎧ object-reference ⎫  ⎧ "method-name-1" ⎫
        ⎨ class-name       ⎬  ⎨ identifier      ⎬
        ⎩ SELF             ⎭  ⎩                 ⎭
        [ USING data-name-1 ... ]
        [ RETURNING data-name-2 ... ]
```

Code that invokes a factory method

```
Environment Division.
Object Section.
Class-Control.
    BookInv is class "bookinv".
Data Division.
Working-Storage Section.
    .
    05  bookInvObj          usage is object reference.
    .
Procedure Division.
    .
    invoke BookInv "New" returning bookInvObj.
```

Code that invokes an object method

```
Working-Storage Section.
    .
    05  on-hand-adjustment  pic s9(03).
    05  on-hand-qty         pic s9(05).
    .
    05  bookInvObj          usage is object reference.
    .
Procedure Division.
    .
    invoke bookInvObj "adjust-on-hand"
                      using on-hand-adjustment
                      returning on-hand-qty.
```

Description

- You use the Invoke statement to invoke a factory method or a class method. To invoke a factory method, you name the class that contains the method on the Invoke statement. To invoke an object method, you name the field that contains the handle for the object on the Invoke statement.

- After the class name or handle, you specify the name of the method to be invoked. You can do that by enclosing the name in quotes or by specifying the name of a field that contains the method name.

- To send data to the method, you include the Using clause with the names of one or more fields that contain the data to be sent. If the method returns data, you include the Returning clause with the names of one or more fields where you want to store the returned data.

- You can also invoke a method from within the object that contains the method. To do that, you specify the word SELF instead of a class name or object reference.

Figure 22-10   How to invoke a method

A book inquiry application

To illustrate the object-oriented concepts and COBOL statements you've learned about in this chapter, the topics that follow present a complete application. This application will perform the same function as the interactive inquiry program presented in figure17-6. If you haven't read that chapter, you may want to review the specifications and code for this program before you continue. Then, you can compare that program to the object-oriented version that's presented next.

The design of the book inquiry application

One of the most difficult tasks of designing an object-oriented application is deciding what each class should contain. In theory, a class should be designed around data. Then, the methods in that class should perform functions on that data. In practice, though, that's not always the case. Instead, many classes are defined based on their functions. Because of that, we won't try to explain how you determine what classes an application should contain. Instead, we'll just present an application design and let you draw your own conclusions.

Figure 22-11 presents the design of a book inquiry application. The function of this application is to accept an item number from the user, retrieve the data for that item from an inventory master file, and then display that information on the screen. To do that, this application has been divided into a main program, called a *driver program*, and four classes: the book manager class (BookMng), the file manager class (BookFM), the book inventory class (BookInv), and the user interface class (BookUI).

As you'll see in a moment, the driver program simply starts the inquiry process. To do that, it creates a book manager object that contains the logic for this application. Because this object will manage the operation of this program, the class it's created from is typically called the *manager class*.

The book manager class manages the interactions with all the other classes. For example, after it creates an object from the file manager class, it sends file I/O requests to that object. The file manager class contains a description of the file along with methods that can be used to open and close the file (open-file and close-file) and create a book inventory object for a selected item (create-book). The create-book method actually reads the record, creates a new book inventory object for that record, and uses the set-book-info method of that object to populate it.

Notice that the file manager object returns the handle for the book inventory object to the book manager object. That way, the book manager object can request information directly from the book inventory object. It does that by using the get-desc-info and get-inv-info methods of that object.

The last class in this diagram, the user interface class, contains all the code for interacting with the user. It's used by the book manager class to display information on the screen and to accept information from the user.

The design of the book inquiry application

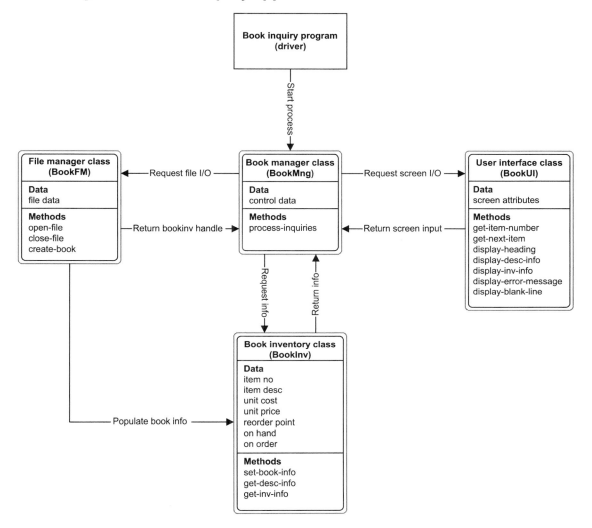

Description

- To design an object-oriented application, you break it down into classes. Each class should operate on a related set of data or perform a related set of functions, and it should be defined so it's reusable.

- A fully object-oriented application typically includes a *driver program*. The main function of this program is to instantiate a class that will manage the execution of the application and then invoke a method of the newly created object that contains the high-level logic for that application.

- The class that manages an application can be called a *manager class*. The manager class typically contains a single method for each application it manages.

Figure 22-11   The design of the book inquiry application

As you study this diagram, keep in mind that it's based on the needs of a single application. So it doesn't take into account any related data or functions that might be needed by other applications in the system. If it did, each class would include more functions, some classes would include more data, and more classes would probably be required. Even so, this design should serve to illustrate the concepts of object-oriented programming. You'll better understand how this design works, though, after you see the code for this application.

The code for the book inquiry program

Figure 22-12 presents the code for the book inquiry program, which is the driver program for the book inquiry application. As you can see in the Class-Control paragraph, this program will interact with a single class: the book manager class. As you'll see in a moment, the book manager class contains all the logic for this application.

The first Invoke statement in the Procedure Division of this program creates a book manager object. Then, the second Invoke statement invokes the process-inquiries method of that object. This method contains the procedural code that manages the operation of this application. It continues to execute until the user indicates that no more items are to be displayed. At that point, control returns to the book inquiry program. Then, this program executes a Stop Run statement and the program ends.

The book inquiry program

```
Identification Division.

Program-id. Bookinq.

Environment Division.

Object Section.

Class-Control.
    BookMng is class "bookmng".

Data Division.

Working-Storage Section.

01   handles.
     05   bookMngObj        object reference.

Procedure Division.

     invoke BookMng "New" returning bookMngObj.
     invoke bookMngObj "process-inquiries".
     stop run.
```

Figure 22-12   The COBOL code for the book inquiry program

The code for the book manager class

Figure 22-13 presents the code for the book manager class. This is the class that's used from the book inquiry program to create a book manager object. This class contains the main logic of this application.

To start, you should notice that the Class-Control paragraph of this class declares five classes. Two of those classes are the book manager class itself and the Base class that it inherits. The other three are the user interface, file manager, and book inventory classes that this application uses.

The object definition for the book manager class consists of a Data Division and a Procedure Division. Within the Data Division, the Working-Storage Section defines the data that will be used by the objects created from this class. That includes handles for all of the objects it will reference; a switch that will indicate when the program should end; an error message field that will be used to hold an error message that's sent to the user interface object; and book data that will be sent to the book inventory object. Because this data is defined within the Data Division of the object, it's available to all the object's methods. In this case, though, the object contains a single method. The definition of this method is presented on page 2 of this listing.

The book manager class   **Page 1**

```
Identification Division.
Class-id.  BookMng
           inherits from Base.

Environment Division.
Object Section.
Class-Control.
    BookMng is class "bookmng"
    BookUI  is class "bookui"
    BookFM  is class "bookfm"
    BookInv is class "bookinv"
    Base    is class "Base".

Object.
    Data Division.
    Working-Storage Section.

    01  handles            object reference.
        05  bookMngObj.
        05  bookUIObj.
        05  bookFMObj.
        05  bookInvObj.

    01  switches.
        05  end-of-inquiries-switch    pic x(01)  value "N".
            88  end-of-inquiries                  value "Y".

    01  error-message                  pic x(50).

    01  book-data.
        05  bk-item-number             pic x(05).
        05  bk-descriptive-data        pic x(50).
        05  bk-inventory-data          pic x(15).
```

Figure 22-13   The COBOL code for the book manager class (part 1 of 2)

The process-inquiries method contains the main logic for this application. Like a traditional COBOL program, it's controlled by a Perform Until statement that's executed repeatedly. In this case, this statement is executed until the user indicates that there are no more inquiries. Before this statement is executed, though, four Invoke statements are executed.

The first Invoke statement in this method creates a new user interface object (bookUIObj), and the second method creates a new file manager object (bookFMObj). Then, the third Invoke statement invokes the open-file method of the file manager object to open the inventory master file. Finally, the fourth Invoke statement invokes the display-heading method of the user interface object to display heading data on the screen.

The inline Perform Until statement starts by invoking the get-item-number method of the user interface object to accept an item number from the user. Next, that item number is checked to see if it's equal to 99999. If it is, it indicates that the program should end. Then, the end-of-inquiries switch is turned on and the Perform Until statement ends.

If the item number isn't equal to 99999, the program continues by invoking the create-book method of the file manager object. As you'll see in a moment, this method reads the record for the specified item from the inventory master file and then creates a new book inventory object that contains the data for that item. Then, the create-book method in the file manager object returns the handle that's assigned to the book inventory object to the book manager object. To accomplish that, the Invoke statement that invokes the create-book method includes a Returning clause that names the field that will contain the pointer to that object.

The If statement that follows this Invoke statement tests if the value of this pointer is null. If it is, it indicates that the item wasn't found in the inventory master file. Then, an appropriate message is moved to the error-message field, and the display-error-message method of the user interface object is invoked to display this message.

If this pointer isn't null, the program continues by invoking the display-blank-line method of the user interface object to blank out line 23 of the screen. That's done in case any error messages were displayed along the way. Then, the get-desc-info of the book inventory object is invoked to get the descriptive data for the item, and the display-desc-info method of the user interface object is invoked to display that data. Next, the get-inv-info method of the book inventory object is invoked to get the inventory data for the item, and the display-inv-info method of the user interface object is invoked to display that data.

After the data for the item is displayed, the get-next-item method of the user interface object is invoked. This method accepts an entry from the user that indicates whether the data for another item should be displayed. If not, the Perform statement ends and the final Invoke statement invokes the close-file method of the file manager object to close the inventory master file. Otherwise, the display-heading method of the user interface object is invoked to redisplay the headings and clear the screen. Then, the statements within the Perform Until statement are executed again.

The book manager class   **Page 2**

```
      Procedure Division.
**************************************************************
      Method-ID. "process-inquiries".
      Procedure Division.

          invoke BookUI "New" returning bookUIObj.
          invoke BookFM "New" returning bookFMObj.

          invoke bookFMObj "open-file".
          invoke bookUIObj "display-heading".

          perform until end-of-inquiries
              invoke bookUIObj "get-item-number"
                  returning bk-item-number
              if bk-item-number = "99999"
                  set end-of-inquiries to true
              else
                  invoke bookFMObj "create-book"
                      using bk-item-number
                      returning bookInvObj
                  if bookInvObj = null
                      move "Inventory record not found."
                          to error-message
                      invoke bookUIObj "display-error-message"
                          using error-message
                  else
                      invoke bookUIObj "display-blank-line"
                      invoke bookInvObj "get-desc-info"
                          returning bk-descriptive-data
                      invoke bookUIObj "display-desc-info"
                          using bk-descriptive-data
                      invoke bookInvObj "get-inv-info"
                          returning bk-inventory-data
                      invoke bookUIObj "display-inv-info"
                          using bk-inventory-data
                      invoke bookUIObj "get-next-item"
                          returning end-of-inquiries-switch
                      if not end-of-inquiries
                          invoke bookUIObj "display-heading"
                      end-if
                  end-if
              end-if
          end-perform.

          invoke bookFMObj "close-file".

      End Method "process-inquiries".

**************************************************************
  End Object.
  End Class BookMng.
```

Figure 22-13   The COBOL code for the book manager class (part 2 of 2)

At this point, you may be wondering why the code in the book manager class isn't just included in the driver program. The answer is that by putting this code in a separate class, this class can serve as the manager for more than one program. If, for example, the book inventory system included a book maintenance program, the book manager class could include another method that controlled the operation of that program. That makes sense because that method would use some of the same control data and classes that the process-inquiries method uses.

The code for the file manager class

The code for the file manager class is presented in figure 22-14. This class contains code that performs the I/O functions on the inventory master file. Because of that, it contains a Select statement for that file along with a FD statement and record description. Notice that these statements are coded within the definition of the class and not the object. With Micro Focus COBOL, you can't code these statements within an object definition, even though they're included in an object that's created from this class. The COBOL-2002 standards, though, indicate that these statements should be coded within the object, which makes more sense.

The object definition in the file manager class contains a Procedure Division that includes three methods. The first method, open-file, opens the inventory master file, and the second method, close-file, closes that file. The third method, create-book, creates and populates a new book inventory object. To do that, it starts by reading a record from the inventory master file using the item number that's passed to it by the book manager class. If a record isn't found with that item number, the Invalid Key clause of the Read statement sets the field that holds the handle for the book inventory object to null. Notice that you must use a Set statement to work with that field since it contains an object reference. When that field is returned to the book manager object, the object can determine that the item wasn't found because its handle has a null value.

If the Read statement is successful, the New method of the book inventory class is invoked to create a book inventory object. Then, the Invoke statement that follows invokes the set-book-info method of that object to populate it with the data for the book. When the method ends, it returns the handle for the book inventory object to the book manager object so it can refer to that object directly.

Note that every time the create-book method is invoked, it creates a new book inventory object. Because the same field is used to hold the handle for that object, though, the pointer to the previous object is lost and the memory that object occupied is released. If you ever need to work with two objects created from the same class at the same time, you can do that by assigning the handle for each object to a different field.

The file manager class

```
Identification Division.
Class-id.  BookFM
           inherits from Base.
Environment Division.
Input-Output Section.
File-Control.
    select invmast assign to "c:\cobol\data\invmasti.dat"
                   organization is indexed
                   access is random
                   record key is im-item-no.
Object Section.
Class-Control.
    BookFM  is class "bookfm"
    BookInv is class "bookinv"
    Base    is class "Base".
Data Division.
File Section.
fd  invmast.
01  inventory-master-record.
    05  im-item-no            pic x(05).
    05  im-descriptive-data   pic x(50).
    05  im-inventory-data     pic x(15).
Object.
    Procedure Division.
*****************************************************************
    Method-ID. "open-file".
    Procedure Division.
        open input invmast.
    End Method "open-file".
*****************************************************************
    Method-ID. "close-file".
    Procedure Division.
        close invmast.
    End Method "close-file".
*****************************************************************
    Method-ID. "create-book".
    Data Division.
    Linkage Section.
    01  ls-item-no     pic x(05).
    01  ls-bookInvObj  object reference.
    Procedure Division using ls-item-no
                       returning ls-bookInvObj.
        move ls-item-no to im-item-no.
        read invmast
            invalid key
                set ls-bookInvObj to null
            not invalid key
                invoke BookInv "New"
                    returning ls-bookInvObj
                invoke ls-bookInvObj "set-book-info"
                    using inventory-master-record
        end-read.
    End Method "create-book".
*****************************************************************
End Object.
End Class BookFM.
```

Figure 22-14   The COBOL code for the file manager class

The code for the book inventory class

The code for the book inventory class is presented in figure 22-15. Notice that the object that's defined by this class contains a Data Division. Then, the Working-Storage Section of this division contains the definitions of the fields for a book. Because these fields are defined within the object, they can be accessed by any of the methods defined by this class.

The Procedure Division of the object contains the definitions of three methods. The first method, set-book-info, receives book data sent to it by the file manager object. The definitions for this data are defined in the Linkage Section of this method. Then, the method moves those fields to the fields in the Data Division of the object so they will be available the next time any of the methods of this object are invoked.

The second method, get-desc-info, moves the descriptive data for a book from the Data Division of the object to the Linkage Section of this method. Then, that data is returned to the book manager object that invoked it. Similarly, the get-inv-info method returns the inventory data for a book to the book manager object. Although these two methods could have been combined into a single method, we chose to separate them to make this class more flexible.

The book inventory class

```
Identification Division.
Class-id.  BookInv
           inherits from Base.
Environment Division.
Object Section.
Class-Control.
    BookInv    is class "bookinv"
    Base       is class "Base".
Object.
    Data Division.
    Working-Storage Section.
    01  book-data.
        05  bk-item-no                pic x(05).
        05  bk-descriptive-data.
            10  bk-item-desc           pic x(40).
            10  bk-unit-cost           pic 9(03)v99.
            10  bk-unit-price          pic 9(03)v99.
        05  bk-inventory-data.
            10  bk-reorder-point       pic s9(05).
            10  bk-on-hand             pic s9(05).
            10  bk-on-order            pic s9(05).
    Procedure Division.
****************************************************************
    Method-ID. "set-book-info".
    Data Division.
    Linkage Section.
    01  ls-book-data.
        05  ls-item-no            pic x(05).
        05  ls-descriptive-data   pic x(50).
        05  ls-inventory-data     pic x(15).
    Procedure Division using ls-book-data.
        move ls-book-data to book-data.
    End Method "set-book-info".
****************************************************************
    Method-ID. "get-desc-info".
    Data Division.
    Linkage Section.
    01  ls-descriptive-data.
        05  ls-item-desc      pic x(40).
        05  ls-unit-cost      pic 9(03)v99.
        05  ls-unit-price     pic 9(03)v99.
    Procedure Division returning ls-descriptive-data.
        move bk-descriptive-data to ls-descriptive-data.
    End Method "get-desc-info".
****************************************************************
    Method-ID. "get-inv-info".
    Data Division.
    Linkage Section.
    01  ls-inventory-data.
        05  ls-reorder-point   pic s9(05).
        05  ls-on-hand         pic s9(05).
        05  ls-on-order        pic s9(05).
    Procedure Division returning ls-inventory-data.
        move bk-inventory-data to ls-inventory-data.
    End Method "get-inv-info".
****************************************************************
End Object.
End Class BookInv.
```

Figure 22-15   The COBOL code for the book inventory class

The code for the user interface class

The code for the user interface class is listed in figure 22-16. This class controls all interactions with the user by displaying data on the screen and accepting data from the screen. To do that, it uses the enhanced Accept and Display statements that are presented in chapter 17. You can refer back to that chapter if you have any trouble understanding how these statements work.

The Data Division of the object definition for this class includes just three 78-level items in the Working-Storage Section. These items define the three colors that will be used to display data on the screen.

The Procedure Division of the object contains a number of methods. Because these methods use mostly standard COBOL statements, you shouldn't have any trouble understanding how they work. The main focus here, then, will be on how these methods interact with the book manager object that invokes them.

The first method, get-item-number, accepts an item number from the user. If the user enters a value other than Space, that value is returned to the book manager object using the ls-item-number field that's defined in the Linkage Section of the object. Otherwise, an error message is displayed and the user is prompted to enter a item number.

Notice that the display-error-message method that's used to display the error message is defined within the user interface object. Because of that, the Invoke statement that invokes this method uses the word SELF instead of the object name.

The next method, get-next-item, asks the user if he or she wants to display the data for another item. If the user enters Y or N, the ls-end-of-inquiries switch that's defined in the Linkage Section of the method is set to the opposite value, and that value is returned to the book manager object that invoked the method. That object can then use this switch to determine if processing should continue or the program should end. If the user enters a value other than Y or N, an error message is displayed. Once again, the method that's used to display this method is defined within the user interface object, so the word SELF is used on the Invoke statement to identify that method.

The display-heading method displays the program name on the first line of the screen, clears the screen, and sets the foreground and background colors for the screen. Then, it displays a message that directs the user what to do. This method is invoked by the book manager class when the program first starts and each time the user indicates another item is to be displayed. Notice that this method neither receives nor returns data. It simply performs its function and then returns control to the book manager object.

The display-desc-info method receives the descriptive data for an item from the book manager object and displays it on the screen. Similarly, the display-inv-info method receives the inventory data for an item and displays it on the screen. Notice that both of the methods move the data that's passed to it to formatted fields in working storage so they're displayed properly.

The user interface class
Page 1

```
Identification Division.
Class-id.  BookUI
           inherits from Base.
Environment Division.
Object Section.
Class-Control.
    BookUI is class "bookui"
    Base   is class "Base".

Object.
    Data Division.
    Working-Storage Section.
    78  black               value 0.
    78  white               value 7.
    78  bright-white        value 15.

    Procedure Division.
**********************************************************
    Method-ID. "get-item-number".
    Data Division.

    Local-Storage Section.
    01  switches.
        05  valid-entry-switch      pic x(01) value "N".
            88  valid-entry                   value "Y".
    01  error-message               pic x(50).

    Linkage Section.
    01  ls-item-number              pic x(05).

    Procedure Division returning ls-item-number.

        move "N"    to valid-entry-switch.
        move spaces to ls-item-number.
        perform until valid-entry
            display "Item number. . . . . " at line 5  column 1
            display "Enter 99999 to end."   at line 24 column 1
            accept ls-item-number at line 5 column 22
                with prompt
            if ls-item-number = space
                move "An item number is required." to
                    error-message
                invoke self "display-error-message"
                    using error-message
            else
                set valid-entry to true
            end-if
        end-perform.

    End Method "get-item-number".
```

Figure 22-16   The COBOL code for the user interface class (part 1 of 4)

The display-error-message method receives an error message from the object that invokes it and displays that message on the screen. As you've already seen, this method is invoked by both the get-item-number and get-next-item methods within the user interface object. It's also invoked by the book manager class when an inventory record for the item number entered by the user isn't found in the inventory master file.

The last method in the user interface class is the display-blank-line method. This method simply displays spaces in line 23, the line where error messages are displayed. It's invoked from the book manager class if a record is found with the item number that's entered by the user to blank out any error messages that may have been displayed. Like the display-heading method, it neither receives nor returns data.

Now that you've seen all the code for this application, you should have a pretty good understanding of how it works. In general, the code should be relatively easy to understand. It's keeping the objects, data, and methods straight that's the difficult part of object-oriented programming. But if you design your classes so that each one either operates on a pre-defined grouping of data, like a record, or performs a set of related functions, like managing file I/O operations or user interaction, you'll be well on your way to developing useful object-oriented programs.

Practical guidelines for using object-oriented programming

After reviewing the object-oriented program presented in this chapter, you may be wondering whether object-oriented programming is worth the trouble. After all, the four-page program that was presented in chapter 17 took nine pages of code when it was converted to object-oriented code. Keep in mind, though, that if you define your classes with reusability in mind, you should be able to use the same classes and methods for this application in other applications.

Also keep in mind that object-oriented COBOL isn't an all or nothing prospect. In other words, you can use it when it makes sense, and use standard COBOL when it doesn't. The next time you design a new application, then, you should ask yourself if any of the code can be put into a class so that it can be reused by other applications. If the answer is yes (and your manager doesn't have any objections), you should give object-oriented programming a try.

Two situations where object-oriented programming almost always makes sense were illustrated by the application you just saw. First, a file manager class like the one in this application could be used to perform the file I/O for any file. That makes sense because most programs require file I/O.

Another situation is illustrated by the book inventory class in our sample application. A class like this can hold the data for a single record from any file. Then, its methods can perform any required operations on that data, like setting, retrieving, and updating data as well as performing calculations on the data. Together, a data manager class like this and a file manager class could be used to perform the operations on a file for any application.

The user interface class   **Page 2**

```
************************************************************
      Method-ID. "get-next-item".
      Data Division.
      Local-Storage Section.

      01  switches.
          05  next-item-switch    pic x(01) value " ".
              88  next-item                 value "Y".

      01  error-message           pic x(50).

      Linkage Section.
      01  ls-end-of-inquiries-switch    pic x(01)  value "N".

      Procedure Division returning ls-end-of-inquiries-switch.

          move " " to next-item-switch.
          perform until next-item-switch = "Y" or "N"
              display "Do you want to display another item?"
                  line 24 column 1
              accept next-item-switch at line 24 column 38
                  with foreground-color bright-white upper
              evaluate next-item-switch
                  when "Y"
                      move "N" to ls-end-of-inquiries-switch
                  when "N"
                      move "Y" to ls-end-of-inquiries-switch
                  when other
                      move "You must enter a 'Y' or 'N'."
                          to error-message
                      invoke self "display-error-message"
                          using error-message
              end-evaluate
          end-perform.

      End Method "get-next-item".

************************************************************
      Method-ID. "display-heading".
      Procedure Division.

          display "Inventory inquiry" at line 1 column 1
              with blank screen
              foreground-color black
              background-color white.
          display "Type an item number. Then press Enter."
              at line 3 column 1.

      End Method "display-heading".
```

Figure 22-16   The COBOL code for the user interface class (part 2 of 4)

The user interface class

```
***************************************************************
    Method-ID. "display-desc-info".
    Data Division.
    Local-Storage Section.
    01   screen-display-fields.
         05   unit-cost              pic zzz.zz.
         05   unit-price             pic zzz.zz.
    Linkage Section.
    01   ls-descriptive-data.
         05   ls-item-desc      pic x(40).
         05   ls-unit-cost      pic 9(03)v99.
         05   ls-unit-price     pic 9(03)v99.

    Procedure Division using ls-descriptive-data.
         move ls-unit-cost  to unit-cost.
         move ls-unit-price to unit-price.
         display "Description:"     line 7   column 1.
         display ls-item-desc       line 7   column 22.
         display "Unit cost:"       line 8   column 1.
         display unit-cost          line 8   column 22.
         display "Unit price:"      line 9   column 1.
         display unit-price         line 9   column 22.

    End Method "display-desc-info".
***************************************************************
    Method-ID. "display-inv-info".
    Data Division.
    Local-Storage Section.
    01   screen-display-fields.
         05   reorder-point         pic zz,zzz.
         05   on-hand               pic zz,zzz.
         05   on-order              pic zz,zzz.
    Linkage Section.
    01   ls-inventory-data.
         05   ls-reorder-point  pic s9(05).
         05   ls-on-hand        pic s9(05).
         05   ls-on-order       pic s9(05).

    Procedure Division using ls-inventory-data.
         move ls-reorder-point to reorder-point.
         move ls-on-hand       to on-hand.
         move ls-on-order      to on-order.
         display "Reorder point:"    line 10 column 1.
         display reorder-point       line 10 column 22.
         display "On hand:"          line 11 column 1.
         display on-hand             line 11 column 22.
         display "On order:"         line 12 column 1.
         display on-order            line 12 column 22.

    End Method "display-inv-info".
```

Figure 22-16   The COBOL code for the user interface class (part 3 of 4)

The user interface class

```
*****************************************************************
      Method-ID. "display-error-message".
      Data Division.
      Linkage Section.
      01  ls-error-message          pic x(50).

      Procedure Division using ls-error-message.

          display ls-error-message at line 23 column 1
              with foreground-color bright-white beep.

      End Method "display-error-message".

*****************************************************************
      Method-ID. "display-blank-line".
      Procedure Division.

          display spaces at line 23 column 1.

      End Method "display-blank-line".

*****************************************************************
  End Object.
  End Class BookUI.
```

Figure 22-16   The COBOL code for the user interface class (part 4 of 4)

Beyond that, if you're charged with the task of designing a small and manageable system, you may want to try implementing it entirely with object-oriented COBOL. If you do, think carefully about what data each class should contain and what operation it should perform. And always keep reusability in mind since that's the biggest advantage to using object-oriented COBOL.

Perspective

If this was your first introduction to object-oriented programming, you may be surprised at how different it is from structured programming. Although the code itself isn't that different—you still use COBOL statements like If and Perform Until statements—it's a whole new way of thinking about data and operations.

Now, the question is how well object-oriented COBOL will be accepted by COBOL shops in the years to come. Will it replace structured programming? Will it be used in combination with structured programming? Will it be rejected as too theoretical, too difficult, or too impractical? Because COBOL has a lengthy tradition of structured programming with billions of lines of structured code currently in operation, the one prediction we will make is that the changes won't take place quickly.

Summary

- An *object* contains data and *methods* that operate on that data. This combination of data and methods is called *encapsulation*.

- An object is an *instance* of a *class*. A class contains the definitions of the data and methods that each object that's created from the class will contain.

- An object can contain data that's available to all of its methods. Each method within the object can also contain data that can be used only by that method.

- *Inheritance* lets you base a new class on an existing class. The inherited class is called a *superclass*, and the class that inherits it is called a *subclass*.

- *Polymorphism* lets you use the same name for a method in different objects. The objects can be created from the same class or from different classes.

- You use the Invoke statement to invoke a method of an object. This statement can send data to and receive data from the object it's invoking.

- You can use the Invoke statement to invoke a factory method or an object method. A *factory method* is a method you can refer to directly from the class that defines it rather than from an object that's created from the class.

- To refer to a class from a COBOL program, you use its name. To refer to an object from a COBOL program, you use its *handle*. A handle contains a reference that points to the location of the object in memory.

Terms

object-oriented programming
OOP
object-oriented COBOL
OO COBOL
object
method
encapsulation
instance
class
instantiation

handle
inherit
inheritance
subclass
superclass
polymorphism
factory
driver program
manager class

Objectives

- Given complete specifications, modify an existing object-oriented application so it performs additional operations.

- In general terms, explain what an object is and how you can use it from a COBOL program.

- In general terms, describe the contents of a class and explain what it means to instantiate a class.

- Explain the principles of encapsulation, inheritance, and polymorphism.

- Describe the statement you use to interact with the methods of an object.

- In general terms, explain how you define a class.

Exercise 22-1 Experiment with object-oriented COBOL

In this exercise, you'll compile the classes and program that make up the book inquiry application presented in this chapter so you can see how an object-oriented program works. Then, you'll modify this application so it displays the total cost of a book in addition to the other information for the book.

Compile and run the book inquiry application

1. Copy the files from chapter 22 into c:\cobol so they're in your default folder.

2. Open the class named bookmng for edit, compile it, and close it, Then, repeat this step for the other classes in this application: bookdm, bookinv, and bookui.

3. Open the program named bookinq for edit and compile it. Then, close the program, open it for execution, and run it to see how it works. When you're done, close the program.

Modify the book inquiry application

4. Open the class named bookinv for edit. Then, add a method named calc-total-cost to this class that calculates the total cost of a book by multiplying the on-hand quantity for the book by its unit cost. This method should return the result of this calculation to the invoking program. When, you're done, compile the class and then close it.

5. Open the class named bookui for edit. Then, add a method named display-total-cost to this class that displays the heading "Total cost:" in column 1 of line 14 and the total cost of a book in column 15 of that line. This method should receive the total cost from the invoking program. Be sure that the method formats this field so it's displayed properly. When you're done, compile the class and then close it.

6. Open the class named bookmng for edit. Then, add code that invokes the two methods you added to the bookinv and bookmng classes. To do that, you'll need to define a new field in the Working-Storage Section of the object that will hold the total cost value. When you're done, compile the class and then close it.

7. Open the program named bookinq for execution and run it. Enter a valid item number (like 10001) and press the Enter key. Is the total cost of this book displayed correctly? If not, make the necessary corrections to the classes, recompile them, and then run this application again. When it works correctly, close it and exit from Personal COBOL.

Student projects

The exercises in the chapters give you a chance to practice the critical skills of each chapter. So if you do all of the exercises for all of the chapters, you practice the skills that you need for developing any program that you're asked to write. To give you the maximum amount of practice in a minimum amount of time, though, none of the exercises asks you to develop a complete project.

In contrast, this appendix provides the specifications for complete projects. For each chapter, there are one or more projects that ask you to apply what you've learned to applications that are different than those in the chapters. This gives you a chance to prove that you can apply what you've learned to any project that you're assigned.

When there are two or more projects for a chapter, we suggest that you choose the one that's most challenging. If you're using this book in a course, though, your instructor will probably assign specific projects to you. Your instructor may also make changes to the specifications for a project or add enhancements that make the project more difficult.

Once you see what these projects ask you to do, you'll get ideas of your own for other projects. You'll also get ideas for enhancements that will make the projects more challenging. The more you program, of course, the better you'll get...so be sure to develop a full range of projects.

Guidelines that apply to all of the projects

Copy the CD ROM files to your C drive

- Before you do any of the projects that require files, you should copy the folders and files of the CD ROM to your C drive. Then, all of the CD ROM files will be stored in a folder structure that starts with c:\cobol.

- After you copy the CD ROM files to your C drive, the data files that you need for the projects will be stored in c:\cobol\data. The extension used for these files is dat.

- After you copy the CD ROM files to your C drive, the copy member files that you can use with the projects will be stored in c:\cobol\copy. The extension for these files is cpy.

Don't enter the record descriptions into your programs

- On the next two pages, you'll see two record descriptions that are used by the projects. These record descriptions are stored in files called *copy members*. These files are stored in the c:\cobol\copy folder and have cpy as the extension.

- One way to get the record descriptions in these copy members into your programs is to type them in. That, however, is both time consuming and error-prone. As a result, you should use one of the alternatives that follow.

- If you haven't read chapter 11 yet, use copy and paste techniques to copy a record description from its copy member file into your program.

- If you have read chapter 11, use the Copy statement to copy the copy member into your program.

Always start a new program from an old program

- As this book has emphasized, you should always start a new program from an old one. At first, you can start your new programs from programs that you have worked on in the exercises. Later on, though, you should start your new programs from programs of your own. Eventually, you should have a set of your own programs that you can use for starting new programs.

Use consistent names for your programs

- To keep the names for your programs simple and consistent, we recommend that you name each program SP (student project) followed by the project number. For instance, you can use SP02-3 as the program name for project 2-3 and SP10-1 as the name for project 10-1.

The record description for the student master file

```
01  STUDENT-MASTER-RECORD.
    05  SM-STUDENT-ID                   PIC 9(09).
    05  SM-STUDENT-STATUS               PIC X(01).
        88  ENROLLED                    VALUE "E".
        88  INACTIVE                    VALUE "I".
    05  SM-STUDENT-NAME-AND-ADDRESS.
        10  SM-STUDENT-NAME             PIC X(25).
        10  SM-DATE-OF-BIRTH.
            15  SM-DOB-YEAR             PIC 9(04).
            15  SM-DOB-MONTH            PIC 9(02).
            15  SM-DOB-DAY              PIC 9(02).
        10  SM-STUDENT-ADDRESS          PIC X(25).
        10  SM-STUDENT-CITY             PIC X(11).
        10  SM-STUDENT-STATE            PIC X(02).
        10  SM-STUDENT-ZIP-CODE         PIC 9(05).
        10  SM-STUDENT-ZIP-CODE-EXT     PIC 9(04).
    05  SM-STUDENT-PROGRESS-SUMMARY.
        10  SM-CLASS-STANDING           PIC 9(01).
            88  FRESHMAN                VALUE 1.
            88  SOPHOMORE               VALUE 2.
            88  JUNIOR                  VALUE 3.
            88  SENIOR                  VALUE 4.
        10  SM-MAJOR                    PIC X(04).
        10  SM-UNITS-COMPLETED          PIC 9(03).
        10  SM-TOTAL-GRADE-POINTS       PIC 9(03).
        10  SM-UNITS-IN-PROGRESS        PIC 9(03).
```

Copy member name and path

```
c:\cobol\copy\stumast.cpy
```

Disk file name and path

```
c:\cobol\data\stumast.dat
```

88 levels

- Several of the definitions in the record description are at the 88 level, which isn't presented until chapter 5. Until you read that chapter, then, you should know that these levels indicate what the values in the fields above can be; they don't require any additional bytes of storage.

- The 88 levels for sm-class-standing, for example, just indicate that this one-digit field can store values of 1, 2, 3, and 4, which stand for freshman, sophomore, junior, or senior class standing.

File sequence

- The primary sequence of the records in this file is by sm-class-standing. This means that all the freshmen are first in the file, followed by sophomores, juniors, and seniors.

- The records are also in sequence in two other ways. First, the records are in sequence by sm-student-id within sm-class-standing. Second, the records are in sequence by sm-student-id within sm-major within sm-class-standing. In the real world, the same file of records couldn't be in sequence in both of these ways, but we set up the data this way so you could use one file for preparing two different types of summary reports.

The record description for the course registration file

```
01  COURSE-REGISTRATION-RECORD.
    05  CR-COURSE-KEY.
        10  CR-DEPARTMENT-CODE         PIC X(04).
        10  CR-COURSE-NUMBER           PIC 9(03).
        10  CR-SECTION-NUMBER          PIC 9(02).
    05  CR-COURSE-INFORMATION.
        10  CR-COURSE-TITLE            PIC X(20).
        10  CR-COURSE-START-DATE.
            15  CR-COURSE-START-YEAR   PIC 9(04).
            15  CR-COURSE-START-MONTH  PIC 9(02).
        10  CR-COURSE-UNITS            PIC 9(01).
        10  CR-COURSE-DAYS             PIC 9(01).
    05  CR-REGISTRATION-INFORMATION.
        10  CR-TEACHER-NUMBER          PIC 9(03).
        10  CR-STUDENT-INFORMATION.
            15  CR-STUDENT-ID          PIC 9(09).
            15  CR-STUDENT-NAME        PIC X(25).
            15  CR-CLASS-STANDING      PIC 9(01).
                88  FRESHMAN           VALUE 1.
                88  SOPHOMORE          VALUE 2.
                88  JUNIOR             VALUE 3.
                88  SENIOR             VALUE 4.
            15  CR-MAJOR               PIC X(04).
    05  CR-GRADING-INFORMATION.
        10  CR-6-WEEKS-GRADE           PIC X(01).
        10  CR-12-WEEKS-GRADE          PIC X(01).
        10  CR-FINAL-EXAM-GRADE        PIC X(01).
        10  CR-SEMESTER-GRADE          PIC X(01).
```

Copy member name and path

```
c:\cobol\copy\crsereg.cpy
```

Disk file name and path

```
c:\cobol\data\crsereg.dat
```

88 levels

- In chapter 5, you'll learn what the 88 levels mean. For now, you should know that the 88 levels for cr-class-standing just indicate that this one-digit field can store values of 1, 2, 3, and 4, which stand for freshman, sophomore, junior, or senior class standing.

File sequence

- The primary sequence of the records in this file is by cr-class-standing. This means that all the freshmen are first in the file, followed by sophomores, juniors, and seniors.

- The records are also in sequence in two other ways. First, the records are in sequence by cr-student-id within cr-class-standing. Second, the records are in sequence by cr-student-id within cr-major within cr-class-standing. In the real world, the same file of records couldn't be in sequence in both of these ways, but we set up the data this way so you could use one file for preparing two different types of summary reports.

About the projects for chapter 2

These projects require the COBOL skills that you learned in chapter 1 and the program development skills that you learned in chapter 2. These projects are simply designed to get you going and to give you some ideas for creating projects of your own.

Project 2-1   Calculate grade point average

This interactive program accepts user entries for grade points and credits. For each set of entries, the program should calculate the grade point average (GPA) by dividing grade points by credits and rounding to two decimal places. The interactive session should be something like this:

```
------------------------------------------------
Calculate another GPA (Y/N)?
Y
------------------------------------------------
Enter the number of grade points for the semester.
41
Enter the number of credits taken.
15
The grade point average is 2.73.
------------------------------------------------
Calculate another GPA (Y/N)?
N
End of session.
------------------------------------------------
```

Project 2-2   Calculate totals and averages

This program accepts a series of numeric entries. For each series, the program should calculate the total and average of the numbers. The interactive session should be something like this:

```
------------------------------------------------
End program (Y/N)?
N
------------------------------------------------
Enter a series of numbers that range from 1-999.
Press the Enter key after each entry.
To end the series, enter 0.
------------------------------------------------
13
871
411
12
0
------------------------------------------------
The total of the numbers is     1,307
The average of the number is      326.75
------------------------------------------------
End program (Y/N)?
Y
End of session.
```

About the projects for chapters 3, 4, and 5

The goal of chapters 3, 4, and 5 is to teach you how to prepare report-preparation programs the way the best professionals prepare them. As a result, the projects that follow ask you to prepare a variety of reports that require a variety of design structures and logical approaches.

Project 3-1   Prepare a student listing

This program reads the student master file and prepares a listing of students.

Files used by the program

Filename	Description	Mode
STUMAST	Student master file	Input
STULIST	Student listing	Printer output

Specifications

- Print one student line on the report for each record in the student master file.
- The student ID and student name should be taken from the master record. The GPA should be calculated by dividing the total grade points in the record by the units completed.
- The data in the class column should be derived from the number that's stored in the class standing field in the student master record where 1 = FRESHMAN, 2 = SOPHOMORE, 3 = JUNIOR, and 4 = SENIOR.
- The total number of students in the listing should be printed at the end of the report.

Print chart

```
DATE:    99/99/9999     STUDENT LISTING                PAGE:  ZZZ9
TIME:    99:99                                         SP03-1R

STUDENT  ID      STUDENT NAME                  CLASS         GPA
-------- ---     --------------------------    --------      ----

999-99-9999      XXXXXXXXXXXXXXXXXXXXXXXXX      XXXXXXXX      9.99
999-99-9999      XXXXXXXXXXXXXXXXXXXXXXXXX      XXXXXXXX      9.99

TOTAL STUDENTS:  ZZ,ZZ9
```

Project 3-2 Prepare an honor student report

This program reads the student master file and creates an honor student report.

Files used by the program

Filename	Description	Mode
STUMAST	Student master file	Input
HONORRPT	Honor student report	Printer output

Specifications

- The report should include only those students with a GPA of 3.5 or higher.
- The student ID and student name should be taken from the master record. The GPA should be calculated by dividing the total grade points in the record by the units completed.
- The data in the class column should be derived from the number that's stored in the class standing field in the student master record where 1 = FRESHMAN, 2 = SOPHOMORE, 3 = JUNIOR, and 4 = SENIOR.
- If a student has a GPA of 3.8 or higher, the report should print RANKING SCHOLAR to the right of the student's GPA.
- The total the number of students listed and the number of ranking scholars should be printed at the end of the report.

Print chart

```
    1234567890123456789012345678901234567890123456789012345678901234567890123
 1 DATE:   99/99/9999               HONOR STUDENT REPORT          PAGE:  ZZZ9
 2 TIME:   99:99                                                  SP03-2R
 3
 4 STUDENT ID      STUDENT NAME                        CLASS        GPA
 5 -----------     --------------------------------    ---------    ----
 6
 7 999-99-9999     XXXXXXXXXXXXXXXXXXXXXXXXX            XXXXXXXXX    9.99    XXXXXXXXXXXXXXXX
 8 999-99-9999     XXXXXXXXXXXXXXXXXXXXXXXXX            XXXXXXXXX    9.99    XXXXXXXXXXXXXXXX
 9
10 TOTAL STUDENTS:      ZZ,ZZ9
11 RANKING SCHOLARS:    ZZ,ZZ9
12
```

Project 4-1 Prepare a student roster

This program reads the student master file and creates a student roster. This report includes summary lines for each class (freshman, sophomore, junior, and senior).

Files used by the program

Filename	Description	Mode
STUMAST	Student master file	Input
SLSTROST	Single line student roster	Printer output

Specifications

- Print one student line for each record in the student master file. These records are in sequence by class standing.

- When the class changes, print the total number of students in the class and the grade point average for the class in two lines as shown in the print chart. For readability, skip a line before and after these summary lines.

- These printed fields should be taken from the master record: student ID, student name, units completed, and units in progress. The GPA should be calculated by dividing the total grade points by the units completed.

- The data in the class column should be derived from the number that's stored in the class standing field in the student master record where 1 = FRESHMAN, 2 = SOPHOMORE, 3 = JUNIOR, and 4 = SENIOR.

- At the end of the report, print the total number of students and the grade point average for all of the students as shown in the print chart. Your program should skip two lines before printing them.

Print chart

```
DATE:    99/99/9999                    STUDENT ROSTER                          PAGE:  ZZZ9
TIME:    99:99                                                                  SP04-1R

                                                               UNITS      UNITS IN
CLASS            STUDENT ID    STUDENT NAME                    COMPLETED  PROGRESS        GPA
-  -  -  -  -    -  -  -  -    -  -  -  -  -  -  -  -  -  -     -  -  -  -  -  -  -  -    -  -  -

XXXXXXXXX        999-99-9999   XXXXXXXXXXXXXXXXXXXXXXXXXXX        ZZ9        ZZ9          9.99
                 999-99-9999   XXXXXXXXXXXXXXXXXXXXXXXXXXX        ZZ9        ZZ9          9.99
                 999-99-9999   XXXXXXXXXXXXXXXXXXXXXXXXXXX        ZZ9        ZZ9          9.99

TOTAL STUDENTS IN CLASS:  ZZ,ZZ9
CLASS GPA:                 9.99


STUDENT TOTAL:  ZZ,ZZ9
STUDENT GPA:     9.99
```

Project 4-2   Prepare a multi-line student roster

This program reads the student master file and prepares a student roster that includes the complete address for each student. This report also includes summary lines for each class (freshman, sophomore, junior, and senior).

Files used by the program

Filename	Description	Mode
STUMAST	Student master file	Input
MLSTROST	Multi-line student roster	Printer output

Specifications

- Print three student lines for each record in the student master file, and skip one line after the lines for each student.

- The student records are in sequence by class standing. When the class changes, print the total number of students in the class and the grade point average for the class in two lines as shown in the print chart.

- The students for each class should start on a new page. The fourth heading line on this page should include the class name: FRESHMAN, SOPHOMORE, JUNIOR, or SENIOR.

- These printed fields should be taken from the master record: student ID, student name, units completed, and units in progress. The GPA should be calculated by dividing the total grade points by the units completed.

- At the end of the report, print the total number of students and the grade point average for all of the students as shown in the print chart. This should be on the same page as the totals for the senior class with two lines skipped before the total lines.

Print chart

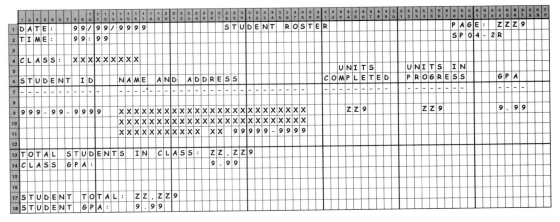

Project 4-3 Prepare a student roster summary

This program reads the student master file and prepares a student roster summary with one summary line for each class.

Files used by the program

File	Description	Mode
STUMAST	Student master file	Input
SRSRPT	Student roster summary	Printer output

Specifications

- The student records are in sequence by class standing.
- For each class, this program should print one line that summarizes the number of students, units completed, units in progress, and class GPA.
- At the end of the report, print grand totals for number of students, units completed, and units in progress. Also print the GPA for all the students.

Print chart

```
    DATE:      99/99/9999    STUDENT ROSTER SUMMARY           PAGE:    ZZZ9
    TIME:      99:99                                          SP04-3R

                  NUMBER OF        UNITS        UNITS IN
    CLASS         STUDENTS      COMPLETED      PROGRESS        GPA
    - - - - - - - -   - - - - - - - -   - - - - - - - -   - - - - - - - -   - - - -

    FRESHMAN         ZZ,ZZ9       ZZZ,ZZ9        ZZZ,ZZ9        9.99
    SOPHOMORE        ZZ,ZZ9       ZZZ,ZZ9        ZZZ,ZZ9        9.99
    JUNIOR           ZZ,ZZ9       ZZZ,ZZ9        ZZZ,ZZ9        9.99
    SENIOR           ZZ,ZZ9       ZZZ,ZZ9        ZZZ,ZZ9        9.99
                     ======       =======        =======        ====

    TOTALS:          ZZZ,ZZ9      ZZZ,ZZ9        ZZZ,ZZ9        9.99
```

Project 5-1   Prepare a two-level student registration report

This program reads the course registration file and prepares a student registration report. This two-level report includes unit totals for each student and for each class.

Files used by the program

File	Description	Mode
CRSEREG	Course registration file	Input
REG1RPT	Student registration report	Printer output

Specifications

- The course registration file is in sequence by student ID within class standing.
- When the student ID changes, this program should print the total units for the student with one line skipped after this total.
- When the class standing number changes, the program should print the total number of students in the class and the total units for all these students with one line skipped before this total and two lines after.
- The data in the class column should be derived from the number that's stored in the class standing field in the course registration record where 1 = FRESHMAN, 2 = SOPHOMORE, 3 = JUNIOR, and 4 = SENIOR.
- At the end of the report, print the total number of students in the report and total number of units with two lines skipped before.

Print chart

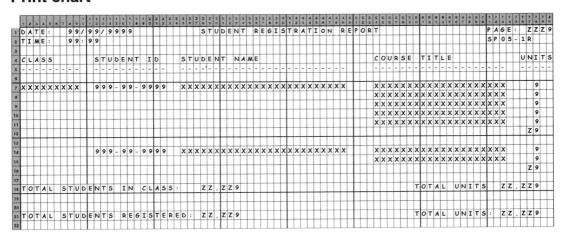

Project 5-2   Prepare a three-level student registration summary

This program reads the course registration file and prepares a student registration summary. This three-level report includes summary lines that show the class counts and unit totals for each student, for each major, and for each class.

Files used by the program

File	Description	Mode
CRSEREG	Course registration file	Input
REG2RPT	Student registration summary	Printer output

Specifications

- The course registration file is in sequence by student ID within major within class standing.
- When the student ID changes, this program should print one summary line for the student that includes the total units for the student.
- When the major changes, the program should print a summary line for that major.
- When the class number changes, the program should print a summary line for that class.
- At the end of the report, print the total number of students in the report and total number of units.

Print chart

About the projects for section 2

The chapters in section 2 present skills that can be applied to all types of programs, not specific types of programs. As a result, it's hard to design realistic projects for each of the chapters in this section. Instead, the projects for these chapters just force you to use the skills presented in the chapters...sometimes with a spirit of fun.

Project 6-1   Apply computational usage to an old program

Modify any one of the programs you've already developed so the proper usage is applied to all fields in working storage that are used in arithmetic operations or numeric comparisons. For Micro Focus Personal COBOL, that usage should be Computational. From this point on, you should use the proper usages in all of your new programs too.

Project 7-1   Develop a number guessing game

This is a simple interactive program that uses the Random function to generate a number from 1 through 100. The user is then given seven tries to guess what that number is. The interactive session should be something like the one that follows, but you can enhance it to make it more fun.

The interactive session

```
Guess what number I'm thinking of between 1 and 100.
10
Too low!
50
Too high!
25
Too high!
17
Ding! Ding! Ding! You guessed it in 4 tries!
Want to play again? Yes or No?
Yes
```

Specifications

*   To generate a random number between 1 and 100, multiply the Random function by 100 because this function returns a decimal fraction between 0 and 1. To make this number different every time the user plays the game, you should code the function with one argument. That argument should be the hours and minutes that you get when you use the Current-Date function.
*   Allow only seven tries. If the user doesn't guess the number by then, display the number along with an appropriate message.

Project 8-1 Prepare a student age listing

This program reads the student master file and prepares a listing of the senior students that includes their current ages as well as their projected ages at graduation. This forces you to work with dates. If you prefer to do this on an interactive basis instead of preparing another report, you can do project 8-2 instead.

Files used by the program

File	Description	Mode
STUMAST	Student master file	Input
AGELIST	Student age listing	Printer output

Specifications

* The second heading line of the report should include a graduation date like 06/21/2001. Then, the report should list the projected age of each senior at this graduation date.

* At the end of the report, the report should include the number of graduating seniors as well as the average graduation age.

Print chart

Project 8-2 Project graduation age and days until graduation

This interactive program should accept two entries from the user: (1) date of birth and (2) projected graduation date. The program should then display (1) the projected age of the user upon graduation and (2) the number of days until graduation. You design the interactive session.

Project 9-1 Translate English to Pig Latin

This interactive program translates any word the user enters into Pig Latin.

The interactive session

```
----------------------------------------
Enter any word to see what it looks like in
Pig Latin.
To quit, type Uitqay.
----------------------------------------
string
The Pig Latin equivalent is: Ingstray
----------------------------------------
unstring
The Pig Latin equivalent is: Unstringlay
----------------------------------------
Uitqay
Oodbyegay!
```

Specifications

- If the word starts with a consonant, move the consonants before the first vowel to the end of the word and add *ay*. If the word starts with a vowel, just add *lay* to the end of the word.

- The word entered can be up to 15 characters long, and the Pig Latin equivalent can be up to 18 characters long. The Pig Latin equivalent should start with an uppercase letter and be followed by all lowercase letters. If a user enters more than one word, translate just the first word.

- To end the program, the user must type the word Uitqay, which is Pig Latin for Quit.

Project 9-2 Unstring name, number, and password

This interactive program should accept one line of user entries that contains last name, account number, and password in this format:

```
Menendez,123-45,jtb
```

The program should then unstring the entries, store them properly in their own fields, and display them. To make this user friendly, the program should unstring the three items whether they're separated by commas or by commas and spaces. You design the interactive session.

- The last name must be one or two words followed by a comma. The program should convert this name to all capital letters and store it in an alphanumeric field.

- The account number must be five digits with one hyphen somewhere between the first and last digit. The program should extract the hyphen and store the five digits in a numeric field.

- The password can be up to eight characters. The program should convert any letters in this field to capitals.

Project 10-1   Use a state table to validate state and zip codes

This interactive program accepts a two-character state code and a five-digit zip code from the user. It then checks the validity of these fields and displays a message that says whether or not they're valid. This type of editing routine should be used in all programs that validate input data.

Specifications

* A copy member for a state table is available in a file named stattbl.cpy that's stored in the c:\cobol\copy folder. If you haven't read chapter 11 yet, you can use cut and paste techniques to copy the code for this table into your program. Otherwise, you can use the Copy statement to copy it.

* If you study the code for this table, you'll see that it consists of 50 occurrences of state code, the lowest valid zip code for that state, and the highest valid zip code for that state. As a result, you can use it to validate the state and zip code entries.

* If a state code is in the table, it's valid. Then, if the zip code is in the range of the lowest and highest zip code for that state, it is valid.

* Develop a simple interactive session that tests your validation routine.

Project 10-2   Prepare GPA range summary

This program prepares a summary of the number of students in each GPA range. To prepare this summary, you need to read all of the records in the student master file and use that data to create a table in working storage. After all the records have been read, the program prints the data in the table as indicated by the print chart.

Print chart

```
         1111111111222222222233333333334444444444 5
12345678901234567890123456789012345678901234567890
 1 DATE:   99/99/9999   GPA RANGE SUMMARY   SP10-2R
 2 TIME:   99:99
 3
 4                                   NUMBER OF
 5         GPA RANGES                STUDENTS
 6         ----------                ---------
 7
 8         3.5 - 4.0                    ZZ9
 9         3.0 - 3.4                    ZZ9
10         2.5 - 2.9                    ZZ9
11         2.0 - 2.4                    ZZ9
12         1.5 - 1.9                    ZZ9
13         1.0 - 1.4                    ZZ9
14         BELOW 1.0                    ZZ9
15
16         TOTAL STUDENTS:           Z,ZZ9
```

Project 11-1 Use copy members

Go back to any one of the programs you developed that uses the student master file. Then, delete the code for its record description, and replace that code with a Copy statement that copies the description into your program. From this point on, you should use Copy statements in any program for which there are copy members.

Project 11-2 Create a subprogram that converts numbers to words

This subprogram should receive a four-digit number and return a word description of the value. If, for example, the subprogram receives the number 1423, it should return these words:

```
One-thousand four-hundred twenty-three
```

This type of subprogram is sometimes used in check printing programs. To test this subprogram, you need to write an interactive program like the one that follows.

```
-------------------------------------------------------
Enter a 1 to 4-digit number.
1423
The number is: One-thousand four-hundred twenty-three
-------------------------------------------------------
Convert another number?
N
End of session.
```

Project 11-3 Create a subprogram that unstrings name, number, and password

If you've read chapter 9, you're ready to create a subprogram that unstrings three fields that are separated by commas. This subprogram should receive one alphanumeric field that contains the unstrung fields and return the three fields. The details for this routine are given in project 9-2. If you've done that project, you can convert its code to the subprogram, and modify the interactive session so it tests the subprogram. Otherwise, you need to create your own test program.

Project 11-4 Create a subprogram for state and zip code validation

If you've read chapter 10, you're ready to create a subprogram that receives a state code and a zip code and returns the values in two switches. The first switch indicates whether the state code was valid. The second switch indicates whether the zip code was valid.

To do this validation, you can use the copy member for the state table that's described in project 10-1. If you've done that project, you can convert its code to the subprogram, and you can use the interactive session to test your subprogram. Otherwise, you need to create your own test program.

About the projects for section 3

The goal of this section is to teach you how to develop programs that update and maintain master files as well as prepare reports that require input data from two or more files. The projects that follow give you a chance to test those skills.

Some of the projects for this section and for section 4 use an indexed version of the student master file. The key for this file is the student ID. Project 14-1 asks you to write a program that creates this file. If you're not assigned to do this project, though, you can use the file named stumasti.dat that's in the c:\cobol\data folder.

Project 13-1   Prepare student registration report

This program reads the course registration file and the student master file to create a student roster report.

Files used by the program

File	Description	Mode
CRSEREG	Course registration file	Input
STUMAST	Student master file	Input
REG3RPT	Student registration report	Printer output

Specifications

- The student address, city, state, and zip code come from the student master file. The other fields come from the course registration file. Both files are in sequence by student ID, and you need to use matching record logic to prepare this report.

- If you want to make this program more difficult, you can develop a two-level report with summary totals by class standing as well as by student. For each class, you can skip to the top of the next page and print the class name in the heading of the report as shown in the print chart for project 4-2.

- If you want to use line sequential files instead of standard sequential files, they are available in the c:\cobol\data folder with these names: stumastl.dat and crseregl.dat.

Print chart

Project 13-2 Update the student master file

This program updates the student master file with grade point information that's supplied by the course registration file. The result is a new student master file that contains the updated information.

Files used by the program

File	Description	Mode
CRSEREG	Course registration file	Input
STUMAST	Old student master file	Input
NEWMAST	New student master file	Output
ERRTRAN	Missing students report	Printer output

Specifications

- The course registration file can have more than one record for each student in the master file.

- For each student record that's matched by a course registration record, add the number of course units to the units completed field, and add the calculated course grade points to the total grade points field.

- To calculate the course grade points, multiply the numeric grade by the course units. To get the numeric grade, convert the letter to a number using a four point system: A=4, B=3, C=2, D=1 and F=0.

- If a course registration record does not have a matching student ID in the student master file, print the error transaction as a line on in the ERRTRAN report. You decide the print layout.

- If you want to use line sequential files instead of standard sequential files as input, they are available in the c:\cobol\data folder with these names: stumastl.dat and crseregl.dat.

Project 13-3 Maintain the student master file

Write a program that maintains just the name and address fields in the student master file. For this program, you design the layout of the transaction file, and you create the test data. If you're using Micro Focus Personal COBOL, use a line sequential file for the maintenance transaction, and use NotePad to create the test file. Note, however, that your program doesn't have to provide for deleting or adding records to the file.

If you want to use a line sequential file instead of a standard sequential file as input, it is available in the c:\cobol\data folder with this name: stumastl.dat.

Project 14-1   Create an indexed student master file

Write a program that converts the sequential student master file to an indexed file. The key for the file is the student ID. Save this file as stumasti.dat in the c:\cobol\data folder.

Files used by the program

File	Description	Mode
STUMAST	Sequential student master file	Input
STUMASTI	Indexed student master file	Output

Project 14-2   Prepare student registration report

Prepare the report that's shown for project 13-1. This time, though, use the indexed student master file instead of the sequential student master file. Then, read the course registration file sequentially as you prepare the report, but read the student master file randomly whenever you need to get the address data for a student.

Files used by the program

File	Description	Mode
CRSEREG	Course registration file	Input
STUMASTI	Indexed student master file	Input
REG4RPT	Student registration report	Printer output

Project 14-3   Update the student master file

This program updates the indexed student master file with grade information from the sequential course registration file.

Files used by the program

File	Description	Mode
CRSEREG	Course registration file	Input
STUMASTI	Indexed student master file	Input-Output
ERRTRAN	Missing students report	Printer output

Specifications

- The course registration file will be read sequentially and the indexed student master file will be read and updated randomly.
- The other specifications for this program are the same as those for project 13-2.
- When you want to return the student master file to its original data, you can rerun the program that you developed for project 14-1.

Project 16-1 Prepare a student listing in descending GPA sequence

This program prepares a student listing after the student master file has been sorted into descending sequence by GPA. As a result, the student listing is in that sequence.

Print chart

```
      DATE:    99/99/9999  STUDENT LISTING BY GPA      PAGE:  ZZZ9
      TIME:    99:99                                   SP16-1R

      GPA     STUDENT ID     STUDENT NAME              CLASS
      ----    -----------    --------------------------  --------

      9.99    999-99-9999    XXXXXXXXXXXXXXXXXXXXXXXXXX  XXXXXXXX
      9.99    999-99-9999    XXXXXXXXXXXXXXXXXXXXXXXXXX  XXXXXXXX

      TOTAL STUDENTS:  ZZ,ZZ9
```

Project 17-1 Display the student master data

This interactive program should use the full-screen features of Micro Focus COBOL to display the data in the indexed version of the student master file.

Specifications

- When the user enters a student ID and presses Enter, the program should read the student master record with that ID and display the student data. If the record can't be found, the program should display an appropriate message.

- You design the screen layout and colors and the way the interactive session works using the standards presented in chapter 17. To design the layout, you can use your word processing program with the font set to a mono-spaced font like Courier New. If you want to use our Word form, you'll find it at c:\cobol\extras\screen layout.

- At the least, you should display these fields: student ID, name, date of birth, address, city, state, zip, status, class, major, units completed, total grade points, units in progress, and GPA. Whenever possible, expand codes like status and class into words so they're more meaningful.

Project 17-2 Maintain the student master file

Write an interactive program that maintains just the name and address fields in the indexed student master file. This program should use the full-screen features of Micro Focus COBOL to display and accept data. You design the screen layout and colors and the way the interactive session works using the standards presented in chapter 17. Note, however, that your program doesn't have to provide for deleting or adding records to the file.

Index

C

For more on Murach products, visit us at
www.murach.com

Micro Focus Personal COBOL

Compiler and Animator on CD ROM
 with a Getting Started booklet and a COBOL reference manual $50.00

Books for COBOL programmers

Murach's Structured COBOL with CD ROM	$62.50
DB2 for the COBOL Programmer, Part 1 (Second Edition)	$45.00
DB2 for the COBOL Programmer, Part 2 (Second Edition)	45.00
CICS for the COBOL Programmer, Part 1 (Second Edition)	$42.50
CICS for the COBOL Programmer, Part 2 (Second Edition)	42.50
The CICS Programmer's Desk Reference (Second Edition)	49.50
MVS JCL (Second Edition)	$49.50
MVS TSO, Part 1 (Second Edition)	42.50
MVS TSO, Part 2 (Second Edition)	42.50

Books for Visual Basic and Access developers

Murach's Visual Basic 6	$45.00
Client/Server Programming: Access 97	40.00

*Prices are subject to change. Please visit our web site or call for current prices.

Our unlimited guarantee...when you order directly from us

You must be satisfied with our books. If they aren't better than any other
programming books you've ever used...both for training and reference....you
can send them back for a full refund. No questions asked!

Your opinions count

If you have any comments on this book, I'm
eager to get them. Thanks for your feedback!

To comment by

E-mail: murachbooks@murach.com
Web: www.murach.com
Postal mail: Mike Murach & Associates, Inc.
     2560 West Shaw Lane, Suite 101
     Fresno, California 93711-2765

To order now,

Call toll-free
 1-800-221-5528
 (Weekdays, 8 am to 5 pm Pacific Time)

Fax: 1-559-440-0963

Web: www.murach.com

Mike Murach & Associates, Inc.
Practical computer books since 1974

What the CD ROM contains

- All of the complete programs that are used as examples in the book.
- All of the programs and data that you need for doing the exercises at the end of each chapter on your own PC.
- Our LISTMODS program, which you can use for generating a structure listing from a structured COBOL program.
- All of the data and copy members that you need for doing the student projects.
- A generic version of the exercises presented throughout this book.
- A Readme.doc or Readme.txt file that lists the folders and files on the CD ROM and describes how you can use them.

How to install the CD ROM files on your PC

- Copy the top-level folder on the CD ROM to your C drive. That will copy all the files to a folder structure that starts with c:\cobol.
- Open the c:\cobol\readme.doc or readme.txt file for other installation instructions.

What compiler the CD ROM programs are designed for

- To get the most from this book, we recommend that you buy and install Micro Focus Personal COBOL on your PC. This inexpensive product is an outstanding training tool. Chapter 2 shows you how to use it, and the exercises at the end of each chapter are tuned to it.
- All of the programs on the CD ROM are written in standard COBOL so you can use them with any COBOL compiler. You can also use the exercises with any COBOL compiler. Since the exercises in the book contain operational directions that are specific to Micro Focus Personal COBOL, though, you may want to use the generic version of the exercises on this CD if you're using another compiler.

How to buy Micro Focus Personal COBOL

- Call us at 1-**800**-221-5528 or visit our web site at www.murach.com to buy Personal COBOL. It comes with a Getting Started book and a complete COBOL reference manual (see the preceding page).
- If you're using this book as part of a course, you should be able to buy Micro Focus Personal COBOL in your bookstore.

How to install and set up Micro Focus Personal COBOL

- The Getting Started book that comes with Personal COBOL describes the installation process. In brief, you run the setup.exe program that's on the Personal COBOL CD ROM and then follow the instructions on the screen.
- Chapter 2 in this book shows you how to set the defaults for this compiler, and the exercises for that chapter walk you through these procedures.